Network
Management
Principles and Practice

Management should go in
Before the network goes on

Network Management
Principles and Practice

Mani Subramanian
Georgia Institute of Technology
Indian Institute of Technology Madras
NMSWorks Software Private Limited

With contributions from

Timothy A. Gonsalves
Indian Institute of Technology Madras

N. Usha Rani
NMSWorks Software Private Limited

Chennai • Delhi

Managing Editor - Acquisitions: Sojan Jose
Managing Editor - Production: M. E. Sethurajan

ISBN 978-81-317-3404-9

First Impression, 2011

Published by Dorling Kindersley (India) Pvt. Ltd., licensees of Pearson Education in South Asia.

Head Office: 7th Floor, Knowledge Boulevard, A-8(A), Sector-62, Noida 201 309, India.
Registered Office: 11 Community Centre, Panchsheel Park, New Delhi 110 017, India.

Composition by Sigma Business Process, Chennai
Digitally Printed in India by Saurabh Printers Pvt. Ltd. in the year of 2013.

Pearson Education Inc., Upper Saddle River, NJ
Pearson Education Ltd., London
Pearson Education Australia Pty, Limited, Sydney
Pearson Education Singapore, Pte. Ltd
Pearson Education North Asia Ltd, Hong Kong
Pearson Education Canada, Ltd., Toronto
Pearson Educacion de Mexico, S.A. de C.V.
Pearson Education-Japan, Tokyo
Pearson Education Malaysia, Pte. Ltd

In loving memory of
Appa Mahadevan
Amma Kalyani

Affectionately dedicated to
Ruth, Ravi, and Meera Subramanian
for sustained support and persistent patience

With deep appreciation to
Stimulating Students
Who led me to learn by teaching

Endorsements

"I have been using the first edition since 2003 as core management principles and practical topics discussed therein made it an extremely useful reference even for practitioners. I am happy to note that the second edition is making the contents of the textbook even more applicable in the current technological context by incorporating management of Optical & MPLS networks widely deployed in the telecommunications network, discussing broadband wireless networks management that are now ubiquitous and the evolution of standards and technologies governing the actual implementation of the NMS itself. The addition of discussions around Cygnet NMS to illustrate the NMS architecture concepts and implementation considerations are quite useful. I am sure the book will serve the needs of both students in academics as well as the telecom and networking professionals."

.Nagarajan, Sankar
Head, NMS R&D Services, Tech Mahindra, Chennai, India

"Many congratulations! It is a wonderful book with lots of minute details on Network Management. I am sure it will be a ready handbook for the student/professional communities.

My sincere thanks for your time and effort in bringing out the second edition of the textbook."

Seetharaman, V.
Head, ITMC & Cable NOC, Bharti Airtel Limited, Chennai, India

"Professor Subramanian has a remarkable ability to set complex network engineering and associated network management problems in context with well-written explanations and real-world examples that deal with the varied demands placed on converging telecommunications networks and the design and operation of the underpinning management systems and protocols.

This book will be extremely useful resource for graduate and postgraduate students on CS/EE courses including those studying in their first year of PhD in Telecommunications Engineering, as it provides a fantastic coverage of a wide range of fundamental network management issues. I for one will be using it for my graduate students."

Parr, Gerrard
School of Computing and Information Engineering, University of Ulster, Coleraine campus, Londonderry, Ireland

"Dr. Subramanian's *Network Management: Principles and Practice* provides the most thorough treatment of network management to date. There is no fluff in this book. It is for the serious, interested reader. It proceeds from the ground up, starting with common network management protocols and continuing to cover telecommunications management and broadband network management, focusing on WANs, optical networks, wireless networks, and home networks. Each chapter builds nicely upon previous chapters so that there is a logical delivery of information. Chapter 9, "Network Management Tools, Systems, and Engineering" is a very useful, practical chapter. It provides the reader with the know-how to perform hands-on network management with various management tools. Chapter 10 covers the classic model of the Telecommunications Management Network, indispensable for understanding network management. Chapter 11 covers other important aspects of network management, including fault management, performance management, security management, policy-based management, and service level management. Further, Chapter 11 includes a section on event correlation methods, typically not found in books on network management, and this is refreshing. These two chapters provide a solid foundation for understanding the management of WANs, optical networks, wireless networks, and home networks in the subsequent chapters. Chapter 16 covers forward-looking topics in network management, including web-based enterprise management and XML-based management approaches. There are appendices on Project Suggestions and Laboratory Tutorials that render the book quite well-suited for use in a course on network management. All in all, Dr. Subramanian's book provides a serious, first-rate treatment of the subject."

Lundy Lewis

Department Chair & Professor, Southern New Hampshire University, Manchester, USA

"This book fills a long-standing need. While there is an abundance of courses and textbooks that deal with typical topics in networking, there is a lack of such books for Network Management. Often, concepts and technologies related to Network Management are relegated to the last few chapters. This book brings out the fact that there is a wealth of detail in this area, which is important for practitioners as well as students.

This book gives comprehensive details of all aspects of network management, in different types of contemporary networks. Reading it would save practitioners considerable time and effort, which they might otherwise put into reading diverse online sources. This book also provides the syllabus structure required for a full-fledged course on Networking Management. It would be appropriate for students at the undergraduate as well as postgraduate levels."

Sridhar Iyer

Indian Institute of Technology Bombay, Mumbai, India

"It is a very comprehensive book on Network Management Systems addressing the needs of academia, industry both R&D and Operations. Coming from a person who has worked on all these functions in telecoms, the good thing about the second edition is the coverage of various technologies like Wireless, broadband, home networking and the challenges these technologies pose to the NMS."

Chalapathi Rao

Vice President & Head Global Delivery, Tata Communications Transformation Services Ltd., Chennai, India

"Mani Subramanian's book has been of great help in our undergraduate Network Management course.

The book provides both a top-down view on Network Management approaches and a bottom-up view of the management information available in almost any kind of network technology and environments. In particular, it offers quick and visual orientation in the jungle of MIBs available in all kinds of equipment.

The new edition kept the spirit of the first edition, but enhanced it significantly with new and helpful visualisations, examples and contemporary management scenarios.

The presentation is interspersed with the author's long-standing experience with Network Management and its tools, which helps the reader to gain a deep understanding of the reasoning behind Network Management models, protocols, services and tools."

Markus Fiedler
Blekinge Institute of Technology, Karlskrona, Sweden

"This edition takes off from the previous one with a renewed perspective on network management, incorporating relevant developments over the past decade. The treatment of the topic beginning with a problem statement sets the scene for a detailed coverage on network management systems and their associated protocols. Mapping of TMN and eTOM gives a well-rounded view of both the technical and business process aspects of network management for the telecom operator. Real industry examples provide the much-needed meeting ground of theory and practical implementations. Dr. Subramanian's experience with the implementation of network management in major telcos lends authenticity to the treatment of this interesting subject. To summarize, the book would be valuable to students and professionals alike."

Aiyappan Pillai
Head, CNMS, Tata Communications Ltd., Mumbai, India

Brief Contents

Contents

Preface

Network-centric World and Role of Network Management

The world in the information era has become network-centric. Daily life, both personal and institutional, is network-centric. Century-old telephone technology has brought us today to the converged telecommunications and data communications technology era. We are linked to and interface with the globally "flat-world" via e-lifeline. The information era has built a world of information networks and systems that we need to operate, administer, maintain, and provision on an on-going basis. That is our challenge.

Areas of management of networks, systems, and applications in data and telecommunication services are not only the responsibility of telecommunications and networking industries and standards bodies but also of the academic world. Students graduating from technical colleges and universities are expected to be prepared to use a network and also to design and to manage one. The existing procedure to design and test some key networks is heuristic. Personnel with experience, and sometimes without, design networks and test them in live situations. A corporation hardly functions today without the deployment of local area networks (LANs) in their networking environment. The majority of homes in developed nations have a home network distributing voice, video, and data information. With the proliferating use of the Internet and Web technology, the subject of networking and network management has become part of the academic curriculum. This textbook, introduced ten years ago, has been part of this evolution. This new edition brings new technologies and services to undergraduate and graduate classrooms in the broad arena of what is known as network management.

Justification for a Textbook on Network Management

Over a decade ago when I started teaching a course on network management, there was a need for a textbook that satisfied quarter/semester requirements. The adoption of this book by colleges and universities across the world has partially filled that void. Just as networking education has been brought from the graduate to the undergraduate level, this edition of the textbook has been upgraded so that early parts of the book can be used at the junior and the senior undergraduate level and latter parts at the graduate level. It also addresses the audience of self-learners who want to get into or gain knowledge of network management.

Once again, a note about the title of this book: As noted in the earlier edition, the title does not truly reflect the contents of the book because we want to keep it succinct. The book covers management principles, practices, and technologies for managing networks, systems, applications, and services. The book is designed to be self-contained, so that the student does not have to traverse in and out of this book's domain. An attempt has been made to strike the right balance between theoretical background and practical aspects of networking. The treatment of practical aspects includes some real-world examples and "war stories." If "a picture is worth a thousand words," this book contains about a million. Just as a programming course requires hands-on programming exercises, so does a network management course. So we have added laboratory tutorials to the appendix, which supplement classroom teaching.

A major addition to the book is the expanded treatment of broadband network management. It covers "triple play" services of voice, video, and data communications. It spans the network over the segments of wide area network (WAN), access networks to home, and home distribution networks including LANs. Multimedia communications is covered from the aspects of wired transmission media of cable, digital subscriber line, and optical fiber as well as fixed and mobile wireless.

This book exposes the student to current network management technology. At the completion of a course using this book, the student could either enter the industry with adequate networking knowledge or graduate school to pursue further research and specialization.

About the Contents

The book is divided into four parts. Part I deals with background material on networking and networking technologies. Part II addresses network management architectures and protocols. The focus is on SNMP and IP network management. Part III extends network management to the management of telecommunications, which includes networks, systems, operations and business services, and management applications. The last, and final, Part IV concludes with the management of broadband networks and the latest trends in management technology.

Part I consists of Chapters 1 and 2. Chapter 1 presents an overview of networking and network management. It is intended not only as a background and top-down information, but also as a motivation for the student. Chapter 2 reviews networking technology with a slant on management aspects. The course, for which this textbook is intended, assumes that the student has basic knowledge of data communications and networking. However, we review them briefly in Chapters 1 and 2. It is extremely difficult to cover much more than the basics of protocols, algorithms, and procedures of transport protocol layers 2, 3, and 4, as well as basic rudiments of components of LAN and WAN networks in such a course. Not much technology can be covered, and network management depends strongly on managing network components that are based on an ever-evolving technology, hence the presence of Chapter 2. It can be either skipped or covered in parts by the instructor. Relevant sections could also be used when dealing with subjects in Parts II, III, and IV. However, it would be useful as reference material for non-classroom learners who want an introduction to networking and network management.

Chapters 3 through 9 form Part II. Basic foundations of models that are needed to build various network management architectures and protocols are covered. OSI-based network management is rarely used, but has some strong fundamental concepts. For completeness of the subject, it is included in Appendix A. SNMP-based protocols that manage TCP/IP networks are covered in Chapters 4 through 8. Chapters 4 and 5 are devoted to learning the concepts and use of SNMP (version 1) in network management. Chapters 6 and 7 deal with the additional specifications defined in versions 2 and 3. Chapter 8 extends network management using remote monitoring capabilities. Chapter 9 discusses networking and network management tools. The architecture and features of some of the widely used network and system management systems are also covered.

Network management is more than just managing the network infrastructure. Part III addresses this from the service, business, and applications points of view. Chapter 10 extends the management area to cover broader aspects of network management from managing network elements and networks to service and business management as addressed in Telecommunications Management Network (TMN) standards. The knowledge acquired on management tools and systems, as well as on principles in Part II, is applied to practical applications in managing fault, configuration, performance, security, and accounting, which forms the contents of Chapter 11.

The demarcation of telecommunications and data communications is becoming increasingly fuzzy in broadband communications. In Part IV, the broadband network is segmented into WAN, access network, and home distribution network. Chapter 12 deals with WAN. IP technology has been extensively dealt with in Parts I and II. The management of ATM network, MPLS network, and optical SONET/SDH/DWDM network management is covered in Chapter 12. Chapter 13 addresses wired broadband access networks in bringing services from core WAN to home. Management of cable, DSL, and PON are the three technologies that we cover. Fixed and mobile wireless access network management form the subject matter of Chapter 14. Having brought voice, video, and data of broadband service to home, it needs to be distributed inside customer premises and managed. This is the topic of discussion in Chapter 15.

The impact of emerging technologies in a Web-based and object-oriented management system is the future of management technology, which is addressed in Chapter 16.

Suggestions for Course Syllabus

Parts I and II along with the Laboratory Tutorials in Appendix C form a unit for undergraduate courses. Parts III and IV are suitable for graduate-level courses with senior-level students admitted with the consent of the instructor.

The complete contents of the book are more than can be covered in a quarter or even a semester course. The instructor may do a "mix and match" between chapters to suit local needs if SNMP basics and some of the broadband network management are to be covered in one semester. Independent of the choice, a project to accompany the course is recommended, and suggestions are given in Appendix B.

For a dedicated course on network management, there are several choices. If the focus is on SNMP management, then Chapters 6 through 8 covering SNMPv2, SNMPv3, and RMON, respectively, can be used. That can be followed with network management tools and systems (Chapter 9) and applications (Chapter 11).

If telecommunications is emphasized (this is more likely in computer engineering schools), then it would be good to include Telecommunications Management Network (Chapter 10).

If broadband services are taught at the school, then Part IV (Chapters 12–16) could be included.

Finally, if the school has a research program on network management, it is suggested that in addition to the special areas of interest, management applications in Chapter 11 be dealt with in depth. In addition, adequate treatment of Advanced Management Topics (Chapter 16) is strongly suggested.

To the Instructor

This textbook is designed as a dual-level book. It can be used for undergraduate courses at the junior or the senior level or for graduate-level courses. It assumes that the student has taken a prerequisite course in either data or telecommunication network or has equivalent knowledge. However, the book does review networking from a management focus prior to dealing directly with the main subject of network management.

With the prolific growth of networking, network management is expected to become part of the academic curriculum, and this book will be useful for both Computer Science and Electrical and Computer Engineering schools that specialize in networking.

Online Supplements: Solutions to exercises are available to instructors from the Pearson representative. Visual aids in the format of PowerPoint slides for instructors and students are available to all from the Pearson website that would facilitate teaching and note-taking in the class.

The book could also be used as a reference material if you are teaching a Continuing Education course on network management. The PowerPoint slides will come in handy as classroom aids. I have found that students like to take home knowledge in the form of a book in addition to the student manual. The author welcomes suggestions and material to be added and may be reached at manims@ieee.org.

To the Student

Although the book is written as a textbook to be adopted for a course, additional information is provided in the book that would serve as a reference book for students after graduation. For example, basic information is provided along with references to serve as a springboard to access additional in-depth details on any specialized management topic.

The book is also geared toward self-motivated engineers in the industry who are eager to learn network management. If the engineer has access to network resources, many of the hands-on exercises could be practiced. At the minimum, it would provide enough tools and knowledge for the frustrated worker when he or she cannot access the network resources and does not know why.

Grateful Acknowledgements

The major impetus for the contents of this book has come from students over the course offerings since 1996. It has been reviewed at various levels and to various depths by many students.

My thanks flow profusely to Professor Timothy Gonsalves and Dr. Usha Rani for making major contributions to Chapters 9 and 16, respectively. We have shared together teaching the Network Management course at Indian Institute of Technology Madras. I thank Professor Gerard Paar for motivating me to come out with a second edition; and it is unfortunate that he could not participate as a contributing author due to other commitments. I owe gratitude to several persons at NMSWorks who have helped in various ways in the preparation of the manuscript. My special thanks to Binu Raghavan for generating topological views of CygNet NMS that is customized for the textbook presentation, to Madangopal and Adithyan for SDH exercises, and to Santosh Chaudhari for help with network load statistics figures.

Many reviewers' comments and suggestions have contributed to the richness of the contents of the first edition that form the basis of this edition. I owe special gratitude to Lundy Lewis, who has made numerous and specific suggestions for improvement in the first edition. The results of interviews described in Chapter 1 generated positive feedback from reviewers and students; and I thank the following at Georgia Tech for consenting to be interviewed: Cas D'Angelo, Ron Hutchins, Dave Miller, John Mize, and John Mullin. Some of the case histories were provided by Rob Beverly, Ron Hutchins, and Dave Miller. Brandon Rhodes and Oleg Kolesnikov provided some interesting practical exercises to be included in the book.

My thanks go to Sojan Jose, Commissioning Editor, M. E. Sethurajan, Senior Production Editor, and Jennifer Samuel Sargunar, Associate Production Editor, of Pearson Education for their ever-willing cooperation in successfully seeing this second edition through to completion.

I am indebted to the Indian Institute of Technology Madras for providing time off for me to come out with the second edition. I also want to thank Professors Ashok Jhunjhunwala, Timothy Gonsalves, and Bhaskar Ramamurthy of TeNeT Group for providing me with an environment to fulfill my desire of the long-needed upgrade of the book.

My wife, Ruth, continued her contributing role to the book by inputting revisions, acting as the local copy editor, and being production manager of manuscripts. Thank you again, Ruth.

Mani Subramanian

About the Author

Mani Subramanian is a Chair Professor at Indian Institute of Technology Madras where he teaches courses on Network Management and Broadband Communication Systems. He is also the Director of NMSWorks Software Solutions Private Ltd., Chennai, India. He initiated a network management program at Georgia Institute of Technology in 1996, where he is presently on the Adjunct Faculty. The first edition of his book, published in 2000, is currently adopted as a textbook in over fifteen countries and translated into Chinese for Higher Education in China. For over 45 years, he has led research and development at several IT corporations including Bell Laboratories, has been in the faculty at three universities, and has founded network management companies in the broadband arena. As an elected Director of the Network Management Forum, he was responsible for the first release of OSI NM specifications. Dr Subramanian received his Ph.D. from Purdue University.

PART I

Background

Chapter 1 presents an overview of telecommunications, data communications, and network management. It is a broad review of networking and network management. It starts with an analogy of the telephone network. Telephone network almost always works, and there are reasons for its achieving quality and reliability. You will learn the relationship between data communications and telecommunications and how the distinction between the two is slowly disappearing. The influence of desktop computing and distributed computing environment based on client–server architecture has revolutionized computer communication. The Internet is a worldwide fabric and you will learn to appreciate how information travels across it around the globe. Basics of communication protocols and architecture are presented along with various standards. Select equivalent applications are used as illustrations comparing the Internet and OSI protocols.

Components of network management are described and complemented by interviews with network managers, whose experiences emphasize the need for network management and a network operations center. Network management is more than just managing networks. Network management is presented from the perspectives of service management, operations support systems, and business management. The platform for a network management system is discussed based on client–server architecture. Chapter 1 concludes with a note on future trends in network management technology.

Chapter 2 focuses on network technology. You may skip this chapter if you are familiar with the practical aspects of networking. If you are knowledgeable on principles of data communication, this chapter will help you appreciate the technological aspects of it. You will learn how various topologies are implemented in LAN and WAN networks. Basics of Ethernet, Token Ring, and FDDI networks are described from a practical point of view. Of these, Ethernet is the most widely deployed LAN today. LAN evolution from basic Ethernet to Gigabit Ethernet with half- and full-duplex configurations is presented. Switched Ethernet adds capability to expand the bandwidth and the flexibility of LAN. Virtual LAN is implemented using a switched Ethernet hub accomplishing flexibility in administration of workstations across multiple LANs. You will learn the various network components—hubs, bridges, routers, gateways, and protocol converters—that need to be managed. A brief review of wide area networking and transmission technology is also presented. Broadband technology is briefly described in this chapter, but a detailed discussion of it will be done in Part IV while addressing the management of broadband networks and services.

Data Communications and Network Management Overview

OBJECTIVES

- Telecommunications overview
- Data communications overview
- Evolution of converged networks
- Desktop processors and LAN technology
- Client–Server architecture in networking
- Internet and intranet
- Network communication protocols
- OSI and Internet standards
- Broadband networks and services
- Need for network management and NMS

- Operations, Administration, Maintenance, and Provisioning
- Network management architecture and organization
- Concept of Network Operations Center
- Perspectives of network management
- Network management system
- Look-ahead of network management technology

This chapter demonstrates the necessity of network system and service management in providing information technology (IT) services. The challenges that IT managers face are presented to motivate the student to get excited about network management. We start with the history of computer communication, walk you through some real-world case histories, and then present an overview of various aspects of network management.

The telephone system is known to be very reliable and dependable. One can make a telephone call from anywhere to anywhere at any time of the day and be reasonably sure that the connection will be made and the quality of connection will be good. This is partly due to the efficient management of the telephone network. Section 1.1 introduces the concept of management for the success of telephone network by using Operation Support Systems (OSSs).

Computer communication initially used the telephone network to carry digital data. There was a clear demarcation between the traditional telecommunication network and computer communication network. The evolution of early computer communication networks is dealt with in Section 1.2.

Computer communication technology radically changed with the advent of desktop computing power and distributed computing environments (DCEs) using local area networks (LAN) as described in Section 1.3. Global communication using Internet became a reality with the introduction of TCP/IP-based networks. Section 1.4 describes Internet and intranet followed by a discussion in Section 1.5 on the importance of communication protocols and standards.

The next phase in the evolution of IT was the introduction of broadband services. Voice, video, and data could be delivered on the same medium to homes. This has revolutionized the access network to home and the distribution network at customer premises. It has also initiated improvement in the core wide area network (WAN). Section 1.6 addresses these issues.

Networking is full of "war stories" as experienced by IT managers. Sections 1.7 and 1.8 present case histories experienced by IT managers and the challenges they face in today's computer and telecommunication environment. Interviews with them emphasize the importance of network and system management tools. Section 1.9 describes network management that comprises operations, administration, maintenance, and provisioning. Three groups perform these functions: Engineering, Operations, and Installation and Maintenance (I&M). Section 1.10 focuses on Network Management System (NMS) and relationships between its various components. Besides managing network components, application system resources also need to be managed. This is the subject of Section 1.11.

Network management technology is still in an evolutionary mode as network and software technologies advance. Section 1.12 briefly addresses NMS platforms based on Microsoft Windows and UNIX operating system. The future directions of network management technology form the content of Section 1.13. As with all chapters in the book, a summary section and exercises conclude this chapter.

1.1 ANALOGY OF TELEPHONE NETWORK MANAGEMENT

The need for data or computer communication network management is best illustrated by an analogy of telephone network management. The high degree of reliability of the telephone network is evidenced by the following illustration. We can pick up a telephone, call anybody, anytime, anywhere in the world, and be almost sure to be connected to the destination. It is reliable and dependable; and the quality and speed of connection are good. It is reliable because it almost always provides service of voice communication that we expect of it. It is dependable because we can be fairly sure that it works when we need it, especially in an emergency situation, such as 911 calls in the USA or military defense situations. The quality of service is generally good; and we can have a conversation across the world with the same clarity that we have when we call our neighbor.

The present-day telephone network is referred to as Public-Switched Telephone Network (PSTN), and is probably the best example of traffic engineering providing guaranteed Quality of Service. The reason for such reliability, dependability, and quality is more than careful planning, design, and implementation of a good telephone network using good and reliable components. The key is management and operation of the network. Much of the management of the network is so well automated that it becomes part of the operation. Let us first look at the telephone network architecture and then at some of the operations support systems that manage it. In the 1970s the telecommunications industry switched to digital services, which followed much the same pattern as voice services and conceived a vision of end-to-end circuit-switched services, known as the Broadband Integrated Services Digital Network (B-ISDN). B-ISDN is now being replaced by Internet and Broadband Service.

The architecture of a telephone network is hierarchical as shown in Figure 1.1 [AT&T 1977]. There are five levels of network switches and three types of trunks that connect these switches. A trunk is a logical link between two switches and may traverse one or more physical links. The end office (Class 5), which is lowest in the hierarchy, is the local switching office. The customer's telephone or Private Branch Exchange (PBX) is connected to the end office via a dedicated link called "loop." The other four higher levels of switches (Class 4 through Class 1) are tandem or toll switches carrying toll (long-distance) calls. Because of the advance in switching technology and economy of transmission, Classes 1 through 4 have been merged into a single class referred to as Class 4. A direct trunk connects two end offices, a toll-connecting trunk connects an end office to any toll office, and a toll (internal) trunk connects any two toll offices.

From the local Class 5 office to the called party's Class 5 office, there are multiple routes. A circuit connection is set up either directly using a local trunk or via higher-level switches and routers. Primary and secondary routes are already programmed into the switch. If the primary route is broken or facilities over the primary route are filled to capacity, an alternate route is automatically assigned. For example, on Mother's Day, which is the busiest telephone-traffic day of the year in the United States, a call to the neighboring town could travel clear across the country and back if that's the route where adequate bandwidth is available. Let us remember that there is a 3-hour time difference between the two coasts, and traffic in the West Coast starts 3 hours later than the East Coast.

To ensure the quality of service in a telephone network, operations support systems are implemented. They constantly monitor the various parameters of the network. For example, to ensure that there is adequate bandwidth to carry the traffic over the facilities, a traffic measurement system constantly measures traffic over switch appearances. The results are analyzed for facility-planning purposes. They also provide real-time input to a NMS when there is excessive blocking (traffic over the capacity of the trunk group) in any link.

The quality of the call, measured in terms of signal-to-noise (S/N) ratio, is measured regularly by a trunk maintenance system. This system accesses all the trunks in an office during the night and does a loop-back test to the far end. The results are analyzed in the morning and corrective actions taken. For example, if the S/N ratio of a trunk is below the acceptance level, the trunk is removed from service before the customer experiences poor performance.

For a given region, there is a network operations center (NOC) where the global status of the network is monitored. Traffic patterns are constantly observed and corrective operations are taken, if needed, in real time. The NOC is the nerve center of telephone network operations.

It is worth noting that the telephone network is managed from the users' perspective, and not from that of the system or the service provider, even though the objectives of both are the same. However,

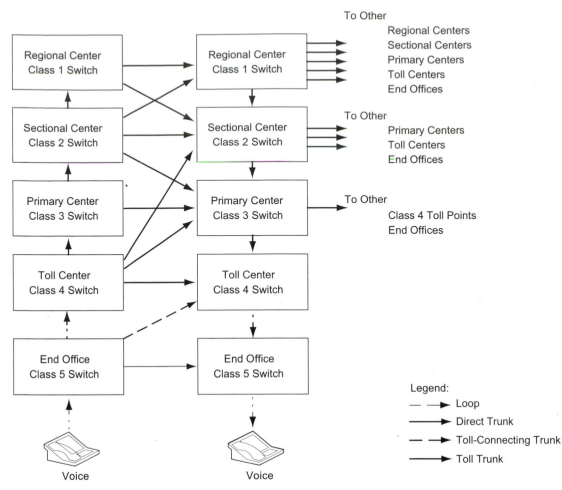

Figure 1.1   Telephone Network Model

with emphasis on the user's point of view, the first objective in operations is restoration of service and then the quality and economy of service. Thus, isolation of the problem and providing alternative means of service, by either manual or automated means, become more important than fixing the problem.

To manage a network remotely, i.e., to monitor and control network components from a central location, network management functions need to be built into the components of the network as much as possible. In that sense, network component designs should include network management functions as part of their requirements and specifications.

The computer or data communication network has not matured to the same extent as the telephone network. Data communications technology is merging with telephone technology. Data and modern telecommunication networks are evolving into broadband communication networks and are more complicated than the plain old telephone service (POTS). Analog audio and video services are migrating to digital services. The analog hierarchy of low-to-high bandwidth signals is being transmitted across the globe using a Synchronous Digital Hierarchy (SDH) mode.

Network management and operations of these digital networks are continuously being developed as new technologies emerge. Further, the telephone industry all over the world had been monopolistic and thus single-vendor oriented. This is no longer true. Digital-based computer communications started as a private industry and is hence multivendor oriented. Unfortunately, this has produced enormous problems to users because network components supplied by different vendors do not always communicate with each other. The network or information systems manager, who has the responsibility of keeping the service alive all the time, has been confronted with resolving the issue as new technology and new vendor products emanate. This situation has been recognized by various industrial and standard groups and is being continuously addressed.

1.2 DATA (COMPUTER) AND TELECOMMUNICATION NETWORK

Network communications technology deals with the theory and application of electrical engineering, computer engineering, and computer science to all types of communication over networks. It also addresses accessing of databases and applications remotely over LANs as well as switched and private lines. A basic network can be viewed as interconnected nodes and links as shown in Figure 1.2. A link carries information from one node to another that is directly connected to it. A node behaves as an end (terminating or originating) node, or an intermediate node, or both. If the node behaves as an end node, information either originates or terminates there. An intermediate node redirects the information from one link to another. End-office nodes mentioned in Section 1.1 behave as end nodes. A node can drop and add information channels and at the same time switch information transparently between two links. Each end node has a connection to a user interface if the information originates or terminates there. This interface could use any type of equipment—audio, video, or Data Terminating Equipment (DTE). A DTE is any equipment that generates or accepts digital data.

Data can be transmitted either in an analog or digital format. The analog data are sent either as a baseband (e.g., voice data from the switching office to the customer premises) or on top of a carrier (e.g., cable TV). Digital data are either directly generated by the user equipment (e.g., computer terminal) or as analog data and are converted to digital data (e.g., Integrated Services Digital Network (ISDN) connection to customer premises). The latter scenario of the ability to handle integrated digital and analog signals is becoming extremely important as in the case of multimedia broadband services. Management considerations associated with them are also very challenging, as we will see in Part IV. Long-distance data transmission today is mostly digital due to its superior price and performance.

Data are sent from the originating to the terminating node via a direct link or via a tandem of links and intermediate nodes. Data can be transmitted in one of three modes: circuit switched, message switched, or packet switched. In the circuit-switched mode, a physical circuit is established between the originating and terminating ends before the data are transmitted. The circuit is released or "torn down" after completion of transmission.

In message-switched and packet-switched modes, data are broken into packets and each packet is enveloped with destination and originating addresses. The message-switched mode is used to send long messages, such as email. The packet-switched mode is used to transmit small packets used in applications such as interactive communication. Bridges and routers open each packet to find the destination address and switch the data to the appropriate output links. The path between the two ends may change during the transmission of a message because each packet may take a different route. They are reassembled in

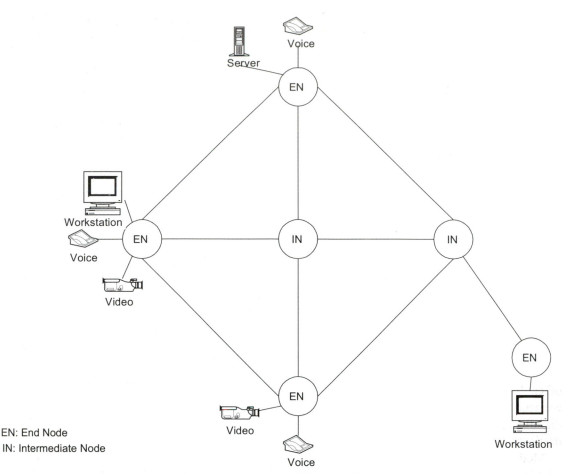

Figure 1.2 Logical Network Model

the right order at the receiving end. The main difference between message and packet switching is that in the former, data are stored by the system and then retrieved by the user at a later time (e.g., email). In the packet-switched mode, packets are fragmented and reassembled in almost real time. They are stored in the system only long enough to receive all the packets in the message. In Europe, X.25 packet-switched network was extensively used in Public-Switched Data Network (PSDN).

Network communications are commonly classified as either data communications or telecommunications. This classification is based on historical evolution. The telephone network, which came into existence first, was known as a telecommunication network. It is a circuit-switched network that is structured as a public network accessible by any user. The telephone network represents a telecommunication network. The organization that provides this service is called a telecommunication service provider (e.g., AT&T, British Telecom, NTT, BSNL, etc.).

With the advent of computers, the terminology data communication network came into vogue. It is also sometimes called computer communication network. The telecommunications infrastructure was, and is, still used for data communications. Figure 1.3 shows an early configuration of terminal-to-host and host-to-host communications, and how data and telecommunication networks interface with each

Data Communication Network

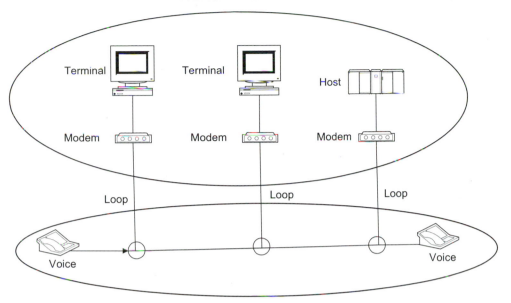

Telecommunication Network

Figure 1.3   Analog and Data Telecommunication Networks

other. To interface, a terminal or host connected to an end-office switch communicates with the host connected to another end-office switch by modems at each end. Modems transfer information from digital to analog at the source (telephone networks carried analog signals) and back to digital at the destination.

Modern telecommunication networks mostly carry digital data. The nodes in Figure 1.4 are digital switches. Analog signals from telephones are converted to digital signals either at the customer premises or the central office. Figure 1.4 shows a corporate or enterprise environment in the stage of the evolution of data and telephone communications. A number of telephones and computer terminals at various corporate sites are connected by telecommunication network. Telephones are locally interconnected to each other by a local switch, PBX, at the customer premises, which interfaces digitally to the telephone network. The computer terminals are connected to a communication controller, such as a digital multiplexer, which provides a single interface to the telephone network.

With the advent of desktop computers and LAN, data communication was revolutionized. Desktop computers could communicate with each other over the LAN. This led to a Distributed Computing Environment (DCE), which is discussed in the next section.

1.3   DISTRIBUTED COMPUTING ENVIRONMENT

Figure 1.5 shows a LAN with hosts and workstations. Let us observe that they are workstations with processing power and not just dumb terminals as described in the previous section. Any workstation can communicate with any host on the LAN. There can be a large number of workstations and hosts depending on the type of LAN. DTEs connected to different LANs that are geographically far apart can

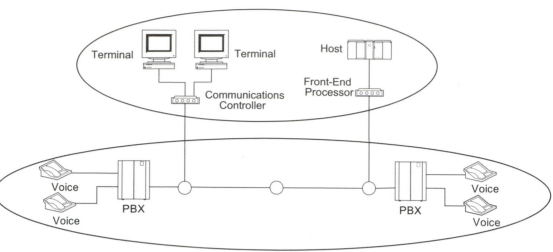

Figure 1.4 Digital Data and Telecommunication Networks

communicate via telecommunication network, either public or private switched. The system of links connecting remote LANs is called a WAN. A LAN is physically connected to a WAN by a bridge or a router as shown in Figure 1.5(b). We will discuss the types of LANs and WANs in Chapter 2. First, we want to bring out two important aspects of DCE in this section.

The first aspect is the question of whether the different platforms and applications running on DCEs have the ability to communicate with each other. In the early stage of communication network evolution, proprietary interfaces between platforms and processes were implemented by telecommunication service providers and computer vendors to communicate autonomously within each of their networks. For example, Bell System, a monopolistic telecommunication service provider, and IBM, the largest computer vendor, established transmission, switching, and interface standards and manufactured their own communications equipment to meet them. They made significant contributions to the standards bodies to make such specifications the industry standards. For customer premises equipment (CPE) interface, specifications are published for them to interface cleanly with the network. For example, Bell System published specifications for Customer Service Unit (CSU) for customer equipment to interface with the network. However, as the telecommunications industry rapidly grew, national and international standards needed to be established for communication between equipment provided by various vendors. Protocols and database standards for handshaking and information exchange are discussed in the following sections. For now, we will assume that the different processors and processes running on them could communicate with each other.

The second aspect of DCE is the ability of processors attached to LANs to do multiple functions. They could continue, as dumb terminals did, to request a host to perform the functions and return the results. Alternatively, they could request some special functions to be performed by a host—and it could be any processor in the network—and receive the results. In this scenario, the processor that requests a service is called the client; and the processor that provides the service is called the server. Such a configuration is termed a client–server environment. Although the terminology of client and server is

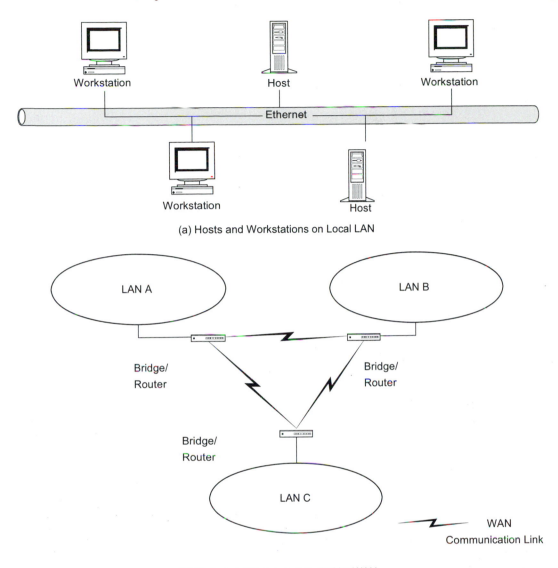

(a) Hosts and Workstations on Local LAN

(b) Remote LANs Interconnected by WAN

Figure 1.5 DCE with LANs and WANs

commonly associated with the processors, the more accurate definition should be associated with the processes. Thus, the process that initiates a transaction to run an application in either a local or a remote processor is called the client. The application process that is invoked by a client process is called the server. The server returns the results to the client. The application designed to take advantage of such a capability in a network is called a client–server architecture. With such an interpretation, the client and server processes can coexist in the same processor or in different processors.

We will now go into some detail on the salient characteristics and features of client–server architecture and models, as they are very pertinent to network management applications and architecture. A simple client–server model is shown in Figure 1.6. There is apt to be confusion between which is a client

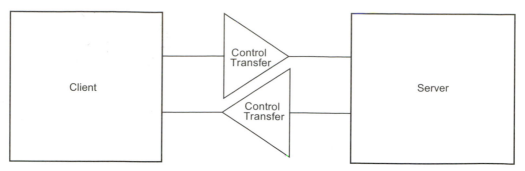

Figure 1.6 Simple Client–Server Model

and which is a server in distributed computing architecture. The best way to distinguish between the two is to remember that the client initiates the request and the server responds.

The client initiates a request to the server and waits. The server executes the process to provide the requested service and sends the results to the client. It is worth noting that the client cannot initiate a process in the server. Thus, the process should have already been started in the server and be waiting for requests to be processed.

A real-world analogy to the client–server operation is a post office. The clerk behind the counter is ready and waiting for a client. She is a server. When a customer walks in and initiates a transaction, for example, ordering stamps, the clerk responds. The customer is the client. After the clerk gives the stamps to the customer, i.e., she has delivered the results, the customer leaves and the clerk, as a server, goes into a waiting mode until the next client initiates a transaction.

As with any system, delays and breakdowns of communication need to be considered in this model. The server may be providing the service to many clients that are connected to it on a LAN, as shown in Figure 1.7(a). Each client's request is normally processed by the server according to the FIFO rule—first in first out. This delay could be minimized, but not eliminated, by concurrent processing of requests by the server. It is also possible that, due to either the communication link or some other abnormal termination, the server may never return the result to the client. The application on the client should be programmed to take care of such deficiencies in communication.

Since the client and application are processes running in a DCE, each of them can be designed to execute a specific function efficiently. Further, each function may be under the jurisdiction of different departments in an organization. An example of this is shown in Figure 1.7(b). joe.stone@source.com (Joe Stone's user id) using a client in a network sends a message to sally.jones@dest.com (Sally Jones' user id) on the network. The message first goes to the mail server on the network. Before it can process the request, the mail server needs to know the network address of sally.jones, which is dest.com. Therefore, it makes a request to the domain name server (DNS) on the network for routing information for the address of dest.com. When it receives that information, it sends out joe.stone's message via the bridge connected to the network. It then sends a message to joe.stone on the client stating that the message has been sent (or not sent because the dest.com address does not exist in the DNS). In this example, the mail server behaves both as a server and as a client. The three processes in this scenario, namely the client, the mail server, and the DNS, are considered cooperative computing processes and may be running in three separate platforms on remote LANs connected by a WAN. Communication between these processes is called peer-to-peer communication. We will soon learn how network management fits into such a model and manages components on the network that perform cooperative computing using peer-to-peer

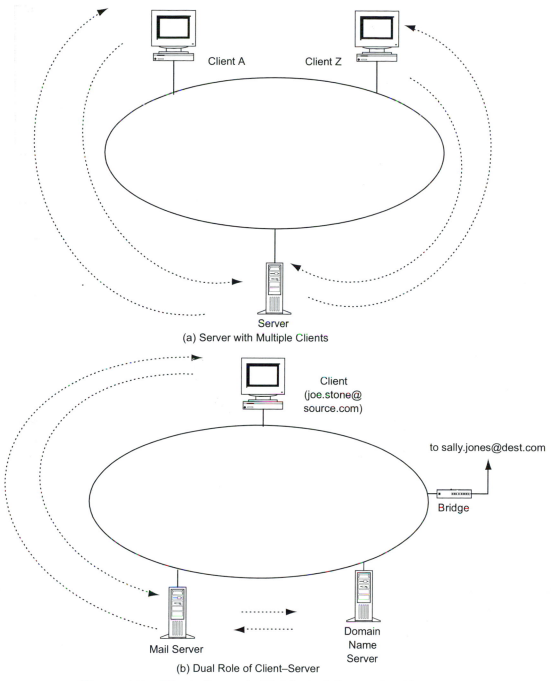

(a) Server with Multiple Clients

(b) Dual Role of Client–Server

Figure 1.7 Client–Server in Distributed Computing Environment

communication. However, before we pursue that, let us first look at a new dimension that the DCE has caused networking to mushroom into—the Internet.

1.4 TCP/IP-BASED NETWORKS: INTERNET AND INTRANET

Transmission Control Protocol/Internet Protocol (TCP/IP) is a suite of protocols that enable networks to be interconnected. It forms the basic foundation of the Internet. Architecture and protocols are discussed in detail in Section 1.5. We will briefly describe the role TCP/IP plays in Internet. Nodes in the network route packets using network protocol, IP, a connectionless protocol. That means there is no guarantee that the packet will be delivered to the destination node. However, end-to-end communication can be guaranteed by using the transport protocol, TCP. Thus, if a packet is lost by IP, the acknowledgement process of TCP ensures successful retransmission of the packet.

TCP/IP suite of protocols contains more than TCP and IP protocols. TCP is a connection-oriented protocol. A complement to TCP is User Datagram Protocol (UDP), which is a connectionless protocol. Much of Internet traffic really uses UDP/IP due to the reliability of data transmission. For example, email and management messages are carried by connectionless transmission.

The Internet is a network of networks. Just as we can communicate over the telecommunication network using the telephone from anywhere to anywhere in the world today, we can now communicate worldwide over the computer network via email. We looked at the example of Joe Stone sending a message to Sally Jones in the previous section, Figure 1.7(b). Let us expand that example and visualize that Joe Stone, who is at the College of Computing building of Georgia Institute of Technology, is sending an email to Sally Jones at her home in Australia. Sally is connected to an Internet service provider, ostrich.com. Similar to a unique telephone number that each station has in the telephone world, each person has a unique address in the computer communication network. Joe's email address is joe@cc.gatech.edu and Sally's address is sally@ostrich.com.au.

Figure 1.8 shows an Internet configuration for our scenario. Assume that Joe is at Workstation A on LAN A sending the email to Sally at Workstation Z that is "teleconnected" to her Internet service provider's email server on LAN Z. Two servers shown on LAN A are mail server and DNS. It should be noted that the servers do not have to be on the same LAN as the sender's LAN, as shown in Figure 1.8. The two servers cooperatively transmit the email message to LAN C on the computer network made up of bridges and routers. The link between LAN A and LAN C could be a WAN. Information is transported exclusively based on TCP/IP-based protocols. We will explain TCP/IP protocol in Section 1.5.2.

Information from LAN C progresses via gateways and WANs to the computer communications network in Australia, as shown in Figure 1.8. The WAN network shown is composed of a series of networks, not all necessarily using TCP/IP protocol. Gateways between them serve as the interfaces between dissimilar and independent autonomous networks and perform many functions including protocol conversions. Autonomous networks have little knowledge of each other's attributes, configurations, and addresses and yet communication is automatically taken care of by a hierarchy of Internet servers along the path.

Joe's email message finally reaches the email server on LAN Z in Australia and is stored there until Sally retrieves it via her Internet link with an Internet service provider's server. In fact, email messages are transmitted by a "store-and-forward" scheme all along the path. In addition, the final stage in the Internet link uses a TCP/IP suite of protocols.

Thus, via the Internet, any user can communicate with any other user in any part of the world as long as both are connected to a network that is part of the Internet. This has also revolutionized the software user interface providing capabilities like web pages so that you can gather information about anything in the world instantly through the Internet.

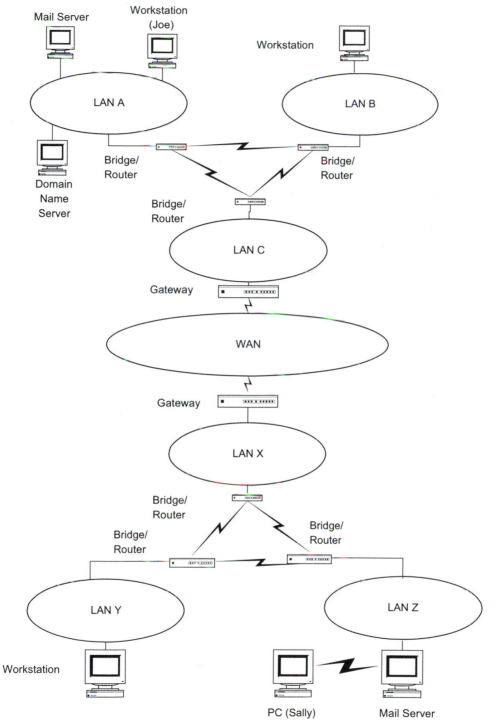

Figure 1.8 Internet Configuration

Another perspective of the Internet is to view it as a layered architecture, as shown in Figure 1.9. This architecture shows the global Internet as concentric layers of workstations, LANs, and WANs interconnected by fabrics of Medium Access Controls (MACs), switches, and gateways. Workstations belong to the user plane, LANs to the LAN plane, and WANs to the WAN plane. The interfaces are defined as the fabrics. MAC fabric interfaces the user plane to the LAN plane. LAN and WAN planes interface through switching fabric. WANs in the WAN plane interface with each other via the gateway fabric.

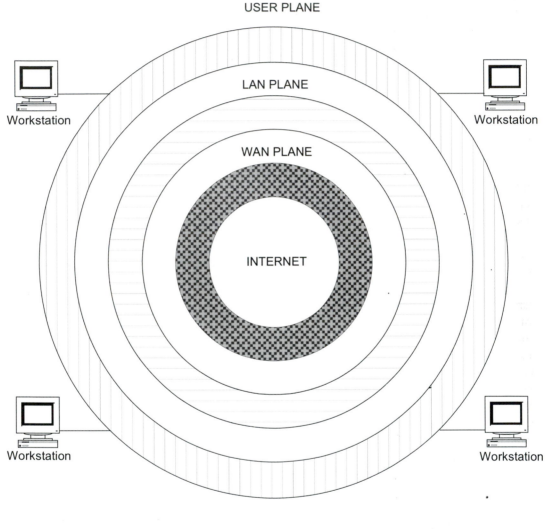

Figure 1.9 Internet Fabric Model

The user's workstation interfaces to a LAN via a MAC, which will be explained in Chapter 2. LANs interface to a WAN by a switching fabric of bridges, routers, and switches. Each WAN may be considered as an autonomous network, and hence needs a gateway to communicate with another WAN. Gateway fabric interconnects different WANs. Thus, a single Internet plane at the core of the model multiplies into millions and millions of users at the user plane, with virtually no limits in sight.

Communication between two users in the user plane, i.e., logical link connection on the user plane, takes the following path. The physical path traverses the MAC fabric, the LAN plane, the switching fabric, the WAN plane, and the gateway fabric to the core and then returns to the user plane going through all the planes and interface fabrics in reverse.

The huge success of Internet technology has spawned intranet technology. The main distinction between the two is similar to that between public and private switched networks. An intranet is a private network and access to it is controlled by the enterprise that owns it, whereas the Internet is public.

The impact of the Internet in networking is enormous. How do we manage the Internet? For example, if an email does not reach its destination, how do we detect where the communication broke down? How do we take advantage of Internet capabilities to implement network management? We have not yet defined network management and how it fits into the client–server environment. However, before we define what network management is, let us briefly look at the protocols and protocol architecture that enable successful communication between different components on the network.

1.5   COMMUNICATION PROTOCOLS AND STANDARDS

Consider a fax machine and a modem bought from a local store successfully sending a fax to a modem and fax machine anywhere in the world, even though each fax machine and attached modem were manufactured by local vendors. Likewise, isn't it a technological miracle that two computers located anywhere in the world can transmit messages to each other as long as each is connected to the Internet? The key to the practical success of these and other such technologies is the interoperability of the two end devices. More and more vendors in more and more countries have recognized that in this world of shrinking cyberspace and advancing modern communication technology, interoperability is the key to the success of their business.

Universal interoperability is achieved when all participants agree to establish common operational procedures. In communications lingo, commonality can be interpreted as standards and procedures as protocols. Let us consider the scenario of Joe sending an email from Georgia Institute of Technology (GA Tech) in Atlanta to a colleague in a Japanese Telecommunications Company (JTC) in Tokyo. Joe composes the message on his computer terminal and sends it to his colleague (yoho@jtc.com.jp). Joe's message with his user id (joe@cc.gatech.edu) and IP address (169.111.103.44) goes through several changes before it is transmitted on the physical LAN medium at GA Tech. The message goes to its College of Computing (cc)'s email server, which obtains the IP address of the destination and sends the message out on the Internet. The message traverses several nodes and links and arrives at the post office box of Yoho's mail server at JTC. She establishes a session in her computer and gets the complete message that Joe transmitted. In this scenario, Joe's message is wrapped with several layers of control information at various times and is broken down into packet units and reassembled at the destination. All these steps happen each time without any loss or error in the message due to standardization and modular (layered) architecture of data communication protocols. As we will soon learn in this section, the popularity of Internet as a peer-to-peer network has been made possible by the peer-to-peer protocol TCP/IP suite.

Architecture can be defined as modeling a system into functional components and the relationship among them. Thus, communication architecture describes the functional components of communication network as well as the operational interface between them. Operational procedures—both intra- and inter-modules—are specified in terms of protocols. Just as human communication is made mutually understandable by speaking a common language, communication protocols are standardized for service interfaces from the perspectives of both a service provider and a service user. If different vendors implement the same standards in their system components, then communication between their different components can be universal. Standardization of protocols involves agreement in the physical characteristics and operational procedures between communication equipment providing similar functions. Thus, looking at our example, all fax machines are able to communicate with each other because all vendors have implemented standards recommended by International Telecommunication Union—Telecommunications Sector (ITU-T). Similarly, email exchange across the world is possible because most vendors have adopted Internet standard Simple Mail Transport Protocol (SMTP) in their software. However, there are email software packages other than SMTP, and the user has to install a gateway in those systems to convert back and forth between SMTP and the vendor-specific proprietary protocol. For example, IBM Lotus uses cc:mail (now defunct), and any network that uses cc:mail has to implement a gateway to send an email over the Internet. Note that there are different mail protocols (SMTP, IMAP, POP, etc.), which have different procedures. We will now look at the details of communication architecture.

1.5.1 Communication Architectures

Communication between users (human beings using a system) and applications (programs that run in a system) occurs at various levels. They can communicate with each other at the application level, the highest level of communication architecture. Alternatively, they can exchange information at the lowest level, the physical medium. Each system can be broadly subdivided into two sets of communication layers. The top set of layers consists of application layers and the bottom set transport layers. The users—and users include application programs—interface with the application level layer, and the communication equipment interfaces with the physical medium. The basic communication architecture is shown in Figure 1.10. In Figure 1.10(a), the two end systems associated with the two end nodes communicate directly with each other. Direct communication occurs between the corresponding cooperating layers of each system. Thus, transport layers can exchange information with each other, and so can the application layers and the users.

This can be illustrated with a real-life example. A hearing-impaired person, accompanied by an interpreter, attended one of my classes. As I lectured, the interpreter translated to the student using sign language. If the student had a question, the interpreter translated the information from sign language, orally to the class and me. In this illustration, the hearing-impaired student and I are at the application layer. The interpreter did the protocol conversion at the application layer level. The transport layer is the aural and visual media.

Figure 1.10(b) shows the end systems communicating via an intermediate system N, which enables the use of different physical media for the two end systems. System N converts the transport layer information into the appropriate protocols. Thus, system A could be on a copper wire LAN and system Z could be on a fiber optic cable.

Various standard organizations propose, deliberate, and establish standards. One of the internationally renowned standard organizations is International Standards Organization (ISO). ISO has developed a highly modular, or layered, architecture for communication protocols that is called the Open Systems

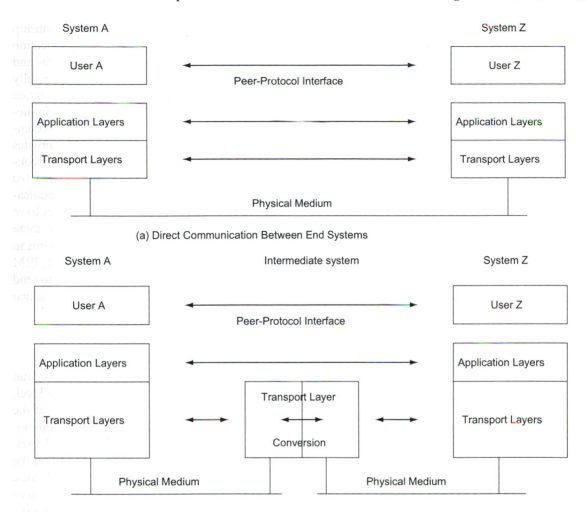

(a) Direct Communication Between End Systems

(b) Communication Between End Systems via an Intermediate System

Figure 1.10 Basic Communication Architecture

Interconnection (OSI) Reference Model, published as OSI RM—ISO 7498. This model was developed based on the premise that the different layers of protocol provide different services; and that each layer can communicate with only its own neighboring level. Two systems can communicate on a peer-to-peer level, that is, at the same level of the protocol. The OSI protocol architecture with all seven layers is shown in Figure 1.11. Table 1.1 describes the salient features of, and services provided by, each layer. Layers 1–4 are the transport system protocol layers and layers 5–7 are application support protocol layers.

OSI protocol architecture truly enables building systems with open interfaces so that networks using systems from different vendors are interoperable. Figure 1.12 expands the basic communication architecture shown in Figure 1.10 to an OSI model. Figure 1.12(a) is a direct end-to-end communication model. The corresponding layers in the two systems communicate with each other on a peer-to-peer protocol interface associated with those layers. In Figure 1.12(b), the end systems communicate with each other by going through an intermediate node/system. Again, notice that the physical media

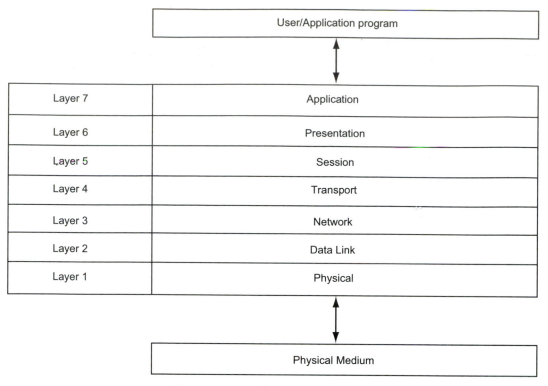

Figure 1.11 OSI Protocol Layers

connected to the end systems could be different. The intermediate system is involved only up to the first three layers in the process. Layers 4–7 are not involved in the intermediate system. This is analogous to a mail container with letters enclosed in envelopes being transported from one town to another town anywhere in the world. It does not matter what network of intermediate cities (nodes) it goes through, or what network of transportation media—surface, air, or water—it takes to get to the destination. The letter in the envelope and contents of packages are untouched at the transfer points and are only handled by the sender and the receiver, i.e., user applications.

The message in each layer is contained in message units called protocol data unit (PDU). It consists of two parts—protocol control information (PCI) and user data (UD). PCI contains header information about the layer. UD contains the data that the layer, acting as a service provider, receives from or transmits to the upper layer/service user layer. The PDU communication model between two systems A and Z, including the users at the top and the transmission medium at the bottom of the PDU layers, is shown in Figure 1.13. As you can see, the size of the PDU increases as it goes towards lower layers. If the size of the PDU exceeds the maximum size of any layer specifications, it is then fragmented into multiple packets. Thus, a single application layer PDU could multiply into several physical PDUs.

1.5.2   Protocol Layers and Services

We will now go into some detail regarding services provided by the seven layers of OSI protocols.

Table 1.1 OSI Layers and Services

LAYER NO.	LAYER NAME	SALIENT SERVICES PROVIDED BY THE LAYER
1	Physical	–Transfers to and gathers from the physical medium raw bit data
		–Handles physical and electrical interfaces to the transmission medium
2	Data link	–Consists of two sublayers: Logical link control (LLC) and Media access control (MAC)
		–LLC: Formats the data to go on the medium; performs error control and flow control
		–MAC: Controls data transfer to and from LAN; resolves conflicts with other data on LAN
3	Network	Forms the switching/routing layer of the network
4	Transport	–Multiplexing and de-multiplexing of messages from applications
		–Acts as a transparent layer to applications and thus isolates them from the transport system layers
		–Makes and breaks connections for connection-oriented communications
		–Data flow control in both directions
5	Session	–Establishes and clears sessions for applications, and thus minimizes loss of data during large data exchange
6	Presentation	–Provides a set of standard protocols so that the display would be transparent to syntax of the application
		–Data encryption and decryption
7	Application	–Provides application-specific protocols for each specific application and each specific transport protocol system

Layer 1, physical layer, is responsible for physically placing the electrical signal on the physical medium and picking up the signal from it. It controls and manages the physical and electrical interfaces to the physical medium including the connector or the transceiver. The physical medium could be copper in the form of a twisted pair or coaxial cable, optical fiber, or wireless media such as radio, microwave, or infrared. The signal could be either analog or digital. There are various protocol standards for a physical-layer interface depending on the transmission medium and the type of signal. The two classes of standards have been established by ITU-T and Electronics Industries Association (EIA).

Layer 2 is the data link control layer, or data link layer for short. Data communication between two DTEs is controlled and managed by this layer. Note that in contrast to a byte-oriented transmission across a computer bus, the data communication is a serial-bit-oriented stream. The data link layer needs to do basic functions: first establish and clear the link, and second transmit the data. Besides these, it also does error control and data compression. Flow control on data link layer is done on a hop-to-hop basis.

For point-to-point communication using a dedicated facility, like the loop link from a customer telephone to the telephone company switching office, the data link control is simple and straightforward to implement. However, if the DTE is connected to a LAN, or which is shared transmission media and is

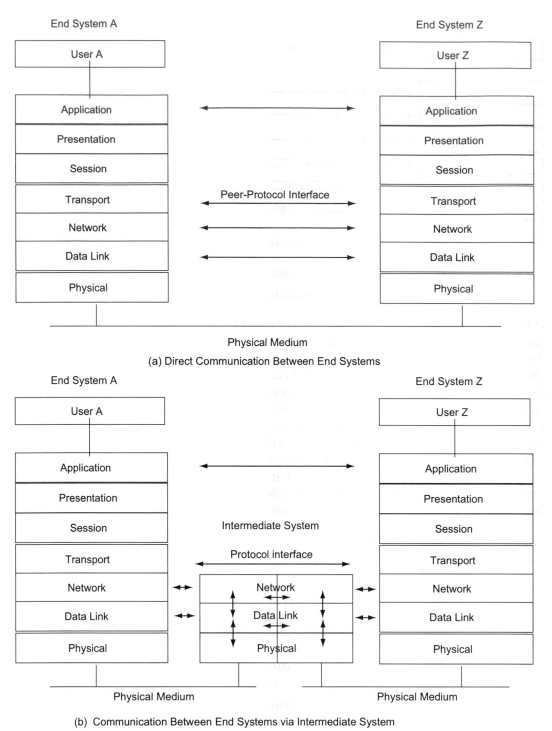

(a) Direct Communication Between End Systems

(b) Communication Between End Systems via Intermediate System

Figure 1.12   OSI Communication Architecture

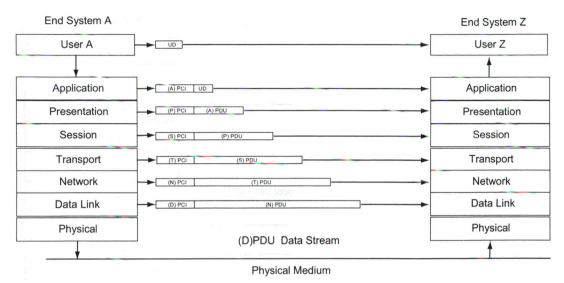

Figure 1.13 PDU Communication Model between End Systems

accessed simultaneously by many users, then the data link control becomes more complex. In the case of point-to-multipoint transmission, the head end controls the access of the medium. LAN is a distributed environment and thus access control is distributed. In an OSI-layered model, the data link layer is divided into two sublayers—logical link control (LLC) and media access control (MAC), as shown in Figure 1.14. The lower MAC layer controls the access and transmittal of data to the physical layer in an algorithmic manner. There are three basic types of LANs. Ethernet LAN is a bus type and the media is accessed using a distributed probabilistic algorithm, Carrier Sensing Multiple Access with Collision Detection (CSMA/CD). The second type of LAN is a ring type used in token ring (TR) and Fiber Distributed Data Interface (FDDI). A deterministic token-passing algorithm is used in this case. The third type of LAN is deployed in wireless medium and is referred to as wireless LAN or WLAN. The probabilistic algorithm, Carrier Sensing Multiple Access with Collision Avoidance (CSMA/CA), is used to access the medium. Random-access protocol will be covered in Chapter 2.

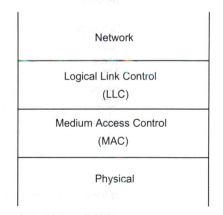

Figure 1.14 Sublayer Structure of a Data Link Protocol Layer

LLC performs link management and data transfer. Link management includes formatting the data to go on the medium, performing error control, and flow control. If there is security required, it could be included in the LLC sublayer.

The network layer is the third layer in the OSI protocol stack. It controls and manages the switching fabric of the network. It provides both connectionless network service (CLNS) and connection-oriented network service (CONS). The former is used when lower layers are highly reliable, such as LANs and bridges, as well as when messages are short. CONS is the method for transmitting long messages, such as file transfer. It is also used when the transmission medium is not reliable. It subdivides the transport PDUs into frames of appropriate size based on transmission parameters. The destination address of each packet is read in both CLNS and CONS at the network layer and routed on the appropriate link.

A router, or a routing bridge, at the nodes of a network performs the function of routing and switching data. Any subnetwork of the node is under the control of that router. The subnetwork(s) can be anything from a simple-single segment LAN to complex subnetworks operating under a proprietary protocol. OSI architectural model handles this by dividing the network layer into three sublayers as shown in Figure 1.15. The top sublayer is the Subnetwork-Independent Convergence Protocol (SNICP) layer that interfaces to the transport layer. The Internet communicates between nodes using Internet address and SNICP. The nodes in turn communicate with subnetworks using the Subnetwork-Dependent Convergence Protocol (SNDCP), which depends on the subnetwork protocol and could be any proprietary protocol. In such a situation, the SNDCP communicates with its data link layer via the third network sublayer, the Subnetwork-Dependent Access Protocol (SNDAP). This subnetwork architecture isolates transport and the above layers from the subnetwork dependencies. It also enables communication between a DTE on the Internet and a DTE on a subnetwork node, as shown in Figure 1.16. Figure 1.16(a) depicts network configuration in which DTE-A connected to end node A communicates with DTE-N1 connected to subnetwork node N1 via the intermediate system gateway node N.

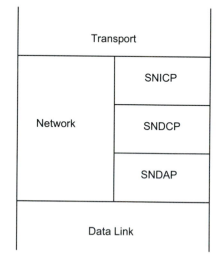

SNICP: Subnetwork-Independent Convergence Protocol

SNDCP: Subnetwork-Dependent Convergence Protocol

SNDAP: Subnetwork-Dependent Adapter Protocol

Figure 1.15 Sublayer Structure of a Network Protocol Layer

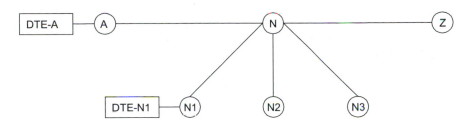

A–N–Z Standard Network

N–N1–N2–N3 Subnetwork Under Node N

(a) Network Configuration

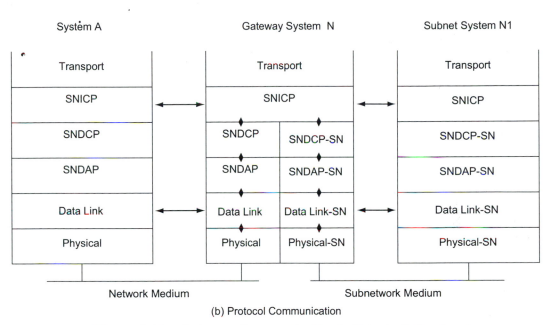

(b) Protocol Communication

Figure 1.16 Gateway Communication to Private Subnetwork

Figure 1.16(b) describes the path of communication through different protocol layers from the originating end system to the terminating end system via the intermediate node gateway. The formats of the PDUs are identical in all three systems at SNICP layer levels and above. Access networks having their own addressing scheme using Network Address Translator (NAT) or Dynamic Host Configuration protocol (DHCP) can be implemented using this scheme.

The most used network protocol is the Internet Protocol (IP) and has been popularized by the Internet. It is part of the Internet suite of the TCP/IP and is a CLNS protocol. In OSI terminology, it is called ISO-IP or ISO CLNP. A connection-oriented OSI protocol is X.25 PLP, Packet Layer Protocol.

A popular scheme of implementing private subnetwork is to establish a network with a private IP address, such as 10.x.y.z. In this instance, the gateway node, known as NAT, converts the global IP address to the local proprietary IP address, for example, LAN Z in Figure 1.8.

The transport layer is the fourth layer of the OSI protocol. It multiplexes the UD provided by application layers and passes packets to the network layer. Its service is independent of the network on which the packets are transmitted. The transport layer can again be connectionless or connection oriented and is implemented in both Internet and OSI protocols. As mentioned earlier, TCP is a component of the IP suite and is connection oriented. The connectionless transport protocol in a TCP/IP suite is called the UDP. Flow control is also implemented in transport layers and functions as data rate manager between application programs and the network layer. ISO has five transport layer specifications, TP0 to TP4. TP4 is analogous to TCP.

Layers 5–7 are application layer protocols. Except in the OSI Reference Model, the three application layers are not clearly separated and independent. Let us look at each layer as if they were independent, like in the OSI model, to understand their specific functions and services provided. An application process communicates with another application process during a session. The session layer services establish communication at the beginning of the session, monitor, synchronize, and error correct the information exchanged during the session, and then release the logical link at the end of the session. It is very strongly related to the presentation layer, which is the medium of presentation of the context of the message to the user or application program. In that sense, the presentation layer is a context-sensitive layer. It can be interpreted as the common language and image that the users at both ends of the system use and understand—shared semantics of the two end users. A common abstract syntax that is used for semantics is Abstract Syntax Notation Number One (ASN.1). Although the primary function of the presentation layer is the conversion of syntax, data encryption and data compression are also generally done in that layer.

The top and the seventh protocol layer is the application layer. The application process interfaces with the application support processes that are provided by this layer. Like the other two layers in the set of application layers (session and presentation), it is strongly coupled with the rest of the application layers. In the OSI Reference Model, one can separate these processes from the presentation and session layers, but in other models there is no clear distinction of the functions. Figure 1.17 presents a comparison of the models—OSI Reference Model and Internet model.

The Internet model does not specify the two lower layers although it is obvious that they use distributed LAN and WAN configurations. The transport and network layers form the suite of TCP/IP protocols that we mentioned earlier. Application layers are combined into application-specific protocols.

Figure 1.18 shows a comparison of four common application-specific protocols in OSI and Internet models. There are more OSI application-specific protocols, which we will not discuss here. All application-specific protocol services in OSI are sandwiched between the user and presentation layers. In the Internet model, they are sandwiched between the user and the transport layer. The boxes on the right-hand side of Figure 1.18 describe the comparable services offered in the two models. A user interfaces with a host as a remote terminal using Virtual Terminal (VT) in the OSI model and TELNET in the Internet model. File transfers are accomplished using File Transfer Access and Management (FTAM) in the OSI model and File Transfer Protocol (FTP) in the Internet. The most common used mail service function in the Internet is Simple Mail Transfer Protocol (SMTP). A similar protocol in the OSI model is the Message-Oriented Text Interchange Standard (MOTIS). Network management is accomplished using the Common Management Information Protocol (CMIP) in the OSI model and the Simple Network Management Protocol (SNMP) in the Internet. We will extensively discuss the details of SNMP in this book. CMIP is briefly discussed in Appendix for completeness. However, it is important to understand the overall picture of protocol layers and other application protocols to appreciate network management functions that are accomplished using network management protocols.

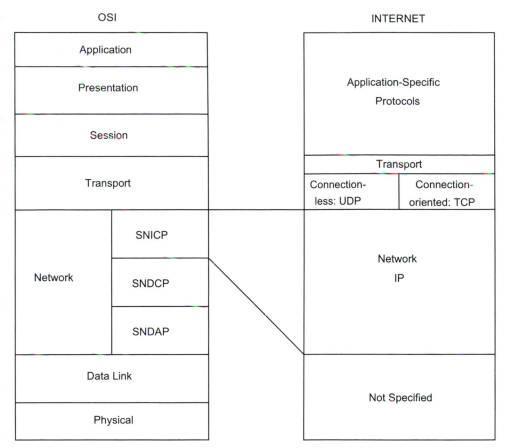

Figure 1.17 Comparison of OSI and Internet Protocol Layer Models

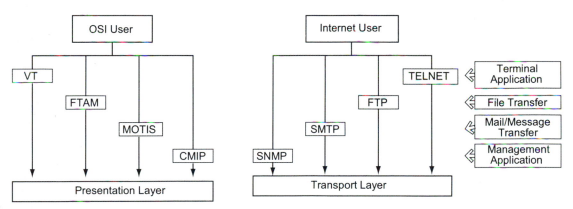

Figure 1.18 Application-Specific Protocols in OSI and Internet Models

1.6   NETWORKS, SYSTEMS, AND SERVICES

We described a network comprising nodes and links in Section 1.2. The physical embodiment of a network can be defined as a system. Thus, the nodes and links are components of a network system. Just as a network can be subdivided into subnetworks, a system comprises subsystems. A system or subsystem is made up of network elements. Network elements can be either active or passive. Thus, a router is an active network element, whereas a splitter or a combiner that divides or combines signal energy is a passive element. A link could also be an active or a passive component. In the case of an active transmission link, it can be subdivided into active nodes and passive transmission media.

Services are functions that users derive out of networks and systems. Networks and systems exist to provide service to the users. Service providers provide telecommunication services to subscribers and customers using networks and systems.

1.6.1 Broadband Networks, Systems, and Services

A broadband communication system can be defined as one that provides broadband service to homes and enterprises. The common interpretation of this definition in practice varies in different countries as well as among various service providers. In the most comprehensive definition of the term, we will define broadband communication system as one that provides voice, video, and data services over the same medium to customer premises. Broadband service comprising audio, video, and data is also known as multimedia service.

Audio service includes telephone, telephone conference, and radio broadcast. Although the end terminals could be either analog or digital devices, information is carried digitally in the context of broadband service. A system providing this service is truly a real-time information system.

Video service includes broadcast television, interactive television, video-on-demand, and video conference services. Video service could be either real-time or quasi (near) real-time service. Once again, the presentation could be on either analog or digital terminals.

Data service includes numerous applications, which can be classified into three categories: store-and-forward, audio streaming, and video streaming. Some examples of store-and-forward service are email, messaging, and Web-based applications. Audio and video broadcast and streaming services mentioned above such as MP3 and video-on-demand can in a sense be considered under this category. They are not sensitive to absolute delay time between the source and the destination, but are affected by delay variations or jitter.

Broadband services are provided using broadband networks. There are numerous types of networks to choose from depending on what segment and what type of service one needs. It is like ordering ice cream in an ice-cream parlor—cone or cup, hard or soft, size small/medium/large, choice of flavor, choice of topping, etc.

The three segments of broadband network are WAN, broadband access network, and CPE network. In broadband terminology, the CPE network is also called home network when the customer premises is a residence. Network segments and choices in various segments are shown in Figure 1.19.

The WAN and access network interface with each other via the edge router. The demarcation point between the access network and CPE network is shown as the residential gateway. Although this is the logical demarcation point, the physical demarcation point between the access network of the service provider and the customer-owned CPE, or home network, could be different. As an example in the cable network, the demarcation point is called Network Interface Unit (NIU) or Network Interface Device (NID) and is the physical termination of the cable access network outside the house. The residential gateway may or may not exist, and if it does, it is a part of CPE network.

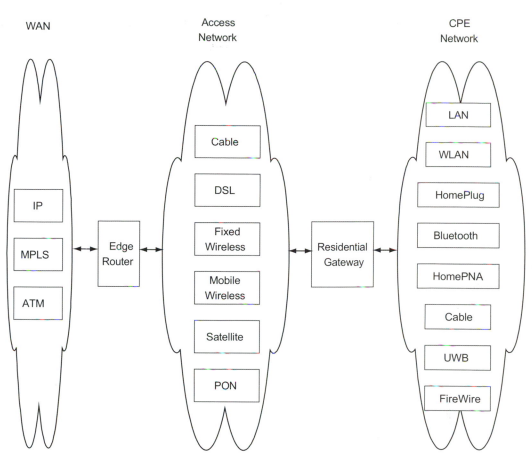

Figure 1.19 Broadband Network Segments and Technologies

1.6.2 Wide Area Networks

The four leading networks and protocols that are used in broadband WAN are Internet using Asynchronous Transfer Mode (ATM), Synchronous Optical Network (SONET), IP, and Multiprotocol Label Switching (MPLS) network.

ATM network: ATM network is ideally suited for WAN or core network. It has fast layer 2 switches that can be configured to function in parallel and thus can process high data rate cell-oriented packets. Latency can be set in ATM switches by setting priorities to the different services—real-time and non-real-time—being provided. Further, traffic performance is increased by establishing Virtual Path–Virtual Circuit (VP–VC).

Four classes of traffic have been defined in ATM network to implement quality of service. Constant bit rate (CBR), real-time variable bit rate (VBR-RT), non-real-time variable bit rate, (VBR-NRT), and available bit rate (ABR) or user bit rate (UBR). Transmission of voice is assigned CBR. An example of VBR-NRT is transmission of still images. Data traffic and store-and-forward traffic get the lowest priority, ABR.

SONET: An optical fiber medium can be used to carry multiplexed lower bandwidth signals implementing SDH. This mode of transmission is known as SONET. The optical transmission network contains regenerators, digital cross-connect elements, and add-and-drop multiplexers (ADM). Modern optical networks use dense wavelength division multiplexers (DWDM) and very high bandwidth signals can be transmitted through this optical network.

Internet: The Internet backbone WAN using IP is highly matured, has a full set of application-oriented features, and can interface with access and CPE network in a more seamless manner. However, its main drawback is that it is difficult to meet quality-of-service requirements needed for multimedia broadband service. Because of its variable packet size and packets choosing possible alternate paths between the source and the destination, the performance of routers and other transmission devices is not as efficient as in an ATM network.

Quality of service in IP-oriented WAN traffic is improved by implementing one of two different approaches. They are integrated service [RFC 2205] and differentiated service [RFC 2474]. In one form of implementation, *Intserv* packets in the Internet are classified into three classes: guaranteed, controlled or predictive, and best effort. *Intserv* reserves bandwidth from the source to the destination on a per-flow basis for a guaranteed class-of-service call or session using reservation protocol, RSVP. Once the reserved path with the necessary bandwidth is established, data are transmitted. The bandwidth is released after the call/session is completed. *Intserv* is not an efficient scheme for establishing quality of service in the backbone network as there is no guarantee that the resources will be available when needed. Further, the scheme does not scale well.

In the differentiated service, *diffserv*, packets belonging to the same class are grouped at each hop and then prioritized. There are four classes and each class has three subclasses for dropping packets—low, medium, and high. The present trend in providing quality of service for backbone is to use differentiated service complemented with some form of reservation capabilities of RSVP.

MPLS network: MPLS attempts to combine the benefits of ATM quality of service with feature benefits of the IP-based Internet. Conventional routers examine the packet headers and classify them into forwarding equivalence classes (FEC). They are then assigned the next hop. In MPLS this is done once, possibly at the ingress router, and a label is attached to it. At each router, only the label lookup is done for determining the next hop. Label lookup can also be done using a switch. A router that supports MPLS is known as a Label Switching Router (LSR). MPLS can support any network layer protocol. RFC 3031 describes MPLS architecture for an IP network layer protocol.

1.6.3   Broadband Access Networks

Figure 1.20 shows six types of broadband access networks that provide broadband service to homes, Small Office Home Office/Small and Medium Enterprise (SOHO/SME), and enterprises. The core network is IP/ATM/MPLS WAN. The link from the head end or the edge router to business customers is shown as an optical carrier-n (OC-n) link, although it could be any other transport scheme. Hybrid fiber coax (HFC) cable network and Digital Subscriber Line (DSL) network are the matured access networks. Fixed wireless is being offered as point-to-multipoint service or meshed network, WiMax, to metropolitan areas. Mobile wireless could be offered using either 3G technology or wireless LAN. The former has the limitation on data rate and the latter on range. Fiber network as Passive Optical Network (PON) is still in an embryonic stage for economic reasons.

Cable Access Network has its head end interfacing to the edge router. Analog and digital signals from various services are multiplexed at the head end and are converted from an electrical signal to optical wavelength signals. The optical signal is then carried over fiber up to an intermediate point, optical node, where it is down-converted to radio frequency and transmitted the rest of the way to the customer

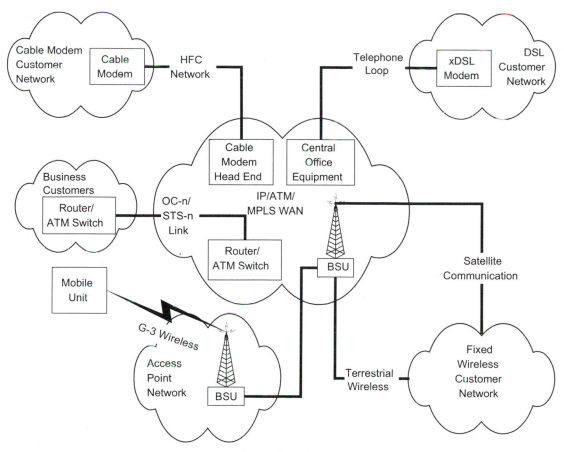

Figure 1.20   Broadband Access Networks

premises over two-way coaxial cable, hence the term hybrid fiber coax (HFC). At the customer premises, the TV analog signal is split from the digital data. The latter is demodulated to a baseband digital signal using a cable modem and is fed to the digital devices, such as computer and appliances.

Digital Subscriber Line access network uses a telephone line and can be deployed using different implementations, referred to as XDSL. Of these, Asymmetric DSL (ADSL) shown in Figure 1.20 is the most prevalent deployed all over the world. Although cable network is more commonly used in the United States by a ratio of approximately 2 to 1, the reverse is the case in the rest of the world. The technology uses the existing unshielded twisted-pair (UTP) wire that carries the **analog** voice to transmit data in addition to voice. The voice is carried as an analog signal at the low end of the frequency spectrum (0–4 kHz) and the digital data over the higher band of the spectrum. It is termed asymmetric as the downstream data rate (from the central office to customer premises) is much higher than the upstream (from customer premises to the central office) data rate. The analog voice and digital data are separated at both ends of the access network using a filter, and the digital data are modulated and demodulated at both ends using ADSL modems. At the central office, voice circuit interfaces with the central office switch and the digital data with the edge router.

Wireless Access Networks: Figure 1.20 shows three types of wireless access networks. The terrestrial wireless network, also known as fixed wireless, is a point-to-multipoint transmission. A base station with multiple antennas covers multiple sectors, each serving many subscribers. The two well-known deployed technologies are Multichannel Multipoint Distribution Service (MMDS) for rural areas and WiMax for urban areas. Satellite wireless systems are primarily used for one-way television broadcasting service. Mobile wireless has limited bandwidth and is currently used in phones such as smart phones, providing broadband service.

1.6.4   Home/CPE Networks

CPE network in enterprise environment is either an IEEE 802.3-based Ethernet LAN or IEEE 802.11-based wireless LAN, also known as WiFi, or a hybrid of both. Home network provides the opportunity to utilize multiple technologies besides Ethernet LAN and WiFi. HomePNA is implemented using twisted-pair telephone cable medium, HomePlug takes advantage of power line wiring in the house, and cable utilizes the television coaxial cable. FireWire is also a wired medium and is based on IEEE 1394 protocol to transmit high-speed digital data. Universal Serial Bus (USB) is used for low data rate peripherals. Wireless home network technologies include Bluetooth and ultra-wide band (UWB) personal area networks (PANs) for short distances.

1.6.5   Quality of Service in Broadband Systems

Quality of service could be interpreted in technical terms in many different ways. However, from the users' point of view, people are used to reliable, dependable, and good quality analog telephone and television service. They expect the same quality of service when the telecommunication and cable services are extended to broadband service that includes voice, video, and data. Networking technology has to prioritize real-time voice and video traffic over store-and-forward data traffic, and provide the end-to-end quality of service. For real-time applications of voice and video, the delay and jitter should be imperceptible. Service should be highly dependable (always available) and reliable (quality is consistent). Monitoring and managing these parameters is a challenge for network management.

1.6.6   Security and Privacy in Broadband Systems

With universal ID and multiple service providers delivering multiple services on shared media to multiple subscribers, the security and privacy of information becomes a primary concern. This is especially critical with e-business over the Internet. Besides implementing security and privacy—authentication, authorization, and encryption—of the data and management information, there has to be a cultural change in the perception of the subscribers that the information link is secure.

1.7   CASE HISTORIES ON NETWORK, SYSTEM, AND SERVICE MANAGEMENT

Network Management is more than just managing the network. In standards bodies it is referred to as Operations, Administration, Maintenance, and Provisioning (OAMP). Of course, networking and network management existed before network management became a formalized discipline. Network management and its complementary functions of system management and application management are all means to the end of service management in providing the subscriber or customer quality of service. As one IT manager commented, the configuration and use of a NMS formalizes what a network administrator would have otherwise done. The network administration "war stories" in the following subsections illustrate that network management (especially without proper tools) could present a challenge to IT managers.

1.7.1 Case History 1: Importance of Topology ("Case of the Footprint")

A stable corporate network consisting of several minicomputers and about 100 desktop workstations and personal computers suddenly started "crashing" frequently (a legacy network example). How often have we heard a network coming down without any apparent reason? Here is how one Vice President of Information Systems describes an incident.

Part of the network went down in the engineering area one morning. Since there were a whole series of users and at that time we were not using a STAR (hub) topology, but rather the old-fashioned serial topology (where all the users were daisy chained to the coax), we suspected a break in the chain, probably at a transceiver tap. Lacking sophisticated NMS tools, Information Systems personnel started walking the hallways asking the users if anyone had just been doing anything out of the ordinary, which might have broken the chain and caused the problem.

The guys came back and reported that no one had said that they had "done anything." So I (VP) started back down the halls with the guys and peeked into each office. Finally, I stopped and said "Let's look up in the ceiling here." Sure enough, we found a transceiver that someone had been fooling with and that was not properly connected, which had caused the break. Once connected, the network segment came back up.

The guys asked "Why did you say—try here?" particularly since the engineer in that office claimed ignorance. I calmly pointed to a dusty image of a sneaker footprint on the engineer's desk and the ceiling tile that was ajar above the desk and said—"you need to use all the diagnostic tools at your disposal!"

1.7.2 Case History 2: Centrally Managed Network Issues

There are numerous war stories that we can describe relating to heavy load on a NMS managing the network and network elements. We will choose one that illustrates several issues related to network design, configuration, and maintenance. An integrated network management system (INMS) was integrating alarms from multiple element management systems (EMSs) in a service provider network. Each EMS manages a domain of network elements and passes the relevant events to the INMS as shown in Figure 1.21. The service provider is able to monitor in its centrally located NOC faults occurring in its global network. As simple as this sounds, its implementation could be extremely complex. Let us consider a simple real-world situation in which a few EMSs were integrated into an INMS and the alarm occurrence time in the INMS was at variance with the individual EMSs.

Each EMS records and displays the receipt time of the alarm. The same is transmitted to the INMS. It was observed that the indication of the time at which the alarm occurred was significantly different in INMS from that indicated in the EMSs that were sending the alarms. The alarm occurrence time was considerably delayed, sometimes by hours, in INMS. The challenge in a centrally managed network is to

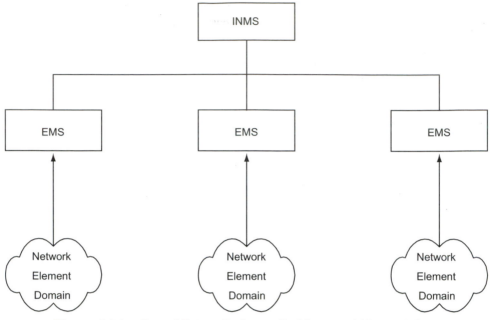

Figure 1.21   Case History 2: Centrally Managed Network Issues

find the root cause of the problem. Is it network delay? Is the delay due to excessive number of events? Is it due to input/output (I/O) limitation of the input port of the INMS? Is it due to I/O output port of EMS? Is it in the software of either EMS or INMS or both? If it is in the INMS software, should the filtering of unnecessary events at the input take care of the problem? The answers to most of these questions were affirmative for each, but to a varying degree in each case. The predominant cause is the stress on NMSs, although it can be traced sometimes to network elements in the various domains. Transmission of unnecessary alarms also causes a stress on the network and networks have gone down due to uncontrolled generations of network management messages.

1.7.3   Transaction Delays in Client–Server Network

In current national and global enterprise organizations, application servers serve thousands of clients over international networks. In a study of banking industry, transaction delays were measured and analyzed to determine the root cause of the delay as reported by tellers of branches. The propagation time of individual transactions was monitored as they traversed through the LAN networks and servers of the branches, through the WAN, and centrally processed by an application server. Some of the transactions were discovered to time-out due to long transaction delays. Study results identified the source of the problem to be gateways and applications; and appropriate actions were initiated to resolve the problem. This case illustrates the need for management of end-to-end communication and the influence of network components, applications, and client–server architecture in a network.

1.7.4   Service Impact in End-to-End Service of Customers

End-to-end communication is further illustrated by the need to proactively identify the service of the customers affected by a network element failure. This is illustrated by the following case. In an optical fiber transport network using TDM SDH network element that carries thousands of channels, the failure of a single component affects services of hundreds of customers. An end-to-end communication breakdown is to be traced to the failure of a single or multiple network elements by root cause analysis and dynamically determine all clients whose services are impacted. The service provider detects the problem even before customer complaints are received and informs the customers that the problem is already being addressed to restore service as soon as possible.

1.7.5   Some Common Network Problems

The most common and serious problems in network are connectivity failures and are handled under the category of fault management. Fault is generally interpreted as failures in accessing networks and systems by users. Network failure is caused more often by a node failure than failure of passive links (except when it is cut by construction crew). Even node failures are more often limited to specific interface failures. When this happens, all downstream systems from that interface are inaccessible. Such failures are associated with failure of the network interface card.

Node failures manifest as connectivity failures to the user. There are networking tools available to the manager to localize the fault, as we shall learn in Chapter 9 on Network Management Systems and Tools.

Another cause of network connectivity failure is procedural, but very common. Network connectivity is based on the IP address, which is a logical address assigned by the network administrator. The IP address is uniquely associated with a physical MAC address of the network component. However, mistakes are made in assigning duplicate IP addresses, especially in an enterprise environment with multiple system administrators.

A host or system interface problem in a shared medium can bring the entire segment down, sometimes intermittently, as shown in Case History 1 above. This could be a nightmare for the network manager to isolate without causing interruption in service. A network manager uses intuitive knowledge to look for patterns such as change in configuration, addition of new equipment or facility, etc. in resolving such problems.

Intermittent problems could also occur due to traffic overload causing packet loss. Sometimes the management system may indicate failures, when in actuality data traffic is flowing normally. Performance monitoring tools could be useful in tracking such problems.

Power hits could reset network component configuration, causing network failure. The network has a permanent configuration (default) and a dynamic configuration (run-time), and thus a power hit could change the configuration.

Finally, there is the non-problem, which really means that the cause of failure is a mystery. There is nothing else that a network manager could do except turn the system off and then on. Bingo! The problem is resolved.

Performance problem could also manifest as network delay and is more an annoyance to the network manager, who needs to separate network delay from the application program or application processes delay. Then the network manager has to convince the user and then the person responsible for the application to rectify the situation.

With the ever-increasing size of the network and connectivity to the Internet, security violation in network management is a frequently encountered problem. This is more a policy problem than technical, which we will address in Chapter 11 when we discuss security management.

1.8   CHALLENGES OF IT MANAGERS

Managing a corporate network is becoming harder as it becomes larger and more complex. When we talk about network management, it includes not only components that transport information in the network, but also systems that generate traffic in the network. What use is a computer network if there are no systems in the network to provide service to users? The systems could be hosts, database servers, file servers, or mail servers. In the client–server environment, network control is no longer centralized, but distributed. Computer and telecommunication networks are merging fast into converged network with common modes and media of transportation and distribution. As in the case of broadband networks, the IT manager needs to maintain both types of networks. Thus, the data communications manager functions and telecommunication manager functions have been merged to that of the IT manager. With the explosion of information storage and transfer in the modern information era, management of information is also the responsibility of the IT manager, with the title of CIO, Chief Information Officer. For example, the IT manager needs to worry in detail about who can access the information and what information they can access, i.e., authentication and authorization issues of security management. The corporate network needs to be secured for privacy and content, using firewalls and encryption. Technology is moving so fast and corporate growth is so enormous, that a CIO has to keep up with new technologies and the responsibility for financial investment that the corporation commits to. This amounts to millions of dollars, and the success or failure of making the right guess—not choice—could make or break the CIO's job. Notice that the word "guess" was used instead of "choice" deliberately because it is not always clear which of the options are a dead end, and hence need to be avoided. Since they are not obvious, the IT manager needs to make provisions for contingencies to change direction when the IT industry does.

A good example of indeterminacy in the fast-moving technology industry was competition between the two technologies of Ethernet and ATM to desktop. ATM was predicted to be the way to go a few years ago. However, this has not been the case because of the development of enhanced capability and speed of Ethernet. Another current example related to this is the decision that one has to make in the adoption and deployment of WAN—whether it should be IP, ATM, or MPLS.

Perspectives of Network Managers In order to appreciate challenges that IT managers face, several of them were interviewed by the author. They face network administration and management problems day in and day out. These are the folks who carry a cell phone with them all the time since most corporate networks run 24/7—i.e., available 24 hours a day 7 days a week! The questions that were posed, with a summary of the answers edited for the current status of IT, follow. They are not an exhaustive list of questions and answers, since that would make the contents of a separate book, but are only intended to indicate the complexity of managing a network and thus motivate a student in networking. Notice that it is not just a technical function, as Case History 1 exemplifies. Also, even use of the best NMS does not solve the problems associated with building and maintaining a network, but it is a necessary tool. Thus, learning network management involves more than understanding network and network management protocols. The author's recent in-depth study of service providers also raises similar comments.

General

- People expect a network to function like a telephone network.
- Reliability in a data network as in a telephone is unrealizable. The telephone network was monopolistic and had expensive redundancy. The data network is ad hoc, decentralized, has loosely

specified interfaces, and has dynamic routing. Thus, it is a lot more flexible than the telephone network though less reliable.

- Designing, deploying, and managing networks that can handle real-time and non-real-time data.
- Integration of multivendor and multitechnology equipment and their network management systems.

1. **What are your top challenging activities in managing the network?**

- Rapid advance of technology
- Problem analysis—needs human intuition and skill besides sophisticated management tools
- Anticipate customer demands
- Acquire and retain human resources
- Manage client–server environment in converged networks
- Networking with emerging technology necessitates the need for continuing education
- Collaborative research between academic institutions and industry
- Maintain reliability, that is, make changes, upgrades, etc. without disrupting the network and impacting business
- Diagnose problems or outages in a non-disruptive manner (without impacting other users on the network)
- Estimate the value of a technology transition. For example, should one transition over to accommodate the increasing number of IP addresses with IPv6 or continue with IPv4 with Network Address Translation (NAT) as a hierarchical addressing scheme?

2. **Which elements of managing your network require most of your time? What percentage of time do you spend on maintenance compared to growth?**

- A 30–80% growth, 20–70% maintenance based on the organization.
- Configuring the management system itself takes most of the time.
- Expanding the network.
- Gathering and analyzing statistics for upper management review to conduct business.

3. **How did you or would you manage your network without an NMS?**

- Reactively, not proactively; firefighting
- Troubleshooting tools, e.g., sniffer, ping, etc.
- Home-grown systems using an open source, e.g., Multi Router Traffic Grapher (MRTG)
- Rely on consultant advice and technical information for growth decisions

4. **Do you need an NMS? Why?**

- For proactive management of network
- Verify customer configuration
- Diagnose problems
- Provide statistics on performance
- Help remove bottlenecks
- NMS formalizes the manual practice of network management
- NMS products reflect the company's practice that develops them
- To see the trend in growth

5. **What problems would you expect the NMS to resolve, and how?**

- Enhance customer satisfaction by meeting the Service Level Agreement (SLA)
- Save time and people resource and thus enhance productivity

- Turn-around shorter for resolution of problems
- Gather statistics and predict trends for planning purposes
- Document events
- Troubleshooting
- Remove constraints and bottlenecks
- Fault isolation
- Expect the NMS to do a root cause analysis and pinpoint failures

We will now briefly introduce the subject of network management functions and system in the following sections.

1.9 NETWORK MANAGEMENT: GOALS, ORGANIZATION, AND FUNCTIONS

Network Management can be defined as Operations, Administration, Maintenance, and Provisioning (OAMP) of network and services. The Operations group is concerned with daily operations in providing network services. The network Administration is concerned with establishing and administering overall goals, policies, and procedures of network management. The Installation and Maintenance (I&M) group handles functions that include both installation and repairs of facilities and equipment. Provisioning involves network planning and circuit provisioning, traditionally handled by the Engineering or Provisioning department. We will describe each of these functions in this section. Although we continue to use the terminology of network management, in the modern enterprise environment this addresses all of IT and IT services.

1.9.1 Goal of Network Management

The goal of network management is to ensure that the users of network are provided IT services with a quality of service that they expect. Toward meeting this goal, the management should establish a policy to either formally or informally contract an SLA with users.

From a business administration point of view, network management involves strategic and tactical planning of engineering, operations, and maintenance of network and network services for current and future needs at minimum overall cost. There needs to be a well-established interaction between the various groups performing these functions.

Figure 1.22 presents a top-down view of network management functions. It comprises three major groups: (i) network and service provisioning, (ii) network and service operations, and (iii) network I&M. It is worth considering the different functions as belonging to specific administrative groups, although there are other ways of assigning responsibilities based on local organizational structure. Network provisioning is the primary responsibility of the Engineering group. The Customer Relations group deals with clients and subscribers in providing services planned and designed by the Engineering group. Network I&M is the primary responsibility of the Plant Facilities group. Interactions between the groups are shown in Figure 1.23. Normal daily operations are the function of the Network Operations group, which controls and administers a NOC. This is the nerve center of network management operations. The functions of NOC are primarily concerned with network operations; its secondary responsibilities are network provisioning and network I&M. The associated service operations are handled by a subscriber operation center (SOC) and customer relations management (CRM). Our focus here is on NOC.

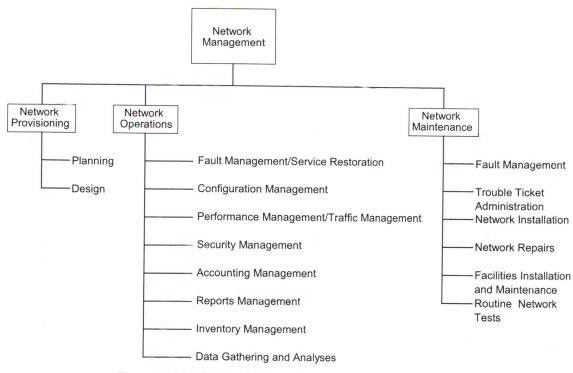

Figure 1.22 Network Management Functional Groupings

1.9.2 Network Provisioning

Network Provisioning consists of network planning and design and is the responsibility of the Engineering group. The Engineering group keeps track of new technologies and introduces them as needed. What is needed and when it is needed are determined from analysis of traffic and performance data provided by the network operations. New or modifications to network provisioning may also be initiated by management decisions. Planning and efficient use of equipment can be achieved with good inventory management of current and future modifications of network configuration by the Network Provisioning group.

Network management tools are helpful to the Engineering group in gathering statistics and studying trends in traffic patterns for planning purposes. Automated operations systems help in the design of circuits and measuring the performance tune-up.

1.9.3 Network Operations and NOC

The functions of network operations listed in Figure 1.22 are administered by the NOC. They are concerned with daily operations of the network and providing network services. ISO has defined five OSI network management applications, which are fault, configuration, performance, security, and account management. They are also responsible for gathering statistics and generating reports for management, system support, and users. NMS and tools are a necessity for NOC operations. They are used in various management applications described below.

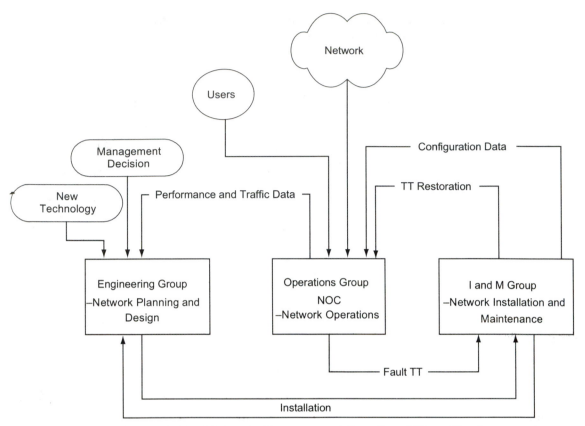

Figure 1.23 Network Management Functional Flow Chart

Fault Management/Service Restoration: Whenever there is a service failure, it is NOC's responsibility to restore service as soon as possible. This involves detection and isolation of the problem causing the failure, and restoration of service. In several failure situations, the network will do this automatically. This network feature is called self-healing. In other situations, NMS can detect failure of components and indicate with appropriate alarms. Restoration of service does not include fixing the cause of the problem. That responsibility usually rests with the I&M group. A trouble ticket is generated and followed up for resolution of the problem by the I&M group.

Trouble Ticket Administration: Trouble ticket administration is the administrative part of fault management and is used to track problems in the network. All problems, including non-problems, are to be tracked until resolved. Periodic analysis of the data, which are maintained in a database, is done to establish patterns of the problems for follow-up action. There are trouble-tracking systems to automate the tracking of troubles from the automatic generation of a trouble ticket by an NMS to the resolution of the problem.

Configuration Management: There are three sets of configuration of the network. One is the static configuration and is the permanent configuration of the network. However, it is likely that the current running configuration, which is the second, could be different from that of the permanent configuration.

Static configuration is one that the network would bring up if it is started from an idle status. The third configuration is the planned configuration of the future when the configuration data will change as the network is changed. This information is useful for planning and inventory management. The configuration data are automatically gathered as much as possible and are stored by NMSs. NOC has a display that reflects the dynamic configuration of the network and its status.

The status of the network is displayed by a NMS and indicates any failure of components of the network, as well as the traffic pattern and performance. Any configuration changes needed to relieve temporary congestion in traffic are made by NOC and are reflected in the dynamic display at NOC.

Performance Management: Data need to be gathered by NOC and kept updated in a timely fashion in order to perform some of the above functions, as well as tune the network for optimum performance. This is part of performance management. Network statistics include data on traffic, network availability, and network delay. Traffic data can be captured based on volume of traffic in various segments of the network. They can also be obtained based on different applications such as Web traffic, email, and network news, or based on transport protocols at various layers such as TCP, UDP, IP, IPX, Ethernet, TR, FDDI, etc. Traffic statistics are helpful in detecting trends and planning future needs. Performance data on availability and delay are useful for tuning the network to increase the reliability and to improve its response time.

Security Management can cover a very broad range of security. It involves physically securing the network, as well as access to the network by users. Access privilege to application software is not the responsibility of NOC unless the application is either owned or maintained by NOC. A security database is established and maintained by NOC for access to the network and network information. There are other aspects of security management such as firewalls and cryptography, which will be introduced later in Chapter 11.

Accounting Management administers cost allocation of the usage of network. Metrics are established to measure the usage of resources and services provided.

Since the network consists of components manufactured by multiple vendors, commonality in the definition and relationship of component attributes is needed. This is defined by Management Information Base (MIB), which we will discuss in Part II. Some of the data acquisition has to be manual (because of legacy systems), but most data can and should be acquired in an automated mode. The SNMP is the most popular protocol to acquire data automatically using protocol- and performance-analyzing tools.

As part of implementing the above standards, we need to ensure that adequate reports are generated and distributed to relevant personnel. There are, in general, three classes of reports: systems, management, and user. System reports are needed for network operations to track activities. Management reports go to the managers of network management group to keep them informed about the activities and performance of NOC and the network. User reports are distributed to users on a periodic basis or are available on-line to let them know the status of network performance.

1.9.4 Network Installation and Maintenance

The Network I&M group takes care of all activities of installation and maintenance of equipment and transmission facilities. This group is the service arm of the Engineering group for installation and fixing troubles for network operations. The group works closely with the Help Desk in responding to the problems reported from the field.

Having introduced what network management is from an operations, administration, maintenance, and planning viewpoint, let us next consider the architecture and organization of an NMS.

1.10   NETWORK MANAGEMENT ARCHITECTURE AND ORGANIZATION

We need to distinguish at the outset the difference between network management and network system and service management. Remember that a user may not make that distinction when he or she cannot access an application on a server from a client application in his or her workstation. This could be either due to a problem in the application program in the server affecting one or more clients or due to a transport problem from the client workstation to the server platform. The former is a network system problem affecting the service offered and falls under the category of network system and service management. The latter is a connectivity problem and falls under network management. We can generalize system and service management as the management of systems and system resources in the network and services offered by the network. Network management is concerned with network resources such as hubs, switches, bridges, routers, and gateways, and the connectivity among them via a network. It also addresses end-to-end connectivity between any two processors (not application processes) in the network.

As we saw in Section 1.1, a network consists of network components and their interconnection. Each vendor, who manufactures a network component or a set of network components, is best qualified to develop an NMS to manage that product or set of products. This involves getting data from each instance of that component in the network to one or more centralized locations and displaying their status on an NMS; for example, failure of a bridge. This would set up an alarm in the NMS to alert operations personnel of the failure. This would enable operations personnel to follow up on the problem and restore service, even before the user calls in a complaint.

As mentioned above, each type of component is managed most efficiently by its respective management system. There is need for an NMS to manage all the components that are connected to a network. Again, it is relatively simple for a vendor to develop an NMS to manage a network comprising only their components. However, a user, such as a global corporation, buys components from many different vendors, and the information systems manager of the corporation has the responsibility of maintaining the network of all vendor components. This might require the installation of multiple NMSs for an enterprise or an NMS that can manage multiple vendor components of a network. Thus, common management system, as well as the integration of different management systems and the interoperability between them, has played a major role in the network management arena. Standards organizations and industrial communities have established standards for this purpose, which are still evolving. The two major management standards are the Internet developed by the Internet Engineering Task Force (IETF) and OSI developed by the ISO. We will look at the former in detail in this book. There are also standards that are developed by industrial consortiums associated with specific technologies, such as DSL Forum and CableLabs.

Network management dumbbell architecture for interoperability is shown in Figure 1.24(a) where two vendor systems A and B exchange common management messages. The messages consist of management information data (type, id, and status of managed objects, etc.) and management controls

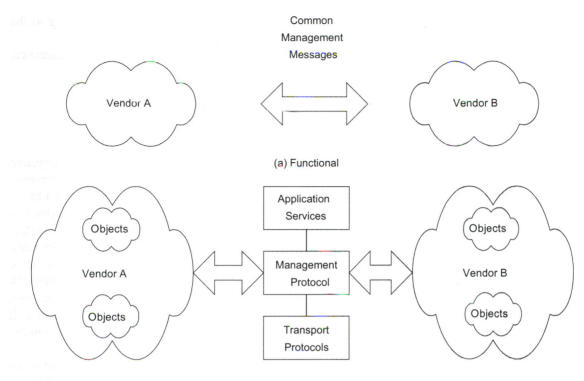

(a) Functional

(b) Services and Protocols

Figure 1.24 Network Management Dumbbell Architecture

(setting and changing configuration of an object). The protocols and services associated with dumb bell architecture are presented in Figure 1.24(b). Application services are the management-related applications such as fault and configuration management. Management protocols are CMIP for the OSI model and SNMP for the Internet model. Transport protocols are the first four OSI layers for the OSI model and TCP/IP over any of the first two layers for the Internet model.

Figure 1.25 models a hierarchical configuration of two network agents monitoring two sets of managed objects. The agent could be an embedded agent in a network element or an EMS communicating with agents embedded in the network elements. An NMS is at the top of the hierarchy. Each network agent monitors its respective objects. Either in response to a polled query from the NMS or triggered by a local alarm, the agent communicates to the NMS the relevant data.

Peer networks can communicate network management messages and controls between each other, as shown in Figure 1.26. An example where such a configuration could be implemented would be two NMSs associated with two telecommunication networks belonging to two network service providers; for example, an interexchange carrier and a local access provider. As the two NMSs communicate with each other, each NMS can superimpose the data from the other and present an integrated picture to the network administrator.

We want to make one final note before we leave this section. Some of the issues associated with the management of telecommunication network by the telecommunication service providers are unique and involve more than just management of networks. This has given birth to the Telecommunication Management Network (TMN) framework and related standards. We will address these in Chapter 10.

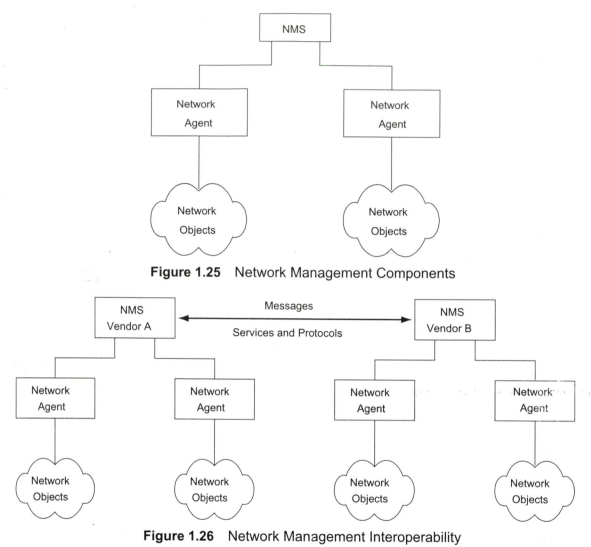

Figure 1.25 Network Management Components

Figure 1.26 Network Management Interoperability

1.11 NETWORK MANAGEMENT PERSPECTIVES

As we said earlier, the NMS primarily manages the networks that transport information. However, from a user's perspective, networks are means to an end, namely to have access to information across the networks. Thus, the users' needs require a total solution to manage the networks, system resources, and applications that run on systems. Applications could be specific user applications, or general-purpose servers such as file servers, database servers, and DNSs. Software products have since been developed to address such system-wide solutions.

An IT manager is interested in more than managing networks, systems, and applications. He or she would like to automate other functions such as back up of databases and programs, downloading of software updates from a central location, and a host of other support functions. These are required to run an IT operation efficiently and in a cost-effective manner.

Another area of system management is logging and archiving of events. This is illustrated by a case history when the system performance during normally slow activity time at night was poor. Further probing the system resources indicated that the system was busy with processes being executed from outside the institution. The system had been "compromised," i.e., had been broken into. The intruder could manipulate the normal system resource tools so as to hide the intruder programs. The intruder was finally discovered from the archival system log.

Solutions to the total IT services are currently being offered by commercial vendors. We will discuss them along with network and system management tools and systems in Part III of the book. We will present here a high-level view of some of the alternate perspectives of the broad aspects of network management.

1.11.1 Network Management Perspective

Domains: The network management overview given so far in the chapter can be perceived as management of a domain. The domain can be any of a selected group of parameters having common attributes. Thus, a geographical domain refers to the subdivisions of a large geographical region. For example, in India the telecommunication administration is divided into circles, and each circle maintains its own telecommunication network.

Another classification of a domain can be based on vendor products. Thus, we could have different vendors' management systems managing their respective products. A third perspective of looking at domains can be from the technology perspective. For example, IP-based products, telecommunication products, broadband communication products, and digital transport products such as SDH could each define a domain managed by a separate NMS, as well as a different administrative group.

Protocols: Network management can be perceived from the protocol used to manage the network such as Internet-based SNMP and OSI-based Common Management Information Protocol/Common Management Information Service Element (CMIP/CMISE). Traffic use of various protocols at each protocol layer can be monitored.

Network and Transmission Technologies: An end-to-end network system could be viewed as comprising multiple network technologies traversing different transmission media and carrying information in different transmission modes, each managed from a different network management perspective. Thus, an end-to-end communication, which can be represented as a logical circuit, could be made up of network elements comprising IP-based routers and ATM-based switches. It can traverse globally through coaxial cable in an access network, wireless transmission over continents, fiber optic cable over land on a WAN and twisted copper wire at home. The transmission mode could be digital TDM, or ATM, or a broadband access mode. An integrated NMS is used to manage end-to-end availability of a circuit that deploys multivendor and multitechnology network elements.

1.11.2 Service Management Perspective

The network is used to provide service to customers and consequently what needs to be managed are the services. The real concern of service providers is more about service management. Providing quality of service to satisfy the customers' needs requires network management. However, while network management focuses on the physical network, service management focuses on services offered over the network and those services meeting customer needs and satisfaction. Various quality of service (QoS) parameters are defined and an SLA is reached between the service provider and the customer. There are several OSSs that provide different types of service management.

Communication services can be offered as public switched network services, Internet services, virtual private network, real-time interactive audio and video services, and others too numerous to list. Computing services are offered to clients using applications running on servers. These servers and applications running on them need to be managed centrally by the service provider or enterprise that owns them. This management is also known as enterprise management. It monitors the health of system resources, as well as the applications that run on them. There are managed service offerings available to manage multiple enterprise networks from a common management facility.

1.11.3   OSS Perspective

While the EMS, NMS, and enterprise management system are designed to manage the network and network resources, OSSs support the operation of network and service management systems. In Section 1.9 we described the supporting functions of networking needed to provide communication services as operations, administration, maintenance, and provisioning (OAMP).

Provisioning System: The logical and physical network has to be provisioned to provide the desired service to the customer. An OSS, provisioning management system, does this function using several other OSSs such as the inventory management system, the service order system, and the element and NMSs. Provisioning management includes circuit provisioning, service provisioning, and network provisioning.

Inventory Management System includes inventory of equipment and facilities. We can generalize equipment as active components forming nodes of a network and facilities as passive components linking the nodes.

Customer Relations Management (CRM) operation support system manages complaints reported by the customers. A proactive approach to CRM is the service provider calling the customer on detecting a service outage indicated by NMS.

Trouble Ticket and Work Force Management manages the troubles detected by the NMS and generates work **order** in the Work Force Management System. Various OSSs help with the remote testing, either on-demand or automated, in installation and maintenance.

IP Telecommunication Application Management: The traditional analog services of voice and video are now offered as digital services. Such services as voice-over-IP and video-over-IP applications require not only management of data, but also connection management. Sessions that are equivalent to a circuit need to be established and managed.

1.11.4   e-Business Management

The e-business management and privacy requirements are associated with e-commerce applications. This includes application management in Internet retail activities, as well as banking automated teller machines.

1.12   NMS PLATFORM

NMSs and tools are available in various platforms—hardware and operating system. Popular high-end systems are housed on UNIX-based servers. Low-end NMSs run either on Windows or Linux-based platforms.

Most high-end NMSs are equipped with remote client capability and can be accessed either via Java client or Web browser. Client platforms are either Windows or UNIX based.

Common troubleshooting and monitoring of network element parameters could be done by using simple networking and network management tools. These are part of TCP/IP stack. For example, network connectivity could be tested using *ping* and *traceroute* commands in UNIX and *tracert* in Microsoft Windows. We will discuss NMSs and tools in detail in Chapter 9.

1.13   CURRENT STATUS AND FUTURE OF NETWORK MANAGEMENT

Current NMSs are based on SNMP protocol. Most commercial network components have embedded SNMP agents. Because of the universality of the IP, transport of management information for SNMP management, which is TCP/IP-based, is automatically resolved. In addition, most of the popular host-operating systems come with TCP/IP protocol suite and thus are amenable to SNMP management.

Current NMSs, however, suffer from several limitations. One of the limitations of SNMP-based management system is that values of managed objects should be defined as scalar values. OSI-based management protocol, CMIP, is object oriented. However, it has not been successful due to the complexity of specifications of managed objects and the limitation of large memory in computer systems in the past. Another limitation of SNMP-based management is that it is a poll-based system. In other words, NMS polls each agent as to its status, or for any other data that it needs for network management. Only a small set of transactions is initiated by a management agent to an NMS as alarms. To detect a fault quickly, or to obtain good statistics, more frequent polling of agents needs to be done by the NMS, which adds to network traffic overhead. There is an alternative solution to this problem, which is deployment of remote monitors as discussed in Chapter 8.

Some of the above constraints in SNMP-based management have been overcome by emerging advanced network management discussed in Chapter 16. Object-oriented technology has reached a matured stage, and the hardware capacity to handle object-oriented stacks is now commercially available. Thus, object-oriented network management is being reconsidered. This has potential application in Telecommunications Management Network discussed in Chapter 10. Network management systems are currently built with object-oriented protocols and schema, such as Common Object Request Broker Architecture (CORBA) protocol and Extended Markup Language (XML) schema.

An active network, which is the direction of next generation network, would include embedded network management applications. Besides the advancement of research and development in network management in standards, protocols, methodology, and new technology, there is considerable activity in management applications, which form the topic of Chapter 11. Of particular significance are event correlation technology in fault management, and secured network and communication in security management.

With the proliferation of the Internet, secured network and communication has become extremely important. Existing management standards do not go far enough in this. However, security management has taken on the role of a special topic in network management. Topics of high interest in this field are firewalls that establish secure networks and cryptography that assure secure communication.

IT itself is exploding and gives rise to new challenges for expanding the horizon of network management. Transport of voice, video, and data is integrated in broadband multimedia services. Broadband multimedia service is based on ATM, IP, and MPLS in a WAN and several emerging access technologies such as HFC, Asymmetric Digital Subscriber Loop (ADSL), and fixed and mobile wireless. Quality of Service in integrated services is important. Managing these new service offerings forms the content of Part IV.

Another re-emerging technology for network management is the wireless technology. This is being widely deployed for WAN, mobile, broadband access, and home networks. Much work on standardization of management of this technology needs to be done in this area.

Summary

We presented in this chapter an overview of data and telecommunication networks, as well as converged networks and how these networks are managed. The telephone network was shown as a model to be followed in accomplishing a reliable, dependable, and quality data communication network. We explained the difference between data communication and telecommunication networks, although this distinction is fast disappearing. Desktop processors and LAN technology have contributed to the client–server distributed computing environment, which has changed the future direction of data communication.

We briefly talked about the Internet and intranet in today's environment. Adoption of standards has played a significant part in the popularity of the Internet. OSI and IPs play an important part in data communication today. We also treated difficulties associated with real-time and non-real-time management of different segments of broadband networks and services. We have presented some practical day-to-day experiences of network managers, including "war stories" to make us realize the importance of network management.

We saw a bird's-eye view of network management and described how network components and networks are managed by network management systems. We extended the concept of network management to managing networks and systems and all of IT services. The future direction of IT management is undergoing changes due to advancements in software and IT. Possible future directions in network management technology were addressed at the end of the chapter.

Exercises

Note for Problems 1–4: It is important that a network administrator be familiar with both the protocols employed in the network and the tools with which its operation may be investigated. There are several tools that are fundamental for administration of an IP network; the after used ones are *ping*, *nslookup*, and *traceroute*. These commands should be available on UNIX platforms. You may get the syntax of their usage by logging into a UNIX system and accessing the on-line manual by invoking the command *man commandname*. Similar tools or commands are available in Windows 95/NT machines (*ping*, *tracert*, *nslookup* either built in or external software) connected to the Internet. Problems 1–7 are intended to familiarize you with exploring a network. You should be able to do these exercises using the commonly available networking tools and on the Internet using websites such as whois.domaintools.com and iternic.net.

In doing these exercises, if you have a problem reaching the destination host, you may use any other equivalent destination site. It is important for you to learn to use tools and interpret results.

1. Who is the primary Internet service provider (ISP) in your institution? Find another institution served by the same ISP by using a traceroute tool.

2. Educational institutions in your state or province are networked. Discover that network by tracing the route from your institute or organization to other institutes or organizations.

3. Draw the route diagram identifying each node for the following data obtained using a trace routing tool. What is the average time a packet takes to travel from noc2 host to *netman* host?

   noc2% traceroute netman.cc.gatech.edu

   traceroute to netman.cc.gatech.edu (130.207.8.31), 30 hops max, 40 byte packets

   main-rtr.gcatt.gatech.edu (199.77.147.1) 1.045 ms 1.012 ms 0.971 ms.

   130.207.251.2 (130.207.251.2) 2.198 ms 1.404 ms 1.837 ms.

   netman.cc.gatech.edu (130.207.8.31) 3.528 ms 1.671 ms 1.602 ms.

4. Between which two hosts on the route between your site and www.president.lv is the largest geographic distance probably traversed? Support your answer with evidence.

5. Ping ns1.bangla.net in this exercise. State what data you gathered and how it determined your conclusion.

   (a) Measure the percent packet loss between a host at your site and the machine ns1.bangla. net, and record the time of your measurement.

   (b) Then determine where along the route to ns1.bangla.net the packets are getting lost.

6. For each host on the route between your location and ns1.bangla.net (or any other foreign country), determine the name of the administrative contact responsible for it (use *whois* command from your UNIX system or from internic.net). List these names alongside the hosts. If you can't find an administrative contact for some of the hosts, then at least state what you did find.

7. You can discover the hosts in your subnetwork by using the ping command with your network IP address and host address of decimal 255. Discover all the hosts in the subnetwork that you are logged on.

8. In Problem 5, identify the gateway from your subnetwork to others.

9. Identify the hosts in the neighboring subnetworks and draw the configuration of interconnected subnetworks.

10. The email system is based on client–server architecture. Send an email to a wrong node address (for example, misspelling the remote node address). Explain the error message(s) that you get and the servers that you get them from.

11. Send an email to a remote site with a wrong user id, but correct node address. Explain the error message(s) that you get and the servers that you get them from.

12. Explain the decimal notation in representing the classes of IPv4 addresses. Give an example for each class.

13. You are given a class B IP address of 145.45.x.y for your network node. As a network engineer, you are asked to configure your network for 126 subnets. (Remember that 0 and 1 are reserved.)

    (a) How would you configure your address for subnets and hosts?

    (b) What is the maximum number of hosts that each subnet can accommodate?

14. An IP network is connected to a Novell IPX network via a gateway as shown. Draw the protocol layers of the gateway in Figure 1.27.

15. MBI Corporation uses cc:mail, which is not Internet standard. The company also uses Novell LAN. Novell has Internet Exchange Protocol, IPX (connectionless datagram service), as its equivalent to Internet TCP/IP. As you know well, most of the global email traffic is on the Internet with SMTP as the mail protocol. Figure 1.28 shows the high-level configuration of the two networks connected through a gateway. Fill in the protocol layers of the gateway.

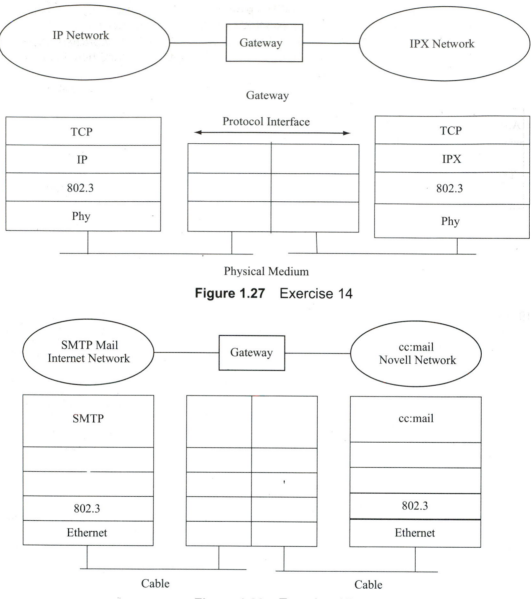

Figure 1.27 Exercise 14

Figure 1.28 Exercise 15

16. Picture a scenario where you are downloading a file from a server, located in Europe, which has an X.25 protocol based on the OSI Reference Model. Its physical medium interface is X.21. Your client machine is connected to the Internet with Ethernet as the physical medium.

(a) Draw the details of the communications network in Figure 1.29(a) using bridges, routers, and a gateway between the server and the client.

(b) Complete the protocol architecture in Figure 1.29(b) for the intermediate gateway system.

17. In Case History 2 described in Section 1.7.2, the delay in alarm indication in INMS was attributed to several possible causes. Give an example for each of these causes.

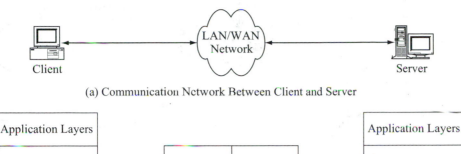

(a) Communication Network Between Client and Server

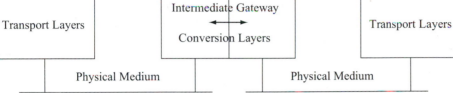

(b) Communication Between End Systems via an Intermediate System

Figure 1.29 Exercise 16

18. As a network engineer in a Network Operations Center, you are following up on two trouble tickets. You do not have a network management system and you have to use the basic network tools to validate the problem before you can resolve them. Please explain what tools you would use in each case and how it would validate the customer complaint

(a) Trouble Ticket 100: Customer says that when he receives messages, the message is periodically missing some characters.

(b) Trouble Ticket 101: Customer in Atlanta complains that when she tries to log into the system *server.headquarters.com* in New York, she gets disconnected with a time-out. However, her colleague in her New York office reports that he is able to access the system.

Review of Information Network and Technology

OBJECTIVES

- Network components and technologies to be managed:
  - Network topologies: LAN and WAN
  - Wired LAN topology: Bus, Ring, Star, and Hybrid Hub
  - Wireless LAN
  - WAN topology: Mesh and Tree
  - Fixed and mobile wireless networks
  - Fiber networks
- Ethernet LAN:
  - Physical media and MAC protocol
  - 10 and 100 Mbps; 1 and 10 Gbps Ethernet LAN
  - Switched and Duplex Ethernet LANs
- Virtual LAN
- Token-Ring LAN
- FDDI
- Network components:
  - Bridges
  - Routers
  - Gateways
- Circuit switching and packet switching
- Transmission technology:
  - Transmission media: Wired and wireless
  - Transmission modes
  - Multiplexing: TDM and WDM
  - SONET and SDH
- Multimedia networks and services

In Chapter 1 we learned that a network comprises nodes and links. Nodes are switches, bridges, routers, or gateways. Links comprise Local Area Networks (LANs), Wide Area Networks (WANs), Access Networks, or Customer Premises Equipment (CPE)/Home Networks. In this chapter we will review these components from the perspectives of concept, technology, and management. We will limit our review here to Internet-based components and some of the telecommunication components. Components associated with broadband-specific networks will be covered in detail when we address them in later chapters.

Section 2.1 presents various network topologies of LANs and WANs. In Section 2.2 we start with basic Ethernet and then traverse the development of Ethernet, Fast Ethernet, Gigabit Ethernet, and switched Ethernet. Token Ring was the most commonly used LAN in the IBM mainframe environment. Fiber-optic technology uses Token-Ring architecture to develop Fiber Distributed Data Interface (FDDI). Flexibility of LAN facilities has been significantly increased by the development of virtual LANs (VLANs). Wireless LAN (WLAN) has become an important component of the modern network.

Network node components form the contents of Section 2.3. We start by describing the implementation of LAN as a discrete component, a hub. LANs are interconnected by bridges. A bridged network is made up of remote bridges in a tree topology. LANs can also be connected in a mesh WAN topology using routers as nodal components. Autonomous WANs with diverse networking protocols are interconnected with gateways that do protocol conversion at network layers and above. Half-bridge/half-router configuration is used for Internet point-to-point communication link. The discussion of Section 2.3 ends with a switching component and the part it plays in WAN topology. Wide area network is briefly discussed in Section 2.4. It is the telecommunication network that computer (or data) communication traverses a long distance.

Section 2.5 addresses transmission technology. It comprises wired and wireless technology that transports information over LANs and WANs. The mode of transmission may be either analog or digital; and a message may be transmitted in either mode, or part of the way in analog mode and the rest in digital. This becomes especially true in broadband multimedia services where data, voice, and video are integrated into a common service, Integrated Services Digital Network (ISDN). Broadband network made up of hybrid technologies is introduced in Section 2.6 for completeness and is discussed in detail in Part IV.

2.1 NETWORK TOPOLOGY

A LAN is a shared medium serving many Digital/Data Terminal Equipments (DTEs) located in close proximity, such as in a building. LANs could also be deployed in a campus environment connecting many buildings.

Three topologies are associated with LANs: bus, ring, and star topology. There exists a fourth pseudo-topology that combines a star topology with either of the other two and is known as a hub. A hub plays an important role in networking as we will soon learn.

LAN topology depicts the configuration of how DTEs are interconnected. Different protocols are used in different topological configurations. Bus architecture is implemented in LANs using Ethernet protocol. Token Ring and FDDI configurations use the ring topology. FDDI can cover a much larger geographical area than Token Ring on copper. Fiber ring topology has been extended to Synchronous Optical Network (SONET) and Resilient Packet Ring (RPR). SONET and RPR can be considered geographical extensions of LAN to WAN, also known as Metropolitan Area Network (MAN), and use different protocols. A star topology is used in cabling infrastructure and is ideally suited for hub implementation, or for WLAN using an access point (AP).

WANs are configured using either the mesh or the tree topology. The mesh topology is the most common form for Internet routing. The tree topology is employed in network using brouters, which are bridged routers that do the routing function at OSI layer 2. It is also known as spanning-tree configuration.

The three LAN topologies and hub configuration are shown in Figure 2.1. In the bus topology, Figure 2.1(a), all DTEs are on a shared bus and have equal access to the LAN. However, only one DTE can have control at any one time. A randomization algorithm determines which DTE has control of the LAN at any given time. This topology is used in Ethernet LAN. Because collisions occur when more

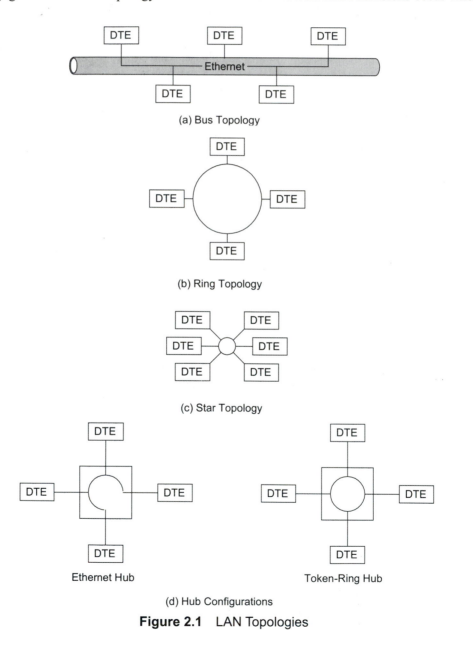

(a) Bus Topology

(b) Ring Topology

(c) Star Topology

Ethernet Hub

Token-Ring Hub

(d) Hub Configurations

Figure 2.1   LAN Topologies

than one station tries to seize the LAN at or about the same time, the bus LAN usually functions at much less than full efficiency. Ethernet protocol is specified by IEEE 802.3 standard.

Figure 2.1(b) shows the ring topology and was most popularized by IBM's Token-Ring LAN. In this topology, each active DTE connected to the ring takes turns in sending information to another DTE in the ring, which may be either a receiving host or a gateway to an external network. At the time a DTE communicates over the ring, it is in control of the ring and control is managed by a token-passing system. The DTE holds on to the token while it is sending data and releases it to its downstream neighbor (round-robin) after its turn is finished. Thus, the process in this topology is deterministic and LAN operates at almost full bandwidth efficiency. IEEE 802.5 standard specifies token-ring protocol. FDDI technology also uses ring configuration, implementing IEEE 802.4 standard.

Figure 2.1(c) represents a star topology that was once used in star LAN. However, it is at present used in a hybrid mode, as discussed in the next paragraph. In the star topology, all DTEs are connected to a central node and interconnected in one of two modes. They can be connected in a broadcast configuration. In this configuration, all the other DTEs receive data transmitted by a DTE. This would be similar to a bus topology. In the second configuration, DTEs are connected to the central node, but are interconnected on a pair-wise basis selectively. In this situation, multiple conversations can occur concurrently between various DTEs passing through the central node.

As mentioned earlier, a hub configuration uses a star topology in combination with either a bus or a token-ring topology. The hub configurations shown in Figure 2.1(d) are the most popular LAN implementation. The hub is also known as a Layer-2 switch. It is a hybrid between (c) and either (a) or (b). DTEs are electronically connected to each other at the central node in either the bus or the ring topology. If they are connected in a broadcast configuration for an Ethernet LAN, it is called an Ethernet hub. If DTEs are connected in a ring topology for use with token-ring LAN, it is called a token-ring hub.

WAN differs from LAN in that it links networks that are geographically separated by a long distance. Typically, the WAN link connects nodes made up of switches, bridges, and routers.

WANs are connected in either a mesh or a tree topology, as shown in Figure 2.2. The mesh topology, Figure 2.2(a), provides multiple paths between nodes. Thus, a message between nodes N1 and N6 may traverse the paths N1–N2–N5–N6, N1–N3–N5–N6, N1–N2–N3–N5–N6, N1–N3–N2–N5–N6, N1–N4–N5–N6, N1–N4–N3–N5–N6, and N1–N3–N4–N5–N6. This allows packets belonging to a message to traverse different paths, thus balancing traffic load. It further provides redundancy for reliability of service. However, a broadcast message from N1 to all other nodes will be rebroadcast by neighboring nodes N2, N3, and N4 to all other nodes. This could cause flooding on the network and looping of

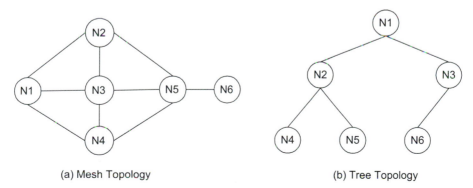

(a) Mesh Topology   (b) Tree Topology

Figure 2.2   WAN Topologies

packets, which needs to be carefully addressed. Flooding is a node receiving the same packets multiple times, and looping is a packet going around nodes in a loop, such as N2–N3–N1–N2 or N4–N3–N2–N1–N4 paths. A mesh topology is usually implemented using switches and routers.

A tree topology is shown in Figure 2.2(b). It appears as a hierarchical architecture. The tree structure starts with a node, called the header node, and branches out to other nodes in a tree structure. There can be no closed loops in the network. However, paths between nodes may be longer. For example, the packet from N4 to N6 has to traverse the top of the hierarchy N1 and then down to N6. The tree topology is simpler to implement than the mesh topology and uses bridges at the OSI data link layer.

2.2   LOCAL AREA NETWORKS

There are two types of LANs that are deployed, bus based or ring based. The most common bus-based LAN is Ethernet and is the most widely deployed LAN. Ring-based LANs are Token Ring and FDDI.

A representation of a campus network with different LANs is shown in Figure 2.3. The backbone of the campus network is a fiber network 10.10.0.0. The notation of the fourth decimal position being 0 is used to represent the network address. Ethernet LAN (10.1.2.0) is connected to the backbone via a router. Workstations on this LAN have the fourth decimal position in their IP addresses from 2 to 5. IP addresses 10.1.2.1 and 10.1.2.6 are the interface addresses to the router and the bridge.

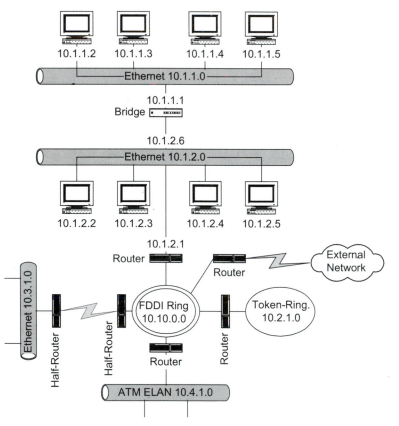

Figure 2.3   Campus Network of LANs

The second Ethernet LAN (10.1.1.0) is connected to the first Ethernet (10.1.2.0) via a bridge. IP addresses 10.1.1.2 to 10.1.2.5 are interfaces to workstations and the IP address 10.1.1.1 is the interface to the bridge. Notice that all external traffic from 10.1.1.0 Ethernet has to traverse 10.1.2.0 Ethernet LAN. 10.2.1.0 is a token-ring LAN connected to the backbone FDDI ring via a router. Two other LANs that are connected to the backbone are ATM Emulated LAN (ELAN) (10.4.1.0) via a router and an Ethernet LAN (10.3.1.0) via two half routers. The two half routers are connected via a dial-up link. It should be pointed out that most campus networks currently deploy high-speed Ethernet over fiber medium and LANs are exclusively Ethernet LANs. We will review LANs in this section and network components in Section 2.3.

2.2.1   Ethernet

Ethernet uses bus architecture with Carrier Sense Multiple Access with Collision Detection (CSMA/CD). DTEs are all connected to the same bus and transmit data in a multiple access mode. In other words, several DTEs can start transmitting frames at the same time. A frame comprises user data that are encapsulated with a header containing the source and destination address. A DTE starts transmitting when there is no carrier sensed on the bus. The transmitted signal travels in both directions on the physical medium. While transmitting, if a collision with another frame is detected, the DTE stops transmitting and attempts again after a certain period. Thus, the mode of transmission is a broadcast type with probabilistic collision of the signal.

A good analogy to understand the collision phenomenon is to envision a hollow pipe with holes all along representing stations. There is a person at each hole representing a station. The ends of the pipe are sealed and do not reflect sound. Let us suppose Joe starts speaking at a hole near one end of the pipe. He makes sure that he does not hear anybody speaking before he starts (carrier sensing). Once he starts talking, he has to make sure that nobody else starts talking until he finishes. He does this by continuing to talk and at the same time listening for other messages on the pipe. If he hears nobody else, then there is no collision. If he hears somebody else, then his message has collided with another person's message; and they both have to start over again. The longest time that Joe has to wait is for a voice to reach him from a person speaking at a hole near the other end of the pipe; and that person starts speaking just before Joe's voice reaches him. From this analogy, we can calculate that the minimum duration of time that Joe has to keep talking to ensure that there is no collision is the round-trip propagation time of his voice along the length of the pipe. Thus, there is a minimum frame size for Ethernet packets, which is 64 bytes. It is left as Exercise 1 for the student to prove this.

IEEE and ISO standards have been developed for Ethernet second layer MAC. They are IEEE 802.3 and ISO 8802.3, respectively. According to these standards, a physical coaxial segment can be a maximum of 500 meters; and there can be a maximum of 100 DTEs connected to it. A maximum of five segments can be connected with four repeaters to form one Ethernet LAN. However, if there are branches in the LAN, as in a tree structure, then any one total Ethernet segment should obey the above rule.

The data rate on an Ethernet bus is normally 10 Mbps (million bits per second). When traffic on the bus reaches about 40% to 70% of the maximum data rate of 10 Mbps, depending on the packet size, performance degrades significantly due to an increased collision rate. The bus medium can either be thick (0.4" diameter, but this is no longer deployed) or thin (0.25" diameter) coaxial cable; and DTEs are tapped on to the bus in a T-connection. There is a maximum segment length for LAN depending on the medium. This is listed in Table 2.1. There is also a limit on the length of the drop cable—the cable from the LAN tap to the

Table 2.1 Ethernet LAN Topology Limits

TYPE	DESCRIPTION	SEGMENT LENGTH	DROP CABLE LENGTH
10Base2	Thin coax (0.25")	200 meters	Not allowed
10Base5	Thick coax (0.4")	500 meters	Twisted pair: 50 meters
10Base-T	Hub topology	N/A	Twisted pair: 100 meters
10Base-F	Hub topology	N/A	2-kilometer fiber

connector on the network interface card (NIC) of the DTE. This is also shown in Table 2.1. As can be seen from the table, the original segment length defined for 10Base5 determined the minimum packet size of 64 bytes. However, with different configurations shown in the table (10Base2, 10Base5, 10Base-T, and 10Base-F), segment lengths and drop lengths vary based on the medium. However, the minimum packet size is still maintained at 64 bytes.

Ethernet LANs used to be configured by running coaxial cable around the DTEs with each DTE being tapped on to the cable. This could cause a great deal of management problem in tracking a faulty DTE. It is also difficult to isolate a DTE that caused heavy load on the LAN, or a killer DTE that has a problem and brings the network down frequently. It is likely that sometimes the maximum length of Ethernet LAN could have exceeded the allowable limit. The network could then crash intermittently at the limit length. It could also have an intermittent problem when traffic on the LAN exceeds the threshold. These problems have been eliminated by setting up the Ethernet LAN in a hub configuration, as shown in Figure 2.1(d). All DTE links, "drops," are brought to a hub located in a central wiring closet and connected to a dedicated port of the hub. DTEs are connected inside the hub in an Ethernet configuration with active electronics. Problems associated with a DTE can now be isolated to a port in this configuration and resolved in a much easier fashion.

2.2.2 Fast Ethernet

The hub technology described above led to the development of Fast Ethernet technology. Fast Ethernet operates at a speed of 100 Mbps data rate on an unshielded twisted pair (UTP) cable and is called 100Base-T. The maximum length from the hub to the DTE is specified as a 100-meter or a 200-meter round trip. This produces a maximum path delay, which is the delay between two DTEs of 400 meters, plus a repeater delay of one repeater instead of four repeaters. This is less than one-tenth the delay in straight Ethernet MAC specifications (5,000 meters) with four repeaters. Thus, speed can be increased ten times from 10 Mbps to 100 Mbps. However, to be consistent with IEEE 802.3 standards, an additional sublayer, convergence layer, needs to be introduced in the physical layer above a physical medium-dependent (PMD) sublayer (similar to what we saw in the OSI network layer). This is shown in Figure 2.4. The physical medium should be capable of carrying a 100-Mbps data rate signal over the maximum length of the drop cable, which is 100 meters. Category 3 UTP cable cannot carry such a high data rate. Hence, four pairs of UTP cables are used to distribute the data, each pair carrying 25 Mbps. Hence, the terminology 100Base-T4 is used, that is, 100 Mbps carried over four twisted pairs. This limitation could be overcome by using two pairs of Category 5 UTP cable in full-duplex mode configuration, which we will discuss in Section 2.2.4. The minimum packet size of 64 bytes is maintained for Fast Ethernet.

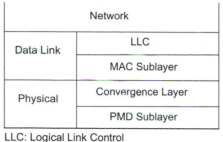

Network		
Data Link	LLC	
	MAC Sublayer	
Physical	Convergence Layer	
	PMD Sublayer	

LLC: Logical Link Control
MAC: Medium Access Control
PMD: Physical Medium Dependent

Figure 2.4   100Base-T Fast Ethernet Protocol Architecture

2.2.3 Gigabit Ethernet

With the successes of Ethernet and fiber-optic communications, the logical evolution in Ethernet technology led to the development of Gigabit Ethernet, Ethernet operating at 1 Gbps (gigabits per second). Gigabit Ethernet is one hundred times the speed of regular Ethernet, ten times that of Fast Ethernet, and faster than FDDI operating at 150 Mbps.

Along with the development of Gigabit Ethernet, a parallel task was undertaken to double the bandwidth of Ethernet by full-duplex operation. We have so far considered only half-duplex operation in the CSMA/CD scheme. We will first describe Gigabit Ethernet in the CSMA/CD half-duplex mode in this section and consider the full-duplex mode for all types of Ethernet in the following subsection.

An approach similar to that of Fast Ethernet was taken to make Gigabit Ethernet compatible with the existing Ethernet network. IEEE 802.3z protocol, whose architecture is shown in Figure 2.5, maintains the data link layer components, logical link control (LLC) and the media access control (MAC) the same, and modifies the physical layer. Physical layer architecture combines the physical interface of the high-speed FibreChannel (developed for fiber-optic communication) with that of IEEE 802.3 Ethernet frame format. It consists of four sublayers: physical medium-dependent (PMD), physical medium attachment (PMA), convergence, and reconciliation, which interfaces with the MAC layer.

Gigabit Ethernet specification initially permits use of three physical media. They are: long-wave laser over single-mode and multimode fiber, 1000Base-LX; short-wave laser over multimode fiber, 1000Base-SX; balanced shielded 150-ohm copper cable; and UTP cable, 1000Base-T.

Both short-wave (780 nanometer, light frequency) and long-wave (1300 nanometer, near-infra-red frequency) lasers are specified to be transmitted over multimode fiber, whereas only long-wave laser specification addresses transmission over single-mode fiber. There is no support for short-wave laser over single-mode fiber. This is based on cost performance. Long-wave laser over single-mode fiber (1300 nanometer laser over 9 micron fiber) can be used up to a ten-kilometer distance, whereas multimode fiber typically extends up to two kilometers. Commercially available multimode fibers are 50 and 62.5 microns in diameter with fiber connectors that can be plugged into equipment. Table 2.2 summarizes approximately the various combinations of media, mode, and drop length (one-way). Attenuation is in the range of 0.25 to 0.5 decibels per kilometer, after which regeneration or amplification may be required.

In Figure 2.5 the PMA is a serializer/deserializer that handles multiple encoding schemes of the upper convergence layer. The encoding scheme is different between optical (8B/10B) and copper media

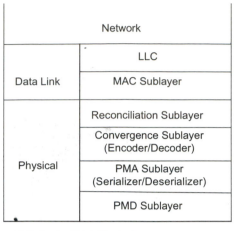

LLC: Logical Link Control
MAC: Medium Access Control
PMA: Physical Medium Attachment
PMD: Physical Medium Dependent

Figure 2.5 IEEE 802.3z Gigabit Ethernet Protocol Architecture

in the convergence layer. The reconciliation layer is a Media-Independent Interface (MII) between the physical media and the MAC layer of the data link control layer.

An added complication of going to 1 Gbps speed is the minimum frame size. Original Ethernet specifications, based on 2500 meters in length with four repeaters, each producing approximately a 5-microsecond delay and 10-Mbps data rate, required a minimum of a 64-byte frame, shown in Figure 2.6(a) to detect any collision. The time to accommodate the 64-byte frame is defined as the slot time, which is 51.2 microseconds. An idle time of 96 bits was allowed between frames, as shown in Figure 2.6(b). Fast Ethernet with a 100-meter drop, 100-Mbps data rate, and one repeater (minimum time each packet needs to traverse in a hub configuration) would take a little over five microseconds. Thus, a slot time of 5.12 microseconds with a 64-byte minimum frame size meets the minimum 64-byte slot size, as shown in Figure 2.6(c), to be compatible with original Ethernet specifications. A round-trip delay in Gigabit Ethernet is primarily determined by the repeater delay. To be backward compatible with original Ethernet specifications based on CSMA/CD, the minimum packet size was extended to 512 bytes, but the minimum frame size was still kept as 64 bytes. For small frames, a carrier extension was allowed, as shown in Figure 2.6(d), to increase the number of bytes in a slot to 512 bytes corresponding to 4.096 microseconds.

Table 2.2 Gigabit Ethernet Topology Limits

	9 MICRON SINGLE MODE	50 MICRON SINGLE MODE	50 MICRON MULTIMODE	62.5 MICRON MULTIMODE	BALANCE SHIELDED CABLE	UTP
1000Base-LX	10 km	3 km	550 m	440 m	–	–
1000Base-SX	–		550 m	260 m	–	–
1000Base-CX	–		–	–	25 m	–
1000Base-T	–		–	–	–	100 m

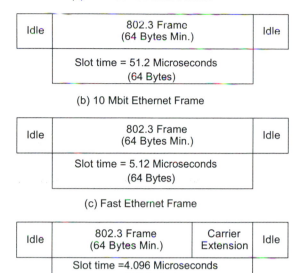

(a) IEEE 802.3 Frame Format

(b) 10 Mbit Ethernet Frame

(c) Fast Ethernet Frame

(d) Gigabit Ethernet Frame

Figure 2.6 Ethernet Formats and 802.3 Frame

An additional modification was made to Gigabit Ethernet specifications to permit bursts of frames to be transmitted by a single station. This is called packet bursting. Devices could send bursts of small packets and utilize full bandwidth capacity. In such a situation, the transmitting station should not allow idle time between frames. This feature improves the efficiency of transmission, especially in the backbone configuration.

With increased data rate capability, Gigabit Ethernet can transport multimedia service that includes voice, video, and data. Quality of Service (QoS) that can establish priority of service to accomplish real-time transmission is an essential requirement for implementation of multimedia service. IEEE 802.1p specifying the class of service (CoS) meets this requirement in a limited way. In addition, Resource Reservation Protocol (RSVP) can be used for advance reservation of bandwidth for this purpose.

2.2.4 Full-Duplex Ethernet

We have so far discussed in the last two subsections increasing the bandwidth of Ethernet by two orders of magnitude by migrating from 10 Mbps Ethernet to Gigabit Ethernet. We will now discuss how data rates of Ethernet, Fast Ethernet, and Gigabit Ethernet could be doubled by migrating from a half-duplex to a full-duplex configuration.

As mentioned in the previous subsection, CSMA/CD configuration is a half-duplex operation. This means that the signal could traverse only in one direction at a given time in the cable to avoid collision with another signal. In Section 2.2.1, we gave the analogy of speaking into a hollow pipe to demonstrate the collision. Let's extend that analogy to the case where there are two hollow pipes and the sound is allowed

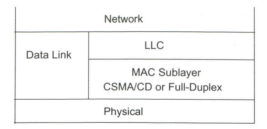

Figure 2.7 IEEE 802.3 x Protocol Architecture

to travel only in one direction. One pipe carries sound in one direction, and the other in the opposite direction. In this case, each person can be speaking on one pipe and receiving a message from somebody else on the other pipe at the same time. This analogy applies to the switched LAN where each station is connected to the hub by two channels. This is the basic concept of a full-duplex configuration. Carrier Sense Multiple Access with Carrier Detection (CSMA/CD) does not apply in this configuration.

With an active LAN implementation with repeaters and the sophistication of electronics in a hub, CSMA/CD restriction could be removed and a hub with a full-duplex operation could be implemented. IEEE 802.3x specifications, shown in Figure 2.7, were developed for this purpose. Using this scheme, the bandwidth could be doubled for each type of Ethernet configuration. Thus, the Ethernet full-duplex configuration could handle 20 Mbps, Fast Ethernet 200 Mbps, and Gigabit Ethernet 2000 Mbps. The full-duplex configuration is generally used in point-to-point communication. This feature can be turned on or off in configuring the hub. For a point-to-point link, an optional flow control feature specified in IEEE 802.3x can be exercised. The receiver can send a "pause frame" to the transmitter to control the flow in case of congestion.

Because of the 802.3x protocol extension, the notation for Ethernet type is modified with an "x" extension. Thus, 10Base-T, 100Base-T, and 100Base-F are modified to be 10Base-Tx, 100Base-Tx, and 100Base-Fx. The Gigabit Ethernet types already denoted ending in x, the option being set to either full- or half-duplex.

Limitations in Gigabit Ethernet implementation to be compatible with original Ethernet with CSMA/CD are removed in full-duplex implementation. Thus, the carrier extension, slot time extension, or packet bursting is not applicable. The Ethernet 96-bit interface gap (idle time between frames) and 64-byte minimum packet size would still apply.

2.2.5 Switched Ethernet

Another outcome of hub technology is the switched Ethernet. Instead of just the broadcast mode inside the hub, packets are opened to see the destination address and passed through to the appropriate destination port. The switch hub can be implemented as a learning device by reading the source address and thus building a routing table to speed up the process. Pairs of DTEs can communicate with each other in parallel as long as they are different DTE pairs and consequently, multiples of 10-Mbps channels are traversing the Ethernet hub at the same time. This is shown in Figure 2.8. There will, however, be a collision if a DTE receives packets from two other DTEs simultaneously and needs resolution.

Not all ports in a switched hub have to operate at the same data rate. A typical arrangement will be for one port to operate at a high data rate and will be connected to a server DTE, with other ports connected to client DTEs. A switched hub in a client–server configuration is shown in Figure 2.9 with the server operating at 100 Mbps and the clients at 10 Mbps.

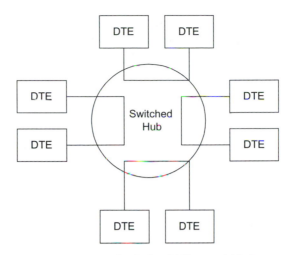

Figure 2.8   Switched Ethernet Hub

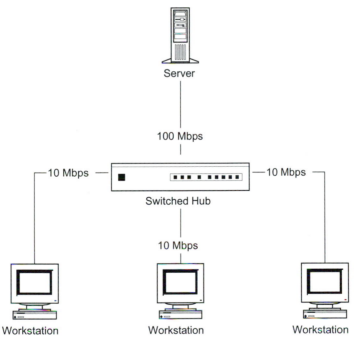

Figure 2.9   Switched Hub in a Client–Server Configuration

2.2.6   10-Gigabit Ethernet

A 10-Gigabit Ethernet or 10GbE or 10 GigE is the fastest of Ethernet standards. It combines the technology of standard Ethernet, full-duplex Ethernet, and switched Ethernet to create a LAN hub with nominal data rate of 10 Gbps over fiber, IEEE 802.3AE, and over copper UTP as specified by IEEE 802.3an standard. A 10-Gigabit Ethernet LAN does not follow the CSMA/CD protocol [Wikipedia1]. The 10-Gigabit Ethernet standard encompasses a number of different physical layer standards, with each physical port in a device supporting any of the many different modules that support different LAN or WAN PHY standards.

2.2.7 Virtual LAN

Another advantage of the switched Ethernet is the capability to establish VLAN. Using a network management system, any port can be assigned to any LAN, and thus LAN configurations can be changed without physically moving equipment. In a corporate environment, this has the advantage of grouping personnel, for example, into different administrative groups with shared LAN without physically moving their location.

As an illustration, MAC addresses for hosts in Figure 2.10 could be assigned to two different LANs. Switching occurs by the switch opening the packet received on a port, reading the OSI layer-2 MAC address, and then transmitting it on another port that may be connected to a different LAN at a different speed. We thus have switched a packet from one LAN to another, which is the function of a bridge that we will discuss in Section 2.3.2. However, it is worth noting here that the workstations that are physically connected to a switched hub belong to two LANs, each being defined as a Virtual LAN (VLAN).

The concept of VLANs is shown in Figure 2.10. The router directs all packets destined for subnets 200.100.150.1 and 200.100.160.1 to the same port on the router. They arrive at the switched hub and are routed to DTE 1 through DTE 5. Each of the five DTEs shown in the figure could be assigned an IP address belonging to either 200.100.150.1 or 200.100.160.1 and thus will be intermingled between the two VLANs. If DTE 1 and DTE 3 both belong to 200.100.150.1 VLAN, then traffic emanating from DTE 1 destined for DTE 3 would have been switched within the same VLAN. DTE 1 could be assigned an IP address 200.100.150.2 and DTE 3 could be assigned address 200.100.160.2. In this case, they belong to different VLANs. MAC addresses remaining fixed (they are assigned in the factory); the packet is now switched between the two VLANs.

Service providers now offer VLAN capability that is spread across a geographically wide area and traverses through switching offices and WAN.

2.2.8 Token Ring

Although Token-Ring LAN is a legacy LAN, we will describe it here as its ring configuration, and fail-safe redundancy aspects have been adopted in later versions of LAN and MAN, such as FDDI and RPR,

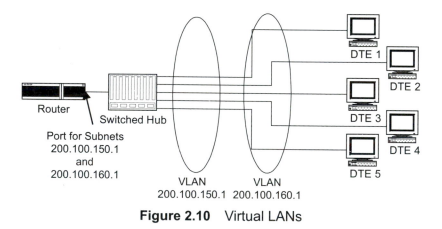

Figure 2.10 Virtual LANs

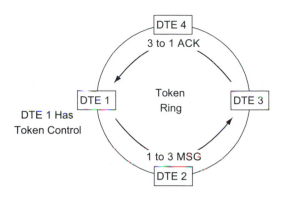

Figure 2.11 Token-Ring LAN

respectively. Token Ring uses the ring topology and is specified by IEEE 802.5 protocol. There is no segment length limit as in Ethernet LAN. All DTEs are connected in a serial fashion in a ring shown in Figure 2.11.

A token is passed around (counterclockwise in Figure 2.11) in a unidirectional mode; and the DTE that has the token is in control of the LAN. Let us consider in Figure 2.11 a situation where DTE 4 has just completed transmission of a message and has released the token. DTE 1 is waiting to pass a message to DTE 3. As soon as the token is received, DTE 1 holds on to the token and transmits its message to DTE 3. The message has the source and destination addresses. DTE 2 looks at the destination address and does not pick up the message. DTE 3 examines the destination address, and realizes that the message is for itself. It then picks up the message and retransmits it with acknowledgment marked in the trailer of the message format. The frame goes around to DTE 1 with DTE 4 just passing the message through. Recognizing that the message has been received, DTE 1 releases the control token and now DTE 2 has a chance to send a message. If the message was not accepted by DTE 3 for any reason, such as a corrupt message, then the message trailer is so marked and appropriate action is taken by DTE 1.

As can be seen, in the token-ring LAN, MAC is deterministic in contrast to the probabilistic nature in Ethernet LAN. Standards that specify token-ring MAC are IEEE 802.5 and ISO 8803.5. This is good configuration for heavily loaded networks.

The maximum size of a frame is not limited by the 802.5 standard. However, in order that no one station monopolizes the ring, the maximum token holding time by any station is configured, which determines the maximum frame size. The minimum frame size is the size of the token. The ring should be long enough to accommodate the entire token; otherwise, the token starts wrapping itself around and all the stations are in an idle mode.

Because of the serial configuration, it is important that any failure of DTE, or turning the DTE off, should not halt the operation of LAN. One scheme to prevent this failure is to design the Token-Ring NIC to create a short whenever there is a failure or it is turned off. This is analogous to serially connected Christmas tree lights. When one bulb burns out, the bulb shorts the connection so that the rest of the lights continue to be lit.

If there is a break in the link segment of the ring, the downstream DTE sends a beacon to the others indicating a failure. For example, if the link between DTE 4 and DTE 1 breaks, DTE 1 will send the beacon.

Ring failure can be permanently resolved by a dual-ring configuration, where the second ring is redundant, as shown in Figure 2.12(a). Let us assume that the normal mode of operation is along the inner ring and the token is going around in the counterclockwise direction. The outer ring is the redundant ring and acts as backup. Figure 2.12(b) shows the situation where DTE 1 has failed. DTE 2 does not receive

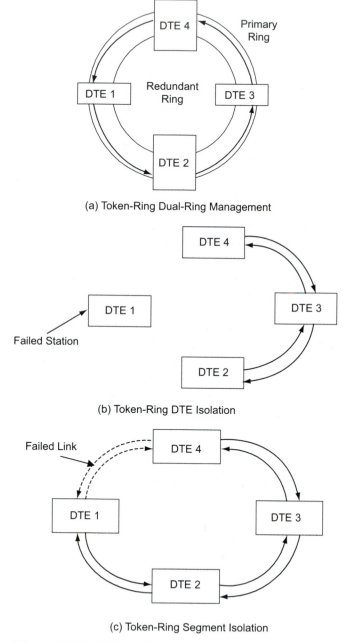

(a) Token-Ring Dual-Ring Management

(b) Token-Ring DTE Isolation

(c) Token-Ring Segment Isolation

Figure 2.12   Token-Ring Dual-Ring Configurations

the signal from DTE 1. DTE 2 will send a beacon. Under this condition, DTE 2 and DTE 4 go into a loop-back condition. DTE 4 receives the token on the inner ring and forwards it on the outer ring to DTE 3. DTE 2 receives the token on the outer ring and forwards it on the inner ring.

Figure 2.12(c) shows the situation where the section of the ring between DTE 4 and DTE 1 is broken. DTE 1 sends a beacon. DTE 4 and DTE 1 perform loop-backs and the continuity of the rings among all four stations is established using both inner and outer rings.

2.2.9 FDDI

Fiber Distributed Data Interface (FDDI) LAN came into being to take advantage of fiber-optic transmission media for LAN technology. It operates at a data rate of 100 Mbps and can include up to 500 DTEs in a single segment of 100-kilometer length without repeaters. Separation between neighboring stations on the cable can be up to 2 kilometers. A fiber-optic cable has the advantage of low-noise interference compared to copper cable, and hence FDDI is ideally suited for a campus backbone network. As mentioned earlier, FDDI is configured as a ring topology and has a token for medium access control. Thus, it follows IEEE 802.5 token-ring standard, but with some significant differences. It is adopted as an international standard by ISO 9314 and American National Standards Institute (ANSI) H3T9.5.

Figure 2.13(a) shows the network configuration of FDDI. It is usually implemented as a dual ring for high reliability. One ring is termed as primary and the second one as secondary. Stations can be connected to the ring either as a single attached station (SAS) to the primary ring, or as a dual attached station (DAS) to both rings. A hierarchical topology can be created using concentrators, as shown in Figure 2.13(b). Concentrators permit the attachment of only SASs, but are economical for wiring and expansion of the FDDI network.

Although the topology of FDDI is similar to the Token Ring, the control token-passing algorithm is different. In the Token Ring, only one DTE utilizes the ring at any given time, whereas in FDDI there can be many frames traversing the ring with communication between multiple pairs of stations.

2.2.10 Wireless LAN

Wireless LAN (WLAN) growth has been very rapid and is being deployed at homes, enterprises, and public places. WiFi, as it is popularly known, is an IEEE 802.11 protocol LAN. 802.11b and 802.11g operate at a 2.4-GHz band and 802.11a operates at a 5-GHz band. IEEE 802.11 working groups have been making amendments to 802.11 to address scalability, provisioning, performance, QoS, and security issues. We will address these along with management issues in Chapter 15 on Home Networking.

The prevalent configuration for deployment of WiFi is a hierarchical configuration, also known as infrastructure configuration. This is shown in Figure 2.14. WLAN may be visualized as a wireless interface to a wired network. Thus, in Figure 2.14, the Access Point (AP) converts the IEEE 802.3 Ethernet protocol on a wired medium to IEEE 802.11 WiFi protocol over a wireless medium. The wired interface is connected to the external network via either a router or a layer-2 switch.

Stations 1, 2, and 3 in Figure 2.14 can be either fixed or mobile or any combination. A typical configuration in a laptop computer is either a removable interface card or built in. Communication between wireless stations passes through the AP, which is also the controller. The range of WiFi is limited, and the area that is under the control of an AP is called the basic service area. The stations associated with a basic service area are usually connected by a wired network to another basic service area.

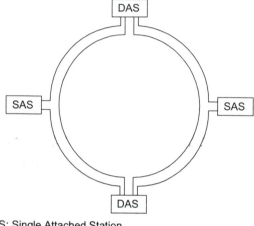

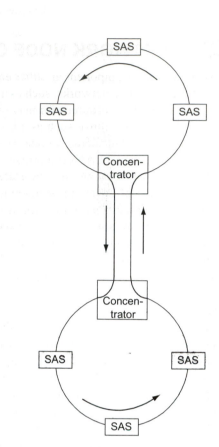

SAS: Single Attached Station
DAS: Dual Attached Station

SAS: Single Attached Station

(a) Dual-Ring FDDI Network Configuration

(b) FDDI Configuration with Concentrators

Figure 2.13   FDDI Configurations

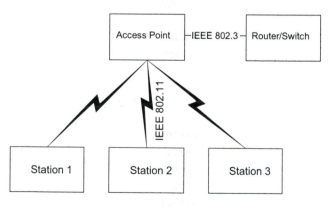

Figure 2.14   Wireless LAN: Hierarchical Topology

A second WLAN topology is the ad hoc network configuration. In this configuration, wireless stations communicate with each other on a peer-to-peer level with one of the stations acting as the controller, or a beacon as it is called.

2.3   NETWORK NODE COMPONENTS

A network node is a component at either end of a network link, such as a hub or a router. It is also a device that connects two networks, such as a bridge connecting two LANs, or a gateway connecting two autonomous networks. Resources for network node are hubs, switches, bridges, routers, and gateways, or a combination of the above such as a brouter (bridged router) and a switched hub. A DTE, such as a workstation, is not considered a node. However, a workstation that has two network interface cards (NICs) connecting to two LANs is a bridge and is considered a node. Hubs are platforms housing one or more functions. Switches now use solid-state devices. Progress in solid-state technology has contributed to the advancement of switching technology that includes an ATM switch. Other network nodes are smart switches with built-in intelligence of various degrees.

In a simplistic view, a node can be looked at as a switch, a bridge, a router, or a gateway. The basic concepts of the four primary nodal components are shown in Figure 2.15. Figure 2.15(a) shows a switch, where inputs and outputs are of the same format. For example, if the input format is an ATM format, the output is also an ATM format. The switch can be used to switch both analog and digital data. When used in the analog mode, as in circuit switching, a call is set up first (connection through the switch is made) and then the analog signal is passed through. The switch is insensitive to the information content. When it is used in the digital mode, it is used as a packet switch. Each input packet is looked at and then switched to the appropriate output port based on content.

A bridge can be viewed as an intelligent packet switch at the data link layer and is shown in Figure 2.15(b). Besides switching input packets to appropriate output ports, it can filter those packets as well. This is useful for connecting two LANs. If traffic is pertinent to the LAN only, it is filtered out. If it is to be delivered outside the LAN where it was generated, then it is switched through the bridge. In an intelligent bridge, knowledge can be learned over time by the bridge as to which packets should be delivered to which ports. Input and output protocols, in practice, are usually the same. However, some bridges can also do protocol conversion, as we will learn in Section 2.3.2.

A router cannot only do all the functions of a switch and a bridge but also route packets to the appropriate port in the correct direction of its destination. It functions at the network layer. Thus, in Figure 2.15(c), input packets from a node in an IP network are sent out as IP packets to another node in the same network or to some other network.

Not all networks use the same protocol. In this case, a gateway is used to convert one protocol format to another protocol format. In Figure 2.15(d), a gateway is shown between an IP network and an X.25 network.

2.3.1   Hubs

Figure 2.16 shows the role of various components in a network. The router, the gateway, and the half-router function at the network layer and route packets. Bridges, local and remote, operate at the data link layer and connect two LANs. Hubs are used to build LANs as we learned in the previous section. We will review various network components in this section.

As mentioned earlier, a hub is a platform with multiple ports. It is implemented to perform some specific functions or a combination of functions. For example, it could house a simple LAN or multiple LAN segments. It can perform a switching function and thus act as a switched LAN. When it switches between LANs, it performs a bridge function. In this section, we will consider a hub used to implement LAN.

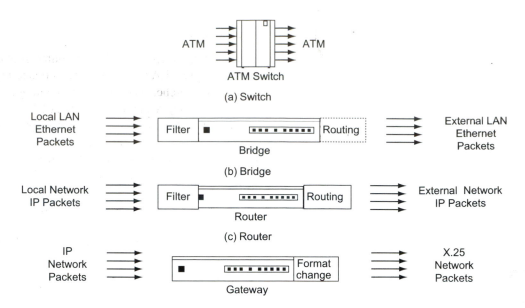

Figure 2.15   Basic Network Node Components

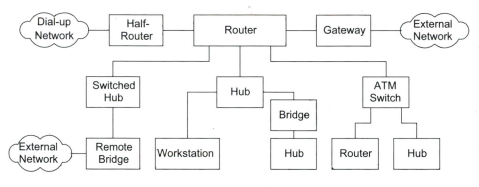

Figure 2.16   Networked Components

Hubs can be looked at as active LANs—DTEs connected with repeaters in a LAN configuration. Limitations of length and number of stations that are imposed on LANs are overcome by "homing" the wiring from the DTEs to the hub in the wiring closet and connecting them in the topology desired. The only limitation is the drop length from the hub to the station, such as the 100-meter maximum length in Ethernet configuration. Any DTE can be connected to any port of the hub. Stacking hubs and daisy chaining them can increase the number of ports. DTE configurations can be changed from a centrally located hub. Further, any DTE could easily be disconnected from the LAN for troubleshooting without impacting the operation of other stations.

Hubs can be stacked to increase the number of ports as shown in the stacked hub configuration in Figure 2.17. Stackable hubs have a common backplane. Thus, it is equivalent to increasing the number of ports in a hub. For example, two 16-port hubs will behave as a 32-port hub.

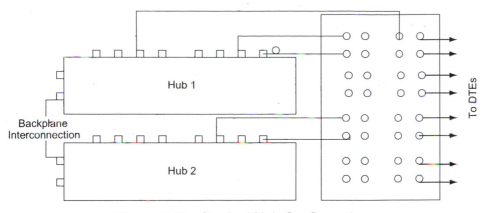

Figure 2.17 Stacked Hub Configuration

2.3.2 Bridges

Bridges are used to interconnect LANs. Three types of local bridges connecting two LANs are shown in Figure 2.18. Figure 2.18(a) shows a simple bridge configuration connecting two Ethernet LANs. This configuration can be looked at as two LANs connected by a repeater, except that now traffic among DTEs in one LAN does not go over to the other LAN. The only traffic that is exchanged between the two LANs via the bridge is that which requires inter-LAN communication. Figure 2.18(b) shows several LANs connected by a multiport bridge. In this case, the bridge opens the packet, reads the MAC address, and switches the packet to the appropriate port that is the path to the destination address. Usually the bridge is a self-learning bridge. It looks at all the packets that are received and records the source address and the port where it was received in a table. It uses this table to transmit packets. If a destination address is not in the table, it does a flooding on all ports and discovers the correct port to add to the table. The table is periodically (less than a few minutes) purged of inactive addresses.

A bridge switches data packets between LANs and to accomplish this has a store-and-forward capability. Local bridges are usually developed as a single protocol device, and have the primary features of switching and filtering out intra-LAN traffic. However, because of the store-and-forward capability in a bridge, additional features could be incorporated to convert protocol. Figure 2.18(c) shows a multiport, multiprotocol bridge configuration, where Ethernet and token-ring LANs are interconnected. Protocol conversion is done at OSI layer 2.

2.3.3 Remote Bridge

Figure 2.18 shows bridges in local LAN configurations. This implies that LANs are brought to a centralized wiring closet and are interconnected via a bridge. Figure 2.19 shows a remote bridge configuration, where two bridges at remote locations are linked via a WAN. WAN architecture mostly uses routers. However, using a remote bridge and a leased dedicated telecommunication link, we can connect remote LANs.

LANs can be connected with bridges that are networked using either the tree topology or the mesh topology. Bridged networks operate at the data link layer. There are two network-routing algorithms used in bridged networks—the spanning-tree algorithm for bridging Ethernet LANs and the source-routing algorithm for bridging token-ring LANs.

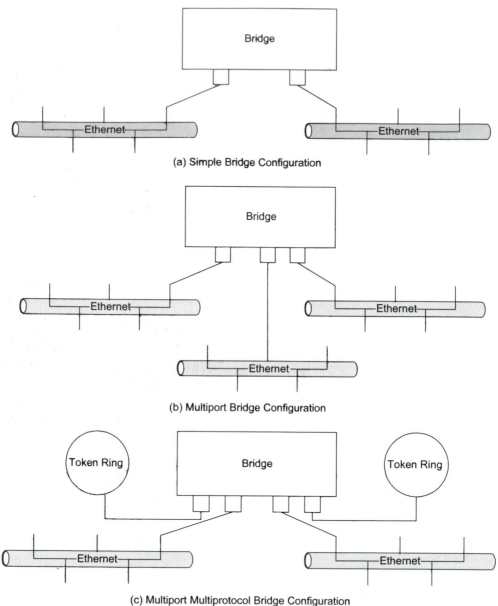

(a) Simple Bridge Configuration

(b) Multiport Bridge Configuration

(c) Multiport Multiprotocol Bridge Configuration

Figure 2.18 Local Bridge Configurations

2.3.4 ## Transparent Bridge

Figure 2.20 shows four LANs networked using three bridges in a tree topology. Each bridge has knowledge only of its neighbor and is transparent to other bridges and LANs, as described below, hence the name transparent bridge.

The transparent bridge uses a routing algorithm, called a spanning-tree algorithm. A spanning-tree algorithm builds and stores a table of ports associated with destination addresses. When a packet

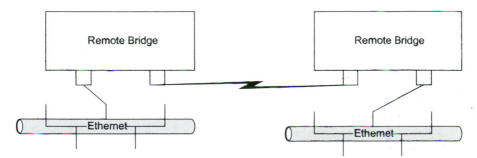

Figure 2.19 Remote Bridge

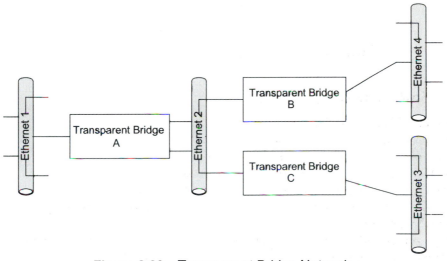

Figure 2.20 Transparent Bridge Network

arrives, the bridge sends the packet on another port to its destination. The bridge has no knowledge as to exactly where the destination LAN is. It only has knowledge of the neighboring node responsible for that destination address.

The transparent bridge learns routing information by a backward learning process. That is, when a packet arrives at a port, it notes the source address of the packet and associates that address with that port in its routing table. It then forwards the packet to the port associated with that destination. If the destination address is not in its routing table, it does a broadcast message to acquire the address.

As shown in Figure 2.20, the topology of the transparent bridge network is the tree topology, which means that there are no closed loops. One of the nodes acts as the header node, which is transparent bridge A in the figure. Although there may physically be more than one path between two LANs, the spanning-tree algorithm eliminates all but one link during the operation. For example, if transparent bridge B had links to both Ethernet 3 and Ethernet 4, then that would form a closed loop, Ethernet 3– transparent bridge B–Ethernet 2–transparent bridge C–Ethernet 3. The spanning-tree algorithm would prevent transparent bridge B from sending or receiving packets on its link to Ethernet 3.

Let us track a message from a host attached to LAN 3 sending a message to LAN 4. It takes the path all the way up the tree to the header bridge A, and then traverses down the other half of the tree to LAN 4. Thus, the header bridge normally needs to handle more traffic than other nodes.

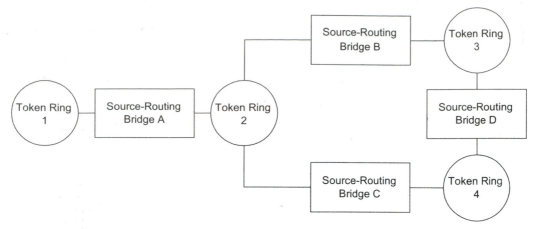

Figure 2.21 Source-Routing Bridge Network

2.3.5 Source-Routing Bridge

A source-routing bridge is used to network token-ring LANs, as shown in Figure 2.21. In the source-routing algorithm used in a bridged token-ring network, the source is aware of the entire path to the destination. In addition to the destination address, the source inserts the route that the packet should take in the packet. Thus, intermediate nodes make no decision as to the path that the packet takes. This is the reason that the token-ring bridge is called a source-routing bridge. The routing table can be stored either centrally on a server or in each source-routing bridge. The route is determined by broadcast packets flooding the entire network.

Comparing a source-routing bridge with a transparent bridge, the latter is more robust and reliable, whereas the former is faster. Thus, changes in the network due to addition or deletion of hosts, or due to failures, are tracked easier than in a source-routing bridge. In a source-routing bridge, the entire routing table has to be rediscovered, which is a heavy resource-consumption process.

Bridges are used for special-purpose networks and have several limitations. Due to dissimilarity in the routing algorithm, communication between media using different protocols becomes difficult, for example between Ethernet and Token Ring or FDDI. Besides, routing algorithms are difficult to create and to maintain. Routers, which operate at the network layer, are designed for routing and hence are better suited for this purpose. Routers and gateways can route packets between different media and different networks (using different network protocols) in a transparent manner. We will now discuss the role of routers in networking.

2.3.6 Routers

Routers and gateways form the backbone of networking. Although we have shown alternative ways of networking with bridges in the previous section—sometimes cheaper and a short cut to establish enterprise networking—the clean approach to establishing computer networks is with the use of routers.

A router, as the name indicates, routes packets through the network. Each router in a computer network has some knowledge of possible routes that a data packet could take to go from the source to the destination. It has the high-level data on what is the best overall route, as well as detailed local data on the best path for the next hop in the link. This is built into a routing table that it periodically updates

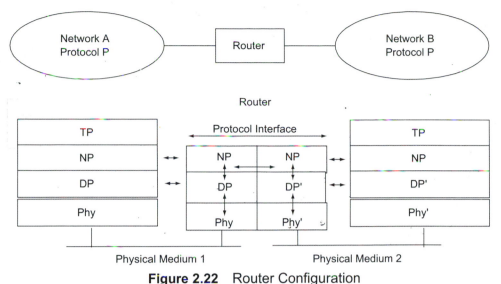

Figure 2.22   Router Configuration

and stores in its database. The router employs a broadcast scheme using an Address Resolution Protocol (ARP) to determine the port associated with destination addresses. The router may also read the contents of a data packet arriving at a given port to determine its source and destination address, as well as what type of data it is and when it was received. It then, using the routing table, intelligently routes it to one or more output ports toward its destination address. The output goes to a single port if it is a data packet going between a source and a destination; or the output is directed to multiple ports if it is a broadcast or multicast type of packet. Figure 2.22 shows a router configuration with protocol architecture. Notice that network layers have the same protocols (NP). However, the data link layer protocol (DP) and physical layer protocol (Phy), as well as the physical media 1 and 2, could be different.

Routers permit loops in their topology and thus are more universal than bridges. This enables load balancing of traffic as well as self-healing of the network in case of a link or router failure. Routers have various algorithms to optimize load balancing of traffic and economize on cost. Several routing algorithms are in use. Of those, open shortest path first (OSPF) is the most widely used. In this algorithm, each router broadcasts route–request packets on the links that it is connected to. Other routers in the network acknowledge the request and repeat the process. Thus, a distributed routing database is built using an algorithm for the shortest path and is kept updated whenever there is a change in network configuration.

Network managers can build routing tables for optimizing their network performance with respect to several parameters, such as least-cost route, delay, bandwidth, etc. The performance of a bridged network is better than a router network due to the additional network layer in the latter case. Hence, a bridged network is used in some special applications where speed is of importance. However, routers are specifically designed based on a network layer, whose main purpose is networking. Thus, degradation in performance using routers over bridges is a small price to pay for the far-reaching benefits we achieve.

2.3.7   Gateways and Protocol Converters

A gateway connects two autonomous networks. Each autonomous network is self-contained in all aspects—routing algorithms, protocol, domain name servers, and network administration procedures and policies. When such an autonomous network communicates with another autonomous network, it

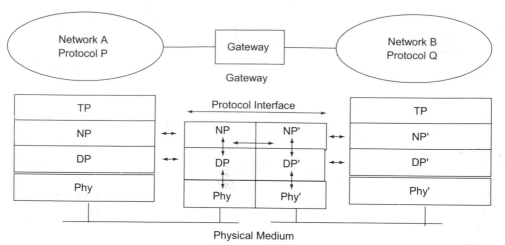

Figure 2.23 Gateway Configuration

traverses a gateway, as shown in Figure 2.23. Generally, the protocol conversion is done at the network layer as shown in the figure.

Since protocol conversion for a gateway is done at the network layer, it could generally be combined with a routing function. Thus, a router with protocol conversion could also be considered a gateway. Node N in Figure 1.16 that connects an IP network with a proprietary subnetwork is an example of this. Node N not only does protocol conversion, but also has the routing table containing information on both networks. In this scheme, Node N would have an IP address, but nodes N1, N2, and N3 may follow a proprietary addressing scheme.

A protocol converter, shown in Figure 2.24, does protocol conversion at the application layer. The protocol converter used to be distinguished from a gateway, but this is no longer the case. Gateway

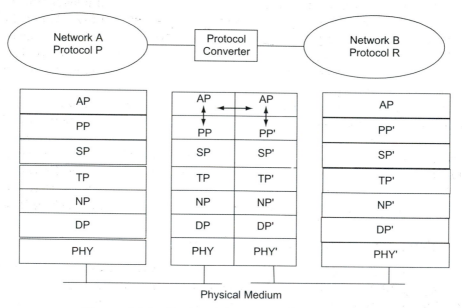

Figure 2.24 Protocol Converter Configuration

is the generic term that is currently in vogue. An example of this would be a protocol converter that would be used between two email systems. Let us consider a company that uses X.400, an ITU-T messaging system. When a person wants to send an email on the Internet to another person, who is using Internet standard Simple Mail Transfer Protocol (SMTP), a protocol converter (gateway) converts X.400 protocol to SMTP.

2.3.8 Multiprotocol Routers and Tunneling

An alternative to the use of gateway to communicate between autonomous networks is tunneling using multiprotocol router. Tunneling is generally used when the source and destination stations are on similar networks, but the data have to traverse intermediate network systems, which may be using different protocols. In this case, the data frame does not go through a protocol conversion in the intermediate networks, but is encapsulated and "tunneled" through as pass-through traffic.

Figure 2.25 shows communications between two Ethernet LANs on IP networks. One of them could be in the USA and the other in India. However, the data have to go through Europe, which is on a X.25 packet-switched data network. The multiprotocol router at the near end encapsulates the IP packet in an X.25 frame and transmits it to the far-end multiprotocol router. The far-end multiprotocol router de-encapsulates the frame and routes it as an IP packet again. The path through Europe behaves very similar to a serial link.

Another application for tunneling is when a station with an IP address belonging to a LAN wants to communicate with another LAN in a distant location, but from a location other than the local LAN. This would be the situation if the station were a portable PC and the person traveling needs to communicate from a foreign location. Let us picture the scenario where Joe wants to communicate from Seattle in northwest United States to Sally at Los Angeles on the West Coast of the United States. Joe's PC belongs to a network domain in New York, which is in the East Coast of the United States. The initial message is routed to the server of the LAN that the station belongs to, in this case New York. The server, recognizing that the station is currently outside of its domain, locates the foreign agent who handles the domain that Joe is currently at and informs Joe and the foreign agent. From then on, the sender "tunnels" the packets directly to the user via the foreign agent.

2.3.9 Half-Bridge Configuration of Router

There are situations where it is desired to have point-to-point communication. For example, when a residential station communicates with an Internet Service Provider (ISP), Point-to-Point Protocol (PPP) could be used. It provides a standard method for multiprotocol datagrams over point-to-point links. This method of communication has been extended to PPP Multilink Protocol (MP). Using MP, datagrams

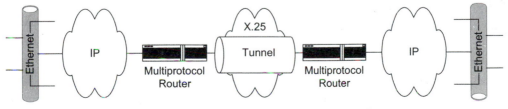

Figure 2.25 Tunneling Using Multiprotocol Routers

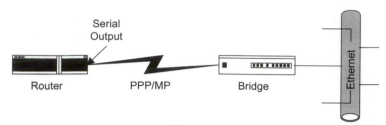

Figure 2.26 Half-Bridge Configuration

could be split, sequenced, transmitted over multiple parallel links, and recombined to construct the original message. This increases the bandwidth and efficiency of point-to-point link communication.

With the expanding universe of the Internet, there are small corporations, as well as small ISPs, who would like to establish dial-up serial links. They require connections to the Internet from their local LAN only when they need them. Typically, they do not need permanent dedicated links. A number of proprietary PPP protocols are currently in use. The most common protocol is the Serial Link Internet Protocol (SLIP) for UNIX. IETF has standardized the Internet DP to be used with point-to-point links. Half-bridge provides a method to connect the LAN via a bridge to a router.

Figure 2.26 shows a half-bridge configuration. The router port connecting to the bridge is configured as a serial interface to the PPP half-bridge. The interface functions as a virtual node on the Ethernet subnetwork on the bridge. The serial interface has an IP address associated with the Ethernet subnetwork. Thus, if the Ethernet subnetwork address is 155.55.123.1, the serial interface on the router could be assigned an IP address 155.55.123.5.

When a packet destined to the Ethernet arrives at the router, it is converted to Ethernet packets, encapsulated in PPP frames, and sent on the Ethernet bridge link. In the reverse direction, Ethernet packets encapsulated in PPP frames are extracted by the router, which converts them to IP packets, and routes them on the Internet.

2.3.10   Edge Routers

Edge routers may in general be considered as those elements that perform routing functions at the edge of a network. In other words, they are ingress and egress network elements of a typical WAN. Depending on the application, the functions of this router vary. For example, if it is an edge router to access network, it needs to handle the "triple play" function of real and non-real time traffic. If it is for an MPLS application, it serves the function of an MPLS edge router, which we will learn more about in Chapter 12.

2.3.11   Switches

It would have been logical for us to start reviewing the switch component before we discussed bridges and routers as network components. However, we have chosen to delay its discussion up to now for a good reason, as it logically flows into discussing WANs.

Switches operate at the physical layer of the OSI Reference Model that we discussed in Section 1.5.1. In Section 2.3 we described a switch as a component that makes a physical connection between input and output ports and that the bits and bytes coming in go out exactly the same way. Bridges and routers use the switching function when they route packets.

Most switching technology is based on solid-state technology, and the speed of switching is getting faster and faster. This enables networks to achieve a digital rate of gigabits per second. The performance of a network is determined by how fast we can switch and multiplex data using switches (and consequently in routers and bridges). More importantly, end-to-end performance of the network depends on the speed, latency, and latency variation in transporting data from the source to the destination. Voice, video, and data have different quality-of-service requirements. Based on these requirements, different types of end-to-end circuits are established using switches.

The switching function accomplished in establishing circuits can be classified into circuit switching and packet switching depending on how it is used. Telephone communication uses circuit switching. A physical path from end-to-end is established prior to talking, which is termed call setup. During the actual telephone conversation, the path remains connected whether there is a conversation actually happening or not. That is, the allocated bandwidth for the path is wasted during the idle time of the conversation. Thus, when you are on the telephone and the other party gives you a telephone number, you may say "Please wait while I get a paper and pencil to write." The facilities remain idle during that time and could have been used by others. A "nailed up circuit," where a permanent path is established for the session, is good for voice and video communications where latency and latency variations are intolerable.

Computer traffic is bursty in nature and lends itself more to packet switching. It would be a waste of bandwidth to use circuit switching for computer data networks. Packet switching utilizes the facilities and, hence, the bandwidth available more efficiently. Data are framed into packets and each packet is switched independently. Data from multiple sources are multiplexed and thus the total available bandwidth is shared.

Packet switching is used in routers. The maximum size of the packet is limited to make the router efficient. Packet sizes can vary from source to source, as well as from the same source. The message from a single source is divided into multiple packets and transmitted over the network to the destination. Each packet may take a different path from the source to the destination and may arrive out of sequence. Thus, they have to be reordered at the destination. This is termed datagram service and is shown in Figure 2.27(a). The message from DTE A has been split into three packets. Packets 1 and 3 take path A–B–D, and Packet 2 travels path A–C–B–D. At DTE Z, Packets 1 and 3 arrive before Packet 2 and hence have to be reassembled in the correct order.

It is desirable in many situations, such as in broadband service using ATM (covered in Section 2.6), to have all the packets from a given source to a given destination take the same path. This is analogous to circuit switching in that the path is fixed for the entire session. The concept of session is the same as in circuit switching. A virtual path–virtual circuit is established during the call setup between the source and the destination and a "virtual circuit identification" (one for each hop) is associated with the channel carrying the traffic. The path and circuit identifications are termed virtual as they resemble the operation in circuit switching, but different in that the connection is not physical. Figure 2.27(b) shows the virtual circuit path for the same message as in Figure 2.27(a) from DTE A to DTE Z. Packets arrive in the correct order at DTE Z in this situation. Although the initial call setup is an overhead, subsequent data transmission is faster than in datagram service. We will discuss more how the virtual path–virtual circuit configuration is used in Asynchronous Transfer Mode (ATM) service in Chapter 12.

Circuit and packet switching are applicable to a WAN, which we will review now.

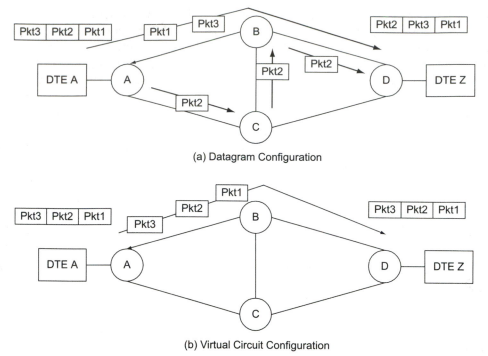

(a) Datagram Configuration

(b) Virtual Circuit Configuration

Figure 2.27 Packet Switch Configurations

2.4 WIDE AREA NETWORKS

The main difference between a WAN and a LAN is the geographical separation between sources and destinations. If the end stations are within a building or campus of buildings, it is still considered a LAN with a possible high-speed backbone LAN, such as FDDI.

As we saw in Section 1.2, computer communication network rides on top of telecommunication network, which is a WAN. Although most telephone and video communications traversing the WAN are still circuit switched, data traffic generated by computer communications is packet switched. We previously discussed two kinds of packet-switched services—datagram service and virtual circuit service.

Virtual circuit can be established on a session basis or on a permanent basis. The former is called a switched virtual circuit (SVC) and the latter a permanent virtual circuit (PVC). Geographically distributed organizations would lease PVCs from public service providers to handle large amounts of traffic. Otherwise, SVC service is used more often. Public telecommunication service providers offer these services. However, private corporations, using their own switches and leased lines from public service providers, set up large enterprise data networks.

We can partition WAN from a network management perspective into two sections and analyze the components and services that need to be managed in each. The two end sections of WAN are the subscriber loop sections, where information flows from central offices of the service provider(s) to customers' premises. The other section is transmission between switching offices.

Subscriber loop sections could be either passive, such as dedicated pairs of wires from the central office to the customer premises, or active links such as coaxial cable interspersed with amplifiers to boost the signal along the way. In either case, a digital subscriber line (DSL) terminates in a network interface unit (NIU) at the customer premises. Examples of NIU are Channel Service Unit (CSU) for interfacing DSL with analog equipment at customer premises, and Digital Service Unit (DSU) for DSL interface with digital equipment. The responsibility of the service provider is up to the NIU. Thus, components that need to be managed are the NIUs and the active components on the loop transmission line.

The transmission section consists of link transmission facilities and nodal components. These are between central offices in the case of a public switched network, and between the routers of service providers in private networks. We have looked at nodal components already. We will now consider transmission media and modes of LANs and WANs.

2.5 TRANSMISSION TECHNOLOGY

2.5.1 Introduction

Transmission technology deals with transmission media and transmission modes. We will look at transmission media first and then at transmission modes.

A transmission medium consists of the link that carries data between two physical systems. There is a coupling mechanism—a transceiver (denoting transmitter and receiver) that delivers to and receives data from the medium. Transmission media can be broadly classified into wired media and wireless media. Transportation of information is accomplished using physical transmission facilities, such as wires and optical fiber, or via wireless media using technology like radio frequency spectrum, infrared, and light waves. In the former case information is transmitted from point to point, whereas in the latter case it is generally done on a broadcast basis.

Both wired and wireless transmissions are used for local as well as WANs. The physical connection and the electronics of the transceiver play an important part in LAN, as they determine how fast and accurately information can be transmitted to and received from the various transmission media. We observed that the bandwidth of all types of Ethernet LANs could be doubled by changing from simplex to duplex configuration. In fact, advancement of new technologies depends on enhancements to existing ones. For example, ATM to the desktop has been aborted because of Ethernet technology's increased ability to handle large bandwidth (in gigabits per second) to the desktop. We also saw in Section 2.3.1 how hub technology has increased throughput in handling a large number of stations on a LAN.

Wireless LAN has so far found only limited use for high-speed communication. However, wireless technology is very extensively used for laptops, mobile communication, satellite transmission, and television access in rural areas.

2.5.2 Wired Transmission

Wired transmission technology uses three media: coaxial cable, twisted-pair cable, and optical fiber. The key parameters to look for in choosing the transmission medium are the following: loss of signal, insensitivity to environmental noise sources (such as cross talk and spurious radio frequency signals generated by appliances), bandwidth handling capability, and transmission delay. The selection of the medium is also determined by the type of stations on the medium and their access control mechanism. We listed the limitations and capabilities of various LAN media for Ethernet LAN in Tables 2.1 and 2.2.

There are two types of coaxial cables—thick and thin. The thick cable is 0.4 centimeters in diameter and is not used anymore. The thin coaxial cable is 0.25 centimeters in diameter and is present in legacy systems or small LANs, where it can be economically installed without a hub.

A twisted-pair cable consists of a pair of wires that are twisted. The gauge of the wire and the type of twist determine the quality of transmission. They are available as unshielded twisted pair (UTP) and shielded twisted pair (STP). Obviously, the latter reduces the interference of radio frequency noise better than the former. Most twisted-pair cabling that is used in LAN is Category 5 (cat-5) UTP. With cat-5 cable, the drop length for IEEE 802.3 LAN given in Table 2.1 can be extended from 100 to 150 meters at 100 Mbps. cat-6a cable extends the data rate to 10 Gbps.

The fiber-optic medium provides the best quality transmission. Of course, it is the most expensive. However, it is economical when LANs need to be networked in a campus environment or building with multiple stories. As shown in Tables 2.1 and 2.2, point-to-point drop for Ethernet could be as high as 2 kilometers, and in Gigabit Ethernet, we can extend it up to 9 kilometers.

It is worth noting the importance of cabling in geographically placed network components. As we all know, implementers always try to stretch the limits of specifications or economize in the installation process. For example, the maximum distance for a cat-3 cable would be stretched beyond the standard distance of 100 meters. Alternatively, instead of cabling all workstations using cat-5 and optical fibers to a central location where patch panels and hubs are collocated, hubs would be distributed to economize in cabling cost and only cat-3 cable is used. However, there is a price to pay in operations and maintenance for this approach since hubs could not be shared and any failure of a remote hub would take much longer for service restoration.

Wired WAN media comprises bundles of twisted pairs (such as in T1 and loop facilities), coaxial cable for analog transmission (for example, N1), and optical fiber (underwater sea cable).

2.5.3   Wireless Transmission Media

Wireless medium is used in WLAN as well as in mobile and satellite communications.

Wireless LAN uses input sources such as a hand-held portable communication device or a computer with a wireless antenna. Wireless LAN technology focuses primarily on transmitting data from portable stations to a wired LAN access point by radio frequency, infrared, or optical transmission. Since the range of transmission is limited for all these, they all function within a given region or cell. If the portable station is a moving target, then the signal has to be handed over from one cell to another cell.

Two fast-growing segments of wireless technology in the non-LAN environment are of interest for data communication. They are Personal Communication Services (PCS) and digital cellular services. Both of these are based on cell-based technology. Data are transmitted by wireless to local cell antennas from where they go to the central location by wired network. PCS is all-digital technology. It operates at lower power (100 watts) and antennas are more closely spaced (1/2 to 1 mile). The digital cellular technology, although analog, carries digitized signal. It needs higher-power antennas, which are separated farther apart (several miles).

Another area of wireless technology is broadband multimedia services. Multimedia is transmitted using satellite wireless technology from a central office to the customer's premises. The return path is via telephone lines.

2.5.4   Transmission Modes

The data transmission mode can be either digital or analog. Narrow-band LAN technology uses digital mode of transmission. Broadband and WAN technologies employ both analog and digital modes of transmission. When information is transmitted in an analog transmission mode, it can be transmitted in either baseband or on a carrier.

In a physical medium, digital transmission is a series of ones and zeros. A physical medium is shared by multiple sources to transport information to multiple destinations. The distinction between various transmission technologies is how information between pairs of end users is coded to share the same medium. They should be multiplexed and de-multiplexed efficiently at the nodes to provide the least and as constant a delay as possible, as well as high throughput.

Figure 2.28 shows three basic modes of transmission. They are Time Division Multiplexing (TDM) transmission, packet transmission, and cell transmission. T1 is the early implementation of TDM digital transmission in the United States by the Bell System. Figure 2.28(a) shows TDM transmission of T1 carrier, which carries 24 voice channels. The T1 carrier has a bandwidth of 1.544 MHz and is equally divided among 24 voice channels, each with a bandwidth of 64 kHz. The top of Figure 2.28(a) shows how the 1.544 MHz transmission "pipe" is divided into 24 small dedicated pipes among the 24 channels. The bottom half of the figure shows the multiplexing of the 24 channels as bit stream on the physical medium. They are multiplexed cyclically from Channel 1 through Channel 24. The maximum bandwidth available for each channel is 64 kHz, but it is all available during a complete session. A session is defined as the duration from establishment of a connection to tearing it down between a pair of users.

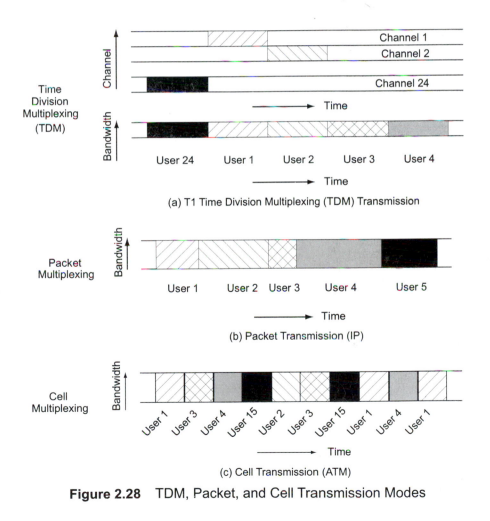

(a) T1 Time Division Multiplexing (TDM) Transmission

(b) Packet Transmission (IP)

(c) Cell Transmission (ATM)

Figure 2.28 TDM, Packet, and Cell Transmission Modes

Notice that all channels have equal bandwidth and occupy the same slot in the transmission channel. When the receiver synchronizes to the transmitter, it is able to de-multiplex the channels, but both the transmitter and the receiver know exactly which slot each user's data occupy. Since a physical connection is set up between the two end stations prior to data transmission, the time delay is constant, which is essential for voice and video transmission. Nodes in the network using TDM are circuit switches. As mentioned in Section 2.3.11, the end-to-end connection is physical. The video channel, which requires more bandwidth (exact bandwidth depends on compression of data and quality of service required), occupies more channels.

Figure 2.28(b) shows the packet transmission mode. We notice that packets of different users are randomly multiplexed. While each user's data is traversing the medium, the full bandwidth of the medium is available to it. This is in contrast to TDM, where only a fraction of the medium bandwidth is available to any user. It can also be noticed that the size of all the user packets need not be the same. Another noticeable factor is that since the circuit connection is not pre-established, each packet contains addresses of the originator and the destination. We briefly described a packet switch in Section 2.3.11. Obviously, packet switches are used with packet transmission. A packet switch at each node looks at the address of the destination and routes it using the appropriate path. Each packet can take a different route depending on the availability of links and bandwidth based on different algorithms used. The packets may arrive out of sequence at the receiver, and the end-to-end transmission time for each packet is different. This transmission mode is acceptable for data transmission, but not for voice and video. Data transmission can tolerate bursty traffic.

The cell transmission mode, shown in Figure 2.28(c), combines the best of the above modes of transmission. The packets are all of the same size and are small in size. Each packet has the full bandwidth of the medium and the packets are statistically multiplexed. The packets all take the same path as in the circuit-switched TDM mode, using the virtual path–virtual circuit concept. This mode of transmission is called the ATM and is one of the fundamental concepts of ATM technology.

A recent development in WAN transport technologies is the evolution of the multiprotocol label switching (MPLS) transmission mode using the MPLS protocol. It can be visualized as an enhancement over IP and ATM protocols and backward compatible with either of them. A label, called the MPLS label, is inserted between layer 2 and layer 3, as shown in Figure 2.29. Thus, for an IP-based protocol,

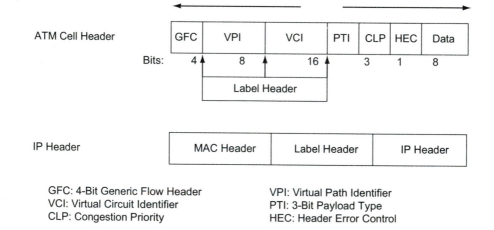

Figure 2.29   MPLS Transmission Mode

the MPLS label is inserted between the IEEE 802.3 MAC header and the network layer IP header. In the case of the ATM protocol, MPLS shim without the TTL field replaces VPI and VCI fields. The MPLS transmission mode attempts to take advantage of the richness of IP characteristics and high performance of ATM.

An IP-based network is feature rich because of its extensive implementation and compatibility with Ethernet LAN. It routes packets intelligently. However, it is slow in performance as it has to open each packet at layer 3 to determine its next hop and its output port. Simultaneous transport of real-time and non-real-time traffic is difficult.

In contrast to IP, the ATM protocol is a high-performance cell-based protocol switching cells at layer 2. It is capable of handling real-time and non-real-time traffic simultaneously, and thus is superior to the IP-based network. However, its address incompatibility with the popular Ethernet LAN, along with difficult end-to-end circuit provisioning, has limited its usage at the customer premises network and hence related applications.

In general, the packet header contains forwarding equivalence class (FEC) information to choose the next hop in a router. In so far as the forwarding decision is concerned, all packets belonging to a particular FEC are assigned the same path leaving the node. The MPLS label is a short, fixed length, locally significant identifier, which is used to identify an FEC.

An MPLS protocol is being deployed in a convergent network for broadband services handling real-time and non-real-time traffic simultaneously, thus achieving high quality of service transport. It can be deployed in the legacy network of either IP or ATM base.

Currently most information is transmitted in digital mode. The legacy digital system is a T-based hierarchy (T1, T3…) in North America and an E-based hierarchy (E1, E2...) in the UK and Europe and uses packet or frame technology. The later implementation of digital mode of transmission in many WANs is the Synchronous Optical Network (SONET), which is addressed in the next section. More recently, the WAN transmission mode has started migrating to MPLS over IP.

We can visualize the above transmission modes as modes of transmission at the basic or atomic level (although not quite true). Each of the modes—TDM, ATM cell mode, IP packet mode, MPLS packet mode—is transmitted using its own protocol. Thus, they can be considered as modes based on protocol. However, modern transmission technology is capable of carrying a large amount of information; i.e., large bandwidth of information; and this should be taken advantage of in designing transmission systems. For instance, optical fiber can carry a terahertz (THz) bandwidth signal. However, the quality of the signal transmission gets worse when the signal bandwidth is large. It is due to network element limitations and propagation constraints. Fortunately, we can transmit a large amount of information using the same physical medium by employing the multiplexing principle discussed in TDM. In T1 or E1 TDM, 24 or 32 channels can be multiplexed by logically partitioning the physical medium into 24 or 32 channels.

Using multiplexing approach, the physical optical-fiber medium can be used to carry multiplexed lower bandwidth signals using Synchronous Digital Hierarchy (SDH). This mode of transmission is known as SONET in North America and SDH in Europe and Asia and is discussed more in Chapter 12. Nodes in the optical transmission network are used to regenerate the signal using regenerators, change path by using optical or digital cross-connect network elements, and drop and add lower-level digital signals at various intermediate points along the path by using Add–Drop Multiplexers (ADM). Figure 2.30 shows a SONET transmission mode. The lower-speed digital signals DS1/E1, DS1C, DS2, designated as Virtual Tributaries (VTs) are multiplexed into a VT Group. A SONET frame comprises an overhead and synchronous payload called a synchronous payload envelope (SPE). The speed of digital data

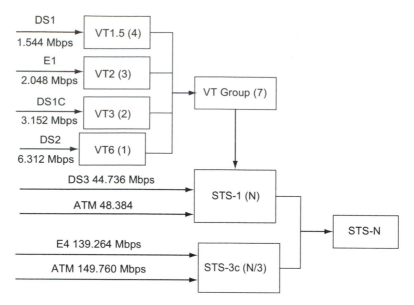

Figure 2.30 SONET Transmission Mode

is synchronized using a SONET basic signal rate of 51.84 Mbps called synchronous transport signal level-1 (STS-1). Higher-rate signals STS-N are generated by interleaving bytes from lower-level STS-1s. The numbers in parentheses in Figure 2.30 indicate the number of input signals that need to be multiplexed.

In Figure 2.30, STS-1 comprises seven VT Group signals, or a DS3 signal, or a 48-Mbps ATM signal. STS-3 SONET signal, also known as STM-1 in SDH, is made up of a 150-Mbps ATM or E4 signal. Transmission rates for SONET/SDH signals are presented in Table 2.3.

The second method of the increasing capacity of information in an optical transmission medium is to take advantage of the optical wavelength of transmission. This is known as wavelength division multiplexing (WDM). This is identical to frequency division multiplexing at (relatively) lower frequencies. Information can be transmitted over multiple wavelengths using multiple transmission protocols, as shown in Figure 2.31. In order to illustrate this point, transmission modes shown in Figure 2.28 are depicted in Figure 2.31 as components in the WDM transmission, each submode traversing at a different wavelength. Several hundreds of tens-of-gigabits signals can be transmitted over the long-haul WAN and short-haul MANs.

Table 2.3 SONET/SDH Transmission Rates

SONET SIGNAL	SDH SIGNAL	BIT RATE (Mbps)
STS-1		51.84
STS-3	STM-1	155.52
STS-12	STM-4	622.08
STS-24		1,244.16
STS-48	STM-16	2,488.32
STS-192	STM-64	9,953.28
STS-768	STM-256	39,814.32

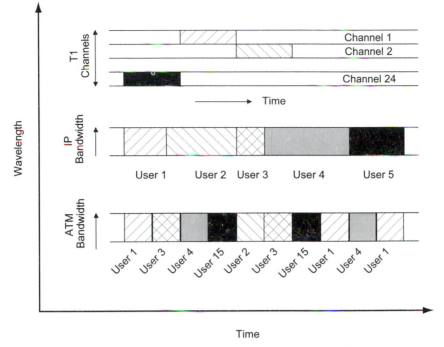

Figure 2.31 Multiwavelength Fiber: WDM

<table>
<tr><td>2.6</td><td></td></tr>
</table>

2.6 INTEGRATED SERVICES: ISDN, FRAME RELAY, AND BROADBAND

Integrated Services Digital Network (ISDN) can be divided into narrow band and broadband ISDN. Broadband ISDN is called broadband services. ISDN was introduced by Bell System to integrate voice and data over telephone loop facilities. The same principle is used in integrating voice, video, and data and providing them as broadband multimedia service.

The early form of integrated services network is Basic ISDN. It is a full-duplex digital interface between the subscriber and the central office. It consists of two basic channels, 56-kilobaud rate each, combined with an 8-kilobaud signaling channel, referred to as 2B+D.

Basic ISDN was extended to T1 and E1 rates of 1.544 Mbps and 2.048 Mbps. This is called the Primary ISDN interface. The T1 interface carries 24 channels and the E1 interface 32 channels.

With the improved quality of transmission media, the ISDN concept was extended from the subscriber interface to a WAN. To achieve near real-time quality for voice, the performance of WAN needs to be improved. This was done by a frame relay service, which eliminates hop-to-hop flow and error controls in a traditional packet switching network, including X.25. Flow and error controls are relegated to higher layers at the ends of a link. The frame relay access speed can go up to 2 Mbps.

However, on-line videos require a much larger bandwidth than could be achieved with frame relay. This has led to early implementation of broadband ISDN, or, as mentioned in the beginning of this section, more succinctly, broadband network. Broadband network and service have contributed significantly to advances in three areas. They are ATM (Asynchronous Transfer Mode), SONET (Synchronous Optical

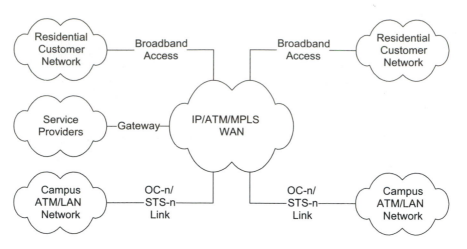

Figure 2.32 Broadband Services Network

Network)/SDH (Synchronous Digital Hierarchy), and broadband access technology. In Chapter 12, we will discuss ATM, which is a cell-based transmission mode, and SONET, which is a digital hierarchy adopted universally.

Broadband access technology, which addresses the link from the central office to the customer's premises, is implemented using one of three technologies. Hybrid fiber coax (HFC) technology is a two-way interactive multimedia communication system using fiber and coaxial cable facilities and cable modems. The second technology uses a DSL. There are several variations of implementing this, generically referred to as xDSL. For example, ADSL stands for asymmetric DSL. The third technology uses wireless transmission from the switching office or head end to the customer's premises via satellite transmission. We will learn in detail about broadband service and access network technologies in Part IV.

Figure 2.32 shows a broadband services network. The WAN is IP, ATM, or MPLS. The WAN is linked to the customer's premises using either optical links, OC-n (Optical Carrier-n)/STS (Synchronous Transport Signal), or one of the three access technologies (HFC, xDSL, or wireless). The customer network consists of two classes, residential customers and corporate customers with a campus-like network. Residential customers are either residential homes or small and medium enterprises (SMEs) that use broadband services, but do not maintain high-speed access network to WAN. Service providers perform that function bringing radio, video, Internet, and other services to homes. Multiple services are multiplexed by multiple service operators (MSO) and are piped to the customer's premises via common facilities. Service providers interface with each other via gateways, which could be either generalized routers or ATM switches.

▉▶ Summary

In this chapter we learned network concepts and technologies that would help us understand network management in Parts II, III, and IV.

Network topologies can be classified as LAN and WAN topologies. There are three network topologies associated with wired LANs. They are bus, ring, and star. The most predominant commercially employed LANs are a hybrid of the star topology with either the bus or the ring topology—the hub topology.

WAN is implemented using either a mesh or a tree topology. Mesh topology is the common implementation and is the topology of the Internet. Tree topology is used when a network is made up of bridges.

We discussed different types of common LAN implementation—Ethernet, Fast Ethernet, Gigabit Ethernet, switched hub, Token Ring, and FDDI. Of these, IEEE 802.3 Ethernet LAN is the predominant type. This uses CSMA/CD MAC protocol. We addressed the introduction of full-duplex types of Ethernet that double the bandwidth. Ethernet can be implemented using various types of transmission media—coaxial cable, UTP, and optical fiber. Fast Ethernet at 100 Mbps and Gigabit Ethernet at 1 Gbps speed can be implemented by employing hub technology. Switched hub multiplies the throughput by simultaneous conversations between pairs of nodes. Virtual LANs, implemented using switched hub, enable logical association of workstations with VLANs.

Token Ring and FDDI both use deterministic MAC and hence are more efficient over random access Ethernet. IEEE 802.5 defines the speed of the Token Ring as either 4 Mbps or 16 Mbps.

FDDI is based on IEEE 802.5 protocol and operates at 100 Mbps. It is typically used for backbone LAN. Because of the need for reliability of the backbone, FDDI can be configured as a dual ring with DAS, in contrast to a single ring with SAS.

Network nodes comprise hubs, bridges, routers, gateways, and switches. Hubs play a significant role in forming LANs as discussed above. Bridges function at the data link layer and can be interconnected to form a network. A network consisting of Ethernet bridges is called a transparent bridge network and should meet the criterion of not having any loop in the network. In contrast, a network made up of Token-Ring bridges, source routing bridges, can have loops in the network. This is because the source specifies the route in the data packet and intermediate nodes do not make any routing decisions.

Routers and gateways function at the network layer. Routers and gateways form the backbone of the Internet. The difference between a router and a gateway is that the former just routes, whereas the latter does protocol conversion. If protocol conversion is done at the application layer, it is called a protocol converter.

Packet switching is the switching of data packets. Packet switches, in general, perform datagram service. That means each packet of the same message can take different routes and may arrive out of sequence. Hence, they have to be reassembled at the receiver in the correct sequence.

We can also configure packet switches to form a virtual circuit. In this case, all packets of a session between the source and the destination take the same path in the network and arrive in the same sequence that they were sent. A virtual circuit can be established on a per-session basis, in which case, it is called a switched virtual circuit (SVC). The virtual circuit is set up and torn down each time. In contrast, for a permanent virtual circuit (PVC), call setup is done and left there permanently.

A WAN is established using either SVC or PVC. WAN is distinguished from LAN by large geographical separation between the source and the destination. It is generally carried over the facilities of telecommunications network.

In discussing transmission technology, we covered wired and WLAN technologies. The role of coaxial cable, twisted-pair cable, and optical fiber was reviewed. LAN transmits data in digital format. WAN and broadband technology services transmit information in both digital and analog modes. We addressed the various transmission modes of TDM, cell, and packet technologies. Optical-fiber technology was presented, which can carry information in the tens of gigahertz bandwidth in the SONET/SDH and WDM transmission modes.

We ended our discussion of network technology by introducing ISDN and broadband multimedia services. They handle voice, video, and data transmission in an integrated manner. The WAN in broadband services is ATM-based SONET and the access to customer premises uses HFC, xDSL, or wireless technology.

Exercises

1. The maximum allowed segment for Ethernet is 500 meters and the maximum number of segments that can be connected by repeaters is limited to five. The minimum length of the frame that can be transmitted is the sum of the round-trip delay and the repeater delays. Assume that the speed of transmission on the cable is 200 meters/microsecond and that the total round-trip delay in traversing all the repeaters is 25 microseconds. Show that the minimum frame size (number of bits per frame) of an Ethernet frame is 64 bytes.

   Note: The maximum frame size is 1,518 bytes.

2. Gigabit Ethernet using CSMA/CD is specified to have a 100-meter drop cable. Show that this corresponds to a slot time of 512 bytes to detect collision. Assume a repeater delay of two microseconds.

3. The Engineering Department of 12 persons in a small corporation is on a regular 10Base-T Ethernet LAN hub with 16 ports. The busy group started complaining because of the slow network performance. The network was operating at 50% utilization, whereas 30% utilization is acceptable. If you are the Information Technology Engineer of the corporation and have to resolve the problem technically,

   (a) Describe four choices for resolving the problem, maintaining the LAN as Ethernet LAN.

   (b) State the advantages and disadvantages of each approach.

4. In Exercise 3, you are told by the IT Manager that the problem is to be resolved by using bridges and the existing hub that could be configured for four subnets. A good rule of thumb is that a LAN utilization of 4% yields good and satisfactory performance. Assume that 12 workstations are functioning at a peer-to-peer level with distribution of traffic between any two stations being the same. What would your new configuration be?

5. Design an Ethernet LAN using a 10/100 Mbps switched Ethernet hub to handle the following specifications:

   Number of clients = 16 operating at 10 Mbps

   Number of server = 1

   50% of the traffic is directed to the server

   Draw the configuration and indicate the transmission modes (half-duplex or duplex) on the ports.

6. Repeat Exercise 4 if the traffic to the server increases to 80.

7. Two virtual LANs, 145.50.50.1 belonging to NM lab and 145.50.60.1 belonging to Networking lab, each have three workstations. The former has workstations 140.50.50.11-13 and the latter 140.50.60.21-23. They are connected to a switched hub as shown in Figure 2.10 on ports 2 through 7. The NICs associated with ports are made by Cabletron and their MAC addresses start with the vendor's global prefix 00-00-D (hexadecimal notation) and end with 11, 12, 13, 21, 22, and 23 (same as the fourth decimal position of the IP address).

   (a) Create a conceptual matrix table, as shown below, which would be generated by the hub that relates the IP address, the MAC address, and the port number.

IP ADDRESS	MAC ADDRESS	PORT NUMBER

   (b) The workstation 23 is moved from Networking lab to NM lab. Show the appropriate parameter changes on the hub and the workstation.

8. In Exercise 7, Port 1 of the hub is connected to a router as shown in Figure 2.10. The IP and MAC addresses associated with the NIC on the hub interfacing to the router are 145.50.50.1

and 00-00-100-00-00-01 and that with the NIC on the router interfacing with the switched hub of 130.30.40.1 and 00-00-10-00.00-64. Extend the matrix of Exercise 7(a) to include Port 1, using the same convention for the MAC address.

9. In Exercise 8, the router is connected to the switched hub by a single physical cable. The router maintains two sets of tables, one to determine the subnets on its network and other to determine the host on the subnet as shown below. The third decimal of the IP address is allocated to subnet designation.

Network Table

NETWORK	SUBNET	HOST
145.50	50	0
...	...	0
145.50	60	0

Subnet Address Tables

NETWORK	SUBNET	HOST	PORT
145.50	50	1	1
145.50	50	11	1
"	"	12	1
"	"	13	1
145.50	60	1	1
"	"	21	1
"	"	22	1
"	"	23	1

(a) What is the mask used by the router to filter the subnet?

(b) Show how two packets arriving in the router and addressed to 145.50.50.11 and 145.50.60.21 are directed to the switched hub by using the above table.

10. Design a client–server network with two servers operating at 100Base-T Fast Ethernet speed and the clients operating at regular 10Base-T Ethernet speed using a 10/100 Mbps NIC. The hub is located in a wiring closet, but the servers and clients are not. Assume that a satisfactory performance is achieved at 40% utilization of the LAN.

11. Which of the following is correct? The maximum throughput of an 8-port switched hub over an 8-port non-switched hub is:

    (a) the same

    (b) 2 times

    (c) 4 times

    (d) 8 times

12. It is assumed in Exercise 11 that the LAN operates at maximum utilization. However, a regular LAN can degrade in performance to an intolerable level at 50% utilization. What is the approximate (ignore contention of more than one station trying to reach the same destination at the same time) percentage utilization improvement of a 12-port switched hub Ethernet LAN over a non-switched hub Ethernet LAN?

13. The minimum size of the frame in a token-ring LAN is determined by the token size, which is 3 bytes long and should be contained in the ring under idle condition. Assume a 16-Mbps LAN and the speed of transmission as 200 meters/microsecond.

    (a) What should be the minimum length of the ring in meters?
    (b) Each station normally adds a bit delay in processing the data. What is the additional length gained by adding one station at a time?

14. Repeat Exercise 13 for an FDDI ring. Assume the speed of transmission as 300 meters/microsecond.

15. Explain the reason why the performance of an Ethernet LAN decreases with increase in the number of stations on the LAN, whereas it increases (at least initially) with the increase in the number of stations in a token-ring LAN.

16. Draw network configuration and protocol layer interface architecture for a multiprotocol bridge that interconnects an Ethernet LAN to a token-ring LAN.

17. A short message is transmitted from a source at Switch A to a destination at Switch Z. The shortest path traverses through 5 intermediate switches. A switch causes an average delay of 5 milliseconds to process a packet. Assume all the packets of the message leave at approximately the same time (although they leave sequentially), as the duration of the message is short compared to the transmission delay in the switches.

    (a) A ssume the message is sent as a datagram and the datagram packets take multiple paths, each packet traversing the shortest path going through 5 intermediate switches and the longest path going through 10 intermediate switches. Calculate the latency time if the packet reassembling time is ignored at the destination.
    (b) What is latency if a virtual circuit is established along the shortest path?

18. How many (a) E1 channels and (b) DS1 (T1) channels comprise an STM-1 SDH signal?

PART II

SNMP and Network Management

Part II, comprising Chapters 3–9, is devoted to understanding the principles of network and system management. Chapters 3–7 discuss the management of a TCP/IP network using Simple Network Management System (SNMP) versions 1, 2, and 3. Remote monitoring, which is also part of SNMP management, is discussed in Chapter 8.

In Chapter 3, technical foundations on standards, models, and language, which are needed to build network management based on various standards, are introduced. Network management standards that are currently used are SNMP (Internet), CMIP (OSI), TMN, IEEE, and Web-based Management. Of these, SNMP is the most widely deployed management system due to its truly simple architecture and implementation. An overview of models and concepts of network management is covered. Specifications of most protocols are done using ASN.1 syntax, which is discussed in some detail.

There are three versions of SNMP-based protocols that manage TCP/IP networks. SNMPv1 is covered in Chapters 4 and 5. Chapter 4 is devoted to the organization and information models of SNMP in network management. System architecture and SNMP messages are presented. The structure of management information (SMI) is presented using ASN.1 syntax. The definition of SNMP objects and their organization in the structure of management information base (MIB) are described. Chapter 5 covers SNMP communication protocol. Message data structures are presented along with the message protocol operations and SNMP MIB.

Learning Chapters 4 and 5 would help the reader to understand the basic principles behind SNMP network management. Case histories and practical examples punctuate the presentation. When the book is used as a textbook for a course, this should provide adequate background for the student to select a project for the course if the course includes a project as part of its requirements. I strongly recommend it—especially for an undergraduate course. A list of projects, which have been used in senior undergraduate and graduate classes, is presented in Appendix B.

Chapter 6 addresses SNMPv2. SNMPv2 adds several significant enhancements to SNMPv1, including efficient transferring of bulk data between systems. One of the intended major enhancements, namely security considerations, was postponed from SNMPv2 to SNMPv3. In Chapter 7, we cover security and privacy, as well as generalized SNMP architecture and applications, which are part of SNMPv3 specifications.

The SNMP management system is based on polling. Remote monitoring of network components using probes and sending only relevant data to the network management system is the goal of RMON discussed in Chapter 8.

Chapter 9 is devoted to networking tools, management tools, and management systems. You will learn some basic networking tools that are part of the operating system, which would be of immense help in day-to-day use and operations of the network. SNMP command tools are convenient tools that can be used for network management even without having a network management system. We have earlier learned the immense benefits of MIBs in network management. Hence, MIBs have to be designed well, which is covered in MIB engineering. The design of the network management system for various vertical network applications, as well as for performing various functions, is covered in detail. After learning these tools, we will cover network management systems ranging from low-end to high-end solutions. We will dwell in more detail on the mid-range enterprise network management systems with examples of commercial systems that are in widespread use.

Basic Foundations: Standards, Models, and Language

In Part I we had an overview of networking and management of network and systems. We learned about network technology and components that need to be managed. There are several management standards and models in existence for managing networks, systems, and services. We can understand and appreciate them better by first looking at the commonality among them, and then the differences that distinguish them. These goals form the objectives of this chapter.

We will consider the foundations that are needed to build various network management models and protocols. We will survey the network management standards and present the general architecture of the network management models in Section 3.1.

The International Standards Organization (ISO) has defined a generalized model that addresses all aspects of network management. We will cover the three models of the architecture in Sections 3.3 through 3.5, which deal with organization, information, and communication. Then we will learn the basics of the formal language, ASN.1, and the data structure that is used for management systems to store management information and communicate with each other in Sections 3.6 through 3.8.

All the above three models are designed for management applications to manage networks, systems, and services. The fourth model, functional model, addresses these in Section 3.9. The applications fall into the categories of fault, configuration, performance, security, and accounting.

In a global perspective, three areas of network need managing. They are network, systems, and services; inter-layer protocols; and intra-layer protocols. In this book our focus will be on network and system management aspects. We define network management as management of the network comprising nodes and links, and system management as managing system resources, such as central processor usage, disk usage, and application processes. Service management deals with services provided by organizations to customers. Service management is an extension of network and systems.

The two leading models of network management are the Internet model and the Open System Interconnection (OSI) model. The Internet model is the most widely used for network management. It is a simple scalar model and hence easy to implement. The OSI model, which is object oriented, is more complex and harder to implement. However, with the matured state of object-oriented technology and the convergence of data and telecommunications technologies, object-oriented implementation of network management has come into vogue. We will address this in Chapter 16. A higher-level management network called the Telecommunications Management Network (TMN) is also based on the OSI model. It addresses all levels of management including service and business aspects. We will study TMN in Chapter 10.

In this book we will be concerned primarily with the study of Internet-based SNMP model. The OSI model is discussed in Appendix A.

3.1   NETWORK MANAGEMENT STANDARDS

There are several network management standards that are in use today.

Table 3.1 lists four standards, along with a fifth class based on emerging technologies, and their salient points. The first four are the OSI model, the Internet model, TMN, and IEEE LAN/MAN. A detailed treatment of the various standards can be found in [Black, 1995]. The first category in Table 3.1, Open System Interconnection (OSI) management standard, is the standard adopted by the International Standards Organization (ISO). The OSI management protocol standard is Common Management Information Protocol (CMIP). The OSI management protocol has built-in services, Common Management Information Service (CMIS), which specify the basic services needed to perform the various functions. It is the most comprehensive set of specifications and addresses all seven layers. OSI specifications are structured and deal with all seven layers of the OSI Reference Model. The specifications are object oriented and hence managed objects are based on object classes and inheritance rules. Besides specifying the management protocols, CMIP/CMIS also address network management applications. Some of the

Table 3.1   Network Management Standards

STANDARD	SALIENT POINTS
OSI/CMIP	• International standard (ISO/OSI)
	• Management of data communications network—LAN and WAN
	• Deals with all seven layers
	• Most complete
	• Object oriented
	• Well structured and layered
	• Consumes large resource in implementation
SNMP/Internet	• Industry standard (IETF)
	• Originally intended for management of Internet components, currently adopted for WAN and telecommunication systems
	• Easy to implement
	• Most widely implemented
TMN	• International standard (ITU-T)
	• Management of telecommunications network
	• Based on OSI network management framework
	• Addresses both network and administrative aspects of management
	• eTOM industry standard for business processes for implementing TMN using NGOSS framework
IEEE	• IEEE standards adopted internationally
	• Addresses LAN and MAN management
	• Adopts OSI standards significantly
	• Deals with first two layers of OSI RM
Emerging Technologies	• Web-Based Enterprise Management (WBEM)
	• Java Management Extension (JMX)
	• XML-based Network Management
	• CORBA-based Network Management

major drawbacks of the OSI management standard were that it was complex and that the CMIP stack was large. Although these are no longer impediments to the implementation of the CMIP/CMIS network management, SNMP is the protocol that is extensively deployed.

In contrast to the CMIP protocol, the Simple Network Management Protocol (SNMP) presented in Table 3.1 is truly simple as its name indicates. It started as an industry standard and has since become very much like standard specifications of a standards organization. The Internet Engineering Task Force (IETF) is responsible for all Internet specifications including network management. The managed objects are defined as scalar objects in SNMP. It was primarily intended to manage Internet components, but is now used to manage WAN and telecommunications systems. It is easy to implement and is the most widely implemented network management system today. We will discuss SNMP management in more detail in this book.

The third category in Table 3.1, TMN, is designed to manage the telecommunications network and is oriented toward the needs of telecommunications service providers. TMN is ITU-T (International Telecommunications Union—Telecommunications) standard and is based on OSI CMIP/CMIS specifications. TMN extends the concept of management beyond managing networks and network components. Its specifications address service and business considerations (M3000). Chapter 10 is devoted to the discussion of TMN.

Enhanced Telecommunications Operations Map (eTOM) is a guidebook for business processes in the telecommunications industry. It is an extension of TMN. It is being developed by TeleManagement Forum (TM Forum) as component of NGOSS (New Generation OSS) [Reillly and Creaner, 2005]. The main difference between the TMN and eTOM approaches is that the former has been developed starting from networks and network equipment (bottom up), while eTOM is a top–down approach. The eTOM framework has been incorporated within the TMN framework as a set of standards (M.3050.x).

The IEEE standards for Local Area Network (LAN) and Metropolitan Area Network (MAN) specifications shown in Table 3.1 are only concerned with OSI layers 1 (physical) and 2 (data link). Those specifications are structured similar to OSI specifications. Both OSI/CMIP and Internet/SNMP protocols use IEEE standards for the lower layers. The IEEE 802.x series of specifications define the standards for the various physical media and data link protocols. IEEE 802.1 specifications present overview, architecture, and management. The IEEE 802.2 standard specifies the Logical Link Control (LLC) layer. As we saw in Chapter 1 (Figure 1.14), the LLC layer provides transparency of the various physical media and protocols to the network layer. The others in series are for specific media and protocols. For example, 802.3 specifications are for Ethernet LANs.

The last category in Table 3.1 addresses several emerging management technologies. One of them is based on using Web technology, Web server for the management system and Web browsers for network management stations. In Web-based management, the organization model uses Web server–Web browser architecture. Much of the object-oriented technology, such as hypermedia server, CORBA-oriented transportation, and client–server push-technology influence the Web-based management.

The Web-Based Enterprise Management (WBEM) standard is developed by the Desktop Management Task Force (DMTF). It is based on the Common Information Model (CIM) data model transported using CIM Operations over HTTP.

The Java Management Extension [JMX] is an open Java technology for management. It defines management architecture, application programming interfaces (APIs), and management services under a single umbrella specification. It was developed under Sun Microsystems's JMAPI (Java Management API) initiative.

XML is a meta-markup language standardized by the Worldwide Web Consortium (W3C) for document exchange in the Web. XML-based network management is based on a network management method, which defines management information by XML and the exchange of data for management in the form of an XML document, and it uses an XML document-processing standard method for processing data.

Common Object Request Broker Architecture (CORBA)-based Network Management is an object-oriented client–server model that uses CORBA. The objects are defined using Interface Description Language (IDL) and uses a distributed managed objects architecture.

With the Web-based management system, not only can object-oriented technology be implemented but also the dedicated workstation constraint is removed by the use of a Web browser. However, which object-oriented technology should an IT manager choose? There is no clear-cut answer to this question, and different vendors have implemented NMSs using different technologies for different applications.

3.2 NETWORK MANAGEMENT MODELS

The OSI network model is an ISO standard and is most complete of all the models. It is structured and it addresses all aspects of management. Figure 3.1 shows an OSI network management architectural model that comprises four models. They are the organization model, the information model, the communication model, and the functional model. Although, the above classification is based on the OSI architectural model, and only parts of it are applicable to other models, it helps us understand the holistic picture of different aspects of network management.

The organization model describes the components of a network management system, their functions, and their infrastructure. The organization model is defined in ISO 10040 OSI Systems Management Overview. It defines the terms object, agent, and manager.

The OSI information model deals with the structure and the organization of management information. ISO 10165 specifies the Structure of Management Information (SMI) and the information database, management information base (MIB). SMI describes how the management information is structured and MIB deals with the relationship and storage of management information.

The third model in OSI management is the communication model. There are three components to this—management application processes that function in the application layer, layer management between layers, and layer operation, which is within the layer. We will focus on the application processes in this book.

The functional model is the fourth component of OSI management, which deals with the user-oriented requirements of network management. As mentioned in Chapter 1, there are five functional application areas defined in OSI, namely configuration, fault, performance, security, and accounting. These are defined as system management functions in OSI.

As mentioned earlier, only OSI presents the most complete model for network management, while the others either deal with only a subset or are still in the process of development of standards. Although a discussion of OSI management is not part of this book, it is briefly covered in Appendix A for completeness of the subject. OSI deals with all seven networking layers. Besides, as we shall see in Chapter 10, it lends itself to addressing service and business management that are more than just networking. The second standard listed in Table 3.1 is SNMP/Internet standard. IETF does not define architecture for the SNMP management model explicitly. However, it does exist implicitly. The organization, information, and communication models are similar to OSI models. The SNMP network management model addresses the functional model in terms of operations, administration, and security. SNMP-based management is widely used for campus-wide networks, although enterprise-wide networks are also managed by using distributed configurations of SNMP-based network management systems (NMSs). SNMP-based management systems, tools, and applications are addressed in Chapter 9. The third standard listed in Table 3.1 is the TMN, which is based on the OSI model. Thus, the four models apply to TMN. The focus of the TMN standard is towards managing telecommunications networks. As mentioned earlier,

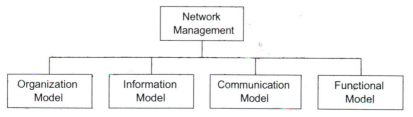

Figure 3.1 OSI Network Management Model

it extends the application functions of OSI further into business and service considerations. Operations systems support service and business management. The fourth standard in Table 3.1 is the IEEE Standard on management and is dedicated to the management of layers 1 and 2 of the OSI Reference Model. It is applicable to LAN and MAN. LAN refers to local area network and MAN (Metropolitan Area Network) refers to metropolitan (intra-city) network. It also addresses standards on broadband network management, which is of great relevance to the current technology. Broadband management is covered in Part IV. Since it deals only with physical and data link layers, it is primarily concerned with the communication model.

In Web-based and object-oriented management, the organization model uses Web server–Web browser architecture. Much of the object-oriented technology, such as hypermedia server, CORBA-oriented transportation, and client–server push-technology are influencing Web-based management. Applications developed under Web-based management could still fall under the OSI functional model. We will now look at each of the models.

3.3 ORGANIZATION MODEL

The organization model describes the components of network management and their relationships. Figure 3.2 shows a representation of a two-tier model. Network objects consist of network elements such as hosts, hubs, bridges, routers, etc. They can be classified into managed and unmanaged objects or elements. The managed elements have a management process running in them called an agent. The unmanaged elements do not have a management process running in them. For example, one can buy a managed or unmanaged hub. Obviously the managed hub has management capability built into it and hence is more expensive than the unmanaged hub, which does not have an agent running in it. The manager communicates with the agent in the managed element.

The manager manages the managed element. As shown in Figure 3.2, there is a database in the manager, but not in the agent. The manager queries and receives management data from the agent, processes them, and stores them in its database. The agent can also send a minimal set of alarm information to the manager unsolicited.

Figure 3.3 presents a three-tier configuration. The intermediate layer acts as both agent and manager. As manager, it collects data from the network elements, processes them, and stores the results in its database. As agent, it transmits information to the top-level manager. For example, an intermediate

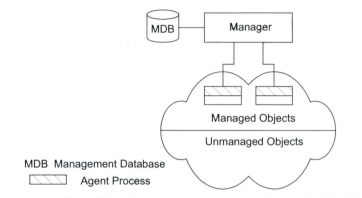

Figure 3.2 Two-Tier Network Management Organization Model

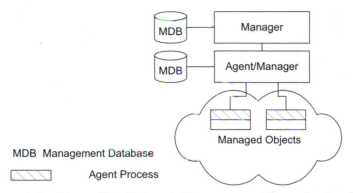

Figure 3.3   Three-Tier Network Management Organization Model

system is used for making statistical measurements on a network and passes the information as needed to the top-level manager. Alternatively, an intermediate NMS could be at a local site of a network and the information is passed on to a remote site.

Network domains can be managed locally; and a global view of the networks can be monitored by a manager of managers (MoM), as shown in Figure 3.4. This configuration uses an enterprise NMS and is applicable to organizations with sites distributed across cities. It is also applicable to a configuration where vendor management systems manage the domains of their respective components, and MoM manages the entire network.

Network management systems can also be configured on a peer-to-peer relationship as shown in Figure 3.5. This is the dumbbell architecture shown in Figure 1.24. We can recognize the similarity between this and the client–server architecture where a host serves as both a client and a server. An example of such a situation would be two network service providers needing to exchange management information

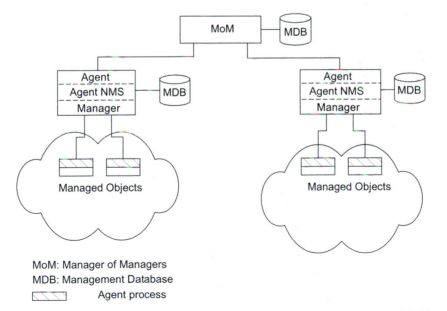

Figure 3.4   Network Management Organization Model with MoM

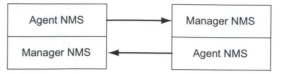

Figure 3.5   Dual Role of Management Process

between them. From the user's point of view, the information traverses both networks and needs to be monitored end-to-end.

In the above discussion, we have used the term network management system (NMS) to mean a system that runs a management process, not just a managed object. Thus, the agent and the manager devices are defined as agent NMS and manager NMS, as shown in Figure 3.4 and Figure 3.5.

3.4   INFORMATION MODEL

An information model is concerned with the structure and storage of information. Let us consider, for example, how information is structured and stored in a library and is accessed by all. A book is uniquely identified by an International Standard Book Number (ISBN). It is a ten-digit number identification that refers to a specific edition of a specific book. For example, ISBN 0-13-437708-7 refers to the book "Understanding SNMP MIBs" by David Perkins and Evan McGinnis. We can refer to a specific figure in the book by identifying a chapter number and a figure number; e.g., Fig. 3.1 refers to Figure 1 in Chapter 3. Thus, a hierarchy of designation {ISBN, Chapter, Figure} uniquely identifies the object, which is a figure in the book. "ISBN," "Chapter," and "Figure" define the syntax of the three pieces of information associated with the figure; and the definition of their meaning in a dictionary would be the semantics associated with them.

The representation of objects and information that are relevant to their management forms the management information model. As discussed in Section 3.3, information on network components is passed between the agent and management processes. The information model specifies the information base to describe managed objects and the relationship between managed objects. The structure defining the syntax and semantics of management information is specified by Structure of Management Information (SMI). The information base is called the Management Information Base (MIB). The MIB is used by both agent and management processes to store and exchange management information. The MIB associated with an agent is called an agent MIB and the MIB associated with a manager is designated as the manager MIB. The manager MIB consists of information on all the network components that it manages; whereas the MIB associated with an agent process needs to know only its local information, its MIB view. For example, a county may have many libraries. Each library has an index of all the books in that location—its MIB view. However, the central index at the county's main library, which manages all other libraries, has the index of all books in all the county's libraries—global manager MIB view.

Figure 3.6 expands the network configuration that is shown in Figure 3.2 to include the MIB that is associated with the manager. Thus, the manager has both the management database (MDB) and the MIB. It is important to distinguish between the two. The MDB is a real database and contains the measured or administratively configured value of the elements of the network. On the other hand, the MIB is a virtual database and contains the information necessary for processes to exchange information among themselves.

Let us illustrate the distinction between MIB and MDB by considering the scenario of adding a component to the network. Assume that all the hubs in the network are made by a single vendor,

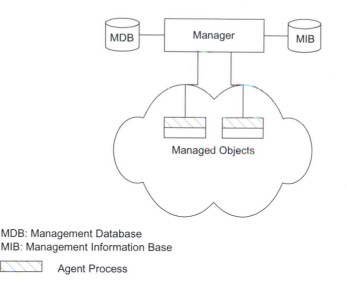

MDB: Management Database
MIB: Management Information Base

 Agent Process

Figure 3.6 Network Configuration with Data and Information Base

say Cabletron. The manager in Figure 3.6 has knowledge about the Cabletron hub and its associated parameters in its MIB; and the values associated with the parameters with the hubs are in its MDB. For example, the number of ports in the hub is a parameter associated with the hub (MIB information); and if they are 12-port hubs, the values associated with the number of ports are 12 (MDB information). Suppose we now add another Cabletron hub to the network. The manager would discover the newly added hub during its next discovery process, which could be just a broadcast ping from the manager. The new hub is another instance of the hub with a new IP address, and its MIB information is already in the manager's MIB. Its address and the number of ports associated with it are added to MDB by the manager querying the agent.

Now, let us add a 3Com hub to the network. Let this be the first time that a 3Com hub is added to the network. The manager would recognize the addition of a new component to the network by the periodic broadcast ping of the network by the manager. However, it would not know what component has been added until the MIB information on the 3Com hub is added to the manager's MIB. This information is actually compiled into the manager's MIB schema. After the information on the 3Com hub has been added to the manager's MIB, it can send queries to the agent residing in the 3Com hub. It then retrieves the values for the type of hub, the number of ports, etc. and adds them to its MDB.

The MIB that contains data on managed objects need not be limited to just physical elements. For example, in network management, management information extends information beyond that associated with the description of network elements or objects. Here are some examples of information that can be stored in the MIB.

Network Elements: hubs, bridges, routers, transmission facilities, etc.
Software Processes: programs, algorithms, protocol functions, databases, etc.
Administrative Information: contact person, account number, etc.
In fact, any type of information could be included as an object in the MIB.

3.4.1 Management Information Tree

The managed objects are uniquely defined by a tree structure specified by the OSI model and are used in the Internet model. Figure 3.7 shows the generic representation of the tree, defined as the Management Information Tree (MIT). There is a root node and well-defined nodes underneath each node at different levels, designated as Level 1, Level 2, etc. Each managed object occupies a node in the tree. In the OSI model, the managed objects are defined by a containment tree representing the MIT.

Figure 3.8 shows the internationally adopted OSI MIT. The root node does not have an explicit designation. The root has three nodes in the layer beneath it—iso, ccitt (itu), and iso–ccitt, (iso–itu). The iso defines the International Standards Organization and ccitt, or itu, defines the International Telecommunications Union (the old name is ccitt). The two standards organizations are on the first layer defining managing objects under them. The joint iso–itu node is for management objects jointly defined by the two organizations. The number in each circle identifies the designation of the object in each layer. Thus, iso is designated as 1, org as 1.3, dod, Department of Defense, as 1.3.6, and the internet as 1.3.6.1. All Internet-managed objects will be that number followed by more dots and numbers. It is to be noted that the names of the nodes are all in lowercase letters as a convention, which we will formally define in Section 3.6.

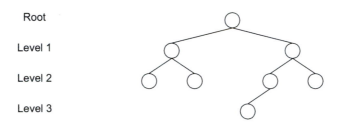

Figure 3.7   Generic Representation of the Management Information Tree

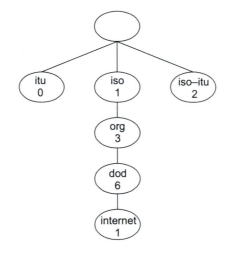

Figure 3.8   OSI Management Information Tree

3.4.2   Managed Object Perspective

Although a managed object need not be a physical object that can be seen, touched, or felt, it is convenient to use a physical representation to understand the characteristics and operations associated with a managed object. Let us consider an object, which is circular in shape. We can define the object in English language syntax as *circle*. To associate a meaning with the object name, *circle*, we can use Webster's dictionary *definition* "a plane figure bounded by a single curved line every point of which is equally distant from the point at the center of the figure." In other words, the definition is a textual description of the object. The object can be viewed and its parameters changed by people who have *access* to it. The *access* privilege could be limited to just accessing it or performing some action on it; for example, resetting a counter value to two. These are all defined as *access* attributes. If we envision a scenario in which the object is used by a nursery school to explain shapes to children, it should at least have some basic shapes, such as a circle, a square, etc. We can define the basic objects that are required of a group (of objects) as the status of the object—whether it is mandatory or optional to have (implement) that object. This attribute of the object is defined as the *status* of the object. There could be many types of objects in the nursery school that are circular in shape. There is a unique identification and name (*object identifier* and *descriptor*) associated with each of them, such as a ring, a donut, etc. There could be many instances of ring and donut; but we are only addressing the types of object, not instances of them here. We have thus defined the five basic attributes of a managed object type from the Internet perspective. They are *name, definition, syntax, access, and status*.

A pictorial view of a circular object in the Internet is shown in Figure 3.9(a).

A managed object in the Internet is defined by five parameters [RFC 1155]. They are:

- *object identifier*   unique ID
  and *descriptor*   and name for the object
- *syntax*   used to model the object
- *access*   access privilege to a managed object
- *status*   implementation requirements
- *definition*   textual description of the semantics of object type

A modification of this is specified in RFC 1212, as we shall see in the next chapter.

The Internet object model is a scalar model and is easy to understand, as seen above. In contrast, the OSI perspective of a managed object is complex and has a different set of characteristics. We will extend the above analogy of the circular object in a nursery to illustrate an OSI perspective.

Figure 3.9(b) presents the conceptual OSI representation of the various characteristics of a managed object. As mentioned earlier, OSI specifications are object oriented, and hence a managed object belongs to an object class. The left side of Figure 3.9(b) presents the same circular object in the OSI model. The definition of an object in an object-oriented perception would include both the shape and values. Thus, the *attribute* of the object is a circle with given dimensions. The *attribute* of an object defines the external perspective of the object. It undergoes an *operation* "push." Push is not really an OSI operational entity, but is used here to illustrate the concept. The *behavior* of the object is to change its shape or attribute from a circle to an ellipse. It then sends *notifications* to the relevant community informing of its change. Thus, the characteristics of an OSI managed object are:

- *object class*   managed object
- *attributes*   attributes visible at its boundary
- *operations*   operations that may be applied to it

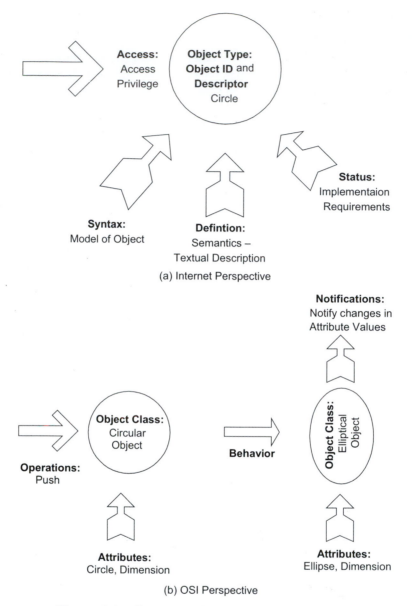

Figure 3.9 Conceptual Views of Managed Object

- *behavior*   behavior exhibited by it in response to an operation
- *notifications*   notifications emitted by the object

It is hard to compare the characteristics of a managed object in the Internet and OSI models on a one-to-one basis, as they are very much different. However, it can be observed in the conceptual models in Figure 3.9 that the OSI characteristics—*operations*, *behavior*, and *notification*—are a part of the Internet communications model. Operation in the Internet is done by get and set commands. Notification is done by response and alarm messages. The *syntax* characteristic of the Internet is part of OSI *attributes*.

Characteristics	Example
Object type	PktCounter
Syntax	Counter
Access	Read-only
Status	Mandatory
Description	Counts number of packets

(a) Internet Perspective

Characteristics	Example
Object class	Packet Counter
Attributes	Single-valued
Operations	get, set
Behavior	Retrieves or resets values
Notifications	Generates notifications on new value

(b) OSI Perspective

Figure 3.10   Packet Counter as an Example of a Managed Object

The *access* characteristic of the Internet is a part of the security function in the OSI functional model. The *status* characteristic of the Internet is handled by conformance as a part of application services in OSI. Further, in OSI we can create and delete objects, while these concepts do not exist in the Internet. Objects in early SNMP management are assumed to exist for management purposes.

Figure 3.10 shows the comparison between Internet and OSI specifications for the object, packet counter. An example of a packet counter as a managed object in the Internet model is given in Figure 3.10(a). The *object type* (we will define *object id* later) is PktCounter. The *syntax* is Counter. The *access* mode is read-only. The *status* implementation is mandatory, which mandates that this object must be implemented if the group it belongs to is implemented. The *description* provides the semantics that the packet counter counts the number of packets.

The example of the same counter as a managed object in the OSI model is given in Figure 3.10(b). The counter is defined as an *object class, Packet Counter.* It could be related to either a sub- or super-class. The *attribute* value is single-valued. We can perform get and set *operations* on its *attribute*. Its *behavior* to a set operation would be to reset the counter, or just retrieve data if the operation is get. The new value is sent out as *notification.*

3.5   COMMUNICATION MODEL

We have discussed in the previous section how information content is defined (SMI) and stored (MIB). We will now address the model associated with how the information is exchanged between systems. Management data are communicated between agent and manager processes, as well as between manager processes. Three aspects need to be addressed in the communication of information between two entities: transport medium of message exchange (transport protocol), message format of communication (application protocol), and the actual message (commands and responses). Let us illustrate this by an example of Azita buying a car from an automobile salesperson, Roberto.

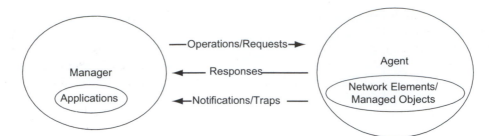

Figure 3.11 Management Communication Model

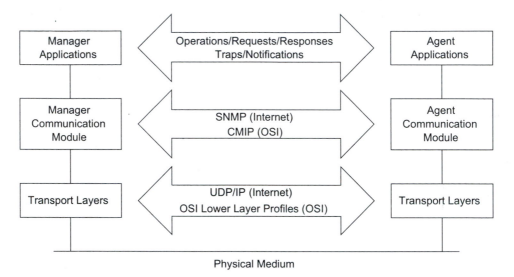

Figure 3.12 Management Communication Transfer Protocols

Azita could go to the automobile dealer and communicate in person with Roberto. Alternatively, she could communicate with Roberto via the Internet. In the former, visual and audio media are the transport mechanisms, and electronic exchange is used in the latter. The communication at the application level could be exchanged in English, Spanish, or any other mutually understandable language between the two. This would be the application-level protocol that is decided between Azita and Roberto. Finally, there are messages exchanged between Azita and Roberto. For example, Azita could request what cars are available and Roberto would respond with the cars that are in stock. Azita could then set a price range and Roberto responds with cars that match the price range. These exchanged messages are the commands/requests/operations and responses/notifications. They can be considered services requested by Azita and provided by Roberto.

Figure 3.11 presents the communication model. The applications in the manager module initiate *requests* to the agent in the Internet model. It is part of the *operations* in the OSI model. The agent executes the request on the network element; i.e., managed object, and returns *responses* to the manager. The traps/notifications are the unsolicited messages, such as alarms, generated by the agent.

Figure 3.12 presents the communication protocol used to transfer information between managed object and managing processes, as well as between management processes. The OSI model uses CMIP along with CMIS. The Internet uses SNMP for communication. The services are part of operations using requests, responses, and alarm notifications.

OSI uses both connection-oriented and connectionless protocols for transportation. For example, the TP4 transport layer protocol riding on top of the x.25 protocol could be used for connection-oriented transporting and application messages. TP4 over Connectionless Network Protocol is used for connectionless transportation. The Internet uses connectionless UDP/IP protocol for transporting messages.

CMIP and SNMP specify the management communication protocols for OSI and Internet management. CMIP is addressed in Appendix A. SNMP is extensively covered throughout the book.

The application processes invoke the management communication layer protocols. OSI deals with messages in the specification of managed objects. Managed objects and their attributes could be manipulated by operations. Basic application service modules are defined by CMIS. In the Internet, operations are executed by SNMP messages.

3.6   ABSTRACT SYNTAX NOTATION ONE: ASN.1

In both the information model and the communication model, discussed in the previous sections, we have addressed functions. In these models, SMI needs to be specified syntactically and semantically, which will be the content of this section.

It is important for communication among systems that a formalized set of rules is agreed upon on the structure and meaning of the language of communication, namely syntax and semantics of the language. There are numerous sets of application and transport protocols. Thus, it is beneficial to choose a syntactical format for the language that specifies the management protocol in the application layer, which is transparent to the rest of the protocol layers. One such format is an old and well-proven format, Abstract Syntax Notation One, ASN.1. We will introduce ASN.1 here to the extent needed to understand its use in network management. The reader is referred to other references [Cassel and Austing, 1996; Larmouth, 1997; Stallings, 1998] for greater depth on the subject.

ASN.1 is more than just syntax. It is a formal language developed jointly by CCITT (now ITU-T) and ISO for use with application layers for data transfer between systems. It is also applicable within the system for clearly separating the abstract syntax and the transfer syntax at the presentation layer. We define the *abstract syntax* as the set of rules used to specify data types and structures for the storage of information. The *transfer syntax* represents the set of rules for communicating information between systems. Thus, the abstract syntax would be applicable to the information model discussed in Section 3.4 and the transfer syntax to the communication model discussed in Section 3.5. The abstract syntax can be used with any presentation syntax, the latter depending on the medium of presentation. The abstract syntax in ASN.1 makes it independent of the lower-layer protocols. ISO 8824/X.208 standards specify ASN.1. The algorithm to convert the textual ASN.1 syntax to machine-readable code is defined in ISO 8825/X.209 standards. It is called Basic Encoding Rules (BER).

3.6.1   Terminology, Symbols, and Conventions

ASN.1 syntax is based on the Backus system and uses the formal syntax language and grammar of Backus–Nauer Form (BNF), which looks like:

        \<name\> ::= \<definition\>

where the notation "\<entity\>" denotes an "entity" and the symbol "::=" represents "defined as."

Let us illustrate the Backus system by developing a simple arithmetic expression <SAE> [Maurer, 1977]:

We can define an entity <digit> as

<digit> ::= 0 | 1 | 2 | 3 | 4 | 5 | 6 | 7 | 8 | 9

where the symbol "|" represent "or." We can also define an operation entity <op> as

<op> ::= + | - | x | /

The definitions on the right side are called *primitives*. Using these primitives, we can construct more entities. Thus, an entity *number* can be constructed from the primitive, <digit>

<number> ::= <digit> | <digit><number>

For example, the number 9 is the digit 9; the number 19 is the concatenation of the digit 1 and the number 9; and the number 219 is the concatenation of digit 2 with the number 19.

We can now construct a simple arithmetic expression <SAE> from the primitives and the construct <number>. Thus,

<SAE> ::= <number> | <SAE> | <SAE><op><SAE>

The format of each line is defined as a *production* or *assignment*.

Let us consider an example with the following two assignments:

<BooleanType> ::= BOOLEAN

<BooleanValue> ::= TRUE I FALSE

The expression on the left side specifies the name of the type and the right side is the definition or value of the type. Thus, BooleanType is defined as BOOLEAN and BooleanValue is defined as either TRUE or FALSE. The above example illustrates the two basic parameters associated with an entity, namely, *data type* and *value*. The first line is called *data type assignment* and it defines the name of the entity; and the second line, value assignment, specifies the assigned value to the data type. Thus, in the above example the entity BOOLEAN can have assigned values of TRUE or FALSE. Entities that are all in capital letters, such as TRUE and FALSE, are called *keywords*.

A group of assignments makes up an ASN.1 module. For example, a name consists of first, middle, and last names, and they can be specified as:

```
person-name    Person-Name::=
          {
          first      "John",
          middle    "I",
          last      "Smith"
          }
```

Here person-name, beginning with lowercase letters, is the name of the data type. Person-Name is a module and begins with capital letters. The module comprises three assignments, whose names are first, middle, and last with values "John," "I," and "Smith."

Figure 3.13 and Figure 3.14 show two examples of ASN.1 data type definition [Larmouth, 1997]. They are two ASN.1 modules defining data types personnelRecord and trade-Message. Because they are modules, they start with capital letters. PersonnelRecord describes the personnel record of an employee in a global corporation. The Trade-Message is a module specifying a list of invoices defining customer name, part numbers, quantity, charge, and security authentication.

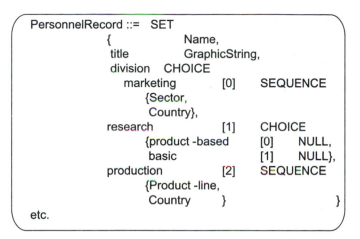

```
PersonnelRecord ::=  SET
                {                   Name,
                    title           GraphicString,
                    division   CHOICE
                        marketing          [0]      SEQUENCE
                            {Sector,
                             Country},
                        research           [1]      CHOICE
                            {product -based        [0]      NULL,
                             basic                 [1]      NULL},
                        production         [2]      SEQUENCE
                            {Product -line,
                             Country       }                          }
        etc.
```

Figure 3.13 ASN.1 Data Type Definition Example 1

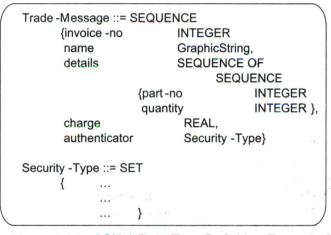

```
Trade -Message ::= SEQUENCE
            {invoice -no             INTEGER
             name                    GraphicString,
             details                 SEQUENCE OF
                                            SEQUENCE
                    {part -no                INTEGER
                     quantity                INTEGER },
             charge                  REAL,
             authenticator           Security -Type}

Security -Type ::= SET
        {       ...
                ...
                ...        }
```

Figure 3.14 ASN.1 Data Type Definition Example 2

Note that in the examples of Figure 3.13 and Figure 3.14, the data types are built-up from primitive data types: INTEGER, REAL, NULL, and GraphicString. GraphicString is one of several Character-String type primitives. These examples present three kinds of data types, which are built using three construction mechanisms:

alternatives:	CHOICE
list:	SET and SEQUENCE
repetition:	SET OF and SEQUENCE OF

These constructs are used to build structured data types. Just as we saw in the <SAE> example earlier, all data types are built from the ground up using primitive (also called atomic) entities. ASN.1 definition allows both backward and forward references, as well as in-line definition. For instance, in Figure 3.13 the data types Name, Sector, Country, and Product-line are defined externally either before or after the module defining PersonnelRecord. The data type whose name is title is defined in-line as the data type GraphicString. It could have been defined as data type Title as follows:

title   Title::= GraphicString

Let us analyze the three construct types. In PersonnelRecord, the person works in one of the three divisions—marketing, research, or production. This is built using CHOICE construction. Notice that in each of those divisions, research could be either product-based or basic.

The constructs SET and SEQUENCE are list builders. The PersonnelRecord module is a set of data types, Name, GraphicString, Sector, Country, etc., which are all different data types. Since they are different and each is uniquely associated with a name, they can be encoded and transmitted in any order. For example, they could be arranged in any of the following orders:

"Smith", "Manager", {"North", "Chile"}
"Manager", "Smith", {"North", "Chile"}
{"North", "Chile"}, "Manager", "Smith"
etc.

Notice that "North" and "Chile" are always in the same order. This is because it is a list built with SEQUENCE construction, and the order in the list should be maintained.

The third type of construction is the repetitive types SET OF and SEQUENCE OF. In the example on TradeMessage in Figure 3.14, the SEQUENCE OF construction is shown. The "details" in the invoice are a repetition of data consisting of the ordered list (SEQUENCE construct) of part number and quantity in each invoice. The repetitive records themselves are ordered in a SEQUENCE OF construction. This means that the data will be transmitted in the order in which they are entered. The encoding scheme will preserve that order while transmitting the data from one process to another. For example, if data are entered for *details* in Figure 3.14 as a sequence {part-no, quantity} in the order {1, 5}, {60, 3}, {120, 40}, they will be transmitted in that order by the sending process. If they had been a SET OF construct instead of a SEQUENCE OF construct for *details* in Figure 3.14, the order is irrelevant. The order in this case for the example could be encoded and transmitted by the sending process as any of the combinations, {1, 5}, {60, 3}, {120. 40}; or {60, 3}, {1, 5}, {120, 40}; or {120, 40}, {1, 5}, {60, 3}; etc. without relevance to the order.

The NULL data type used in Figure 3.13, PersonnelRecord, is a placeholder. No value needs to be associated with it except indicating that such a data type exists.

We observe in the PersonnelRecord example in Figure 3.13 that some assignments have integers in square brackets. For instance,

{product-based [0] NULL,
 basic   [1] NULL}

These are called *tags*. The definition of a tag is introduced in ASN.1 to uniquely identify a data type and will be discussed in detail later.

We have used several symbols and primitive data types including *keywords* in the preceding examples. A complete list of ASN.1 symbols is shown in Table 3.2.

Table 3.3 lists some of the frequently used ASN.1 keywords. The reader is directed to the reference [Perkins and McGinnis, 1997] for a more complete list.

As we said earlier, we can group assignments that are related to each other; this group is called a module. A formal definition of a module is as follows:

<module name> DEFINITIONS ::= BEGIN
        <name> ::= <definition>
        <name> ::= <definition>
END

Table 3.2 ASN.1 Symbols

SYMBOL	MEANING
::=	Defined as or assignment
I	Or, alternatives, options of a list
-	Signed number
--	Following the symbol are comments
{ }	Start and end of a list
[ ]	Start and end of a tag
( )	Start and end of a subtype
..	Range

Table 3.3 ASN.1 Keywords

KEYWORD	BRIEF DESCRIPTION
BEGIN	Start of an ASN.1 module
CHOICE	List of alternatives
DEFINITIONS	Definition of a data type or managed object
END	End of an ASN.1 module
EXPORTS	Data types that can be exported to other modules
IDENTIFIER	A sequence of non-negative numbers
IMPORTS	Data types defined in external modules
INTEGER	Any negative or non-negative number
NULL	A placeholder
OBJECT	Used with IDENTIFIER to uniquely identify an object
OCTET	Unbounded 8-bit bytes (octets) of binary data
OF	Used with SET and SEQUENCE
SEQUENCE	Ordered list maker
SEQUENCE OF	Ordered array of repetitive data
SET	Unordered list maker
SET OF	Unordered list of repetitive data
STRING	Used with OCTET for denoting a string of octets

For example, a MIB definition module will look like:

```
RFC1213-MIB DEFINITIONS ::= BEGIN
   …
   …
   …
END
```

The terms DEFINITIONS, BEGIN, and END are primitives and are called keywords in ASN.1. They are built-in expressions and have special meaning. The DEFINITIONS indicate that the named module,

Table 3.4 ASN.1 Data Type Conventions

DATA TYPES	CONVENTION	EXAMPLE
Object name	Initial lowercase letter	sysDescr, etherStatsPkts
Application data type	Initial uppercase letter	Counter, IpAddress
Module	Initial uppercase letter	PersonnelRecord
Macro, MIB module	All uppercase letters	RMON-MIB
Keywords	All uppercase letters	INTEGER, BEGIN

RFC 1213-MIB, is being defined. The body of a module always starts with BEGIN and ends with END. Grouping assignments into modules has the great advantage that modules can be imported into and exported from other modules. Thus, they are reusable.

We notice in the examples described so far in this section that we have used both lowercase and uppercase letters. There are ASN.1 conventions to designate the data. These are shown in Table 3.4.

3.6.2   Objects and Data Types

We will now use ASN.1 notation to define the various data types and apply them to describe objects in the context of SMI and MIB.

We observed in Section 3.6.1 that the data type could be either a simple type (also called primitive, atomic, or basic), or it could be structured. In addition, we talked about tag designation, which uniquely identifies the data type irrespective of the syntax version. In general, data types are defined based on structure and tag. The structure is subdivided into four categories. The tag is subdivided into class and tag number. This is shown in Figure 3.15. An object can be uniquely defined by its tag, namely class and tag number. For exchange of information between systems, the structure information is also included.

The four categories of data type structure, shown in Figure 3.15 are, *simple type*, *structured type*, *tagged type*, and *other type*.

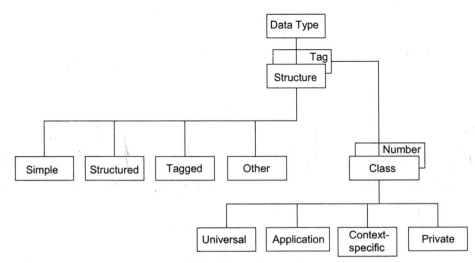

Figure 3.15   ASN.1 Data Type Structure and Tag

A *simple type* is one for which the values are specified directly. For example, we can define a page of a book as PageNumber of simple type, which can take on any integer value. INTEGER is a *simple type*. Thus,

PageNumber ::= INTEGER

Similarly, we can define the chapter number of the book as

ChapterNumber ::= INTEGER

Values for PageNumber can be specified as 1, 2, 3,... and for ChapterNumber as 1, 2, 3,...

A data type is defined as a *structured type* when it contains other types. Types that are within a *structured type* are called *component types*. In the above example, a page number of a book could be defined as a *structured type* by a SEQUENCE construction of ChapterNumber and PageNumber component data types. Let us call it BookPageNumber.

BookPageNumber ::= SEQUENCE
{ChapterNumber, Separator, PageNumber}

where Separator is a data type with value "-." BookPageNumber is a *structured type*. Values for BookPageNumber would then be like 1-1, 2-3, or 6-25.

We can define all the pages of the book as a collection of individual pages. If we want to define them in a sequential order from the first page of the first chapter to the last page of the last chapter, we would use a SEQUENCE OF construction. Let us call it BookPages.

BookPages ::= SEQUENCE OF { BookPageNumber}

We could define the same in an alternative manner as

BookPages ::= SEQUENCE OF
{
SEQUENCE
{ChapterNumber, Separator, PageNumber}
}

The above two definitions have identical meaning. Values for BookPages would then be 1-1, 1-2, 1-3, …, 2-1, 2-2, 2-3,... The ordering of the values is by the order in which the data are specified and not by sorting of the component data types in the structured construct.

The pages of a book could also be specified as a collection of individual pages in random order. The *structured type* for BookPages would then be constructed with the SET OF data type construct:

BookPages ::= SET OF
{
SEQUENCE
{ChapterNumber, Separator, PageNumber}
}

Note that we could not have used a SET OF construct for BookPageNumber as the order of the chapter number, separator, and page number is important to keep. However, we could have used the SET construct to define BookPages as

BookPages ::= SET {ChapterNumber, Separator, PageNumber}

and assigned values 1-2, 2-3, 1-1, ... in a random order. The order of the values in the transmission of data between the sender and the receiver is unimportant. Thus, SET is distinguished from SEQUENCE in two respects. First, the data types should all be distinct; and second, the order of values in SET is of no consequence, whereas it is critical in a SEQUENCE construct. It is also worth noting that the component data types in a SEQUENCE construct need not be distinct since the order is preserved.

Tagged type is a type derived from another type and is given a new tag id. Although a data type has a unique tag associated with it, a tag data type is defined to distinguish types within an application. For instance, in Figure 3.14 although "invoice-no" is an INTEGER type, which we will soon learn as a universal class with a tag number [1], it could have been assigned a local tag id. This is sometimes done to improve the efficiency of encoding.

The fourth and last category of structure is *other type*, which is a data type that is not pre-defined. It is chosen from CHOICE and ANY types, which are contained in other types. Type CHOICE defines the selection of one value from a specified list of distinct types. Thus, in Figure 3.13, "research" uses a CHOICE construct to select one of the two alternatives between "product-based," and "basic." We can represent them with specific values instead of NULL, as follows:

```
research        Research ::= CHOICE
                  {
                      product-based        ProductType,
                      basic                VisibleString
                  }
                  ProductType ::=        VisibleString
```

Type ANY is always supplemented with any valid ASN.1 type defined in another module. We have given two representations for Research, the one above and the other in Figure 3.13. We could give a definition of these two options by defining Research as follows:

```
Research ::= CHOICE
    {
    product-based   ANY,
    BASIC           ANY
    }
```

This definition using ANY specifies that the "product-based" entity could be either a NULL or a ProductType data type, and similarly "basic" could be either VisibleString or NULL.

Figure 3.15 shows two perspectives of data type—*structure* and *tag*. The structure that we have so far described addresses how the data type is constructed. On the other hand, *tag* uniquely identifies the data type. It is required for encoding the data types for communication. Every data type except CHOICE and ANY has a tag associated with it. Tag has two components—*class* and *tag number*. There are four classes of tag. They are: *Universal, Application, Context-specific*, and *Private*; and each data type belonging to each class is assigned a unique number.

The *universal class* is the most commonly used class, and the ASN.1 list of *universal class* assignments is given in Table 3.5. A core set of assignments is used in all applications. Data types belonging to the *universal class* are application-independent. It is similar to the use of a global variable in a software program, and is applicable anywhere in a program. It need not be defined repeatedly in the subroutines of the program. BOOLEAN and INTEGER are examples of a *universal class*, whose tag numbers are [1] and [2], respectively.

Table 3.5 Universal Class Tag Assignments

TAG	TYPE NAME	SET OF VALUES
Universal 1	BOOLEAN	TRUE or FALSE
Universal 2	INTEGER	0, Positive and negative numbers
Universal 3	BIT STRING	A string of binary digits or null set
Universal 4	OCTET STRING	A string of octets or null set
Universal 5	NULL	Null, single-valued
Universal 6	OBJECT IDENTIFIER	Set of values associated with the object
Universal 7	Object description	Human readable text describing the object
Universal 8	EXTERNAL	The type is external to the standard
Universal 9	REAL	Real numbers, expressed in scientific notation Mantissa × Base^{exponent}
Universal 10	ENUMERATED	Specified list of integers
Universal 11	ENCRYPTED	Encrypted information
Universal 12–15	Reserved for future use	
Universal 16	SEQUENCE and SEQUENCE OF	Ordered list of types
Universal 17	SET and SET OF	Unordered list of types
Universal 18	NumericString	Digits 0–9, space
Universal 19	PrintableString	Printable characters
Universal 20	TeletexString	Character set specified by CCITT Recommendation T.61
Universal 21	VideotexString	Character set specified by CCITT Recommendation T.100 and T.101
Universal 22	IA5String	International Alphabet 5, which is equivalent to ASCII
Universal 23	UTCTime	Time format YYMMDDHHMM[SS][local time differential from universal standard time]
Universal 24	GeneralizedTime	Time format YYYYMMDDHHMM[SS][local time differential from universal standard time]
Universal 25	GraphicString	Graphic character set specified by ISO 8824
Universal 26	VisibleString	Character set specified by ISO 646, equivalent to ASCII
Universal 27	GeneralString	General character string
Universal 28	CharacterString	Character set
Universal 29–	Reserved for future use	

Tags belonging to the *application class* are specific to applications. Examples of application-specific tag numbers are used in examples in Figure 3.13. A universal class tag number can be overridden with an application-specific *tag number*. Types in two different applications can have the same application-specific tag, but carry two different meanings.

Application-specific assignments are classified as such. For instance, in the above example of Book-PageNumber, if we assign PageId, ChapterNumber, PageNumber, and the tags APPLICATION 1, 2, and 3, respectively, the assignment will read

PageId ::= [APPLICATION 1] SEQUENCE {

[APPLICATION 2] ChapterNumber,

[APPLICATION 3] PageNumber}

When defining large modules, the structure can become large. We can introduce descriptive names and comments on the structure for easy reading. Let us expand the above example as follows:

PageId ::= [APPLICATION 1] SEQUENCE {

        chapter-number   [APPLICATION 2] ChapterNumber,

        page-number   [APPLICATION 3] PageNumber}

-- page numbers are grouped by chapter numbers

The descriptive words "chapter number" and "page number" do not affect the result when encoding this structure, neither do the comments following the "--".

In the previous example, both **PageNumber** and ChapterNumber have **INTEGER** values. **INTEGER** can be classified as either **UNIVERSAL 2** or **APPLICATION 3**. This could be encoded either way. The efficiency of encoding can be improved if we had added the data designation **IMPLICIT** as below:

PageNumber ::= [APPLICATION 3] IMPLICIT INTEGER

Such an expression forces the encoding to follow the local tag assignment.

The *context-specific type*, a subset of an application, is limited to that application. Thus, in Example 1 of Figure 3.13, research has a tag [1] associated with the application of PersonnelRecord and under that application, research has two context-specific tags [0] and [1] for product-based and basic.

The *private type* is used extensively by vendors of network products. A vendor is assigned a node on the MIT, and all branches and leaves under that node will be assigned a private data type by the vendor.

Before leaving the subject of tags, it is worth noting a special case of data type **INTEGER**. It is an **ENUMERATED** type and is similar to **INTEGER**. For example, we can define the colors of the rainbow as **ENUMERATED** type integers.

RainbowColors ::= ENUMERATED

    {

                violet   (0)

                indigo (1)

                blue   (2)

                green   (3)

                yellow (4)

                orange (5)

                red   (6)

    }

In this case, when a value of 5 is designated for the object type **RainbowColors**, it is implied that it is orange. **RainbowColors** could take on only the seven integer values defined.

An example for the **ENUMERATED** type for **INTEGER** from SNMP MIB, which we will cover in Chapter 5, *error status* in a *get-response* message is:

```
ErrorStatus ::=
        INTEGER{
                NoError(0)
                tooBig(1)
                noSuchName(2)
                badValues(3)
                readOnly(4)
                genErr(5)
                }
```

A subtype data type is derived from a parent type. For example, in the PageNumber example, if we limit the maximum page number to 255 (based on 2^8), then the assignment would read

PageNumber ::= Integer (0..255)

The parenthesis indicating that it is a subtype expression (see Table 3.2), where the integer range is from 0 to 255.

Let us conclude this section with a real-life example in network management of a data type, which is the address translation table in SNMP IP MIB. An entry in the table is of data type IpNetMediaEntry, which is a sequence of four managed objects with associated data types as shown below. Each of the four objects starts with a lowercase letter, and the associated data type with either a capital letter or is all capital letters.

```
IpNetMediaEntry ::=SEQUENCE {
        ipNetToMedialfIndex             INTEGER
        ipNetToMediaPhysAddress         PhysAddress
        ipNetToMediaNetAddress              IpAddress
        ipNetToMediaType                INTEGER}
```

3.6.3   Object Name

In a MIB, there is an identifier for each occurrence of an object. In the ASN.1 notation, it is the OBJECT IDENTIFIER. The object identifier for the Internet shown in Figure 3.8 is

internet OBJECT IDENTIFIER ::= {iso(1) org(3) dod(6) internet(1)}

Thus, the object identifier for the Internet has the value 1.3.6.1, which we discussed in Section 3.5.1. The MIT shown in Figure 3.8 has been extended to include the class private type in the MIB and is shown in Figure 3.16. Thus, the object identifier for private enterprise IBM is 1.3.6.1.4.1.2.

3.6.4   An Example of Use of ASN.1 from ISO 8824

Figure 3.17 shows the ASN.1 structure for a personnel record. Part (a) shows the informal description, part (b) shows the ASN.1 description of the record, and part (c) shows the description of the record value. There are several salient points to note in this example. First, there are no simple types in this example such as the page number defined in Section 3.6.3. The data type, Name, does not have an associated object name, although we could define one, for example, personnel-name. In such a case, the second line in Figure 3.17(b) would read

personnel-name   Name

PersonnelRecord is a structured data type, SET with the basic component types Name, EmployeeNumber, Date, Name (nameOfSpouse), and ChildInformation. ChildInformation itself is a

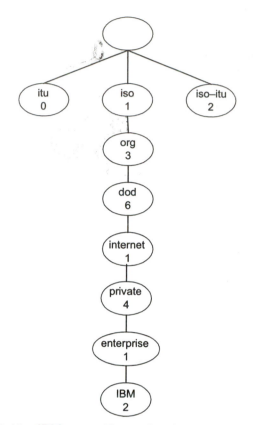

Figure 3.16 IBM as an Example of a Private Class in MIT

structured data type, a SET consisting of Name and Date as component types. A third structured data type that we notice is SEQUENCE for the data type Name with VisibleString as the component types.

The SEQUENCE type is used for Name and the SEQUENCE OF type is used for children, which contains component type SEQUENCE. Thus, the first occurrence of Name in PersonnelRecord is a SEQUENCE construct, and the same construct is embedded in children, which is a SEQUENCE OF construct. Thus, we see a nested structure in this example.

The structure for PersonnelRecord is a structured type and it could have been defined without the data designation IMPLICIT as well as the local tag [APPLICATION 0]. However, as mentioned in Section 3.6.2, the local tag type has been used to improve the efficiency of coding. Further use of the IMPLICIT designation makes the coding more efficient in that it will be encoded with the [APPLICATION 2] tag and not the UNIVERSAL tag, which is also applicable. In this situation, it would not be encoded as UNIVERSAL type 1.

3.7 ENCODING STRUCTURE

The ASN.1 syntax containing the management information is encoded using the BER defined for the transfer syntax. The ASCII text data are converted to bit-oriented data. We will describe one specific encoding structure, called TLV, denoting Type, Length, and Value components of the structure. This is shown in Figure 3.18. The full record consists of type, length, and value.

```
Name:                  John P Smith
Title:                 Director
Employee Number        51
Date of Hire:          17 September 1971
Name of Spouse;        Mary T Smith
Number of Children     2
Child Information
       Name            Ralph T Smith
       Date of Birth   11 November 1957
Child Information
       Name            Susan B Jones
       Date of Birth   17 July 1959
```
(a) Informal description of personnel record

```
PersonnelRecord ::= [APPLICATION 0] IMPLICIT SET {
        Name,
        title [0] VisibleString,
        number EmployeeNumber,
        dateOfHire [1] Date,
        nameOfSpouse [2] Name,
        children [3] IMPLICIT  SEQUENCE OF ChildInformation DEFAULT { } }
ChildInformation ::= SET {
        Name,
        dateOfBirth [0] Date }
Name ::= [APPLICATION 1] IMPLICIT SEQUENCE {
        givenName VisibleString,
        initial VisibleString,
        familyName VisibleString }

EmployeeNumber ::= [APPLICATION 2] IMPLICIT INTEGER

Date ::=  [APPLICATION 3] IMPLICIT VisibleString     -- YYYYMMDD
```
(b) ASN.1 description of the record structure

```
{                          {givenName "John", initial "T", familyName "Smith"},
title                      "Director"
number                     "51"
dateOfHire                 "19710917"
nameOfSpouse               {givenName "Mary", initial "T", familyName "Smith"},
children
{ {                        {givenName "Ralph", initial "T", familyName "Smith"},
   dateOfBirth             "19571111"},
   {                       {givenName "Susan", initial "B", familyName "Jones"}
   dateOfBirth             "19590717"}}}
```
(c) ASN.1 description of a record value

Figure 3.17   ISO 8824 Example of Use of ASN.1

The type has three subcomponents—class, P/C, and tag number. P/C specifies whether the structure is primitive, i.e., a simple type or a construct, anything other than a simple type. It is encoded as a 1-byte (an octet) field. The two most significant bits (7th and 8th bit) specifying the class are coded as per values

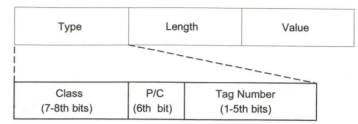

Figure 3.18 TLV Encoding Structure

defined in Table 3.6. The value of P/C is 0 for Primitive and 1 for Construct. The lowest 5 bits (1–5) designate the tag value in binary. For example, INTEGER, from Table 3.5, belongs to a universal class with a tag value of 2 and is a primitive data type. Hence, the type is 00000010.

The length specifies the length of the value field in the number of octets. The length is defined as a series of octets. It is either one octet (short) or more than one octet (long). The most significant bit (8th bit) is set to 0 for a short length with the low 7 bits indicating the length of the value. If the value field is longer than 127 (maximum specified by 7 bits), then the long form is used for length. The 8th bit of the first octet is marked as 1 and the rest of the seven bits of the first octet indicate how many octets follow to specify the length. For example, a value length of 128 would look like

10000001 10000000

The value field is encoded based on the data type. It is a multiple number of octets. The simplest data type value to encode is an OCTET STRING. An octet string of '0C1B'H (the string is designated with apostrophes on both sides and an H denoting hexadecimal notation) would look like

00001100 00011011

The complete TLV for the string of octets '0C1B'H is made up from universal (00) Primitive (0) data type of a tag value of 4 with a one-octet length field to indicate that there are two octets of value field. It is

00000100 00000010 00001100 00011011

The integer value is encoded using a twos-complement form. For a positive value, the actual value is the binary representation with the most significant always being 0 to indicate a positive sign. If the integer exceeds 127, an additional octet of 0s is prefixed. Thus, a value of 255 is written as 00000000 11111111, with the leading 0 indicating the positive sign bit. For a negative integer, the absolute value of the integer is written in a binary form. The leading sign bit should be 0 to indicate the positive sign. Invert all the 1s to 0s and all the 0s to 1s. Then add 1 to the inverted binary digits. The leading sign bit will automatically become 1, indicating a negative integer. For example, a –5 will start as 00000101.

Table 3.6 Value of Class in Type

CLASS	8TH BIT	7TH BIT
Universal	0	0
Application	0	1
Context-specific	1	0
Private	1	1

Inverting the bits and adding 1, it becomes 11111011. Refer to Perkins and McGinnis [1997] for the encoding of other values.

3.8   MACROS

The data types and values that we have so far discussed use ASN.1 notation of syntax directly and explicitly. ASN.1 language permits extension of this capability to define new data types and values by defining ASN.1 macros. The ASN.1 macros also facilitate grouping of instances of an object or concisely defining various characteristics associated with an object.

The structure of a macro takes the form shown in Figure 3.19.

As can be observed from Table 3.4, the keyword for a macro is all in capital letters. TYPE NOTATION defines the syntax of the new types and VALUE NOTATION defines the syntax of the new values. The auxiliary assignments define and describe any new types identified.

The **OBJECT-IDENTITY** macro is used to define information about an **OBJECT IDENTIFIER** assignment. Figure 3.20 shows an example from RFC 2578 of creating an Internet object using an **OBJECT-IDENTITY** macro. The two syntactical expressions **STATUS** and **DESCRIPTION** are mandatory and the type ReferPart is optional. The value in **VALUE NOTATION** defines the object identifier.

As an example of the usage of the **OBJECT-IDENTITY** macro, let us consider a registration authority that registers all computer science courses that are offered in the College of Computing. Suppose we

```
<macroname> MACRO ::=

BEGIN

        TYPE NOTATION ::=  <syntaxOfNewType>

        VALUE NOTATION ::= <syntaxOfNewValue>

        <auxiliaryAssignments>

END
```

Figure 3.19   Structure of an ASN.1 Macro

```
OBJECT-IDENTITY  MACRO
BEGIN
TYPE NOTATION ::=
"STATUS" Status
"DESCRIPTION"Text
ReferPart
VALUE NOTATION ::=
value(VALUE OBJECT IDENTIFIER)
Status ::= "current" | "deprecated" | "obsolete"
ReferPart ::= "REFERENCE" Text I empty
Text ::= "value (IASString)"
END
```

Figure 3.20   OBJECT-IDENTITY Macro [RFC 1902]

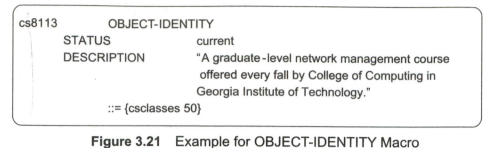

Figure 3.21 Example for OBJECT-IDENTITY Macro

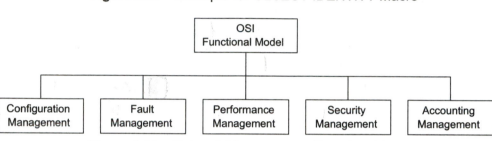

Figure 3.22 Network Management Functional Model

want to formally register the network management course *cs8113* under the object descriptor *csclasses* as the 50th subnode. We can specify an ASN.1 OBJECT-IDENTITY macro shown in Figure 3.21. The object identifier *cs8113* has a value {csclasses 1}. Its status is current and has a description explaining the course offering.

3.9 FUNCTIONAL MODEL

The functional model component of an OSI model addresses user-oriented applications. They are formally specified in the OSI model and are shown in Figure 3.22. The model consists of five models: configuration management, fault management, performance management, security management, and accounting management. Part III of the book is devoted to the application aspects of network management.

Configuration management addresses the setting and changing of configurations of networks and network components. Relevant management information is embedded in managed objects, such as switches, hubs, bridges, and routers. Configuration management involves setting up these parameters. For example, alarm thresholds could be set to generate alarms when packet loss exceeds a defined value. Information on the object name and contact person to be contacted when the component fails could be entered in the management agent. The configuration data are gathered automatically by, and are stored in, the NMS at the network operations center (NOC). NMS displays in real-time the configuration of the network and its status.

Fault management involves detection and isolation of the problem causing the failure in the network. An NMS constantly monitors and displays in real-time major and minor alarms based on the severity of failures. Restoration of service is done as soon as possible and it could involve reconfiguration of the network, which is part of configuration management. In several failure situations, the network could do this automatically. This network feature is called self-healing. In other situations, restoration of service does not include fixing the cause of the problem. A trouble ticket is generated and followed up for resolution of the problem using a trouble ticket administration system.

This is the trouble ticket administration of fault management and is used to track problems in the network. All problems—including non-problems—are to be tracked until resolved. Periodic analysis of the data, which are maintained in a database, is done to establish patterns of the problems for follow-up action. There are trouble-tracking systems to automate the tracking of troubles from the automatic generation of a trouble ticket by an NMS to the resolution of the problem.

Performance management is concerned with the performance behavior of the network. The status of the network is displayed by a network-monitoring system that measures the traffic and performance statistics on the network. Network statistics include data on traffic volume, network availability, and network delay. Traffic data can be captured based on the traffic volume in various segments of the network. Data need to be gathered by the NOC and updated in a timely fashion in order to administer performance management. Any configuration changes needed to relieve temporary congestion in traffic are made by the NOC. Permanent relief is engineered by the addition of equipment and facilities as well as policy changes. Performance-monitoring tools can gather statistics of all protocol layers. We can analyze the various application-oriented traffic such as Web traffic, Internet mail, file transfers, etc. The statistics on applications could be used to make policy decisions on managing the applications. Performance data on availability and delay are useful for tuning the network to increase the reliability and to improve its response time.

Security management covers a broad range of security aspects. It involves physically securing the network, access to the network resources, and secured communication over the network. A security database is established and maintained by the NOC for access to the network and network information. Any unauthorized access to the network resources generates an alarm on the NMS at the NOC. Firewalls are implemented to protect corporate networks and network resources from being accessed by unauthorized personnel and programs, including virus programs. Secured communication is concerned with the tampering of information as it traverses the network. The content of the information should neither be accessed nor altered by unauthorized personnel. Cryptography plays a vital part in security management.

Accounting management administers cost allocation of the usage of network. Metrics are established to measure the usage of resources and services provided. Traffic data gathered by performance management serve as input to this process.

Another dimension of application management is concerned with service and business management, which we discuss in Chapter 7. Service and business management is directed toward service providers, in order for them to accomplish customer satisfaction and to ensure the profitability of business. The traffic statistics, trouble ticket administration data, and accounting management results are inputs to service and business management.

■ Summary

The foundations of standards, models, and language needed to delve into the study of network management have been addressed in this chapter. These are the four network management models—OSI, Internet, Telecommunications Network Management, and IEEE 802—and a fifth emerging one using Web technology.

The OSI management model categorizes the four functions of network management into four models. They are configuration, information, communication, and application functions. Each of these has been addressed in detail. Some parts of the OSI model are applicable to the other three management models.

The organization model describes the management process in the network element, called the agent process, and the management process in the manager. We presented the two-tier and three-tier architectural models and the relationship between them.

The information model addresses the SMI that enables processes running in different components in the network to exchange management data. We defined the management object for both OSI and Internet/SNMP management models.

The two primary communications protocols are CMIP in OSI and SNMP in the Internet.

We discussed the syntactical format, Abstract Syntax Notation One, and how it is applied to defining managed objects. We presented the terminology, symbols, and conventions used in ASN.1, and then defined the various categories and structure of data types. We defined the managed objects in OSI and SNMP/Internet management models in adequate detail so that we should be prepared to study SNMP management in the next two chapters. We briefly covered how ASN.1 is applied to specifying the management information tree and MIB by giving some specific examples.

The text-oriented ASN.1 specifications need to be encoded for transmission of data between systems. We discussed the most widely adopted encoding scheme, the Basic Encoding Rules.

We defined the extension to ASN.1 in defining an ASN.1 macro and presented an example from the SNMP management model used to create a new object.

The application functions are subdivided into five categories of management: configuration, fault, performance, security, and accounting. We have addressed each function briefly in this chapter.

Exercises

1. What are the standards used for the various layers in an Ethernet-based network that is managed by the Internet management protocol? Assume that Ethernet runs on 10 Mbps on an unshielded twisted pair cable.

2. Consider a network of multivendor network components. Hubs are made by Cabletron and are managed by Cabletron's Spectrum NMS (network management system). Routers are made by Cisco and are managed by CiscoWorks NMS. The entire network is managed by general-purpose NMS such as HP OpenView Network Node Manager. Draw a two-tier management network that performs configuration and fault management. Explain the rationale for your configuration.

3. Redraw the management network configuration of Exercise 2 as a three-tier configuration. What are the requirements on the three-tier network management system?

4. Explain succinctly the difference between the database of a network management system and its MIB. How do you implement each in a network management system?

5. You have been assigned the responsibility of adding a new vendor's components with its own network management system to an existing network managed by a network management system. Identify the three sets of functions that you need to do to fulfill your task.

6. Write an ASN.1 module that specifies DaysOfWeek as SEQUENCE type with each day of the week (day1, day2, ...) as the type VisibleString. Write the ASN.1 description

   (a) for the structure and
   (b) for the value

7. Repeat Exercise 6 defining DaysOfWeek as an ENUMERATED data type, with values from 0 to 6.

8. The following is the informal record structure of my home address:

Name	Mani M. Subramanian
Address	1652 Harts Mill Road
City	Atlanta
State	GA
Zip Code	30319

Write for your record:

(a) the informal record structure

(b) ASN.1 description of the record structure

(c) the record value for your home address

9. Given the definition

```
class ::= SET {
        name            VisibleString
        size            INTEGER
        graduate                BOOLEAN
        }
```

which of the following set of values is (are) compatible with the above ASN.1 record structure?

(a) "CS4803B," FALSE, 28

(b) CS8113B, TRUE, 28

(c) "CS4803B," 28, TRUE

(d) CS4803B, 28, TRUE

10. (a) Describe a list and an ordered list in ASN.1 syntax

(b) Identify the differences between them

(c) Differentiate between list construction and repetitive construction using examples

11. In a ballroom dance, the conductor asks the guests to group themselves into couples made up of a male and a female (order does not matter) for a dance. Write an ASN.1 module for danceGroup with data type DanceGroup that is composed of data type Couple; couple is constructed using male and female.

12. A high school class consists of four boys and four girls. The names of the boys with their heights are Adam (65"), Chang (63"), Eduardo (72'), and Gopal (62"). The names of the girls are Beth (68"), Dipa (59"), Faye (61"), and Ho (64"). For each of the following cases, write an ASN.1 description for record values by selecting appropriate data types. Start with data type **Studentinfo**, listing information on each student.

(a) A random list of the students

(b) An alphabetized list of students

(c) Sorted line up of students with increasing height

(d) Any one student to be a class representative to the faculty meeting

(e) Two groups, each of boys and girls only

13. In Section 3.6.2, we defined the tag for Chapter-number type as APPLICATION 2. Encode this chapter (3) in TLV format.

14. You are establishing a small company with your network managed by a network management system. Give an example of each of the five functional applications that you would implement.

SNMPv1 Network Management: Organization and Information Models

OBJECTIVES

- *ETF SNMP standard*
  - *History*
  - *RFC, STD, and FYI*
- *Organization model*
  - *2- and 3-tier models*
  - *Manager and agent*
- *Management messages*

- *Structure of management information, SMI*
- *Object type and instance*
- *Scalar and aggregate managed objects*
- *Management information base, MIB*
- *NMS physical and virtual databases*
- *IETF MIB-2 standard*

SNMP management is also referred to as Internet management. We have chosen to call it SNMP management since it has matured to the level that it manages more than the Internet, for example, intranet and telecommunications networks. Any network that uses TCP/IP protocol suite is an ideal candidate for SNMP management. SNMP network management systems (NMSs) can manage even non-TCP/IP network elements through proxy agents.

SNMP management is the most widely used NMS. Most network components that are used in enterprise network systems have network agents built in them that can respond to an SNMP NMS. Thus, if a new component, such as a host, a bridge, or a router that has an SNMP agent built in, is added to a managed network, the NMS can automatically start monitoring the added component. The ease of adding components and configuring them for management has contributed to the acceptance and popularity of the SNMP management system. To quote Marshall Rose [Rose, 1996], who is one of the early architects of SNMP management, the fundamental axiom is, "the impact of adding network management to managed nodes must be minimal, reflecting a lowest common denominator."

SNMP management got started as an interim set of specifications, the ultimate standard being OSI management. Since that did not materialize, SNMP specifications were enhanced by the development of SNMPv2 and SNMPv3. The first version of SNMP is informally referred to as SNMPv1, as it is titled in this chapter. SNMPv2 and SNMPv3 are covered in Chapters 6 and 7, respectively.

We start by giving a real-world example of a managed network in Section 4.1 and show the kind of detailed information one could gather from an NMS. We then learn what SNMP management is and how that enables us to obtain that kind of information. The history of SNMP management goes back to 1970 in managing the Internet. The Internet Engineering Task Force (IETF) has the responsibility to develop Internet standards including network management standards. The standards documents are available free in Request for Comments documents (RFCs). These are covered in Sections 4.2 and 4.3.

The SNMP management model is introduced in Section 4.4 and addresses primarily organization, information, and communication. An NMS comprises management process, agent process, and network elements. We discuss various possible configurations in Section 4.5. There are three messages transmitted by the manager and two by the agent for a total of five messages. Management data are obtained by the manager by polling the agents. Agents respond with requested data. They also generate a few alarms when needed. This simple architecture of SNMP management is described in Section 4.6.

SNMP information model, described in Section 4.7, comprises the Structure of Management Information (SMI) and the Management Information Base (MIB). SMI uses ASN.1 syntax to define managed objects. SMIv1 documented the specifications distinct from the formal ASN.1 definition as it was then expected that OSI would be the future standard. However, that did not happen. Hence, SMIv2 merged the two parts into a concise document. The MIB defines the relationship between managed objects and groups of related objects into MIB modules. MIB-II is a superset of MIB-I and is used in SNMPv1.

SNMP architecture, administration, and access policies, which fall under the communication model, are discussed in the next chapter.

4.1 MANAGED NETWORK: CASE HISTORIES AND EXAMPLES

Let us look at some of the real-world experiences that demonstrate the power of network management before learning how it is accomplished. As with any good technology, the power of technology could result in both positive and negative results. Atomic energy is a great resource, but an atomic bomb is not! An NMS is a powerful tool, but it could also bring your network down, when not "managed" properly.

As part of my experience in establishing a network operations center, as well as in teaching a network management course, we made several visits to see how various corporations and institutions manage their networks. One of the visits was to an AT&T Network Control Center, which monitored the network status of their network in the entire eastern half of the United States. We could see the network of nodes and links on a very large screen, mostly in green indicating that the network was functioning well. The display screen would automatically refresh every few minutes. We saw nodes or links change color to yellow or red, indicating a minor or major alarm. We would also then see them turn back to green without interference by any human being. What we were seeing was monitoring of a national network from a central monitoring center. Monitoring was done by the NMSs and operations support systems without any human intervention. Even the healing of the network after a failure was accomplished automatically—self-healing network as it is called. Any persistent alarm was pursued by the control center, which tested the network remotely using management tools to isolate and localize the trouble. It was an impressive display of network management capability.

In another visit to a major international news network world headquarters, we were shown the monitoring of not only network failures, but also the performance of networks around the globe. Network Operations Center personnel were able to look at networks in various continents separately, as well as in the global integrated network. The system was putting out not only alarms, but also the cause of the failure, which was accomplished using artificial intelligence built in the system.

On a more intimate level, one of the directors of Information Technology was narrating his experience of resolving a network failure problem using the discovery tool that identified new components in the network. A newly added host interface card was the culprit! This was done from a network operations center, without sending an engineer to the remote site.

There is also another side to the power of this awesome discovery tool, which was an experience of another network manager. He was once asked by one of the departments in the campus to shut off the discovery tool as it was flooding the network and degrading performance. Thus, powerful network management tools also need to be managed to avoid degradation of network performance. There are horror stories of the network coming down when turning on NMSs.

When asked what is the most benefit that he got out of an NMS, one of the managers answered that it is the consistency of administering, for example, configuring the network. This came across as an extremely interesting comment to me as I was once involved in automating the installation and maintenance of a telephone network. One of the operating telephone company managers, who helped in specifications then, commented that what we were trying to accomplish was an impossible task. He said that there were no standard operations procedures for the company that could be automated, and even in one single operations center, no two groups were following the same procedures! Believe it or not, the project was a success.

Let us now illustrate what an NMS could do by monitoring a subnetwork using a commercial NMS. The addresses of network components have been intentionally modified for security reasons.

Figure 4.1 shows a managed LAN that was discovered by an NMS. We show here only a subnetwork of a larger network managed by the NMS. As we mentioned above, an NMS can automatically discover any component in the network as long as the component has a management agent. The management agent could be as simple as a TCP/IP suite that responds to a ping by the NMS. However, agents in the modern network components are more sophisticated. We will study how NMS does an autodiscovery of elements in the network in Chapter 12. Let us accept for now that it has been accomplished somehow.

The managed subnetwork that we are discussing here is an Ethernet LAN that is shown below the backbone cloud in Figure 4.1. It consists of a router and two hubs and is connected to the backbone network. The LAN IP address is 172.16.46.1, and the two hub addresses have been configured as 172.16.46.2 and 172.16.46.3. The LAN IP address, 172.16.46.1, is the address assigned to the interface card in the router. Interface cards in the router and the interface card in each of the hubs are connected by a cat-5 cable forming the Ethernet LAN.

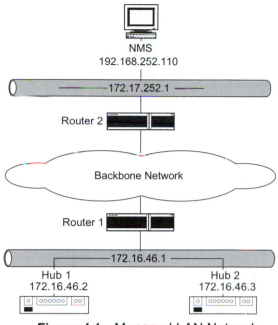

Figure 4.1 Managed LAN Network

The NMS, whose IP address is 192.168.252.110, is physically and logically located remotely from the 172.16.46.1 LAN. It is configured on the LAN 192.168.252.1 and is connected to the backbone network. Information system managers establish conventions to designate a network and a subnetwork. A 0 in the fourth decimal position of an IP address designates a network, and a subnetwork is designated with a 1 in the fourth position of the dotted decimal notation. Thus, 172.16.46.1 is a LAN subnetwork in the network 172.16.46.0.

Once network components have been discovered and mapped by the NMS, we can query and acquire information on system parameters and statistics on the network elements. Figure 4.2 presents system information on three network elements in the managed LAN gathered by the NMS sending specific queries asking for system parameters.

Figure 4.2(a) shows that the network element is designated by 172.16.46.2. No specific title or name has been assigned to it. System description indicates that it is a hub made by a 3Com vendor, with its model and software version. It also gives the system object ID and how long the system has been up without failure. The format of the System ID follows the format shown in Figure 3.10 with the 3Com node under enterprises node being 43. The last three node numbers, 1.8.5, following 43 describe the private MIB of 3Com. The *System Up Time* indicates that the system has been operating without failure for over 286 days. The number in parenthesis is in units of one hundredths of a second. Thus, the hub designated by the IP address 172.16.46.2 has been up for 2,475,380,437 hundredths of seconds, or for 286 days, 12 hours, 3 minutes, 24.37 seconds. System Description and System Object ID are factory set and the rest are user settable.

Figure 4.2(b) shows similar parameters for the second hub, 172.16.46.3, on the LAN. Figure 4.2(c) presents system information sent by the router on the network to the NMS's queries. The system name for the router has been configured and hence the query received the response of the name, router1. gatech.edu.

Title: System Information   : 172.16.46.2
Name or IP Address: 172.16.46.2

System Name   :
System Description   : 3Com LinkBuilder FMS, SW version:3.02
System Contact   :
System Location   :
System Object ID   : .iso.org.dod.internet.private.enterprises.43.1.8.5
System Up Time   : (2475380 437) 286 days, 12:03:24.37

(a) System Information on 172.16.46.2 Hub

Title: System Information: 172.16.46.3
Name or IP Address: 172.16.46.3

System Name   :
System Description   : 3Com LinkBuilder FMS, SW version:3.12
System Contact   :
System Location   :
System Object ID   : .iso.org.dod.internet.private.enterprises.43.1.8.5
System Up Time   : (3146735182) 364 days, 4:55:51.82

(b) System Information on 172.16.46.3 Hub

Title: System Information: router1.gatech.edu
Name or IP Address: 172.16.252.1

System Name   : router1.gatech.edu
System Description   : Cisco Internetwork Operating System Software
                     : IOS (tm) 7000   Software (C7000 -JS-M), Version
                     : 11.2(6),RELEASE SOFTWARE (ge1)
                     : Copyright (c) 1986 -1997 by Cisco Systems, Inc.
                     : Compiled   Tue 06 -May-97 19:11 by kuong
System Contact
System Location   :
System Object ID   : iso.org.dod.internet.private.enterprises.cisco.ciscoProducts.
                       cisco 7000
System Up Time   : (315131795) 36 days, 11:21:57.95

(c) System Information on Router

Figure 4.2   System Information Acquired by an NMS

Figures 4.3(a), (b), and (c) present the data acquired by the NMS from the interface cards on the two hubs and the router, which are on LAN 172.16.46.1. They are addresses associated with each interface. At the top of each figure are the titles and IP address or name of the network interface card used by the NMS to access the network component. Thus, in Figure 4.3(a), the title and the name or IP address are 172.16.46.2. Note that the IP address 172.16.46.3 is the address as seen by the NMS traversing the router. In Figure 4.3(b), the IP address 172.16.46.3 is the access address of the second hub on the

Title: Addresses: 172.16.46.2
Name or IP Address: 172.16.46.2

Index	Interface	IP Address	Network Mask	Network Address	Link Address
1	3Com	172.16.46.2	255.255.255.0	172.16 46.0	0x08004E07C25C
2	3Com	192.168.101.1	255.255.255.0	192.168.101.0	<none>

(a) Addresses on 172.16.46.2 Hub Ports

Title: Addresses: 172.16.46.3
Name or IP Address: 172.16.46.3

Index	Interface	IP Address	Network Mask	Network Address	Link Address
1	3Com	172.16.46.3	255.255.255.0	172.16 46.0	0x08004E0919D4
2	3Com	192.168.101.1	255.255.255.0	192.168.101.0	<none>

(b) Addresses on 172.16.46.3 Hub Ports

Title: System Information: router1.gatech.edu
Name or IP Address: 172.16.252.1

Index	Interface	IP Address	Network Mask	Network Address	Link Address
23	LEC.1.0	192.168.3.1	255.255.255.0	192.168.3.0	0x00000C3920B4
25	LEC.3.9	192.168.252.1	255.255.255.0	192.168.252.0	0x00000C3920B4
13	Ethernet2/0	172.16.46.1	255.255.255.0	172.16.46.0	0x00000C3920AC
16	Ethernet2/3	172.16.49.1	255.255.255.0	172.16.49.0	0x00000C3920AF
17	Ethernet2/4	172.16.52.1	255.255.255.0	172.16.52.0	0x00000C3920B0
9	Ethernet1/2	172.16.55.1	255.255.255.0	172.16.55.0	0x00000C3920A6
2	Ethernet 0/1	172.16.56.1	255.255.255.0	172.16.56.0	0x00000C39209D
15	Ethernet2/2	172.16.57.1	255.255.255.0	172.16.57.0	0x00000C3920AE
8	Ethernet1/1	172.16.58.1	255.255.255.0	172.16.58.0	0x00000C3920A5
14	Ethernet2/1	172.16.60.1	255.255.255.0	172.16.60.0	0x00000C3920AD

(c) Addresses on Router Ports (Partial List)

Figure 4.3 Addresses Information Acquired by an SNMP NMS

172.16.46.1 LAN. Figure 4.3(c) shows the title and name or IP address as router1.gatch.edu. By using a network lookup command, the IP address of router1.gatech.edu can be recognized as 172.16.252.1. This is the backbone interface address of the router and is the interface on the router as seen by the NMS traversing the backbone network.

In Figures 4.3(a), (b), and (c), we notice that there are six columns of data. The first column is the index, which identifies the row in the matrix. Each row is a collection of various addresses associated with an interface. The second column describes the port id. For example, hubs 1 and 2 have 3Com cards in them. Column 2 of Figure 4.3(c) identifies the card and the port of the interface. For example, the row with index 2 identifies Ethernet 0 card/port 1. The IP address of the interface card is presented in the third column of the matrix. The IP address in the third column and the network mask address in the fourth column are "and-ed" in modula-2 arithmetic to obtain the network address presented in the fifth column. This implies that all packets destined for network address 172.16.46.0 will be accepted by hub 1. The sixth and the last column in Figure 4.3, the link address, contains the MAC address. In the first row of Figure 4.3(a), 08004E07C25C is the MAC address of the hub 1 interface card. Link addresses in the second rows of Figures 4.3(a) and (b) are presented as "none," as they are non-LAN interfaces.

The Figure 4.3(c) matrix has many rows, as it is a router with many interface cards, each with multiple ports. For example, each Ethernet card has four physical ports. LEC 1.0 and LEC 3.9 are ATM LAN Emulation Card interfaces.

4.2   HISTORY OF SNMP MANAGEMENT

SNMP management began in the 1970s. Internet Control Message Protocol (ICMP) was developed to manage Advanced Research Project Agency NETwork (ARPANET). It is a mechanism to transfer control messages between nodes. A popular example of this is Packet Internet Groper (PING), which is part of the TCP/IP suite now. We learned to use this in the exercises in Chapter 1. PING is a very simple tool that is used to investigate the health of a node and the robustness of communication with it from the source node. It started as an early form of network-monitoring tool.

ARPANET, which started in 1969, developed into the Internet in the 1980s with the advent of UNIX and the popularization of client–server architecture. Data were transmitted in packet form using routers and gateways. TCP/IP-based networks grew rapidly, mostly in defense and academic communities and in small entrepreneurial companies taking advantage of the electronic medium for information exchange. National Science Foundation officially dropped the name ARPANET in 1984 and adopted the name Internet. Note that the Internet is spelled with a capital I and is limited to a TCP/IP-based network. An Internet Advisory Board (IAB) was formed to administer Internet activities, which are covered in the next section.

With the growth of the Internet, it became essential to have the capability to remotely monitor and configure gateways. Simple Gateway Monitoring Protocol (SGMP) was developed for this purpose as an interim solution. The IAB recommended the development of SNMP that is a further enhancement of SGMP. Even SNMP management was intended to be another interim solution, with the long-term solution being migration to the OSI standard CMIP/CMIS. However, due to the enormous simplicity of SNMP and its extensive implementation, it has become the de facto standard. SNMPv2 was developed to make it independent of the OSI standard, as well as adding more features. SNMPv2 has only partially overcome some of the limitations of SNMP. The final version of SNMPv2 was released without one of its major enhancements on its security feature due to strong differences in opinion. SNMPv3 addresses the security feature.

4.3   INTERNET ORGANIZATIONS AND STANDARDS

4.3.1   Organizations

We mentioned in the previous section that the IAB recommended the development of SNMP. The IAB was founded in 1983 informally by researchers working on TCP/IP networks. Its name was formally changed from the Internet Advisory Board to the Internet Architecture Board in 1989 and was designated with the responsibility to manage two task forces—the Internet Engineering Task Force (IETF) and the Internet Research Task Force (IRTF).

The IRTF is tasked to consider long-term research problems in the Internet. It creates focused, long-term, and small research groups working on topics related to Internet protocols, applications, architecture, and technology.

With the growth of the Internet, the IETF organization has grown to be the protocol engineering, development, and standardization arm of the IAB.

The Internet Network Information Center (InterNIC) is an organization that maintains several archives that contain documents related to the Internet and the IETF activities. They include among other documents, Request for Comments document (RFC), Standard RFC (STD), and For Your Information RFC (FYI). The latter two are subseries of RFCs (more about these in the next section).

The Internet Assigned Numbers Authority (IANA) is the central coordinator for the assignment of unique parameter values for Internet protocols. It is the clearinghouse to assign and coordinate use of numerous Internet protocol parameters. The Internet protocol suite contains numerous parameters, such as Internet addresses, domain names, autonomous system numbers (used in some routing protocols), protocol numbers, port numbers, MIB object identifiers (including private enterprise numbers), and many others. The common use of Internet protocols by the Internet community requires that these values be assigned uniquely. It is the task of IANA to make those unique assignments as requested and to maintain a registry of currently assigned values.

4.3.2   Internet Documents

Originally, RFC was just what the name implies—Request for Comments. Early RFCs were messages between ARPANET architects about how to resolve certain problems. Over the years, RFC has become more formal. It had reached the point that they were being cited as standards, even when they were not. To help clear up some confusion, there are now two special subseries within the RFCs: FYIs and STDs. The "For Your Information" RFC subseries was created to document overviews and topics that are introductory. Frequently, FYIs are created by groups within the IETF User Services Area. The STD RFC subseries was created to identify those RFCs that do in fact specify Internet standards. Every RFC, including FYIs and STDs, has an RFC number by which they are indexed and can be retrieved. FYIs and STDs have FYI numbers and STD numbers, respectively, in addition to RFC numbers. This makes it easier for a new Internet user, for example, to find all of the helpful, informational documents by looking for the FYIs among all the RFCs. If an FYI or STD is revised, its RFC number will change, but its FYI or STD number will remain constant for ease of reference.

RFC documents are available in public libraries and can be accessed via the Internet. Some sources that are in the public domain to access RFC and other Internet documents are:

> ftp://ftp.internic.net/rfc
> ftp://nic.mil/rfc
> ftp.nic.it
> http://nic.internic.net/

A novice to SNMP management could easily be confused as to which RFC document refers to what, namely, SMI, MIB, and SNMP, etc. It is confusing because the management field and associated documents are continuously evolving. Figure 4.4 portrays a high-level view of various document paths and

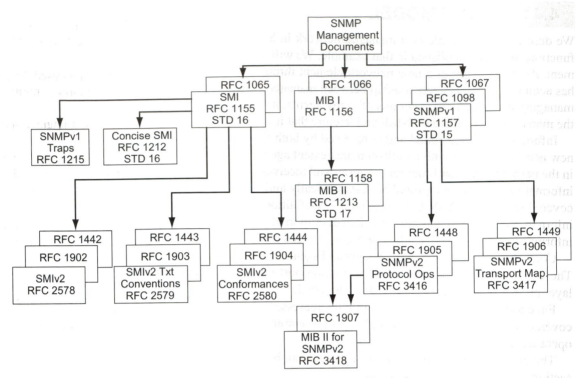

Figure 4.4 SNMP Document Evolution

documents that are relevant to SNMPv1 and SNMPv2. Documents associated with SNMPv3 will be described in Chapter 7. It is not intended to be a complete list, but to identify major core documents. There are three series of RFC and STD documents. They are: SMI, MIB, and SNMP Protocol. There are three standard documents, STD 15, 16, and 17 that have been approved by the IETF. STD 15/RFC 1157 defines the SNMP protocol. RFCs 1905, on protocol operations, and 1906, on transport mappings, are expanded updates of RFC 1157. These have been updated to RFC 1448 and RFC 1449 and subsequently, with the evolution of SNMPv3, to RFC 3416 and RFC 3417, respectively. In Figure 4.4, RFCs in the back of the cascades are earlier versions of the draft that have become obsolete. For example, RFC 1448 has been replaced by RFC 1905.

Structure of Management Information (SMI) forms the contents of RFC 1155, shown in Figure 4.4. A more concise version of SMI is given in RFC 1212 and is a supplement to RFC 1155. They both comprise STD 16 document. RFC 1155 did not address trap events, which is covered in RFC 1215.

SMIv2 is next in the evolution of SMI specifications, which are covered as STD 58 with the three documents RFC 2578–RFC 2580 describing SMIv2 data definition language, textual conventions, and conformance, respectively.

MIB has gone through a few iterations. RFC 1213/STD 17 is the version that is currently in use. It is backward compatible with MIB I specified in RFC 1156, which is obsolete now. Legacy systems that have implemented MIB I can continue to be used with MIB II implementation.

SNMP protocol has gone through modification and is part of SNMPv2. RFC 1907 is an early version of MIB II for SNMPv2 and the latest version is RFC 3418, which has gone through only minor changes from RFC 1907.

4.4   SNMP MODEL

We described an example of a managed network in Section 4.1. We saw that numerous management functions were accomplished in that example. We will now address how this is done in SNMP management. An NMS acquires a new network element through a management agent or monitors the ones it has acquired. There is a relationship between manager and agent. Since one manager is responsible for managing the designated functions of many agents, it is hierarchical in structure. The infrastructure of the manager–agent and the SNMP architecture that it is based on form the organization model.

Information is transmitted and is received by both the manager and the agent. For example, when a new network element with a built-in management agent is added to the network, the discovery process in the network manager broadcasts queries and receives positive response from the added element. The information must be interpreted both semantically and syntactically by the agent and the manager. We covered the syntax, ASN.1, in Section 3.7. Definition of semantics and syntax form the basis of the information model. We present a detailed definition of a managed object, rules for the SMI, and a virtual information database, MIB, which groups managed objects and provides a relational framework.

Communication between the manager and agents has to happen before information can be exchanged. The TCP/IP protocol suite is used for the transport mechanism. SNMP is defined for the application layer protocol and will be presented in Chapter 5.

Functions and services are not explicitly addressed in SNMP management. Security management is covered in the administration model as part of communication. Services are covered as part of SNMP operations.

The organization model, which has gone through an evolutionary process, is described in the next section.

4.5   ORGANIZATION MODEL

The initial organization model of SNMP management is a simple two-tier model. It consists of a network agent process, which resides in the managed object, and a network manager process, which resides in the NMS and manages the managed object. This is shown in Figure 4.5(a). Both the manager and the agent are software modules. The agent responds to any management system that communicates with it using SNMP. Thus, multiple managers can interact with one agent as shown in Figure 4.5(b)

We can question the need of multiple managers in a system when it is easy to monitor all objects in a network with standard messages. However, to configure a system in detail, more intimate knowledge of the object is needed, and hence an NMS provided by the same vendor would have more capabilities than another vendor's NMS. Thus, it is common practice to use an NMS to monitor a network of multiple

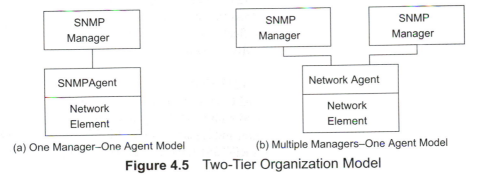

(a) One Manager–One Agent Model   (b) Multiple Managers–One Agent Model

Figure 4.5   Two-Tier Organization Model

vendor products, and several vendors' NMSs to configure respective network elements. Further, during fault tracking, a vendor's NMS can probe in more depth the source of failure—even to the level of identification of a component on a printed circuit board.

In two-tier models, the network manager receives raw data from agents and processes them. It is sometimes beneficial for the network manager to obtain pre-processed data. For example, we may want to look at traffic statistics, such as input and output packets per second, at an interface on a node as a function of time. Alternatively, we may want to get the temporal data of data traffic in a LAN. Instead of the network manager continuously monitoring events and calculating the information—for example, data rate—an intermediate agent called Remote Monitoring (RMON) is inserted between the managed object and the network manager. This introduces a three-tier architecture as shown in Figure 4.6. The network manager receives data from managed objects, as well as from the RMON agent about the managed objects. The RMON function, implemented in a distributed fashion on the network, has greatly increased the centralized management of networks.

A pure SNMP management system consists of SNMP agents and SNMP managers. However, an SNMP manager can manage a network element, which does not have an SNMP agent. Figure 4.7 shows

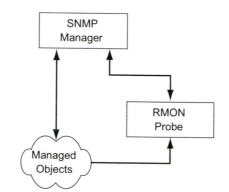

Figure 4.6   Three-Tier Organization Model

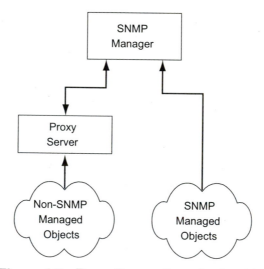

Figure 4.7   Proxy Server Organization Model

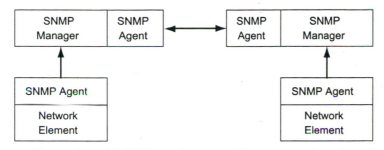

Figure 4.8 NMS Behaving as a Manager and an Agent

the organizational model for this case. This application occurs in many situations, such as legacy systems management, telecommunications management network, managing wireless networks, etc. In all these cases, they are part of an overall network that have to be managed on an integrated basis. As an example in a legacy case, we may want to manage outside plant and customer premises equipment for a Hybrid Fiber Coax (HFC) access system in broadband services to home. There are amplifiers on the outside cable plant, which do not have SNMP agents built in them. The outside cable plant uses some existing cable technology and has monitoring tools built into it, as for example transponders that measure various amplifier parameters. Information from the amplifiers could be transmitted to a central (head end) location using telemetry facilities. We can have a proxy server at the central location that converts data into a set that is SNMP compatible and communicates with the SNMP manager.

An SNMP management system can behave as an agent as well as a manager. This is similar to client–server architecture, where a host can function as both a server and a client (see Figure 1.8). In Figure 4.6, RMON, while collecting data from network objects, performs some functions (network monitoring) of a network manager. However, pre-processed data by RMON may be requested by the network manager or sent unsolicited by RMON to the network manager to integrate with the rest of the network data and to display it to the user. In the latter situation, RMON acts as a network agent. Another example of a system acting as both an agent and a manager is when two NMSs managing two autonomous networks exchange information with each other when the networks are connected via a gateway. This model is presented in Figure 4.8 and is applicable to two telecommunication service providers managing their respective wide area networks. To provide end-to-end service to customers, service providers may need to exchange management information between them.

4.6 SYSTEM OVERVIEW

Now that we have learned the relationship between the network (management) agent and manager and the different ways they can be configured, let us consider SNMP management from a system point of view. We have opted to do this prior to discussing details of the other three models—information, communication, and functional, because it would help us to understand them better if we have the big picture first.

Figure 4.9 shows SNMP network management architecture. It portrays the data path between the manager application process and the agent application process via the four transport function protocols—UDP, IP, Data Link Control (DLC), and Physical (PHY). The three application layers above the transport layer are integrated in the SNMP process.

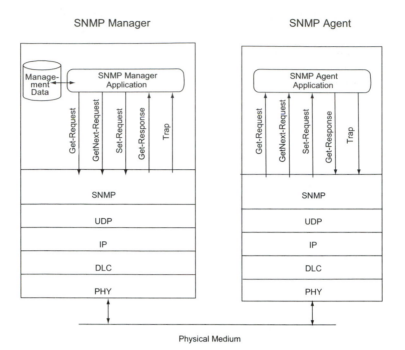

Figure 4.9 SNMP Network Management Architecture

As we stated in Chapter 1, the Internet is only concerned with the TCP/IP suite of protocols and does not address layers above or below it. Thus, layers 1 (PHY) and 2 (DLC) in the transport layers can be anything of users' choice. In practice, SNMP interfaces to the TCP/IP with UDP as the transport layer protocol.

RFC 1157 describes SNMP system architecture. It defines SNMP "by which management information for a network element may be inspected or altered by logically remote users." Two companion RFCs are RFC 1155, which describes the structure and identification of management information, and RFC 1156, which addresses the information base that is required for management.

As the name implies, SNMP protocol has been intentionally designed to be simple and versatile; this surely has been accomplished as indicated by its success. Communication of management information among management entities is realized through exchange of just five protocol messages. Three of these (get-request, get-next-request, and set-request) are initiated by the manager application process. The other two messages, get-response and trap, are generated by the agent process. Message generation is called an event. In the SNMP management scheme, the manager monitors the network by polling the agents as to their status and characteristics. However, efficiency is increased by agents generating unsolicited alarm messages, i.e., traps. We will summarize the messages here and describe structures associated with their Packet Data Units (PDUs) later. RFC 1157 defines the original specifications.

The get-request message is generated by the management process requesting the value of an object. The value of an object is a scalar variable. System group parameters in Figure 4.2 are single-instance values and are obtained using the get-request message.

The get-next-request, or simply called get-next, is very similar to get-request. In many situations, an object may have multiple values because of multiple instances of the object. For example, we saw in

Figure 4.3 that an interface could have multiple addresses associated with a given row. Another example is the routing table of a router, which has multiple values (instances) for each object. In such situations, get-next-request obtains the value of the next instance of the object.

The set-request is generated by the management process to initialize or reset the value of an object variable. The configuration parameters in Figure 4.2 that are settable can be set using the set-request message.

The get-response message is generated by an agent process. It is generated only on receipt of a get-request, get-next-request, or set-request message from a management process. The get-response process involves filling the value of the requested object with any success or error message associated with the response.

The other message that the agent generates is trap. A trap is an unsolicited message generated by an agent process without any message or event arriving from the manager process. It occurs when it observes the occurrence of a preset parameter in the agent module. For example, a node can send traps when an interface link goes up or down. Or, if a network object has a threshold value set for a parameter, such as the maximum number of packets queued up, a trap could be generated and transmitted by the agent application whenever the threshold is crossed in either direction.

The SNMP manager, which resides in the NMS, has a database that polls managed objects for management data. It contains two sets of data—one on information about the objects, MIB, and a second on the values of the objects. These two are often confused with each other. MIB is a virtual data (information) base and is static. In fact, it needs to be there when an NMS discovers a new object in the network. It is compiled in the manager during implementation. If information about the managed object is not in the manager, it could still detect the object but would mark it as unidentifiable. This is because the discovery process involves a broadcast PING command by the NMS and responses to it from network components. Thus, a newly added network component would respond if it has a TCP/IP stack that normally has a built-in ICMP. However, the response contains only the IP address. MIB needs to be implemented in both the manager and the agent to acquire the rest of the information, such as the system group information shown in Figure 4.2.

The second database is dynamic and contains measured values associated with the object. This is a true database. While MIB has a formalized structure, the database containing actual values can be implemented using any database architecture chosen by the implementers.

It is worth noting in Figure 4.9 that the SNMP manager has a database, which is the physical database, and the SNMP agent does not have a physical database. However, both have MIBs, which are compiled into the software module and are not shown in the figure.

4.7 INFORMATION MODEL

The information model deals with SMI and MIB, which are discussed in the following subsections.

4.7.1 Introduction

Figure 4.9 shows the information exchange between the agent and the manager. In a managed network, there are many managers and agents. For information to be exchanged intelligently between manager and agent processes, there has to be common understanding on both the syntax and semantics. The syntax used to describe management information is ASN.1 and a general introduction to it was given in Chapter 3. In this section, we will address SNMP-specific syntax and semantics of management information.

We discussed the types of messages in the previous section and will discuss more in Chapter 5 when we consider the communication model. In this section we will address the specification and organizational aspects of managed objects. This is called the Structure of Management Information, SMI, and is defined in RFC 1155. Specifications of managed objects and the grouping of, and relationship between, managed objects are addressed in the MIB [RFC 1213].

There are generic objects that are defined by IETF and can be managed by any SNMP-compatible NMS. Objects that are defined by private vendors, if they conform to SMI defined by RFC 1155 and MIB specified by RFC 1213, can also be managed by SNMP-compatible NMSs. There are other RFCs that address specialized network objects, such as FDDI [RFC 1285], OSPF [RFC 1253], ATM [RFC 1695], etc. Private vendor objects are specified in private MIBs provided by vendors for their specific products.

4.7.2   Structure of Management Information

A managed object can be considered to be composed of an object type and an object instance, as shown in Figure 4.10. SMI is concerned only with the object type and not the object instance. That is, the object instance is not defined by SMI. For example, Figures 4.2(a) and (b) present data on two 3Com hubs. They are both identical hubs, except for a minor software release difference. The object types associated with both hubs are represented by the identical object ID, iso.org.dod.internet.private.enterprises.43.1.8.5. Hub 1 with an IP address 172.16.46.2 is an instance of the object.

Figure 4.11 shows the situation where there are multiple instances of an object type. In Figures 4.2(a) and (b), hub 1 with an IP address 172.16.46.2 and hub 2 with an IP address 172.16.46.3 are two instances of the object.

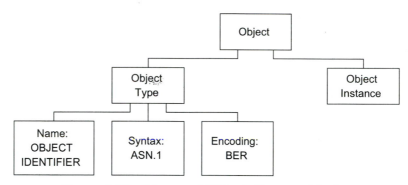

Figure 4.10   Managed Object: Type and Instance

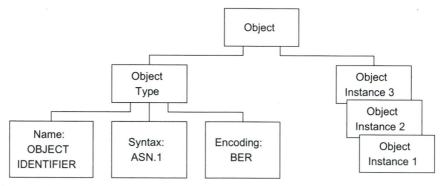

Figure 4.11   Managed Object: Type with Multiple Instances

A managed object need not be just a network element, it could be any object. For example, the Internet as an organization has an object name, "internet," with OBJECT IDENTIFIER 1.3.6.1. Of course, there can only be one instance of it! Thus, a managed object is only a means of identifying an object, whether it is physical or abstract.

The object type, which is a data type, has a name, a syntax, and an encoding scheme as discussed in Section 3.7. The name is represented uniquely by a descriptor and an object identifier. The syntax of an object type is defined using the abstract data structure ASN.1. Basic encoding rules (BER) have been adopted as the encoding scheme for transfer of data types between agent and manager processes, as well as between manager processes. We will next discuss each of these for SNMP-managed objects in detail.

Names. Every object type, i.e., every name, is uniquely identified by a DESCRIPTOR and an associated OBJECT IDENTIFIER. DESCRIPTOR and OBJECT IDENTIFIER are in uppercase since they are ASN.1 keywords. The DESCRIPTOR defining the name is mnemonic and is all in lowercase letters—at least it begins with lowercase letters, as we just described the Internet object as "internet." Since it is mnemonic and should be easily readable, uppercase letters can be used as long as they are not the beginning letter. For example, the object IP address table is defined as *ipAddrTable*. OBJECT IDENTIFIER is a unique name and number in the Management Information Tree (MIT), as we discussed in Section 3.4.1. We will henceforth use the term Management Information Base (MIB) for the Internet MIT. Thus, the Internet MIB has its OBJECT IDENTIFIER 1.3.6.1, as shown in Figure 3.5. It can also be defined in a hybrid mode, for example,

internet OBJECT IDENTIFIER ::= {iso org(3) dod(6) 1 }.

Information inside the curly brackets can be represented in various ways. This is shown in Figure 4.12. We can use any combination of the unique name and the unique node number on the management tree.

Any object in the Internet MIB will start with the prefix 1.3.6.1 or *internet*. For example, there are four objects under the *internet* object. These four objects are defined as:

directory	OBJECT IDENTIFIER ::= {internet 1}
mgmt	OBJECT IDENTIFIER ::= {internet 2}
experimental	OBJECT IDENTIFIER ::= {internet 3}
private	OBJECT IDENTIFIER ::= {internet 4}

The first line in this example states that the object, directory, is defined as the first node under the object internet. The four subnodes under the "internet" node are shown in Figure 4.13. We will discuss objects in the MIB tree in the next section.

The *directory*(1) node is reserved for future use of OSI Directory in the Internet. The *mgmt*(2) node is used to identify all IETF recommended and IAB-approved subnodes and objects. As of now the only

```
internet OBJECT IDENTIFIER ::= { iso(1) org(3) dod(6) internet(1) }
internet OBJECT IDENTIFIER ::= { 1 3 6 1 }
internet OBJECT IDENTIFIER ::= { iso org  dod internet }
internet OBJECT IDENTIFIER ::= { iso org  dod(6) internet(1) }
internet OBJECT IDENTIFIER ::= { iso(1) org(3) 6 1 }
```

Figure 4.12 Different Formats of Declaration of OBJECT IDENTIFIER

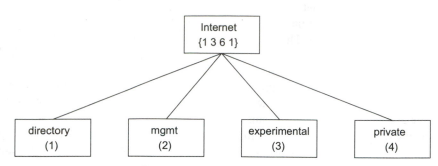

Figure 4.13   Subnodes under Internet Node in SNMPv1

node connected directly to {internet 2} is *mib-2*. As we said earlier, MIB-2 is a superset of MIB-1, and hence *mib-2* is the only node under {mgmt} as shown below:

mib-2   OBJECT IDENTIFIER ::= {mgmt 1}

The *experimental*(3) node was created to define objects under IETF experiments. For example, if IANA has approved a number 5 for an experimenter, we would use the OBJECT IDENTIFIER {experimental 5}.

The last node is *private*(4). This is a heavily used node. Commercial vendors can acquire a number under enterprises(1), which is under the private(4) node. Thus, we have

enterprises   OBJECT IDENTIFIER ::= {private 1}
or
enterprises   OBJECT IDENTIFIER ::= {1 3 6 1 4 1}

Figure 4.14 shows an example of four commercial vendors—Cisco, HP, 3Com, and Cabletron who are registered as nodes 9, 11, 43, and 52, respectively, under enterprises(1). Nodes under any of these nodes are entirely left to the discretion of the vendors.

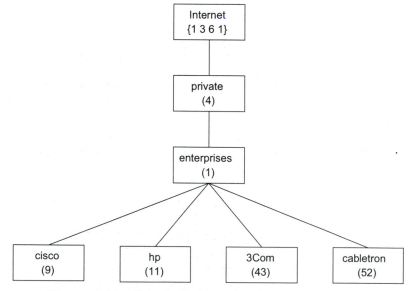

Figure 4.14   Private Subtree for Commercial Vendors

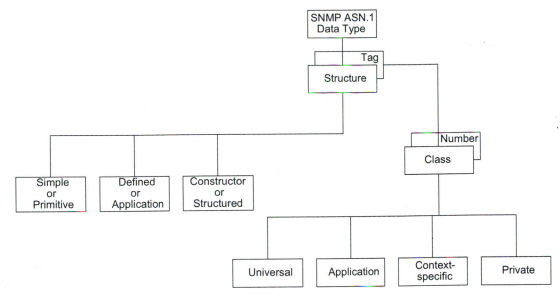

Figure 4.15 SNMP ASN.1 Data Type

Syntax. ASN.1 syntax that was introduced in Section 3.7 is used to define the structure of object types. Not all constructs of ASN.1 are used in TCP/IP-based SNMP management. Figure 4.15 shows the TCP/IP-based ASN.1 data type. It is very similar to Figure 3.15, but only has three categories under structure.

The three structural types shown in Figure 4.15 are simple, constructor, and defined types, as defined in RFC 1155. Other common terms used for these are primitive (or atomic), structured, and application types, respectively, as shown in Figure 3.9. The tagged type is not explicitly used in TCP/IP management, although the IMPLICIT and EXTERNAL keywords are utilized for derived application data types.

SNMP ASN.1 data types are listed in Table 4.1. All data types except SEQUENCE and SEQUENCE OF are called base types.

Primitive or simple types are atomic in nature and are: INTEGER, OCTET STRING, OBJECT IDENTIFIER, and NULL. These are also referred to as non-aggregate types.

INTEGER has numerous variations based on the sign, length, range, and enumeration. The reader is referred to Perkins and McGinnis [1997] for a detailed presentation on the subject. When the integer value is restricted by a range, it is called a subtype, as presented in the comments column of Table 4.1, as INTEGER (n1..nN).

The data type ENUMERATED was specified in Section 3.6.2 as a special case of INTEGER data type. In SNMP management, it is specified as INTEGER data type with labeled INTEGER values. The following example of error-status in GetResponse associated with GetRequest-PDU illustrates the use of it. Each enumerated INTEGER has a name associated with it:

```
error-status INTEGER {
        noError(0)
        tooBig(1)
        genErr(5)
        authorizationError(16)
}
```

Table 4.1 SNMP-based ASN.1 Data Type Structure

STRUCTURE	DATA TYPE	COMMENTS
Primitive types	INTEGER	Subtype INTEGER (n1..nN)
		Special case: Enumerated INTEGER type
	OCTET STRING	8-bit bytes binary and textual data
		Subtypes can be specified by either range or fixed
	OBJECT IDENTIFIER	Object position in MIB
	NULL	Placeholder
Defined types	NetworkAddress	Not used
	IpAddress	Dotted decimal IP address
	Counter	Wrap-around, non-negative integer, monotonically increasing, max $2^{32}-1$
	Gauge	Capped, non-negative integer, increase or decrease
	TimeTicks	Non-negative integer in hundredths of second units
	Opaque	Application-wide arbitrary ASN.1 syntax, double-wrapped OCTET STRING
Constructor types	SEQUENCE	List maker
	SEQUENCE OF	Table maker

Any non-zero value indicates the type of error encountered by the agent in responding to a manager's message. As a convention, the value 0 is not permitted in the response message. Thus, a noError message is filled with NULL.

The OCTET STRING data type is used to specify either binary or textual information that is 8 bits long. Just as in INTEGER data type, a subtype in OCTET STRING can be specified. In fact, the subtype value can either be ranged, fixed, or a choice between them. Some examples of the subtype are:

```
OCTET STRING (SIZE 0..255)
OCTET STRING (SIZE 8)
OCTET STRING (SIZE 4 | 8)
OCTET STRING (SIZE 0..255 | 8)
```

The combination keyword OBJECT IDENTIFIER, as we discussed before, is the object position in the MIB. The fourth primitive type listed in Table 4.1 is NULL and is also a keyword. SNMPv1 keywords are listed in Table 4.2.

The second category of data types shown in Figure 4.15 and Table 4.1 consists of **defined types**. These are application-specific data types, and are also SNMP-based types. They are defined using primitive types. The primitive types used are NetworkAddress (not used in SNMP management), IpAddress, Counter, Gauge, and TimeTicks. The base type, Opaque, is used to specify octets of binary information. It is intended for adding new base types to extend SNMP SMI. Other application-wide data types can be constructed as long as they are IMPLICITly defined using these application data types.

Table 4.2 SNMPv1 Keywords

ACCESS
BEGIN
CHOICE
Counter
DEFINITIONS
DEFVAL
DESCRIPTION
END
ENTERPRISE
FROM
Gauge
IDENTIFIER
IMPORTS
INDEX
INTEGER
IpAddress
NetworkAddress
OBJECT
OBJECT-TYPE
OCTET
OF
Opaque
REFERENCE
SEQUENCE
SIZE
STATUS
STRING
SYNTAX
TRAP-TYPE
TimeTicks
VARIABLES

NetworkAddress is a choice of the address of the protocol family. For us, it is the TCP/IP-base Internet family, which uses the base type IpAddress.

IpAddress is the conventional four groups of dotted decimal notation of IPv4; for example, 190.146.252.255. The 32-bit string is designated as OCTET STRING of length 4 in network byte order.

Counter is an application-wide data type and is a non-negative integer. It can only increase in value up to a maximum of $2^{32}-1$ (4,294,967,295) and then wraps around starting from 0. The counter type is useful for defining values of data types that continually increase, such as input packets received on an interface or output packet errors on an interface.

The data type **Gauge** is also a non-negative integer, but its value can move either up or down. It pegs at its maximum value of $2^{32}-1$ (4,294,967,295). Gauge is used for data types whose value increases or decreases, such as the number of interfaces that are active in a router or hub.

TimeTicks is a non-negative integer and measures time in units of hundredths of a second. Its value indicates in hundredths of a second the number of units of time between the current instant and the time it was initialized to 0. The maximum value is $2^{32}-1$ (4,294,967,295). The system up time in Figure 4.2 is an example of this.

Opaque is an application-wide data type that supports the capability to pass arbitrary ASN.1 syntax. It is used to create more data types based on previously defined data types. This is extensively used in private vendors defining new data types in their products. When it is encoded, it is double wrapped, meaning the TLV (tag, length, and value) for the new definition is wrapped around the TLV of the previously defined type. Its size is undefined in SNMPv1, which causes some problem in its implementation. It is limited in SNMPv2.

The Opaque data type can be defined both IMPLICITly and EXPLICITly. By use of EXTERNAL type, encoding other than ASN.1 may be used in opaquely encoded data.

The third and last type of structure shown in Figure 4.15 is **constructor** or **structured type**. SEQUENCE and SEQUENCE OF are the only two constructor data types in Table 4.1 that are not base types. They are used to build lists and tables. Note that the constructs SET and SET OF, which are in ASN.1, are not included in the SNMP-based management syntax. SEQUENCE is used to build a list and SEQUENCE OF is used to build a table. We can conceptualize the list as values in a row of a table.

The syntax for list is

   SEQUENCE { <type1>, <type2>,..., <typeN> }

where each type is one of ASN.1 primitive types.

The syntax for table is

   SEQUENCE OF <entry>

where <entry> is a list constructor.

Illustrations of building list and table are shown in Figures 4.16(a) and (b). Figure 4.16(a) shows the object *ipAddrEntry* as an entry that is created from a list of objects. The list of objects in Figure 4.16(a) is 1 through 5 in the table. They are all basic types and each row of an object has the object name, OBJECT IDENTIFIER and *ObjectSyntax*. For example, object 1 on row 1 is the IP address defined as *ipAdEntAddr*. It has an OBJECT IDENTIFIER {ipAddrEntry 1} and syntax IpAddress. Note that there are two data types (ObjectSyntax) in the table, namely IpAddress and INTEGER. Thus, data types can be mixed in building a list. However, they are all basic data types and not constructor types.

The sixth object in the table is the object *ipAddrEntry* and is made up of the list of the first five objects. Construction for that is a SEQUENCE data type structure as shown. In Figure 4.16(a), the object *ipAdEntReasmMaxSize* has the syntax INTEGER(0..65535), which denotes that it is a subtype and the integer can take on values in the range from 0 to 65535.

Figure 4.16(b) shows the seventh object, *ipAddrTable*. It is node 20 under ip node and has a SEQUENCE OF construct. The *ipAddrTable* table is made up of instances of *ipAddrEntry* object.

Encoding. SNMPv1 has adopted BER with its TLV for encoding information to be transmitted between agent and manager processes. We covered this in Section 3.8 and illustrated a few ASN.1 data types. SNMP data types and tags are listed in Table 4.3. Encoding rules for various types follow.

OBJECT IDENTIFIER is encoded with each subidentifier value encoded as an octet and concatenated in the same order as in the object identifier. Since a subidentifier could be longer than an octet length, the

	Object	OBJECT IDENTIFIER	ObjectSyntax
1	ipAdEntAddr	{ipAddrEntry 1}	IpAddress
2	ipAdEntIfIndex	{ipAddrEntry 2}	INTEGER
3	ipAdEntNetMask	{ipAddrEntry 3}	IpAddress
4	ipAdEntBcastAddr	{ipAddrEntry 4}	INTEGER
5	ipAdEntReasmMaxSize	{ipAddrEntry 5}	INTEGER
6	ipAddrEntry	{ipAddrTable 1}	SEQUENCE

```
List:    IpAddrEntry    ::=
             SEQUENCE    {
                 ipAdEntAddr              IpAddress
                 ipAdEntIfIndex           INTEGER
                 ipAdEntNetMask           IpAddress
                 ipAdEntBcastAddr         INTEGER
                 ipAdEntReasmMaxSize      INTEGER (0..65535)
             }
```

(a) Managed Object IpAddrEntry as a List

	Object Name	OBJECT IDENTIFIER	Syntax
7	ipAddrTable	{ip 20}	SEQUENCE OF

```
Table:  IpAddrTable ::=
            SEQUENCE OF IpAddrEntry
```

(b) Managed Object ipAddrTable as a Table

Figure 4.16   Example of Building a List and a Table for a Managed Object

Table 4.3   SNMP Data Types and Tags

TYPE	TAG
OBJECT IDENTIFIER	UNIVERSAL 6
SEQUENCE	UNIVERSAL 16
IpAddress	APPLICATION 0
Counter	APPLICATION 1
Gauge	APPLICATION 2
TimeTicks	APPLICATION 3
Opaque	APPLICATION 4

most significant bit (8th bit) is set to 0, if the subidentifier is only one octet long. The 8th bit is set to 1 for the value that requires more than one octet and indicates more octet(s) to follow. An exception to the rule of one or more octets for each subidentifier is the specification of the first two subidentifiers. For example, *iso(1)* and *standard(3)* {1 3}, are coded as 43 in the first octet of the value. As an illustration, let us consider the object identifier *internet* {1 3 6 1}. The first octet of the TLV is the UNIVERSAL 6 tag, and the second octet defines the length of the value, which consists of three octets (43, 6, and 1). Thus, the encoded format is:

> 00000110 00000011 00101011 00000110 00000001

IP Address is encoded as straight octet strings. Counter, Gauge, and TimeTicks are coded as integers. Opaque is OCTET STRING type.

4.7.3 Managed Objects

In Chapter 3 we briefly looked at the perspective of a managed object in an SNMP management model and compared it to the OSI model. We will now specify in detail the SNMP data type format that would serve the basis for defining managed objects. We will address managed objects in the MIB in Section 4.7.4.

Structure of Managed Objects. Managed object, as we saw in Section 3.4.2, has five parameters. They are textual name, syntax, definition, access, and status as defined in RFC 1155. For example, *sysDescr* is a data type in the MIB that describes a system. Specifications for the object that describes a system are given in Figure 4.17.

As we notice in Figure 4.17, the **textual name** for an object type is mnemonic and is defined as OBJECT DESCRIPTOR. It is unique and is made up of a printable string beginning with a lowercase letter, *sysDescr*, in our example. OBJECT DESCRIPTOR defines only the object type, which is a data type. We will henceforth use the term *object type* and not *data type* when referring to a managed object. OBJECT DESCRIPTOR does not specify instances of a managed object. Thus, it describes what type of object it is and not the occurrence or instantiation of it, as we pointed out in Section 4.7.2. In Figures 4.2(a) and (b), the system description for the two hubs is 3Com LinkBuilder FMS with an appropriate software version. They both could be of the same software version and hence could be identical. Identification of each instance is left to the specific protocol that is used, and is not part of the specifications of either SMI or MIB. Thus, instances of the two hubs in Figures 4.2(a) and (b) are identified with their respective IP addresses, 172.16.46.2 and 172.16.46.3.

Associated with each OBJECT DESCRIPTOR is an OBJECT IDENTIFIER, which is the unique position it occupies in the MIB. In Figure 4.17, *sysDescr* is defined by OBJECT IDENTIFIER {system 1}.

```
OBJECT:
        sysDescr:          { system 1 }
        Syntax:            DisplayString (SIZE (0..255))
        Definition:        "A textual description of the entity. This value
                           should include the full name and version
                           identification of the system's hardware type,
                           software operating system, and networking
                           software. It is mandatory that this contain only
                           printable ASCII characters."
        Access:            read-only
        Status:            mandatory
```

Figure 4.17 Specifications for System Description

Syntax is the ASN.1 definition of the object type. The syntax of s*ysDescr* is OCTET STRING.

A **definition** is an accepted textual description of the object type. It is a basis for the common language or semantics to be used by all vendors. It is intended to avoid confusion in the exchange of information between the managed object and the management system, as well as between various NMSs.

Access is the specification for the privilege associated with accessing the information. It is one of read-only, read-write, write-only, or not-accessible. The first two choices are obvious and the third choice, not-accessible, is applicable, for example, in specifying a table. We access the values of the entries in the table and not the table itself, and hence it is declared not-accessible. The access for *sysDescr* is read-only. Its value is defined by the system vendor during the manufacturing process.

Status specifies whether the managed object is current or obsolete. A managed object, once defined, can only be made obsolete and not removed or deleted. If it is current, the implementation of it is specified as either mandatory or optional. Thus, the three choices for status are mandatory, optional, and obsolete. The status for *sysDescr* is mandatory.

Related objects can be grouped to form an **aggregate object type**. In this case the objects that make up the aggregate object type are called subordinate object types. The **subordinate object type** could either be simple (primitive type) or an aggregate type. However, it should eventually be made up of simple object types.

Macros for Managed Objects. In order to encode the above information on a managed object to be processed by machines, it has to be defined in a formalized manner. This is done using macros. Figure 4.18(a) shows a macro where an object type is represented in a formal way [RFC 1155]. A macro always starts with the name of the type—in this case, OBJECT-TYPE—followed by the keyword MACRO, and then the definition symbol. The right side of the macro definition always starts with BEGIN and ends with END.

The body of the macro module consists of three parts: type notation, value notation, and supporting productions. TYPE NOTATION defines the data types in the module and VALUE NOTATION defines the name of the object. Thus, in the example of Figure 4.18, the notations SYNTAX, ACCESS, and STATUS define the data types Object Syntax, Access, and Status. The notation for value specifies the Object Name. Supporting productions in Figure 4.18 define the allowed values for access and status. Access can only be one of any of the four options: read-only, read-write, write-only, or not-accessible. Allowed values for Status are mandatory, optional, or obsolete.

```
OBJECT-TYPE MACRO ::=
BEGIN
        TYPE NOTATION ::= "SYNTAX" TYPE (TYPE ObjectSyntax)
                "ACCESS" Access
                "STATUS" Status
        VALUE NOTATION ::= value (VALUE ObjectName)
        Access ::= "read-only" | "read-write" | "write-only" | "not-accessible"
        Status ::= "mandatory" | "optional" | "obsolete"
END
```

(a) An OBJECT-TYPE Macro [RFC 1155]

Figure 4.18   Scalar OBJECT-TYPE Macro and Example

```
sysDescr OBJECT-TYPE
        SYNTAX Display String (SIZE (0..255))
        ACCESS read-only
        STATUS mandatory
        DESCRIPTION
                "A textual description of the entity. This value should include the full
                name and version identification of the system's hardware type,
                software operating system, and networking software. It is
                mandatory that this contain only printable ASCII characters."
::= {system 1 }
```

(b) A Scalar or Single Instance Macro: sysDescr [RFC 1213]

Figure 4.18 (continued)

Figure 4.18(b) [RFC 1213] shows the application of the macro to a scalar, single-instance managed object, *sysDescr*, which is one of the components of the system group in the MIB, as we shall see in the next section. Its OBJECT IDENTIFICATION is {system 1}. DESCRIPTION defines the textual description of the object.

Aggregate Object. An aggregate object is a group of related objects. Figure 4.19 shows an example of an aggregate managed object, *ipAddrTable*, which we briefly considered as an example of structured data type in Figure 4.16. This is the IP address table that defines the IP address for each interface of the managed object. Objects 1 through 5 represent simple data types that make up an entry in a table. The textual name of the entry is *ipAddrEntry*. Thus, object 1 with the OBJECT DESCRIPTOR, *ipAdEntAddr*, is the first element of the entry, *ipAddrEntry*, and is given the unique OBJECT IDENTIFICATION, {ipAddrEntry 1}. This represents the IP address and has the syntax IpAddress, a keyword listed in Table 4.2. The access privilege to it is read-only and every managed object and management system is required to implement it.

Object 2 is *ipAdEntIfIndex* and is the second subordinate object type of *ipAddrEntry*. It identifies the instance of occurrence of the entry in the table. It references the values of other elements associated with the interface for that entry occurrence. Although a single element is adequate to uniquely identify the occurrence of an entry in this table, we will see later that there could be more than one element needed in other tables. The syntax of *ipAdEntIfIndex* is INTEGER, a primitive data type. Access and status are read-only and mandatory.

Objects 3, 4, and 5, *ipAdEntNetMask*, *ipAdEntBcastAddr*, and *ipAdEntReasmMaxSize*, respectively, specify the subnet mask, broadcast address information, and the size of the largest datagram. The definition for each describes what the object is.

Object 6 is the managed object, *ipAddrEntry*, which consists of the subordinate object types of 1 to 5 above. It describes the complete set of information consisting of the five fields needed for an entry in the IP interface address table. The syntax for *ipAddrEntry* is a SEQUENCE data type consisting of the five data types. Each data type is identified with its OBJECT DESCRIPTOR and syntax. Note that the access for *ipAddrEntry* is non-accessible. *ipAddrEntry* is itself a subordinate object type of the managed object, *ipAddrTable*. It is the first (and only) element of *ipAddrTable* and has the OBJECT IDENTIFICATION {*ipAddrTable* 1}.

OBJECT 1
        ipAdEntAddr   { ipAddrEntry 1 }
    Syntax   IpAddress
    Definition   "The IP address to which this entry's information pertains"
    Access   read-only
    Status   mandatory

OBJECT 2
        ipAdEntIfIndex   { ipAddrEntry 2 }
    Syntax   INTEGER
    Definition   "The index value which uniquely identifies the interface to which this entry is applicable. The interface identified by a particular value of this index is the same interface as identified by the same value of ifIndex. "
    Access   read-only
    Status   mandatory

OBJECT 3
        ipAdEntN etMask   { ipAddrEntry 3 }
    Syntax   IpAddress
    Definition   "The subnet mask associated with the IP address of this entry. The value of the mask is an IP address with all the network bits set to 1 and the host bits set to 0."
    Access   read-only
    Status   mandatory

OBJECT 4
        ipAdEntBcastAddr   { ipAddrEntry 4 }
    Syntax   INTEGER
    Definition   "The value of the least-significant bit in the IP broadcast address used for sending datagrams on the (logical) interface associated with the IP address of this entry. For example, when the Internet standard all-ones broadcast address is used, the value will be 1. This value applies to both the subnet and network broadcasts addresses used by the entity on this (logical) interface. "
    Access   read-only
    Status   mandatory

Figure 4.19   Specifications for an Aggregate Managed Object: ipAddrTable

OBJECT 5

	ipAdEntR easmMaxSize	{ ipAddrEntry 5 }
Syntax	INTEGER (0..65535)	
Definition	"The size of the largest IP datagram which this entity can reassemble from incoming IP fragmented datagrams received on this interface."	
Access	read-only	
Status	mandatory	

OBJECT 6

	ipA ddrEntry	{ ipAddrTable 1 }
Syntax	ipAddrEntry ::= SEQUENCE {	
	ipAdEntAddr	IpAddress,
	ipAdEntIfIndex	INTEGER,
	IpAdEntNetMask	IpAddress,
	IpAdEntBcastAddr	INTEGER,
	ipAdEntReasmMaxSize	INTEGER (0..65535)
Definition	"The addressing information for one of this entitys'IP addresses."	
Access	not -accessible	
Status	mandatory	

OBJECT 7

	ipAddrTable	{ ip 20 }
Syntax	SEQUENCE OF IpAddrEntry	
Definition	"The table of addressing information relevant to this entity's IP addresses."	
Access	not -accessible	
Status	m andatory	

Figure 4.19 (continued)

ipAddrTable is the OBJECT DESCRIPTOR for the IP address table, which has a unique place in the MIB tree with the OBJECT IDENTIFIER {ip 20}. We will see how the managed object *ip* group fits in the MIB tree in the next section. The syntax of *ipAddrTable* is the structure SEQUENCE OF the data type *ipAddrEntry*. Again, the access is not-accessible.

As an example of the use of the above specifications in a table, let us consider the following entry in an IP address table:

OBJECT 1	{ipAdEntAddr } = { internet "123.45.2.1".}
OBJECT 2	{ipAdEntIfIndex} = { "1" }
OBJECT 3	{ipAdEntNetMask} = { internet "255.255.255.0" }
OBJECT 4	{ipAdEntBcastAddr} = { "0" }
OBJECT 5	{ipAdEntReasmMaxSize} = { "12000" }

The value of *ipAdEntIfIndex* for this entry in the IP address table is equal to 1, and the IP address defining this interface is 123.45.2.1 using the Internet-specific protocol. The value associated with network mask is 255.255.255.0, with *ipAdEntBcastAddr* 0, and with the maximum size of the packet 12,000.

Figure 4.20 [RFC 1213] presents the macro for the IP address table, a multiple-instance presented in Figure 4.17. The text following "--" are comments and not encoded. The module starts at the highest level defining the *ipAddrTable*, then follows up with *ipAddrEntry* and finally defines the subordinate object types of *ipAddrEntry*. Note that there is an additional clause, INDEX, in the *ipAddrEntry* macro in Figure 4.20. This uniquely identifies the instantiation of the entry object type in the table. Thus,

```
-- the IP address table
-- The IP address table contains this entity's IP addressing information.

        ipAddrTable OBJECT-TYPE
            SYNTAX  SEQUENCE OF IpAddrEntry
            ACCESS  not-accessible
            STATUS  mandatory
            DESCRIPTION
                "The table of addressing information relevant to this entity's IP addresses."
            ::= { ip 20 }

        ipAddrEntry OBJECT-TYPE
            SYNTAX  IpAddrEntry
            ACCESS  not-accessible
            STATUS  mandatory
            DESCRIPTION
                "The addressing information for one of this entity's IP addresses."

            INDEX   { ipAdEntAddr }
            ::= { ipAddrTable 1 }

        IpAddrEntry ::=
            SEQUENCE {
                ipAdEntAddr
                    IpAddress,
                ipAdEntIfIndex
                    INTEGER,
                ipAdEntNetMask
                    IpAddress,
                ipAdEntBcastAddr
                    INTEGER,
                ipAdEntReasmMaxSize
                    INTEGER (0..65535) }

        ipAdEntAddr OBJECT-TYPE
            SYNTAX  IpAddress
            ACCESS  read-only
            STATUS  mandatory
            DESCRIPTION
                "The IP address to which this entry's addressing information pertains."
```

Figure 4.20 Aggregate Managed Object Macro: ipAddrTable [RFC 1155]

```
                  ::= { ipAddrEntry 1 }
                  ipAdEntIfIndex OBJECT-TYPE
                  SYNTAX  INTEGER
                  ACCESS  read-only
                  STATUS  mandatory
                  DESCRIPTION
```
"The index value which uniquely identifies the interface to which this entry is applicable. The interface identified by a particular value of this index is the same interface as identified by the same value of *ifIndex*."
```
                  ::= { ipAddrEntry 2 }

                  ipAdEntNetMask OBJECT-TYPE
                  SYNTAX  IpAddress
                  ACCESS  read-only
                  STATUS  mandatory
                  DESCRIPTION
```
"The subnet mask associated with the IP address of this entry. The value of the mask is an IP address with all the network bits set to 1 and all the host bits set to 0."
```
                  ::= { ipAddrEntry 3 }

                  ipAdEntBcastAddr OBJECT-TYPE
                  SYNTAX  INTEGER
                  ACCESS  read-only
                  STATUS  mandatory
                  DESCRIPTION
```
"The value of the least-significant bit in the IP broadcast address used for sending datagrams on the (logical) interface associated with the IP address of this entry. For example, when the Internet standard all-ones broadcast address is used, the value will be 1. This value applies to both the subnet and network broadcasts addresses used by the entity on this (logical) interface."
```
                  ::= { ipAddrEntry 4 }

                  ipAdEntReasmMaxSize OBJECT-TYPE
                  SYNTAX  INTEGER (0..65535)
                  ACCESS  read-only
                  STATUS  mandatory
                  DESCRIPTION
```
"The size of the largest IP datagram which this entity can reassemble from incoming IP frag-mented datagrams received on this interface."
```
                  ::= { ipAddrEntry 5 }
```

Figure 4.20   (continued)

ipAdEntAddr object uniquely identifies the instantiation. We will discuss this more in the next section on columnar objects.

We have so far presented the SMI as it was originally developed in RFC 1155. This helped us understand the two aspects of an object module: specifications and formal structure. Obviously, there is duplication in this. It was originally developed this way to eventually migrate to OSI specifications. However, with the reality that the OSI standards were not implemented and SNMP standards had been deployed extensively, the specifications and formal structure were combined into a concise definition of object macro, described in RFC 1212. It is presented in Figure 4.21.

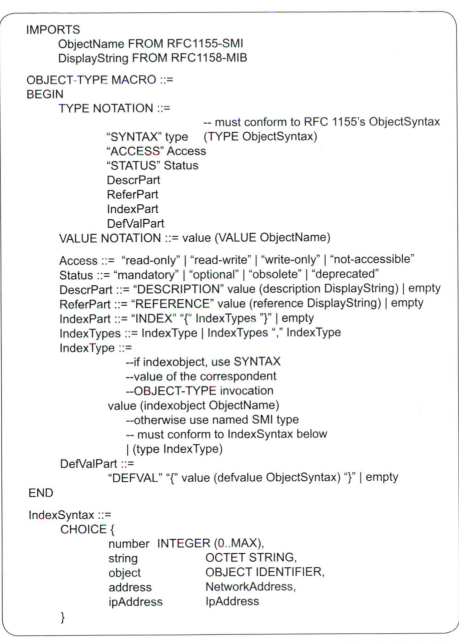

```
IMPORTS
        ObjectName FROM RFC1155-SMI
        DisplayString FROM RFC1158-MIB

OBJECT-TYPE MACRO ::=
BEGIN
        TYPE NOTATION ::=
                                        -- must conform to RFC 1155's ObjectSyntax
                "SYNTAX" type    (TYPE ObjectSyntax)
                "ACCESS" Access
                "STATUS" Status
                DescrPart
                ReferPart
                IndexPart
                DefValPart
        VALUE NOTATION ::= value (VALUE ObjectName)

        Access ::=  "read-only" | "read-write" | "write-only" | "not-accessible"
        Status ::= "mandatory" | "optional" | "obsolete" | "deprecated"
        DescrPart ::= "DESCRIPTION" value (description DisplayString) | empty
        ReferPart ::= "REFERENCE" value (reference DisplayString) | empty
        IndexPart ::= "INDEX" "{" IndexTypes "}" | empty
        IndexTypes ::= IndexType | IndexTypes "," IndexType
        IndexType ::=
                        --if indexobject, use SYNTAX
                        --value of the correspondent
                        --OBJECT-TYPE invocation
                value (indexobject ObjectName)
                        --otherwise use named SMI type
                        -- must conform to IndexSyntax below
                        | (type IndexType)
        DefValPart ::=
                "DEFVAL" "{" value (defvalue ObjectSyntax) "}" | empty
END

IndexSyntax ::=
        CHOICE {
                number  INTEGER (0..MAX),
                string          OCTET STRING,
                object          OBJECT IDENTIFIER,
                address         NetworkAddress,
                ipAddress       IpAddress
        }
```

Figure 4.21   OBJECT-TYPE Macro: Concise Definition [RFC 1212]

Note that there is the definition of imports from other modules. Also, there are additional clauses, ReferPart, IndexPart, and DefVal, and their associated value definitions. The REFERENCE clause is a textual reference to the document from which the object is being mapped. The INDEX clause is the columnar object identifier, which as we said, will be discussed in the next section under columnar objects. DEFVAL is the default value to the object, if applicable.

Aggregate Object as Columnar Object. The aggregate object that was discussed above has been formally defined as columnar objects in RFC 1212. SNMP operations apply exclusively to scalar operations. This means that a single scalar value is retrieved or edited on a managed object with any one operation. However, managed objects do have multiple instances within a system and need to be represented formally. An aggregate object type comprises one or more subtypes; and each subtype could have multiple instances, with a value associated with each instance.

It is convenient to conceptually define a tabular structure for objects that have multiple values, such as the IP address table. Such tables can have any number of rows including none, with each row containing one or more scalar objects. This is shown in Figure 4.22(a). Table T contains subordinate object Entry E

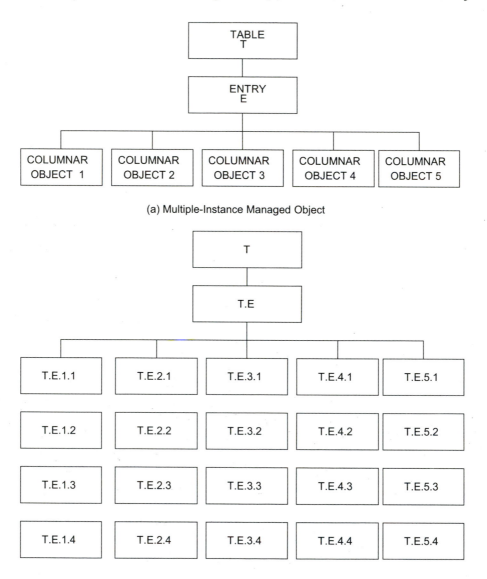

(a) Multiple-Instance Managed Object

(b) Example of a 5-Columnar Object with 4 Instances (Rows)

Figure 4.22   Numbering Convention of a Managed Object Table

that is a row in the table. Since the table is a SEQUENCE OF construction with entry E as components, there are multiple entries in the table; i.e., there are multiple rows in the table. Entry E is a SEQUENCE construct consisting of subordinate objects, columnar objects 1 through 5, in Figure 4.22(a).

Figure 4.22(b) shows a five-columnar object with four instances, i.e., four rows. It is important to note the convention used in denoting each object in the rows. The columnar objects in each row are denoted by the concatenation of the object identifier of the table, the entry, and then the object, and lastly by the row number. Note that the last two numbers are not like what we would normally think of as a row and column sequence in a matrix representation. It is more like column and row designation. Thus, the third occurrence (third row) of the fourth columnar object (fourth column) is T.E.4.3. The value for the row number is the value of the index of the table. For example, *ipAdEntAddr*, which is the IP address, is the index for the IP address table example shown in Figure 4.20. Hence, the value of *ipAdEntAddr* will determine the row of the table.

Let us apply this conceptual table to the IP address table example we have been following. This is shown in Figure 4.23. Figure 4.23(a) presents the detail of the columnar object, *ipAdEntBcastAddr*, which is the fourth columnar object under *ipAddrEntry*, which is a subordinate object of *ipAddrTable*. The OBJECT IDENTIFIER of the *ipAddrTable* in the MIB is 1.3.6.1.2.1.4.20. The *ipAddrEntry* is node 1 under it and *ipAdEntBcastAddr* is the fourth node under *ipAddrEntry*. Thus, the columnar object identifier of *ipAdEntBcastAddr* is {1.3.6.1.2.1.4.20.1.4}.

Figure 4.23(b) shows the tabular presentation of an IP address table. The table shows four rows and six columns. Each of the four rows in the IP address table indicates a set of values associated with each instance of *ifAddrEntry* in the table.

The first column in Figure 4.23(b) is the row number, which is added to the other five columns (column 2 through 6) that represent the five columnar objects of the IP address table. We have added the first column of the row number for easy explanation only; it is not part of the managed objects. The first columnar object *ipAdEntAddr* is in bold letters to indicate that it is the index for the table. As each row in an aggregate object table is uniquely identified by the INDEX clause of the OBJECT-TYPE macro, each row in our example is uniquely identified by indexing the value of *ipAdEntAddr*. The second row is the columnar object *ipAdEntIfIndex*. Note that *ipAdEntIfIndex*, which is the same as the *ifNumber* of the Interfaces group, is not an index, but just an object associated with each row of the table. The last three columns in Figure 4.23(b) represent the columnar objects *ipAdEntNetMask*, *ipAdEntBcastAddr*, and *ipAdEntReasmMaxSize*.

Figure 4.23(c) shows the representation of the object identifier associated with each instance. There are four instances illustrated in the figure. The first column is the columnar object identifier, the second column is the row number shown in Figure 4.23(b), and the last column is the object identifier for the instance of the columnar object. Let us first look at the first row of Figure 4.23(c). We want to represent the object identifier associated with the columnar object *idAdEntAddr* for the specific occurrence presented in the second row of Figure 4.23(b). The object identifier *ipAdEntAddr* in the first row of Figure 4.23(c) is its columnar object identifier 1.3.6.1.2.1.4.20.1.1. It is suffixed with the value of the table index field *ipAdEntAddr* 123.45.3.4. The resultant object identifier 1.3.6.1.2.1.4.20.1.1.123.45.3.4 is shown in the first row of the last column of Figure 4.23(c).

The second entry in Figure 4.23(c) illustrates the object identifier 1.3.6.1.2.1.4.20.1.2.165.8.9.25 for the columnar object *ipAdEntIfIndex* for the instance indicated in the third row of Figure 4.23(b). The third and fourth entries in Figure 4.23(c) illustrate the object identifier values of *ipAdEntBcastAddr* and *ipAdEntReasmMaxSize* for rows 1 and 4 of Figure 4.23(b), respectively.

```
ipAddrTable {1.3.6.1.2.1.4.20}
        ipAddrEntry (1)
                ipAdEntAddr (1)
                ipAdEntIfIndex (2)
                ipAdEntNetMask (3)
                ipAdEntBcastAddr (4)
                ipAdEntReasmMaxSize (5)


Columnar object ID of ipAdEntBcastAddr is (1.3.6.1.2.1.4.20.1.4):


iso org dod internet mgmt mib ip ipAddrTable  ipAddrEntry ipAdEntBcastAddr
 1   3   6     1     2   1  4     20             1               4
```

(a) Columnar Objects under ipAddrEntry

Row	ipAdEntAddr	ipAdEntIfIndex	IpAdEntNetMask	IpAdEntBcast Addr	IpAdEntReasmMax Size
1	123.45.2.1	1	255.255.255.0	0	12000
2	123.45.3.4	3	255.255.0.0	1	12000
3	165.8.9.25	2	255.255.255.0	0	10000
4	9.96.8.138	4	255.255.255.0	0	15000

(b) Object Instances of ipAddrTable (1.3.6.1.2.1.4.20)

Columnar Object	Row # in (b)	Object Identifier
ipAdEntAddr 1.3.6.1.2.1.4.20.1.1	2	{1.3.6.1.2.1.4.20.1.1.123.45.3.4}
ipAdEntIfIndex 1.3.6.1.2.1.4.20.1.2	3	{1.3.6.1.2.1.4.20.1.2.165.8.9.25}
ipAdEntBcastAddr 1.3.6.1.2.1.4.20.1.4	1	{1.3.6.1.2.1.4.20.1.4.123.45.2.1}
IpAdEntReasmMaxSize 1.3.6.1.2.1.4.20.1.5	4	{1.3.6.1.2.1.4.20.1.5.9.96.8.138}

(c) Object ID for Specific Instances

Figure 4.23   Multiple-Instance Managed Object: ipAddrTable

The formalized definitions of SMI as presented in STD 16/RFC 1155 are shown in Figure 4.24. In addition to the definition of the object type macro, it also specifies the exports of names and object types, as well as the Internet MIB, which is addressed in the next section.

```
RFC1155-SMI DEFINITIONS ::= BEGIN

        EXPORTS -- EVERYTHING
                internet, directory, mgmt, experimental, private, enterprises,
                OBJECT-TYPE, ObjectName, ObjectSyntax, SimpleSyntax,
                ApplicationSyntax, NetworkAddress, IpAddress, Counter, Gauge,
                TimeTicks, Opaque;

        -- the path to the root

        internet          OBJECT IDENTIFIER ::= { iso org(3) dod(6) 1 }

        directory         OBJECT IDENTIFIER ::= { internet 1 }
        mgmt              OBJECT IDENTIFIER ::= { internet 2 }
        experimental      OBJECT IDENTIFIER ::= { internet 3 }
        private           OBJECT IDENTIFIER ::= { internet 4 }

        enterprises       OBJECT IDENTIFIER ::= { private 1 }

        -- definition of object types

        OBJECT-TYPE MACRO ::=
BEGIN
        TYPE NOTATION ::= "SYNTAX" type (TYPE ObjectSyntax)
                          "ACCESS" Access
                          "STATUS" Status
        VALUE NOTATION ::= value (VALUE ObjectName)

        Access ::= "read-only" | "read-write" | "write-only" | "not-accessible"
        Status ::= "mandatory" | "optional" | "obsolete"
END

        -- names of objects in the MIB

        ObjectName ::=
            OBJECT IDENTIFIER

        -- syntax of objects in the MIB

        ObjectSyntax ::=
            CHOICE {
                simple
                    SimpleSyntax,

        -- Note that simple SEQUENCEs are not directly mentioned here to keep things
        simple (i.e., prevent misuse). However, application-wide types, which are IMPLIC-
        ITly encoded simple SEQUENCEs, may appear in the following CHOICE.

                application-wide
                    ApplicationSyntax
            }
```

Figure 4.24 SMI Definitions [RFC 1155]

```
            SimpleSyntax ::=
               CHOICE {
                 number
                    INTEGER,
                 string
                    OCTET STRING,
                 object
                    OBJECT IDENTIFIER,
                 empty
                    NULL
               }

         ApplicationSyntax ::=
            CHOICE {
              address
                 NetworkAddress,
              counter
                 Counter,
              gauge
                 Gauge,
              ticks
                 TimeTicks,
              arbitrary
                 Opaque

-- Other application-wide types, as they are defined, will be added here.
            }

-- application-wide types

NetworkAddress ::=
   CHOICE {
     internet
        IpAddress
   }
IpAddress ::=
   [APPLICATION 0]        -- in network-byte order
      IMPLICIT OCTET STRING (SIZE (4))
Counter ::=
   [APPLICATION 1]
      IMPLICIT INTEGER (0..4294967295)
Gauge ::=
   [APPLICATION 2]
      IMPLICIT INTEGER (0..4294967295)
TimeTicks ::=
   [APPLICATION 3]
      IMPLICIT INTEGER (0..4294967295)
Opaque ::=
   [APPLICATION 4]        -- arbitrary ASN.1 value,
      IMPLICIT OCTET STRING   -- "double-wrapped"
END
```

Figure 4.24   (continued)

4.7.4   Management of Information Base

As stated in Section 4.7.1, MIB-II specified in RFC 1213 is the current standard, STD 17. It is a superset of MIB-I or simply MIB, as it was then addressed in RFC 1156. We will present here MIB-II information. Both MIB-I and MIB-II can be implemented in SNMPv1. MIB is organized such that implementation can be done on an as-needed basis. The entire MIB does not have to be implemented in either the manager or the agent process.

Let us remember that MIB is a virtual information store (base). Managed objects are accessed via this virtual information base. Objects in the MIB are defined using ASN.1. In the previous section, we discussed the SMI, which defines the mechanism for describing these objects. The definition consists of three components: *name* (OBJECT DESCRIPTOR), *syntax* (ASN.1), and *encoding* (BER).

Objects defined in MIB-II have the OBJECT IDENTIFIER prefix:

mib-2   OBJECT IDENTIFIER ::= {mgmt 1}

MIB-II has an additional attribute to the status of a managed object. The new term is "deprecated." This term mandates the implementation of the object in the current version of MIB-II, but is most likely to be removed in future versions. For example, *atTable* is deprecated in MIB-II.

Object Groups. Objects that are related are grouped into object groups. Notice that this grouping is different from the grouping of object types to construct an aggregate object type. Object groups facilitate logical assignment of object identifiers. One of the criteria for choosing objects to be included in standards is that it is essential for either fault or configuration management. Thus, if a group is implemented in a system by a vendor, all the components are implemented, i.e., status is mandatory for all its components. For example, if the External Gateway Protocol (EGP) is implemented in a system, then all EGP group objects are mandatory to be present.

The MIB module structure consists of the module name, imports from other modules, and definitions of the current module. The basic ASN.1 structure is shown in Figure 4.25.

There are 11 groups defined in MIB-II. The tree structure is shown in Figure 4.26, and Table 4.4 presents the name, object identification (OID), and a brief description of each group. It can be observed that these groups are nodes under the MIB object *mib-2* whose OBJECT IDENTIFIER is 1.3.6.1.2.1.

The System group contains objects describing system administration. The Interfaces group defines interfaces of the network component and network parameters associated with each of those interfaces. The Address translation group is a cross-reference table between the IP address and the physical address. IP, ICMP, TCP, UDP, and EGP groups are the grouping of objects associated with the respective protocol of the system. The group, CMOT, is a placeholder for future use of the OSI protocol, CMIP over TCP/IP. The Transmission group was created as a placeholder for network transmission-related parameters and was a placeholder in RFC 1213. Numerous transmission systems and objects have been developed under this group since then. SNMP group is the communication protocol group associated with SNMP

```
<module name > DEFINITIONS ::= BEGIN
         <imports>
         <definitions>
END
```

Figure 4.25   MIB Module Structure

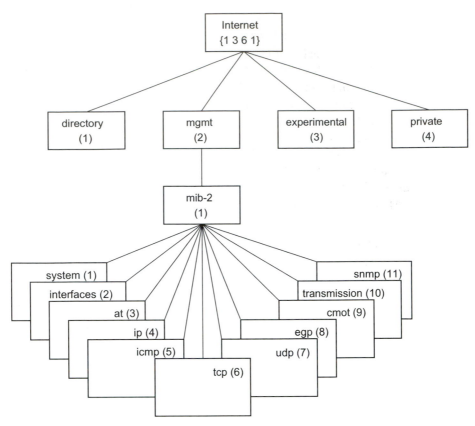

Figure 4.26 Internet MIB-II Group

Table 4.4 MIB-II Groups

GROUP	OID	DESCRIPTION (BRIEF)
system	mib-2 1	System description and administrative information
interfaces	mib-2 2	Interfaces of the entity and associated information
at	mib-2 3	Address translation between IP and physical address
ip	mib-2 4	Information on IP protocol
icmp	mib-2 5	Information on ICMP protocol
tcp	mib-2 6	Information on TCP protocol
udp	mib-2 7	Information on UDP protocol
egp	mib-2 8	Information on EGP protocol
cmot	mib-2 9	Placeholder for OSI protocol
transmission	mib-2 10	Placeholder for transmission information
snmp	mib-2 11	Information on SNMP protocol

management. We will now learn more about some of these groups. It should be noted that there are more groups defined under the Internet node, which we will address in Chapter 5.

The following sections describe details of each group except for CMOT, transmission, and SNMP. The CMOT group is a placeholder and is not yet defined. The Transmission group is based on the transmission media underlying each interface of the system; the corresponding portion of the Transmission group is mandatory for that system. The SNMP group will be addressed in Chapter 5 as part of the communication model.

Although there are many more groups in MIB-II, details on only the generic groups directly related to physical properties of basic network elements (System and Interfaces) and the managed objects associated with Internet protocols (IP, TCP, and UDP) are presented here. They are intended to familiarize the reader quickly with how to read and interpret RFCs specifying MIBs. It is strongly recommended that you refer to the RFC for detailed specifications on each group and understand the structure of each MIB group.

Some examples associated with managed objects in the group are presented along with a description of the group in order to appreciate the significance of each MIB. In Chapter 9 we will learn to use the SNMP command using SNMP tools and retrieve the values associated with managed objects.

System Group. The System group is the basic group in the Internet standard MIB. Its elements are probably the most accessed managed objects. After an NMS discovers all the components in a network or newly added components in the network, it has to obtain information on the system it discovered, such as system name, object ID, etc. The NMS will initiate the get-request command on the objects in this group for this purpose. Data on the systems shown in Figure 4.2 were obtained by the NMS using this group. The group also has administrative information, such as contact person and physical location that helps a network manager.

Implementation of the System group is mandatory for all systems in both the agent and the manager. It consists of seven entities, which are presented in Figure 4.27 and Table 4.5. The vendor of the equipment programs the system description (*sysDescr*) and OBJECT IDENTIFIER (*sysObjID*) during manufacturing. System up time is filled in hundredths of a second dynamically during operation. Network management systems usually convert this into a readable format of days, hours, and minutes in their presentation, as shown in Figure 4.2. Although system services (*sysServices*) object is mandatory to be implemented, most NMSs do not show the information automatically.

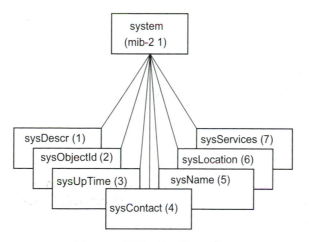

Figure 4.27   System Group

Table 4.5 System Group

ENTITY	OID	DESCRIPTION (BRIEF)
sysDescr	system 1	Textual description
sysObjectID	system 2	OBJECT IDENTIFIER of the entity
sysUpTime	system 3	Time (in hundredths of a second since last reset)
sysContact	system 4	Contact person for the node
sysName	system 5	Administrative name of the system
sysLocation	system 6	Physical location of the node
sysServices	system 7	Value designating the layer services provided by the entity

Interfaces Group. The Interfaces group contains managed objects associated with the interfaces of a system. If there is more than one interface in the system, the group describes the parameters associated with each interface. For example, if an Ethernet bridge has several network interface cards, the group would cover information associated with each interface. However, the Interfaces MIB contains only generic parameters. In the Ethernet example, there is more information associated with the Ethernet LAN, which is addressed in the MIB specifications of the particular medium, as in Definitions of Managed Objects for the Ethernet-like Interface types [RFC 2358]. An NMS would combine information obtained from various groups in presenting comprehensive data to the user.

The Interfaces group specifies the number of interfaces in a network component and managed objects associated with each interface. Implementation of Interfaces group is mandatory for all systems. It consists of two nodes as shown in Figure 4.28 and Table 4.6. The number of interfaces of the entity is defined by *ifNumber*, and the information related to each interface is defined in the Interfaces table, *ifTable*.

Each interface in the Interfaces table can be visualized as being attached to either a subnetwork or a system. The term **subnetwork** is not to be confused with the term **subnet**, which refers to an addressing partitioning scheme in the Internet suite of protocols. The index for the table is just one entity, specified by *ifIndex*, as shown below in the definition of the *ifEntry* module under *ifTable*.

```
IfEntry  OBJECT-TYPE
         SYNTAX      ifEntry
         ACCESS      not-accessible
         STATUS      mandatory
         DESCRIPTION
                 "An interface entry containing objects at the subnetwork layer and below for a
                 particular interface."
         INDEX  {ifIndex}
         ::= {ifTable 1}
```

The index is also shown in bold letters in the figure and the table.

The entity *ifType* describes the type of data link layer directly below the network layer. It is defined as an enumerated integer. Examples of these are: ethernet-csmacd(7), iso88025-tokenRing(9). See RFC 1213 for the specified type of standard interfaces.

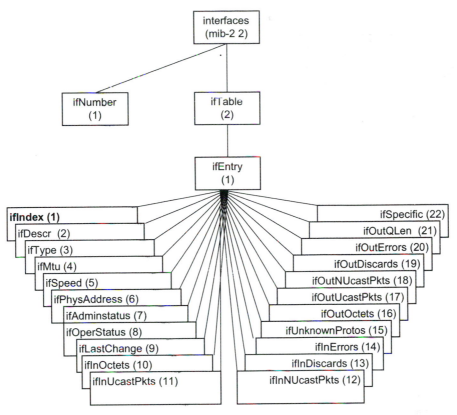

Figure 4.28 Interfaces Group

The administrative and operational status that is indicated by object identifiers 7 and 8 should agree with each other when the system interface is functioning as administered.

Object identifiers 11–15 refer to the measurements (with counter syntax) on inbound traffic and object identifiers 16–21 to measurements on outbound traffic.

An example of use of Interfaces MIB would be to measure the incoming and the outgoing traffic rate on a given interface of an Ethernet hub. We can specify a port on an Ethernet network interface card by the value of *ifIndex* and query (*get-request*) the number of input unicast packets (*ifInUcastPkts*) and the number of output unicast packets (*ifOutUcastPkts*) every second. Remember that we get the reading of two counters, which are incremented with every packet coming in or going out of the port from the management agent associated with the port. We would then take the difference in the consecutive counter reading to derive the packet rate of traffic with time.

Interface Sublayers. One of the strengths of an IP network layer protocol is that it is designed to run over any network interface. IP considers any and all protocols it runs over as a single "network interface" layer. The Interfaces group defines a generic set of managed objects such that any network interface can be managed in an interface-independent manner through these managed objects. The Interfaces group provides the means for additional managed objects specific to particular types of network interface (e.g., a specific medium such as Ethernet or Time Division Multiplex (TDM) channels) to be

Table 4.6 Interfaces Group

ENTITY	OID	DESCRIPTION (BRIEF)
ifNumber	interfaces 1	Total number of network interfaces in the system
ifTable	interfaces 2	List of entries describing information on each interface of the system
ifEntry	ifTable 1	An interface entry containing objects at the subnetwork layer for a particular interface
ifIndex	ifEntry 1	A unique integer value for each interface
ifDescr	ifEntry 2	Textual data on product name and version
ifType	ifEntry 3	Type of interface layer below the network layer defined as an enumerated integer
ifMtu	ifEntry 4	Largest size of the datagram for the interface
ifSpeed	ifEntry 5	Current or nominal data rate for the interface in bps
ifPhysAddress	ifEntry 6	Interface's address at the protocol layer immediately below the network layer
ifAdminStatus	ifEntry 7	Desired status of the interface: up, down, or testing
ifOperStatus	ifEntry 8	Current operational status of the interface
ifLastchange	ifEntry 9	Value of sysUpTime at the current operational status
ifInOctets	ifEntry 10	Total number of input octets received
ifInUcastPkts	ifEntry 11	Number of subnetwork unicast packets delivered to a higher-layer protocol
ifInNUcastPkts	ifEntry 12	Number of non-unicast packets delivered to a higher-layer protocol
ifInDiscards	ifEntry 13	Number of inbound packets discarded irrespective of error status
ifInErrors	ifEntry 14	Number of inbound packets with errors
ifInUnknownProtos	ifEntry 15	Number of unsupported protocol packets discarded
ifOutOctets	ifEntry 16	Number of octets transmitted out of the interface
ifOutUcastPkts	ifEntry 17	Total number of unicast packets that higher-level layer requested to be transmitted
ifOutNUcastPkts	ifEntry 18	Total number of non-unicast packets that higher-level layer requested to be transmitted
ifOutDiscrds	ifEntry 19	Number of outbound packets discarded irrespective of error status
ifOutErrors	ifEntry 20	Number of outbound packets that could not be transmitted because of errors
ifOutQLen	ifEntry 21	Length of the output queue in packets
ifSpecific	ifEntry 22	Reference to MIB definitions specific to the particular media used to realize the interface

defined as extensions to the Interfaces group for media-specific management. Since the standardization of MIB-II, many such media-specific MIB modules have been defined. Concurrently, the Interfaces group has evolved to accommodate the additional managed objects that need to be specified in a data link layer (DLL)– Layer 2.

DLL can be visualized, in general, as comprising several sublayers. These can either be horizontally stacked or vertically sliced (or "stacked"), as shown in Figures 4.29(a) and (b), respectively. An example of the former is an interface with PPP running over a High data rate Digital Subscriber Line (HDSL) link, which uses an RS232-like connector. An example of the latter is a cable access link with a downstream channel and several upstream channels.

Since the simplistic model of a single conceptual row in the *ifTable* in the Interfaces group, an additional MIB group, *ifMIB* (mib-2 31) was created. This is not shown in Figure 4.26, which is the original MIB-II Group. It is shown in Figure 4.30. The first subnode of *ifMIB* is *ifMIBObjects*. There are other subnodes under *ifMIB* and the reader is referred to [RFC 2863] for details. Under the subnode *ifMIBObjects (ifMIB 1)*, there are three tables *ifXTable (ifMIBObjects 1)*, *ifStackTable (ifMIBObjects 2)*, and *ifRcvAddressTable (ifMIBObjects 4)*. Including the *ifTable (interfaces 2)*, there are four generic Interfaces group tables under the two MIBs, *interfaces* and *ifMIB,* which we should be concerned with in defining managed objects in the DLL layer. In addition to this, there are device-specific interface MIBs, such as Ethernet-like managed objects (*transmission 7*) that we would discuss under each subject as we deal with them. It is worth noting that specifications for *ifMIB* have gone through a series of documentation—RFC 1229, RFC 1573, RFC 2233, and RFC 2863—each obsolescing the previous version.

Figure 4.29   Interface Sublayers

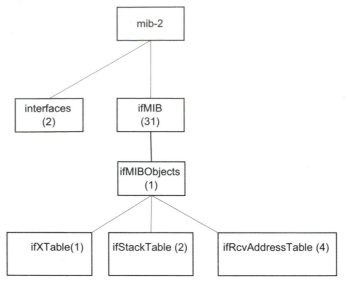

Figure 4.30 Interfaces Groups

ifXTable contains objects that have been added to the Interface MIB group as a result of the Interface evolution effort, or replacements for objects of the original (MIB-II) *ifTable* that were deprecated because the semantics of the said objects have significantly changed. It is an augmentation of *ifTable*. How two tables are augmented in SMI to appear as a single table is described in Chapter 6 under SNMP2.

ifStackTable contains objects that define relationships among sublayers of an interface. Each sublayer is *defined* as an *ifType* and is represented by a conceptual row in the *ifTable*. Because of the addition of such conceptual rows, the value of *ifIndex* is no longer constrained. In other words, it can be stated that the index of a conceptual row no longer has to be less than or equal to the value of *ifIndex*. The upper layer in the *ifStackTable, ifStackHigherLayer,* is the sublayer above the sublayer under consideration and carries the value of the *ifIndex* of that sublayer. If there is no interface sublayer above, i.e., it interfaces directly with the network layer, then the *ifIndex* value is zero. Similarly, *ifStackLowerLayer* is the lower interface sublayer, it has a corresponding *ifIndex* value of that row. If it interfaces directly with the physical medium, its value is zero.

ifRcvAddressTable contains objects that are used to define media-level addresses, which this *interface* will receive, such as a port ID. This table is a generic table.

Address Translation Group. The Address Translation group consists of a table that converts NetworkAddress to a physical or subnetwork address for all interfaces of the system. For example, in Ethernet the translation table is ARP cache. Since in MIB-II each protocol group contains its own translation table, this is not needed and hence its status is deprecated. It is mandatory to be implemented to be backward compatible with MIB-I.

IP Group. The Internet is based on IP protocol as the networking protocol. This group has information on various parameters of the protocol. It also has a table that replaces the Address Translation table. Routers in the network periodically execute the routing algorithm and update its routing table, which are defined as managed objects in this group. We will discuss the contents of this group in detail now.

The IP group defines all the parameters needed for the node to handle a network layer IP protocol either as a host or as a router; implementation is mandatory. Figure 4.31 and Table 4.7 present the tree structure and details of the entities, respectively. The group contains three tables, IP address table, IP routing table, and IP Address Translation table.

We can use the IP MIB to acquire any information associated with the IP layer. For example, to learn the value of the managed object, *ipForwarding* will indicate whether the node is acting as just a router or a gateway between two autonomous networks. We can measure IP datagrams received that are in error, such as those with wrong addresses (*ipInAddrErrors*).

The three tables belonging to the IP group are shown in Figure 4.32 (IP Address Table), Figure 4.33 (IP Routing Table), and Figure 4.34 (IP Address Translation Table). Table 4.8 shows the entity table for the IP address table. The index for the table, *ipAdEntAddr*, is shown in bold letters.

In Figure 4.23(b), we illustrated an example of four instantiations (rows) associated with the IP address table. The IP address table MIB shown in Figure 4.32 and Table 4.8 is used to retrieve data from the router. It could be retrieved using *get-request* or *get-next-request* commands.

The IP routing table is shown in Figure 4.33 and Table 4.9. It contains an entry for each route presently known to the entity. Multiple routes, up to five, to a single destination can appear in the table, but access to such multiple entries is dependent on the table-access mechanism defined by the network management protocol. Routes are indicated by the entities, *ipRouteMetricN*, where *N* is any integer from 1

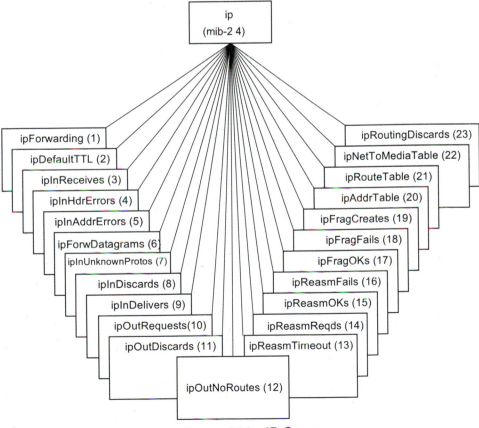

Figure 4.31 IP Group

Table 4.7 IP Group

ENTITY	OID	DESCRIPTION (BRIEF)
ipForwarding	ip 1	Node acting as a gateway or not
ipDefaultTTL	ip 2	Time-to-Live field of the IP header
ipInReceives	ip 3	Total number of input datagrams received from interfaces, including those in error
ipInHdrErrors	ip 4	Number of datagrams discarded due to header errors
ipInAddrErrors	ip 5	Number of datagrams discarded due to address errors
ipForwDatagrams	ip 6	Number of input datagrams attempted to forward to the destination; successfully forwarded datagrams for source routing
ipInUnknownProtos	ip 7	Number of locally addressed datagrams received successfully but discarded due to unsupported protocol
ipInDiscards	ip 8	Number of input datagrams discarded with no problems (e.g. back of buffer space)
ipInDelivers	ip 9	Total number of input datagrams successfully delivered to IP user protocols
ipOutRequests	ip 10	Total number of IP datagrams that local IP user protocols supplied to IP
ipOutDiscards	ip 11	Number of no-error IP datagrams discarded with no problems (e.g. lack of buffer space)
ipOutNoRoutes	ip 12	Number of IP datagrams discarded because no route could be found to transmit them to their destination
ipReasmTimeOut	ip 13	Maximum number of seconds that received fragments are held while they are awaiting reassembly
ipReasmReqds	ip 14	Number of IP datagrams received needing reassembly
ipReasmOKs	ip 15	Number of successfully reassembled datagrams
ipReasmFails	ip 16	Number of failures detected by the IP reassembly algorithm (not discarded fragments)
ipFragOKs	ip 17	Number of successfully fragmented datagrams
ipFragFails	ip 18	Number of IP datagrams not fragmented due to "Don't Fragment Flag" set
ipFragCreates	ip 19	Number of datagram fragments generated as a result of fragmentation
ipAdddrTable	ip 20	Table of IP addresses
ipRouteTable	ip 21	IP routing table containing an entry
ipNetToMediaTable	ip 22	IP Address Translation table mapping IP addresses to physical addresses
ipRoutingDiscards	ip 23	Number of routing entries discarded even though they were valid

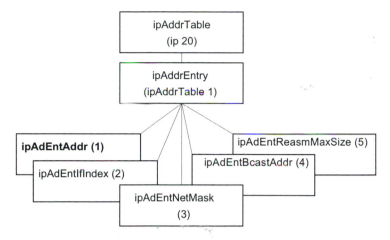

Legend: INDEX in bold

Figure 4.32 IP Address Table

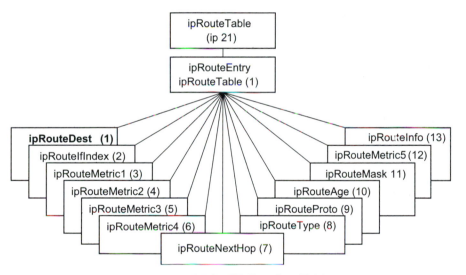

Figure 4.33 IP Routing Table

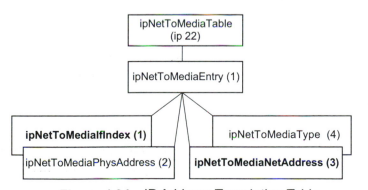

Figure 4.34 IP Address Translation Table

Table 4.8 IP Address Table

ENTITY	OID	DESCRIPTION (BRIEF)
ipAddrTable	ip 20	Table of IP addresses
ipAddrEntry	IpAddrTable 1	One of the entries in the IP address table
ipAdEntAddr	IpAddrEntry 1	The IP address to which this entry's addressing information pertains
ipAdEntIfIndex	IpAddrEntry 2	Index value of the entry, same as ifIndex
ipAdEntNetMask	IpAddrEntry 3	Subnet mask for the IP address of the entry
ipAdEntBcastAddr	IpAddrEntry 4	Broadcast address indicator bit
ipAdEntReasmMaxSize	IpAddrEntry 5	Largest IP datagram that can be reassembled on this interface

Table 4.9 IP Routing Table

ENTITY	OID	DESCRIPTION (BRIEF)
ipRouteTable	ip 21	IP routing table
ipRouteEntry	ipRouteTable 1	Route to a particular destination
ipRouteDest	ipRouteEntry 1	Destination IP address of this route
ipRouteIfIndex	ipRouteEntry 2	Index of interface, same as ifIndex
ipRouteMetric1	ipRouteEntry 3	Primary routing metric for this route
ipRouteMetric2	ipRouteEntry 4	An alternative routing metric for this route
ipRouteMetric3	ipRouteEntry 5	An alternative routing metric for this route
ipRouteMetric4	ipRouteEntry 6	An alternative routing metric for this route
ipRouteNextHop	ipRouteEntry 7	IP address of the next hop
ipRouteType	ipRouteEntry 8	Type of route
ipRouteProto	ipRouteEntry 9	Routing mechanism by which this route was learned
ipRouteAge	ipRouteEntry 10	Number of seconds since routing was last updated
ipRouteMask	ipRouteEntry 11	Mask to be logically ANDed with the destination address before comparing with the ipRouteDest field
ipRouteMetric5	ipRouteEntry 12	An alternative metric for this route
ipRouteInfo	ipRouteEntry 13	Reference to MIB definition specific to the routing protocol

to 5. An entry 0.0.0.0 in *ipRouteDest* is considered a default route. The index for the table is *ipRoute Dest*. As in the IP address table, the *ipRouteIfIndex* has the same value as the *ifIndex* of the Interfaces table.

Figure 4.34 and Table 4.10 show the IP Address Translation table. It contains cross-references between IP addresses and physical addresses, such as MAC address of Ethernet interface cards. In some

Table 4.10   IP Address Translation Table

ENTITY	OID	DESCRIPTION (BRIEF)
ipNetToMediaTable	ip 22	Table mapping IP addresses to physical addresses
ipNetToMediaEntry	IpNetToMediaTable 1	IP address to physical address for the particular interface
ipNetToMediaIfIndex	IpNetToMediaEntry 1	Interfaces on which this entry's equivalence is effective; same as ifIndex
ipNetToMediaPhysAddress	IpNetToMediaEntry 2	Media-dependent physical address
ipNetToMediaNetAddress	IpNetToMediaEntry 3	IP address
ipNetToMediaType	IpNetToMediaEntry 4	Type of mapping; validates with ipNetToMediaType object

situations, such as DDN-X.25 where this relationship is algorithmic, this table is not needed and hence has zero entries. Indices for this table consist of two entities, *ipNetToMediaIfIndex* and *ipNetToMediaNetAddress*. Again, the *IpNetToMediaIfIndex* has the same value as *ifIndex* in the Interfaces group.

Baker [RFC 1354] has proposed an improved implementation of the IP routing table, called the IP Forwarding Table shown as an MIB tree in Figure 4.35 and the associated table in Table 4.11. The routing table that was originally proposed in RFC 1213 is inconsistent with SNMP protocol in that no specific policy was defined to choose the path among multiple choices in the IP route table. RFC 1354 has fixed this deficiency. Besides, it has added next hop autonomous system number, useful to the administrators of regional networks.

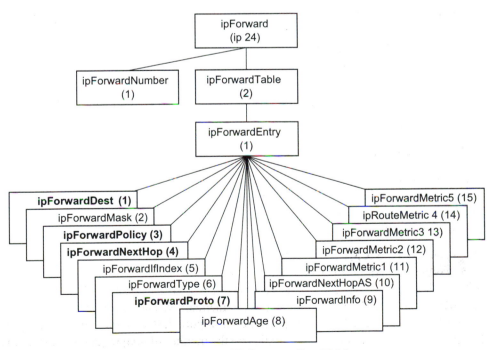

Figure 4.35 IP Forwarding Table

Table 4.11 IP Forwarding Table

ENTITY	OID	DESCRIPTION (BRIEF)
ipForward	ip 24	Contains information on IP forwarding table; deprecates IP routing table
ipForwardNumber	ipForward 1	Number of entries in the IP forward table
ipForwardTable	ipForward 2	Routing table of this entity
ipForwardEntry	IpForwardTable 1	A particular route to a particular destination under a particular policy
ipForwardDest	IpForwardEntry 1	Destination IP route of this address
ipForwardMask	IpForwardEntry 2	Mask to be logically ANDed with the destination address before comparing with the ipRouteDest field
ipForwardPolicy	IpForwardEntry 3	Set of conditions that selects one multipath route
ipForwardNextHop	IpForwardEntry 4	Address of the next system
ipForwardIfIndex	IpForwardEntry 5	ifIndex value of the interface
ipForwardType	IpForwardEntry 6	Type of route: remote, local, invalid, or otherwise; enumerated integer syntax
ipForwardProto	IpForwardEntry 7	Routing mechanism by which this route was learned
ipForwardAge	IpForwardEntry 8	Number of seconds since routing was last updated
ipForwardInfo	IpForwardEntry 9	Reference to MIB definition specific to the routing protocol
ipForwardNextHopAS	IpForwardEntry 10	Autonomous system number of Next Hop
ipForwardMetric1	IpForwardEntry 11	Primary routing metric for this route
ipForwardMetric2	IpForwardEntry 12	An alternative routing metric for this route
ipForwardMetric3	IpForwardEntry 13	An alternative routing metric for this route
ipForwardMetric4	IpForwardEntry 14	An alternative routing metric for this route
ipForwardMetric5	IpForwardEntry 15	An alternative routing metric for this route

The entity *ipForwardPolicy* defines the general set of conditions that would cause the selection of one multipath route over others. Selections of path can be done by the protocol. If it is not done by the protocol, it is then specified by the IP Type-of-Service (TOS) Field, which is a part of the IP type of service field. See Baker [RFC 1354] for more details.

ICMP Group. We used the ICMP to do some of the networking exercises in Chapter 1. It is part of the TCP/IP suite of protocols. All parameters associated with ICMP protocol are covered in this group.

As mentioned in Section 4.2, ICMP is a precursor of SNMP and a part of the TCP/IP suite. It is included in MIB-I and MIB-II and implementation is mandatory. The ICMP group contains statistics on ICMP control messages of ICMP and is presented in Figure 4.36 and Table 4.12. The syntax of all entities is read-only counter. For example, statistics on the number of *ping* requests (icmp echo request) sent might be obtained from the counter reading of *icmpOutEchoes*.

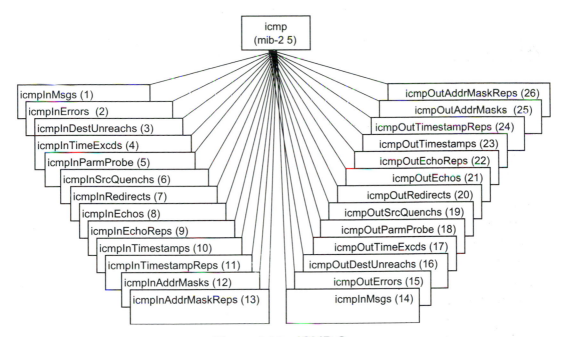

Figure 4.36 ICMP Group

Table 4.12 ICMP Group

ENTITY	OID	DESCRIPTION (BRIEF)
icmpInMsgs	icmp 1	Total number of ICMP messages received by the entity including icmpInErrors
icmpInErrors	icmp 2	Number of messages received by the entity with ICMP-specific errors
icmpInDestUnreachs	icmp 3	Number of ICMP Destination Unreachable messages received
icmpInTimeExcds	icmp 4	Number of ICMP Time Exceeded messages received
icmpInParmProbs	icmp 5	Number of ICMP Parameter Problem messages received
icmpInSrcQuenches	icmp 6	Number of ICMP Source Quench messages received
icmpInRedirects	icmp 7	Number of ICMP Redirect messages received
icmpInEchos	icmp 8	Number of ICMP Echo (request) messages received
icmpInEchoReps	icmp 9	Number of ICMP Echo Reply messages received
icmpInTimestamps	icmp 10	Number of ICMP Timestamp (request) messages received
icmpInTimestampReps	icmp 11	Number of ICMP Timestamp Reply messages received
icmpInAddrMasks	icmp 12	Number of ICMP Address Mask Request messages received

Table 4.12 (continued)

ENTITY	OID	DESCRIPTION (BRIEF)
icmpInAddrMaskReps	icmp 13	Number of ICMP Address Mask Reply messages received
icmpOutMsgs	icmp 14	Total number of ICMP messages attempted to be sent by this entity
icmpOutErrors	icmp 15	Number of good ICMP messages not sent, does not include the ones with errors
icmpOutDestUnreachs	icmp 16	Number of ICMP Destination Unreachable messages sent
icmpOutTimeExcds	icmp 17	Number of ICMP Time Exceeded messages sent
icmpOutParmProbs	icmp 18	Number of ICMP Parameter Problem messages sent
icmpOutSrcQuenchs	icmp 19	Number of ICMP Source Quench messages sent
icmpOutRedirects	icmp 20	Number of ICMP Redirect messages sent
icmpOutEchos	icmp 21	Number of ICMP Echo (request) messages sent
icmpOutEchoReps	icmp 22	Number of ICMP Echo Reply messages sent
icmpOutTimestamps	icmp 23	Number of ICMP Timestamp (request) messages sent
icmpOutTimestampReps	icmp 24	Number of ICMP Timestamp Reply messages sent
icmpOutAddrMasks	icmp 25	Number of ICMP Address Mask Request messages sent
icmpOutAddrMaskReps	icmp 26	Number of ICMP Address Mask Reply messages sent

TCP Group. The transport layer of the Internet defines Transmission Control Protocol (TCP) for a connection-oriented circuit and User Datagram Protocol (UDP) for a connectionless circuit. We will describe the TCP group in this section and UDP in the next subsection.

The TCP group contains entities that are associated with the connection-oriented TCP. They are present only as long as the particular connection persists. It is mandatory to implement this group. The entities are shown in Figure 4.37 and Table 4.13. It contains one table, the TCP connection table, which is presented in Figure 4.38 and Table 4.14. The table entry has four indices to uniquely define it in the table. They are: *tcpConnLocalAddress, tcpConnLocalPort, tcpConnRemAddress*, and *tcpConnRemPort* and are identified in boldface. One may obtain all TCP active sessions from this table with addresses and ports of local and remote entities.

UDP Group. The UDP group contains information associated with the connectionless transport protocol. Its implementation is mandatory. Figure 4.39 and Table 4.15 present the UDP group tree structure and entities, respectively. The group contains a UDP listener table, shown as part of Figure 4.39 and Table 4.15. The table contains information about the entity's UDP end-points on which a local application is currently accepting datagrams. Indices for the table entry are *udpLocalAddress* and *udpLocalPort*, and are indicated in bold letters.

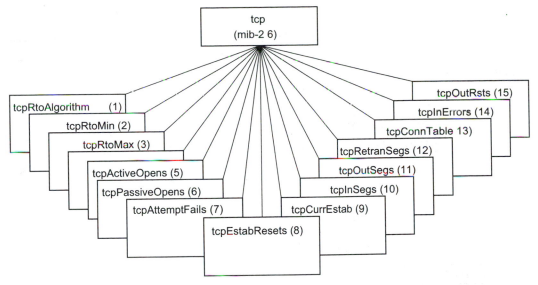

Figure 4.37 TCP Group

Table 4.13 TCP Group

ENTITY	OID	DESCRIPTION (BRIEF)
tcpRtoAlgorithm	tcp 1	Timeout algorithm for retransmission of octets
tcpRtoMin	tcp 2	Minimum value for timeout in milliseconds for retransmission
tcpRtoMax	tcp 3	Maximum value for timeout in milliseconds retransmission
tcpMaxConn	tcp 4	Maximum number of TCP connections
tcpActiveOpens	tcp 5	Number of active connections made CLOSED to SYN-SENT state
tcpPassiveOpens	tcp 6	Number of passive connections made LISTEN to SYN-RCVD state
tcpAttemptFails	tcp 7	Number of failed attempts to make connection
tcpEstabResets	tcp 8	Number of resets done to either CLOSED or LISTEN state
tcpCurrEstab	tcp 9	Number of connections for which the current state is either ESTABLISHED or CLOSED-WAIT
tcpInSegs	tcp 10	Total number of segments received including with errors
tcpOutSegs	tcp 11	Total number of segments sent excluding retransmission
tcpRetransSegs	tcp 12	Total number of segments retransmitted
tcpConnTable	tcp 13	TCO connection table
tcpInErrs	tcp 14	Total number of segments received in error
tcpOutRsts	tcp 15	Number of segment sent containing RST flag

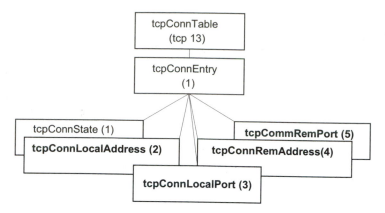

Figure 4.38 TCP Connection Table

Table 4.14 TCP Connection Table

ENTITY	OID	DESCRIPTION (BRIEF)
tcpConnTable	tcp 13	TCO connection table
tcpconnEntry	TcpConnTable 1	Information about a particular TCP connection
tcpConnState	TcpConnEntry 1	State of the TCP connection
tcpConnLocalAddress	TcpConnEntry 2	Local IP address
tcpConnLocalPort	TcpConnEntry 3	Local port number
tcpConnRemAddress	TcpConnEntry 4	Remote IP address
tcpConnRemPort	TcpConnEntry 5	Remote port number

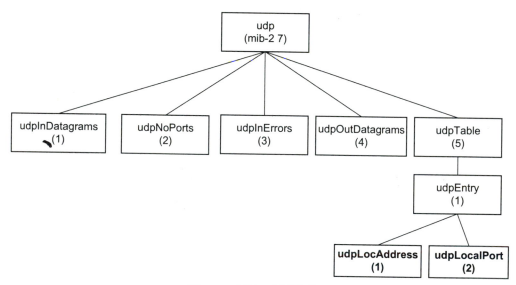

Figure 4.39 UDP Group

Table 4.15   UDP Group

ENTITY	OID	DESCRIPTION (BRIEF)
udpInDatagrams	udp 1	Total number of datagrams delivered to the users
udpNoPorts	udp 2	Total number of received datagrams for which there is no application
udpInErrors	udp 3	Number of received datagrams with errors
udpOutDatagrams	udp 4	Total number of datagrams sent
udpTable	udp 5	UDP Listener table
udpEntry	udpTable 1	Information about a particular connection or UDP listener
udpLocalAddress	udpEntry 1	Local IP address
udpLocalPort	udpEntry 2	Local UDP port

▊ Summary

We have learned the basic functions of SNMP management in this chapter. Advanced functions are covered in the next chapter. The subject matter included in this chapter has been approved as a standard by IETF and implemented by most vendors.

We briefly learned the historical development of SNMP standards and documents. They grew more out of practical necessity than the need for setting standards. The Internet Engineering Task Force is the standards organization and RFC, STD, and FYI are IETF documents on standards development.

SNMP management is organized as two-tier management, in which a manager process and an agent process communicate with each other. The agent process resides in the network element. The manager process is built in network management stations. The agent process does not perform any analysis, which is done in the manager. The two-tier structure can be extended to three-tier by sandwiching a proxy agent, or RMON, between the manager and the agent.

All management operations are done using five messages in SNMPv1, which is the current standard. They are get-request, get-next, set-request, get-response, and trap. The first three are sent from the manager to the agent, and the last two are sent by the agent to the manager.

Messages are exchanged according to specifications defined in the Structure of Management Information (SMI). It is composed of name, syntax, and encoding rules. The name is a unique name for the managed object and an associated unique object identifier. The syntax uses Abstract Syntax Notation 1 (ASN.1) language. Encoding is done using basic encoding rules (BER).

Objects or entities can be composed of other scalar objects. Multiple instances of a managed object, such as the IP address table, are handled by defining tables and columnar objects in the table. Managed objects are organized in a virtual database, called the Management Information Base (MIB). It is distinct from the management database that contains values for managed objects. Managed objects are grouped in the MIB according to their function. MIB-II, which is a superset of MIB-I, consists of 11 groups. Several groups have since been added to the MIB, although they have not been approved as a standard.

▊ Exercises

1. Refer to Figure 4.3 to answer the following questions:
   (a) What are the classes of networks shown in Figure 4.3(a)?
   (b) Explain the function of a network mask.

(c) In Figure 4.3(c), network addresses 172.16x.0 are subnets derived from the network address 172.160.0. Explain how IP address bits are split between subnet and host addresses.

2. Access Simple Gateway Monitoring Protocol (SGMP) RFC 1028 on the Internet. Describe the four message types defined in the document. (You do not have to present the structure of the message.)

3. Present OBJECT IDENTIFIER for the object sun.products in two different formats, one in all mnemonic and the other in all numeric.

4. Represent the objects as OBJECT IDENTIFIERs starting from the root for the three network components in Figure 4.2.
   (a) Hub in Figure 4.2(a) in hybrid format
   (b) Hub in Figure 4.2(b) in numeric format
   (c) Router in Figure 4.2(c) in hybrid format

5. Encode IP Address 10.20.30.40 in TLV format.

6. Refer to RFC 1213 for the following exercise:
   (a) Write the ASN.1 specifications for *sysServices.*
   (b) Illustrate the specifications with values for a bridge.
   (c) Illustrate the specifications with values for a router.

7. Write the object DESCRIPTOR and syntax of the following SNMP managed entities:
   (a) IP address 125.52.66.24
   (b) A row in the Interfaces table (the row specifications only, not the objects in the row)
   (c) MAC address of an interface card

8. In Exercise 4 of Chapter 1, you measured the percent packet loss using Ping tool, which depends on the ICMP group. Name the MIB objects that are used in the procedure and present the macros for the OBJECT TYPE.

9. Explain how you would determine whether a device is acting as a host or as a router using an SNMP command.

10. Refer to the IP Address Translation table shown in Figure 4.34 and Table 4.10, as well as the numbering convention shown in Figure 4.22 to answer the following questions:
    (a) List the columnar objects under *ipNetToMediaEntry.*
    (b) Draw an object instance table for *ipNetToMediaTable* as in Figure 4.23(b) without the row column. Fill three rows of data using MIB specifications.
    (c) Redraw the table in (b), now filling each cell in the table with an object instance identifier. Use *N* = 1.3.6.1.2.1.4.22.1 for *ipNetToMediaEntry* in the table.

11. You own a specialty company, ABC (Atlanta Braves Company), which sells hats and jackets. You obtained an OBJECT IDENTIFIER 5000 under *enterprises* node from IANA. You have two branch locations. Each has an inventory system that can be accessed by the IP address; which have the following OBJECT DESCRIPTORS:

branch1 - 100.100.100.15
branch2 - 100.100.100.16

Each branch has two types of products whose inventory are

    hats
    jackets

Hats are all of the same size and the inventory is a scalar value, hatQuantity.
Jackets come in different sizes and the inventory is maintained in a table, jacketTable, whose columnar objects are

jacketSize (index)

jacketQuantity

Create a MIB module for your company. The objective is to find the inventory of any specific product while sitting in your office as president of the company.

(a) Draw a MIB subtree.

(b) Write a MIB module.

12. A network manager discovers that a network component is performing poorly and issues an order to the technician to replace it. Which MIB group contains this information for the technician to find out the physical location of the component?

13. How would you use one of the standard MIB objects to determine which one of the stations in a LAN is functioning as a bridge to the external network?

14. TCP is a connection-oriented protocol and UDP is a connectionless protocol. Identify differences in the two MIBs that exemplify this difference.

15. What OBJECT TYPE would you use to identify the address of the neighboring gateway from your local gateway?

16. An IT manager gets complaints from users that there is excessive delay in response over the Ethernet LAN. The manager suspects that the cause of the problem is excessive collisions on the LAN. She gathers statistics on collisions using the dot3StatsTable and localizes the problem to a single faulty network interface card. Explain how she localized the problem. You may use RFC 2358 to answer this exercise.

17. FDDI is heavily used as a backbone network in a corporate complex.

(a) Draw a MIB tree for FDDI MIB. Limit your tree to the top five groups.

(b) Develop a three-column table presenting entity, OID, and brief descriptions of the groups and tables under each group.

18. Two new managed objects, *ifName* and *ifAlias* were introduced in *ifMIB* module. Explain the purpose of these new managed objects in network management and give an example for each case.

19. Illustrate (a) the PPP over HDCL and (b) the cable access link with one downstream and two upstream channels using the interface sublayers shown in Figure 4.29.

SNMPv1 Network Management: Communication and Functional Models

OBJECTIVES

- *Communication model: Administrative and messages*
- *Administrative structure*
  - *Community-based model*
  - *Access policy*
  - *MIB view*
- *Message PDU*
- *SNMP protocol specifications*
- *SNMP operations*
- *SNMP MIB*
- *SNMP functional model*

We have covered the organization and information models of SNMPv1 in the previous chapter. In this chapter we will address the SNMPv1 communication and functional models. Although SNMPv1 does not formally define the functional model, applications are built in the community-based access policy of the SNMP administrative model.

5.1   SNMP COMMUNICATION MODEL

The SNMPv1 communication model defines specifications of four aspects of SNMP communication: architecture, administrative model that defines data access policy, SNMP protocol, and SNMP MIB. Security in SNMP is managed by defining community, and only members belonging to the same community can communicate with each other. A manager can belong to multiple communities and can thus manage multiple domains. SNMP protocol specifications and messages are presented. SNMP entities are grouped into an SNMP MIB module.

5.1.1   SNMP Architecture

The SNMP architectural model consists of a collection of network management stations and network elements or objects. Network elements have management agents built in them, if they are managed elements. The SNMP communications protocol is used to communicate information between network management stations and management agents in the elements.

There are three goals of the architecture in the original specifications of SNMP [RFC 1157]. First, it should minimize the number and complexity of management functions realized by the management agent. Secondly, it should be flexible for future expansion (addition of new aspects of operation and management). Lastly, the architecture should be independent of architecture and mechanisms of particular hosts and gateways.

Only non-aggregate objects are communicated using SNMP. The aggregate objects are communicated as instances of the object. This has been enhanced in SNMPv2, as we shall see in the next chapter. Consistent with the rest of SNMP standards, ASN.1 transfer syntax and BER encoding scheme are used for data transfer SNMP.

SNMP monitors the network with the five messages shown in Figure 4.9; and we discussed them in Section 4.6. They comprise three basic messages: set, get, and trap. Information about the network is primarily obtained by the management stations polling the agents. The get-request and get-next-request messages are generated by the manager to retrieve data from network elements using associated management agents. The set-request is used to initialize and edit network element parameters. The get-response-request is the response from the agent to get and set messages from the manager. The number of unsolicited messages in the form of traps is limited to make the architecture simple and to minimize traffic.

There are three types of traps—generic-trap, specific-trap, and time-stamp, which are application specific. The generic-trap type consists of *coldStart, warmStart, linkDown, linkUp, authenticationFailure, egpNeighborLoss,* and *enterpriseSpecific.* The specific-trap is a specific code and is generated even when an *enterpriseSpecific* trap is not present. An example of this would be to gather statistics whenever a particular event occurs, such as use by a particular group. The time-stamp trap is the time elapsed between the last initialization or re-initialization of the element and the generation of the trap.

SNMP messages are exchanged using a connectionless UDP transport protocol in order to be consistent with simplicity of the model, as well as to reduce traffic. However, the mechanisms of SNMP are suitable for a variety of protocols.

5.1.2 Administrative Model

Although the topic of administrative models should normally be discussed as part of security and privacy under the functional model, at this point it helps to understand the administrative relationship among entities that participate in the communication protocol in SNMP. Hence, we will discuss it now.

In RFC 1157 the entities residing in management stations and network elements are called SNMP application entities. Peer processes, which implement SNMP, and thus support SNMP application entities, are termed protocol entities. We will soon discuss protocol entities in detail. First, let us look at the application entities.

We will refer to the *application entity* residing in the management station as the SNMP manager, and the application entity in the element as the SNMP agent. The pairing of the two entities is called an SNMP community. The SNMP community name, called the *community,* is specified by a string of octets. Multiple pairs can belong to the same community. Figure 5.1 shows multiple SNMP managers communicating with a single SNMP agent. While an SNMP manager is monitoring traffic on an element, another manager may be configuring some administrative information on it. A third manager can be monitoring it to perform some statistical study. We also have the analogous situation where a manager communicates with multiple agents.

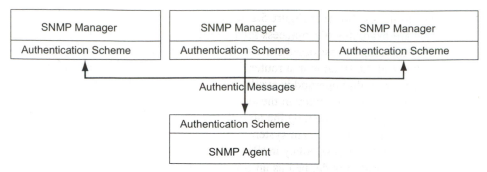

Figure 5.1 SNMP Community

With one-to-many, many-to-one, and many-to-many communication links between managers and agents, a basic authentication scheme and an access policy have been specified in SNMP. Figure 5.1 shows the *authentication scheme*, which is a filter module in the manager and the agent. The simplest form of authentication is the common community name between the two application entities. Encryption would be a higher level of authentication in which case both the source and the receiver know the common encryption and decryption algorithms.

The SNMP authorization is implemented as part of managed object MIB specifications. We discussed MIB specifications for managed objects in Chapter 4, and will discuss MIB specifications for SNMP protocol in Section 5.1.4. A network element comprises many managed objects—both standard and private. However, a management agent may be permitted to view only a subset of the network element's managed objects. This is called the community *MIB view*. In Figure 5.2 the SNMP agent has a MIB view of objects 2, 3, and 4, although there may be other objects associated with a network element. In addition to the MIB view, each community name is also assigned an *SNMP access mode*, either READ-ONLY or READ-WRITE, as shown in Figure 5.2. A pairing of SNMP MIB views with an SNMP access code is called a *community profile*.

A community profile in combination with the access mode of a managed object determines the operation that can be performed on the object by an agent. For example, in Figure 5.2, an SNMP agent with READ-WRITE SNMP access mode can perform all operations—get, set, and trap—on objects 2, 3, and 4. On the other hand, if the SNMP agent has READ-ONLY access mode privilege, it can only perform get and trap operations on objects 2, 3, and 4. Object 1 has a "not-accessible" access mode and hence no operation can be performed on it.

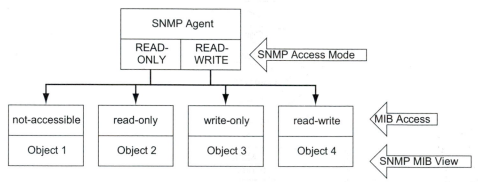

Figure 5.2 SNMP Community Profile

There are four access modes shown in Figure 5.2. They are not-accessible, read-only, write-only, and read-write. The tables are examples of no-access mode. One can only access scalar objects associated with the entities under the table. Most objects available for the public community are read-only, such as the interface statistics and the IP table in a router. These are the get and trap operations. If the access mode is defined as read-write, that operand is available for all three operations of get, set, and trap. An example of read-write access is *sysContact* in the system group. The write-only access mode is used to set the operand value of a get MIB object by the network manager, for example *sysDescr* in the system group. This is done in network management systems as implementation-specific.

We can now define an SNMP access policy in SNMP management. A pairing of an SNMP community with an SNMP community profile is defined as an SNMP access policy. This defines the administrative model of SNMP management. Figure 5.3 shows an example of three network management systems in three network operation centers (NOC) having different access to different community domains. Agents 1 and 2 belong to Community 1. However, they do have two different community profiles, community profiles 1 and 2. Manager 1, which is part of Community 1, can communicate with both Agents 1 and 2. However, it cannot communicate with Agents 3 and 4 belonging to Community 2. Manager 2 has access to them as it also belongs to Community 2. Agent 3 has community profile 3 and Agent 4 has community profile 4. Manager 3 has access to both Community 1 and 2 and hence can communicate with all the agents. We can picture an enterprise network management fitting this scenario. If a corporation has two operations in two cities, Manager 1 in NOC 1 and Manager 2 in NOC 2 are responsible for managing their respective domains. A top view of the overall operations can be viewed and managed by NOC 3 in the headquarters operation.

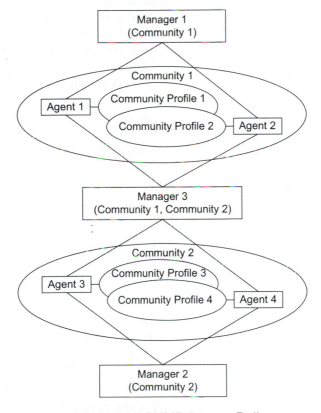

Figure 5.3 SNMP Access Policy

A practical application of the SNMP access policy can be envisioned in an enterprise management system of a corporation with headquarters in New York and domains or network sites in New York and San Francisco. Let Manager 1 and Community 1 be associated with San Francisco, and Manager 2 and Community 2 with New York. Let Manager 3 be the overall network management system, the Manager of Managers (MoM). Manager 1 manages Agents 1 and 2 associated with network elements in San Francisco. Manager 2 manages the New York network domain. Manager 1 does not have the view of New York and Manager 2 cannot perform operations on network elements belonging to the San Francisco domain. Manager 3 has both community names defined in its profile and hence has the view of the total enterprise network in New York and San Francisco.

The SNMP access policy has far-reaching consequences beyond that of servicing a TCP/IP-based Internet SNMP community. It can be extended to managing non-SNMP community using the SNMP proxy access policy. The SNMP agent associated with the proxy policy is called a proxy agent or commercially, a proxy server. The proxy agent monitors a non-SNMP community with non-SNMP agents and then converts objects and data to SNMP-compatible objects and data to feed to an SNMP manager.

Figure 5.4 shows an illustration of SNMP and non-SNMP communities being managed by an SNMP manager. A practical example of this would be a network of LAN and WAN. LAN could be a TCP/IP network with SNMP agents. WAN could be an X.25 network, which is not an Internet model, but can be managed by a proxy agent and integrated into the overall management system.

5.1.3   SNMP Protocol Specifications

Peer processes, which implement SNMP, and thus support SNMP application entities, are termed *protocol entities*. Communication among protocol entities is accomplished using messages encapsulated in a UDP datagram. An SNMP message consists of a version identifier, an SNMP community name, and a protocol data unit (PDU). Figure 5.5 shows the encapsulated SNMP message. The version and community names are added to the data PDU and along with the application header is passed on to the transport layer as SNMP PDU. The UDP header is added at the transport layer, which then forms the transport PDU for the network layer. The addition of the IP header to the Transport PDU forms the Network PDU for the data link layer (DLC). The network or DLC header is added before the frame is transmitted on to the physical medium.

An SNMP protocol entity is received on port 161 on the host except for trap, which is received on port 162. The maximum length of the protocol in SNMPv1 is 484 bytes (1,472 bytes now in practice). It

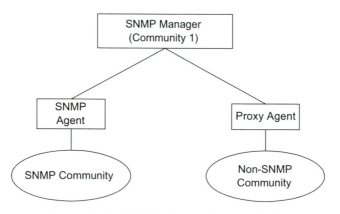

Figure 5.4   SNMP Proxy Access Policy

						Data

Data PDU

Application PDU

		Application Header	Version	Community	Data PDU

Transport PDU

	UDP Header	Application PDU	

Network PDU

IP Header	Transport PDU

Data Link PDU

DLC Header	Network PDU

Figure 5.5 Encapsulated SNMP Message

is mandatory that all five PDUs be supported in all implementations: GetRequest-PDU, GetNextRequest-PDU, GetResponse-PDU, SetRequest-PDU, and Trap-PDU. One of these five data PDUs is the data PDU that we start with at the top in Figure 5.5. RFC 1157-SNMP Macro definition is given in Figure 5.6.

```
RFC1157 SNMP DEFINITIONS ::= BEGIN

IMPORTS
        ObjectName, ObjectSyntax, NetworkAddress, IpAddress, TimeTicks
            FROM RFC1155  -SMI
--top-level message
        Message ::=
            SEQUENCE {
                version       -- version
                 INTEGER {          -1 for this RFC
                    version-1(0)
                },
                community   -- community name
                 OCTET STRING,
                data         -- e.g., PDUs if trivial
                 ANY         -- authentication is being used
                }
-- protocol data units
        PDUs ::=
            CHOICE {
                get-request
                get-next-request       GetRequest-PDU,
                get-response           GetNextRequest-PDU,
                set-request            GetResponse-PDU,
                trap                   SetRequest-PDU,
                }                      Trap-PDU
-- the individual PDUs and commonly used data types will be defined later
END
```

Figure 5.6 RFC 1157-SNMP Macro

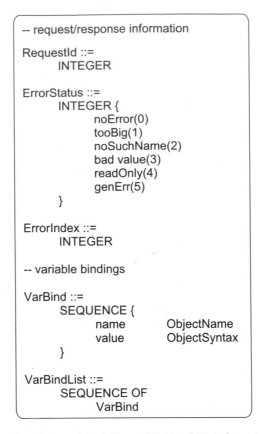

```
-- request/response information

RequestId ::=
        INTEGER

ErrorStatus ::=
        INTEGER {
                noError(0)
                tooBig(1)
                noSuchName(2)
                bad value(3)
                readOnly(4)
                genErr(5)
        }

ErrorIndex ::=
        INTEGER

-- variable bindings

VarBind ::=
        SEQUENCE {
                name        ObjectName
                value       ObjectSyntax
        }

VarBindList ::=
        SEQUENCE OF
                VarBind
```

Figure 5.7 Get and Set Type PDU ASN.1 Construct [RFC 1157]

Basic operations of the protocol entity involve the following steps as a guide to implementation [RFC 1157]. The protocol entity that generates the message constructs the appropriate data PDU as an ASN.1 object. It then passes the ASN.1 object along with a community name and the transport addresses of itself and the destination (e.g., 123.234.245.156:161) to the authentication scheme. The authentication scheme returns another ASN.1 object (possibly encrypted). The protocol entity now constructs the message to be transmitted with the version number, community name, and the new ASN.1 object, then serializes it using the BER rules, and transmits it.

The reverse process goes on at the receiver. The message is discarded if an error is encountered in any of the steps. A trap may be generated in case of authentication failure. On successful receipt of the message, a return message is generated, if the original message is a get-request.

A managed object is a scalar variable and is simply called a variable. Associated with the variable is its value. The pairing of the variable and value is called *variable binding* or *VarBind*. The data PDU in the message contains a VarBind pair. For efficiency sake, a list of VarBind pairs can be sent in a message. The ASN.1 construct for get and set type of messages is shown in Figure 5.7 and a conceptual presentation in Figure 5.8. The *VarBindList* contains n instances of VarBind (pairs).

The PDU type for the five messages are application data types, which are defined in RFC 1157 as:

get-request   [0]
get-next-request   [1]

PDU Type	RequestID	Error Status	Error Index	VarBind 1 Name	VarBind 1 Value	...	VarBind n Name	VarBind n Value

Figure 5.8   Get and Set Type PDUs

set-request   [2]
get-response   [3]
trap   [4]

In Figure 5.8 *RequestID* is used to track a message with the expected response or for loss of a message (remember UDP is unreliable). Loss-of-message detection is implementation specific, such as time out if no response is received for a request within a given time. A non-zero *ErrorStatus* is used to indicate that an error occurred. The convention is not to use 0 if no error is detected. *ErrorIndex* is used to provide additional information on the error status. The value is filled with NULL in those cases where it is not applicable, such as in get-request data PDU. Otherwise, it is filled with the *varBind* number where the error occurred; for   example, 1 if the error occurred in the first *varBind*, 5 if the fifth *varBind* had an error and so on.

Figure 5.9 shows the structure for a trap PDU, which contains *n VarBind*s, i.e., *n* managed objects. The enterprise [RFC 1155] and agent-address pertain to the system generating the trap. The generic-trap consists of seven types as listed in Table 5.1. The integer in parenthesis associated with each name indicates the enumerated INTEGER. The specific-trap is a trap that is not covered by the *enterpriseSpecific* trap. Time-stamp indicates the elapsed time since last re-initialization.

PDU Type	Enterprise	Agent Address	Generic-Trap Type	Specific-Trap Type	Time-Stamp	VarBind 1 Name	VarBind 1 Value	...	VarBind n Name	VarBind n Value

Figure 5.9   Trap PDU

Table 5.1   Generic Traps

GENERIC-TRAP TYPE	DESCRIPTION (BRIEF)
coldStart(0)	Sending protocol entity is reinitializing itself; agent configuration or protocol entity implementation may be altered
warmStart(1)	Sending protocol entity is reinitializing itself; agent configuration or protocol entity implementation not altered
linkDown(2)	Failure of one of the communication links
linkUp(3)	One of the links has come up
authenticationFailure(4)	Authentication failure
egpNeighborLoss(5)	Loss of EGP neighbor
enterpriseSpecific(6)	Enterprise-specific trap

5.1.4 SNMP Operations

SNMP operations comprise get and set messages from the manager to the agent, and get and trap messages from the agent to the manager. We will now look at these operations in detail in this section.

GetRequest PDU Operation. Figure 5.10 shows a sequence of operations in retrieving the values of objects in a System group. It starts with the get-request operation using a GetRequest PDU from a manager process to an agent process and the get-response from the agent with a GetResponse PDU. The message from the manager starts from the left side and ends at the agent process on the right side of the figure. The message from the agent process starts on the right side of the figure and ends at the manager process on the left side of the figure. The sequence of directed messages moves with time as we move down the figure. Messages depicted represent the values of the seven objects in the System group.

The manager process starts the sequence in Figure 5.10 with a GetRequest PDU for the object *sysDescr*. The agent process returns a GetResponse PDU with a value "SunOS." The manager then sends a request for *sysObjectID* and receives the value "E:hp." The exchange of messages goes on until the value of 72 for the last object in the group *sysServices* is received.

GetNextRequest PDU Operation. A get-next-request operation is very similar to get-request, except that the requested record is the next one to the OBJECT IDENTIFIER specified in the request. Figure 5.11 shows the operations associated with retrieving data for the System group by the manager process using the get-next-request. The first message is a GetRequest PDU for *sysDescr* with the response returning the value "SunOS." The manager process then issues a GetNextRequest PDU with the OBJECT IDENTIFIER *sysDescr*. The agent processes the name of the next OBJECT IDENTIFIER *sysObjectID* and its value "E:hp." The sequence terminates when the manager issues a get-next-request for the object identifier next to *sysServices*, and the agent process returns the error message "noSuchName."

The System group example we just looked at is a simple case where all the objects are single-valued scalar objects. Let us now consider a more complex scenario of a MIB that contains both scalar and aggregate objects. A generalized case of a conceptual MIB comprising three scalar objects and a table is

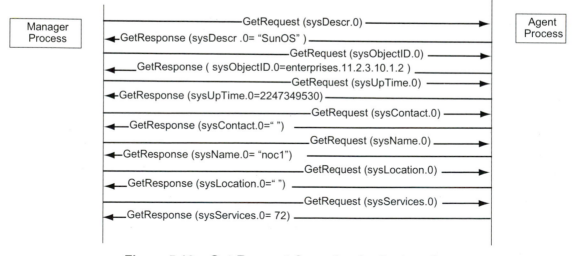

Figure 5.10 Get-Request Operation for System Group

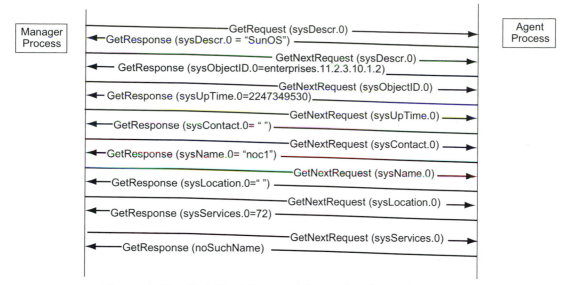

Figure 5.11 Get-Next-Request Operation for a System Group

shown in Figure 5.12. The first two objects A and B are single-valued scalar objects. They are followed by an aggregate object represented by the table T with an entry E and two rows of three columnar objects, T.E.1.1. through T.E.3.2. The MIB group ends with a scalar object Z.

Figure 5.13 shows the use of nine get-request messages to retrieve the nine objects. The left side of the figure shows the sequential operation for getting the MIB shown on the right side of the figure. The MIB shown is the same as in Figure 5.12, now drawn to follow the sequence of operations. We observe

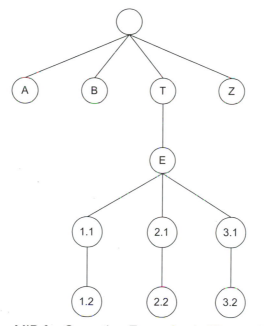

Figure 5.12 MIB for Operation Examples in Figures 5.13 and 5.15

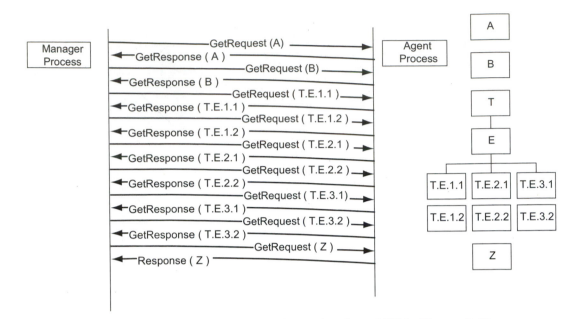

Figure 5.13 Get-Request Operation for a MIB in Figure 5.12

a few hidden assumptions in retrieving the data using the get-request operations. First, we need to know all the elements in the MIB including the number of columns and rows in the table. Second, we traversed the MIB from top to bottom, which is really from right to left in the MIB tree structure. Third, we retrieved the data in the table by traversing all the instances of a columnar object. The number of instances or rows in a table could be dynamic and is not always known to the management process. Thus, if the manager had issued a request for the object T.E.1.3 after acquiring T.E.1.2, it would have received an error message from the agent process. This is when get-next-request is very useful. However, we need to have a convention on the definition of what the next object in a MIB tree is, especially on the table representing an aggregate object. In SNMP, objects are retrieved using lexicographic convention. We will first explain what this convention is before using the get-next-request operation to retrieve the same MIB group data.

The increasing order of entity used in SNMP operations is in lexicographic order. Let us understand lexicographic order by considering a simple set of integers shown in Table 5.2. The left side is a sequence of numerically increasing integer numbers, and the right side is lexicographically increasing order for this sequence. We notice that in the lexicographic order, we start with the lowest integer in the leftmost character, which in our case is 1. Before increasing the order in the first position, we select the lowest integer in the second position from the left, which is 11. There are two numbers (1118 and 115) that start with 11. We anchor at 11 for the first two positions and then move on to select the lowest digit in the third position, which is 111. We then move to the fourth position and obtain 1118 as the second number. Now, return to the third position and retrieve 115 as the third number. Having exhausted 1s (ones) in positions two to four, select 2 for the second position, and retrieve 126 as the next number. We continue this process until we reach 9.

We will now apply the lexicographic sequence to ordering object identifiers in a MIB. Instead of each character being treated as a literal, we treat each node position as a literal and follow the same rules. An example illustrating this is given in Table 5.3. The MIB associated with this example is shown in

Table 5.2 Lexicographic-Order Number Example

NUMERICAL ORDER	LEXICOGRAPHIC ORDER
1	1
2	1118
3	115
9	126
15	15
22	2
34	22
115	250
126	2509
250	3
321	321
1118	34
2509	9

Figure 5.14. It can be noticed that the lexicographically increasing order of node traces the traversal of the tree starting from the leftmost node 1. We traverse down the path all the way to the leftmost leaf 1.1.5, keeping to the right whenever a fork is encountered. We then move up the tree and take a right on the first fork. This leads us to the leaf node 1.1.18. Thus, the rule at a forked node is to always keep to the right while traversing down and while going up. Thus, we are always keeping to the right if you imagine ourselves walking along the tree path and looking in the forward direction. We turn around when we reach a leaf.

Returning to get-next-request operation, the get-response message contains the value of the next lexicographic object value in each VarBind. If the request VarBind contains a scalar, non-tabular object,

Table 5.3 MIB Example for Lexicographic Ordering

1
1.1
1.1.5
1.1.18
1.2
1.2.6
2
2.2
2.10
2.10.9
3
3.4
3.21
9

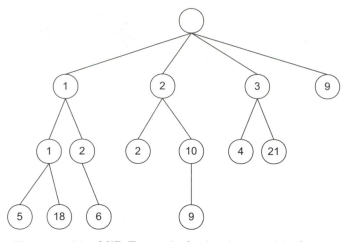

Figure 5.14 MIB Example for Lexicographic Ordering

the response contains the next scalar, non-tabular value, or the first columnar object value of a table, if it is the next lexicographic entity. Figure 5.15 shows the principle of operation of the functioning of get-next-request and response. We use the same MIB view that we had in Figure 5.12 using get-request operation. The manager process starts the operation with a get-request message for object A and receives the response with the value of A filled in. Subsequent requests from the manager are get-next-request type with the object ID of the just received ones. Responses received are the next object ID with its value. Operations continue until Z is received. The subsequent request receives a response with an error message "noSuchName."

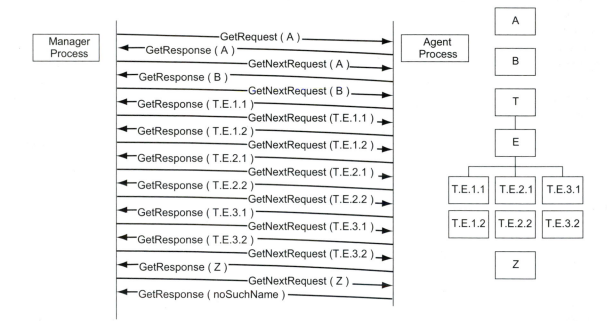

Figure 5.15 Get-Next-Request Operation for a MIB in Figure 5.12

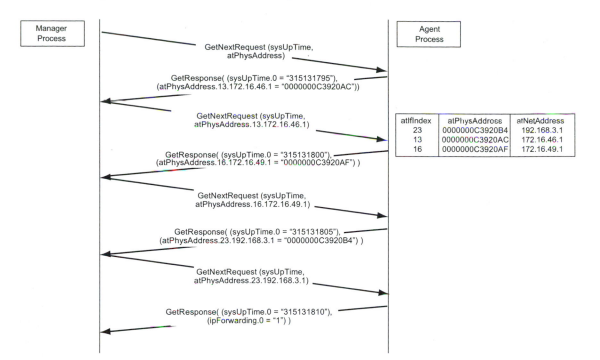

Figure 5.16 GetNextRequest Example with Indices

There are several advantages in using get-next-request. First, we do not need to know the object identifier of the next entity. Knowing the current OBJECT IDENTIFIER, we can retrieve the next one. Next, in the case of an aggregate object, the number of rows is dynamically changing. Thus, we do not know how many rows exist in the table. The get-next-request resolves this problem.

There is also another advantage of the get-next-request. We can use this to build a MIB tree by repeating the request from any node to any node. This is called MIB walk, and is used by a MIB browser in NMS implementation.

Figure 5.16 shows a faster method to retrieve an aggregate object. It shows an Address Translation table with a matrix of three columnar objects, *atIfIndex*, *atPhysAddress*, and *atNetAddress*. The objects *atIfIndex* and *atNetAddress* are the indices that uniquely identify a row. There are three rows in the table. If we use the get-next-request operation shown in Figure 5.15, it would take us ten message exchanges. The *VarBindList* comprises two VarBind name–value pairs, *sysUpTime* and *atPhysAddress*, suffixed with the values of *atIfIndex* and *atNetAddress*. Instead of issuing ten get-next-requests with a single VarBind in the message, the manager generates four GetNextRequest PDUs with a list of two VarBind fields. Although the Address Translation table is relatively stable, in general, a table is dynamic, and hence the time-stamp is requested by including *sysUpTime*.

In this method, the manager has to know the columnar objects of the table. The first query message retrieves the indices automatically. For the Address Translation table, the *atIfIndex* and *atNetAddress* are indices. This is shown in the request and response message OIDs. The first get-next-request message does not contain any operand value. The next three contain the value returned by the response. The fourth and last get-next-request brings the object, *ipForwarding*, which is the first element in the

IP group, which is the next group in Internet MIB. This is because all table entries in the Address Table have been retrieved. It is up to the manager process to recognize this and terminate the process. If the table contained more columns, the *VarBindList* could be expanded and values for all the objects in the next row obtained with each request.

There are more details to this PDU operation and the reader is referred to the references Perkins and McGinnis [1997], RFC [1905], and Stallings [1998].

SNMP PDU Format Examples. We will now look at the PDU for the System group example shown in Figure 5.10 using a sniffer tool. Sniffer is a management tool that can capture packets going across a transmission medium. We have used this tool to "sniff" some SNMP messages to display how messages actually look. We are presenting a series of messages that query a system for its system group data (Figure 5.17). This corresponds to the data shown in Figure 5.10. We then set the missing values for a couple of entities in the group (Figures 5.18 and 5.19) and finally reexamine them (Figure 5.20).

Figure 5.17(a) shows a GetRequest message for the system group values going from the manager, noc3.gatech.btc.gatech.edu (noc3, for short), to the agent, noc1.btc.gatech.edu (noc1, for short). The first line shows that it was sent at 13:55:47 from port 164 of noc1 to snmp port of noc3. The tool that was used has actually translated the conventional port number 161 to snmp. The community name is public and the GetRequest message is 111 bytes in length. The SNMP version number is not filled in.

```
13:55:47.445936 noc3.btc.gatech.edu.164 > noc1.btc.gatech.edu.snmp:
Community = public
GetRequest(111)
Request ID = 1
system.sysDescr.0
system.sysObjectID.0
system.sysUpTime.0
system.sysContact.0
system.sysName.0
system.sysLocation.0
system.sysServices.0
```

(a) Get-Request Message from Manager-to-Agent (Before)

```
13:55:47.455936 noc1.btc.gatech.edu.snmp > noc3.btc.gatech.edu.164:
Community = public
GetResponse(172)
Request ID = 1
system.sysDescr.0 =      "SunOS noc1 5.5.1 Generic_103640-08 sun4u"
system.sysObjectID.0 = E:hp.2.3.10.1.2
system.sysUpTime.0 = 247349530
system.sysContact.0 =      ""
system.sysName.0 =      "noc1 "
system.sysLocation.0 =      ""
system.sysServices.0 = 72
```

(b) Get-Response Message from Agent-to-Manager (Before)

Figure 5.17   Sniffer Data of Get Messages (Incomplete Data in Agent)

13:56:24.894369 noc3.btc.gatech.edu.164 > noc1.btc.gatech.edu.snmp:
Community = netman
SetRequest(41)
Request ID = 2
system.sysContact.0 = "Brandon Rhodes"

13:56:24.894369 noc1.btc.gatech.edu.snmp > noc3.btc.gatech.edu.164:
Community = netman
GetResponse(41)
Request ID = 2
system.sysContact.0 = "Brandon Rhodes"

Figure 5.18   Sniffer Data of Set-Request and Response for System Contact

13:56:27.874245 noc3.btc.gatech.edu.164 > noc1.btc.gatech.edu.snmp:
Community = netman
SetRequest(37)
Request ID = 3
system.sysLocation.0 = "BTC NM Lab"

13:56:27.884244 noc1.btc.gatech.edu.snmp > noc3.btc.gatech.edu.164:
Community = netman
GetResponse(37)
Request ID = 3
system.sysLocation.0 = "BTC NM Lab"

Figure 5.19   Sniffer Data of Set-Request and Response for System Location

14:03:36.788270 noc3.btc.gatech.edu.164 > noc1.btc.gatech.edu.snmp:
Community = public
GetRequest(111)
Request ID = 4
system.sysDescr.0
system.sysObjectID.0
system.s ysUpTime.0
system.sysContact.0
system.sysName.0
system.sysLocation.0
system.sysServices.0

(a) Get-Request Message from Manager-to-Agent (After)

Figure 5.20   Sniffer Data of Get Messages (Complete Data in Agent)

14:03:36.798269 noc1.btc.gatech.edu.snmp > noc3.btc.gat ech.edu.164:
Community = public
GetResponse(196)
Request ID = 4
system.sysDescr.0 =   "SunOS noc1 5.5.1 Generic_103640 -08 sun4u"
system.sysObjectID.0 = E:hp.2.3.10.1.2
system.sysUpTime.0 = 247396453
system.sysContact.0 = "Brandon Rhodes"
system.sysName.0 = "noc1"
system.sysLocation.0 = "BTC NM Lab"
system.sysServices.0 = 72

(b) Get-Response Message from Agent-to-Manager (After)

Figure 5.20 (continued)

The seven object IDs from *system.sysDescr.*0 to *system.sysServices.*0 all end with zero to indicate that they are single-valued scalar objects. The agent, noc1, sends a GetResponse message of 172 bytes with values filled in for all seven objects. The GetResponse message is shown in Figure 5.17(b). Notice that the values for *sysContact* and *sysLocation* in GetResponse are blank as they have not been entered in the agent. In addition, the request number identified in the GetResponse PDU is the same as the one in the GetRequest PDU.

Figure 5.18 shows the use of the SetRequest message to write the *sysContact* name in noc1 whose value is "Brandon Rhodes." Notice that the community name is changed to netman. The community of netman has the access privilege to write in noc1, and the object, *system.sysContact*, has the read-write access for the netman community. The agent, noc1, makes the change and sends a GetResponse message back to noc3. Figure 5.19 shows a similar set of messages for setting the entity *sysLocation* with the value "BTC NM Lab."

Figures 5.20(a) and (b) are a repetition of Figure 5.14 of the GetRequest and GetResponse messages. We now see the completed version of the system group data.

5.1.5 SNMP MIB Group

Figure 5.21 shows the MIB tree for the SNMP group, and Table 5.4 gives the description of the entities. Note that OID 7 and OID 23 are not used. The number of transactions in the description column in the table indicates ins and outs of the SNMP protocol entity. All entities except *snmpEnableAuthenTraps* have the syntax, Counter. The implementation of the SNMP group is mandatory—obviously!

5.2 FUNCTIONAL MODEL

There are no formal specifications of functions in SNMPv1 management. Application functions are limited, in general, to network management in SNMP and not to the services provided by the network.

There are five areas of functions (configuration, fault, performance, security, and accounting) addressed by the OSI mode. Some configuration functions, as well as security and privacy-related issues, were addressed as part of the SNMP protocol entity specifications in the previous section. For

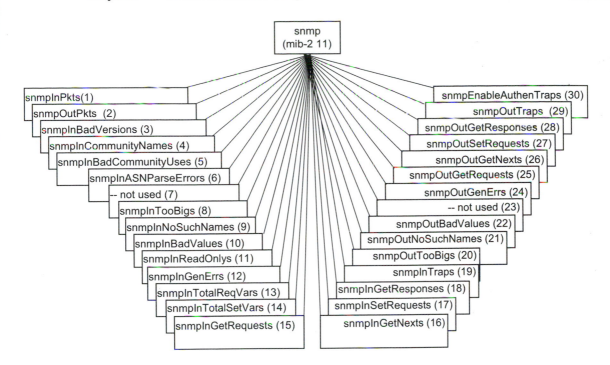

Figure 5.21 SNMP Group

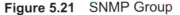

example, the override function of traps is one of the objects in the SNMP group, which has the access privilege of read and write and hence can be set remotely. Security functions are built in as part of the implementation of the protocol entity. Community specifications and authentication scheme partially address these requirements.

The write access to managed objects is limited to implementation in most cases. Thus, configuration management in general is addressed by the specific network management system or by the use of console or telnet to set configurable parameters. We saw the use of the configuration management function in the examples shown in Figures 5.18 and 5.19.

Fault management is addressed by error counters built into the agents. They can be read by the SNMP manager and processed. Traps are useful to monitor network elements and interfaces going up and down.

Performance counters are part of the SNMP agent MIB. It is the function of the SNMP manager to do performance analysis. For example, counter readings can be taken at two instances of time and the data rate calculated. The intermediate manager/agent, such as RMON, can perform such statistical functions, as we will see in the next chapter.

The administrative model in protocol entity specifications addresses security function in basic SNMP.

The accounting function is not addressed by the SNMP model.

Table 5.4 SNMP Group

ENTITY	OID	DESCRIPTION (BRIEF)
snmpInPkts	snmp (1)	Total number of messages delivered from transport service
snmpOutPkts	snmp (2)	Total number of messages delivered to transport service
snmpInBadVersions	snmp (3)	Total number of messages from transport service that are of unsupported version
snmpInBadCommunityNames	snmp (4)	Total number of messages from transport service that are of unknown community name
snmpInBadCommunityUses	snmp (5)	Total number of messages from transport service, not allowed operation by the sending community
snmpInASNParseErrs	snmp (6)	Total number of ASN.1 and BER errors
	snmp (7)	Not used
snmpInTooBigs	snmp (8)	Total number of messages from transport service that have 'tooBig' errors
snmpInNoSuchNames	snmp (9)	Total number of messages from transport service that have 'noSuchName' errors
snmpInBadValues	snmp (10)	Total number of messages from transport service that have 'badValue' errors
snmpInReadOnlys	snmp (11)	Total number of messages from transport service that have 'readOnly' errors
snmpInGenErrs	snmp (12)	Total number of messages from transport service that have 'genErr' errors
snmpInTotalReqVars	snmp (13)	Total number of successful Get-Request and Get-Next messages received
snmpInTotalSetVars	snmp (14)	Total number of objects successfully altered by Set-Request messages received
snmpInGetRequests	snmp (15)	Total number of Get-Request PDUs accepted and processed
snmpInGetNexts	snmp (16)	Total number of Get-Next PDUs accepted and processed
snmpInSetRequests	snmp (17)	Total number of Set-Request PDUs accepted and processed
snmpInGetResponses	snmp (18)	Total number of Get-Response PDUs accepted and processed
snmpInTraps	snmp (19)	Total number of Trap PDUs accepted and processed
snmpOutTooBigs	snmp (20)	Total number of SNMP PDUs generated for which error-status is 'tooBig'
snmpOutNoSuchNames	snmp (21)	Total number of SNMP PDUs generated for which error-status is 'noSuchName'
snmpOutBadValues	snmp (22)	Total number of SNMP PDUs generated for which error-status is 'badValue'
	snmp (23)	Not used
snmpOutGenErrs	snmp (24)	Total number of SNMP PDUs generated for which error-status is 'genErr'
snmpOutGetRequests	snmp (25)	Total number of SNMP Get-Request PDUs generated
snmpOutGetNexts	snmp (26)	Total number of SNMP Get-Next PDUs generated
snmpOutSetRequests	snmp (27)	Total number of SNMP Set-Request PDUs generated
snmpOutGetResponses	snmp (28)	Total number of SNMP Get-Response PDUs generated
snmpOutTraps	snmp (29)	Total number of SNMP Trap PDUs generated
snmpEnableAuthenTraps	snmp (30)	Override option to generate authentication failure traps

◼️ Summary

All management operations are done using five messages in SNMPv1. They are get-request, get-next-request, set-request, get-response, and trap. The first three are sent from the manager to the agent and the last two are sent by the agent to the manager.

The SNMP communication model deals with the administrative structure and the five SNMP message PDUs. The administrative model defines the community within which messages can be exchanged. It also defines the access policy as to who has access privilege to what data. The five protocol entities are defined in ASN.1 format and macros. We learned SNMP operations by tracing messages exchanged between manager and agent processes. We then looked inside PDU formats for various messages to learn the data formats.

There is no formal specification for the functional model in SNMP management. However, management functions are accomplished by built-in schemes and managed objects. The administrative model in SNMP and the operations using managed objects are employed to accomplish various functions.

◼️ Exercises

1. Three managed hubs with interface id 11–13 (fourth decimal position value) in subnetwork 200.100.100.1 are being monitored by a network management system (NMS) for mean time between failures using the *SysUpTime* in *system {internet. mgmt.mib-2.system}* group. The NMS periodically issues the command get-request *object-instance community OBJECT IDENTIFIER* Fill the operands in the three set of requests that the NMS sends out. Use "public" for the *community* variable.

2. You are assigned the task of writing specifications for configuring SNMP managers and agents for a corporate network to implement the access policy. The policy defines a community profile for all managed network components where a public group (community name *public*) can only look at the System group, a privileged group (community name *privileged*) that can look at all the MIB objects, and an exclusive group (community name *exclusive*) that can do a read-write on all allowed components. Present a figure (similar, but not identical, to the flow chart shown in Figure 5.2) showing the paths from the SNMP managers to managed objects of a network component.

3. Fill in the data in the trap PDU format shown in Figure 5.9 for a message sent by the hub shown in Figure 4.2(a) one second after it is reset following a failure. Treat the trap as generic and leave the specific trap field blank. The only *varBind* that the trap sends is *sysUpTime*. (Refer to RFC 1157 and RFC 1215.)

4. An SNMP manager sends a request message to an SNMP agent requesting *sysUpTime* at 8:00 A.M. Fill in the data for the fields of an SNMP PDU shown in Figure 5.5. Please use "SNMP" for the application header, enumerated INTEGER 0 for version-1, and "public" for community name.

5. In Exercise 4, if the SNMP manager sent the request at 8:00 A.M. and the SNMP agent was reset at midnight after a failure, fill in the fields for the SNMP PDU on the response received.

6. An SNMP manager sends a request for the values of the *sysUpTime* in the System group and *if Type* in the Interfaces group for *ifNumber* value of 3. Write the PDUs with the fields filled in for

   (a) the get-request PDU, and
   (b) the get-response PDU with noSuchName error message for *ifType*

7. The following data response information is received by the manager for a get-request with a *varBindList*. Compose

   (a) the get-request PDU, and
   (b) the get-response PDU

OBJECT	VALUE
Error Status	Too big
Error Index	udpInErrors
udpInDatagrams	500,000
udpNoPorts	1,000
udpInErrors	5000
udpOutDatagrams	300,000

8. Draw the message sequence diagram similar to the one shown in Figure 5.10 for the hub example given in Figure 4.2(a). Assume that a separate get-request message is sent for each data value.

9. Repeat Exercise 7 with a VarBindList. Use the format of Figure 5.16.

10. For the UDP Group MIB shown in Figure 4.39, assume that there are three rows for the columnar objects in the *udpTable*. Write the OBJECT IDENTIFIER for all the objects in lexicographic order.

11. Draw the message sequence diagram for the following *ipNetToMediaTable* retrieving all the values of objects in each row with single get-next-request commands, similar to the one shown in Figure 5.16. The indices are *ipNetToMediaIfIndex* and *ipNetToMediaNetAddress*. Ignore obtaining *sysUpTime*.

ipNetToMedia IfIndex	IpNetToMediaPhys Address	ipNetToMediaNet Address	ipNetTo MediaType
25	00000C3920B4	192.68.252.15	4
16	00000C3920AF	172.16.49.1	4
9	00000C3920A6	172.16.55.1	4
2	00000C39209D	172.16.56.1	4

12. Compose data frames for SNMP PDUs for the example shown in Figure 5.16 for the following two cases:

   (a) The first GetNextRequest (*sysUpTime*, *atPhysAddress*) and the GetResponse.
   (b) The second GetNextRequest and GetResponse with values obtained in (a).

13. A data analyzer tool is used to look at a frame of data traversing a LAN. It is from the station *noc3* in response to a request from *noc1*. Use the following system status to answer this question.

   Version = 0
   Community = netman

OBJECT	VALUE	UNITS
Request ID	100	
Error Status	Too big	udpInErrors too high
Error Index	udpInErrors	
sysUpTime	1,000,000	hundredths of a second
udpInDatagrams	500,000	datagrams
udpNoPorts	1,000	datagrams
udpInErrors	5000	datagrams
udpOutDatagrams	300,000	datagrams

Compose the expected data frames for SNMP PDU types. Your frames should look like the ones shown in Figure 5.17.

(a) Get Request from the manager to the managed object.
(b) Get Response from the managed object to the manager.

SNMP Management: SNMPv2

OBJECTIVES

- *Community-based security*
- *SNMPv2 enhancements*
  - *Additional messages*
  - *Formalization of SMI*
- *Get-bulk request and information-request*

- *SNMP MIB modifications*
- *Incompatibility with SNMPv1*
- *Proxy server*
- *Bilingual manager*

SNMPv1, which was originally called SNMP, was developed as an interim management protocol with OSI as the ultimate network management protocol. A placeholder, CMOT (CMIP over TCP/IP), was created in the Internet Management Information Base (MIB) for migrating from SNMP to CMIP. But the "best-laid plans…" never came about. SNMP caught on in the industry. Major vendors had incorporated SNMP modules in their network systems and components. SNMP now needed further enhancements.

Version 2 of Simple Network Management Protocol, SNMPv2, was developed when it became obvious that OSI network management standards were not going to be implemented in the near future. The working group that was commissioned by the IETF to define SNMPv2 released it in 1996. It is also a community-based administrative framework similar to SNMPv1 defined in STD 15 [RFC 1157], STD 16 [RFC 1155, 1212], and STD 17 [RFC 1213]. Although the original version was known as SNMP, it is now referred to as SNMPv1 to distinguish it from SNMPv2.

6.1 MAJOR CHANGES IN SNMPv2

Several significant changes were introduced in SNMPv2. One of the most significant changes was to improve the security function that SNMPv1 lacked. Unfortunately, after significant effort, due to lack of consensus, this was dropped from the final specifications, and SNMPv2 was released with the rest of the changes. The security function continued to be implemented on an administrative framework based on the community name and the same administrative framework as in SNMPv1 was adopted for SNMPv2. SNMPv2 Working Group has presented a summary of the community-based Administrative Framework for the SNMPv2 framework, and referred to it as SNMPv2C in RFC 1901. RFC 1902 through RFC 1907 present the details on the framework. There are significant differences between the two versions of SNMP, and unfortunately version 2 is not backward compatible with version 1. RFC 1908 presents implementation schemes for the coexistence of the two versions.

The basic components of network management in SNMPv2 are the same as version 1. They are the agent and the manager, both performing the same functions. The manager-to-manager communication, shown in Figure 4.8, is formalized in version 2 by adding an additional message. Thus, the organizational model in version 2 remains essentially the same. In spite of the lack of security enhancements, major improvements to the architecture have been made in SNMPv2. We will list some of the highlights that would motivate the reader's interest in SNMPv2.

Bulk Data Transfer Message: Two significant messages were added. The first is the ability to request and receive bulk data using the get-bulk message. This speeds up the get-next-request process and is especially useful to retrieve data from tables.

Manager-to-Manager Message: The second additional message deals with interoperability between two network management systems. This extends the communication of management messages between management systems and thus makes network management systems interoperable.

Structure of Management Information (SMI): In SNMPv1, SMI is defined as STD 16, which is described in RFCs 1155 and 1212, along with RFC 1215, which describes traps. They have been consolidated and rewritten in RFCs 1902–1904 for SMI in SNMPv2. RFC 1902 deals with SMIv2, RFC 1903 with textual conventions, and RFC 1904 with conformances.

SMIv2 is divided into three parts: module definitions, object definitions, and trap definitions. An ASN.1 macro, MODULE-IDENTITY, is used to define an information module. It concisely conveys the semantics of the information module. The OBJECT-TYPE macro defines the syntax and semantics of a managed object. The trap is also termed notification and is defined by a NOTIFICATION-TYPE macro.

Textual Conventions are designed to help define new data types. They are also intended to make the semantics consistent and clear to the human reader. Although new data types could have been created using new ASN.1 class and tag, the decision was made to use the existing defined class types and apply restrictions to them.

Conformance Statements help the customer objectively compare features of various products. It also keeps vendors honest in claiming their product as being compatible with a given SNMP version. Compliance defines a minimum set of capabilities. Additional capabilities may be offered as options in the product by vendors.

Table Enhancements: Using a newly defined columnar object with a Syntax clause, *RowStatus*, conceptual rows could be added to or deleted from an aggregate object table. Further, a table can be expanded by augmenting another table to it, which is helpful in adding additional columnar objects to an existing aggregate object.

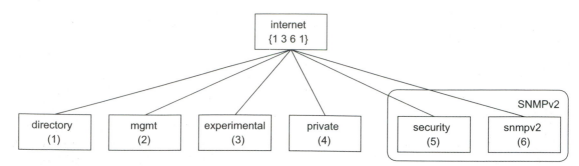

Figure 6.1 SNMPv2 Internet Group

MIB Enhancements: In SNMPv2, the Internet node in the MIB has two new subgroups: security and snmpV2, as shown in Figure 6.1. There are significant changes to System and SNMP groups of version 1. There are changes to the System group made under mib-2 node in the MIB. The SNMP entities in version 2 are a hybrid, with some entities from the SNMP group, and the rest from the groups under the newly created snmpV2 node.

Transport Mappings: There are several changes to the communication model in SNMPv2. Although use of UDP is the preferred transport protocol mechanism for SNMP management, other transport protocols could be used with SNMPv2. The mappings needed to define other protocols on to UDP are the subject of RFC 1906.

6.2   SNMPv2 SYSTEM ARCHITECTURE

SNMPv2 system architecture looks essentially the same as that of version 1, as shown in Figure 4.9. However, there are two significant enhancements in SNMPv2 architecture, which are shown in Figure 6.2. First, there are seven messages instead of five as in Figure 4.9. Second, two manager applications can communicate with each other at the peer level. Another message, report message, is missing from Figure 6.2. This is because even though it has been defined as a message, SNMPv2 Working Group did not specify its details. It is left for the implementers to generate the specifications. It is not currently being used and is hence omitted from the figure.

The messages *get-request*, *get-next request*, and *set-request* are the same as in version 1 and are generated by the manager application. The message, response, is also the same as get-response in version 1, and is now generated by both agent and manager applications. It is generated by the agent application in response to a get or set message from the manager application. It is also generated by the manager application in response to an *inform-request* message from another manager application.

An *inform-request* message is generated by a manager application and is transmitted to another manager application. As mentioned above, the receiving manager application responds with a response message. This set of communication messages is a powerful enhancement in SNMPv2, since it makes two network management systems interoperable.

The message *get-bulk-request* is generated by manager application. It is used to transfer large amounts of data from the agent to the manager, especially if it includes retrieval of table data. The retrieval is fast and efficient. The receiving entity generates and fills data for each entry in the request and transmits all the data as a response message back to the originator of the request.

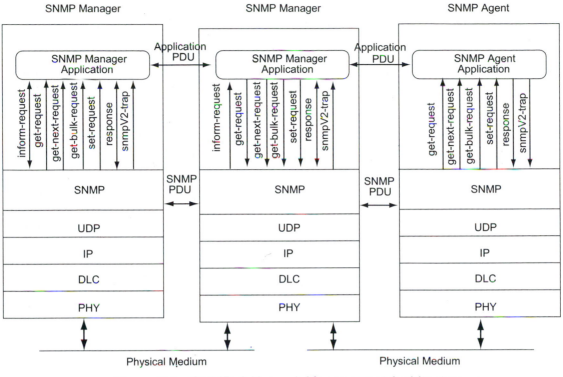

Figure 6.2 SNMPv2 Network Management Architecture

An *SNMPv2-trap event,* known as trap in version 1, is generated and transmitted by an agent process when an exceptional situation occurs. The destination to which it is sent is implementation-dependent. The PDU structure has been modified to be consistent with other PDUs.

Another enhancement in SNMPv2 over version 1 is the mapping of the SNMP layer over multiple transport domains. An example of this is shown in Figure 6.3, in which an SNMPv2 agent riding over a connectionless OSI transport layer protocol, Connectionless-Mode Network Service (CLNS), communicates with an SNMPv2 manager over the UDP transport layer. RFC 1906, which describes transport mappings, addresses a few well-known *transport layer mappings*; others can be added using a similar structure.

Details on the MIB relating to SNMPv2 are covered in Section 6.4 and communication protocol aspects of messages in Section 6.5. Although not a standard, RFC 1283 specifies SNMP over Connection-Oriented Transport Service (COTS), a connection-oriented OSI transport protocol. However, SNMP is not specified over connection-oriented Internet protocol, TCP.

6.3 SNMPv2 STRUCTURE OF MANAGEMENT INFORMATION

There are several changes to SMI in version 2, as well as enhancements to SMIv2 over that of SMIv1. As stated earlier, SMIv2 [RFC 1902] is divided into three parts: module definitions, object definitions, and notification definitions.

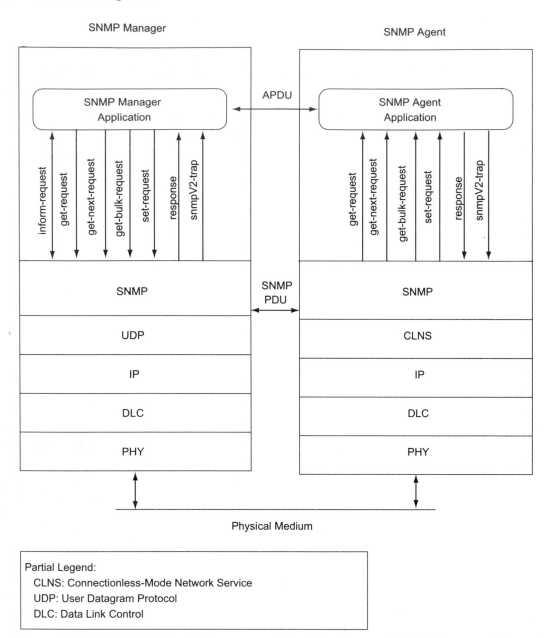

Figure 6.3 SNMPv2 Network Management Architecture on Multiple Transport Domains

We introduced the concept of a module in Section 3.6.1, which is a group of assignments that are related to each other. Module definitions describe the semantics of an information module and are formally defined by an ASN.1 macro, MODULE-IDENTITY.

Object definitions are used to describe managed objects. The OBJECT-TYPE macro that we discussed in Section 4.7.3 is used to define a managed object. OBJECT-TYPE conveys both syntax and semantics of the managed object.

Notification in SMIv2 is equivalent to trap in SMIv1. In SMIv1, trap is formally specified by an ASN.1 macro, TRAP-TYPE. In SMIv2, notification is specified by an ASN.1 macro, NOTIFICATION-TYPE, and conveys both its syntax and semantics.

In addition to the above three parts, there is an additional part defined in SMIv2, which formalizes the assignment of OBJECT IDENTIFIER. Even though we have two assignments in SMIv1, namely, object name and trap, they are not formally structured. In SMIv2, an ASN.1 macro, OBJECT-IDENTITY is introduced for the assignment of object name and notification to OBJECT IDENTIFIER, as shown in Figure 6.4.

6.3.1 SMI Definitions for SNMPv2

Figure 6.4 shows a skeleton of the SMIv2 and the reader is referred to RFC 1902 for a complete set of definitions. We have taken the liberty of presenting the definitions with some additional comments (marked by *) and structural indentations to bring out clearly the BEGIN and END of macros.

Definitions begin with the high-level nodes under the Internet MIB. Two additional nodes, security and SNMPv2, are introduced. The security node is just a placeholder and is reserved for the future. The *snmpV2* node has three subnodes: *snmpDomains*, *snmpProxys*, and *snmpModules*. The MIB tree showing all these nodes defined in SMIv2 is presented in Figure 6.5.

6.3.2 Information Modules

RFC 1902 defines *information module* as an ASN.1 module defining information relating to network management. SMI describes how to use a subset of ASN.1 to define an information module.

There are three kinds of information modules that are defined in SNMPv2. They are MIB modules, compliance statements for MIB modules, and capability statements for agent implementations. This classification scheme does not impose rigid taxonomy in the definition of managed objects. Figure 6.6 shows an example where *conformance information* and *compliance statements* are part of the SNMP group of SNMPv2 MIB. As we shall see later, the SNMP group in SNMPv2 contains some of the objects of version 1 and some new objects and object groups (to be defined later). It also has information on conformance requirements. In the example shown, the mandatory groups in implementing SNMPv2 are *snmpGroup*, *snmpSetGroup*, *systemGroup*, and *snmpBasicNotificationsGroup*. Thus, if a network component vendor claims that its management agent is SNMPv2 compliant, these groups as they are defined in SNMPv2 should be implemented.

MIB specifications contain only compliant statements in them. The *agent-capability statements* are part of implementation in the agent by the vendor. It might be included as part of an "enterprise-specific" module.

The information on SMIv2 has been split into three parts in the documentation. MIB modules for SMIv2 are covered in RFC 1902. The textual conventions to be used to describe MIB modules have been formalized in RFC 1903. The conformance information, which encompasses both compliance and agent capabilities, is covered in RFC 1904.

6.3.3 SNMP Keywords

Keywords used in the specifications of SMIv2 are a subset of ASN.1. But it is a different subset from that of SMIv1. Table 6.1 shows the comparison of keywords used in the two versions. We will address

```
SNMPv2-SMI DEFINITIONS ::=
BEGIN

-- the path to the root
      org          OBJECT IDENTIFIER ::= {iso 3}
                    ...
      private      OBJECT IDENTIFIER ::= {internet 4}
      enterprises  OBJECT IDENTIFIER ::= {private 1}
      security     OBJECT IDENTIFIER ::= {internet 5}
      snmpV2       OBJECT IDENTIFIER ::= {internet 6}
      -- transport domains
      snmpDomains      OBJECT IDENTIFIER ::= {snmpV2 1}
            -- transport proxies
      snmpProxys       OBJECT IDENTIFIER ::= {snmpV2 2}
      --module identities
      snmpModules      OBJECT IDENTIFIER ::= {snmpV2 3}
      -- definitions for information modules
      MODULE-IDENTITY MACRO
      BEGIN
            <clauses> ::= <values>
      END
      -- definitions for OBJECT IDENTIFIER assignments*
      OBJECT-IDENTITY MACRO ::=
      BEGIN
                  <clauses> ::= <values>
      END

            --names of objects
            objectName ::=      OBJECT IDENTIFIER
            notificationName ::= OBJECT IDENTIFIER
      -- syntax of objects
                  <objectSyntax Productions>
                  <dataType Productions>
      -- definition of objects
      OBJECT-TYPE MACRO ::=
      BEGIN
            <clauses> ::= <values>
      END
      -- definition for notification
      NOTIFICATION-TYPE MACRO ::=
      BEGIN
            <clauses> ::= <values>
      END

      -- definition of administration identifiers
            zeroDotZero ::= { 0 0 } -- a value for null identifiers
END
```

Figure 6.4   Definitions of SMI for SNMPv2 (Skeleton)

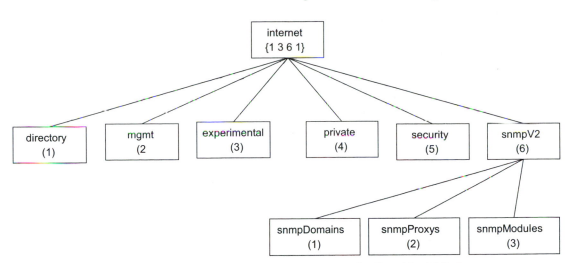

Figure 6.5 SNMPv2 Internet Nodes Defined in SMIv2

the new keywords for specific applications as we discuss them. It is worth noting here that some of the general keywords have been replaced with limited keywords. Thus, Counter is replaced by Counter32, Gauge by Gauge32, and INTEGER by Integer32. The NetworkAddress is deleted from use and only IpAddress is used.

It is also to be noted that reference in IMPORTS clause or in clauses of SNMPv2 macros to an informational module is not through "descriptor" as it was in version 1. It is referenced through specifying its module name, an enhancement in SNMPv2.

It should be observed that the expansion of the ASN.1 module macro occurs during the implementation phase of a product, and not at run-time.

6.3.4 Module Definitions

The MODULE-IDENTITY macro is added to SMIv2 specifying an informational module. It provides administrative information regarding the informational module as well as revision history. SMIv2 MODULE-IDENTITY macro is presented in Figure 6.7.

Figure 6.8 shows an example of a MODULE-IDENTITY macro (a real-world example of a non-existent module) for a network component vendor, InfoTech Services, Inc. (isi), which is updating their private-enterprises-isi MIB module {private.enterprises.isi}.

The last updated clause is mandatory and contains the date and time in UTC time format [RFC 1902]. "Z" refers to Greenwich Mean Time. The Text clause uses the NVT ASCII character set [RFC 854], which is a printable set. All clauses, except the Revision clause, must be present in the macro.

6.3.5 Object Definitions

The OBJECT-IDENTITY macro has been added in SMIv2 and is used to define information about an OBJECT-IDENTIFIER. It is presented in Figure 6.9. The STATUS clause has one of three values: current, deprecated, or obsolete. The value *mandatory* in SMIv1 is replaced with the value *current* in SMIv2. The value *optional* is not used in SMIv2. The new value, *deprecated*, has been added to define

```
SNMPv2-MIB DEFINITIONS ::=
BEGIN
        ...         ...         ...         ...
snmpMIB      MODULE IDENTITY ::= {snmpModules 1}
        ...         ...         ...         ...
snmpMIBObjects   OBJECT IDENTIFIER ::= {snmpMIB 1}

-- the SNMP group
snmp                OBJECT IDENTIFIER ::= {mib-2 11}
snmpInPkts              OBJECT-TYPE ::= {snmp 1}
snmpOutPkts             OBJECT-TYPE ::= { snmp 2}
        ...         ...         ...         ...
snmpSet             OBJECT IDENTIFIER ::= {snmpmibObjects 6}
snmpSetSerialNo         OBJECT-TYPE ::= { snmpSet 1}

-- conformance information
snmpMIBConformance
OBJECT IDENTIFIER ::=  {snmpMIB 2}
snmpMIBCompliances
                OBJECT IDENTIFIER  ::=  {snmpMIBConformance 1}
snmpMIBGroups    OBJECT IDENTIFIER  ::=  {snmpMIBConformance 2}

-- compliance statements

snmpBasicCompliance MODULE-COMPLIANCE
        STATUS      current
        DESCRIPTION
                "The compliance statement for SNMPv2 entities which
                implement the SNMPv2 MIB."
        MODULE      -- this module
            MANDATORY-GROUPS  {snmpGroup, snmpSetGroup,
                                systemGroup,
                                snmpBasicNotificationsGroup}
            GROUP       snmpCommunityGroup
            DESCRIPTION
                "This group is mandatory for SNMPv2 entities which support
                community-based authentication."
        ::= {snmpMIBCompliances  2 }

-- units of conformance
snmpGroup  OBJECT-GROUP   ::= {snmpMIBGroups 8}
snmpCommunityGroup     OBJECT-GROUP ::= {snmpMIBGroups 9}
snmpObsoleteGroup OBJECT-GROUP ::=  {snmpMIBGroups 10}
        ...         ...         ...         ...

END
```

Figure 6.6 Example of the SNMP Group including Conformance and Compliance in SNMPv2 MIB

Table 6.1 SNMP Keywords

KEYWORD	SNMPV1	SNMPV2
ACCESS	Y	Y
AGENT-CAPABILITIES	N	Y
AUGMENTS	N	Y
BEGIN	Y	Y
BITS	N	Y
CONTACT-INFO	N	Y
CREATION-REQUIRES	N	Y
Counter	Y	N
Counter32	N	Y
Counter64	N	Y
DEFINITIONS	Y	Y
DEFVAL	Y	Y
DESCRIPTION	Y	Y
DISPLAY-HINT	N	Y
END	Y	Y
ENTERPRISE	Y	N
FROM	Y	Y
GROUP	N	Y
Gauge	Y	N
Gauge32	N	Y
IDENTIFIER	Y	Y
IMPLIED	N	Y
IMPORTS	Y	Y
INCLUDES	N	Y
INDEX	Y	Y
INTEGER	Y	Y
Integer32	N	Y
IpAddress	Y	Y
LAST-UPDATED	N	Y
MANDATORY-GROUPS	N	Y
MAX-ACCESS	N	Y
MIN-ACCESS	N	Y
MODULE	N	Y
MODULE-COMPLIANCE	N	Y
MODULE-IDENTITY	N	Y
NOTIFICATION-GROUP	N	Y

Table 6.1   (continued)

KEYWORD	SNMPV1	SNMPV2
NOTIFICATION-TYPE	N	Y
NetworkAddress	Y	N
OBJECT	Y	Y
OBJECT-GROUP	N	Y
OBJECT-IDENTITY	N	Y
OBJECT-TYPE	Y	Y
OBJECTS	N	Y
OCTET	Y	Y
OF	Y	Y
ORGANIZATION	N	Y
Opaque	Y	Y
PRODUCT-RELEASE	N	Y
REFERENCE	Y	Y
REVISION	N	Y
SEQUENCE	Y	Y
SIZE	Y	Y
STATUS	Y	Y
STRING	Y	Y
SUPPORTS	N	Y
SYNTAX	Y	Y
TEXTUAL-CONVENTION	N	Y
TRAP-TYPE	Y	N
TimeTicks	Y	Y
UNITS	N	Y
Unsigned32	N	Y
VARIABLES	Y	N
VARIATION	N	Y
WRITE-SYNTAX	N	Y

objects that are required to be implemented in the current version, but may not exist in future versions of SNMP. This allows for backward compatibility during the transition between versions.

Although the REFERENCE clause was used only in an OBJECT-TYPE construct in SMIv1, it is used in many constructs in version 2.

Let us extend our hypothetical example of InfoTech Services and suppose that ISI makes a class of router products. It is given an OBJECT IDENTIFIER as isiRouter OBJECT IDENTIFIER ::= {private. enterprises.isi 1}. The class of router products can be specified at a high level using the OBJECT-IDEN-

```
MODULE-IDENTITY MACRO ::=
BEGIN
        TYPE NOTATION ::=
                            "LAST-UPDATED" value (Update UTCTime)
                            "ORGANIZATION" Text
                            "CONTACT-INFO" Text
                            "DESCRIPTION" Text
                            RevisionPart
        VALUE NOTATION ::=
                            value (VALUE OBJECT IDENTIFIER)
        RevisionPart ::=    Revisions | empty
        Revisions ::= Revision | Revisions Revision
        Revision ::=
            "REVISION" value (UTCTime)
            "DESCRIPTION" Text
        -- uses the NVT ASCII character set
        Text ::= """" string """"
END
```

Figure 6.7 MODULE-IDENTITY Macro

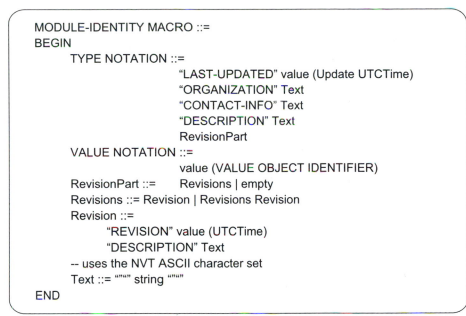

Figure 6.8 Example of MODULE-IDENTITY Macro

TITY macro as shown in Figure 6.10(a). The status of the *isiRouter* is current and is described as an 8-slot IP router. A reference is given for obtaining the details.

A specific implementation of the router in *isiRouter* class of products is *routerIsi123*. This is a managed object specified by the OBJECT-TYPE macro shown in Figure 6.10(b). We are already familiar with the OBJECT-TYPE macro by now.

Let us make sure that we clearly understand the terminology used with the term OBJECT. OBJECT IDENTIFIER defines the administrative identification of a node in the MIB. The OBJECT IDENTITY macro is used to assign an object identifier value to the object node in the MIB. The OBJECT-TYPE is a macro that defines the *type* of a managed object. It is also used to describe a new type of object. As we have learned in the previous chapters, an *object instance* is a specific instance of the *object (type)*. Thus, a specific instance of the *routerIsi123* could be identified by its IP address 10.1.2.3.

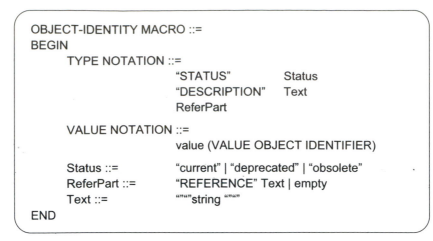

```
OBJECT-IDENTITY MACRO ::=
BEGIN
        TYPE NOTATION ::=
                                "STATUS"            Status
                                "DESCRIPTION"       Text
                                ReferPart

        VALUE NOTATION ::=
                                value (VALUE OBJECT IDENTIFIER)

        Status ::=              "current" | "deprecated" | "obsolete"
        ReferPart ::=           "REFERENCE" Text | empty
        Text ::=                """"string """"
END
```

Figure 6.9 OBJECT-IDENTITY Macro

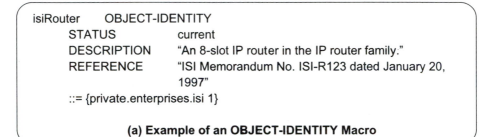

```
isiRouter      OBJECT-IDENTITY
        STATUS              current
        DESCRIPTION         "An 8-slot IP router in the IP router family."
        REFERENCE           "ISI Memorandum No. ISI-R123 dated January 20,
                            1997"
        ::= {private.enterprises.isi 1}
```

(a) Example of an OBJECT-IDENTITY Macro

```
routerIsi123  OBJECT-TYPE
        SYNTAX             DisplayString
        MAX-ACCESS         read-only
        STATUS             current
        DESCRIPTION        "An 8-slot IP router that can switch up to
                           100 million packets per second."
        ::= {isiRouter 1}
```

(b) Example of an OBJECT-TYPE Macro

Figure 6.10 Example of OBJECT-IDENTITY and OBJECT-TYPE Macros

Comparing Figure 6.10(a) with Figure 6.10(b) we observe the difference between OBJECT-IDENTITY and OBJECT-TYPE. The status clause appears in both. The description clause that also appears in both describes different aspects of the object. The OBJECT-IDENTITY describes the high-level description; whereas the OBJECT-TYPE description focuses on the details needed for implementation.

Let us now visualize the router in Figure 6.10 with several slots for interface cards. We want to define the parameters associated with each interface. The parameters that are managed objects (or entities) are defined by an aggregate object, *IfTable*. For example, the *ifNumber* for our router example could be 32 if the router has eight slots and each card has four ports.

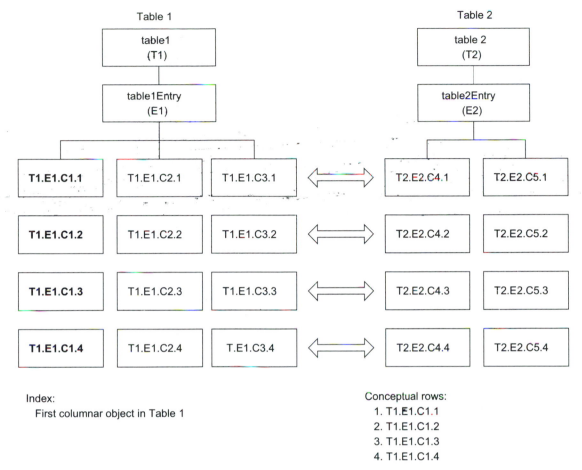

Figure 6.11 Augmentation of Tables

SMIv2 extends the concept table for an aggregate object from a single table to multiple tables. This allows for expansion of managed objects when the number of columnar objects needs to be increased, or when the objects are best organized by grouping them hierarchically. Let us first consider the case of adding columnar objects to an existing table with the following restrictions: (a) the number of conceptual rows is not affected by the addition; (b) there is one-to-one correspondence between the rows of the two tables; and (c) the INDEX of the second table is the same as that of the first table. This is shown in Figure 6.11.

Table 1 is called the aggregate object *table1* and has three columns and four rows; and Table 2 is called the aggregate object *table2* and has two columns and four rows. There is a one-to-one correspondence in rows between the two tables. The row object for table1 is *table1Entry*, and the row object for table 2 is *table2Entry*. The INDEX is defined in Table 1 for both tables and it is the columnar object T1.E1.C1. We are using the notations T1, E1, C1, etc., for easier visual conceptualization of the instance of an object in a table using the prefixes of table ID (e.g., T1) and entry (e.g., E1). The columnar object notation starts with C (e.g., C1). The value or values suffixed with the columnar object identifier uniquely identifies the row. Thus, the list of objects identified by the index T1.E1.C1.2 is the ones in the second rows of

```
table1Entry OBJECT-TYPE
        SYNTAX          TableT1Entry
        MAX-ACCESS      not-accessible
        STATUS          current
        DESCRIPTION     "An entry (conceptual row) in table T1"
        INDEX           {T1.E1.C1}
            ::= { table1 1}
table2Entry OBJECT-TYPE
        SYNTAX          TableT2Entry
        MAX-ACCESS      not-accessible
        STATUS          current
        DESCRIPTION     "An entry (conceptual row) in table T2"
        AUGMENTS        {table1Entry}
            ::= {table2 1}
```

Figure 6.12   ASN.1 Constructs for Augmentation of Tables

Tables 1 and 2. The value of the columnar object T2.E2.C4 in Table T2 corresponding to index T1.E1.C1.2 is T2.E2.C4.2. Table 1 is called the **base table**, and Table 2 is the **augmented table**. The indexing scheme comprises two clauses, the INDEX clause and the AUGMENTS clause. The constructs for the rows of the two tables in Figure 6.11 are shown in Figure 6.12. The object *table1Entry* has the INDEX clause and *table2Entry* has the AUGMENTS clause that refers to *table1Entry*. The combination of the two tables still provides four conceptual rows, T1.E1.C1.1 through T1.E1.C1.4 (identified by the index), the same number of rows as in the base table.

Figure 6.13 shows an example of augmentation of tables. We have augmented *ipAddrTable* in the standard MIB with a proprietary table, *IpAugAddrTable* that could add additional information to the rows of the table. *IpAddrTable* is the base table and *ipAugAddrTable* is the augmented table. In a practical case, the *ipAugAddrTable* could add two more columnar objects defining the board and port number associated with the *ipAdEntIfIndex*.

A table with a larger number of rows (**dense table**) can be augmented to the base table with combined indices of both, as shown in Figure 6.14. The INDEX clause for combining unequal-sized tables is the combined indices; i.e., combined columnar objects as the INDEX clause for the added aggregate object. In Figure 6.14, Table 1 consists of two rows and three columnar objects, T1.E1.C1, T1.E1.C2, and T1.E1.C3, with the first columnar object T1.E1.C1 being the index. Table 2 has four rows and two columnar objects, T2.E2.C4 and T2.E2.C5, with its first columnar object, T2.E2.C4, being the index. The combined index for specifying the aggregate object of Table 2 appended to Table 1 is the set of both first columnar objects, T1.E1.C1 and T2.E2.C4. Table 1 is called the **base table** and Table 2 is called the **dependent table**. As we see in Figure 6.14, the combined base table and the dependent table could have a maximum of 8 conceptual rows (multiplication of the rows of the two tables).

Figure 6.15 shows the constructs for augmenting a dense table to a base table. The two table objects, *table1* and *table2*, are nodes under the node table. The *table1Entry* defines a row in *table1* with the columnar object T1.E1.C1 as the index. The *table2Entry* is a row in *table2*. Its index is defined by the indices of both tables, namely T1.E1.C1 and T2.E2.C3.

We can visualize the application of augmentation of a dense table with an example of a router with multiple slots, each slot containing a particular type of board, for example, LEC and Ethernet shown in

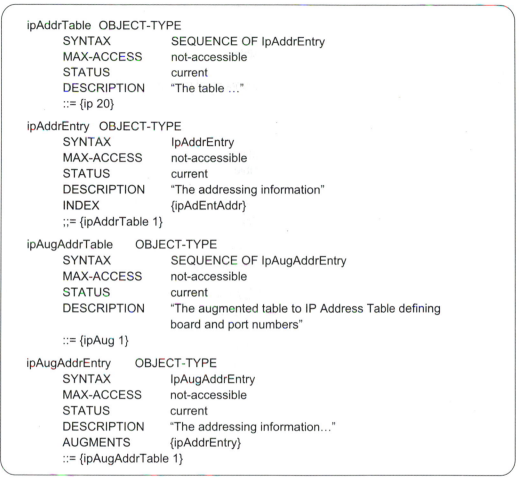

```
ipAddrTable  OBJECT-TYPE
        SYNTAX          SEQUENCE OF IpAddrEntry
        MAX-ACCESS      not-accessible
        STATUS          current
        DESCRIPTION     "The table ..."
        ::= {ip 20}

ipAddrEntry  OBJECT-TYPE
        SYNTAX          IpAddrEntry
        MAX-ACCESS      not-accessible
        STATUS          current
        DESCRIPTION     "The addressing information"
        INDEX           {ipAdEntAddr}
        ;;= {ipAddrTable 1}

ipAugAddrTable    OBJECT-TYPE
        SYNTAX          SEQUENCE OF IpAugAddrEntry
        MAX-ACCESS      not-accessible
        STATUS          current
        DESCRIPTION     "The augmented table to IP Address Table defining
                        board and port numbers"

        ::= {ipAug 1}

ipAugAddrEntry    OBJECT-TYPE
        SYNTAX          IpAugAddrEntry
        MAX-ACCESS      not-accessible
        STATUS          current
        DESCRIPTION     "The addressing information..."
        AUGMENTS        {ipAddrEntry}
        ::= {ipAugAddrTable 1}
```

Figure 6.13   Example of Augmentation of Tables

Figure 4.3(c). The slot and the board type will be defined in Table 1. Each board may have a different number of physical ports. The port configuration is defined by Table 2. By using the combination of the two tables, we can specify the details associated with a given port in a given slot.

The third possible scenario in appending an aggregate object to an existing aggregate object is the case where the augmented table has fewer rows than that of the base table. This is called a **sparse dependent table** case and is shown in Figure 6.16. In this example, the index for the second table is the same as that for the base table and the constructs are similar to the ones shown in Figure 6.12 except that the AUGMENTS clause is substituted with the INDEX clause for *table2Entry*. This is shown in Figure 6.17.

In SNMPv2, operational procedures were introduced for the creation and deletion of a row in a table. However, prior to discussing these procedures, let us first look at the textual convention that was specified to create a new object type in designing MIB modules. We will return to row creation and deletion in Section 6.3.7.

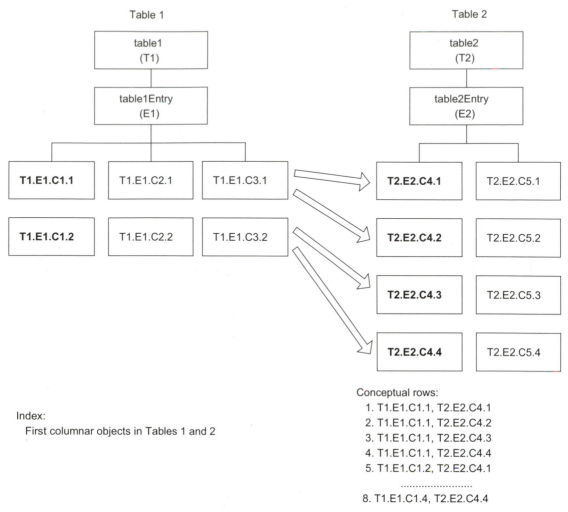

Figure 6.14 Combined Indexing of Tables

6.3.6   Textual Conventions

Textual conventions are designed to help definition of new data types following the structure defined in SMIv2. It is also intended to make the semantics consistent and clear to the human reader. Although new data types could have been created using new ASN.1 class and tag, the decision was made to use the existing defined class types and apply restrictions to them. This is accomplished by defining an ASN.1 macro, TEXTUAL-CONVENTION, in SMIv2.

The TEXTUAL-CONVENTION macro concisely conveys the syntax and semantics associated with a textual convention. SNMP-based management objects defined using a textual convention are encoded by the same Basic Encoding Rules that define their primitive types. However, they do have the special semantics as defined in the macro. For all textual conventions defined in an information module, the name shall be unique and mnemonic, similar to the data type and shall not exceed 64 characters. However, it is usually limited to 32 characters.

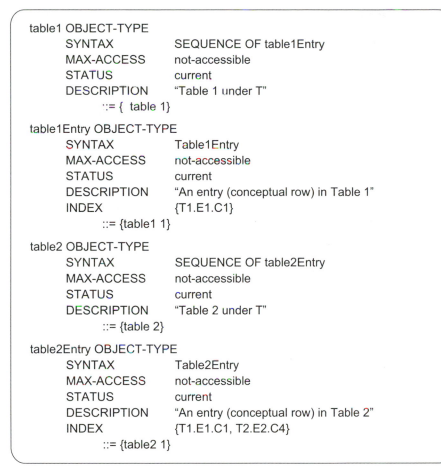

```
table1 OBJECT-TYPE
        SYNTAX              SEQUENCE OF table1Entry
        MAX-ACCESS          not-accessible
        STATUS              current
        DESCRIPTION         "Table 1 under T"
            ::= { table 1}

table1Entry OBJECT-TYPE
        SYNTAX              Table1Entry
        MAX-ACCESS          not-accessible
        STATUS              current
        DESCRIPTION         "An entry (conceptual row) in Table 1"
        INDEX               {T1.E1.C1}
            ::= {table1 1}

table2 OBJECT-TYPE
        SYNTAX              SEQUENCE OF table2Entry
        MAX-ACCESS          not-accessible
        STATUS              current
        DESCRIPTION         "Table 2 under T"
            ::= {table 2}

table2Entry OBJECT-TYPE
        SYNTAX              Table2Entry
        MAX-ACCESS          not-accessible
        STATUS              current
        DESCRIPTION         "An entry (conceptual row) in Table 2"
        INDEX               {T1.E1.C1, T2.E2.C4}
            ::= {table2 1}
```

Figure 6.15   ASN.1 Constructs for Augmenting Dense Table

Let us now compare the definition of a type in SMIv1 with SMIv2. The textual convention was defined in SNMPv1 as an ASN.1 type assignment. For example, the textual convention for data type *DisplayString* in SNMPv1, from RFC 1213, is

```
DisplayString ::= OCTET STRING
-- This data type is used to model textual information taken from the NVT
-- ASCII character set. By convention, objects with this syntax are
-- declared as having
-- SIZE (0..255).
```

The same example of DisplayString in SNMPv2 is defined as:

```
DisplayString ::= TEXTUAL-CONVENTION
        DISPLAY-HINT "255a"
        STATUS          current
        DESCRIPTION "Represents textual information taken from the NVT ASCII character
                    set, as defined in pages 4, 10-11 of RFC 854. ...."
        SYNTAX          OCTET STRING (SIZE (0..255) )
```

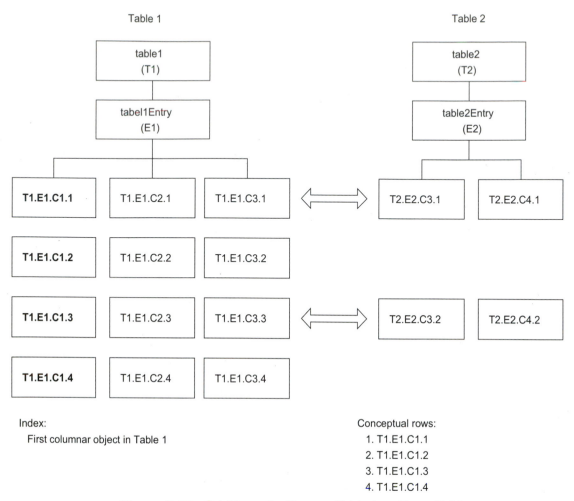

Figure 6.16 Addition of a Sparse Table to a Base Table

As we can see from the above example, the TEXTUAL-CONVENTION in SNMPv2 is defined as data type, and is used to convey the syntax and semantics of a textual convention. The macro for textual conventions is defined in RFC 1903, and a skeleton of it is presented in Figure 6.18. It has the definition of type and value notations with the formalized definition of data types.

All clauses except *DisplayPart* in the TEXTUAL-CONVENTION macro are self-explanatory and represent similar clauses as in SMIv1. The *DISPLAY-HINT* clause, which is optional, gives a hint as to how the value of an instance of an object, with the syntax defined using this textual convention, might be displayed. It is applicable to the situations where the underlying primitive type is either INTEGER or OCTET STRING.

For INTEGER type, the display consists of two parts. The first part is a single character denoting the display format: "a" for ASCII, "b" for binary, "d" for decimal, "o" for octal, and "x" for hexadecimal. It is followed by a hyphen and an integer in the case of decimal display indicating the number of decimal points. For example, a hundredths value of 1234 with DISPLAY-HINT "d-2" is displayed as 12.34.

For OCTET-STRING type, the display hint consists of one or more octet-format specifications. A brief description of each part is shown in Table 6.2. For example, the DISPLAY-HINT "255a" indicates that the *DisplayString* is an ASCII string of up to a maximum of 255 characters.

```
table1 OBJECT-TYPE
        SYNTAX              SEQUENCE OF table1Entry
        MAX-ACCESS          not-accessible
        STATUS              current
        DESCRIPTION         "Table 1 under T"
           ::= { table 1}

table1Entry OBJECT-TYPE
        SYNTAX              Table1Entry
        MAX-ACCESS          not-accessible
        STATUS              current
        DESCRIPTION         "An entry (conceptual row) in Table 1"
        INDEX               {T1.E1.1}
           ::= {table1 1}

table2 OBJECT-TYPE
        SYNTAX              SEQUENCE OF table2Entry
        MAX-ACCESS          not-accessible
        STATUS              current
        DESCRIPTION         "Table 2 under T"
           ::= {table 2}

table2Entry OBJECT-TYPE
        SYNTAX              Table2Entry
        MAX-ACCESS          not-accessible
        STATUS              current
        DESCRIPTION         "An entry (conceptual row) in Table 2"
        INDEX               {table1Entry}
           ::= {table2 1}
```

Figure 6.17   ASN.1 Constructs for Augmenting Sparse Table

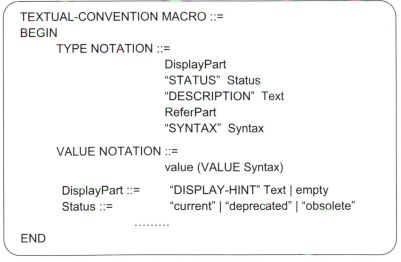

```
TEXTUAL-CONVENTION MACRO ::=
BEGIN
     TYPE NOTATION ::=
                        DisplayPart
                        "STATUS"  Status
                        "DESCRIPTION"  Text
                        ReferPart
                        "SYNTAX"  Syntax

     VALUE NOTATION ::=
                        value (VALUE Syntax)

     DisplayPart ::=    "DISPLAY-HINT" Text | empty
     Status ::=         "current" | "deprecated" | "obsolete"
                    .........
END
```

Figure 6.18   TEXTUAL-CONVENTION Macro [RFC 1903]

Table 6.2   DISPLAY-HINT for Octet-Format

1	(Optional) repeat indicator "*"	An integer, indicated by *, which specifies how many times the remainder of this octet-format should be repeated
2	Octet length	One or more decimal digits specifying the number of octets
3	Display format	"b" for binary, "x" for hexadecimal, "d" for decimal, "o" for octal, and "a" for ASCII for display
4	(Optional) display separator character	A single character other than a decimal digit or "*" produced after each application of the octet specification.
5	(Optional) repeat terminator character	A single character other than a decimal digit or "*" present if display character is present. Produced after the second and third part.

Table 6.3 shows the types for which textual conventions were specified in SMIv2. A brief description for each type is also given. They are applicable to all MIB modules. Only those textual conventions whose status is current are given in the table. One of the important textual conventions is *RowStatus*, which is used for the creation and deletion of conceptual rows, which we will discuss next.

Table 6.3   SMIv2 Textual Conventions for Initial Data Types

DisplayString	Textual information from NVT ASCII character set [RFC 854]
PhysAddress	Media- or physical-level address
MacAddress	IEEE 802 MAC address
TruthValue	Boolean value; INTEGER {true (1), false (2)}
TestAndIncr	Integer-valued information used for atomic operations
AutonomousType	An independently extensible type identification value
VariablePointer	Pointer to a specific object instance; e.g., syscontact.0, ifInOctets.3
RowPointer	Pointer to a conceptual row
RowStatus	Used to manage the creation and deletion of conceptual rows and is used as the value of the SYNTAX clause for the status column of a conceptual row
TimeStamp	Value of sysUpTime at which a specific occurrence happened
TimeInterval	Period of time, measured in units of 0.01 seconds
DateandTime	Date–time specifications
StorageType	Implementation information on the memory realization of a conceptual row as to the volatility and permanency
Tdomain	Kind of transport service
Taddress	Transport service address

6.3.7 Creation and Deletion of Rows in Tables

The creation of a row and deletion of a row are significant new features in SMIv2. This is patterned after a similar procedure that was developed for RMON, which we will cover in Chapter 8. There are two methods to create a row in a table. The first is to create a row and make it active, which is available immediately. The second method is to create the row and make it available at a later time. This means that we need to know the status of the row as to its availability.

The information on the status of the row is accomplished by introducing a new column, called the *status* column. In Table 6.3, we observe that for the textual convention, RowStatus is used as the value of the SYNTAX clause for the *status* column of a conceptual row. Table 6.4 shows the status with enumerated integer syntax for the six states associated with the row status. The last three states, along with the first one (1, 4, 5, and 6), are those that the manager uses to create or delete rows on the agent. The first three states (1, 2, and 3) are those that are used by the agent to send responses to the manager.

The MAX-ACCESS clause is extended to include "read-create" for the *status* object, which includes read, write, and create privileges. It is a superset of read-write. If a *status* columnar object is present, then no other columnar object of the same conceptual row may have a maximal access of "read-write." But it can have objects with maximum access of read-only and not-accessible. If an index object of a conceptual row is also a columnar object (it does not always have to be), it is called *auxiliary object* and its maximum access is made non-accessible. There could be more than one index object to define a conceptual row in a table.

Let us now analyze the create and delete operations using the conceptual table shown in Figure 6.19. The table, *table1*, originally has two rows and three columns. The first column, *status*, has the value of the status of the row as indicated by the enumerated integer syntax of RowStatus textual convention. The second columnar object, *index*, is the index for the conceptual row of *entry1*; and the third columnar object contains non-indexed data. We will illustrate the two types of row-creation and row-deletion operations by adding a third row and then deleting it.

As we notice from Table 6.4, there are two states for RowStatus, *createAndGo* and *createAndWait*, which are action operations. In the former, the manager sends a message to the agent to create a row and make the *status* active immediately. In the latter operation, the manager sends a message to create a

Table 6.4 RowStatus Textual Convention

STATE	ENUMERATION	DESCRIPTION
active	1	Row exists and is operational
notInService	2	Operation on the row is suspended
notReady	3	Row does not have all the columnar objects needed
createAndGo	4	This is a one-step process of creation of a row, immediately goes into the active state
createAndWait	5	Row is under creation and should not be commissioned into service
destroy	6	Same as Invalid in EntryStatus. Row should be deleted

row, but not to make it active immediately. Figure 6.20 shows the Create-and-Go operation. The manager process initiates a Set-Request-PDU to create a conceptual row with the values given for the three columnar instances of the row. The value for the index column is specified by the VarBind *index* = 3. This is suffixed to the other two columnar objects in the new row to be created. The value of *status* is specified as 4, which is the *createAndGo* state as seen in Table 6.4. The *set-request* message also specifies the default value *DefData* for *data.3*, and thus all the information needed to establish the row and

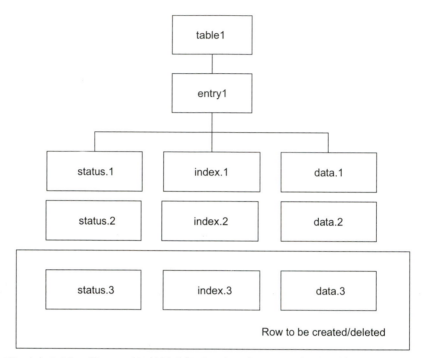

Figure 6.19   Conceptual Table for the Creation and Deletion of a Row

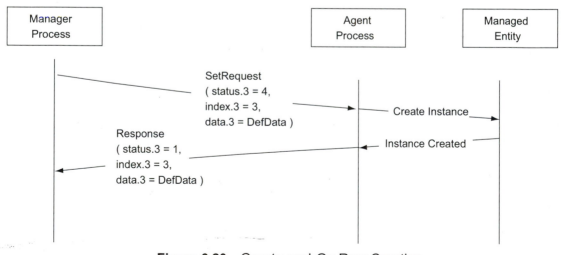

Figure 6.20   Create-and-Go Row Creation

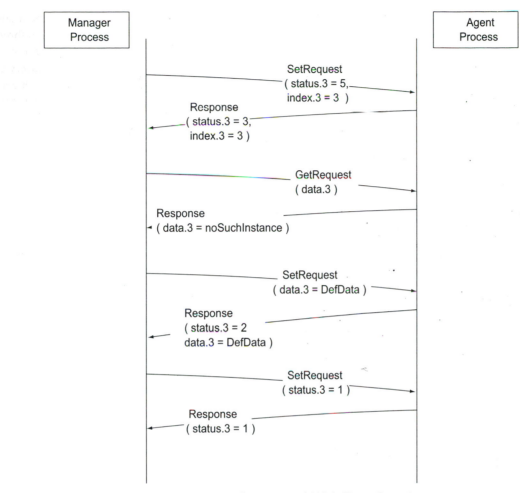

Figure 6.21 Create-and-Wait Row Creation

turn it into an active state is complete. The agent process interacts with the managed entity, creates the instance successfully, and then transmits a response to the manager process. The value of the *status* is 1, which denotes that the row is in an active state. The response also contains the values of the other columnar object instances.

Figure 6.21 presents a scenario for operational sequence in the creation of a row using the Create-and-Wait method. Again, this illustration takes the same scenario of adding the third row to the table shown in Figure 6.17. Only the manager and the agent are shown and not the managed entity in this figure. The manager process sends a Set-Request-PDU to the agent process. The value for *status* is 5, which is to create and wait. The third columnar object expects a default value, which is not in the set-request message. Hence, the agent process responds with a *status* value of 3, which is *notReady*. The manager sends a get-request to get the data for the row. The agent responds with *noSuchInstance* message, indicating that the data value is missing. The manager subsequently sends the value for *data* and receives a response of *notInService* (2) from the agent. The fourth and final exchange of messages in the figure is to activate the row with a *status* value of 1. With each message received from the manager, the agent either validates or sets the instance value on the managed entity.

Table 6.5 Table of States for Row Creation and Deletion

ACTION	A STATUS COLUMN DOES NOT EXIST	B STATUS COLUMN NOTREADY	C STATUS COLUMN NOTINSERVICE	D STATUS COLUMN ACTIVE
Set status column to createAndGo	noError -> D	inconsistent-Value	inconsistent-Value	inconsistent-Value
Set status column to createAndWait	noError, see 1 or wrongValue	inconsistent-Value	inconsistent-Value	inconsistent-Value
Set status column to active	inconsistent-Value	inconsistent-Value or see 2 ->D	noError ->D	noError ->D
Set status column to notInService	inconsistent-Value	inconsistent-Value or see 3 -> C	noError ->C	noError ->C or wrongValue
Set status column to destroy	noError ->A	noError ->A	noError ->A	noError ->A
Set any other column to some value	see 4	noError see 1	noError ->C	see 5 ->D

A summary of possible state transitions is given in Table 6.5. The first column lists the action; and the transitions based on the present state are listed in the next four columns.

1. goto B or C, depending on information available to the agent.
2. If other variable bindings included in the same PDU provide values for all columns, which are missing but are required, then return noError and goto D.
3. If other variable bindings included in the same PDU provide values for all columns, which are missing but are required, then return noError and goto C.
4. At the discretion of the agent, the return value may be either: *inconsistentName*: because the agent does not choose to create such an instance when the corresponding RowStatus instance does not exist, or *inconsistentValue*: if the supplied value is inconsistent with the state of some other MIB object's value, or *noError*; because the agent chooses to create the instance.

   If noError is returned, then the instance of the status column must also be created, and the new state is B or C, depending on the information available to the agent. If *inconsistentName* or *inconsistent Value* is returned, the row remains in state A.
5. Depending on the MIB definition for the column/table, either *noError* or *inconsistentValue* may be returned.

   NOTE: Other processing of the set request may result in a response other than *noError* being returned, e.g., wrongValue, *noCreation*, etc.

The operation of deletion of a row is simple. A *set-request* with a value of 6, which denotes *destroy,* for *status,* is sent by the manager process to the agent process. Independent of the current state of the row, the row is deleted and the response sent back by the agent. The instance in the managed entity is deleted in the process. This is shown in Figure 6.22.

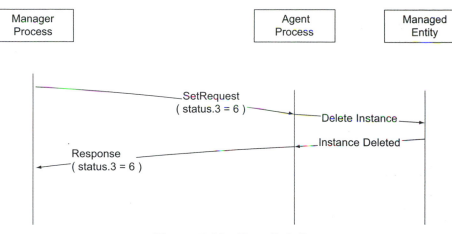

Figure 6.22 Row Deletion

Notification Definitions

The trap information in SMIv1 has been redefined using the NOTIFICATION-TYPE macro in SMIv2. As we will see in Section 6.5, the PDU associated with the trap information is made consistent with other PDUs. The NOTIFICATION-TYPE macro contains unsolicited information that is generated on an exception basis, for example, when set thresholds are crossed. It can be transmitted within either a SNMP-Trap-PDU from an agent or an InformRequest-PDU from a manager. Two examples of a NOT-IFICATION-TYPE macro, drawn from RFC 1902 and RFC 1907 are shown in Figure 6.23. The first example, linkUp, is generated by an agent when a link that has been down comes up.

The OBJECTS clause defines the ordered sequence of MIB objects, which are included in the notification. It may or may not be present. The second example, coldStart, in Figure 6.23, has the OBJECTS clause missing and is not needed.

```
linkUp NOTIFICATION-TYPE
        OBJECTS     {ifIndex}
        STATUS      current
        DESCRIPTION
                "A linkUp trap signifies that the SNMPv2 entity, acting in an agent
                role, recognizes that one of the communication links represented in
                its configuration has come up."
        ::= {snmpTraps 4}


coldStart NOTIFICATION-TYPE
        STATUS      current
        DESCRIPTION
                "A coldStart trap signifies that the SNMPv2 entity, acting in
                an agent role, is reinitializing itself such that its configuration is
                unaltered."
        ::= {snmpTraps 1}
```

Figure 6.23 Examples of NOTIFICATION-TYPE Macro

The other two clauses, STATUS and DESCRIPTION, have the usual mappings.

We have not presented here discussions on refined syntax in some of the macros, as well as extension to informational modules. You are referred to RFC 1902 for a treatment of these, which also discusses the conversion of a managed object from the OSI to the SNMP version.

6.3.9 Conformance Statements

RFC 1904 defines SNMPv2 conformance statements for the implementation of network management standards. A product, generally, is considered to be in compliance with a particular standard when it meets the minimum set of features in its implementation. Minimum requirements for SNMPv2 compliance are called module compliance and are defined by an ASN.1 macro, MODULE-COMPLIANCE. It specifies the minimum MIB modules or a subset of modules that should be implemented. The actual MIB modules that are implemented in an agent are specified by another ASN.1 module, AGENT-CAPABILITIES. For the convenience of defining module compliance and agent capabilities, objects and traps have been combined into groups, which are subsets of MIB modules. Object grouping is defined by an ASN.1 macro, OBJECT-GROUP, and the group of traps is defined by the NOTIFICATION-GROUP macro.

Object Group. The OBJECT-GROUP macro defines a group of related objects in a MIB module and is used to define conformance specifications. It is compiled during implementation, not at run-time. The macro is shown in Figure 6.24. The implementation of an object in an agent implies that it executes the get and set operations from a manager. If an agent in SNMPv2 has not implemented an object, it returns a noSuchObject error message.

```
OBJECT-GROUP MACRO
BEGIN
        TYPE NOTATION ::=
                        ObjectsPart
                        "STATUS" Status
                        "DESCRIPTION" Text
                        ReferPart


        VALUE NOTATION ::=
                        value (VALUE OBJECT IDENTIFIER)


        ObjectsPart ::=        "OBJECTS" "{"objects"}"
        Objects ::=           Object | Objects "," Object
        Object ::=            value (Name  Object Name)
        Status ::=            "current" | "deprecated" | "obsolete"
        ReferPart ::=         "REFERENCE" Text  | empty

        -- uses the NVT ASCII character set
        Text ::=              """" string """"
END
```

Figure 6.24 OBJECT-GROUP Macro

```
systemGroup        OBJECT-GROUP
          OBJECTS     {sysDescr, sysObjectID, sysUpTime, sysContact, sysName,
                      sysLocation, sysServices, sysORLastChange, sysORID,
                      sysORUptime, sysORDesc}
          STATUS      current
          DESCRIPTION     "The system group defines objects that are common
                          to all managed systems."
          ::= {snmpMIBGroups 6}
```

Figure 6.25   Example of an OBJECT-GROUP Macro

The OBJECTS clause names each object contained in the conformance group. Each of the named objects is defined in the same informational module as the OBJECT-GROUP macro and has a MAX-ACCESS clause of "accessible-for-notify," "read-only," "read-write," or "read-create." Every object that is defined in an informational module with a MAX-ACCESS clause other than "not-accessible" is pres-ent in at least one object group. This prevents the mistake of adding an object to an information module, but forgetting to add it to a group.

The STATUS, DESCRIPTION, and REFERENCE clauses have the usual interpretations.

An example of an OBJECT-GROUP, systemGroup in SNMPv2, is shown in Figure 6.25. The system group defines the objects, which pertain to overall information about the system. Since it is so basic, it is implemented in all agent and management systems. All seven entities defined as values for OBJECTS should be implemented. There are some new entities, such as *sysORLastChange*, in the group that were not in SNMPv1. These will be addressed when we discuss SMPv2 MIB in the next section.

Notification Group. The notification group contains notification entities, or what was defined as traps in SMIv1. The NOTIFICATION-GROUP macro is shown in Figure 6.26. The macro is compiled during implementation, not during run-time. The value of an invocation of the NOTIFICATION-GROUP macro is the name of the group, which is an OBJECT IDENTIFIER.

An example of NOTIFICATION-GROUP, *snmpBasicNotificationsGroup*, is shown in Figure 6.27. According to this invocation, the conformance group, *snmpBasicNotificationsGroup*, has two notifications: *coldStart* and *authenticationFailure*.

Module Compliance. The MODULE-COMPLIANCE macro, shown in Figure 6.28, defines the minimum set of requirements for implementation of one or more MIB modules. The expansion of the MODULE-COMPLIANCE macro is done during the implementation and not during run-time. The MODULE-COMPLIANCE macro can be defined as a component of the information module or as a companion module.

The STATUS, DESCRIPTION, and REFERENCE clauses are self-explanatory.

The MODULE clause is used to name each module for which compliance requirements are specified. Modules are identified by the module name and its OBJECT IDENTIFIER. The latter can be dropped if the MODULE-COMPLIANCE is invoked within an MIB module and refers to the encompassing MIB module.

There are two CLAUSES of groups that are specified by the MODULE-COMPLIANCE macro. They are MANDATORY-GROUPS and GROUP. As the name implies, the MANDATORY-CLAUSE

```
NOTIFICATION-GROUP MACRO
BEGIN
      TYPE NOTATION ::=
                              NotificationsPart
                              "STATUS" Status
                              "DESCRIPTION" Text
                              ReferPart


      VALUE NOTATION ::=
                              value (VALUE OBJECT IDENTIFIER)




NotificationsPart ::=         "NOTIFICATIONS" "{"Notifications"}"
Notifications ::=             Notification | Notifications "," Notification
Notification ::=              value (Name NotificationName)


      Status  ::=                     "current" | "deprecated" | "obsolete"
      ReferPart ::=                   "REFERENCE" Text | empty


      -- uses the NVT ASCII character set
      Text ::= """" string """"

END
```

Figure 6.26 NOTIFICATION-GROUP Macro

```
snmpBasicNotificationsGr      oup NOTIFICATION-GROUP
      NOTIFICATIONS               {coldStart, authenticationFailure}
      STATUS                     current
      DESCRIPTION         "The two notifications which an SNMP-2 entity is
                              required to implement."
            ::= {snmpMIBGroups 7}
```

Figure 6.27 Example of a NOTIFICATION-GROUP Macro

modules have to be implemented for the system to be SNMPv2 compliant. The group specified by the GROUP clause is not mandatory for the MIB module, but helps vendors define specifications of the features that have been implemented.

When both WRITE-SYNTAX and SYNTAX clauses are present, restrictions are placed on the syntax for the object mentioned in the OBJECT clause. These restrictions are tabulated in Section 9 of RFC 1902.

The *snmpBasicCompliance* macro is an example of a MODULE-COMPLIANCE macro and is part of the SNMPv2 MIB presented in Figure 6.6. A system is defined as SNMPv2 compliant if and only if *snmpGroup*, *snmpSetGroup*, *systemGroup*, and *snmpBasicNotificationsGroup* are implemented. The GROUP, *snmpCommunityGroup*, is optional.

```
MODULE-COMPLIANCE MACRO
BEGIN
      TYPE NOTATION ::=
                              "STATUS" Status
                              "DESCRIPTION" text
                              ReferPart
                              ModulePart

      VALUE NOTATION ::=
                              value (VALUE OBJECT IDENTIFIER)

      Status  ::=               "current" | "deprecated" | "obsolete"
      ReferPart ::=             "REFERENCE" Text | empty
      ModulePart ::=            Modules | empty
      Modules ::=               Module | Modules Module
      Module ::=                -- name of module --
                                "MODULE" ModuleName
                                Mandatory Part
                                CompliancePart
      ModuleName ::=            moduleReference ModuleIdentifier | empty
-- must not be empty unless contained in MIB module
ModuleIdentifier ::=  value (ModuleID OBJECT IDENTIFIER) | empty
      MandatoryPart ::=         "MANDATORY-GROUPS" "{" Groups"}"
                                | empty

      Groups ::=                Group | Groups "," Group
      Group ::=                 value (Group OBJECT IDENTIFIER)
      CompliancePart ::=        Compliances | empty
      Compliances ::=           Compliance | Compliances compliance
      Compliance ::=            ComplianceGroup | Object
      ComplianceGroup ::=       "GROUP" value (Name OBJECT IDENTIFIER)
                                "DESCRIPTION" Text

      Object ::=                "OBJECT" value (Name ObjectName)
                                SyntaxPart
                                WriteSyntaxPart
                                AccessPart
                                "DESCRIPTION" Text
      --must be a refinement for object's SYNTAX clause
      SyntaxPart ::=            "SYNTAX" type (SYNTAX) | empty
      --must be a refinement for object's SYNTAX clause
WriteSyntaxPart ::= "WRITE-SYNTAX" type (WriteSYNTAX) | empty
      AccessPart ::=            "MIN-ACCESS" Access | empty
      Access ::=                "not-accessible" | "accessible-for-notify" |
                                 "read-only" | "read-write" | "read-create"
                                -- uses the NVT ASCII character set
                                Text ::= """" string """"

END
```

Figure 6.28 MODULE-COMPLIANCE Macro

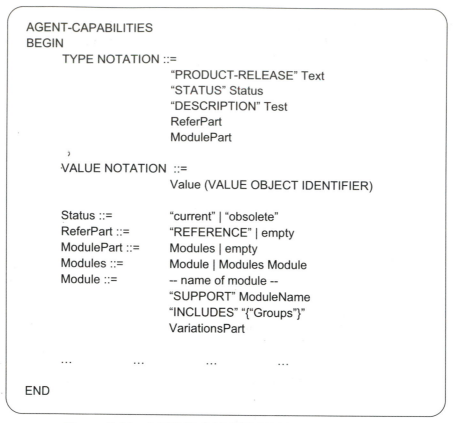

Figure 6.29 AGENT-CAPABILITIES Macro (Skeleton)

Agent Capabilities. The AGENT-CAPABILITIES macro is lengthy and the reader is referred to RFC 1904 for exact specifications. A skeleton of the macro and significant points of the macro are covered here and are shown in Figure 6.29.

The AGENT-CAPABILITIES macro for the router example given in Figure 6.10 is shown in Figure 6.30. Note that *snmpMIB* model, which is SNMPv2-MIB, includes *system* and *snmp* MIBs. Those MIBs and the associated groups are supported by the router. Other standard MIBs and groups supported by the router are indicated in Figure 6.30.

6.4 SNMv2 MANAGEMENT INFORMATION BASE

As mentioned in Section 6.2 and shown in Figure 6.5 two new MIB modules, security and SNMPv2, have been added to the Internet MIB. The SNMPv2 module has three submodules: snmpDomains, snmpProxys, and snmpModules. snmpDomains extends the SNMP standards to send management messages over transmission protocols other than UDP, which is the predominant and preferred way of transportation [RFC 1906]. Since UDP is the preferred protocol, systems that use another protocol need a proxy service to map on to UDP. Not much work has been done on snmpProxys, as of now.

There are changes made to the core MIB-II defined in SNMPv1. Figure 6.31 presents an overview of the changes to the Internet MIB and their relationship. The system module and the *snmp* module under

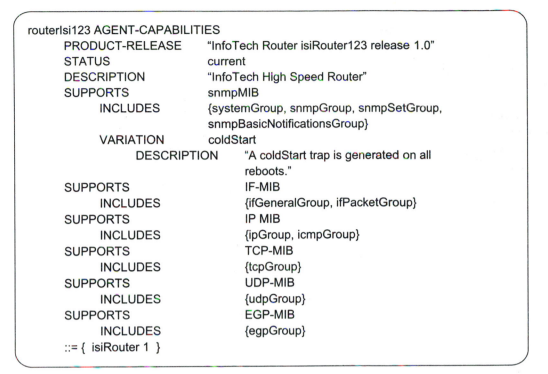

```
routerlsi123 AGENT-CAPABILITIES
        PRODUCT-RELEASE        "InfoTech Router isiRouter123 release 1.0"
        STATUS                 current
        DESCRIPTION            "InfoTech High Speed Router"
        SUPPORTS               snmpMIB
            INCLUDES           {systemGroup, snmpGroup, snmpSetGroup,
                               snmpBasicNotificationsGroup}
            VARIATION          coldStart
                DESCRIPTION        "A coldStart trap is generated on all
                                   reboots."
        SUPPORTS               IF-MIB
            INCLUDES           {ifGeneralGroup, ifPacketGroup}
        SUPPORTS               IP MIB
            INCLUDES           {ipGroup, icmpGroup}
        SUPPORTS               TCP-MIB
            INCLUDES           {tcpGroup}
        SUPPORTS               UDP-MIB
            INCLUDES           {udpGroup}
        SUPPORTS               EGP-MIB
            INCLUDES           {egpGroup}
        ::= { isiRouter 1 }
```

Figure 6.30 Example of an AGENT-CAPABILITIES Macro

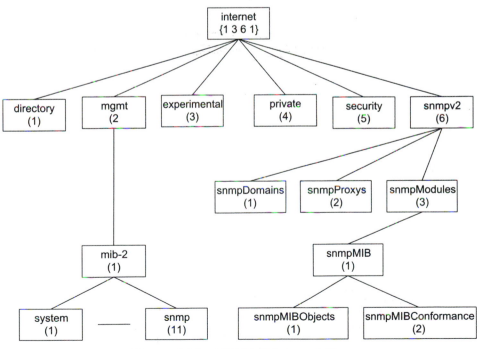

Figure 6.31 SNMPv2 Internet Group

mib-2 have significant changes as defined in RFC 1907. A new module *snmpMIB* has been defined, which is {snmpModules 1}. There are two modules under *snmpMIB*: *snmpMIBObjects* and *snmpMIB-Conformance*.

The MIB module *snmpMIBObjects* addresses the new objects introduced in SNMPv2, as well as those that are obsolete. This is primarily concerned with trap, which has been brought into the same format as other PDUs. Also, many of the unneeded objects in the SNMP group have been made obsolete.

We discussed conformance specifications and object groups in the previous section. These are specified under the *snmpMIBconformance* module. As SNMPv2 is currently defined, there is a strong coupling between system, *snmp*, *snmpMIBObjects*, and *snmpMIBconformance* modules. With this picture in mind, it will be a lot easier to follow RFC 1907, which discusses all these modules.

6.4.1 Changes to the System Group in SNMPv2

There are seven entities or objects in SNMPv2, which are common to a system. Additional information is added to the System group in SNMPv2, which contains a collection of objects that support various MIB modules. These are called object resources and are configurable both statically and dynamically. Figure 6.32 shows the MIB tree for the System group in SNMPv2. The *sysORLastChange* entity and *sysORTable* have been added to the set of objects in the System group. Table 6.6 presents the entity, OID, and a brief description of each entity for the System group.

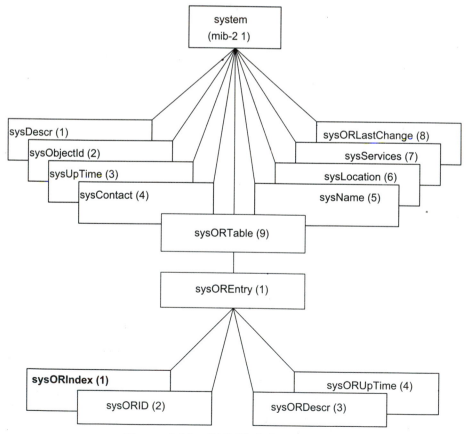

Figure 6.32 SNMPv2 System Group

Table 6.6 SNMPv2 System Group

ENTITY	OID	DESCRIPTION (BRIEF)
sysDescr	system 1	Textual description
sysObjectID	system 2	OBJECT IDENTIFIER of the entity
sysUpTime	system 3	Time (in hundredths of a second since last reset)
sysContact	system 4	Contact person for the node
sysName	system 5	Administrative name of the system
sysLocation	system 6	Physical location of the node
sysServices	system 7	Value designating the layer services provided by the entity
sysORLastChange	system 8	SysUpTime since last change in state or sysORID change
sysORTable	system 9	Table listing system resources that the agent controls; manager can configure these resources through the agent.
sysOREntry	sysORTable 1	An entry in the sysORTable
sysORIndex	sysOREntry 1	Row index, also index for the table
sysORID	sysOREntry 2	ID of the resource module
sysORDescr	sysOREntry 3	Textual description of the resource module
sysORUpTime	sysOREntry 4	System up-time since the object in this row was last instantiated

6.4.2 Changes to the SNMP Group in SNMPv2

The SNMP group in SNMPv2 has been considerably simplified from SNMPv1 by eliminating a large number of entities that were considered unnecessary. The simplified SNMP group is shown in Figure 6.33 (compare with Figure 5.21!). It has only eight entities, six old ones (1,3,4,5,6,30) and

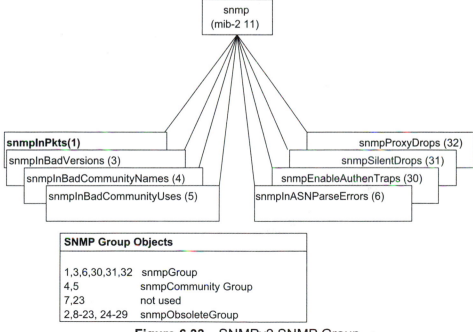

Figure 6.33 SNMPv2 SNMP Group

two new ones (31,32). Figure 6.33 also presents the four groups of all SNMP entities: *snmpGroup*, *snmpCommunityGroup*, *snmpObsoleteGroup*, and the group of two objects, 7 and 23, not used even in version 1. We will soon see that the *snmpGroup* is mandatory to implement for compliance of SNMPv2 and the *snmpCommunityGroup* is optional. The *snmpObsoleteGroup* is self-explanatory.

The SNMPv2 SNMP group table is shown in Table 6.7. All the unused and obsolete entities have been omitted for clarity.

6.4.3 Information for Notification in SNMPv2

Information on traps in SNMPv1 has been restructured in version 2 to conform to the rest of the PDUs. The macro TRAP-TYPE, used in version 1 and described in RFC 1215, has been made obsolete in SNMPv2. At the same time, enhancement to specifications has been made, and the terminology has been generalized to "notification," as the subheading indicates.

The information on notifications is defined under *snmpMIBObjects* and is shown in Figure 6.34. There are three modules under the *snmpMIBObjects* node: *snmpTrap* (4), *snmpTraps* (5), and *snmpSet* (6). The subnode designations 1, 2, and 3 under *snmpMIBObjects* have been made obsolete. A brief description of the subnodes and leaf objects under *snmpMIBObjects* is given in Table 6.8.

The *snmpTrap* group contains information on the OBJECT IDENTIFIERs of the trap and the enterprise responsible to send the trap. A new value, *accessible-for-notify*, has been added to the MAX-ACCESS clause to define objects under *snmpTrap*.

The entities under *snmpTraps* are the well-known traps that are currently in extensive use in SNMPv1. The *snmpSetSerialNo* is a single entity under *snmpSet* and is used by coordinating manager objects to

Table 6.7   SNMPv2 SNMP Group

ENTITY	OID	DESCRIPTION (BRIEF)
snmpInPkts	snmp (1)	Total number of messages delivered from transport service
snmpInBadVersions	snmp (3)	Total number of messages from transport service that are of unsupported version
snmpInBadCommunityNames	snmp (4)	Total number of messages from transport service that are of unknown community name
snmpInBadCommunityUses	snmp (5)	Total number of messages from transport service, of not allowed operation by the sending community
snmpInASNParseErrs	snmp (6)	Total number of ASN.1 and BER errors
snmpEnableAuthenTraps	snmp (30)	Override option to generate authentication failure traps
snmpSilentDrops	snmp (31)	Total number of the five types of received PDUs that were silently dropped due to exceptions in var-binds or max. message size
snmpProxyDrops	snmp (32)	Total number of the five types of received PDUs that were silently dropped due to inability to respond to a target proxy

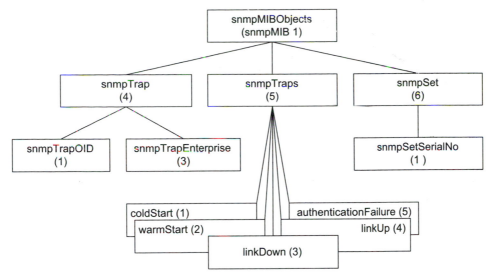

Figure 6.34 MIB Modules under snmpMIBObjects

Table 6.8 snmpMIBObjects MIB

ENTITY	OID	DESCRIPTION (BRIEF)
snmpTrap	snmpMIBObjects 4	Information group containing trap ID and enterprise ID
snmpTrapOID	snmpTrap 1	OBJECT IDENTIFIER of the notification
snmpTrapEnterprise	snmpTrap 2	OBJECT IDENTIFIER of the enterprise sending the notification
snmpTraps	snmpMIBObjects 5	Collection of well-known traps used in SNMPv1
coldStart	snmpTraps 1	Trap informing of a cold start of the object
warmStart	snmpTraps 2	Trap informing of a warm start of the object
linkDown	snmpTraps 3	Agent detecting a failure of a communication link
linkUp	snmpTraps 4	Agent detecting coming up of a communication link
authentificationFailure	snmpTraps 5	Agent reporting receipt of an unauthenticated protocol message
snmpSet	snmpMIBObjects 6	Manager-to-Manager notification messages
snmpSetSerialNo	snmpSet 1	Advisory lock between managers to coordinate set operation

perform the set operation. This is intended as coarse coordination only; fine-grain coordination may require more MIB objects in appropriate groups.

6.4.4 Conformance Information in SNMPv2

Conformance information is defined by the *snmpMIBConformance* module, as shown in Figure 6.35. It consists of two submodules, *snmpMIBcompliances* and *snmpMIBGroups*. The *snmpMIBCompliances* module has been extensively covered in Section 6.3.9. Units of conformance are defined in terms of OBJECT-GROUPS, mentioned in Section 6.3.9. Table 6.9 presents the various OBJECT-GROUPs defined in SNMPv2 and associated OBJECTS for all but *snmpObsoleteGroup*, which is shown in Figure 6.33.

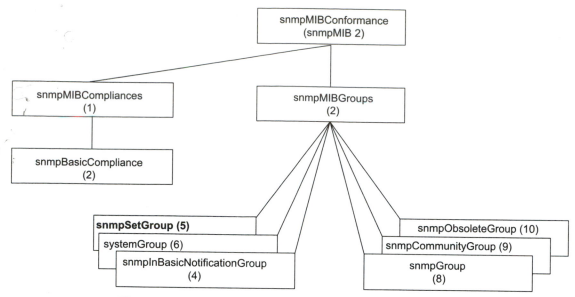

Figure 6.35   MIB Modules under snmpMIBConformance

6.4.5   Expanded Internet MIB-II

As SNMP network management expands covering legacy as well as new technology, MIB modules are continuously increasing. Figure 6.36 shows an expanded MIB-II when SNMPv2 was released and has more modules than those covered in RFC 1213. It is not intended to be an exhaustive list but includes RMON MIB module that we will be addressing in this textbook. Table 6.10 gives a description of each group in the MIB.

6.5   SNMPv2 PROTOCOL

SNMPv2 protocol operations are based on a community administrative model, which is the same as in SNMPv1. This was discussed in Section 5.2.2. We presented SNMPv2 protocol operations from a system architecture view in Section 6.2. In this section we will discuss details of PDU data structures and protocol operations.

6.5.1   Data Structure of SNMPv2 PDUs

The PDU data structure in SNMPv2 has been standardized to a common format for all messages. This improves the efficiency and performance of message exchange between systems. The significant improvement is bringing the trap data structure in the same format as the rest. The generic PDU message structure is shown in Figure 6.37 and is the same as Figure 5.8 of SNMPv1. The PDU type is indicated by an INTEGER. The error-status and error-index fields are either set to zero or ignored in the get-request, get-next-request, and set messages. The error-status is set to zero in the get-response message if there is no error; otherwise the type of error is indicated. The PDU and error-status are listed in Table 6.11. The error-index is set to zero if there is no error. If there is an error, it identifies the first variable binding in the variable-binding list that caused the error message. The first variable binding in a request's variable-binding list is index one, the second is index two, etc.

Table 6.9   SNMPv2 OBJECT-GROUPs

OBJECT-GROUPS	OID	OBJECTS
snmpSetGroup	snmpMIBGroups 5	snmpSetSerialNo
systemGroup	snmpMIBGroups 6	sysDescr
		sysObjectID
		sysUpTime
		sysContact
		sysName
		sysLocation
		sysServices
		sysORLastChange
		sysORID
		sysORUpTime
		sysORDescr
snmpBasicNotification Group	snmpMIBGroups 7	coldStart
		authenticationFailure
snmpGroup	snmpMIBGroups 8	snmpInPkts
		snmpInBadVersions
		snmpInASNParseErrs
		snmpSilentDrops
		snmpProxyDrops
		snmpEnableAuthenTraps
snmpCommunityGroup	snmpMIBGroups 9	snmpInBadCommunityNames
		snmpInBadCommunityUses
snmpObsoleteGroup	snmpMIBGroups 10	Please see Figure 6.33

There is a difference in usage of the error-status and error-index fields between SNMPv1 and SNMPv2. In version 1, any error encountered by the agent in responding to requests from the manager generates a non-zero value in either the error-status field or in both the error-status and error-index fields. Values in variable bindings are returned only under non-error conditions.

However, in SNMPv2, if only the error-status field of the Response-PDU is non-zero, the value fields of the variable binding in the variable-binding list are ignored. If both the error-status field and the error-index field of the Response-PDU are non-zero, then the value of the error-index field is the index of the variable binding (in the variable-binding list of the corresponding request) for which the request failed. Values in other variable bindings in the variable-binding list are returned with valid values and processed by the manager.

The generic PDU format is applicable to all SNMPv2 messages except the Get-Bulk-Request PDU, for which the format is shown in Figure 6.38. It can be seen that the format of the structure is the same in both cases, except that in the get-bulk-request message, the third and fourth fields are different. The third field, the error-status field, is replaced by non-repeaters; and the fourth field, the error-index

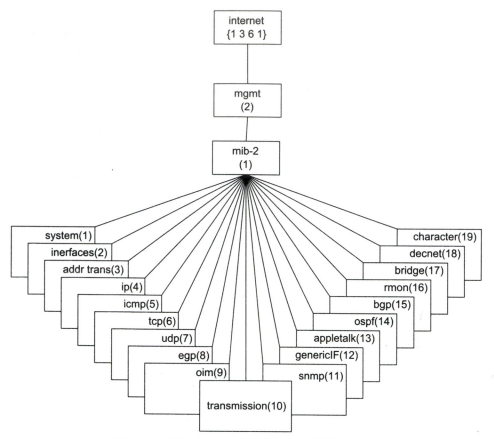

Figure 6.36 Expanded Internet MIB-II Group

Table 6.10 Expanded MIB-II Group

GROUP	OID	DESCRIPTION (BRIEF)
ifMIB	mib-2 31	Extension to interfaces group for new technologies
appletalk	mib-2 13	MIB for appletalk networks
ospf	mib-2 14	Open Shortest Path First routing protocol MIB
bgp	mib-2 15	MIB for Border Gateway Protocol for inter-autonomous network routing
rmon	mib-2 16	MIB for remote monitoring using RMON probe; there are MIBs under this for Ethernet and Token Ring networks
bridge	mib-2 17	MIB for bridges
decnet	mib-2 18	Digital Equipment Corporation DECnet MIB
character	mib-2 19	MIB for ports with character stream output for computer peripheral

PDU Type	RequestID	Error Status	Error Index	VarBind 1 name	VarBind 1 value	...	VarBind n name	VarBind n value

Figure 6.37 SNMPv2 PDU (all but bulk)

Table 6.11 Values for Types of PDU and Error-status Fields in SNMPv2 PDU

FIELD	TYPE	VALUE
PDU	0	Get-Request-PDU
	1	GetNextRequest-PDU
	2	Response-PDU
	3	Set-Request-PDU
	4	obsolete
	5	GetBulkRequest-PDU
	6	InformRequest-PDU
	7	SNMPv2-Trap-PDU
Error Status	0	noError
	1	tooBig
	2	noSuchName
	3	badValue
	4	readOnly
	5	genErr
	6	noAccess
	7	wrongType
	8	wrongLength
	9	wrongEncoding
	10	wrongValue
	11	noCreation
	12	inconsistentValue
	13	resourceUnavailable
	14	commitFailed
	15	undoFailed
	16	authorizationError
	17	notWritable
	18	inconsistentName

field, is replaced by max-repetitions. As we mentioned in Section 6.2, the get-bulk-request enables us to retrieve data in bulk. We can retrieve a number of both non-repetitive scalar values and repetitive tabular values with a single message. Non-repeaters indicate the number of non-repetitive field values

PDU Type	RequestID	Non-Repeaters	Max Repetitions	VarBind 1 name	VarBind 1 value	...	VarBind n name	VarBind n value

Figure 6.38 SNMPv2 GetBulkRequest PDU

requested; and the max-repetitions field designates the maximum number of table rows requested. We will next look at the SNMPv2 operations using PDUs.

6.5.2   SNMPv2 Protocol Operations

There are seven protocol operations in SNMPv2, as discussed in Section 6.2. We will ignore the report operation, which is not used. The messages, *get-request*, *get-next-request*, *set-request*, and *get-response*, are in both SNMPv1 and SNMPv2 versions and operate in a similar fashion. The two additional messages that are in SNMPv2, which are not in version 1, are the *GetBulkRequest* and *InformRequest*. The command, *get-bulk-request*, is an enhancement of *get-next request* and retrieves data in bulk efficiently. This is covered in the next subsection. The *InformRequest* is covered in a subsequent section along with SNMPv2-Trap, which has been modified in version 2.

GetBulkRequest PDU Operation. The *get-bulk-request* operation is added in SNMPv2 to retrieve bulk data from a remote entity. Its greatest benefit is in retrieving multiple rows of data from a table. The basic operation of get-bulk-request is the same as get-next-request. The third and fourth field positions are used in get-bulk-request message PDU as *non-repeaters* and *max-repetitions*, as shown in Figure 6.38. The non-repeaters field indicates the number of non-repetitive (scalar) objects to be retrieved. The max-repetitions field defines the maximum number of instances to be returned in the response message. This would correspond to the number of rows in an aggregate object. The value for the max-repetitions field is operation-dependent and is determined by such factors as the maximum size of the SNMP message, or the buffer size in implementation, or the expected size of the aggregate object table.

The data structure of the response for the get-bulk-request operation differs from other get and set operations. Successful processing of the get-bulk-request produces variable bindings (larger array of Var-BindList) in the response PDU, which is larger than that contained in the corresponding request. Thus, there is no one-to-one relationship between the VarBindList of the request and response messages.

Figure 6.39 shows a conceptual MIB to illustrate the operation of get-next-request and get-bulk-request shown in Figure 6.40 and Figure 6.41. It is similar to Figure 5.12 with two additional rows added to the table. To notice the difference in improvement of get-bulk-request over get-next-request, let us look at Figure 6.40, which shows the sequence of operations for get-next-request for the MIB shown in Figure 6.39. The sequence starts with a get-request message from the manager process with a VarBindList array of two scalar variables A and B. It is subsequently followed by the get-next-request message with three columnar OBJECT IDENTIFIERS T.E.1, T.E.2, and T.E.3. The get-response returns the first instance values T.E.1.1, T.E.2.1, and T.E.3.1. The sequence of operation continues until the fourth instance is retrieved. The last get-next-request message with the OBJECT IDENTIFIERS T.E.1.4, T.E.2.4, and T.E.3.4 generates the values T.E.2.1, T.E.3.1, and Z. This is because there are no more instances of the table. It retrieves the three objects, which are logically the next lexicographically higher objects—namely T.E.2.1 (next to T.E.1.4), T.E.3.1 (next to T.E.2.4), and Z (next to T.E.3.4). The manager would stop the sequence at this message. However, if it continues the operation, it would receive a *noSuchName* error message.

Figure 6.41 shows the sequence of operations to retrieve the MIB shown in Figure 6.39 using the get-bulk message. The entire MIB data are retrieved in two requests. The first message GetBulkRequest (2, 3, A, B, T.E.1, T.E.2, T.E.3) is a request for receiving two non-repetitive objects (the first variable (2) in the request command) and three repetitive instances (the second operand (3) in the command) of the columnar objects (T.E.1, T.E.2, and T.E.3). The response returns values of A and B for the non-repetitive

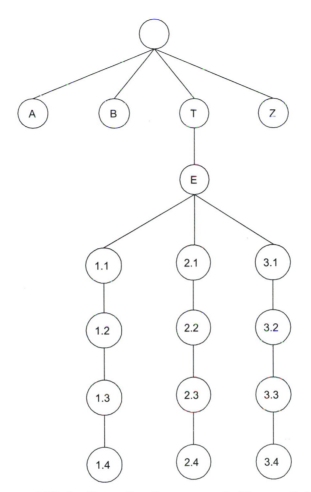

Figure 6.39 MIB for Operation Sequences in Figures 6.40 and 6.41

objects, and the first three rows of the aggregate object table. The second request is for three more rows of the table. Since there is only one more row left to send, the response message contains the information in the last row, the next lexicographic entity, Z, and the error message *endOfMibView*. The manager interprets this as end of the table.

Figure 6.42 shows the retrieval of the Address Translation table shown in Figure 5.16 using the get-bulk-request operation. Instead of four sets of get-next-request and get-response messages, only two get-bulk-request and response messages are needed in the get-bulk-request operation.

SNMPv2-Trap and InformRequest PDU Operations. The SNMPv2-Trap PDU performs the same function as in version 1. As we notice, the name has been changed, as well as its data structure to the generic format shown in Figure 6.37. The variable bindings in positions 1 and 2 are specified as *sysUpTime* and *snmpTrapOID*, as shown in Figure 6.43. The destination(s) to which a trap is sent is implementation-dependent.

A trap is defined by using a NOTIFICATION-TYPE macro. If the macro contains an OBJECTS clause, then the objects defined by the clause are in the variable bindings in the order defined in the

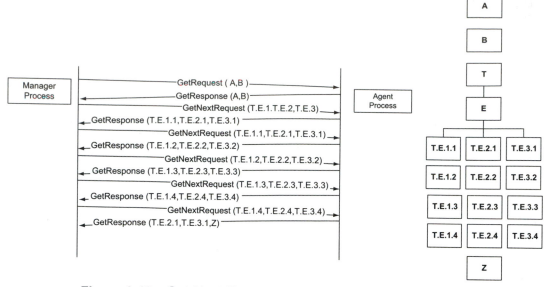

Figure 6.40 Get-Next-Request Operation for MIB in Figure 6.39

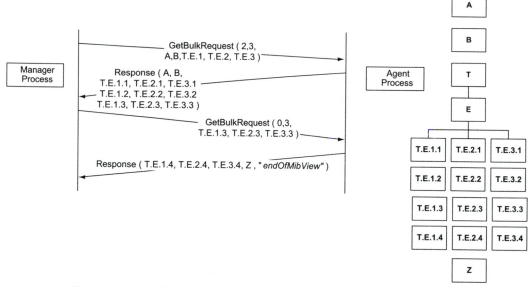

Figure 6.41 Get-Bulk-Request Operation for MIB in Figure 6.39

clause. For example, we may want to know what interface is associated with a *linkUp* trap. In this case the linkUp NOTIFICATION-TYPE would have *ifIndex* as an object in its OBJECTS clause, as shown in Figure 6.44.

An InformRequest PDU is generated by a manager (in contrast to a trap generated by an agent) to inform another manager of information in its MIB view. While a trap is received passively by a manager, an InformRequest generates a response in the receiving manager to send to the sending manager.

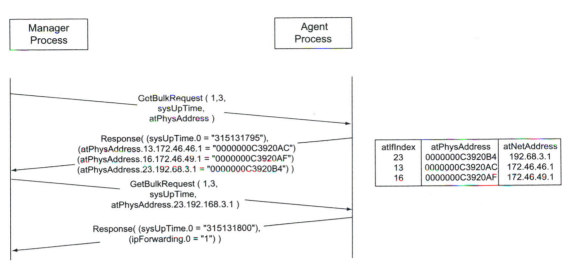

Figure 6.42 Get-Bulk-Request Example

PDU Type	RequestID	Error Status	Error Index	VarBind 1 sysUpTime	VarBind 1 value	VarBind 2 snmpTrapOID	VarBind 2 value	.. .

Figure 6.43 SNMPv2 Trap PDU

```
linkUp NOTIFICATION-TYPE
    OBJECTS          { ifIndex }
    STATUS           current
    DESCRIPTION      "A linkUp trap signifies that the SNSMPv2 entity,
                     acting in an agent role, recognizes that one of the
                     communication links represented in its configuration
                     has come up."
```

Figure 6.44 Example of an OBJECTS Clause in a NOTIFICATION-TYPE Macro

6.6   COMPATIBILITY WITH SNMPv1

An SNMP proxy server, in general, converts a set of non-SNMP entities into a set of SNMP-defined MIB entities. Unfortunately, SNMPv2 MIB is not backward compatible with SNMPv1 and hence requires conversion of messages. SNMPv2 IETF Working Group has proposed [RFC 1908] two schemes for migration from SNMPv1 to SNMPv2: bilingual manager and SNMP proxy server.

6.6.1   Bilingual Manager

One of the migration paths to transition to SNMPv2 from version 1 is to implement both SNMPv1 and SNMPv2 interpreter modules in the manager with a database that has profiles of the agents' version. The interpreter modules do all the conversions of MIB variables and SNMP protocol operations in both directions. The bilingual manager does the common functions needed for a management system. The SNMP

PDU contains the version number field to identify the version (see Figure 5.5). This arrangement is shown in Figure 6.45. This is expensive to implement and maintain. The alternative scheme is to use a proxy server.

6.6.2 SNMP Proxy Server

The SNMPv2 proxy server configuration is shown in Figure 6.46. The requests to and responses from, as well as traps from, SNMPv2 agents are processed by the SNMPv2 manager with no changes. A proxy server is implemented as a front-end module to the SNMPv2 manager for communication with SNMPv1 agents.

Figure 6.47 details the conversions that are done by an SNMP v2–v1 proxy server. The get-Request, GetNextRequest-PDU, and Set-Request-PDU from the SNMPv2 manager are passed through unaltered by the proxy server. There are two modifications done to the GetBulkRequest PDU. The values for the two fields, non-repeaters and max-repetitions, are set to zero and transmitted as GetNextRequest PDU. The GetResponse from SNMPv1 is passed through unaltered by the proxy server to the SNMPv2 manager, unless a response has a *tooBigError* value. In the exception case, the contents of the variable-binding field are removed before propagating the response. The trap from the SNMPv1 agent is prepended with two VarBind fields, *sysUpTime*.0 and *snmpTrapOID*.0, with their associated values and then passed on to the SNMPv2 manager as SNMPv2-Trap PDU.

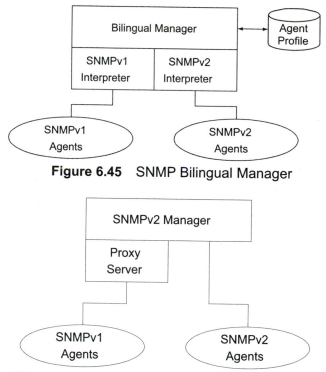

Figure 6.45   SNMP Bilingual Manager

Figure 6.46   SNMPv2 Proxy Server Configuration

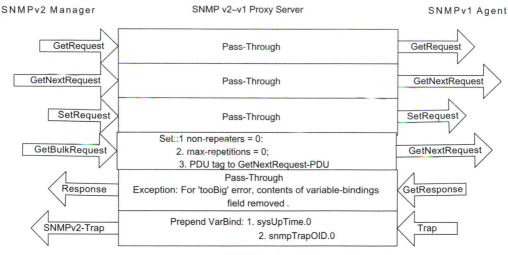

Figure 6.47   SNMP v2–v1 Proxy Server

Summary

A significant number of network management systems and agents that are on the market today use SNMP version 1, referred to as SNMPv1. However, some of the features that have been added to SNMPv1 have been formally defined in SNMPv2. We have learned enhancements in SNMPv2 over that of SNMPv1 in this chapter.

The enhancements to SNMP architecture are the formalization of manager-to-manager communication and the inclusion of traps as part of the SMI and messages, instead of as an appendix to SMI as in SNMPv1. Three additional messages have been added. They are get-bulk-request, inform-request, and report. Only get-bulk-request and inform-request details have been defined and the report is left to the implementers of a system. The report is not used in practice at present.

There are several changes to SMI in SMIv2. Modules are formally introduced using the MODULE-IDENTITY macro. An OBJECT-IDENTITY macro defines the MIB objects; and a NOTIFICATION-TYPE macro defines traps and notifications. SMIv2 has been split into three parts, each being defined in a separate RFC. They are module definitions, textual conventions, and conformance specifications. Module definitions specify the rules for defining new modules. Textual conventions help define precise descriptions of modules for human understanding. Conformance specifications are intended to interpret what the vendor is specifying in the network component with regard to compliance with SNMP management. Object groups are introduced to group a number of related entities. Conformance specifications detail the mandatory groups that should be implemented to be SNMP conformant. The object groups also help vendors define the capabilities of the system when they implement additional groups beyond that of mandatory ones.

Two new modules have been added to the Internet module. They are security and snmpV2. The security module is, as of now, a placeholder in the MIB tree as no consensus could be reached within the working group in defining it. It is specified in SNMPv3, which is covered in Chapter 7. The System and SNMP groups have been modified in the Internet MIB. Additional objects have been added to the System group that supports various MIB modules. A large number of entities have been made obsolete in the SNMP module. Obsolete entities are defined as an obsolete group in the SNMPv2 module. The SNMPv2 module also defines the MIB definition for compliance groups. Object groups defining a collection of related entities are defined to specify vendor compliance and capabilities.

All protocol PDUs, including trap, have been unified into a common data format. The newly introduced get-bulk-request is intended to improve the efficiency of get-next request in SNMPv1 by retrieving data in large quantities. The get-next-request is still maintained in this version. Interoperability between management systems has been facilitated by a new message, inform-request. We have given a conceptual presentation of table management, as this has become important when multiple management systems try to set configuration on an agent at the same time.

The unfortunate part of SNMPv2 is that it is not backward compatible with SNMPv1. Two schemes have been recommended for migrating from version 1 to version 2. Proxy server is the preferred approach over that of a bilingual manager. Proxy server can also be developed for managing non-SNMP agents with an SNMP manager.

Exercises

1. Define the OBJECT-IDENTITY module for the following objects mentioned in Exercise 4.11:
   (a) hats
   (b) jacketQuantity

2. Write the OBJECT TYPE modules for ipAddrTable, ipAddrEntry, and ipAdEntIfIndex in an IP address translation table shown in Figure 4.20 in SMIv2.

3. Add two columnar objects, cardNumber (of interface card) and portNumber (port in the interface card), to an IP address table in a router. The index values for the IP address table rows are 150.50.51.1, 150.50.52.1, 150.50.53.1, and 150.50.54.1. The packets to the first two addresses are directed to ports 1 and 2 of interface card 1. The last two addresses refer to ports 1 and 2 of interface card 2.

   (a) Draw a conceptual base table and an augmented table (ipAug 1).
   (b) Present the ASN.1 constructs for both down to the leaf level of the MIB tree. Limit your leaf for *ipTable* to *ipAdEntAddr* object.

4. Table 6.12 shows the output of a network management system detailing the addresses of a router in a network. Three columnar objects (Index, IP Address, and Physical Address) belong to the Address Translation table, atTable. Treat the other three columns as belonging to an augmented table, atAugTable (atAug 1). Repeat Exercises 3(a) and (b) for this case. Use SMIv2 textual conventions.

Table 6.12   Table for Exercise 4

atIfIndex	intType	intNumber	PortNumber	IP Address atNetAddress	Physical Address atPhysAddress
3	6	0	2	172.46.41.1	00:00:0c:35:C1:D2
4	6	0	3	172.46.42.1	00:00:0c:35:C1:D3
5	6	0	4	172.46.43.1	00:00:0c:35:C1:D4
6	6	0	5	172.46.44.1	00:00:0c:35:C1:D5
2	6	0	1	172.46.63.1	00:00:0c:35:C1:D1
7	15	1	0	172.46.165.1	00:00:0c:35:C1:D8
1	6	0	0	172.46.252.1	00:00:0c:35:C1:D0

5. In Exercise 3, the router interfaces with subnets are reconfigured as virtual LANs. There is only one interface card with two ports handling two subnets each. The packets to the two subnets, 150.50.51.1 and 150.50.52.1, are directed to port 1 of the interface card; and the packets to 150.50.53.1 and 150.50.54.1 are connected to port 2. The second table is the dependent table, ipDepTable (ipDep 1).

(a) Draw a conceptual base table and a dependent table.

(b) Present the ASN.1 constructs for both down to the leaf level of the MIB tree. Limit your leaf for *ipTable* to *ipAdEntAddr* object.

6. A table is used in a corporation for each branch to maintain an inventory of their equipment in the agent system located at the branch. The inventory table is maintained remotely from the central location. Items can be added, deleted, or changed. The objects that make up the table are:

Branch ID	{corp 100}
Table name	invTable
Row name	invEntry
Columnar object 1	invStatus
Columnar object 2	invNumber (index)
Columnar object 3	make
Columnar object 4	model
Columnar object 5	serNumber

(a) Draw the inventory conceptual table.

(b) Write the detailed ASN.1 constructs for the table.

7. In Exercise 6, the following equipment is to be added as the 100th inventory number:

make	Sun
model	Ultra5
serNumber	S12345

(a) Add the conceptual row to the table in Exercise 6(a).

(b) Draw the operational sequence diagram for create-and-go operation to create the new row.

8. In Exercise 6, equipment with the inventory number 50 is no longer in use and is hence to be deleted. Draw the operational sequence to delete the conceptual row.

9. Generate an ASN.1 OBJECT-GROUP macro for Address Translation group in SNMPv2 implementation.

10. Draw request-response messages, as shown in Figure 6.40 and Figure 6.41, to retrieve all columnar objects of the Address Translation group shown in Table 6.13. Assume that you know the number of rows in the table in making requests.

(a) get-next-request and response

(b) get-bulk-request and response

(c) Compare the results of (a) and (b)

Table 6.13 Table for Exercises 10

INDEX	IP ADDRESS	PHYSICAL ADDRESS
3	172.46.41.1	00:00:0c:35:C1:D2
4	172.46.42.1	00:00:0c:35:C1:D3
5	172.46.43.1	00:00:0c:35:C1:D4
6	172.46.44.1	00:00:0c:35:C1:D5
2	172.46.63.1	00:00:0c:35:C1:D1
7	172.46.165.1	00:00:0c:35:C1:D8
1	172.46.252.1	00:00:0c:35:C1:D0

11. Fill in the values for the SNMPv2 Trap PDU shown in Figure 6.43 for a message sent by the hub shown in Figure 4.2(a) one second after it is reset following a failure. (You may want to compare the result with that of Exercise 3 in Chapter 5 for SNMPv1.)

SNMP Management: SNMPv3

OBJECTIVES

- *SNMPv3 features*
  - *Documentation architecture*
  - *Formalized SNMP architecture*
  - *Security*
- *SNMP engine ID and name for network entity*
- *SNMPv3 applications and primitives*
- *SNMP architecture*
  - *Integrates the three SNMP versions*
  - *Message-processing module*
  - *Dispatcher module*
  - *Future enhancement capability*

- *User security model, USM*
  - *Derived from user ID and password*
  - *Authentication*
  - *Privacy*
  - *Message timeliness*
- *View-based access control model, VACM*
  - *Configure set of MIB views for agent with contexts*
  - *Family of subtrees in MIB views*
  - *VACM process*

SNMPv2 was released, after much controversy, as a community-based SNMP framework, SNMPv2C, without any enhancement to security. SNMPv3 was subsequently developed to fulfill that need in SNMP management. Fortunately, SNMPv3 has ended up addressing more than just security. It is a framework for all three versions of SNMP. It is designed to accommodate future development in SNMP management with minimum impact to existing management entities. Modular architecture and documentation have been proposed to accomplish this goal.

The latest set of additional documentation [RFC 3410–3418, 3584] detailing the specifications of SNMPv3 is described in the RFCs listed in Table 7.1. They comprise IETF-adopted standards STD 62.

RFC 3410 provides an overview of SNMPv3 Framework.

Table 7.1   SNMPv3 RFCs

RFC 3410	Introduction and Applicability Statements (not STD)
RFC 3411	Architecture for Describing SNMP Management Frameworks
RFC 3412	Message Processing and Dispatching for SNMP
RFC 3413	SNMPv3 Applications
RFC 3414	User-based Security Model (USM) for SNMPv3
RFC 3415	View-based Access Control Model for SNMP
RFC 3416	Version 2 of the Protocol Operations for SNMP
RFC 3417	Transport Mappings for SNMP
RFC 3418	MIB for SNMP
RFC 3584	SNMPv3 Coexistence and Transition (BCP (Best Current Practices) 74)

RFC 3411 presents an overview of SNMPv3. It defines a vocabulary for describing SNMP Management Frameworks and an architecture for describing the major portions of SNMP Management Frameworks.

RFC 3412 describes message processing and dispatching for SNMP messages. Procedures are specified for processing multiple versions of SNMP messages to the proper SNMP Message Processing Models (MPM) and for dispatching packet data units (PDUs) to SNMP applications. A new MPM for version 3 is proposed in this document.

RFC 3413 defines five types of SNMP applications: command generators, command responders, notification originators, notification receivers, and proxy forwarders. It also defines the Management Information Base (MIB) modules for specifying targets of management operations, for notification filtering, and for proxy forwarding.

RFC 3414 addresses the User-based Security Model (USM) for SNMPv3 and specifies the procedure for providing SNMP message level security. MIBs for remotely monitoring and managing configuration parameters are also specified.

RFC 3415 is concerned with the Access Control Model that deals with the procedure for controlling access to management information. MIB is specified for remotely managing the configuration parameters for the view-based access control model (VACM).

RFC 3416 defines version 2 syntax and procedures for sending, receiving, and processing of SNMP PDUs.

RFC 3417 defines the transport of SNMP messages over various protocols.

RFC 3418 describing the behavior of an SNMP entity obsoletes RFC 1907 MIB for SNMPv2.

RFC 3584 describes the coexistence of SNMPv3, SNMPv2, and SNMPv1. It also describes how to convert MIB modules from SMIv1 format to SMIv2 format.

7.1 SNMPv3 KEY FEATURES

One of the key features of SNMPv3 is the modularization of architecture and documentation. The design of the architecture integrated SNMPv1 and SNMPv2 specifications with the newly proposed SNMPv3. This enables continued usage of legacy SNMP entities along with SNMPv3 agents and manager. That is good news as there are tens of thousands of SNMPv1 and SNMPv2 agents in the field.

An SNMP engine is defined with explicit subsystems that include dispatch and message-processing functions. It manages all three versions of SNMP to coexist in a management entity. Application services and primitives have been explicitly defined in SNMPv3. This formalizes the various messages that have been in use in the earlier versions.

Another key feature is the improved security feature. The configuration can be set remotely with secured communication that protects against modification of information and masquerade by using encryption schemes. It also tries to ensure against malicious modification of messages by reordering and time delaying of message streams, as well as protects against eavesdropping of messages.

The access policy used in SNMPv1 and SNMPv2 is continued and formalized in the access control in SNMPv3, designated VACM. The SNMP engine defined in the architecture checks whether a specific type of access (read, write, create, notify) to a particular object (instance) is allowed.

7.2 SNMPv3 DOCUMENTATION ARCHITECTURE

The numerous SNMP documents have been organized by IETF to follow a document architecture. The SNMP document architecture addresses how existing documents and new documents could be designed to be autonomous and, at the same time, be integrated to describe the different SNMP frameworks. The representation shown in Figure 7.1 reflects the contents of the specifications, but it is another perspective of what is given in RFC [3410]. It can be correlated with what we presented in Figure 4.4. Two sets of documents are of general nature. One of them is the set of documents on roadmap, applicability statement, and coexistence and transition.

The other set of documents, SNMP frameworks, comprises the three versions of SNMP. An SNMP framework represents the integration of a set of subsystems and models. A model describes a specific design of a subsystem. The implementation of an SNMP entity is based on a specific model based on a specific framework. For example, a message in an SNMP manager is processed using a specific message processing mode (we will discuss these later) in a specific SNMP3 framework. The SNMP frameworks document set is not explicitly shown in the pictorial presentation in RFC [2271], as we have done here. RFC [1901] in SNMPv2 and RFC [2271] in SNMPv3 are SNMP framework documents.

The information model and MIBs cover Structure of Management Information (SMI), textual conventions, and conformance statements, as well as various MIBs. These are covered in STD 16 and STD 17 documents along with SMIv2 documents [RFC 2578–2580].

Message Handling and PDU Handling sets of documents address transport mappings, message processing and dispatching, protocol operations, applications, and access control. These would correspond to the SNMP STD 15 documents and the draft documents on SNMPv2 [RFC 1905–1907] shown in Figure 4.9. RFCs [2573–2575] address these in SNMPv3.

7.3 ARCHITECTURE

An SNMP management network consists of several nodes, each with an SNMP entity. They interact with each other to monitor and manage the network and resources. The architecture of an SNMP entity

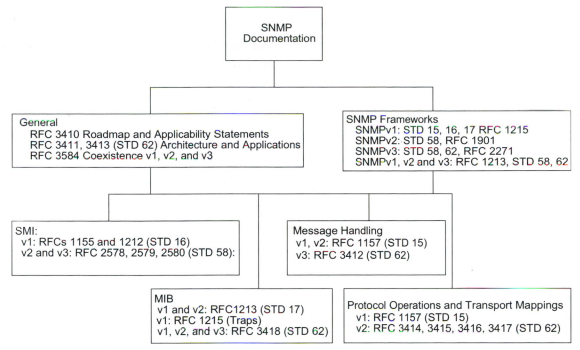

Figure 7.1 SNMP Documentation (Recommended in SNMPv3)

is defined as the elements of an entity and the names associated with them. There are three kinds of naming: naming of entities, naming of identities, and naming of management information. Let us first look at the elements of an entity, including its naming.

7.3.1 Elements of an Entity

The elements of the architecture associated with an SNMP entity, shown in Figure 7.2, comprise an SNMP engine and a set of applications. The SNMP engine, named *snmpEngineID*, comprises a dispatcher, message processing subsystem, security subsystem, and an access control subsystem.

SNMP Engine. As shown in Figure 7.2, an SNMP entity has one SNMP engine, which is uniquely identified by an *snmpEngineID*. The SNMP engine ID is made up of octet strings. The length of the ID is 12 octets for SNMPv1 and SNMPv2, and is variable for SNMPv3. This is shown in Figure 7.3. The first four octets in both formats are set to the binary equivalent of the agent's SNMP management private enterprise number. The first bit of the four octets is set to 1 for SNMPv3 and 0 for earlier versions. For example, if Acme Networks has been assigned {enterprises 696}, the first four octets would read '800002b8'H in SNMPv3 and '000002b8'H in SNMPv1 and SNMPv2.

The fifth octets for SNMPv1 and SNMPv2 indicate the method that the enterprise used for deriving the SNMP engine ID and 6–12 octets function of the method. For a simple entity, it could be just the IP address of the entity.

The fifth octet of the SNMPv3 engine ID indicates the format used in the rest of the variable number of octets. Table 7.2 shows the values of the fifth octet for SNMPv3.

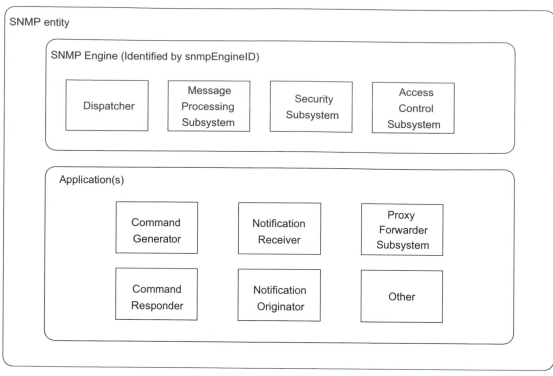

Figure 7.2   SNMPv3 Architecture

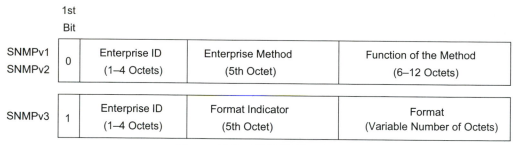

Figure 7.3   SNMP Engine ID

Dispatch Subsystem. There is only one dispatcher in an SNMP engine and it can handle multiple versions of SNMP messages. It does the following three sets of functions. First, it sends messages to and receives messages from the network. Second, it determines the version of the message and interacts with the corresponding MPM. Third, it provides an abstract interface (described in Section 7.3.3) to SNMP applications to deliver an incoming PDU to the local application and to send a PDU from the local application to a remote entity.

The three separate functions in the dispatcher subsystem are accomplished using: (1) a transport mapper; (2) a message dispatcher; and (3) a PDU dispatcher. The transport mapper delivers the message over the appropriate transport protocol of the network. The message dispatcher routes the outgoing and incoming messages to the appropriate module of the message processor. If a message is received for an SNMP version, which is not handled by the message processing subsystem, it would be rejected by the

Table 7.2   SNMPv3 Engine ID Format (5th Octet)

0	Reserved, unused
1	IPv4 address (4 octets)
2	IPv6 (16 octets)
	Lowest non-special IP address
3	MAC address (6 octets)
	Lowest IEEE MAC address, canonical order
4	Text, administratively assigned
	Maximum remaining length 27
5	Octets, administratively assigned
	Maximum remaining length 27
6–127	Reserved, unused
128–255	As defined by the enterprises Maximum remaining length 27

message dispatcher. The PDU dispatcher within an SNMP entity handles the traffic routing of PDUs between applications and the Message Processor Model.

Message Processing Subsystem. The SNMP message processing subsystem of an SNMP engine interacts with the dispatcher to handle version-specific SNMP messages. It contains one or more MPMs. The version is identified by the version field in the header.

Security and Access Control Subsystems. The security subsystem provides security services at the message level in terms of authentication and privacy protection. The access control subsystem provides access authorization service.

Applications Module. The application(s) module is made up of one or more applications, which comprise command generator, notification receiver, proxy forwarder, command responder, and notification originator. The first three applications are normally associated with an SNMP manager and the last two with an SNMP agent. The application(s) module may also include other applications, as indicated by the box, "Other," in Figure 7.2.

7.3.2   Names

Naming of entities, identities, and management information is part of SNMPv3 specifications. We already mentioned the naming of an entity by its SNMP engine ID, *snmpEngineID*. Two names are associated with identities, *principal* and *securityName*. *Principal* is the "who" requesting services. It could be a person or an application. The *securityName* is a human readable string representing a principal. The principal could be a single user; for example, name a network manager or a group of users, such as names of operators in the network operations center. It is made non-accessible. It is hidden and is based on the security model (SM) used. However, it is administratively given a security name; for example, User 1 or Admin, which is made readable by all.

A management entity can be responsible for more than one managed object. For example, a management agent associated with a managed object at a given node could be managing a neighboring node besides its own. Each object is termed *context* and has a *contextEngineID* and a *contextName*. When there is a one-to-one relationship between the management entity and the managed object, *contextEngineID* is the same as *snmpEngineID*. A *scopedPDU* is a block of data containing a *contextEngineID*, a *contextName*, and a PDU. An example of this would be a switched hub where a common SNMP agent in the hub is accessed to manage the interfaces of the hub. The agent would have an *snmpEngineID* and each interface card would have a context Engine ID. In contrast, in a non-switched hub with each interface card being managed individually, the snmpEngineID and contextID are the same.

7.3.3   Abstract Service Interfaces

The subsystems in an SNMP entity communicate with each other across an interface, a subsystem providing a service and the other using the service. We can define a service interface between the two. If the interface is defined such that it is generic and independent of specific implementation, it becomes a conceptual interface, termed *abstract service interface*. These abstract services are defined by a set of primitives that define the services. Figure 7.4(a) shows subsystem A sending a request for service using the primitive *primitiveAB* to subsystem B. The *primitiveAB* is associated with the receiving subsystem B, which is the one that is providing the service in this illustration. A primitive has IN and OUT as operands or parameters, which are data values. These are indicated by a1 and a2, and b1 and b2, respectively. The IN parameters are input values to the called subsystem from the subsystem calling for service. The OUT parameters are the responses expected from the called subsystem to the calling subsystem. The OUT parameters are sent unfilled in the message format by the calling system (remember Get-Request PDU?) and are returned filled (Get-Response) by the called subsystem. When the calling subsystem expects a response from the called subsystem, there are directed messages in both directions with a two-directional arrow coupling the two, as shown in Figure 7.4(a). In this case the primitive *primitiveAB* is only indicated in the forward direction. In addition to returning the OUT parameters, the called subsystem could also return a value associated with the result of the request in terms of *statusInformation* or result, as shown in Figure 7.4(a). Because of the execution of *primitiveAB*, subsystem B may initiate a request for service from another subsystem, subsystem C, using *primitiveBC* over the abstract service interface between subsystems B and C.

In general, except for dispatcher, primitives are associated with the receiving subsystem. Dispatcher primitives are used in receiving messages from and to the application modules, as well as registering and unregistering them, and in transmitting and receiving messages from the network.

Figure 7.4(b) shows the example of the application, command generator, sending a request *sendPdu* (destined for a remote entity) to the dispatcher. The dispatcher, after successful execution of the service requested and sending it on the network, returns to the application *sendPduHandle*. The *sendPduHandle* will be used by the command generator to correlate the response from the remote entity. There are no OUT parameters to be filled in this primitive except the status information. However, the command generator does expect the status information, hence the coupling arrow indicator in the figure. The dispatcher sends an error indicator instead of *sendPduHandle* for the status information if the *sendPdu* transaction is a failure. The dispatcher also generates a request to the MPM, *prepareOutgoingMessage*. The *prepareOutgoingMessage* has both IN and OUT parameters and hence information flows in both directions. The numerous IN and OUT parameters associated with primitives are not identified in the figure for the sake of simplicity.

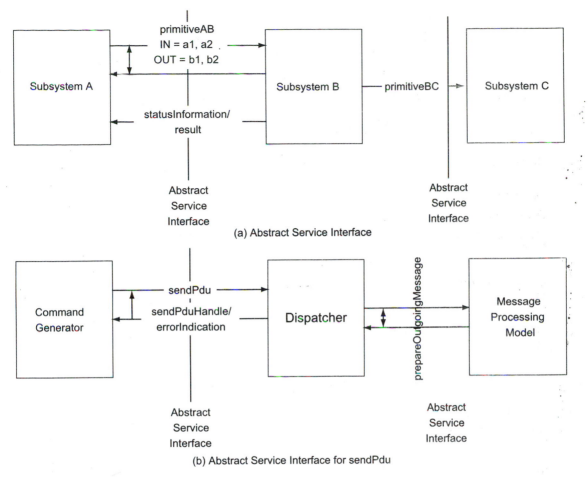

Figure 7.4 Abstract Service Interfaces

Table 7.3 lists the primitives served by the dispatcher, message processing subsystem, security, and access control subsystems. A brief description is presented for each primitive on the service provided and the user of service.

7.4   SNMPv3 APPLICATIONS

SNMPv3 formally defines five types of applications. These are not the same as the functional model that the OSI model addresses. These may be considered as the application service elements that are used to build applications. They are command generator, command responder, notification originator, notification receiver, and proxy forwarder. These are described in RFC 2273.

7.4.1   Command Generator

A command generator application is used to generate get-request, get-next-request, get-bulk, and set-request messages. The command generator also processes the response received for the command sent. Typically, the command generator application is associated with the network manager process.

Table 7.3 List of Primitives

MODULE	PRIMITIVE	SERVICE PROVIDED
Dispatcher	sendPdu	Processes request from application to send a PDU to a remote entity
Dispatcher	processPdu	Processes incoming message from a remote entity
Dispatcher	returnResponsePdu	Processes request from application to send a response PDU
Dispatcher	processResponsePdu	Processes incoming response from a remote entity
Dispatcher	registerContextEngineID	Registers request from a context engine
Dispatcher	unregisterContextEngineID	Unregisters request from a context engine
Message Processing Model	prepareOutgoingMessage	Processes request from dispatcher to prepare outgoing message to a remote entity
Message Processing Model	prepareResponseMessage	Processes request from dispatcher to prepare outgoing response to a remote entity
Message Processing Model	prepareDataElements	Processes request from dispatcher to extract data elements from an incoming message from a remote entity
Security Model	generateRequestMsg	Processes request from message processing model to generate a request message
Security Model	processIncomingMsg	Processes request from message processing model to process security data in an incoming message
Security Model	generateResponseMsg	Processes request from message processing model to generate a response message
Intra-Security Model	authenticateOutgoingMsg	Processes request to authentication service to authenticate outgoing message
Intra-Security Model	authenticateIncomingMsg	Processes request for authentication service to incoming message
Intra-Security Model	encryptData	Processes request from security model to privacy service to encrypt data
Intra-Security Model	decrypt Data	Processes request for privacy service to decrypt an incoming message
Access Control Model	isAccessAllowed	Processes request from application to access and authorize service requested

Figure 7.5 shows the use of the command generator application using the get-request example. In the top half of the figure, the get-request message is sent after it passes through the dispatcher, the MPM, and the SM. The command generator sends the *sendPdu* primitive to the dispatcher, which requests the

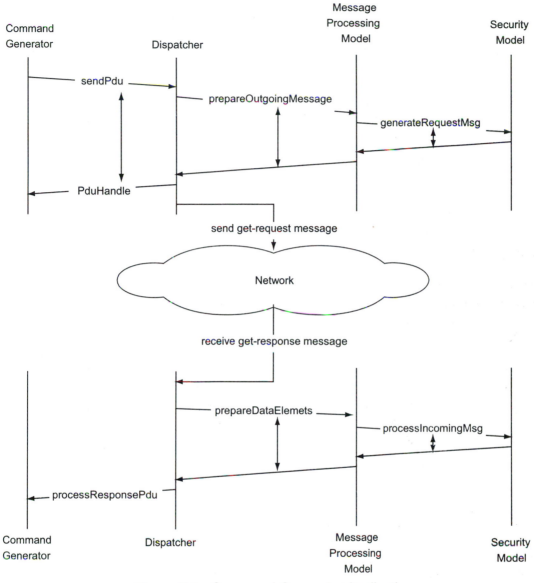

Figure 7.5 Command Generator Application

MPM to prepare an outgoing message. The dispatcher also sends a *sendPduHandle* to the command generator to track the request. The details on the information exchanged between MPM and SM are covered in Section 7.6. The SM is used to generate the outgoing message, including authentication and privacy parameters. The dispatcher then sends the message on the network.

The bottom half of Figure 7.5 presents the role of the command generator when the get-response message is received from the remote entity. The dispatcher receives the message from the network and requests MPM to prepare data elements, which are addressed in Section 7.6. The SM validates the authenticity and privacy parameters. The dispatcher receives the returned message from SM and forwards it to the command generator to process the response.

An example of the command generator transaction is an SNMPv1 get-request command from a network management system (NMS) to an agent requesting the values of System group (see Figure 5.17a). The command generator sends the command and OIDs to the dispatcher along with version number (SNMPv1) and security information. It also sends a tracking ID, *sendPduHandle*, to the NMS. This would be *Request ID* (=1) shown in Figure 5.17(a). When the MPM returns the outgoing message, which could be a secured (authenticated and encrypted) message, the dispatcher delivers it to the network using user datagram protocol (UDP) to be transmitted to the agent. The command generator receives the response from the dispatcher (asynchronously) sent by the agent. The primitive *processResponsePdu* would deliver the PDU containing the values for the System group shown in Figure 5.17(b) to the command generator. The command generator matches the response PDU received with *Request ID* = 1 with the one that was sent.

7.4.2 Command Responder

A command responder processes the get and set requests destined for it and is received from a legitimate non-authoritative remote entity. It performs the appropriate action of get or set on the network element, prepares a get-response message, and sends it to the remote entity that made the request. This is shown in Figure 7.6. In contrast to Figure 7.5, in which the top and bottom half processes run on two remote objects, the top and bottom of Figure 7.6 belong to the same object. Typically, the command responder is in the management agent associated with the managed object.

Before the get-request could be processed by the command-responder application, the context that the SNMP engine is responsible for must register with the SNMP engine. It does this by using the *registerContextEngineID*. Once this is in place, the get-request (same example as used in command generator) is received by the dispatcher, data elements are prepared by the MPM, security parameters are validated by the SM, and the *processPdu* is passed on to the command responder. This set of processes is presented in the top half of Figure 7.6.

Once the request is processed by the Command Responder, it prepares the get-response message as shown in the bottom half of Figure 7.6. The message is passed to the Dispatcher using the *returnResponsePdu*. The MPM prepares the response message, the SM performs the security functions, and the Dispatcher eventually transmits the get-response message on the network.

Continuing the example discussed in Section 7.4.1 for the command generator, the dispatcher in the SNMP agent receives the message. The message is processed by the MPM and the SM and is returned to the dispatcher. Assuming that the managed object has registered its context engine ID with the dispatcher using *registerContextEngineID*, the message is delivered to the command responder using *processPdu*. When the command responder acquires the System group information, it fills the PDU received with System group object values shown in Figure 5.17(b). The *returnResponsePdu* primitive is used by the command generator to deliver the message to the dispatcher. The dispatcher, after processing the get-response message through the MPM and the SM, transmits it across the network using UDP protocol.

7.4.3 Notification Originator

The notification originator application generates either a trap or an inform message. Its function is somewhat similar to the command responder, except that it needs to find out where to send the message and what SNMP version and security parameters to use. Further, the notification generator must determine the *contextEngineID* and context name of the context that has the information to be sent. It obtains

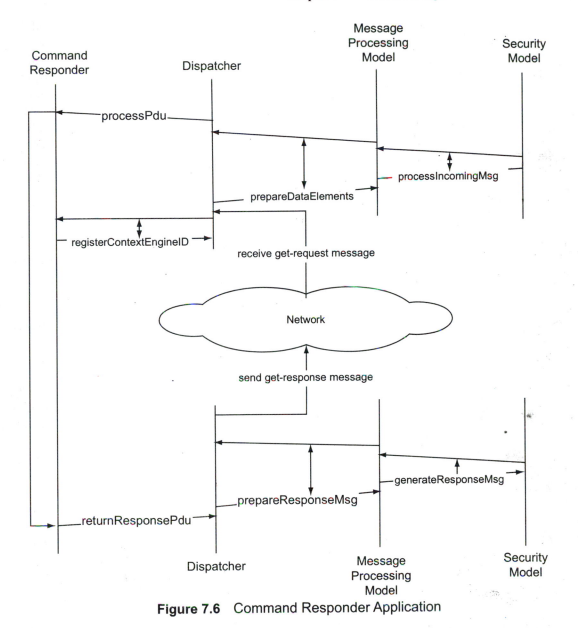

Figure 7.6 Command Responder Application

these data using newly created MIBs for the notification group and the target group, as well as using other modules in the system. We will learn about the new MIBs defining the new groups in Section 7.5. The notification group contains information on whether a notification should be sent to a target and, if so, what filtering should be used on the information. The target that the notification should be sent to is obtained from the target group.

7.4.4 Notification Receiver

The notification receiver application receives SNMP notification messages. It registers with the SNMP engine to receive these messages, just as the command responder does to receive get and set messages.

7.4.5 Proxy Forwarder

The proxy forwarder application performs a function similar to what we discussed in Chapter 6 on the proxy server. However, the proxy definition has been clearly defined and restricted in SNMPv3 specifications. The term "proxy" is used to refer to a proxy forwarder application that forwards SNMP requests, notifications, and responses without regard for what managed objects are contained in those messages. Non-SNMP object translation does not fall under this category. The proxy forwarder handles four types of messages: messages generated by the command generator, command responder, notification generator, and those that contain a report indicator. The proxy forwarder uses the translation table in the proxy group MIB created for this purpose.

7.5 SNMPv3 MANAGEMENT INFORMATION BASE

The new objects defined in SNMPv3 follow the textual convention specified in SNMPv2 and described in Section 6.3. Refer to the RFCs listed in Table 7.1 for complete details on managed objects and MIBs in SNMPv3. We will address a subset of the MIBs here. Figure 7.7 shows the MIB of the new object groups. They are nodes under *snmpModules* {1.3.6.1.6.3}, shown in Figure 6.31. There are seven new MIB groups. The *snmpFrameworkMIB*, node 10 under *snmpModules*, describes the SNMP Management architecture. The MIB group *snmpMPDMIB* (node 11) identifies objects in message processing and dispatching subsystems.

There are three groups defined under *snmpModules* for applications. They are *snmpTargetMIB* (node 12), *snmpNotificationMIB* (node 13), and *snmpProxyMIB* (node 14). The first two are used for notification generator. The *snmpTargetMIB* defines MIB objects, which are used to remotely configure the parameters used by a remote SNMP entity. There are two tables in that MIB, which are of specific interest for us. They are shown in Figure 7.8. The *snmpTargetAddrTable*, which is in *snmpTargetObjects* group, contains the addresses to be used in the generation of SNMP messages. There are nine columnar objects in the table, which are listed in Table 7.4.

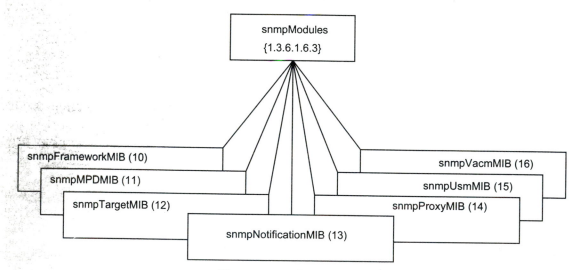

Figure 7.7   SNMPv3 MIB

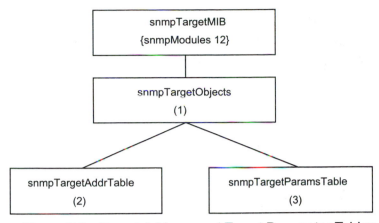

Figure 7.8 Target Address and Target Parameter Tables

Table 7.4 SNMP Target Address Table

ENTITY	OID	DESCRIPTION (BRIEF)
snmpTargetAddrTable	snmpTargetObjects 2	Table of transport addresses
snmpTargetAddrEntry	snmpTargetAddrTable 1	Row in the target address table
snmpTargetAddrName	snmpTargetAddrEntry 1	Locally administered name associated with this entry
snmpTargetAddrTDomain	snmpTargetAddrEntry 2	Transport type of the addresses
snmpTargetAddrTAddress	snmpTargetAddrEntry 3	Transport address
snmpTargetAddrTimeOut	snmpTargetAddrEntry 4	Reflects the expected maximum round-trip time
snmpTargetAddrRetryCount	snmpTargetAddrEntry 5	Number of retries
snmpTargetAddrTagList	snmpTargetAddrEntry 6	List of tag values used to select the target addresses for a particular operation
snmpTargetAddrParams	snmpTargetAddrEntry 7	Value that identifies an entry in the snmpTargetParams Table
snmpTargetAddrStorageType	snmpTargetAddrEntry 8	Storage type for this row
snmpTargetAddrRowStatus	snmpTargetAddrEntry 9	Status of the row

The second table in the *snmpTargetObjects* group is the *snmpTargetParamsTable*. The lead into this table is by using the columnar object *snmpTargetAddrParams* in the *snmpTargetAddrTable*. This contains the security parameters on authentication and privacy. The columnar objects in *snmpTargetParamsTable* are listed in Table 7.5.

The *snmpNotificationMIB* shown in Figure 7.9 deals with MIB objects for the generation of notifications. There are three tables in this group—namely, the notification table, the notification filter profile table, and the notification filter table. They are under the node *snmpNotifyObjects*. The SNMP notification table, *snmpNotifyTable*, is used to select management targets that should receive notifications, as well as the type of notification to be sent. Table 7.6 shows the columnar objects in the group.

The notification profile table group, *snmpNotifyProfileTable*, is used to associate a notification filter profile with a particular set of target parameters. The third group, the notification filter table,

Table 7.5   SNMP Target Parameters Table

ENTITY	OID	DESCRIPTION (BRIEF)
snmpTargetParamsTable	snmpTargetObjects 3	Table of SNMP target information to be used
snmpTargetParamsEntry	snmpTargetParamsTable 1	A set of SNMP target information
snmpTargetParamsName	snmpTargetParamsEntry 1	Locally administered name associated with this entry
snmpTargetParamsMPModel	snmpTargetParamsEntry 2	Message processing model to be used
snmpTargetParamsSecurityModel	snmpTargetParamsEntry 3	Security model to be used
snmpTargetParamsSecurityName	snmpTargetParamsEntry 4	Security name of the principal
snmpTargetParamsSecurityLevel	snmpTargetParamsEntry 5	Level of security
snmpTargetParamsStorageType	snmpTargetParamsEntry 6	Storage type for the row
snmpTargetParamsRowStatus	snmpTargetParamsEntry 7	Status of the row

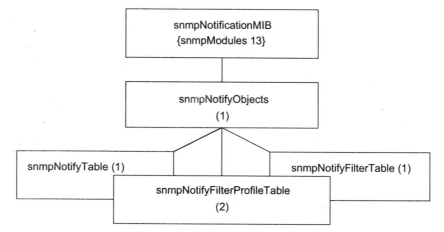

Figure 7.9   SNMP Notification Tables

Table 7.6   SNMP Notification Table

ENTITY	OID	DESCRIPTION (BRIEF)
snmpNotifyTable	snmpNotifyObjects 1	List of targets and notification types
snmpNotifyEntry	snmpNotifyTable 1	Set of management targets and the type of notification
snmpNotifyName	snmpNotifyEntry 1	Locally administered name associated with this entry
snmpNotifyTag	snmpNotifyEntry 2	A single value that is used to select entries in the snmpTargetAddrTable
snmpNotifyType	snmpNotifyEntry 3	Selects trap or inform to send
snmpNotifyStorageType	snmpNotifyEntry 4	Storage type for the row
snmpNotifyRowStatus	snmpNotifyEntry 5	Status of the row

snmpNotifyFilterTable, contains table profiles of the targets. The profile specifies whether a particular target should receive particular information.

The *snmpProxyMIB* is concerned with objects in a proxy forwarding application, such as the SNMPv2 proxy server shown in Figure 6.46. It contains a table of translation parameters used by the proxy forwarder application for forwarding SNMP messages.

The SNMP USM objects are defined in *snmpUsmMIB* module (node 15). Lastly, the objects for VACM for SNMP are defined in the *snmpVacmMIB* module (node 16). We will discuss the details of these MIBs later when we address security in the next section and access control in Section 7.8.

7.6 SECURITY

One of the main objectives, if not the main objective, in developing SNMPv3 is the addition of security features to SNMP management. Authentication and privacy of information, as well as authorization and access controls, have been addressed in SNMPv3 specifications. We will cover the authentication and privacy issues in this section and in Section 7.7. We will deal with access control in Section 7.8.

SNMPv3 architecture permits flexibility to use any protocol for authentication and privacy of information. However, the IETF SNMPv3 working group has specified a USM for its security subsystem. It is termed user-based as it follows the traditional concept of a user, identified by a user name with which to associate security information. The working group has specified HMAC-MD5-96 and HMAC-SHA-96 (see Section 7.7.1 for an explanation) as the authentication protocols. Cipher Block Chaining mode of Data Encryption Standard (CBC-DES) has been adopted for privacy protocol.

We will discuss the general aspects of security associated with the types of threats, the security modules, the message data format to accommodate security parameters, and the use and management of keys in this section. We will specifically address the USM in the next section.

7.6.1 Security Threats

Four types of threats exist to network management information while it is being transported from one management entity to another: (1) modification of information, (2) masquerade, (3) message stream modification, and (4) disclosure. These are shown in Figure 7.10, where the information is transported from management entity A to management entity B. For the first three threats, the signal has to be intercepted by an intruder to tamper with it, whereas for the disclosure threat, the signal can just be tapped and not intercepted.

Modification of information is the threat that some unauthorized user may modify the contents of the message while it is in transit. Data contents are modified, including falsifying the value of an object. It does not include changing the originating or destination address. The modified message is received by entity B, which is unaware that it has been modified. For example, the response by an SNMP agent to a request by an SNMP manager could be altered by this threat.

Masquerade is when an unauthorized user sends information to another assuming the identity of an authorized user. This can be done by changing the originating address. Using the masquerade and modification of information, an unauthorized user can perform operation on a management entity, which he or she is not permitted to do. The SNMP set operation should be protected against this attack.

The SNMP communication uses connectionless transport service, such as UDP. This means that the message could be fragmented into packets with each packet taking a different path. The packets could

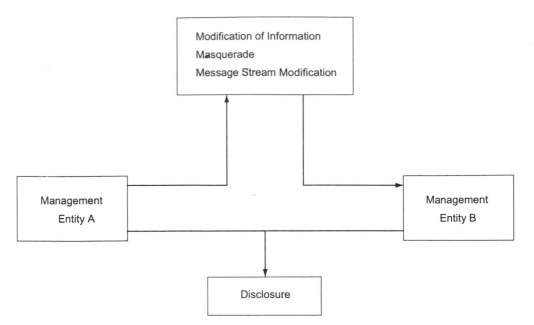

Figure 7.10 Security Threats to Management Information

arrive at the destination out of sequence and have to be reordered. The threat here is that the intruder may manipulate the message stream (**message stream modification**) and maliciously reorder the data packets to change the meaning of the message. For example, the sequence of data of a table could be reordered to change the values in the table. The intruder could also delay messages so that those messages arrive out of sequence. The message could be interrupted, stored, and replayed at a later time by an unauthorized user.

The fourth and last threat that is shown in Figure 7.10 is **disclosure** of management information. The message need not be intercepted for this, but just eavesdropped. For example, the message stream of accounting could be promiscuously monitored by an employee with a TCP/IP dump procedure, and then the information could be used against the establishment.

There are at least two more threats that would be considered as threats in traditional data communication, but the SNMP SM has classified them as being non-threats. The first is denial of service, when an authorized user is denied service by a management entity. This is considered as not being a threat, as a network failure could cause such a denial. It is the responsibility of the protocol to address this issue. The second threat that is not considered a management threat is traffic analysis by an unauthorized user. It was determined by the IETF SNMPv3 working group that there is no significant advantage achieved by protecting against this attack.

7.6.2 Security Model

In normal operational procedures, the MPM in the message processing subsystem interacts with security subsystem models. For example, in Figure 7.2, an outgoing message is generated by an application, which is first handled by a dispatcher subsystem, then by an MPM, and finally by the SM. If the message is to be authenticated, the SM authenticates it and forwards it to the MPM. Similarly for an incoming message, the MPM requests the service of the security subsystem to authenticate the user ID.

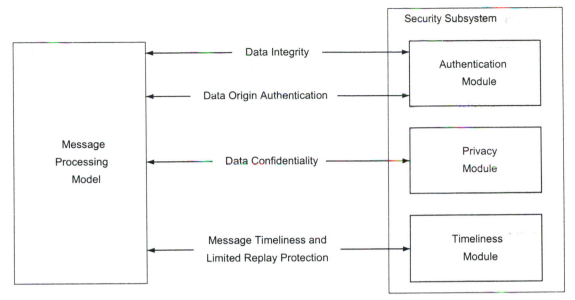

Figure 7.11 Security Services

Figure 7.11 shows the services provided by the three modules in the security subsystem to the MPM. They are the authentication module, the privacy module, and the timeliness module.

Authoritative SNMP Engine. When two management entities communicate, the services provided by each are determined by the role they play, i.e., whether the entity is authorized to perform the service. This led to the concept of authoritative and non-authoritative SNMP engines. This is dependent on which SNMP engine controls the communication between the two entities. SNMPv3 architecture defines that in a communication between two SNMP engines, one acts as an *authoritative engine* and the other as a *non-authoritative engine.* There is a well-defined set of rules as to who is the authoritative SNMP engine for each message that is communicated between two SNMP engines. For get-request, get-next-request, get-bulk-request, set-request or inform messages, the receiver of the message is the authoritative SNMP engine. Since these messages are originated by a manager process in a network management system (NMS), the receiver is the SNMP agent. Thus, the agent is the authoritative SNMP engine. For trap, get-response, and report messages, the sender or the agent is the authoritative SNMP engine. Thus, an SNMP engine that acts in the role of an agent is the designated authoritative SNMP engine. The SNMP engine that acts in the role of a manager is the non-authoritative engine. In general, an SNMP agent is the authoritative SNMP engine in SNMP communication.

An authoritative SNMP engine is responsible for the accuracy of the time-stamp and a unique SNMP engine ID in each message. This requires that every non-authoritative SNMP engine keep a table of the time and authoritative engine ID of every SNMP engine that it communicates with.

Security Authentication. Communication between two entities could satisfy the condition of authoritative and non-authoritative pair. However, it should be the right set of pairs. Thus, the source from which the message is received should be authenticated by the receiver. Further, authentication is needed for the security reasons discussed in Section 7.6.1. Security authentication is done by the authentication module in the security subsystem.

The *authentication module* provides two services, *data integrity* and *data origin authentication*. The data integrity service provides the function of authenticating a message at the originating end and validating it at the receiving end, ensuring that it has not been modified in the communication process by an unauthorized intruder. Authentication validation also catches any non-malicious modification of data in the communication channel. The authentication scheme uses authentication protocols, such as HMAC-MD5-96 or HMAC-SHA-96 in SNMPv3 or any other protocol in place of it.

The second service that is provided by the authentication module is *data origin authentication*. This ensures that the claimed identity of the user on whose behalf the message was sent is truly the originator of the message. The authentication module appends to each message a unique identifier associated with an authoritative SNMP engine.

Privacy of Information. The second module in the security subsystem in Figure 7.11 is the *privacy module*, which provides *data confidentiality service*. Data confidentiality ensures that information is not made available or disclosed to unauthorized users, entities, or processes. The privacy of the message is accomplished by encrypting the message at the sending end and decrypting it at the receiving end.

Timeliness of Message. The *timeliness module* is the third module in the security subsystem and provides the function of checking *message timeliness* and thus prevents message redirection, delay, and replay. Using the concept of an authoritative SNMP engine, a window of time is set in the receiver to accept a message. The travel time between the sender and the receiver should be within this time window interval. The time clock in both the sender and the receiver is synchronized to the authoritative SNMP engine. The recommended value for the window time in SNMPv3 is 150 seconds.

For implementation of the timeliness module, the SNMP engine maintains three objects: *snmpEngineID, snmpEngineBoots,* and *snmpEngineTime*. The *snmpEngineID* uniquely identifies the authoritative SNMP engine. The *snmpEngineBoots* is a count of the number of times the SNMP engine has re-booted or re-initialized since *snmpEngineID* was last configured. The *snmpEngineTime* is the number of seconds since the *snmpEngineBoots* counter was last initialized or reset.

The timeliness module also checks the message ID of a response with the request message and drops the message if they do not match.

We will next look at the message format in SNMPv3 in general, and the security parameters contained in it in particular.

7.6.3   Message Format

The SNMPv3 message format is shown in Figure 7.12. It consists of four groups of data. Details of the fields in each group except security parameters are given in Table 7.7. The first group is a single field, which is the version number and is in the same position as in SNMPv1 and SNMPv2.

Global (header) data defined by the data type header are the second group of data in the message format. They contain administrative parameters of the message, which are message ID, message maximum size, message flag, and message SM. It is worth noting that an SNMP engine can handle many models concurrently in the message processing subsystem. The dispatcher subsystem examines the version number in the message and sends it to the appropriate message processing module in the message subsystem. For example, if the version is set to snmpv2, the SNMPv2 message processing module would be invoked.

The third group of data, security parameter fields, are used by the SM in communicating between sending and receiving entities. The values of the parameters depend on the message SM set in the header data. The parameters are shown in Figure 7.12 and will be discussed in Section 7.7.

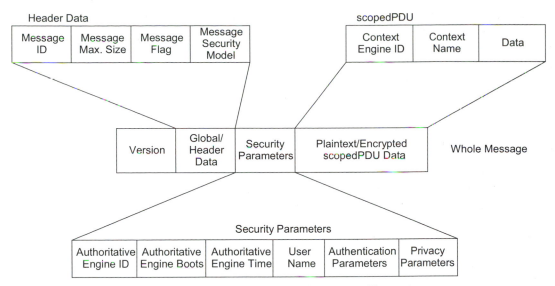

Figure 7.12 SNMPv3 Message Format

Table 7.7 SNMPv3 Message Format

FIELD	OBJECT NAME	DESCRIPTION
Version	msgVersion	SNMP version number of the message format
Message ID	msgID	Administrative ID associated with the message
Message max. size	msgMaxSize	Maximum size supported by the sender
Message flags	msgFlags	Bit fields identifying report, authentication; and privacy of the message
Message security model	msgSecurityModel	Security model used for the message; concurrent multiple models allowed
Security parameters (See Table 7.8)	msgSecurityParameters	Security parameters used for communication between sending and receiving security modules
Plaintext/encrypted scopedPDU data	scopedPduData	Choice of plaintext or encrypted scopedPDU; scopedPDU uniquely identifies context and PDU
Context engine ID	contextEngineID	Unique ID of a context (managed entity) with a context name realized by an SNMP entity
Context name	contextName	Name of the context (managed entity)
PDU	data	Contains unencrypted PDU

The fourth and final group of fields in the whole message record shown in Figure 7.12 is the plaintext/encrypted *scopedPDU* data. The *scopedPduData* field contains either unencrypted or encrypted *scopedPDU*. If the privacy flag is set to zero (no privacy) in the message flag (see header data), then this field contains plaintext *scopedPDU*, which is unencrypted *scopedPDU*. The plaintext *scopedPDU* comprises the context engine ID, context name, and the PDU. A management entity can be responsible for multiple instances of managed objects. For example, in an ATM switch, a single managed entity acts as the agent for all the network interface cards in all its ports. We could treat each interface card as a context with a context engine ID and a context name. Thus, a particular context name, in conjunction with a particular context engine ID, identifies the particular context associated with the management information contained in the PDU portion of the message. The object name for PDU is *data*.

7.7 SNMPv3 USER-BASED SECURITY MODEL

The security subsystem for SNMPv3 is a USM, which is based on the traditional user name concept. Just as we have defined abstract service interfaces between various subsystems in an SNMP entity, we can define abstract service interfaces in USM. They define conceptual interfaces between generic USM services and self-contained authentication and privacy services. There are two primitives associated with authentication service, one to generate an outgoing authenticated message (*authenticateOutgoingMsg*) and another to validate the authenticated incoming message (*authenticateIncomingMsg*). Similarly, there are two primitives associated with privacy services, *encryptData* and *decryptData*, for the encryption of outgoing messages and the decryption of incoming messages. These were included in the list of primitives in Table 7.3.

Services provided by authentication and privacy modules in the security subsystem for outgoing and incoming messages are shown in Figures 7.13 and 7.14, respectively. Looking at the overall picture, the MPM invokes the USM in the security subsystem. The USM in turn invokes, based on the security level set in the message, the authentication and privacy modules. Results are returned to the MPM by the USM.

In Figure 7.13 that shows the process of an outgoing message, we will assume that both privacy and authentication flags are set in the message flag in the header data. The MPM inputs the MPM information, header data, security data, and *scopedPDU* to the security subsystem. The USM invokes the privacy module first, providing the encryption key and *scopedPDU* as input. The privacy module outputs

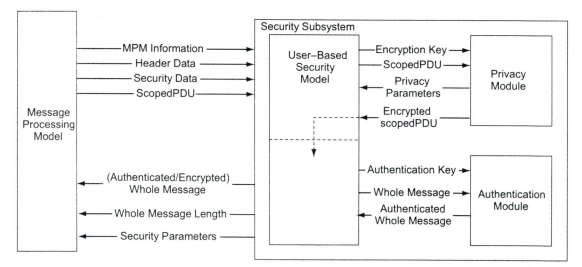

Figure 7.13 Privacy and Authentication Service for an Outgoing Message

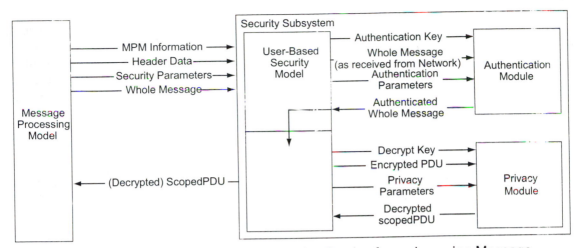

Figure 7.14 Privacy and Authentication Service for an Incoming Message

privacy parameters that are sent as part of the message and the encrypted *scopedPDU*. The USM passes the unauthenticated whole message with encrypted *scopedPDU* to the authentication module along with the authentication key. The authentication module returns the authenticated whole message to USM. The security subsystem returns the authenticated and encrypted whole message along with the message length and security parameters to the MPM.

Figure 7.14 shows the reverse process of an incoming message going through the authentication validation first, and then decryption of the message by the privacy module.

The security parameters used in the SM are shown in Figure 7.12. Table 7.8 lists the parameters and the corresponding SNMPv3 MIB objects. The position of the relevant MIB objects associated with the security parameters belongs to the two modules, *snmpFrameworkMIB* and *snmpUsmMIB*, under *snmpModulesMIB* shown in Figure 7.7. The details of the position of the objects in the MIB are presented in Figure 7.15.

We have already discussed the first three parameters in Table 7.8 associated with engine ID, number of boots, and time since the last boot. They are in the *snmpEngine* group shown in Figure 7.15. The last three parameters in the table are in *usmUserTable* in the *usmUser* group shown in Figure 7.15.

The fourth parameter is the user (principal) on whose behalf the message is being exchanged. The authentication parameters are defined by the authentication protocol columnar object in the *usmUserTable*. The *usmUserTable* describes the users configured in the SNMP engine and the authentication parameters the type of authentication protocol used. Likewise, the privacy parameters describe the type of privacy protocol used.

The *usmUserSpinLock* is an advisory lock that is used by SNMP command generator applications to coordinate their use of the set operation in creating or modifying secrets in *usmUserTable*.

Now that we have a broad picture, let us return to Figure 7.13 and follow through the detailed data flow and processes involved in the USM. Figure 7.13 shows the operation for an outgoing message, which could be either a Request message or a Response message. The MPM inputs information on the *message processing model* to be used (normally SNMP version number), leader data, security data (SM, SNMP engine ID, security name, and security level) and *scopedPDU* to the Security Subsystem (SS). This information is received by the User-base Security Model (UCM) in SS.

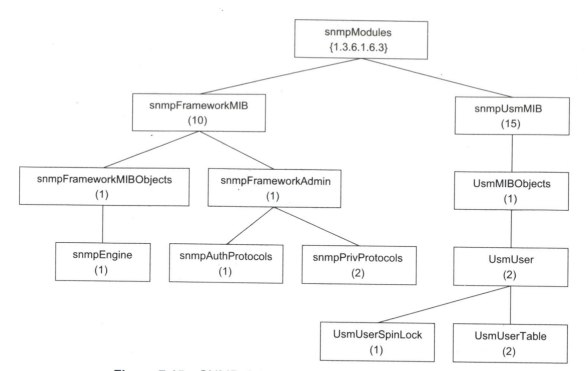

Figure 7.15   SNMPv3 MIB Objects for Security Parameters

Table 7.8   Security Parameters and Corresponding MIB Objects

SECURITY PARAMETERS	USM USER GROUP OBJECTS
msgAuthoritativeEngineID	snmpEngineID (under snmpEngine Group)
msgAuthoritativeEngineBoots	snmpEngineBoots (under snmpEngine Group)
msgAuthoritativeEngineTime	snmpEngineTime (under snmpEngine Group)
msgUserName	usmUserName (in usmUserTable)
msgAuthenticationParameters	usmUserAuthProtocol (in usmUserTable)
msgPrivacyParameters	usmUserPrivProtocol (in usmUserTable)

In the USM, the security-level settings for privacy and authentication determine the modules invoked. The encryption key and *scopedPDU* (context engine ID, context name, and PDU) are fed into the privacy module, which encrypts the PDU and returns the encrypted PDU along with privacy parameters to the calling module, USM.

The USM then communicates with the authentication module. The USM inputs the encrypted whole message along with the authentication key. The authentication module returns the authenticated whole message to USM. The USM passes the authenticated and encrypted whole message, whole message length, and securities parameters back to the MPM.

The operation for an incoming message is shown in Figure 7.14. Inputs to the security subsystem are the MPM information, header data, security parameters for the received message, and the whole message. The output of the security subsystem is *scopedPDU* in plaintext format.

Within the security subsystem, the operational sequence of authentication and privacy for an incoming message are reversed from that of the outgoing message. The message is first sent to the authentication module with the authentication key, the whole message received from the network, and authentication parameters received from the network as inputs. It outputs an authenticated whole message to the calling module in USM. The USM then feeds the decrypt key, privacy parameters, and the encrypted *scopedPDU* and receives in return the decrypted *scopedPDU*. The decrypted *scopedPDU* is then passed on to the message processing module.

7.7.1   Authentication Protocols

The secret to security using the authentication and privacy schemes is the secret key that is shared between the sender and the user. There is a secret key for authentication and a secret key for encryption and decryption. The secret key for the User-based Security Module (USM) is developed from the user password. Two algorithms are recommended in SNMPv3 for developing the key from the password. They are HMAC-MD5-96 and HMAC-SHA-96. The first letter in the designation stands for the cryptographic hash function (H) used for generating the Message Access Code (MAC). The second part in the designation is the hashing algorithm used, the first one being the MD5 hashing algorithm, and the second one the SHA-1 hashing algorithm to generate MAC. The MAC is derived by truncating the hashing code generated to 96 bits as indicated by the last set of characters in the designation.

Authentication Key. The authentication key, the secret key for authentication, is derived from a chosen password of the user. The user in our case is the non-authoritative SNMP engine, which is generally an NMS. In both MD5 and SHA-1 algorithms, the password is repeated until it forms exactly a string of 2^{20} octets (1,048,576 octets), truncating the last repetition, if necessary. This result is called *digest0* [Stallings, 1998]. In the second step, the *digest0* is hashed using either the MD5 or the SHA-1 algorithm to derive *digest1*. MD5 algorithm yields a 16-octet *digest1,* and SHA-1 results in a 20-octet *digest1*. A second string is formed by concatenating the authoritative SNMP engine ID and *digest1*. This string is fed into the respective hashing algorithm to derive *digest2.* The derived *digest2* is the user's authentication key, *authKey*, which is input to the authentication modules shown in Figures 7.13 and 7.14. You are referred to RFC [2104] and Stallings [1998] for details on MD5 and SHA-1 algorithms.

The choice between the 16-octet MD5-based *authKey* and the 20-octet SHA-1-based *authKey* is based on the implementation. In the 20-octet key, it is harder to break the code than in the 16-octet key. However, the processing is faster with the 16-octet key. Further, the same 16-octet key derived from the same password could be used for the privacy key, although it is recommended that the same key not be used for both.

HMAC Procedure. The 96-bit long code MAC is derived using the HMAC procedure described in RFC 2104 and RFC 2274. First, two functions K1 and K2 are derived using *authKey* obtained above, and two fixed but different strings, *ipad* and *opad,* as defined in the following manner. A 64-byte *extendedAuthKey* is derived by supplementing *authKey* with zeros.

> *ipad* = the hexadecimal byte 0x36 (00110110) repeated 64 times
>
> *opad* = the hexadecimal byte 0x5c (01011100) repeated 64 times
>
> K1 = *extendedAuthKey* XOR *ipad*
>
> K2 = *extendedAuthKey* XOR *opad*

HMAC is computed by performing the following nested hashing functions on K1, K2, and *wholeMsg*, which is the unauthenticated whole message shown in Figure 7.13:

H (K2, H (K1, *wholeMsg*))

The first 12 octets of this final digest are the MAC. These are the authentication parameters, *msgAuthenticationParameters,* which are shown in Figure 7.12 and are included as part of the authenticated whole message, *authenticatedWholeMsg* shown in Figure 7.13.

Key Management. A user (NMS) has only one password and hence one *secret* key *digest1* mentioned in the authentication key discussion earlier. However, it communicates with all the authoritative SNMP engines (all the agents in the network). The shared information is again a secret between the two communicating engines. The concept of a localized key is introduced to accomplish this instead of storing a separate password for each pair of communicating engines. A hash function, which is the same hashing function that is used to generate the secret key, is employed to generate the localized key.

Localized key = H (*secret, authoritativeSnmpEngineID, secret*)

where *secret* is the secret key (*digest1*) and the *authoritativeSnmpEngineID* is the SNMP engine ID of the authoritative SNMP engine with which the local user is communicating. This localized key, different for each authoritative engine, is stored in each authoritative engine with which the user communicates. Notice that the localized key is the same as *authKey*.

SNMPv3 permits the operation of changes and modification in a key, but not the creation of keys to ensure that the secret key does not become stale.

Discovery. One important function of an NMS as a user is the discovery of agents in the network. This is accomplished by generating a Request message with a security level of no-authentication and no-privacy, a user name of "initial," an authoritative SNMP engine ID of zero length, and a varBind list that is empty. The authoritative engines respond with Response messages containing the engine ID and the security parameters filled in. Additional information is then obtained via pair-wise communication messages.

7.7.2 Encryption Protocol

The encryption generates non-readable *ciphertext* from a readable text, *plaintext.* The SNMPv3 recommendation for data confidentiality is to use the CBC-DES Symmetric Encryption Protocol. The USM specifications require the *scopedPDU* portion of the message be encrypted. A secret value in combination with a timeliness value is used to create the encryption/decryption key and initialization vector (IV). Again, the secret value is user-based, and hence is associated typically with an NMS. The 16-octet privacy key, *privKey,* is generated from the password as described in the generation of authentication code using MD-5 hashing algorithm.

The first eight octets of the 16-octet privacy key are used to create the DES key. The DES key is only 56 bits long and hence the least significant bit of each octet in the privacy key is discarded. The 16-octet IV is made up of two parts, an 8-octet pre-IV concatenated with an 8-octet *salt.* The pre-IV is the last eight octets of the privacy key. The *salt* is added to ensure that two identical instances of ciphertext are not generated from two different plaintexts using the same key. The *salt* is generated by an SNMP engine by concatenating a 4-octet *snmpEngineBoots* with a locally generated integer. The *salt* is the privacy parameter shown in Figures 7.12, 7.13, and 7.14.

The encryption process first divides the plaintext of *scopedPDU* into 64-bit blocks. The plaintext of each block is XOR-ed with the ciphertext of the previous block, and the result is encrypted to produce a ciphertext for the current block. For the first block, the IV is used instead of the ciphertext of the previous block.

7.8   ACCESS CONTROL

We have covered security considerations in network management with regard to data integrity, message authentication, data confidentiality, and the timeliness of message in the previous two sections. We will now address access control, which deals with who can access network management components and what they can access. In SNMPv1 and SNMPv2, this subject has been covered using the community-based access policy. In SNMPv3, access control has been made more secure and more flexible. It is called VACM.

VACM defines a set of services that an application in an agent can use to validate command requests and notification receivers. It validates command requests as to the sending sources and their access privilege. It assumes that authentication of the source has been done by the authentication module. In order to perform the services, a local database containing access rights and policies has been created in the SNMP entity, called Local Configuration Datastore (LCD). This is typically in an agent or in a manager functioning in an agent role when it communicates with another manager.

The LCD needs to be configured remotely and hence security considerations need to be introduced. A MIB module for VACM has been introduced toward achieving this.

7.8.1   Elements of the Model

Five elements comprise VACM: (1) groups, (2) security level, (3) contexts, (4) MIB views and view families, and (5) access policy. We will define each of them now.

Groups. A group, identified as *groupName*, is a set of zero or more SM (*vacmSecurityModel*)—security name (*vacmSecurityName*) pairs on whose behalf SNMP management objects can be accessed. A security name is a principal as defined in Section 7.3.2 and is independent of the SM used. All elements belonging to a group have identical access rights. Equivalent of a group in SNMPv1 is the community name. Thus, all NMSs (security names) in SNMPv1 (SM) with a community name public (group) would have equal access privilege to an agent.

Security Level. Security level (*vacmAccessSecurityLevel*) is the level of security of the user, namely no authentication–no privacy, authentication–no privacy, and authentication–privacy. This is set by the message flag shown in Figure 7.12. A member using a specific SM and with a given security name in a group could have different access rights by using different security levels.

Contexts. As mentioned in Section 7.3, an SNMP context is a collection of management information accessible by an SNMP entity. An SNMP entity has access to potentially more than one context. Each SNMP engine has a context table that lists the locally available contexts by *contextName*.

MIB Views and View Families. As in SNMPv1 and SNMPv2, access rights to contexts are controlled by a MIB view (see Figure 5.2). A MIB view is defined for each group and it details the set of managed object types (and optionally, the specific instances of object types). Following the approach of the tree-like naming structure for MIB, the MIB view is defined as a combination of a set of *view subtrees*, where each view subtree is a subtree within the managed object naming tree. A simple MIB view could be all nodes defined under an OBJECT IDENTIFIER, for example, *system*. A view subtree is identified by the OBJECT IDENTIFIER value, which is the longest OBJECT IDENTIFIER prefix common to all (potential) MIB object instances in that subtree. For the system example, it is {1.3.6.1.2.1.1}.

An example of a complex MIB view could be all information relevant to a particular network interface. This can be represented by the union of multiple view subtrees, such as a set of *system* and *interfaces* to view all managed objects under the System and Interfaces groups.

A more complex view is a situation where all the columnar objects in a conceptual row of a table appear in separate subtrees, one per column, each with a similar format. Because the formats are similar, the required set of subtrees can be aggregated into one structure, called a *family of view subtrees*. A family of view subtrees is a pairing of an OBJECT IDENTIFIER value (called the family name) together with a bit string value (called the family mask). The family mask indicates which subidentifiers of the associated family name are significant to the family's definition. A family of view subtrees can either be included or excluded from the MIB view.

Access Policy: The access policy determines the access rights to objects as *read-view, write-view,* and *notify-view*. For a given *groupName, contextName, securityModel,* and *securityLevel,* that group's access rights are defined by either the combination of the three views, or *not-accessible*. The read-view is used for get-request, get-next-request, and get-bulk-request operations. The write-view is used with the set-request operation. The notify-view represents the set of object instances authorized for the group when sending objects in a notification.

7.8.2   VACM Process

The VACM process is presented as a flowchart in Figure 7.16. We will explain the process in terms of an SNMP agent with an SNMP engine having responsibility for many contexts. The tables shown in the figure are addressed in the next section on VACM MIB. As RFC 2275 describes, the VACM process answers the six questions related to access of management information. They are:

1. Who are you (group comprising security model and security name)?
2. Where do you want to go (context to be accessed)?
3. How secured are you to access the information (security model and security level)?
4. Why do you want to access the information (to read, write, or send notification)?
5. What object (object type) do you want to access?
6. Which object (object instance) do you want to access?

The first question is answered by the introduction of the group concept. The group that the requester belongs to is determined by the VACM from the SM and the security name. It uses the security-to-group table for validating the principal and deriving the group name.

The second question is answered by checking whether the context that needs to be accessed is within the responsibility of the agent. If the first two questions are answered in the affirmative, then the results of those, namely *group name* and *context name,* along with the *security model* and the *security level* (answer to how), are fed into the "access allowed?" process. It is assumed by VACM that the SM and the security level (the third question) have already been validated by the security module. Given these four

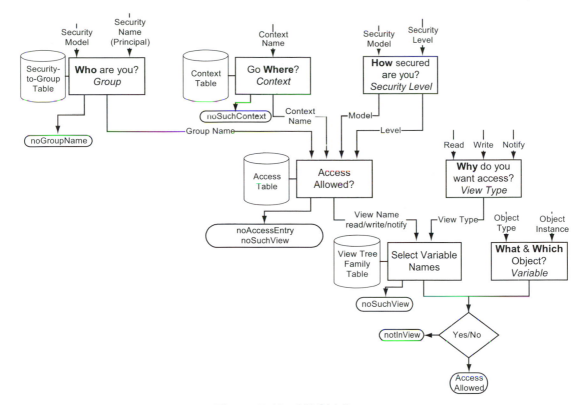

Figure 7.16 VACM Process

inputs as indices, the access table provides the views permitted, *view name*. It comprises one or more of the views, read-view, write-view, and notify-view.

The answer to the fourth question regarding why access is needed is used by the "select variable names" process to select the family of view subtrees eligible to be accessed. The view tree family table is applicable for this selection. A match is made between the result of this process and the answers to the last two questions as to what (object type) and which (object instance), to make a decision on whether access is allowed or not.

Each process puts out an error message based on the validation as shown in Figure 7.16.

7.8.3 VACM MIB

The processes in VACM use the tables to perform the functions mentioned. A VACM MIB has been defined specifying the newly created objects. This is shown in Figure 7.17. The *snmpVacmMIB* is a node under *snmpModules* shown in Figure 7.7. The three tables defining the context, group, and access are nodes under *vacmMIBObjects*, which is a node under *snmpVacmMIB*.

The *vacmContextTable* is a list of *vacmContextNames*. The *vacmSecurityToGroupTable* has columnar objects, *vacmSecurityModel*, *vacmSecurityName*, as indices to retrieve *vacmGroupName*.

The VACM Access Table, shown in Figure 7.18, is used to determine the access permission and the *viewName*. It has *vacmGroupName* from the *vacmSecurityToGroupTable* as one of the indices.

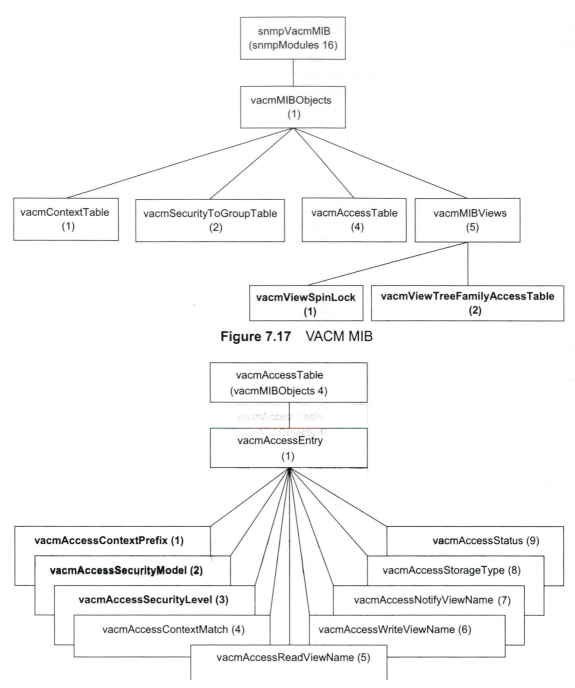

Figure 7.17 VACM MIB

Figure 7.18 VACM Access Table

The other three indices from this table are *vacmAccessContextPrefix*, *vacmAccessSecurityModel*, and *vacmAccessSecurityLevel*. The *viewName* representing the three views, *vacmAccessReadViewName*, *vacmAccessWriteViewName*, and *vacmAccessNotifyViewName*, are retrieved from the table. The *vacmAccessStorageType* and *vacmAccessStatus* are the administrative information objects relating to the storage volatility and the row status.

The *vacmMIBViews*, subnode (5), under *vacmMIBObjects*, shown in Figure 7.19, has the subordinate nodes *vacmViewSpinLock* and *vacmViewTreeFamilyAccessTable*. The *vacmViewSpinLock* is an advisory lock that is used by SNMP command generator applications to coordinate their use of the set operation in creating or modifying views in agents. It is an optional implementation object.

The *vacmViewTreeFamilyTable* describes families of subtrees that are available within MIB views in the local SNMP agent for each context. Each row in this table describes a subtree for a *viewName* and an OBJECT IDENTIFIER. For example, if the "access allowed?" process in Figure 7.16 yields three values for *viewName*, that would result in three conceptual rows in this table. The *vacmViewTreeFamilyViewName* representing the *viewName* is one of the columnar objects and an index in the table. Two indices define a conceptual row in this table. The second is *vacmViewTreeFamilySubtree*. It is a node representing the top of the tree. For example, if the OBJECT IDENTIFIER were 1.3.6.1.2.1.1, it would represent the *system* subtree. The OBJECT IDENTIFIER for the local agent is determined by the highest OBJECT IDENTIFIER that would address all object instances in the local view.

In some situations, we may want to view different subsets of a subtree. In such cases, we can form a family of view subtrees by using a combination of two parameters. The first is the selection of the view, which is done by a family mask defined by *vacmViewTreeFamilyMask*; and the second parameter is the family type defined by *vacmViewTreeFamilyType*, shown in Figure 7.19. The family mask is a bit string that is used with the *vacmViewTreeFamilySubtree*. Using this feature, specific objects in a subtree are selected if the corresponding object identifier matches. If the corresponding bit value is 0 in the family mask, it is considered a wild card and any value of the object identifier would be

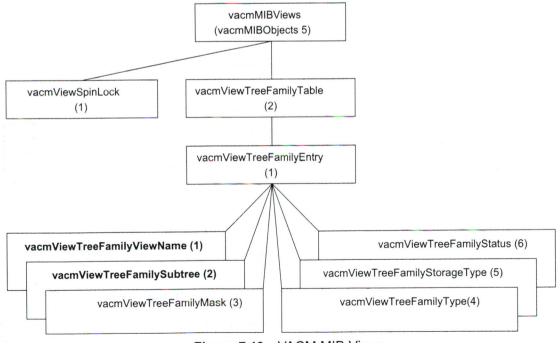

Figure 7.19 VACM MIB Views

selected. After the selection is made, if the family type value is included (1), the view is included. If it is excluded (2), the view is excluded. There is more flexibility in the views by introducing a columnar object *vacmViewTreeFamilyType* that indicates whether a particular subtree in the family of subtrees derived from *vacmViewTreeFamilySubtree* and *vacmViewTreeFamilyMask* is to be included or excluded in a context's MIB view.

As an example of the System group to be included, values for various parameters of the family entry in Figure 7.19 are:

> Family view name = "system"
> Family subtree = 1.3.6.1.2.1.1
> Family mask = ""
> Family type = 1

The zero length string, "", for mask value designates all 1s by convention.

We could extend the view by adding a second row to the table. For example, we could add an SNMP group by adding another row to the table with the family subtree 1.3.6.1.2.1.11.

Suppose we want to add a columnar object to the table. We would add the columnar object with the index added as another row. We could also add all the columnar objects of a conceptual row in a table. A useful convention for doing this is to use the definition of columnar object 0, which designates all columnar objects in a table. For example, {1.3.6.1.2.1.2.2.1.0.5} identifies all columnar objects associated with the 5th interface (corresponding to *ifIndex* value of 5) in the *ifTable*.

If more than one family name is present with the same number of subidentifiers, the lexicographic convention is followed for the predominance among them. This helps in the following way. Suppose we wanted to choose all columnar objects in the above *ifTable* example, except the *ifMtu*, which is the 4th columnar object. We would then choose {1.3.6.1.2.1.2.2.1.4.5} and the Type = 2 to exclude it. Since this is lexicographically higher than {1.3.6.1.2.1.2.2.1.0.5}, this will take precedence. Thus, the combination of the two will select all 5th row objects except *ifMtu*.

Summary

We have reviewed the latest version of SNMP, SNMPv3, in this chapter. The two major features are the specifications for a formalized SNMP architecture that addresses the three SNMP frameworks for the three versions. Two new members, dispatch and message processing modules, are defined. This would enable a network management system to handle messages from and to agents that belong to all three current versions. It would also accommodate future versions, if needed.

The second major feature is the inclusion of security. A security subsystem is defined, which addresses data integrity, data origin authentication, data confidentiality, message timeliness, and limited message replay protection. The authentication module in the security subsystem addresses the first two issues, the privacy module protects data confidentiality, and the timeliness module deals with message timeliness and limited replay protection. The security subsystem is the User-based Security Model (USM). It is derived from the traditional concept of user ID and password.

The access policies of SNMPv1 and SNMPv2 have been extended and made more flexible by the VACM. An SNMP agent handling multiple objects (contexts) can be configured to present a set of MIB views and a family of subtrees in its MIB views. These views can be matched with seven input parameters to determine access permission to the principal. They are the SM (version of SNMP), the security name (principal), the security level (dependent on the authentication and privacy parameters), the context name, the type of access needed, the object type, and the object instance.

Exercises

1. The first four octets of an SNMP engine ID in a system are set to the binary equivalent of the system's SNMP management private enterprise number as assigned by the IANA. Write the first four octets of the SNMP engine ID in hexadecimal notation for the four enterprises, (cisco, hp, 3com, and cabletron,) shown in Figure 4.14 for the following two versions:

   (a) SNMPv1
   (b) SNMPv3

2. Write the full SNMP engine ID for:

   (a) SNMPv1 for a 3Com hub with the IPv4 address 128.64.46.2 in the 6th to 9th octets followed by 0s in the rest.
   (b) SNMPv3 for the Cisco router interface with IPv6 address ::128.64.32.16.

3. Describe the SNMPv3 *scopedPDU* that the SNMP agent (router) responds to NMS with the data shown in Figure 4.2(c).

4. Figure 7.20 shows a generalized time-sequenced operation for get-request message going from a manager to an agent. Complete the primitives in Figure 7.20 explicitly identifying the application modules used.

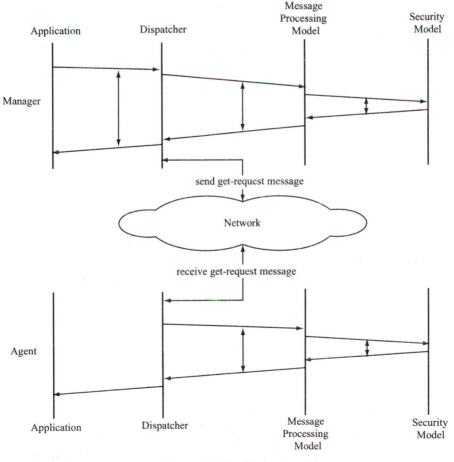

Figure 7.20 Exercise 4

5. Draw the time-sequence operation similar to that in Figure 7.20 detailing the elements of procedure for get-response message from the agent to the manager.
6. Detail the IN and OUT parameters of the *sendPdu* and *prepareOugoingMsg* primitives shown in Figure 7.4(b) by referring to RFC 2271.
7. Identify the authoritative and non-authoritative entities in Figure 7.20.
8. Define the configuration parameters for a notification generator to send traps to two network management systems *noc1* and *noc2* by filling in the objects in the *snmpTargetAddressTable*, *snmpTargetTable*, and *snmpNotifyTable*. Specifications for the two targets are given below. You may use the Appendix of RFC 2273 as a guide to answer this exercise.

	noc1	noc2
messageProcessingModel	SNMPv3	SNMPv3
securityModel	3 (USM)	3 (USM)
secuirtyName	"noc1"	"noc2"
snmpTargetParamsName	"NOAuthNoPriv-noc1"	"NOAuthNoPriv-noc1"
securityLevel	noAuthNoProv(1)	authPriv(3)
transportDomain	snmpUDPDomain	snmpUDPDomain
transportAddress	128.64.32.16:162	128.64.32.8:162
tagList	"group1"	"group2"

9. Access RFC 2274 and list and define the primitives provided by the authentication module at the sending and receiving security subsystems. Describe the services provided by the primitives.
10. Access RFC 2274 and list and define primitives provided by the privacy module at the sending and receiving security subsystems. Describe the services provided by the primitives.
11. Specify the family name, the family subtree, the family mask, and the family type in *vacmViewTreeFamilyTable* for an agent to present a view of:
    (a) the complete IP group
    (b) IP address table (*ipAddrTable*)
    (c) the row in the IP address table corresponding to the IP address 172.46.62.1
12. Write the *vacmViewTreeFamilyTable* for the three rows that present the system group in the IP address table for the row with IP address 172.46.62.1 without the *ipAdEntReasmMaxSize*.

SNMP Management: RMON

OBJECTIVES

- *Remote network monitoring, RMON*
- *RMON1: Monitoring Ethernet LAN and token-ring LAN*
- *RMON2: Monitoring upper protocol layers*
- *Generates and sends statistics close to subnetworks to central NMS*
- *RMON MIBs for RMON group objects*

The success of SNMP management resulted in the prevalence of managed network components in the computer network. SNMPv1 set the foundation for monitoring a network remotely from a centralized network operations center (NOC) and performing fault and configuration management. However, the extent to which network performance could be managed was limited. The characterization of the performance of a computer network is statistical in nature. This led to the logical step of measuring the statistics of important parameters in the network from the NOC and the development of remote monitoring (RMON) specifications.

8.1 WHAT IS REMOTE MONITORING?

We saw examples of SNMP messages going across the network between a manager and an agent in Section 5.1.4. We did this using a tool that "sniffs" every packet that is going across a local area network (LAN), opens it, and analyzes it. It is a passive operation and does nothing to the packets, which continue to proceed to their destinations. This is called monitoring or probing the network and the device that does the function is called the network monitor or the probe. Let us distinguish between the two components of a probe: (1) physical object that is connected to the transmission medium and (2) processor, which analyzes the data. If both are at the same place geographically, it is a local probe, which is how sniffers used to function. We will discuss this further in Chapter 9, when we consider management systems and tools.

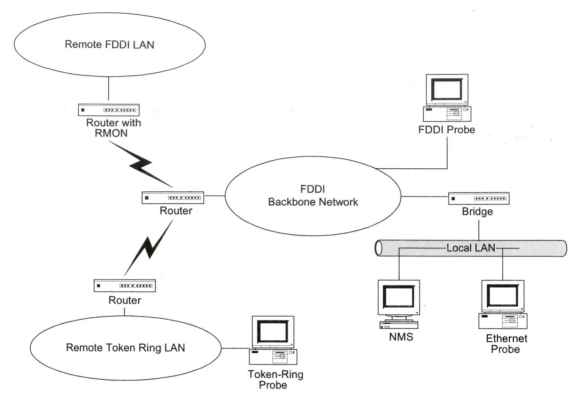

Figure 8.1 Network Configuration with RMONs

The monitored information gathered and analyzed locally can be transmitted to a remote network management station. In such a case, remotely monitoring the network using a probe is referred to as remote network monitoring or RMON. Figure 8.1 shows a fiber-distributed data interface (FDDI) backbone network with a local Ethernet LAN. There are two remote LANs, one a token-ring LAN and another, an FDDI LAN, connected to the backbone network. The network management system (NMS) is on the local Ethernet LAN. There is either an Ethernet probe or an RMON on the Ethernet LAN monitoring the local LAN. The FDDI backbone is monitored by an FDDI probe via the bridge and Ethernet LAN. A token-ring probe monitors the token-ring LAN. It communicates with the NMS via routers and the wide area network (WAN) (shown by the lightening bolt symbol of the telecommunications link). The remote FDDI is monitored by the built-in probe on the router. The FDDI probe communicates with the NMS via the WAN. All four probes that monitor the four LANs and communicate with the NMS are RMON devices.

The use of RMON devices has several advantages. First, each RMON device monitors the local network segment and does the necessary analyses. It relays the necessary information in both solicited and unsolicited fashion to the NMS. For example, RMON could be locally polling network elements in a segment. If it detects an abnormal condition, such as heavy packet loss or excessive collisions, it would send an alarm. Because the polling is local, the information is more reliable. This example of local monitoring and reporting to a remote NMS significantly reduces SNMP traffic in the network. This is especially true for the segment in which the NMS resides, as all the monitoring traffic would otherwise converge there.

The following case history illustrates another advantage. RMON reduces the necessity of agents in the network to be visible at all times to the NMS. One of the NMSs would frequently indicate that one of the hubs would show failure, but the hub recovered itself without any intervention. The performance study of the hub that the LAN was part of indicated that the LAN would frequently become overloaded with heavy traffic, and would have a significant packet loss. That included the ICMP packets that the NMS was using to poll the hub. The NMS was set to indicate a node failure if three successive ICMP packets did not receive responses. Increasing the number of packets needed to indicate a failure stopped the failure indication. This demonstrates the third advantage.

There are more chances that the monitoring packets, such as ICMP pings, may get lost in long-distance communication, especially under heavy traffic conditions. This may wrongly be interpreted by the NMS as the managed object being down. RMON pings locally and hence has less chance of losing packets, thus increasing the reliability of monitoring.

Another advantage of local monitoring using RMON is that individual segments can be monitored on a more continuous basis. This provides better statistics and greater ability for control. Thus, a fault could be diagnosed quicker by the RMON and reported to the NMS. In some situations, a failure could even be prevented by proactive management.

The overall benefits of implementing RMON technology in a network are higher network availability for users and greater productivity for administrators. A study report [CISCO/RMON] indicates increased productivity of several times for network administrators using RMON in their network.

8.2   RMON SMI AND MIB

For a network configuration system, like the one shown in Figure 8.1, to work successfully, several conditions need to be met. Network components are made by different vendors. Even the RMON devices may be from different vendors. Thus, just as in the communication of network management information, standards need to be established for common syntax and semantics for the use of RMON devices. The syntax used is ASN.1. The RMON structure of management information is similar to SMIv2 in defining object types. The Remote Network Monitoring Management Information Base (RMON MIB) defining RMON groups has been developed and defined in three stages. The original RMON MIB, now referred to as RMON1 was developed for Ethernet LAN in November 1991 RFC 1271, but was made obsolete in 1995 RFC 1757. Token-ring extensions to RMON1 were developed in September 1993 [RFC 1513]. The use of RMON1 for remote monitoring was found to be extremely beneficial. However, it addressed parameters at the OSI layer 2 level only. Hence, RMON2 [RFC 2021] was developed and released in January 1997, which addressed the parameters associated with OSI layers 3 through 7.

The RMON group is node 16 under MIB-II (mib-2 16), as shown in Figure 6.36. All the groups under the RMON group are shown in Figure 8.2. It consists of nine Ethernet RMON1 groups (rmon 1 to rmon 9), one token-ring extension group to RMON1 (rmon 10), and nine RMON2 groups (rmon 11–20) for the higher layers.

RMON1 is covered in Section 8.3 and RMON2 in Section 8.4. We will discuss the applications of RMON in Part III when we discuss applications, systems, and tools.

8.3   RMON1

RMON1 is covered by RFC 1757 for Ethernet LAN and RFC 1513. There are two data types introduced as textual conventions, and ten MIB groups (rmon 1 to rmon 10), as shown in Figure 8.2.

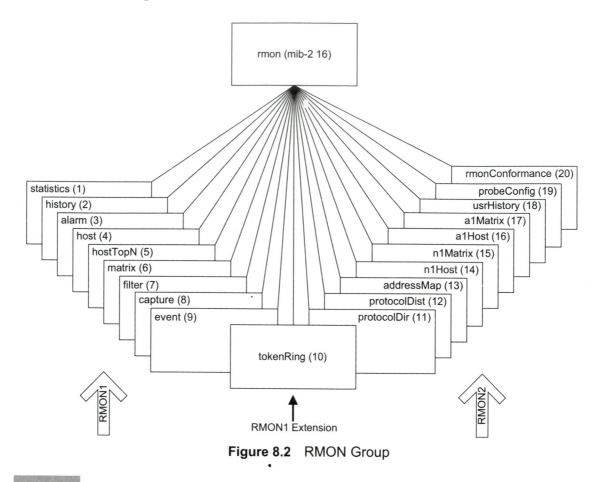

Figure 8.2 RMON Group

8.3.1 RMON1 Textual Conventions

Two new data types that are defined in RMON1 textual conventions are *OwnerString* and *EntryStatus*. Both these data types are extremely useful in the operation of RMON devices. RMON devices are used by management systems to measure and produce statistics on network elements. We will soon see that this involves setting up tables that control parameters to be monitored. Typically, there is more than one management system in the network, which could have permission to create, use, and delete control parameters in a table. Or, a human network manager in charge of network operations does such functions. For this purpose, the owner identification is made part of the control table defined by the *OwnerString* data type. The *EntryStatus* is used to resolve conflicts between management systems in manipulating control tables.

The *OwnerString* is specified in the NVT ASCII character set specified by *DisplayString*. The information content of *OwnerString* contains information about the owner: IP address, management station name, network manager's name, location, or telephone number. If the agent itself is the owner, as for example in the addition of an interface card, the *OwnerString* is set to "monitor."

In order to understand the data type, *EntryStatus*, we need to understand the concept of creation and deletion of rows in tables, which was discussed in Section 6.4.7. For a table to be shared by multiple users, a columnar object *EntryStatus*, similar to *RowStatus* in SNMPv2, is added to the table that

Table 8.1 EntryStatus Textual Convention

STATE	ENUMERATION	DESCRIPTION
valid	1	Row exists and is active. It is fully configured and operational
createRequest	2	Create a new row by creating this object
underCreation	3	Row is not fully active
invalid	4	Delete the row by disassociating the mapping of this entry

contains information on the status of the row. The *EntryStatus* data type can exist in one of four states: (1) *valid*, (2) *createRequest*, (3) *underCreation*, and (4) *invalid*. The four states of *EntryStatus* are shown in Table 8.1. Under the *valid* state condition, the instantiation or row of the table is operational and is probably measuring the number of input octets in the IF group on an interface. Any management system, which is authenticated to use the RMON device, may use this row of data. Of course, if the owner of the row decides to make it invalid, other systems lose the data. The *invalid* state is the way to delete a row. Based on implementation, the row may be immediately deleted and the resource claimed, or it may be done in a batch mode later. If the desired row of information does not already exist, the management system can create a row. The *EntryStatus* is then set to *createRequest*. The process of creation may involve more than one exchange of PDUs between the manager and the agent. In such a situation, the state of the *EntryStatus* is set to *underCreation* so that others won't use it. After the creation process is complete, it is set to the *valid* state.

8.3.2 RMON1 Groups and Functions

RMON in general, and RMON1 specifically, performs numerous functions at the data link layer. Figure 8.3 shows a pictorial representation of RMON1 groups and functions. The data-gathering modules, which are LAN probes, gather data from the remotely monitored network comprising Ethernet and token-ring LANs. The data can serve as inputs to five sets of functions. Three of those comprise monitoring of traffic statistics. The host and conversation statistics group deals with traffic data associated with the hosts, ranking of traffic for the top N hosts, and conversation between hosts. The group of statistical data associated with Ethernet LAN, namely Ethernet statistics and Ethernet history statistics, is addressed by the groups and functions in the Ethernet statistics box. The history control table controls the data to be gathered from various networks. It is also used by the token-ring statistics modules in the token-ring statistics box. Outputs of various modules are analyzed and presented in tabular and graphical forms to the user by the network manager in the NMS.

The filter group is a cascade of two filters. The packet filter filters incoming packets by performing a Boolean and/or XOR with a mask specified. This could be quite complex. The filtered packet stream is considered a channel. We can make further selections based on the channel mask. The filtered outputs may generate either alarms or events. These are reported to the network manager. The output of the data gatherer could also generate an alarm directly.

The output of the filter group could be stored in the packet capture module for further analysis by the network manager. This could be associated with a special study of the traffic pattern or troubleshooting of an abnormality in the network.

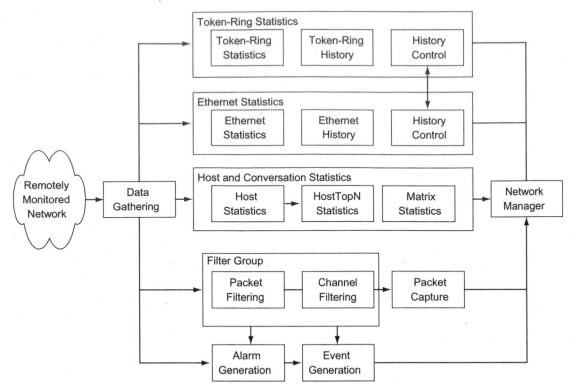

Figure 8.3 RMON1 Groups and Functions

The above functions associated with the various groups are accomplished using ten groups associated with the RMON1 MIB, as shown in Table 8.2. The first nine groups are applicable to common data and to Ethernet LAN, and the tenth group extends it to token-ring LAN. Most of the groups have one or more tables. The groups fall into three categories. The largest category is the statistics-gathering groups. These are the Statistics groups, the History groups, the Host group, the Host Top N group, and the Matrix group. The second category deals with the network event reporting functions. These are the Alarm group and the Event group. The third category deals with filtering the input packets according to selected criteria and capturing the data if desired for further analysis. These are the Filter group and the Packet Capture group. We will consider RMON1 groups and the token-ring extension to RMON1 in Sections 8.3.4 and 8.3.5, respectively.

In Table 8.2, we notice in the Tables column that some of the groups have tables with "2" as part of the name; for example, *etherStats2Table* in the Statistics group. These are additional tables created during RMON2 specifications development and are enhancements to RMON1. Hence, they are included here as part of RMON1. The enhancements to RMON1 include the standard *LastCreateTime* textual convention for all control tables and *TimeFilter* textual convention that provides capability for the filter to handle rows to be used for the index to a table. The *LastCreateTime* enhancement helps keep track of data with the changes in control. The *TimeFilter* enables an application to download only those rows that changed since a particular time. The agent returns a value only if the time mark is less than the last update time.

As an example, let us consider a *fooTable* with two rows and three columnar objects, *fooTimeMark* (with *TimeFilter* as the data type), *fooIndex*, and *foocounts*. The indices defining a row are *fooTimeMark*

Table 8.2 RMON1 MIB Groups and Tables

GROUP	OID	FUNCTION	TABLES
Statistics	rmon 1	Provides link-level statistics	–etherStatsTable
			–etherStats2Table
History	rmon 2	Collects periodic statistical data and stores for later retrieval	–historyControlTable
			–etherHistoryTable
			–historyControl2Table
			–etherHistory2Table
Alarm	rmon 3	Generates events when the data sample gathered crosses pre-established thresholds	–alarmTable
Host	rmon 4	Gathers statistical data on hosts	–hostControlTable
			–hostTable
			–hostTimeTable
			–hostControl2Table
Host Top N	rmon 5	Computes the top N hosts on the respective categories of statistics gathered	–hostTopNcontrolTable
Matrix	rmon 6	Gathers statistics on traffic between pairs of hosts	–matrixControlTable
			–matrixSDTable
			–matrixDSTable
			–matrixControl2Table
Filter	rmon 7	Performs filter function that enables capture of desired parameters	–filterTable
			–channelTable
			–filter2Table
			–channel2Table
Packet capture	rmon 8	Provides packet capture capability to gather packets after they flow through a channel	–buffercontrolTable
			–captureBufferTable
Event	rmon 9	Controls the generation of events and notifications	–eventTable
Token ring	Rmon 10	See Table 8.3	See Table 8.3

and *fooIndex*. Let the *TimeFilter* index start at 0, the last update of *fooCounter* in row #1 occur at time 3, and its value is 5. Assume the update to row #2 occurred at time 5 and the value was updated to 9. This scenario would yield the following instance of *fooCounts* in the *fooTable*:

    fooCounts.0.1   5
    fooCounts.0.2   9

```
fooCounts.1.1    5
fooCounts.1.2    9
fooCounts.2.1    5
fooCounts.1.2    9
fooCounts.3.1    5
fooCounts.3.2    9
fooCounts.4.2    9        (Note that row #1 does not exist for times 4 and 5 since the last update
                          occurred at timemark 3.)
fooCounts.5.2    9
```

(Both rows #1 and #2 do not exist for timemark greater than 5.)

8.3.3 Relationship Between Control and Data Tables

Observing the Tables column in Table 8.2, you will notice several of the groups have a data table and a control table. The data table contains rows (instances) of data. The control table defines the instances of the data rows in the data table and is settable to gather and store different instances of data. The relationship between the control table and the data table is illustrated in a generic manner in Figure 8.4. The value of the *dataIndex* in the data table is the same as the value of *controlIndex* in the control table.

Let us understand how the data table and the control table work together using the matrix group in Table 8.2. We can collect data based on source and destination addresses appearing in the packets on a given interface using the *matrixSDTable* (matrix source–destination table). The control index is an integer uniquely identifying the row in the control table. It would have a value of 1 for the first interface of a managed entity. The value of the columnar object, *controlDataSource*, identifies the source of the data that is being collected. In our example, if the interface #1 belongs to the interfaces group, then *controlDataSource* is *ifIndex.1*.

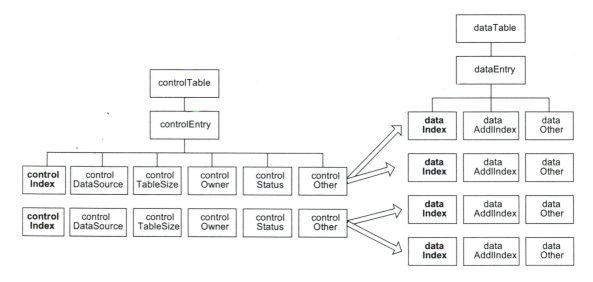

Note on Indices:
Indices marked in bold letter
Value of dataIndex same as the value of controlIndex

Figure 8.4   Relationship Between Control and Data Tables

The *controlTableSize* identifies entries associated with this data source. In our matrix source–destination table example, this would be the source–destination pair in each row of the table.

The *controlOwner* columnar object is the entity or person who created the entry. The entity could be either the agent or NMS, or a management person. The *controlStatus* is one of the entries listed in Table 8.1. The *controlOther* could be any other object.

To uniquely identify a conceptual row in the data table, we may need to specify more indices than the *dataIndex*. This is indicated as *dataAddlIndex* in Figure 8.4. In our matrix source–destination example, additional indices are source and destination address objects. The *dataOther* in the data table indicates data being collected, such as the number of packets.

8.3.4   RMON1 Common and Ethernet Groups

We have so far covered the global picture of RMON1 Ethernet MIB and how data and control tables are related to each other. Let us now address the nine RMON1 common and Ethernet groups.

Statistics Group. The statistics group contains statistics measured by the probe for each monitored Ethernet interface on a device. The *etherStatsTable* in this group has an entry for each interface. Data include statistics on packet types, size, and errors. It also provides capability to gather statistics on the collision of the Ethernet segment. The number of collisions is a best estimate, as the number of collisions detected depends on where the probe is placed on the segment.

The statistics group is used to measure live statistics on nodes and segments. Commercial NMSs include features such as dynamic presentation of various traffic patterns. The number of MIB collisions could also be used for alarm generation when it exceeds a set high threshold value.

History Group. The history group consists of two subgroups: the history control group and the history (data) group. The history control group controls the periodic statistical sampling of data from various types of networks. The control table stores configuration entries comprising interface, polling period, and other parameters. Information is stored in a media-specific table, the history table, which contains one entry for each specific sample. A short-term and a long-term interval, such as 30-second and 30-minute intervals, may be specified to obtain two different statistics. The data objects defined are dropped events, number of octets and packets, different type of errors, fragments, collisions, and utilization.

The history group is extremely useful in tracking the overall trend in the volume of traffic. Since historical data are accumulated at the data link layer, they include traffic caused by all higher-layer protocols. Short-term history statistics can also be used to troubleshoot network performance problems. For example, in one study of traffic pattern that the author participated in, short-term history statistics revealed that a significant volume of "transparent" data was contributed by servers in the network, which were functioning as "mirrors" for a public news service on the Internet. Although the service was considered to be desirable, since it was generated and consumed externally, it behaved somewhat transparently with regard to the local network traffic.

Alarm Group. The alarm group periodically takes statistical samples on specified variables in the probe and compares them with the pre-configured threshold stored in the probe. Whenever the monitored variable crosses the threshold, an event is generated. To avoid excessive generation of events on the threshold border, rising and falling thresholds are specified. This works in the following manner. Suppose an alarm event is generated when the variable crosses the falling threshold while going down in value. Another event would be generated only after the value crosses the rising threshold at least once.

The group contains an *alarm table* that has a list of entries defining the alarm parameters. The columnar objects *alarmVariable* and *alarmInterval* are used to select the variable and the sampling interval. The sampling type is either the absolute or delta value. In the former, the absolute value of the variable at the end of the previous period is stored as an alarm value. In the latter type, the absolute value at the end of a period is subtracted from the beginning of the period and the computed value is stored. These values are compared with the rising and falling thresholds to generate alarms.

An example of an absolute value would be a new interface card on test for infant mortality. The threshold of the sum of outgoing and incoming packets could be set to 1 gigaoctects and the RMON would generate an alarm/event when the threshold is reached. An example of delta type is threshold set to 10,000 packets in a 10-second interval for excessive packet loss.

Host Group. The host group contains information about the hosts on the network. It compiles the list of hosts by looking at the good packets traversing the network and extracting the source and destination MAC addresses. It maintains statistics on these hosts. There are three tables in the group: *hostControlTable*, *hostTable*, and *hostTimeTable*. The *hostControlTable* controls the interfaces on which data gathering is done. The other two tables depend on this information. The *hostTable* contains statistics about the host. The *hostTimeTable* contains the same data as the host table, but is stored in the time order in which the host entry was discovered. This helps in the fast discovery of new hosts in the system. The entries in the two data tables are synchronized with respect to the host in the *hostControlTable*. We can obtain statistics on a host using this MIB.

Host Top N Group. The host top N group performs a report-generation function for ranking the top N hosts in the category of the selected statistics. For example, we can rank–order the top ten hosts with maximum outgoing traffic. The *HostTopNControlTable* is used to initiate generation of such a report.

As an example of the type of data that can be acquired using an RMON probe, Figure 8.5 shows a chart derived using an RMON probe for the output octets of the top ten hosts in a network. The names of the hosts have been changed to generic host numbers for security reasons.

Matrix Group. The matrix group stores statistics on the conversation between pairs of hosts. An entry is created for each conversation that the probe detects. There are three tables in the group. The *matrixControlTable* controls the information to be gathered. The *matrixSDTable* keeps track of the source to destination conversations; and the *matrixDSTable* keeps data based on destination to source traffic. We can obtain a graph similar to Figure 8.5 for the conversation pairs in both directions using this group.

Filter Group. The filter group is used to filter packets to be captured based on logical expressions. The stream of data based on a logical expression is called a "channel." The group contains a filter table and a channel table. The filter table allows packets to be filtered with an arbitrary filter expression, a set of filters associated with each channel. Each filter is defined by a row in the filter table. A channel may be associated with several rows. For each channel, the input packet is validated against each filter associated with that channel and is accepted if it passes any of the tests. A row in the channel table of the filter group includes the interface ID (same as *ifIndex*) with which the channel is associated, along with acceptance criteria. The combination of the filter and channel filtering provides enormous flexibility to select packets to be captured.

Packet Capture Group. The packet capture group is a post-filter group. It captures packets from each channel based on the filter criteria of packet and channel filters in the filter group. The channel filter criteria for acceptance of the filter group output are controlled by the *bufferControlTable* and

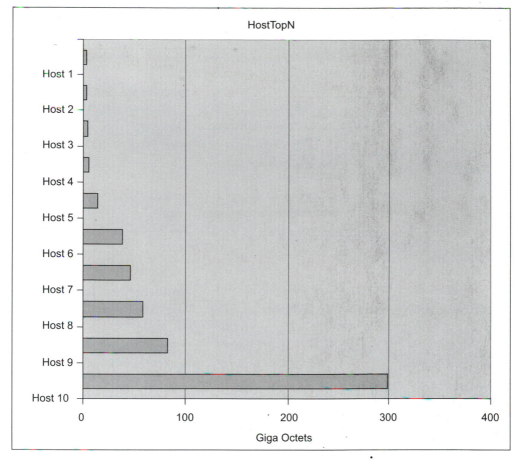

Figure 8.5 HostTop-10 Output Octets

the captured channel data in the *captureBufferTable*. Each packet captured is stored in the buffer as an instance.

Event Group. The event group controls the generation and notification of events. Both the rising alarm and the falling alarm can be specified in the *eventTable* associated with the group. Besides the transmittal of events, a log is maintained in the system.

8.3.5 RMON Token-Ring Extension Groups

As we mentioned earlier, token-ring RMON MIB is an extension to RMON1 MIB and is specified in RFC 1513. Table 8.3 presents the token-ring MIB groups and tables. There are eight groups, each with a data table and two with control tables.

There are two token-ring statistics groups, one at the MAC layer (token-ring statistics group) and a second on packets collected promiscuously (token-ring promiscuous statistics group). They both contain statistics on ring utilization and ring error statistics. The MAC-layer statistics group collects data on token-ring parameters such as token packets, errors in packets, bursts, polling, etc. The promiscuous

Table 8.3 RMON Token-Ring MIB Groups and Tables

TOKEN RING GROUP	FUNCTION	TABLES
Statistics	Current utilization and error statistics of MAC Layer	tokenRingMLStatsTable
		tokenRingMLStats2Table
Promiscuous statistics	Current utilization and error statistics of promiscuous data	tokenRingPStatsTable
		tokenRingPStats2Table
MAC-layer history	Historical utilization and error statistics of MAC layer	tokenRingMLHistoryTable
Promiscuous history	Historical utilization and error statistics of promiscuous data	tokenRingPHistoryTable
Ring station	Station statistics	ringStationControlTable
		ringStationTable
		ringStationControl2Table
Ring station order	Order of the stations	ringStationOrderTable
Ring station configuration	Active configuration of ring stations	ringStationConfigControlTable
		ringStationConfigTable
Source-routing	Utilization statistics of source routing information	sourceRoutingStatsTable
		sourceRoutingStats2Table

statistics group addresses statistics on the number of packets of various sizes and the type of packets as to data—multicast or broadcast. There are two corresponding history statistics groups—current and promiscuous. Each of the four statistics groups has one data table associated with it.

There are three groups associated with the stations on the ring. The ring station group provides statistics on each station being monitored on the ring along with its status. The data are stored in the *ringStationTable*. The rings and parameters to be monitored are controlled by the *ringStationControlTable*. The ring station order group provides the order of the station on the monitored rings and has only a data table. The ring station configuration group manages the stations on the ring.

The last group in the ring groups is the source-routing group. It is used to gather statistics on routing information in a pure source-routing environment.

8.4 RMON2

RMON1 dealt primarily with data associated with the OSI data link layer. The success and popularity of RMON1 led to the development of RMON2. RMON2 [RFC 2021] extends the monitoring capability to the upper layers, from the network layer to the application layer. The term application level is used in the SNMP RMON concept to describe a class of protocols, and not strictly the OSI layer 7 protocol. The error statistics in any layer include all errors below the layer, down to the network layer. For example, the network layer errors do not include data link layer errors, but the transport layer errors include the network layer errors.

Several of the groups and functions in RMON2 at higher layers are similar to that of the data link layer in RMON1. We will discuss the groups and their similarity here. We will cover in detail how protocol analyzer systems incorporate the higher-layer data gathered using RMON2 in Chapter 9 on NMSs and tools.

8.4.1 RMON2 Management Information Base

The architecture of RMON2 is the same as RMON1. RMON2 MIB is arranged into ten groups. Table 8.4 shows the RMON2 MIB groups and tables. We have already discussed enhancements to RMON1 MIB in the previous section.

The protocol directory group is an inventory of the protocols that the probe can monitor. The capability of the probe can be altered by reconfiguring the *protocolDirTable*. The protocols range from the data link control layer to the application layer. This is identified by the columnar object on the unique protocol ID. Each protocol is further subdivided based on parameters, such as fragments. The protocol identifier and protocol parameters are used as indices for the rows of the table. There is one entry in the table for each protocol. The protocols that can be used with the protocol directory have been defined in RFC 2074.

The protocol distribution group provides information on the relative traffic of different protocols either in octets or packets. It collects very basic statistics that would help a NMS manage bandwidth allocation utilized by different protocols. The *protocolDistControlTable* is configured according to the data to be collected and *protocolDistStatsTable* stores the data collected. Each row in the *protocolDist StatsTable* is indexed by the *protocolDistControlIndex* in the *protocolDistControlTable* and *protocol DirLocalIndex* in the *protocolDirTable*. The data table stores the packet and octet counts.

The address map group is similar to the address translation table binding the MAC address to the network address on each interface. It has two tables for control and data.

The network-layer host group measures traffic sent from and to each network address representing each host discovered by the probe, as the host group in RMON1 does.

The network-layer matrix group provides information on the conversation between pairs of hosts in both directions. It is very similar to the matrix tables in RMON1. The group also ranks the top N conversations. It has two control tables and three data tables.

The application layer functions are grouped into two groups, the application-layer host group and the application-layer matrix group. They both calculate traffic by protocol units and use their respective control tables in the network-layer host group and the network-layer matrix group. The application-layer matrix group can also generate a report of the top N protocol conversations.

Alarm and history group information have been combined into the user history collection group in RMON2. This function, normally done by NMSs, can be off-loaded to RMON. It has two control tables and one data table. Data objects are collected in bucket groups. Each bucket group pertains to a MIB object, and the elements in the group are the instances of the MIB object. Users can specify the data to be collected by entering data into *usrHistoryControlTable*, which will then be assembled with rows of instances in the *usrHistoryObjectTable*. Each row in the former specifies the number of buckets to be allocated for each object, and the latter contains rows of instances of the MIB object. The data are stored in *userHistoryTable*. There could be one or more instances of *userHistoryTable* associated with each *usrHistoryObjectTable*.

Table 8.4 RMON2 MIB Groups and Tables

GROUP	OID	FUNCTION	TABLES
Protocol directory	rmon 11	Inventory of protocols	protocolDirTable
Protocol distribution	rmon 12	Relative statistics on octets and packets	protocolDistControlTable
			protocolDistStatsTable
Address map	rmon 13	MAC address to network address on the interfaces	addressMapControlTable
			addressMapTable
Network-layer host	rmon 14	Traffic data from and to each host	n1HostControlTable
			n1HostTable
Network-layer matrix	rmon 15	Traffic data from each pair of hosts	n1MatrixControlTable
			n1MatrixSDTable
			n1MatrixDSTable
			n1MatrixTopNControlTable
			n1MatrixTopNTable
Application-layer host	rmon 16	Traffic data by protocol from and to each host	a1HostTable
Application-layer matrix	rmon 17	Traffic data by protocol between pairs of hosts	a1MatrixSDTable
			a1MatrixDSTable
			a1MatrixTopNControlTable
			a1MatrixTopNTable
User history collection	rmon 18	User-specified historical data on alarms and statistics	usrHistoryControlTable
			usrHistoryObjectTable
			usrHistoryTable
Probe configuration	rmon 19	Configuration of probe parameters	serialConfigTable
			netConfigTable
			trapDestTable
			serialConnectionTable
RMON conformance	rmon 20	RMON2 MIB compliances and compliance groups	See Section 8.4.2

The probe configuration group provides the facility to configure the probe. The data can be accessed using a modem connection. The pertinent data are stored in the *serialConfigTable* and *serialConnectionTable*. The *netConfigTable* contains the network configuration parameters, and the *trapDestTable* defines the destination addresses for the traps.

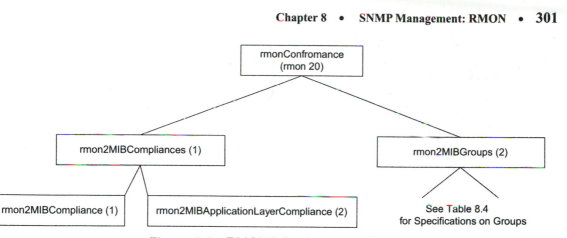

Figure 8.6 RMON2 Conformance Group

8.4.2 RMON2 Conformance Specifications

Conformance specifications were not specified in RMON1. They have been added in RMON2. As shown in Figure 8.6, the RMON2 conformance group consists of two subgroups, rmon2MIBCompliances and rmon2MIBGroups. The compliance requirements are separated into basic RMON2 MIB compliance and application layer RMON2 MIB compliance. Each compliance module defines the mandatory and optional groups. Vendors are required to implement the mandatory groups for compliance; optional groups may be used by vendors to specify additional capabilities.

There are 13 groups in rmon2MIBGroups. They are listed in Table 8.5 along with the mandatory (M) and optional (O) requirements for the basic- and application-level conformance to RMON2. The *rmon1EnhancementGroup* is mandatory for systems that implement RMON1 with RMON2. Notice that *probeConfigurationGroup* is a basic group and hence marked as mandatory, even though it is not specified as such in RFC 2021 definitions. The *rmon1EnhancementGroup* is mandatory for implementation of RMON1. The *rmon1EthernetEnhancementGroup* and *rmon1TokenRingEnhancementGroup* add enhancements to RMON1 that help management stations. The enhancements include filter entry, which provides variable-length offsets into packets and the addition of more statistical parameters.

8.5 ATM REMOTE MONITORING

We will be learning management of ATM in Chapter 9. However, there is a similarity in the use of remote probes for RMON on an ATM network. We will address the commonality and differences here. You may skip this section now, if you so choose, and return to it after you have studied ATM management.

We have thus far learned about RMON and its advantages for gathering statistics on Ethernet and token-ring LANs. RMON1 dealt with the data link layer and RMON2 with higher-level layers. IETF RMON MIBs have been extended to perform traffic monitoring and analysis for ATM networks (see af-nm-test-0080.000 in Table 9.3). Figure 8.7 shows an RMON MIB framework for the extensions, as portrayed by the ATM Forum. Switch extensions for RMON and ATM RMON define RMON objects at the "base" layer, which is the ATM sublayer level. ATM protocol IDs for RMON2 define additional objects needed at the higher-level layers [RFC 2074].

There are several differences between RMON of Ethernet and token ring and monitoring of ATM devices. Extending RMON to ATM requires design changes and new functionality. Particular attention needs to be paid to the following issues: high speed, cell vs. frames, and connection-oriented nature of

Table 8.5 RMON2 Groups and Compliances

OBJECT GROUP	RMON2 MIB	RMON2 MIB APPLICATION LAYER COMPLIANCE
protocolDirectoryGroup	M	M
protocolDistributionGroup	M	M
addressMapGroup	M	M
n1HostGroup	M	M
n1MatrixGroup	M	M
a1HostGroup	N/A	M
a1MatrixGroup	N/A	M
usrHistoryGroup	M	M
probeInformationGroup	M	M
probeConfigurationGroup	M*	M*
rmon1EnhancementGroup	O†	O†
rmon1EthernetEnhancemnetGroup	O	O
rmon1TokenRingEnhancementGroup	O	O

* One of the basic groups in RMON2 and hence is mandatory.

† Mandatory for systems implementing RMON1.

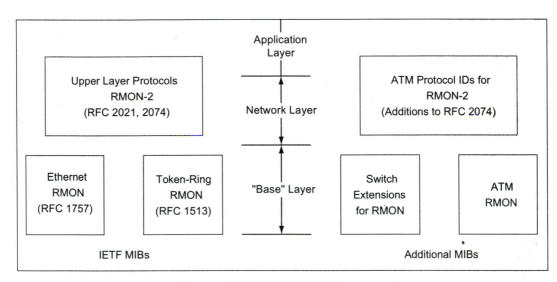

Figure 8.7 RMON MIB Framework

ATM. At the data link sublayer, ATM RMON measures cells instead of packets or frames, and provides cell-based per-host and per-conversation traffic statistics. The high-speed nature of ATM imposes a severe set of requirements in ATM RMON implementation. At the application layer, RMON provides basic statistics for each monitored cell stream, for each ATM host, and for conversation between pairwise hosts. It also provides capability for flexible configuration mechanisms suited to the connection-oriented nature of ATM.

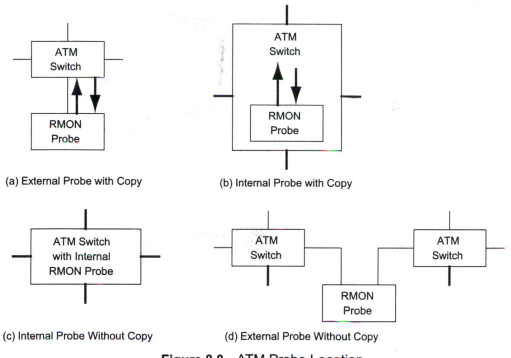

(a) External Probe with Copy

(b) Internal Probe with Copy

(c) Internal Probe Without Copy

(d) External Probe Without Copy

Figure 8.8 ATM Probe Location

There are four different collection perspectives that are possible for ATM RMON, as shown in Figure 8.8. Figure 8.8(a) is a stand-alone probe attached to a single port of a switch. ATM traffic is copied somehow to the RMON probe. Figure 8.8(b) is an embedded probe within a switch, but with no access to the switch fabric. Again, ATM traffic is somehow copied to the RMON probe. Figure 8.8(c) is an embedded probe with access to the switch fabric. However, this type of probe measures traffic at the cell header level only. Figure 8.8(d) is a stand-alone probe, tapping a network-to-network interface between two switches. ATM traffic in both directions is monitored directly without switch intervention. When RMON instrumentation is either embedded into the switch fabric (c) or placed between two switches as in (d), no modification of the circuit is needed. In (a) and (b), circuit steering is needed to copy the cells onto the probe. The two-way arrows in the figures indicate two half-duplex circuits that carry the steered traffic.

The ATM RMON MIB is under the experimental node of the IETF Internet MIB and is shown in Figure 8.9. The functions of the groups and the tables in each group are given in Table 8.6. The MIB contains four groups: *portSelect, atmStats, atmHost,* and *atmMatrix.*

The *portSelect* group addresses port selection. It is used to define the ports to be monitored in a particular statistics, host, or matrix collection. It contains two tables. The *portSelGrpTable* controls the set-up of ports and ATM connection selection criteria used on behalf of any collection associated with entries in this table, such as *atmHostTable.* The *portSelTable* is then used to control the set-up of selection criteria for a single ATM port.

The *atmStats* group collects basic statistics. It counts the total amount of traffic on behalf of one or more *portSelectGroups.* There are two tables in this group: *atmStatsControlTable* and *atmStatsTable.*

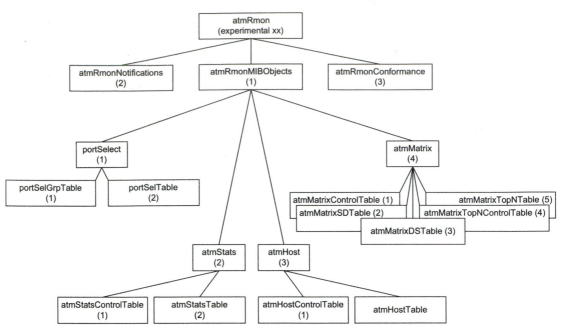

Figure 8.9 ATM RMON MIB

Table 8.6 ATM RMON MIB Groups and Tables

GROUP	OID	FUNCTION	TABLES
portSelect	atmRmonMIBObjects 1	Port selection	portSelGrpTable
			portSelTable
atmStats	atmRmonMIBObjects 2	Basic statistics	atmStatsControlTable
			atmStatsTable
atmHost	atmRmonMIBObjects 3	ATM per-host statistics	atmHostControlTable
			atmHostTable
atmMatrix	atmRmonMIBObjects 4	ATM per-circuit statistics	atmMatrixControlTable
			atmMatrixSDTable
			atmMatrixDSTable
			atmMatrixTopNControlTable
			atmMatrixTopNTable

The *atmHost* group collects per-host statistics. It counts the amount of traffic sent on behalf of each ATM address discovered by the probe, according to associated *portSelectGroup* criteria. It contains a data table and a control table.

The *atmMatrix* group collects per-circuit statistics and reports the top N circuit traffic. It gathers traffic data on a pair-wise source–destination address, according to *portSelectGroup* criteria, in both directions. It contains three data tables and two control tables. The *atmMatrixControlTable* is used to define the source-to-destination (*atmMatrixSDTable*) and destination-to-source (*atmMatrixDSTable*) traffic. The *atmMatrixTopNControlTable* and *atmMatrixTopNTable* are used to analyze and present the top N traffic carriers.

8.6 A CASE STUDY ON INTERNET TRAFFIC USING RMON

A study was undertaken for planning purposes to gather statistics on the Internet growth at the Georgia Institute of Technology. The technical objectives of the study included traffic growth and trend and traffic pattern. The latter was based on (1) weekly and monthly patterns, (2) diurnal patterns, (3) distribution of traffic by users, packet size, and protocol, and (4) source of traffic based on source–destination data.

The network comprised multiple domains of Ethernet and FDDI LANs. The network complex was connected to the Internet via a high-speed gateway. Data were gathered by measurements made on various domains individually, as well as on the gateway.

Various tools were used to gather data, including RMON statistics. Hewlett-Packard's Netmetrix Protocol Analyzer was used for Ethernet LANs. The statistics were gathered using the host top N and history groups to select the top generators of traffic over the period. The matrix group was used to measure incoming and outgoing traffic. The filter and packet capture groups were beneficial in analyzing the type of traffic based on the application level protocol, such as HTTP, NNTP, etc.

Besides the commercial tools, special tools were developed for the study. For example, the commercial probes were not fast enough to measure the packets traversing an FDDI ring. Hence, a promiscuous mode of counting the packets (function of a probe) was developed to measure traffic on the gateway. We will learn more about management tools and their use in management applications in Chapter 9. However, the case study described here is intended to illustrate the importance of gathering statistics and the use of RMON for that purpose.

A partial summary of the results follows. The names in the results have been changed to protect the privacy and security of the institution.

Results

1. **Growth Rate**: Internet traffic grew at a significant rate from February to June at a monthly rate of 9% to 18%.

February to March	12%
March to April	9%
April to May	18%

   Note: There was a sudden drop in June due to end of spring quarter and the beginning of summer quarter.

2. **Traffic Pattern**:
   - Monthly/Weekly: The only discernible variation was lower traffic over weekends.
   - Daily: 2/3 of the top 5% peaks occurred in the afternoon.
   - Users:

Top six domain of users (96%) are

Domain 1	20%
Domain 2	30%
Subdomain 1	(25%)
Subdomain 2	(3%)
Domain 3	34%
Domain 4	7%
Domain 5	3%
Domain 6	2%

Top three hosts sending or receiving data were:

    Newsgroups

    Mbone

    Linux host

What we have learned:

1. The three top groups of users contributing to 84% of the Internet traffic are students (surprise!), Newsgroup services, and Domain 1.
2. The growth rate of Internet use during the study period in the spring quarter was 50%.

◼ Summary

In this chapter we discussed the enhancement to SNMP management by the introduction of remote monitoring, RMON. Remote monitoring is monitoring the network using remotely positioned probes in various segments in the network. RMON1 was initially defined for data link level parameters of Ethernet LAN. It was then extended to token-ring LAN. RMON2 development followed to monitor and produce statistics for parameters associated with the upper layers, from the network to the application level. We will pursue the use of RMON in managing networks from a practical point of view in Part III of this book.

◼ Exercises

1. An NMS connected to a 10-Mbps Ethernet LAN is monitoring a network comprising routers, hubs, and workstations. There are 10,000 nodes in the network to monitor. It sends an SNMP query to each station once a minute and receives a response when the stations are up. Assume that an average frame size is 1,000 bytes long for get-request and response messages.

    (a) What is the maximum traffic load on the LAN that has the NMS?
    (b) Assume that the Ethernet LAN operates at a maximum efficiency of 40% throughput, what is the overhead (SNMP packets/total packets) due to network monitoring?

2. In Exercise 1, assume that the network comprises ten subnetworks, an RMON monitoring each subnet.

    (a) Design a heartbeat monitoring system, using RMONs, that indicates failures to the NMS within a minute of a failure.
    (b) What is the monitoring load on each subnet?
    (c) If the NMS is still expected to detect any failure within 1 minute of occurrence, what is the overhead on the LAN to which the NMS is connected due to this traffic?

3. (a) Describe qualitatively how utilization (number of frames transmitted/number of frames offered) depends on the frame size on an Ethernet LAN.

(b) How would you measure the distribution of the frame size on the LAN?

4. (a) Describe the two methods of measuring collisions on an Ethernet LAN.
   (b) Compare the two methods in terms of what you can measure.

5. Two identical token rings with the same number of stations operate at different efficiencies (ratio of time spent in data transmission to that of the total time). One operates at a higher efficiency than the other. You suspect that it is due to the difference in frame sizes of the data frames in the two rings.

   (a) Why would you suspect the frame size?
   (b) How would you prove your suspicion using RMON?

6. How would you measure the types and distribution of frames in a token-ring LAN?

7. An RMON probe in a network measures Ethernet packets on hub interfaces (*ifIndex*) 1 and 2. The counters are set to zero as the measurement started and interface 1 has counted 1,000 1,500-byte packets and interface 2 has measured 100 64-byte packets. These are stored in rows 1 and 2 of the *protocolDistStatsTable*. They are indexed by the *protocolDistControlIndex* of 1 and 2 and the *protocolDirLocalIndex* of 11 and 12.

   (a) Draw the conceptual rows of the tables involved with the relevant columnar objects and values.
   (b) Write each instance of the columnar object of the data with its associated index and value.

Network Management
Tools, Systems, and Engineering

OBJECTIVES

- *System utilities for management*
  - *Basic networking tools*
  - *SNMP tools*
  - *Protocol analyzer*
- *Measurement of network statistics*
  - *Traffic load*
  - *Protocol*
  - *Data*
  - *Error*
  - *Traffic monitoring using MRTG*
- *MIB engineering*
  - *Limitations of SMI and SNMP*
  - *Counters and rates*
  - *Object-oriented design*
  - *SMI tables*
  - *SMI actions*
  - *Guiding principles for MIB design*

- *Design considerations of NMS*
  - *System and user requirements*
  - *Local and remote management*
  - *Functional requirements*
  - *Architectural aspects*
  - *Key design considerations*
  - *Functional modules and managers*
  - *Root cause analysis*
  - *Distributed network management*
  - *Server and client platforms*
- *Network management systems*
  - *Display of functional views of network management*
  - *Examples of commercial and open source NMSs*
  - *System and applications management*
  - *Enterprise management system*
  - *Telecommunications management system*

Thus far we have covered SNMP standards for IP network management. This includes protocols and Management Information Bases (MIBs). In this chapter we will discuss assorted tools and techniques that can be used for the management of networks using SNMP (and other management protocols).

In Section 9.1 we start with commonly available utilities that can be used for management. This is followed by a discussion of tools for gathering network statistics in Section 9.2. Next, in Section 9.3 we examine the design of MIBs (MIB Engineering), which is important for any vendor of networking equipment. In Section 9.4 we turn to the design of a typical network management system (NMS) server for a large telecom network. In Section 9.5 we outline several commercial and free NMS products for different types of networks.

9.1   SYSTEM UTILITIES FOR MANAGEMENT

A significant amount of network management can be done using operating system (OS) utilities and some freely downloadable SNMP tools. These can be put together quickly using simple scripting languages such as Perl [Cozens; Lidie and Walsh, 2002]. Some of these tools are described below.

9.1.1   Basic Tools

Numerous basic tools are either a part of the OS or are available as add-on applications that aid in obtaining network parameters or in the diagnosis of network problems. We will describe some of the more popular ones here under the three categories of status monitoring, traffic monitoring, and route monitoring.

Network Status Tools. Table 9.1 lists some of the network status-monitoring tools that are available in the Linux/UNIX and Microsoft Windows (XP and Vista) environments. We use Linux and UNIX interchangeably in this section as the same set of basic utilities and tools are available on both. This also applies to Solaris, HP-UX, AIX, MacOS X, and Free BSD.

The command *ifconfig* on a UNIX system is used to assign an address to a network interface or to configure network interface parameters. Usually, one needs to be a super-user (su) in UNIX to set interface parameters. However, it can be used without options by any user to obtain the current configuration of the local system or of a remote system. In this and other commands, you may invoke *man command-name* to obtain the manual page of a command in a UNIX system. An example of *ifconfig* is shown in Figure 9.1.

Table 9.1   Status-Monitoring Tools

NAME	OPERATING SYSTEM	DESCRIPTION
ifconfig	Linux	Obtains and configures networking interface parameters and status
ping	Linux/Windows	Checks the status of node/host
nslookup	Linux/Windows	Looks up DNS for name–IP address translation
dig	Linux	Queries DNS server (supersedes nslookup)
host	Linux	Displays information on Internet hosts/domains

```
netman: ifconfig –a
lo0: flags=849<UP,LOOPBACK,RUNNING,MULTICAST> mtu 8232
        inet 127.0.0.1 netmask ff000000
hme0: flags=863<UP,BROADCAST,NOTRAILERS,RUNNING,MULTICAST>
        mtu 1500 inet 192.207.8.31 netmask ffffff00 broadcast 192.207.8.255
```

Figure 9.1 Example of Interface Configuration (*ifconfig*)

The option –a is for displaying all interfaces. As we can see, there are two interfaces, the loopback interface, lo0, and the Ethernet interface, hme0. Option –a provides information on whether the interface is up or down, what maximum transmission unit (mtu) it has, the Ethernet interface address, etc.

One of the most basic tools is *ping* (packet Internet groper). A frequent use of it is when an execution of a command on a remote station fails. As one of the first diagnostics, we want to ensure that the connection exists, for which the *ping* utility is executed to the remote host. If it fails, then there is a problem with the link. If it passes, then the trouble is with either the application or something else.

You have already used the *ping* tool in the Chapter 1 exercises. It is based on the ICMP echo_request message and is available in both UNIX and Microsoft Windows OSs. "Pinging" a remote IP address verifies that the destination node and the intermediate nodes have live connectivity and provides the round-trip delay time. By pinging multiple times, we can obtain the average time delay, as well as percentage loss of packets, which is a measure of throughput. This feature can be used to check the performance of the connection. There are numerous implementations of ping. Read the manual page for details on the specific implementation on each host.

The UNIX commands, *nslookup*, *host*, and *dig*, are useful for obtaining names and addresses on hosts and domain name servers. A domain name server provides the service of locating IP addresses. The *nslookup* tool is an interactive program for making queries to the domain name server for translating the host name to the IP address and vice versa. The command, by default, sends the query to the local domain name server, but any other server can also be specified. The command *dig* is a more powerful replacement for *nslookup*.

For example, the command *dig nimbus.tenet.res.in* on the host *beluga* yields the result shown in Figure 9.2.

An interpretation of the above result follows. The host, beluga, obtained the IP address of nimbus. tenet.res.in (203.199.255.4) from the domain's name server 203.199.255.3. This information is given in

```
[beluga]~> dig +nocomments nimbus.tenet.res.in
nimbus.tenet.res.in.   604800       IN      A       203.199.255.4
tenet.res.in.          604800       IN      NS      volcano.tenet.res.in.
tenet.res.in.          604800       IN      NS      lantana.tenet.res.in.
volcano.tenet.res.in.  604800       IN      A       203.199.255.3
;; Query time: 2 msec
;; SERVER: 203.199.255.3#53(203.199.255.3)
;; WHEN: Fri Mar  6 14:12:43 2009
;; MSG SIZE  rcvd: 149
[beluga]~>
```

Figure 9.2 Example of Network Address Translation (*dig*)

the first line of the output (the A-record). The *authority* for this information, i.e., the name server(s) for the domain, is given in subsequent NS-records. The name server that responded to this query is given in the comments at the end.

Instead of the host name, the IP address could also be used as the option parameter in the dig command. For example, the command dig +short –x 203.199.255.5 will return the information that this IP address is assigned to *lantana.tenet.res.in. dig* can give very verbose output. The options *+nocomments* and *+short* are used to suppress some of this.

dig or *nslookup* can help when one wants to find all the hosts on a local area network (LAN). This can be done using a broadcast ping on the LAN. We need to know the IP address to execute this command, which we may not know. However, if we know a host name on the LAN, we could obtain the IP address using *nslookup*.

The interactive command *host* can also be used to get the host name using the domain name server. However, with the appropriate security privilege, it can be used to get all the host names maintained by a domain name server. The *dig* and *host* utilities also provide additional data on the hosts, besides host names. Refer to the manual page for details.

Network Traffic-Monitoring Tools. Table 9.2 lists several traffic-monitoring tools. One of the tools is ping, which we have mentioned as a status-monitoring tool in Table 9.1. As we stated earlier, by repeatedly executing ping with a large repeat count (e.g., ping –c 100) and measuring how many of those were successfully received back, we can calculate the percentage of packet loss. Packet loss is a measure of throughput. The example in Figure 9.3 displays zero packet loss when five packets were transmitted and received. It also shows the round-trip packet transmission time.

Another useful tool, heavily based on ping, is called *bing* (point-to-point bandwidth ping). The *bing* utility determines the raw throughput of a link by calculating the difference in round-trip times for different packet sizes from each end of the link. For example, if we want to measure the throughput of a hop or point-to-point link between L1 and L2, we derive it from the results of the measurements of ICMP echo requests to L1 and L2. The difference between the two results yields the throughput of the link L1–L2. This method has the advantage of yielding accurate results, even though the path to the link L1–L2 from the measuring station could have a lower bandwidth than the link L1–L2 for which the measurement is

Table 9.2 Traffic-Monitoring Tools

NAME	OPERATING SYSTEM	DESCRIPTION
ping	UNIX/Windows	Used for measuring round-trip packet loss
bing	UNIX	Measures point-to-point bandwidth of a link
tcpdump	UNIX	Dumps traffic on a network
getethers	UNIX	Acquires all host addresses of an Ethernet LAN segment
iptrace	UNIX	Measures performance of gateways
ethereal, wireshark	Linux/Windows	Graphical tool to capture, to inspect, and to save Ethernet packets

```
netman: ping -s mit.edu
PING mit.edu: 56 data bytes
64 bytes from MIT.MIT.EDU (18.72.0.100): icmp_seq=0. time=42. ms
64 bytes from MIT.MIT.EDU (18.72.0.100): icmp_seq=1. time=41. ms
64 bytes from MIT.MIT.EDU (18.72.0.100): icmp_seq=2. time=41. ms
64 bytes from MIT.MIT.EDU (18.72.0.100): icmp_seq=3. time=40. ms
64 bytes from MIT.MIT.EDU (18.72.0.100): icmp_seq=4. time=40. ms


----mit.edu PING Statistics----
5 packets transmitted, 5 packets received, 0% packet loss
round-trip (ms)  min/avg/max = 40/40/42
```

Figure 9.3 Example of Traffic Monitoring (*ping*)

made. However, there is a practical limit to it (about 30 times). In practice, this means that if you have a 64-kbps connection to the Internet, the maximum throughput of the link you can measure is 2 Mbps.

Other commands examine the packets that traverse the network to provide different outputs. The commands, *tcpdump* and *ethereal* (also known as *wireshark*), put a network interface in a promiscuous mode, in which raw data are gathered from the network without any filtering, and log the data. All of them could generate an output text file, associating each line with a packet containing information on the protocol type, length, source, and destination. Because of the security risk associated with looking at data in a promiscuous mode in these cases, the user ID is limited to super-user. An example of the output of *ethereal* is shown in Figure 9.4. Each line shows information about one packet. Several packets are Address Resolution Protocol (ARP) requests. In these cases, the source MAC address is shown. For ease of reading, the vendor ID of the MAC address is shown in text form, followed by the 24-bit serial number. The three lines in gray scale in the middle of the window show packets belonging to a single HTTP session over a transmission control protocol (TCP) connection. They capture the three-way handshake used by TCP to establish the connection. The first of these packets is a connection request from 10.6.21.59 to the HTTP port on server 10.94.3.215. The server responds with an SYN+ACK, and finally, the initiator ACKs to complete the connection establishment handshake.

For an example of *tcpdump* command output, please see the SNMP get-request and get-response PDUs shown in Figure 5.17 that were obtained using the *tcpdump* tool.

The command *getethers* discovers all host/Ethernet address pairs on the LAN segment (a.b.c.1 to a.b.c.254). It generates an ICMP echo_request message similar to ping using an IP socket. The replies are compared with the ARP table to determine the Ethernet address of each responding system.

The *iptrace* tool uses the NETMON program in the UNIX kernel and produces three types of outputs: IP traffic, host traffic matrix output, and abbreviated sampling of a pre-defined number of packets.

Network Routing Tools. Table 9.3 lists three sets of route-monitoring tools. The *netstat* tool displays the contents of various network-related data structures in various formats, depending on the options selected. The network-related data structures that can be displayed using *netstat* include the routing table, interface statistics, network connections, masquerade connections, and multicast memberships. The example of the routing tables obtained using *netstat* is given in Figure 9.5. It shows the ports associated with various destinations. *netstat* is a useful diagnostic tool for troubleshooting. For example, the routing table information shown in Figure 9.5 informs the network operator which nodes have been

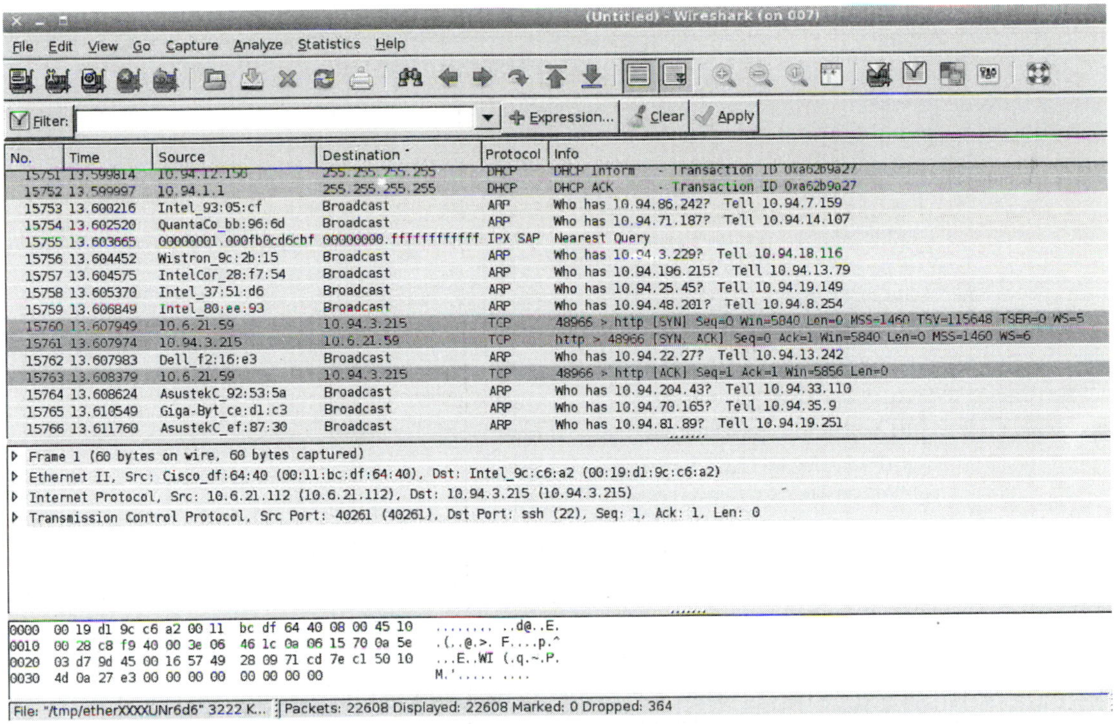

Figure 9.4 Traffic Monitoring using Ethereal (Wireshark)

Table 9.3 Route-Monitoring Tools

NAME	OPERATING SYSTEM	DESCRIPTION
netstat	UNIX	Displays the contents of various network-related data structures
arp rarp	UNIX, Windows	Displays and modifies the Internet-to-Ethernet address translation tables
traceroute tracert	UNIX/Windows	Traces the route to a destination with routing delays

active since the last purge of the table, which is typically in the order of a minute. The most frequently used options of netstat are: −r that obtains the contents of the routing tables; −i that prints the table of all networking interfaces; and −a that prints information about all active Internet connections and UNIX-domain sockets.

The *arp* tool displays and modifies the Internet-to-Ethernet address translation tables (ARP cache) used by the ARP. Some UNIX systems provide an additional tool for manipulating the contents of Ethernet-to-Internet address translation tables (RARP cache). The name of the tool is *rarp* and its use is similar to *arp*.

The third set of routing tools shown in Table 9.3 is *traceroute* (UNIX) or *tracert* (MS Windows), which is the basic tool used most extensively to diagnose routing problems. The tool discovers the route taken by packets from the source-to-destination through each hop. It is very useful in localizing the

```
netstat −r
Routing tables

Internet:
```

Destination	Gateway	Flags	Refs	Use	Netif	Expire
Default	gw.litech.net	UGC	44	541550	de0	
172.16.15.1	gw.litech.net	UGH	0	0	de0	
ah.litech.net	0:80:48:ee:74:b4	UHLW	9	2653683	de0	202
uucp.litech.net	uucp.litech.net	UH	0	0	lo0	
sip-17.litech.net	big	UH	0	5551	ppp3	
dip-244.litech.net	gw.litech.net	UGH	0	2472	de0	
univers-litech-gw	gw.litech.net	UGH	0	47	de0	
194.44.232	gw.isr.lviv.ua	Ugc	0	171831	ppp9	
OSPF-ALL.MCAST.NET	localhost	UH	1	86491	lo0	
OSPF-DSIG.MCAST.NE	localhost	UH	1	25127	lo0	

Figure 9.5 Routing Table using netstat−r

source of route failure. It is also useful in performance/packet delay evaluation as the result gives the delay time to each node along the route. *traceroute* is based on the ICMP time_exceeded error report mechanism. When an IP packet is received by a node with a time-to-live (TTL) value of 0, an ICMP packet is sent to the source. The source sends the first packet with a TTL of zero to its destination. The first node looks at the packet and sends an ICMP packet since TTL is greater than 0. Then, the source sends the second packet with a TTL larger than the TTL needed to get to the first node, and thus *traceroute* acquires the second node. This process continues until all the nodes between the source and the destination have been determined.

Figure 9.6 gives two sample traces taken close to each other in time between the same source *mani. bellsouth.net* and destination *mani.btc.gatech.edu*. We notice significant differences in the route taken, the delay times, and the number of hops. We would expect these differences since each packet in an IP network is routed independently. Each line shows the router that the packet traversed in sequential order. The three time counts on each line indicate the round-trip delay for each router on three attempts made from the source. We notice that there is a jump in the round- trip delay from 2–5 milliseconds to greater than 10 milliseconds when the packet crosses over from the local BellSouth network. In some lines, for example in lines 9 and 13 in Sample 1, one round-trip delay reads high, which could be attributed to the router being busy. In Sample 2, the second half of the route appears congested, indicating consistent large round-trip delays. We also notice that some of the routers respond with their IP address, while others do not. The lines that are marked with asterisks are responses from those routers, which have been administratively prevented from revealing their identity in their responses.

There are also Web-based *traceroute* and *ping* utilities available in some systems. The use of these tools significantly decreases the time necessary to detect and isolate a routing problem because the final decision is based on independent data obtained from various hosts on the net.

```
Tracing route to mani.btc.gatech.edu [199.77.147.96]
over a maximum of 30 hops:

 1    2 ms   3 ms    3 ms  bims008001.bims.bellsouth.net [205.152.8.1]
 2    4 ms   2 ms    3 ms  172.16.11.2
 3    5 ms   4 ms    3 ms  172.16.4.2
 4    5 ms   3 ms    3 ms  bims011033.bims.bellsouth.net [205.152.11.33]
 5    4 ms   4 ms    4 ms  205.152.13.98
 6    *      *       *     Request timed out
 7    5 ms   9 ms   12 ms  205.152.2.249
 8   33 ms  31 ms   31 ms  Hssi0-0-0.GW2.ATL1.ALTER.NET [157.130.65.229]
 9   68 ms  10 ms   11 ms  105.ATM3-0-0.XR1.ATL1.ALTER.NET [146.188.232.66]
10   11 ms  14 ms   12 ms  195.ATM12-0-0.BR1.ATL1.ALTER.NET
[146.188.232.49]
11   16 ms  14 ms   14 ms  atlanta1-br1.bbnplanet.net [4.0.2.141]
12   19 ms  15 ms   17 ms  atlanta2-br2.bbnplanet.net [4.0.2.158]
13   21 ms  56 ms  328 ms  atlanta2-cr99.bbnplanet.net [4.0.2.91]
14   17 ms  18 ms   17 ms  192.221.26.3
15   32 ms  20 ms   18 ms  130.207.251.3
16   20 ms  17 ms   17 ms  mani.btc.gatech.edu [199.77.147.96]
Trace complete
```

Sample 1

```
Tracing route to mani.btc.gatech.edu [199.77.147.96]
over a maximum of 30 hops:

 1    3 ms    3 ms    4 ms  bims008001.bims.bellsouth.net [205.152.8.1]
 2    3 ms    3 ms    2 ms  172.16.11.2
 3    5 ms    4 ms    4 ms  172.16.4.2
 4    5 ms    3 ms    4 ms  bims011033.bims.bellsouth.net [205.152.11.33]
 5    7 ms    4 ms    4 ms  205.152.13.98
 6    *       *       *     Request timed out
 7    9 ms    8 ms    9 ms  205.152.2.249
 8  228 ms  214 ms  191 ms  206.80.168.9
 9  230 ms  246 ms  234 ms  maeeast.bbnplanet.net [192.41.177.2]
10  243 ms  222 ms  212 ms  vienna1-nbr2.bbnplanet.net [4.0.1.93]
11  230 ms  213 ms  202 ms  vienna1-nbr3.bbnplanet.net [4.0.5.46]
12  247 ms  227 ms  236 ms  vienna1-br2.bbnplanet.net [4.0.3.149]
13  228 ms  235 ms  238 ms  atlanta1-br1.bbnplanet.net [4.0.2.58]
14    *     257 ms  238 ms  atlanta2-br2.bbnplanet.net [4.0.2.158]
15  225 ms  234 ms  233 ms  atlanta2-cr99.bbnplanet.net [4.0.2.91]
16  240 ms  229 ms  251 ms  192.221.26.3
17  235 ms  245 ms  225 ms  130.207.251.3
18    *     268 ms  243 ms  mani.btc.gatech.edu [199.77.147.96]
Trace complete
```

Sample 2

Figure 9.6 Examples of Route Tracing (*traceroute*)

9.1.2 SNMP Tools

There are several tools available to obtain the MIB tree structure, as well as its values from a network element. Each of these tools has several implementations. We will not go into specific implementations here, but will describe their functionality. You may obtain details on the use and options from the manual page describing the tool.

SNMP MIB tools are of three types: (1) SNMP MIB browser uses a graphical interface; (2) a set of SNMP command-line tools, which is primarily UNIX- and Linux/FreeBSD-based tools; and (3) Linux/FreeBSD-based tool, *snmpsniff*, which is useful to read SNMP PDUs.

SNMP MIB Browser. An SNMP MIB browser is a user-friendly tool that can be accessed from public software libraries or commercially purchased. All extract MIB-II of SNMPv1 and some can extract SNMPv2 MIB. Some can also acquire private MIB objects. You specify the host name or the IP address first. Then information on a specific MIB object, or a group, or the entire MIB can be requested, depending on the implementation. The response comes back with the object identifier(s) and value(s) of the object(s).

For example, using the graphical MIB browser *tkmib* (http://www.net-snmp.org) and requesting the variable *system.sysDescr* from host 10.65.0.32 yields the response shown in Figure 9.7. The MIB tree is shown in graphical form in the top window. By clicking on a leaf node in the tree and invoking a *get*,

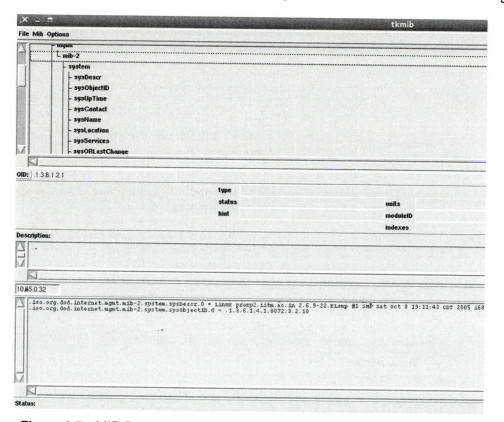

Figure 9.7 MIB Browser Example (*tkmib*) for a System Descriptor Object

199.77.147.182:

sysDescr.0 : SunOS noc5 5.6 Generic_105181-03 sun4u
sysObjectID.0 : 1.3.6.1.4.1.11.2.3.10.1.2
sysUpTime.0 : 8d 22:21:53.74
sysContact.0 :
sysName.0 : noc5
sysLocation.0 :
sysServices.0 : 72
sysORLastChange.0 : 0d 0:00:00.00

Figure 9.8   MIB Browser Example (Text Based) for a System Group

the response from the agent is shown in the bottom panel. We see that the node is a Linux-based proxy server running kernel 2.6.9-22 with symmetrical multiprocessor (SMP) support. Figure 9.8 shows the results obtained by using a text-based browser to retrieve the system group from host 99.77.147.182.

SNMP Command-Line Tools. There are several SNMP command-line tools available in the UNIX, Linux, or FreeBSD and Windows OS environments. Command-line tools generate SNMP messages, which are get, get-next, getbulk, set, response, and trap. Public domain software packages can be downloaded that are capable of operating either as an SNMPv1, SNMPv2, or SNMPv3 manager. A popular suite is available from *http://www.net-snmp.org*. The following commands are described in SNMPv1 format. An option of –v2 or –v3 is used to generate SNMPv2c or SNMPv3, respectively.

SNMP Get Command.

> snmpget [options] host community objectID [*objectID*]

This command communicates with a network object using the SNMP *get-request* message. The *host* may be either a host name or an IP address. If the SNMP agent resides on the host with the matching *community* name, it responds with a *get-response* message returning the value of the *objectID*. If multiple *objectIDs* are requested, a *varBind* clause is used to process the message containing multiple object names (see Figure 4.48). If the get-request message is invalid, the get-response message contains the appropriate error indication.

For example,

> snmpget 199.77.147.182 public system.sysdescr.0

retrieves the system variable system.sysDescr

> system.sysdescr.0 = "SunOS noc5 5.6 Generic_105181-03 sun4u."

The 0 at the end of the *objectID* indicates that the request is for a single scalar variable.

SNMP Get-Next Command.

> snmpgetnext [options] host community objectID [objectID]

The command is similar to *snmpget* except that it uses the SNMP *get-next-request* message. The managed object responds with the expected get-response message on the *objectID* that is lexicographically next to the one specified in the request. This command is especially useful to get the values of variables in an aggregate object, i.e., in a table.

For example,

Snmpgetnext 199.77.147.182 public interfaces.ifTable.ifEntry.ifIndex.1 retrieves

Interfaces.ifTable.ifEntry.ifIndex.2 = "2."

SNMP Walk Command.

       snmpwalk [options] host community [objectID]

The *snmpwalk* command uses *get-next-request* messages to get the MIB tree for the group defined by the *objectID* specified in the request. It literally walks through the MIB. Without the *objectID*, the command displays the entire MIB tree supported by the agent.

SNMP Set Command. The *snmpset* command sends the SNMP set-request message and receives the *get-response* command.

SNMP Trap Command. The *snmptrap* command generates a trap message. Some implementation handles only SNMPv1 traps and others handle SNMPv1, SNMPv2, and SNMPv3 and can be specified in the argument. Note that this acts as an SNMP agent

SNMP Sniff Tool. The SNMP Sniff tool, *snmpsniff*, is similar to the *tcpdump* tool and is implemented in Linux/FreeBSD environment. It captures SNMP packets going across the segment and stores them for later analysis.

9.1.3   Protocol Analyzer

The protocol analyzer is a powerful and versatile network management tool. We will consider it as a test tool in this section, and later on look at its use as a system management tool. It is a tool that analyzes data packets on any transmission line. Although it could be used for the analysis of any line, its primary use is in the LAN environment, which is what we will focus on here. Measurements using the protocol analyzer can be made either locally or remotely. The basic configuration used for a protocol analyzer is shown in Figure 9.9. It consists of a data capture device that is attached to a LAN. This could be a specialized tool, or either a personal computer or workstation with a network interface card. The captured data are transmitted to the protocol analyzer via a dial-up modem connection, a local or campus network, or a wide area network. The protocol analyzer analyzes the data and presents it to the user on a user-friendly interface.

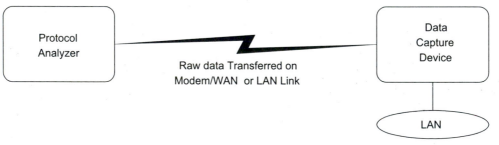

Figure 9.9 Basic Configuration of a Protocol Analyzer

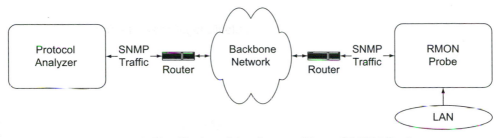

Figure 9.10 Protocol Analyzer with an RMON Probe

The protocol analyzers that are available in the commercial market are capable of presenting a multitude of results derived from the data. Contents of data packets can be viewed and analyzed at all layers of the OSI reference model. The distribution of various protocols at each layer can be ascertained. At the data link layer, besides the statistical counts, the collision rate can be measured for Ethernet LAN. At the transport layer, port information for different applications and sessions can be obtained. The distribution of application-level protocols provides valuable information on the nature of traffic in the network, which can be used for performance tuning of the network.

Numeous commercial and open-source protocol analyzers and sniffers are now available. Sniffer can be used as a stand-alone portable protocol analyzer, as well as on the network HP. NetMetrix protocol analyzer is a software package loaded on to a workstation. It uses LanProbe as the collector device, which can be configured also as an RMON probe. The communication between RMON and the protocol analyzer is based on the SNMP protocol, as shown in Figure 9.10.

A protocol analyzer functioning as a remote-monitoring analyzer collects data using an RMON probe. The raw data that are gathered are pre-analyzed by the RMON and transmitted as SNMP traffic instead of raw data in the basic configuration mentioned earlier. The statistics could be gathered over a time period for analysis or displayed on a real-time basis. In the promiscuous mode, the actual data collected by the probe could be looked at in detail, or statistics at various protocol layers could be displayed. The results are used to perform diagnostics on network problems, such as traffic congestion. They could also be used with the help of the tool to do network management functions such as traffic reroute planning, capacity planning, load monitoring, etc.

Using an RMON probe for each segment of the network and one protocol analyzer for the entire network, as shown in Figure 9.11, the complete network can be monitored. The RMON probe for each type of LAN is physically different. Even for the same type of LAN, we need a separate probe for each segment, which could be expensive to implement.

9.2 NETWORK STATISTICS MEASUREMENT SYSTEMS

One key aspect of network management is traffic management. We will consider performance management as one of the application functions when we deal with them in Chapter 11. However, we will first consider how the basic tools that we discussed in Section 9.1 are used to gather network statistics in the network at various nodes and segments. We will then cover an SNMP tool, Multi Router Traffic Grapher (MRTG), which can be used to monitor traffic.

One of the best ways to gather network statistics is to capture packets traversing network segments or across node interfaces in a promiscuous mode. We have learned that protocol analyzers do just that.

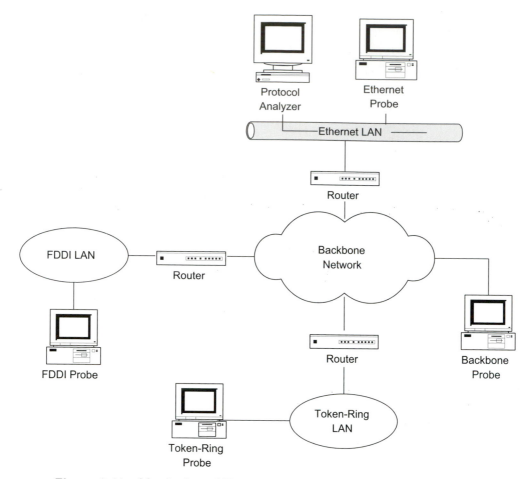

Figure 9.11 Monitoring of Total Network with Individual RMON Probes

Thus, they are good tools to gather network statistics. Another way to gather network statistics is to develop a simple application using a function similar to *tcpdump*, using a high-performance network interface card and processor, and analyze the data for the required statistics. After all, that is the basis on which protocol analyzers are built.

The RMON MIB that we studied in Sections 8.3 and 8.4, along with the SNMP communication protocol, provides a convenient mechanism to build network-monitoring systems. The configurations shown in Figure 9.10 and Figure 9.11 can be used as the network-monitoring system to gather various RMON objects. The RMON1 MIB groups and tables shown in Tables 8.2 and 8.3 are used to gather statistics at the data link layer in Ethernet and token-ring LANs. The RMON2 MIB groups and tables presented in Table 8.4 define parameters for higher-layer statistics.

9.2.1 Traffic Load Monitoring

Traffic load monitoring can be done based on the source, the destination, and the source–destination pair. We may want to balance the traffic load among the various LAN segments, in which case we need to measure the total traffic in each network segment or domain. Data for traffic monitoring can be sampled at the data link layer using the RMON1 MIB history group. Traffic relevant to a host, either as source or as a destination, is available in the host group. Hosts can be ranked on the traffic load that they carry using the *HostTopN* group. In the absence of an RMON probe, there is no convenient way to measure traffic in a segment directly except to compute it externally knowing the hosts in the segment.

Load statistics in an IP network can also be obtained by measuring IP packets at the network layer level. The entities in the network layer host and the network layer matrix groups in RMON2 MIB can be used for this measurement. Figure 9.12, Figure 9.13, and Figure 9.14 show the load statistics measured in a Fiber Distributed Data Interface (FDDI) LAN segment using the NetMetrix protocol analyzer as the Load Monitor and FDDI probe.

In Figure 9.12 there are 1,609 sources that generated data packets. The top ten have been identified, with the highest entry being news-ext.gatech.edu. The entry LOW-CONTRIB is a combination of sources other than those specifically identified. Traffic is measured as the number of octets. Figure 9.13 presents similar statistical data on traffic that is destined to the hosts in the network segment. Figure 9.14 presents the top ten conversation pairs of hosts. Each line identifies the host-pairs, traffic from NetHost1 to NetHost2. Oct1to2 and Oct2to1 denote the traffic in octets from NetHost1 to NetHost2 and NetHost2 to NetHost1, respectively. For example, news-ext.gatech.edu transmitted 3K octets/second of outgoing traffic to and received 60K octets of incoming traffic from howland.erols.net.

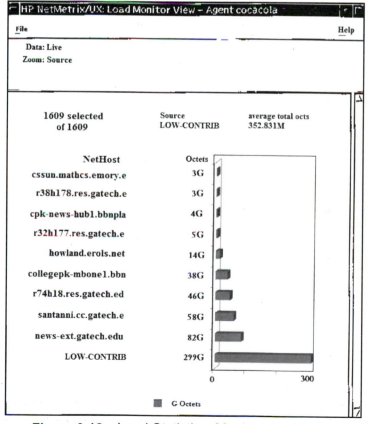

Figure 9.12 Load Statistics: Monitoring of Sources

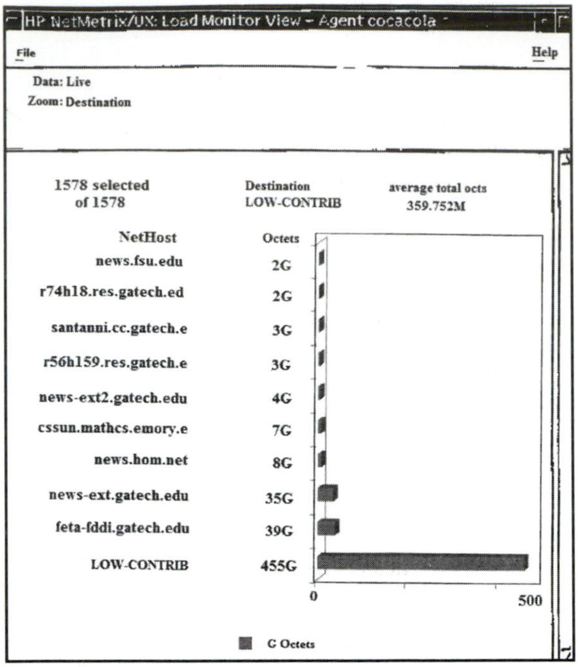

HP NetMetrix/UX: Load Monitor View – Agent cocacola

File   Help

Data: Live
Zoom: Destination

1578 selected of 1578	Destination LOW-CONTRIB	average total octs 359.752M

NetHost	Octets	
news.fsu.edu	2G	
r74h18.res.gatech.ed	2G	
santanni.cc.gatech.e	3G	
r56h159.res.gatech.e	3G	
news-ext2.gatech.edu	4G	
cssun.mathcs.emory.e	7G	
news.hom.net	8G	
news-ext.gatech.edu	35G	
feta-fddi.gatech.edu	39G	
LOW-CONTRIB	455G	

0   500

■ G Octets

Figure 9.13 Load Statistics: Monitoring of Destinations

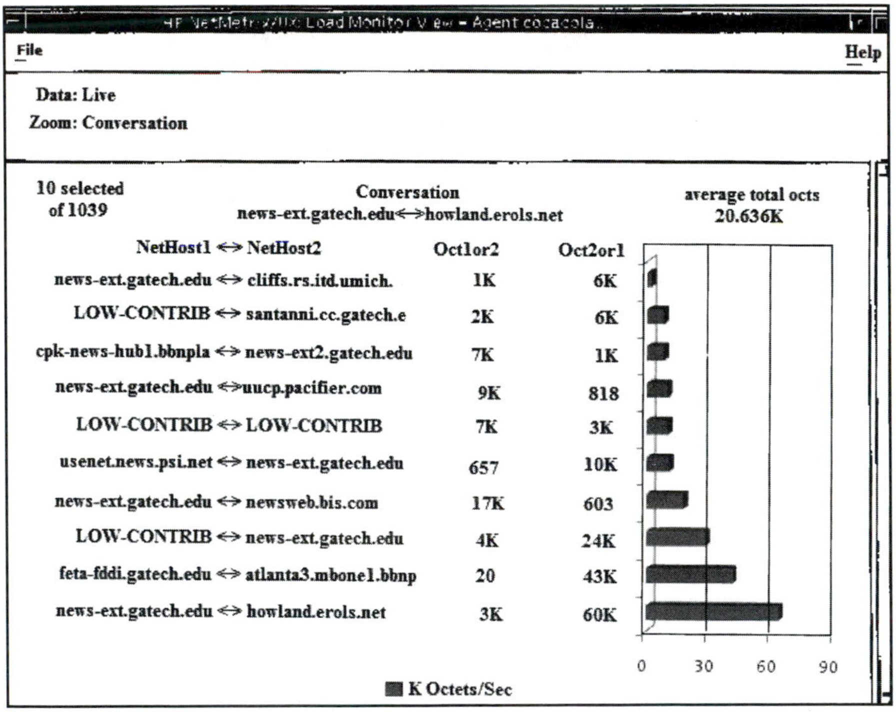

HP NetMetrix/UX: Load Monitor View – Agent cocacola

File   Help

Data: Live
Zoom: Conversation

10 selected of 1039	Conversation news-ext.gatech.edu←→howland.erols.net		average total octs 20.636K

NetHost1 ←→ NetHost2	Oct1or2	Oct2or1	
news-ext.gatech.edu ←→ cliffs.rs.itd.umich.	1K	6K	
LOW-CONTRIB ←→ santanni.cc.gatech.e	2K	6K	
cpk-news-hub1.bbnpla ←→ news-ext2.gatech.edu	7K	1K	
news-ext.gatech.edu ←→uucp.pacifier.com	9K	818	
LOW-CONTRIB ←→ LOW-CONTRIB	7K	3K	
usenet.news.psi.net ←→ news-ext.gatech.edu	657	10K	
news-ext.gatech.edu ←→ newsweb.bis.com	17K	603	
LOW-CONTRIB ←→ news-ext.gatech.edu	4K	24K	
feta-fddi.gatech.edu ←→ atlanta3.mbone1.bbnp	20	43K	
news-ext.gatech.edu ←→ howland.erols.net	3K	60K	

0   30   60   90

■ K Octets/Sec

Figure 9.14 Load Statistics: Monitoring of Conversation Pairs

9.2.2 Protocol Statistics

Packets can be captured by data capture devices based on the filter set for the desired criteria. From the captured data, we can derive protocol statistics of various protocols at each layer of the OSI Reference Model. This is very useful at the application layer level. We can obtain the traffic load for different applications such as file transfer (FTP), Web data (HTTP), and news groups (NNTP). This information can be used for bandwidth management of real-time and non-real-time traffic.

Figure 9.15 shows the distribution of protocols at the data link (top left corner), network (top right corner), transport (bottom left corner), and application (bottom right corner) layers, obtained using NetMetrix LanProbe and a protocol analyzer. Data link and network layers show 100% LLC and IP protocols. The majority of the transport layer protocol packets belong to TCP and the next in order is UDP. The other category is undefined. At the application layer(s), the distribution contains HTTP (Web protocol), NNTP (news protocol), FTP-data, UDP-other, TCP-other, and undefined other. The Georgia Tech Internet backbone network in which the measurements were made carries a complex variety of protocol traffic including multimedia traffic and next generation Internet traffic.

9.2.3 Data and Error Statistics

Data and error statistics can be gathered directly from managed objects using the specifications defined in various MIB groups. The RMON statistics groups for Ethernet [RFC 1757] and token ring [RFC 1513] contain various types of packets and errors in the data link layer. Similar information is available on higher-level layers from specifications detailed in RMON2 [RFC 2021]. Information on statistics can also be gathered for the individual medium from the respective MIBs under the transmission group. For example, statistics on Ethernet can be derived from the Ethernet-like statistics group in Ethernet-like

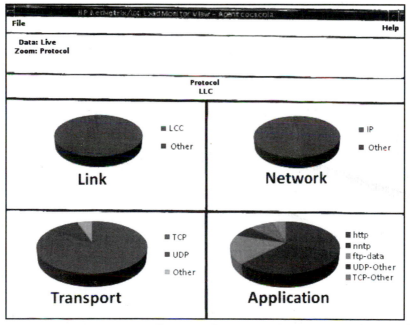

Figure 9.15 Protocol Distribution (NetMetrix)

interface types MIB [RFC 1284], token-ring statistics from IEEE 802.5 MIB [RFC 1748], and FDDI data from FDDI MIB [RFC 1285].

9.2.4   Using MRTG to Collect Traffic Statistics

The MRTG is a tool that monitors traffic load on network links [Oetiker and Rand, http://oss.oetiker. ch/mrtg]. It generates a live visual representation of traffic data by reading the SNMP traffic counters on routers and creates graphs that are embedded into Web pages. These can be monitored using any Web browser. Visual presentations of traffic data are presented as daily view, the last 7 days view, the last 4 weeks view, and the last 12 months view. The generic software can be implemented in either UNIX or Windows NT platform. An example of the views can be seen on http://switch.ch/network/operation/statistics/geant2.html.

9.3   MIB ENGINEERING

In the SNMP model of management, information about each network element is contained in its MIB (Chapter 4). The manager's view of the NE is defined by and is limited to its MIB. The ease of developing management applications depends on how closely the MIB matches the needs of the manager. In most cases, the MIB is hardcoded into the NE by the vendor. Thus, care must be taken in designing the MIB. This is the focus of *MIB engineering*.

There are some commonly used constructs in many MIBs. The use of these *idioms* makes it easier for the manager to understand and use the MIB. The SNMP protocol and structure of management information (SMI), by virtue of their stress on simplicity, have some limitations. Fortunately, there are work-arounds to enable the manager to accomplish complex tasks despite these limitations.

First we cover some basic principles, limitations, and idioms of SMI. We then take a number of frequently occurring requirements and show how to design MIBs for them.

9.3.1   General Principles and Limitations of SMI

SMI provides a very simple view of the network. Every element is completely defined by a set of variables (euphemistically referred to as *objects*), which may take on a limited number of data types. These include scalar or primitive types (Boolean, Integer, IP address, String, Counter, etc.) and three structured or constructed types (arrays, records, and sets).

An *array* is an ordered list of elements all being of the same type. Each element is identified by its index. A *record* is an ordered collection of elements of different types, with each element referred to by name. A *set* is an unordered collection of elements. The elements could either all be of the same type or of different types. E.g., the interfaces table, *ifTable*, is an array with one element for each interface in the node. Each element in the table contains a record with several fields describing the interface (see Figure 4.28).

As an example of a set, suppose the manager wishes to define a trap filter in an agent. The filter consists of a set of conditions that are AND'ed together. Only if all conditions are satisfied, the trap is forwarded. We could define:

        TrapFilter ::= SET OF Conditions

The order of evaluation of the conditions does not matter.

There are restrictions on the construction of types:

- An array can contain a record and vice versa. An array can contain a record that itself contains other records. However, an array cannot contain a record that contains an array
- A record can be defined to hold related variables pertaining to one part of an NE (in one subtree of the MIB). Another record with identical fields but different names must be defined

The SNMP protocol allows a manager to get or set the value of a variable (see Figure 3.9). However, it does not permit a manager to perform an action such as resetting an interface or deleting a file. In object-oriented terms, an SNMP object has member variables and accessor methods, but does not have any general methods to perform actions.

The SNMP protocol supports request response transactions where each transaction can automatically either get or set a limited number of variables. The limit is imposed by the size of an SNMP PDU. It does not allow combining gets and sets in one transaction, nor does it allow a sequence of operations to form a session. SNMP transactions are very limited compared to database transactions. The latter allow a large sequence of select and update queries to be combined in a single transaction, which either succeeds completely or is not executed at all. In addition, access to the relevant parts of the database by other users can be prevented during the transaction.

9.3.2 Counters vs. Rates

Rates are central to network management. Performance is measured largely in terms of rates. For example, the throughput of a link is given in bits/second or packets/second, the throughput of a server in transactions/second, and user behavior in requests/hour.

Rates are also important in some aspects of fault management, specifically in determining when the load on the system is reaching its capacity and hence is liable to fail. For example, if a 1 Mb/s link is subjected to traffic at the rate of 0.98 Mb/s, congestion is very likely with the consequent increase in delays, packet loss, timeouts, and retransmissions. If the congestion persists, it could result in the failure of end applications or the routers at either end of the link. Proactive fault management attempts to spot congestion in its nascent stage and then take congestion avoidance measures to prevent failures. The onset of congestion is indicated by comparing the live throughput with predefined thresholds. The threshold depends on the capability of the router to tolerate temporary overload by means of buffering of packets. Suppose for a router with a 10-packet buffer we set the congestion threshold at 0.8 Mb/s; if the router has a 20-packet buffer, we might increase the threshold to 0.9 Mb/s. The threshold settings depend on the mix of packet sizes and other practical factors. In practice, the threshold is tuned by the operator based on experience.

The manager may also require the counter value. For example, if broadband subscribers are billed based on data transferred, the NMS manager would retrieve the counter of bytes transferred and pass it on to the Billing System.

A counter is a direct performance measure. On a network link, the network interface maintains several counters such as packets and bytes transmitted, packets and bytes received, errors, etc. Whenever a packet is processed, one or more counters are incremented appropriately. These counters are thus available to the NMS agent at no extra cost, are always up to date, and accurate. Hence, the MIB should include the counter. Be mindful that the counter reading wraps around and should be interpreted correctly.

A rate is a derived measure. To determine the transmit rate, we periodically read the transmit octets counter and calculate the rate:

$$\text{Transmit rate} = \frac{\text{transmit octets at } t_2 - \text{transmit octets at } t_1}{t_2 - t_1}$$

The rate depends on the averaging interval $t_2 - t_1$. For example, Figure 9.16 shows a 5-second burst of packets during which 4,000 octets are transmitted. The network is idle for some time thereafter.

Table 9.4 shows the rates calculated over various time intervals. Note that the rate varies quite drastically from 0 to 8,000 b/s. The interval 0–4 is especially troublesome. The counter is 3,000, but the actual number of octets transmitted is 3,500. Even if the Network Interface Card (NIC) has hardware to increment the counter for every octet, this would not be correct because we do not know whether the packet transmission is successful until the end of transmission.

Thus, we see that the derived measure of rate is imprecise and gives different results depending on the averaging interval. Different managers may require different averaging intervals and even one manager may require different averaging intervals at different times. For example, while projecting future growth in network traffic for capacity augmentation, the manager may want a 1-hour average. To monitor congestion in a link, the averaging may be done over 5-minute periods. While troubleshooting some problem, the manager may average over 30-seconds or less to see instantaneous fluctuations.

Normally, the MIB does not include rates. It is left to the manager to poll the counter at the desired periodicity and to compute the rate.

There are a few exceptions. The central processing unit (CPU) load of a server is usually computed using some OS-specific algorithm and the OS may not expose convenient counters. Hence, the agent simply makes available the rates computed by the OS, say the 30-second, 1-minute, and 5-minute load averages. The corresponding counters are not included in the MIB.

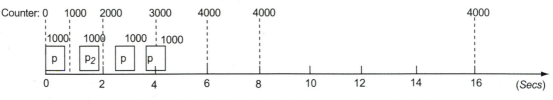

Figure 9.16 Burst of Activity on a Network Link

Table 9.4 Rates Calculated over Various Intervals

INTERVAL (SECONDS) t_1, t_2	COUNTER DIFFERENCE (OCTETS)	RATE (b/s)
0, 2	2,000 – 0	8,000
0, 4	3,000 – 0	6,000
0, 5	4,000 – 0	6,400
0, 10	4,000 – 0	3,200
0, 16	4,000 – 0	2,000
8, 12	4,000 – 4,000	0

9.3.3 Object-Oriented Approach to MIB Engineering

A network element has management parameters pertaining to its configuration, its operation, and its performance. In a complex device such as a server, a backbone router, or a telephone switch, the number of such parameters can easily be in the 1000s. For ease of comprehension, in an object-oriented design related variables are collected into classes. Similar classes are related to one another in an inheritance tree. Given a class definition, instances of the class can be created, referred to as objects [Bahrami, 1999].

SMI provides the MIB group that is a simple form of a class. A MIB group is just a subtree of the MIB tree. The name of the root node of the subtree is the name of the group. Consider MIB-II, which is the standard set of variables implemented by all SNMP nodes (see Section 4.7.4). These variables are grouped into a number of groups such as the system group, the interfaces group, the IP group, and the TCP group (see Figure 4.26).

In an object-oriented language such as C++ or Java, the language supports useful properties of the class. These include encapsulation (variables are private to a class), inheritance (one class inherits the variables and behavior of another class), and so on. We now show how these OO features can be used in information modeling, taking a router with network interfaces as an example.

In SMI, the analogous properties of MIB groups are more a matter of recommended practice. For instance, the TCP group has a count of the number of open connections, *tcpCurrEstab* (see Table 4.13). Normally, this is updated by the TCP code and this variable is considered to be encapsulated within the TCP group. However, it is quite possible for the interfaces code to examine the TCP headers as packets pass through the interface to detect the start/end of a session. The interfaces code could directly manipulate the *tcpCurrEstab* variable in the TCP group. This is a poor practice and is error-prone—a packet could be discarded by the IP layer before it reaches TCP. SMI does not prevent this practice.

Inheritance allows one class to derive some of its properties from a similar (usually more general) class. For instance, an interface has properties such as type, speed, address, and packets sent. An Ethernet interface shares these properties and also has additional properties such as number of collisions. An RS-232 interface has additional properties such as parity. So, it is desirable to derive Ethernet and RS-232 classes from a base interface class as depicted in Figure 9.17.

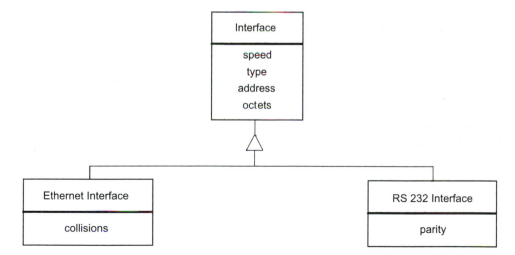

Figure 9.17 Inheritance Used to Define Various Network Interfaces

An Ethernet interface object has the properties speed, type, address, octets, and collisions, while an RS-232 object has the properties speed, type, address, octets, and parity.

Naming. An object-oriented language allows the reuse of the same name in different contexts without any confusion. For instance, given classes Router and Switch, there is no confusion in the use of the same member variable name *numInterfaces*: *Router.numInterfaces* and *Switch.numInterfaces* are clearly distinct. Similarly, grouping of classes into *packages* or *namespaces* permits reuse of class names.

SMI uses a globally unique hierarchy to classify names. Hence, the same name could be used in different subtrees (or groups). The system group in MIB-2 has a *sysDescr* variable. A vendor could have a *sysDescr* variable in its product-specific subtree. They are distinct as *mib-2.system.sysDescr* and *midas. corDECT.sysDescr*, for example.

There are limitations, however. The same name cannot be used twice in the same MIB file. Hence, it is conventional to have a unique prefix for all variables in a MIB group—"sys" for the system group, "if" for the interfaces group, and so on. Thus, we have *mib-2.system.***sysDescr** and *mib-2.interfaces. ifTable.ifEntry.***ifDescr**.

Instantiation. Given a class, many objects of that class can be created or *instantiated*. This can be done statically at compile-time or dynamically at runtime as shown in the C++ code below.

```
Router r1, r2;     //Statically create 2 routers
Router *r3;
. . . .             // Dynamic creation of a 3rd router
if (condition) r3 = new Router;
```

One agent can in general have only one instance of a MIB subtree. In the special case of a subtree that is part of a table, the agent can have multiple instances. See, for example, *ifEntry* in the *interfaces. ifTable*. Even in this case, creation and deletion of rows in the table ("objects") are not as straightforward as the use of *new* and *delete* operators in C++. In SMIv1, row creation is ambiguous and deletion is not supported. In SMIv2, these operations require special fields to be added to the table (see Section 6.3.7).

Recommended Practices. As telecom devices are complex, the object-oriented design of a MIB is highly desirable. SMI has limited support for the object-oriented design of a MIB. Some commonly used practices are as follows:

1. Use of unique prefixes for all variables in a MIB subtree, such as "if" in the interfaces group, "tcp" in the TCP group, and so on. This makes names longer than necessary.
2. Extensive use of tables to allow variable numbers of objects of the same type, e.g., *ifTable, tcpConnTable*, etc.
3. Dynamic creation and deletion of rows (objects) require inclusion of special variables such as *rowStatus* in the row of a table and a variable such as *ifNumber* to count the number of active rows.
4. Copy-and-paste of certain blocks of MIB definition from one file (subtree) to another.

9.3.4   SMI Tables

Besides groups, in SMI, tables are the most commonly used construct for the aggregation of data. SMI tables were introduced in Section 4.7.3 using some examples from MIB-2. An SMI table consists of three levels in the registration tree: table node, entry node, and leaf nodes containing columnar data (see Figure 4.22). For example, in the interface table we have the table node *ifTable*, the entry node *ifTable. ifEntry*, and the data nodes *ifTable.ifEntry.ifIndex.1, ifTable.ifEntry.ifDescr.1,* etc.

Since only a single entry node ever appears under the table node, it is a natural question whether this can be omitted with the data nodes directly under the table node. However, the entry node is essential because of the way SMI defines an index. The entry node describes a complete row and only the node describing a row can specify the index column (see Clause 4.1.6 in RFC 1212). Since the index is essential for specifying a leaf node in a table (one element of the table), every table must have an entry node.

We now turn to the selection of the index field. The index field must enable selection of a unique row. If two or more rows have the same index value, the manager can retrieve only one of the rows. This is a consequence of the form of the SNMP get request in which every data value is obtained by specifying its complete name. The variable binding allows only one data value for one variable name.

Sequence Number as Index. In many cases the rows in the table correspond to sequence-numbered physical entities. For example, a 24-port switch has ports numbered from 0 to 23; and in a router each interface occupies one physical, numbered slot. In such cases it is natural to use this sequence number as the index.

Name as Index. Consider a software application on a server. A unique index can be the name of the application suffixed with the version number. Recall that when a string is used as the index, the ASN.1 encoding of the string is suffixed to the object ID (OID) of the row object to specify a leaf node. Thus, the name of the variable holding the path name of the Apache Web server application in an *appTable* might be *appTable.appEntry.appPath. 'A'.'p'.'a'.'c'.'h'.'e'*. With the usual ASCII codes this would be *appTable.appEntry.appPath.65.112.97.99.104.101*.

OID (Variable Name) as Index. In some tables the index is an OID. Suppose we wish to maintain an inventory table of equipment in a MIB. Each item is identified by its vendor and brand name. Assume that each of these equipments is manageable by SNMP and has a proprietary MIB defined by the vendor. Each such MIB is contained in a MIB group noted in an OID that uniquely identifies the equipment. Consider the corDECT wireless exchange manufactured by Midas Communication Technologies. Midas has been assigned the enterprise node {1 3 6 1 4 1 3794} in the {private enterprises} subtree (see Figure 4.14). corDECT is the first product of Midas and hence has the OID {1 3 6 1 4 1 3794 1}. This OID, encoded in ASN.1, can be used as the index in the inventory table.

Multidimensional Tables. SMI supports only one index for a table. However, this index can be a concentration of several columns, effectively yielding a multidimensional table. An example is the *tcpConnTable* in which the index is the concatenation of local IP address, local port, remote IP address, and remote port. These four quantities together uniquely identify a TCP connection. Thus, the state of connection to a Web server would be given by the variable *tcpConnTable.tcpConnEntry.tcp-ConnState.10.6.21.7.20.27.10.6.21.1.0.80*. Here the host 10.6.21.7 has opened a connection to port 80 on the server 10.6.21.1. The local port is 20 * 256 + 27 = 5147.

Note that the *tcpConnTable* (as also most other such multidimensional tables) is sparse. The total number of possible index values is $2^{32}2^{16}2^{32}2^{16} = 2^{96} \approx 10^{32}$, a truly enormous number. Most hosts have only a few 10s to a few 100s of connections open at a time. Hence, the agent should use some space-efficient data structure such as a hash table or a linked list of linked lists [Horowitz, 1995].

9.3.5 SMI Actions

For managing a network element it is necessary to perform actions such as enable/disable an interface, delete temporary files on a sever, reboot a node, etc. An object in an object-oriented programming language has actions (member functions). SMI "objects" directly only contain data but do not have functions.

In a MIB, an action can be performed by defining appropriate semantics of a variable. The semantics is given by the DESCRIPTION field in the OBJECT-TYPE macro used to specify the variable. The manager can invoke the action by an SNMP set on this "action" variable.

There are two ways in which the agent can inform the manager of the result of the action (analogous to the return value of a function). If the action completes almost immediately, the agent sends the SNMP response only after the completion. The value of the variable in the response indicates the result of the action. An example is the deletion of a file.

Some actions may take an unpredictable amount of time, say formatting a disk. In this case, the agent initiates the action and sends the SNMP response immediately with the value indicating that the action is in progress. When the action completes, the agent updates the same or another variable that can be queried by the manager. An example of the latter is found in the *Interfaces* group in MIB-2. *iftable* has one column *ifAdminStatus*, which the manager sets to *up* or *down* to request a change of status. The actual status is available in *ifOperStatus*. Note carefully the DESCRIPTION fields in the definitions of the variables in Figure 9.18.

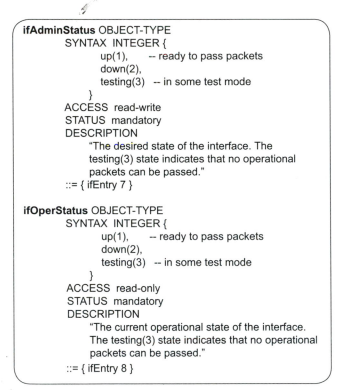

```
ifAdminStatus OBJECT-TYPE
        SYNTAX  INTEGER {
                up(1),      -- ready to pass packets
                down(2),
                testing(3)  -- in some test mode
                }
        ACCESS  read-write
        STATUS  mandatory
        DESCRIPTION
                "The desired state of the interface. The
                testing(3) state indicates that no operational
                packets can be passed."
        ::= { ifEntry 7 }

ifOperStatus OBJECT-TYPE
        SYNTAX  INTEGER {
                up(1),      -- ready to pass packets
                down(2),
                testing(3)  -- in some test mode
                }
        ACCESS  read-only
        STATUS  mandatory
        DESCRIPTION
                "The current operational state of the interface.
                The testing(3) state indicates that no operational
                packets can be passed."
        ::= { ifEntry 8 }
```

Figure 9.18 *ifTable* Variables for Changing the Status of an Interface

9.3.6   SMI Transactions

Suppose a manager needs to perform a complex task consisting of several steps. This may happen, for instance, if there is misrouting of packets to destination 69.96.172.9 by an IP router. The manager may go through the following steps to troubleshoot and fix the problem:

1. Fetch all entries in the routing table with the destination matching any prefix of 69.96.172.9 (such as 69.96.172.xxx,69.96.xxx.xxx) using SNMP Get.
2. Identify the incorrect entry.
3. Change the incorrect entries using SNMP set.
4. Test the new route using ping. If ping fails, repeat steps 1–3.

During this process the manager needs exclusive access to the routing table. If any other manager reads and modifies the same rows, confusion may result. What is required is a transaction that may include a sequence of Gets and Sets to a subtree of the MIB. The SNMP protocol does not support this. Each SNMP request is atomic and independent of all other requests. One request cannot contain both Get and Set. Only a small number of variables can be simultaneously accessed in a request, limited by the SNMP message size of 484 bytes (v1 and v2).

To implement complex transactions without modifying the SNMP standard, we need to add a few variables with special semantics (DECRIPTION field). Assuming that we need to provide transaction-based access to *aRoot* and its subtree, the extra variables are shown in Figure 9.19 and the corresponding declarations are shown in Figure 9.20. Note that aData1, aData2,... are nodes in the protected subtree. The nodes numbered >1000 are nodes added to support transactions.

To initiate a transaction, the manager attempts to set *aLock* to *true*. If the lock was already held by another manager, the set fails with an error. The manager periodically retries the set. When the set succeeds, the agent stores the manager's identification (typically, IP address and port number) in *aManagerInfo*. During the transaction, only this manager is permitted to access the subtree rooted in *aRoot*. In the normal course after completing its work, the manager ends its transaction by setting *aLock* to *false*.

Suppose the manager forgets to release the lock. After *aTimeout* elapses, the lock is automatically freed. There will be a default timeout, which can be modified by the manager, subject to a maximum to prevent hogging of the lock with starvation of other managers. Occasionally, an emergency situation may arise for which an authorized manager may need to preempt the lock. This is done by writing to *aForceUnlock*. The agent will accept the write and replace the current lock owner with the initiator of the forcible unlock, provided the initiator is in a list of authorized managers.

Thus, it is possible to provide complex transactions in which a manager has exclusive access to a subtree of an MIB during a session. This is accomplished within the constraints of SNMP and SMI

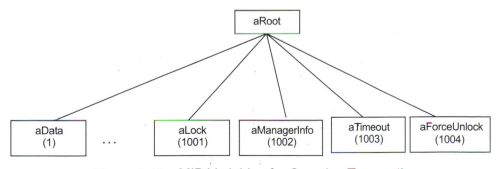

Figure 9.19   MIB Variables for Complex Transactions

```
aLock OBJECT-TYPE
        SYNTAX  Boolean
        ACCESS  read-write
        STATUS  optional
        DESCRIPTION
                "If it is false, set true succeeds and manager info is saved. If
                true, set true by owner succeeds and resets timer. If true, set
                true by other manager fails with badValue(3) error."
        ::= { aRoot 1001 }
aManagerInfo OBJECT-TYPE
        SYNTAX  ManagerInfo
        ACCESS  read-only
        STATUS  optional
        DESCRIPTION
                "Contains the id of the manager who most recently succeeded in
                acquiring aLock."
        ::= { aRoot 1002 }
aTimeout OBJECT-TYPE
        SYNTAX  Time Ticks
        ACCESS  read-write
        STATUS  optional
        DESCRIPTION
                "aLock will be reset aTimeout Ticks after being set."
        ::= { aRoot 1003 }
aForceUnlock OBJECT-TYPE
        SYNTAX  Boolean
        ACCESS  read-write
        STATUS  optional
        DESCRIPTION
                "If set by an authorized manager, alock is reset."
        ::= { aRoot 1004 }
```

Figure 9.20   Declarations for Figure 9.19

by defining a few auxiliary variables. To cater to specific needs, the set of auxiliary variables can be changed, for instance to define separate read and write locks, etc.

9.3.7   Summary: MIB Engineering

In this section we first outlined some of the limitations of SMI and SNMP. We discussed the support provided by SMI for the object-oriented design of complex MIBs. Finally, we presented MIB engineering techniques for handling tables, performing actions, and supporting complex transactions. To learn more about MIB engineering, the next step is to read some of the available MIBs for devices similar to the one at hand and to follow the patterns therein. The guiding principle in MIB engineering is that *the MIB should facilitate the common needs of most managers.*

9.4   NMS DESIGN

We now turn to the design of an NMS server for a large telecom or enterprise network. We first outline the requirements of such an NMS. This determines the architecture. Next, we go into details of the important components of the server.

9.4.1   Functional Requirements

The characteristics of a telecom or large enterprise network were discussed in Chapter 1. Telecom networks today provide a variety of services including voice, data, Internet, and video. A large telecom network serves 10s to 100s of millions of subscribers. For example, India, which has the fastest growing-telecom base in the world, had 413 million subscribers in February 2009 (http://www.telecomindiaonline.com). Its two largest service providers were Bharti Airtel with 90 million and BSNL with 80 million subscribers. India's telecom base is expected to double in the next 4–5 years.

The NMS is expected to support the full range of fault, configuration, accounting, performance, and security (FCAPS) functionality (Section 3.10). Based on these, the key requirements are given below.

Scalability. Typically, such a network has a large number of manageable devices including switches, servers, routers, base stations, multiplexers, etc. These may range in number in the thousands in a large enterprise or Tier-3 telecom network to several million in the largest Tier-1 telecom networks. In most networks, the number of elements grows with time. By scalable we mean that the same NMS can be deployed in networks of different sizes merely by changing the hardware platform. For example, if dual-processor servers with a 2-GB RAM and a 200-GB hard disk are sufficient for a network with N elements, a network with $10N$ elements may require a 16-processor server with a 32-GB RAM and a 1-TB disk. This requires a software design that can exploit the concurrency of the 16-processor server.

Scalability is important to the network administrator. Having invested in one NMS and having developed experience in using it, the administrator would expect the same product to be useable as the network grows in size. For the NMS vendor, scalability is important for a different reason. Developing an NMS is expensive, requiring several years of development by a large team of software engineers. Having invested so much, the vendor would like to maximize its revenue by selling the same product to many customers.

Heterogeneity. As the network evolves over many years, it encompasses a diversity of technologies, vendors, and types of equipment. These may support different management protocols such as SNMPv1, SNMPv2, SNMPv3, CMIP, etc. Some devices may use proprietary protocols. The NMS should easily accommodate this diversity without increasing the complexity faced by the operator.

Geographic Spread. We are interested in managing networks with a wide geographic spread, which has three implications. First, the WAN links used to connect the NMS to distant NEs may have a limited bandwidth, say 64 Kb/s or less, compared to 100 Mb/s or more for a 100m LAN connection. This bandwidth may have to be shared with subscribers' traffic. Hence, the amount of management traffic generated must be limited. Second, the end-to-end delay for an IP packet may be 10s or 100s of milliseconds or even several seconds compared to a submillisecond on a LAN. Third, long-distance links are likely to fail from time to time resulting in temporary disconnection of some parts of the network.

Bursty Load. Some activities such as polling *ifInOctets* for performance reports are done at regular intervals. These present a steady, predictable load to the NMS. Other activities such as handling faults are unpredictable. They are characterized by long periods of quiet with short bursts of activity.

Figure 9.21 shows the number of events generated in a live telecom network, measured at 15-minute intervals during a 24-hour period. The minimum number of events during an interval is 10, the maximum is 947, and the average is 153. See Jagadish and Gonsalves [2009a] for a more extensive discussion of observed fault characteristics of a telecom network.

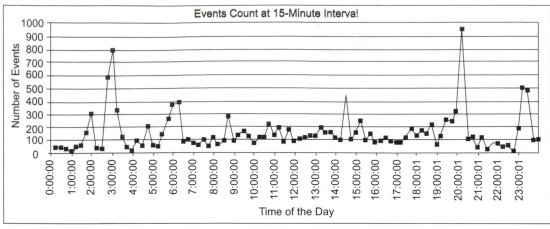

Figure 9.21 Occurrence of Fault Events in a Typical Telecom Network during a 24-Hour Period

It is generally too expensive to dimension the server hardware for the extreme peak load. Hardware is dimensioned well above the average load, but below the peak. NMS software must be designed to handle peak overload conditions gracefully. It may temporarily delay or discard less important events, but it should not fail altogether.

Real-Time Response. Fault notifications require responses within a short time. This may range from under 1 second to 10s of seconds depending on the nature of the event. The response may be an automatic control action by the NMS, or it may involve manual intervention by an operator.

Batch Processing. Performance monitoring, especially for capacity planning, requires a periodic analysis of large volumes of polled data. While imposing a heavy load on the server hardware, this should not be allowed to degrade the real-time response.

Diverse Users. The NMS has a variety of users. These include:

1. *Administrators*: These are experienced and privileged staff who have a high level of responsibility for the management of the network. They may perform sensitive tasks such as bringing a major switch online or offline, reformatting the disk in a server, granting permission to other NMS users. If a mistake is made in any such task, it could have serious repercussions on the operation of the network, even leading to considerable financial loss.
2. *Operators*: Many staff perform routine operational tasks that affect management aspects of the network to a lesser extent. These include generating traffic reports, diagnosing and repairing an individual port in a switch, answering customer queries, etc.
3. *Subscribers/Clients*: Customers of the network may be given access to see the health of their access to the network, to see reports of their SLA agreement such as bandwidth use, etc. They may be able to configure some parameters of their service, e.g., whether or not an email warning is sent when they near their monthly download limit. They cannot change anything else in the network or view other customers' information.

Clearly the NMS must have support for the creation of a large numbers of users, each having different privileges. The menus and commands that are available to each user should be limited to those that are necessary for the role of that user.

Local and Remote Management. Much of network management is performed remotely from the *Network Operations Center (NOC)*. However, there are users who need to use the NMS from other locations. Subscribers may be located anywhere in the network. A technician, who is replacing a faulty hardware unit, may need to login to the NMS from the field location to divert traffic from the faulty unit, configure the replacement unit, and restore traffic routing. Accountants and top management may want to see reports on network resource use, expenses, and generation of revenue from their offices.

Ease of Use. Network administration is faced with two challenges: one is the increasing complexity of network equipment and the other the high attrition rate of technical staff. Hence, it is important for the NMS to have an easy-to-use UI. Increasingly, this is graphical (GUI) and may be browser based. At the same time, experienced users may prefer cryptic commands and keyboard shortcuts that enable them to work faster than with a point-and-click interface.

Security. There are two aspects to security; the first is the security of the network and network elements. This includes providing secure access to network elements for privileged administrators and operators, preventing and detecting malicious attacks such as the denial of service attacks, and monitoring and ensuring the confidentiality of sensitive traffic on the network.

The second aspect is the security of the NMS itself. The NMS perforce has to have access to every network element. It can perform arbitrary configuration of network elements. It stores vast amounts of commercially sensitive data about the network operation. As such, it introduces a single point of vulnerability to the network: a person who can gain unauthorized access to the NMS may well have complete unfettered freedom to tamper with the entire network!

Data Management. With tens of thousands to millions of network elements, each being polled regularly for several variables, the volume of data collected can be very large. If lost, these data can never be recovered. Careful backup of data is essential.

These data need to be kept online for 3–12 months and archived offline for several years. In some countries, preservation of certain network data for several years is mandated by laws and regulations.

For a telecom network with 10 million subscribers, the typical volume of data collected is shown in Table 9.5. (Details of the calculations are given in the exercises at the end of this chapter.)

Note that the disk space requirement is 2–3 times the data volume shown in the table. This is to account for index files created by the database management system (DBMS), temporary copies of data made by the NMS applications, and temporary working space.

9.4.2 Architecture of the NMS Server

We now examine the architecture and major design aspects of the NMS server in light of the requirements discussed in Section 9.4.1. In many cases there is no one correct decision, only design trade-offs where different designers may prefer different choices. This is the nature of real-world design. In these cases, we discuss the range of good choices.

Table 9.5 Typical Data Storage Requirement for a 10m Subscriber Network

PERIOD	1 DAY	1 WEEK	1 MONTH	1 YEAR
Data Volume	2 GB	15 GB	60 GB	750 GB

The NMS server has to handle diverse tasks with very different characteristics. These include polling of performance parameters at regular internals, real-time response to unexpected events, and a good user interface (UI). It has to deal with a plethora of device types. It is a large and complex software application and we hence adopt a *Modular architecture* [Bahrami, 1999]. A set of closely related functions is grouped into a module. These functions interact closely and use shared data structures. The different modules interact relatively infrequently.

A typical architecture for an NMS server is shown in Figure 9.22. This section draws many lessons from the CygNet NMS [Gonsalves, 2000; www.nmsworks.co.in], which has been deployed in several major telecom and enterprise networks.

A number of modules are grouped around a central *managed object database* (*MDB*). The *MDB* contains the configuration information of each managed object. A managed object is typically an NE (router) or a subsystem of an NE (interface of a router). The *MDB* contains the events and performance data of each managed object (MO). The *MDB* must be designed for efficient access to large amounts of data. It contains a code to validate the data and maintain consistency.

The *Discovery Module* is responsible for automatically detecting the presence of new NEs in the network. If these are of interest to the administrator, the discovery module adds corresponding MOs to the *MDB*. The discovery module is a part of the *Configuration Manager*, which also has provision for the manual addition of MOs. The discovery module also detects changes to the configuration of an NE and updates the *MDB* accordingly.

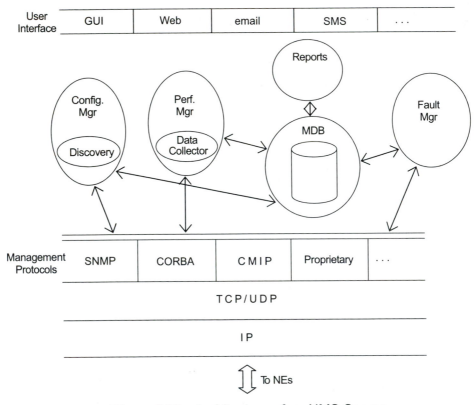

Figure 9.22 Architecture of an NMS Server

The *Fault Manager* (FM) receives notifications of events in NEs. It may also infer faults by analysis of data. For instance, by comparing measured throughput on a link with link capacity, it can detect a congestion fault. The FM notifies the operator through various means such as text, graphics, audio, etc. It may also take automatic corrective action to resolve a fault.

One of the important functions of the *Performance Manager* (PM) is data collection. This is done by periodically polling NEs for relevant performance data. Note that some of these data may be used by the FM as described above. The other important function of the PM is data analysis. Reports are generated to identify bottlenecks, analyze trends in order to plan capacity upgrades, and to tune the network and systems. Anomalies in performance trends may also indicate security problems such as denial of service attack.

Each module has two logical layers. The lower or *core* layer contains the business logic of the module. For example, the logic of sending periodic poll requests, processing the response, and updating the MDB is in the core layer of the PM. The upper layer contains the UI. Typically, this is a graphical user interface (GUI). It may also use text, audio, video, SMS, and so on.

Functional modules communicate with the NEs through the protocol layer. This layer may support a number of common management protocols such as various versions of SNMP, XML, CMIP, and also proprietary protocols.

9.4.3   Key Design Decisions

In this section we describe key design decisions motivated by the requirements in Section 9.4.1. This is followed by a detailed design of the functional modules.

The NMS server has to perform many functions. It deals with real-world entities such as switches, base stations, routers, servers, subscribers, and operators. It needs to handle the properties of these entities and evenly relate to them. It is natural to use an *object-oriented design* [Bahrami, 1999]. Software objects correspond one-to-one to physical objects. This simplifies design, makes it easier to adopt the design to new requirements, and results in more robust software. Most NMSs are written in C++ or Java.

The design needs to be **scalable**. That is, the same software should be able to cater to a network of 100, 1,000, or 1,000,000 elements. The design approach that accomplishes this using the choice of hardware and software is illustrated in Figure 9.23. Scalability can be achieved to a limited extent by using more powerful hardware. Suppose that 100 NEs could be managed using a server with a 1-GHz CPU (Figure 9.23(a)). Replacing the server with a 3-GHz CPU may increase the capacity to 300 NEs (Figure 9.23(b)). Only limited scalability can be achieved by this approach: today, 3 GHz is the practical limit of CPU speeds.

To further increase the capacity, we may consider a server with multiple CPUs sharing memory (a shared memory multiprocessor (SMP)). Such SMPs are available inexpensively with up to eight CPUs. However, a sequential program can use only one CPU. To use multiple CPUs simultaneously, a concurrent software design is needed. This is achieved by using multiple *threads of execution* [Tanenbaum, 2007]. Each thread runs on one CPU and can access the same shared memory. Thus, by redesigning our software to use threads, we could manage $100 \times 3 \times 8 = 2,400$ NEs with an 8-CPU 3-GHz server (Figure 9.23(c)). These capacity increases are the ideal. In practice, the actual increase in capacity will be lower as one thread may wait for another one, or threads conflict to access the same variables.

Beyond a point, an SMP becomes prohibitively expensive. To further increase the capacity, we need to again redesign our software to enable it to run on a cluster of SMPs interconnected by a high-speed

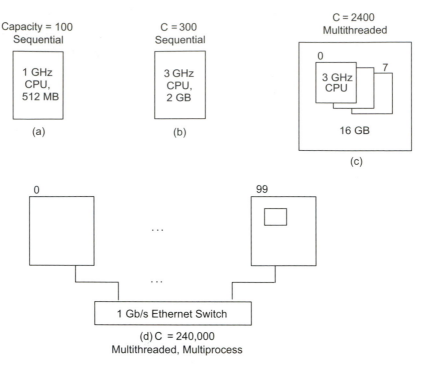

Figure 9.23 Scalable Design Using Threads and Processes

LAN. The software needs to be structured as cooperating *processes* that communicate with one another using interprocess communication (IPC) such as TCP/IP, RPC, Java RMI, or XML/HTTP [Tanenbaum, 2007]. With 100, 8-CPU SMPs connected by a 1-Gb/s Ethernet, the capacity of our server could scale up to $2,400 \times 100 = 240,000$ NEs (Figure 9.23(d)).

Note that the numbers of NEs above are the managed NEs only. The total number including unmanaged PCs, telephones, etc., may be one to three orders of magnitude larger. The actual capacity also depends on the polling interval, etc., so the numbers in Figure 9.23 are indicative only.

The server needs to handle event notification in real time. It also periodically needs to generate reports. To assure that real-time processing is not delayed by periodic batch processing, the former is given higher priority. If the software is structured as *threads and processes*, priorities can be assigned to these and the OS will ensure the real-time response.

With a large number of NEs and data saved online for months to facilitate analysis, the NMS has to deal with enormous volumes of data. Most of the data are structured with well-defined fields such as <NE id, time stamp, OID, value> for a performance parameter. Appending incoming data to a flat file is very efficient. However, retrieval based on criteria is very inefficient. All major NMSs use an R-DBMS for data storage. Examples of commercial R-DBMS products are Oracle, DB2, and SQL server. Opensource MYSQL and PostgreSql products are also commonly used.

We next consider the UI. To minimize training costs and to allow non-technical people (such as accountants and top management) to use the NMS, it is normal to have a *graphical user interface* (GUI). Nowadays, the GUI is often *browser based*. This further reduces the learning curve and ensures that the GUI will run on a wide range of desktop PCs.

The NMS needs to present a large amount of information to the operator. A well-designed GUI can use color-coded symbols and icons to present this information without confusion. Color codes can be used to highlight fault information that needs urgent attention. A judicious use of audio further improves the UI. Network administration is a 24 × 7 activity. Many NMS servers have the ability to notify the operator via SMS, pager, or telephone call with text-to-speech synthesis.

9.4.4 Discovery Module

In a large telecom network, the details of the NEs to be managed need to be entered into the NMS database. Doing this manually is a daunting and error-prone task. The goal of the discovery module is to automate this task. Initially, the discovery module tries to find manageable elements in the network and add their details to the NMS. Subsequently, it periodically checks each NE for any changes in this configuration. The discovery module also tries to determine the topology of the network.

Discovery supplements, but does not replace, manual configuration. For example, the NMS could discover that a router has ten interfaces. Polling intervals for the interface traffic depend on the importance of the connected links. Discovery may set a default polling interval of 15 minutes. An administrator may set the intervals for important interfaces to 5 minutes. For a backup link, the administrator may change the interval to 1 hour.

The strategy used in the discovery process is to check a range of IP addresses for the presence of NEs using the simplest and most generic possible techniques. When an NE is found, the discovery process attempts to find out the type of NE and its characteristics by using more elaborate and specific techniques.

Configuring Discovery. Discovery is controlled by a configuration file, which sets a number of parameters. A basic set of parameters is shown in Table 9.6. Many more parameters could be specified.

Discovery Procedure. The flow chart of the discovery procedure is shown in Figure 9.24. "Check if node present" is normally done using ping. As ping is unreliable, 2–3 ping requests are sent. In some locations, ping may not work because its ICMP echo request and echo response packets are blocked by firewalls. In such cases, attempting to open a TCP connection to a port may be used. This is more expensive in terms of network bandwidth and CPU resources on both ends.

Table 9.6 Basic Discovery Parameters

PARAMETER	VALUE	DESCRIPTION
IP addresses	10.0.0.1–10.0.0.254, 192.168.0.0/24	A range or list of IP addresses
Wait interval	10 seconds	Waiting time between discovery of successive IPs to minimize load on the network
SNMP version	v1	v1, v2c, or v3
SNMP community	"public"	A commonly used value
Discover types	Router, server, switch	Only elements of these types are added to the MDB
Ignore types	PC, UPS	Elements of these types are not added to the MDB

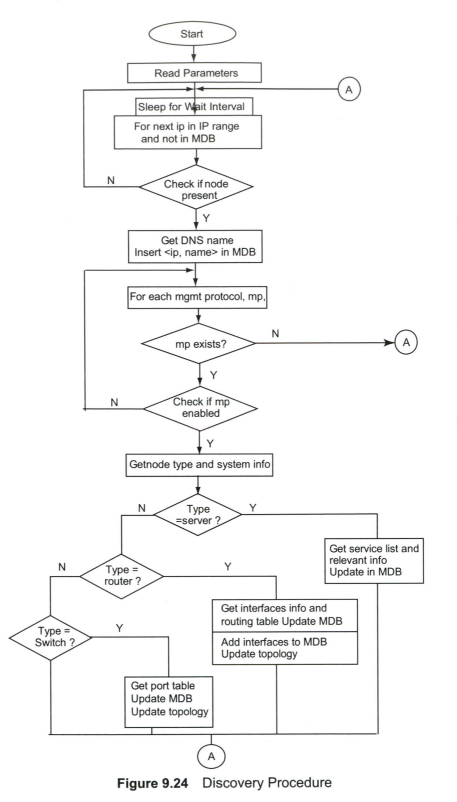

Figure 9.24 Discovery Procedure

SNMPget(ip, v3, auth info, sysObjectId)
If response then node is v3
Else SNMPget(ip, v2c, community, sysObjectId)
If response then node is v2c
Else SNMPget(ip, v1, community, sysObjectId)
If response then node is v1
If node is v1, v2c or v3 then
Lookup sysObjectId to determine type of node
Based on node type, use SNMPget, SNMPgetnext, SNMPgetbulk to retrieve
relevant OIDs and tables.

Figure 9.25 Discovery of an SNMP Node

Inserting a newly discovered element into the MDB usually also involves configuring polling for OIDs dependant on the type of NE, configuring a trap receiver and other event detectors, and adding an icon to the pictorial map of the network. Finally, an administrator may be notified to manually approve and possibly modify the parameters and settings for the new NE.

Checking for which management protocol is enabled is done by sending a series of requests to glean information. For example, a typical sequence for SNMP is shown in Figure 9.25. In the steps that check for the SNMP version, it may be necessary to check for several possible authentication parameters. For example, suppose the read community for PCs in a network is "public," for routers it is "x375tz," and for servers it is "private." For every IP, each of these communities is tried until one is accepted by the agent.

Rediscovery. Periodically, the NMS may check NEs that are in the MDB for any change in their configuration. This process is referred to as rediscovery. Some changes may be detected by the NMS during normal operations. For instance, if the PM is polling an interface on a router and that interface is permanently disconnected. Polls will fail and the FM will show the interface status as down. The operator who disconnected the interface will notice this and delete the interface from the MDB.

Suppose, however, that a new interface is connected to a router. This will not be detected by the polling process. Similarly, new NEs may be connected to the network. A server that was serving as an email relay may be redeployed as a Web server.

Rediscovery follows a simpler flow chart compared to discovery. We already know the management protocol and authentication information and the configuration. Rediscovery mainly involves fetching the configuration information from the NE and comparing it with the details in the MDB. Any new services or subsystems detected are updated in the MDB and notified to an administrator for review. Any removal of existing services or interfaces is presented to an administrator for confirmation before deletion from the MDB.

Topology. The topology of a network depends on the interconnections between routers and switches. Hubs are usually not SNMP-manageable and are not included in topology discovery. During the discovery process, the discovery module determines the type of each NE and hence identifies the routers and switches. It then obtains topology information from the MIB of the router or switch (last two items in Figure 9.25).

In a router, every active interface has an IP address. This is given by the *ipAdEntAddr* MIB variable (Table 4.8). For each interface, the neighbor's IP address can be found in the *ifForwardNextHop* MIB variable (Table 4.11). The variables *ipAdEntIfIndex* and *ipForwardIfIndex* in these two tables form the link. The *ifType* and *ifSpeed* variables in the interface table give the type and speed, respectively, of the link between this router and the neighboring router. Next, the discovery process is applied to each of the neighbors to further extend the topology. Note that to avoid discovering a very large number of nodes, many of which may be outside the domain of the NMS server, discovery may be limited to a certain number of loops. It is also usually limited to the ranges of IP addresses that belong to the organization.

When discovery encounters a layer 2 switch, it can find the number of ports from the *dot1dBase-NumPorts* MIB variable [RFC 1493]. If there are several switches in the network, the spanning tree table (*dot1dStpPortTable*) can be used to find the topology of the extended LAN. Finally, discovery can find the MAC address of machines connected to each port using the forwarding database (*dot1dTp FdbTable*).

Figure 9.26 shows an example topology and information about the network that could be obtained automatically through discovery. The discovery process has created a simple map with each link labeled with its speed and type. The width of the lines is indicative of the link speed. Each interface is labeled with its IP address. The layout of the nodes and links is arbitrary. After discovery, the NMS administrator can manually reposition nodes and links to reflect their geographical positions.

Efficiency Issues. In Figure 9.24 we showed a sequential algorithm that checks one IP address at a time. For any IP that is not in use, the process waits for three pings to timeout, say $3 \times 10 = 30$ seconds. Assume that for each address in use the discovery takes 5 seconds.

Table 9.7 shows the total time taken for discovery for different networks with varying percentages of IPs in use. In the first row, we have one Class C network that has a total of about 250 assignable addresses. Of these, varying percentages are actually used. Likewise, in the second row we have ten Class C networks. Consider the first cell in the table. The total discovery time is calculated as:

Discovery time = Number of IPs in use x success time + number of IPs not in use × timeout time

$$= 250 \times 0.05 \times 5 + 250 \times 0.95 \times 30 \text{ seconds}$$
$$= 62.5 + 7,125 \text{ seconds} \approx 2.0 \text{ hours}$$

The other cells are calculated similarly.

It is clear from Table 9.7 that sequential discovery is practical only for very small networks. During discovery, the discovery module spends most of the time waiting for the response or timeout. The CPU time for each IP that is tested may be at most a few milliseconds, while the network delay may be 100s of milliseconds (success) to 10s of seconds (failure).

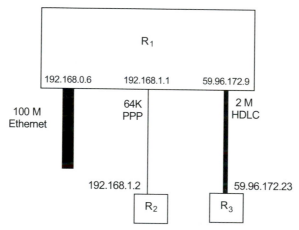

Figure 9.26 Example of Topology Discovery of WAN Links

Table 9.7   Time to Complete Discovery Sequentially

% ADDRESSES IN USE / TOTAL ASSIGNABLE ADDRESSES	5%	20%	50%	100%
1 Class C ~ 250	2.0 hr	1.7 hr	1.2hr	0.3 hr
10 Class C ~ 2,500	20.0 hr	17.4 hr	12.2 hr	3.5 hr
1 Class B ~ 65,000	21.6 dy	18.8 dy	13.2 dy	3.8 dy
16 Class B ~ 1,000,000	332.8 dy	289.4 dy	202.5 dy	57.9 dy

Note: Numbers in italics are days, normal font in hours

Hence, it is feasible to have concurrent testing of several IPs without overloading the NMS server. The discovery module could transmit messages to a number of IPs in quick succession without waiting for replies. Later, when each reply is received, it is matched with the corresponding request and processed appropriately.

Suppose 100 IPs are tested concurrently. The time to complete discovery decreases dramatically as shown in Table 9.8. For small networks, discovery takes a few seconds to a few minutes. For a large network, the time ranges from an hour to 3 days. By increasing the concurrency, we could reduce these times further. For a network with 5% of 1,000,000 IPs in use, i.e., 50,000 NEs, 3 days is acceptable. Keep in mind that the administrator needs to verify and perhaps correct the discovered elements, which would take much longer than 3 days!

Thread Pool or Worker Pool A convenient method of implementing concurrent discovery is by using a pool of worker threads (Figure 9.27). The discovery controller creates *tasks* from the range(s) of IPs to be discovered, each task containing one or a few IPs. It adds these tasks to the *Task Queue*. Next, it creates a number of *worker threads*. Each of the workers picks up a task from the Task Queue when it is free. It executes the sequential discovery algorithm shown in Figure 9.24 for each of the IPs in the task. Whenever a worker completes discovery of the IPs in one task, it takes another task from the queue. Thus, all workers are kept busy until the task queue is empty.

Note that the Task Queue is a shared data structure and must be accessed by only one worker at a time. This exclusive access can be implemented using semaphores or other mutual exclusion mechanisms [Tanenbaum, 2007]. The Task Queue is accessed twice per task, once to add the task and once to remove it. If access to the Task Queue is very frequent, the mutual exclusion overhead could become a bottleneck. To avoid this, the controller normally bundles several IPs in one task. E.g., with 1,000,000 addresses and 1 IP per task, the number of accesses to the Task Queue is 2,000,000. If 250 IPs are bundled per task, the number of tasks is reduced to 4,000 and the number of accesses to only 8,000.

The optimum number of worker threads depends on the range of IPs, the hardware configuration of the NMS server, and the load generated by other modules. For flexibility, upper and lower limits on the number of workers can be configured in the discovery parameters. The controller then adjusts the actual number in the pool dynamically within these limits.

9.4.5   Performance Manager

The PM has two major functions. The first is data collection, which is an online activity. The PM continually monitors network elements for interesting performance-related statistics. These may be processed

Table 9.8 Time to Complete Discovery with Ten Concurrent Threads

	% ADDRESSES IN USE	5%	20%	50%	100%
TOTAL ASSIGNABLE ADDRESSES					
1 Class C ~250		72 s	63 s	44 s	13 s
10 Class C ~2,500		719 s	625 s	438 s	125 s
1 Class B ~65,000		5.2 hr	4.5 hr	3.2 hr	0.9 hr
16 Class B ~1,000,000		79.9 hr	69.4 hr	48.6 hr	13.9 hr

Note: Numbers in italics are hours, normal font in seconds

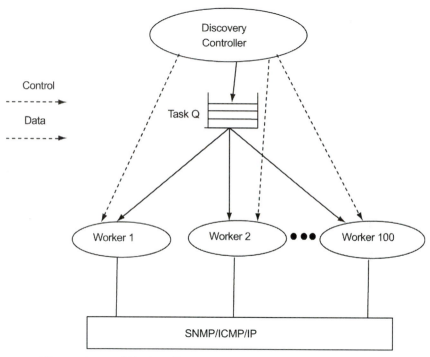

Figure 9.27   Worker Pool Design for Concurrent Discovery

and are stored in a database. Example statistics include traffic on a link (*ifInoctets* and *ifOutoctets*), rate of transactions hitting a server, and CPU utilization of a server.

The other major function is offline *analysis and report generation* based on the collected data. A common requirement is analysis of the utilization of a network link with projection of further growth in traffic. This is used to plan capacity upgradation before the link becomes a bottleneck.

Data Collection. The PM collects data for several reasons. Data may be used for analysis of trends in order to plan capacity upgradation. In this case, the data are not needed immediately. Hence, data collection could be done *offline*. The agent or a lower-level manager polls the variables of interest and accumulates the values in a local file. Periodically, say once a day, a *bulk transfer* of the file to the NMS server is done. We refer to the lower-level manager as the *local data collector* (LDC).

Data collection may be done in order to detect congestion or to implement quality of service (QoS). In these cases, the NMS needs to take immediate action in case of a fault. Hence, *online* data collection is required. Here, the polling is done from the server directly to the agent.

In both cases, polled data are stored in the same database table. Each poll record contains at least the following fields:

- **NE:** identification of the agent, typically the DNS name or the IP address
- **Variable name:** OID or other name
- **Value:** collected value
- **Timestamp:** time of polling

We now consider some important issues in offline and online data collection.

Offline Data Collection. Let us consider the fields in the poll record. The NE *name* used by the LDC and the manager may be different. For example, the NE may have a local IP address that is used by the LDC for its polling, which is put into the local file. When the file is transferred to the manager, the manager needs to modify this to the name used by it for the NE, which may be a global address.

The *timestamp* inserted by the LDC is based on its clock. There may be a skew between this clock and the manager's clock. Since LDCs often run on low-end devices, the clock skew could be very large. The manager needs to estimate the skew and adjust the timestamps accordingly. The situation is made more difficult if the LDC reboots in the middle of the day and skews changes.

Finally, the manager needs to ensure that there are no *duplicate* records or lost records. After transferring the day's file, the LDC should delete it and start a fresh file. However, suppose the LDC does not delete the transferred records. The manager needs to check for duplicates by inserting a unique sequence number in every record.

Online Data Collection. For real-time performance analysis, the PM polls each NE directly for variables of interest. Some issues need to be addressed:

Avoid overloading the server: The PM may be polling several variables in a large number of NEs, e.g., 1,000 routers each having 20 interfaces. There are four variables of interest in each router. Thus, there are 80,000 polls. If polls are synchronized and each is done with a separate packet, the burst of 80,000 replies within a short span could overload the server.

The CPU load depends on the number of packets and the number of variables. In fact the per-packet overhead due to interrupts, etc., is often high. We can reduce the number of packets by combining a number of variables in one SNMP get request. For example, an SNMP get response with one variable may be 65 B long. If we pack four variables for one interface into one packet, the length may increase only to 140 B (compared to $4 \times 65 = 260$ B for 4 packets). Second, the data collector can stagger polls to avoid bursts of packets.

Avoid overloading the network: Suppose that ten of these routers are in a distant part of the network that is connected to the NMS by a 64 kb/s link. Suppose the NMS polls all variables every 30 seconds and it uses one packet of 200 B for each interface. The resultant traffic on the link is $(10 \times 20 \times 200)/30$ B/second $= 10.67$ kb/s. About 16% of the link bandwidth is used for polling only. In addition, traps, accounting, and configuration messages will consume more bandwidth. This can seriously affect subscriber traffic on this link. One solution is to configure different polling rates. Only a few important interfaces are polled every 30 seconds. Other interfaces may be polled once in 5 minutes or 15 minutes. This will reduce polling traffic overhead to a negligible level.

Avoid overloading the agent: A single CPU in a low-end NE often performs the real functions of the NE (routing, switching, printing, etc.) and processing of manager requests. Too many manager requests could overload the CPU and cause its real functions to suffer. Mitigation techniques mentioned above will help this problem also.

Poll Configuration. Different metrics vary at different rates. For a fast-varying metric, say traffic on a backbone link, it may be necessary to poll the counters frequently, say once in 30 seconds–2 minutes. The free disk space on a server varies slowly. We may poll this only once an hour.

Hence, the data collector should allow the poll period to be specified independently for each variable on each NE. There may be several variables being polled on one NE, possibly at different periods. To reduce the CPU and network load, the data collector tries to club several polls into one network packet, e.g., one SNMPget-request command could accommodate 10–20 OIDs and their values.

Dynamic poll periods: Suppose a link is being polled at 15-minute intervals. If it experiences congestion, it is useful to increase the rate of polling to 5 minutes or even 1 minute. It is possible for the data collector to support such dynamic poll periods. However, conditions for changing the poll period are usually related to faults, accounting, etc. Hence, the better design is to have the FM, as part of its handling of the congestion fault, to re-configure the polling period for the variable of interest in the data collector.

A novel design optimizes both the accuracy of the collected data and keeps the network traffic and server load within limits [Jagadish and Gonsalves, 2009b]. The agent or LDC polls data at a high rate and pushes it to the NMS at a possibly lower rate. The LDC evaluates the error between the data that reach the manager and the actual data. It adapts the rate of pushing to the manager to keep the error within a specified accuracy objective. In addition, the NMS sends feedback to the LDC on its load and the importance of this NE in relation to other NEs. This factor, which changes dynamically depending on the faults in the network, is used to further adjust the rate of push.

Concurrency: In a large network, the data collector could be polling several variables in each of 1000s of NEs for a total of 10,000s of polls. If the average polling period is say 300 seconds, the aggregate rate of polling could be 100/second. This could easily overload the CPU. Hence, the data collector for a large network should be multithreaded and possibly multiprocessed. The *worker pool design* introduced in the discovery module (refer Section 9.4.4) is appropriate here also.

Overrun: Ideally each variable is polled at precise intervals. For example, if a variable is configured for a 2-minute polling interval, the polls should take place as shown in Figure 9.28.

In reality, polls may get delayed for a number of reasons. Owing to network loss/congestion, the response to one poll may reach only after the next poll time. The CPU may be overloaded, especially due to a burst of faults. Fault handling is usually a higher priority than polling.

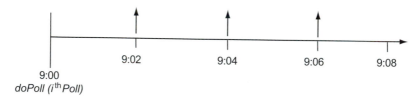

Figure 9.28 Ideal Polling at 2-Minute Intervals

A poll that is scheduled for 9:02, may actually be executed at 09:02:25. In case of severe congestion, the poll may be delayed to 09:04:45, i.e., after the next scheduled poll time. Suppose polls are scheduled at precisely 2-minute intervals, with one poll object being created for each poll. Under overload, a backlog of poll objects could build up in memory. This may slow down the system, further increasing the overload, and affecting the critical fault handling. If the overload persists, the NMS server could even crash.

The solution is to schedule only one poll at a time for each variable. When a poll completes, the next poll is scheduled at the first nominal poll time in the future. In the above example, if the first poll completes at 09:01, the second poll is scheduled at 09:02. However, if the first poll is delayed and completes only at 9:02:23, the second poll is scheduled at 09:04. This tactic of skipping a poll in case of overload ensures that the data collector does not further overload the system. The pseudo-code for static and load-sensitive polling is given in Figure 9.29 and Figure 9.30, respectively.

Database Schema. Polled data are stored in a database for ease of access and analysis. In a large network, with data stored for months or even years, the database size can become very large (see Table 9.9). The database schema need to be carefully designed to ensure good performance even with these very large sizes.

The minimum information stored for each poll of a variable is: NE name, Timestamp, Variable name, and Variable value.

The performance of report generation depends on the indices in the poll records. Of the four fields, it is normal to select records by timestamp (show traffic on 20/06/2008), by NE (show transactions on *www.server.com*), and by variable (show *ifInOctets* on several links). It is rare to select by value. Hence, tables should be indexed on the first three fields.

Assuming 4 B per field and three indices, the size of each poll record is 28 B. To account for the indices and temporary copies, we assume $28 \times 2 = 56$ B per record.

Assuming 10,000 NEs, 10 variables per NE, and an average poll period of 300 seconds, we have an aggregate polling rate of $10,000 \times 10/300 = 333$ polls/second. Database sizes over various periods are shown in Table 9.9.

```
doPoll (iᵗʰ poll)
{
poll for OID
process value
schedule (i+1)ᵗʰ poll at t_start + i × pollInterval
}
```

Figure 9.29 Static Polling can Cause System Overload

```
doPoll (iᵗʰ poll)
{
poll for OID
process value
let k = (t_now - t_start)/pollInterval
        //k is the index of the next nominal poll
Schedule poll at t_start +k × pollInterval
}
```

Figure 9.30 Load-sensitive Polling Algorithm

Table 9.9 Typical Growth of Collected Data

	1 DAY	1 WEEK	1 MONTH	1 YEAR
Number of records	29 m	201 m	863 m	10,501 m
Database size	1.6 GB	11.3 GB	48.3 GB	588 GB

A good DBMS is designed to perform well with the size of one table being up to a few million records and occupying 10s–100s MB of space. Beyond these limits, performance degrades and it is desirable to split the data into multiple tables. On the other side of the coin, having multiple tables makes programming more complex. It is easier to select relevant records from a single table than from a set of tables. DBMS performance also begins to degrade if there are 100s of simultaneously open tables.

The polled data can be divided into multiple tables in several ways:

- One table per NE
- One table per variable (or OID)
- One table per day

Let us examine the performance implications of each of these designs. We consider the number of open tables, the size of each table, the time for insert (done for every poll), and the performance for reports (typically done in batch mode). We also consider the safety of the data.

With one table/NE, the number of open tables is very large as all NEs are being polled, by say 10,000 open tables. The size of each table is modest and insert is fast as there is no conflict between multiple polls. Reports that analyze data across many NEs are tedious to develop. However, reports for one NE access only one table and hence may run efficiently.

Considering one table per variable, the number of tables is large but less than in the above case. The tables are of moderate size resulting in good performance. Insert is fast. Almost any report would need to access many tables, resulting in access conflicts and poorer performance.

One table/day results in only a few 100 tables. Further, all inserts are done in the current day's table only. Most reports analyze past data and hence there is no conflict between such batch reports and the data collector's inserts. A few online reports access the current day's table and cause occasional conflict.

Because of the structure of a DBMS table, even a few bytes of data corrupted in a table or its index could result in loss of the entire table. Hence, having a single table is a poor choice. One table per day is perhaps the best design. Loss of one table does not lead to loss of all information about some important NE. With one table per NE, we could lose all data collected about the most important NE!

Conclusions. Table 9.10 summarizes the different designs and their implications on performance and data safety. For a small network, a single table is a good choice. For large networks, one table/day is often the best choice, though some administrators may prefer one table/NE.

Note that in the 1-table/NE, the NE name is the table name and hence need not be a column (and index). Hence, the space per record is 20 B. Similarly, in the 1 table/variable case, the variable name is the table name.

Some NMS platforms give the administrator the option of configuring the number of tables for data collection and how the polled data are split among these tables. Once the choice is made it is difficult to change as the code for reports depends on the schema. The choice should be made with due diligence.

Table 9.10 Comparison of Different DBMS Schema Designs

	1 TABLE	1 TABLE/ NE	1 TABLE/OID	1 TABLE/DAY
Space/record	28 B	20 B	20 B	20 B
Number of open tables	1	Very large	Large	Few
Insert	Slow	Fast	Fast	Fast
Reports	1 table, conflict with insert	1 table, less conflict	Several tables, some conflict	1 table, conflict for online reports, no conflict for offline reports
Data safety	Poor	Good	Good	Very good

9.4.6 Fault Manager

Fault management is the most important function of the NMS: if the network has faults, performance and accounting become almost irrelevant. Because of the unpredictable nature of faults and their tendency to occur in bursts, the design of the fault management module is especially complex. If it is not done well, the NMS server itself could fail when the network experiences a burst of faults.

We first define the terms used in fault management. We then trace the path of a fault through the system. Finally, we touch on some advanced topics such as root cause analysis (RCA).

Definitions. A *fault* is a problem in a network element or network link. Examples are: a system goes down due to power failure; a link fails due to a cable cut; a disk gets full; and congestion on a link when traffic exceeds some threshold.

When a fault occurs, the NMS may detect it as an *event*. This may be done in different ways by a variety of *event detectors*. One form of event detector is a trap receiver that handles notifications sent by the NE. Another form of event detector is the poll manager detecting that an element is down when a poll fails. This is notified to the FM.

A single fault may result in several events in the NMS. For example, as SNMP traps are unreliable, the agent may send the same trap repeatedly to ensure that the manager receives it. These redundant events are filtered out by the *event correlator*.

When an event first occurs indicating the presence of a new fault in the network, if the fault is of interest to the operator, an *alarm* is created as the manifestation of this fault. The alarm should remain in the NMS as long as the fault persists. The alarm contains all the information about the fault and the actions taken by the operator or the NMS in response. Ideally, for every fault of interest, there should be exactly one alarm in the NMS.

The alarm is brought to the attention of the operator via an *alarm indication*. The indication may be graphical (change of color of an icon on the screen), audio, an SMS, an entry in a log file, etc. The type of indication depends on the importance and urgency of the fault.

Sometimes, one fault may result in events that cannot be easily correlated. For example, if a link fails, the routers on both ends of the link may independently report the fault. This results in two alarms being created in the NMS. Such situations are detected by the *alarm correlator*, which is a high-level analog of the event correlator.

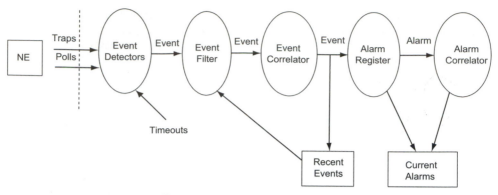

Figure 9.31 Path of an Event through the Fault Manager

Path of an Event in the FM. The first step in fault management is detection of the fault event by the NMS (Figure 9.31). This is done by one or more of a variety of **Event Detectors** in the FM. Different types of events and the corresponding event-detection mechanisms are given below:

1. Notification: This detector receives notification (such as SNMP traps) sent by the NE and converts them into event objects in the NMS.
2. Poll failure: When a status or performance poll request sent by the data collector in the poll manager fails, it indicates a fault in the NE. This is informed to the FM, again by creating an event object.
3. Performance threshold crossing: When the data collector polls for traffic variables such as *ifIn Octets* and *ifOutOctets*, it computes the corresponding rates. If any rate crosses a threshold, a thre-shold event is generated.
4. Internal escalation: When a fault occurs in an important element, the NMS may set a time limit during which the fault must be attended to. If this time limit is exceeded, an event is generated.

The next step is **Event Filtering**. An NE may generate events that are not of interest to the NMS. For example, a router may periodically send a notification about interfaces that have not been configured. Any such event that matches one of a set of conditions configured by the administrator is discarded by the event filter module.

Next, the event is processed by the **Event Correlator**. The event correlator first checks if this event is a duplicate of an event in the *Recent Events Table*. The event may be an exact duplicate (e.g., a router sends a link-down trap every 10 seconds as long as the link is down). The event may be closely similar to recent events (e.g., a link-down trap is received and soon thereafter polling for *ifInOctets* on that interface fails). In either case the duplicate event is discarded.

Since duplicate events may be separated in time, the event correlator must examine all events within a time window. Say, if the polling interval is 300 seconds, the time lag between the trap and the poll failure may be up to 300 seconds. In this case, the event correlator may examine events in a time window of 500 seconds. Of course, using too large a time window would result in the event correlator loading the NMS server unnecessarily.

The event correlator also has to consider the possibility that the link state has changed three times instead of just once. Consider the following sequence of events:

1. 10:31:05: Router7, If3, Link down, Detector: Trap.
2. 10:34:32: Router7, If3, Link down, Detector: Status Poll.

Clearly both events are caused by the same physical fault in Interface 3 of Router7. The first is generated by the trap receiver, the second by the data collector's status polling.

All the fields of the two events match except the timestamps and the event detector. Hence, the event correlator discards event (2). Next consider this sequence:

1. 10:43:08: Router7, If3, Link down, Detector: Trap.
2. 10:44:15: Router7, If3, Link up, Detector: Trap.
3. 10:46:10: Router7, If3, Link down, Detector: Status Poll.

If we simply compare fields as in the previous case, we would conclude that event (3) is a duplicate of event (1) and is to be discarded. However, a closer analysis indicates that the link went down, then came up within a minute and again went down a second time. The second link-down trap evidently did not reach the NMS. Event (3) should be accepted.

These examples indicate that the event correlator should search backwards in the Recent Events Table until one of three conditions is met:

1. It finds a matching event for the same NE and subsystem (such as interface): the new event is discarded.
2. It finds a different event for the same NE and subsystem: the new event is accepted.
3. It reaches the beginning of the time window without finding an event for this NE and subsystem: the new event is accepted.

An event that passes through the event filter and event correlator is now converted into an alarm by the **Alarm Registration** module. The FM has now recognized the existence of a new fault in the network. This alarm will be notified to the operator by suitable alarm indications. The alarm object is used to keep track of actions taken by the operator and NMS until the fault is rectified (discussed below). It is possible that one network fault results in the creation of two or more seemingly unrelated alarm objects. The **Alarm Correlator** and **Root Cause Analysis** modules address this problem. These are discussed at the end of this section.

Alarm Indications. The FM indicates the existence of an alarm to the operator in one or more ways. These include:

- *Visual*: the icon for the concerned NE changes color and may start flashing. A pop-up window may also be used to display information about the alarm
- *Audio*: A tone or other audible indication is played. Using text-to-speech synthesis (TTS), information about the alarm can be conveyed without the operator having to come near the display
- *SMS, phone call*: if the operator is not in the NOC, the NMS could send an SMS or dial out to the operator's phone and play a message (using TTS). This is useful outside normal working hours
- *Email*: if the fault does not require urgent attention, the NMS could send an email to the operator
- *Log*: in all cases, the FM writes a message to a non-volatile log on disk for post-mortem analysis. The log message contains at least a timestamp, name/address of the NE, previous state, new fault state, and descriptive text

For each fault, which one or more of these indications are used depends on the nature of the fault, the severity of the fault, the importance of the faulty subsystem and NE, and other faults that are currently pending.

Consider a router with two links, one is a leased line that connects the campus to the Internet, the other connects to a dial-up modem as a fallback in case the leased line fails. Now, suppose that a periodic

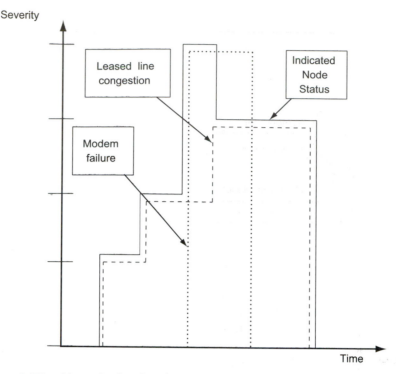

Figure 9.32 Alarm Indication for a Router with Two Simultaneous Faults

self-test of the modem fails—an alarm of critical severity (red indicated by dotted line) is generated (Figure 9.32). Soon after, the leased line experiences congestion of major severity (blue indicated by dashed line). If the color of the router symbol reflects the highest severity of any subsystem, the operator will learn of the modem failure (unimportant as it is not being used) and the congestion on the leased line (quite important) will be hidden. It is clear that the visual alarm indication should reflect the high priority alarm rather than the high severity one, shown by the black line.

Since these priorities are very much dependent on the network, the design of the FM should allow these to be configured by the administrator. Typically, the following configurability is supported:

1. For each <NE, subsystem, event>, set the severity.
2. For each <NE, subsystem, event>, set the priority.
3. For each <NE, subsystem, event, severity>, set the alarm indication(s).
4. For each <NE, subsystem, event, priority>, set the alarm indication(s).

Of course, for ease of use, a good NMS will have pre-configured defaults that satisfy most cases. This configuration of alarms is usually done through a GUI.

Alarm Finite State Machine. As we have already seen, a fault has a lifetime during which it goes through several stages. These include initial occurrence, the operator noticing the fault, corrective action being taken, and clearing of the fault. The fault is represented in the NMS by an alarm object. This alarm object must mirror the physical reality. The most natural design to represent this behavior is a *finite state machine* (FSM).

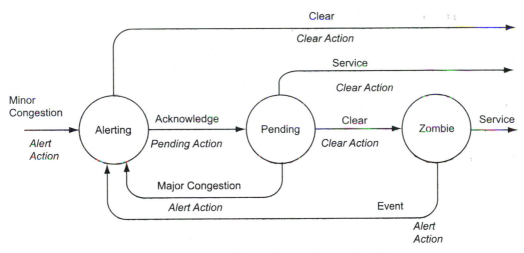

Figure 9.33 Alarm Finite State Machine

An FSM has *states, events,* and *actions.* The object remains in a state for some period of time. During this time it may perform some action continuously. The FSM makes a transition to another state only when an *event* occurs. The transition is (almost) instantaneous and is usually accompanied by some *action.*

Let us consider a typical FSM for a link congestion fault (Figure 9.33). The states are shown by labeled circles. Events are the labels above the transition arcs. Actions are shown in italics below the arcs.

When a minor congestion event is detected by the FM, it creates a new alarm object and puts it in the alerting state. The alert action taken on the transition is to change the color of the icon on the screen (say, to orange), start it flashing, and perhaps start playing an audio message. The flashing and audio playback continue as long as the alarm is in the alerting state to catch the operator's attention.

The next event is the operator *acknowledging* the new alarm. The action taken is to stop the flashing and audio playback. The alarm then moves to the pending state. The operator now starts to take some corrective action. There are several possible events that could occur next.

1. Service: The operator completes the corrective action and indicates that the fault has been serviced. The FM restores the icon color to normal (green) and resolves the alarm object from its action list. Note that the alarm object is usually kept in a history table in the DB for future auditing and analysis.

2. Clear: The fault may clear on its own; say a temporary burst of noise on a link due to operating of welding machines in the vicinity. In this case the icon is also restored to normal. However, the alarm object is kept in memory in a zombie state. This is to give the operator a chance to return to the console and indicate the corrective action taken if any. That is, the operator should service the zombie alarm.

3. Major congestion: The fault may worsen before it is corrected, which typically happens with congestion. The initial event that caused creation of the alarm object may have been a minor congestion, say link utilization exceeding 90%. Before congestion control measures take effect, utilization reaches 95% and a major congestion event is generated. This causes the alarms to go each to the alerting state with the color changing from orange to red.

The FSM design lends itself to systematic, error-free programming. List all states and events. Create a transition table with one column for each state and one row for each event. In each cell of the table, enter the action to be taken and the next state. For certain <state, event> pairs, the action may be to ignore the event. The next state could be the same as the current state. For the FSM in Figure 9.33, the lists of states and events are given in Table 9.11 and Table 9.12, respectively. Note that the diagram in Figure 9.33 is a representation of this table in which impossible or ignored <state, event> pairs are not shown. The corresponding transition table is shown in Table 9.13. In each cell, the action is shown in italics and the next state is shown below that. In some causes, the FSM may transition to different states depending on a condition (e.g., < Altering, Major congestion> and <Pending, Major congestion>).

Alarm Correlator and Root Cause Analysis (RCA). A single fault in a network may cause many alarms in the NMS. These may appear to be unrelated as they are associated with different NEs. Consider an enterprise network with a single WAN link to a branch office. The branch office has a LAN with several servers that are managed by the NMS in the head office (Figure 9.34).

Suppose the WAN link fails. Router R_1 will report a link-down event via a trap. Polling of R_2, S_1, S_2, and S_3 will fail, and the data collector will generate a node failure event for each of these. The operator will see a large number of alarms. The operator may spend time investigating these, or may even decide to ignore them, and hence may miss the important alarm (the link failure in R_1).

Table 9.11   List of Alarm States

STATE	DESCRIPTION
Initial	A new, unused alarm object
Altering	The alarm is registered in the list of active alarms. The FM operator has not yet noticed the alarm. The FM uses various alarm indications to catch the attention of the operator.
Pending	The operator has noticed the alarm. The FM is awaiting the results of corrective actions.
Zombie	The FM is aware that the fault condition is clear. The icon color is normal. The operator has yet to indicate the corrective action taken.
Closed	The operator and the FM are both aware that the fault is closed. The alarm object is returned to the pool of unused alarms and is effectively in the initial state.

Table 9.12   List of FSM Events

EVENTS	DESCRIPTION
Minor congestion	Utilization on a link exceeds 90%
Major congestion	Utilization on a link exceeds 95%
Clear	Utilization on a link falls below 90%
Acknowledge	Operator invokes an FM menu or button to indicate awareness of a new alarm
Service	Operator invokes an FM menu or button to indicate corrective action taken

Table 9.13 Transition Table for Alarm FSM in Figure 9.33

	INITIAL	ALERTING	PENDING	ZOMBIE
Minor congestion	*Alert action* Alerting state	*Null*	*Null*	*Alert action* Alerting state
Major congestion	*Alert action* Alerting state	*If alarm severity is Minor then:* Alerting action Alerting state	*If alarm severity is Minor then:* Alerting action Alerting state	*Alert action* Alerting state
Acknowledge	NA	Pending action Pending state	NA	NA
Service	NA	NA	Clear action Closed state	Clear action Closed state
Clear	Null	*Clear action* Closed state	*Clear action* Zombie state	*Null*

Null: ignore the event
NA: not applicable—this <state, event> pair should never occur. Usually indicates a software bug and should be logged and reported to the software developers.

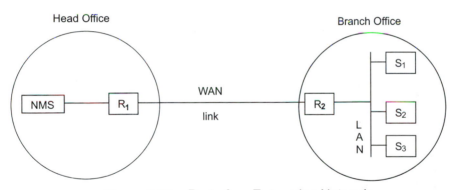

Figure 9.34 Part of an Enterprise Network

We have seen earlier in this section some simple methods to filter and correlate repeated or duplicate events. After the remaining events are registered as alarms, the alarm correlator searches for multiple alarms that arise from the same physical fault. It then suppresses all but one of these to avoid overloading and confusing the operator.

Several correlation techniques are commonly used. All have intelligence or reasoning behind them. The reasoning methods distinguish one technique from another. We will discuss these approaches in Chapter 11.

Similar to the case with event correlation, related alarms may be registered at different times. The range in delays depends on the polling interval and could be several seconds to 10s of minutes. Any alarm correlator could adapt to this delay in two ways: (1) It may favor immediate indication, in which case the operator may initially see the less important alarm, which is replaced shortly thereafter by the more important one. (2) It may opt for consistency in UI and delay indication of any alarm until the end of the correlation window. This could affect fault rectification time and should be limited.

The reasoning-based approaches described in Section 11.4 require a significant amount of operator intervention to ensure that the associated library has sufficient, but not too much, knowledge. Here we describe an efficient *fully automatic* method for detecting the one alarm out of a group of alarms that represents the real fault, i.e., the **root cause** alarm. This method is based only on the topology and state information in the NMS database and uses a novel graph algorithm [Bhattacharya *et al.*, 2005]. It is implemented in the CygNet NMS, which is described in Section 9.5.4.

The goal of RCA is to show only one primary alarm for one fault and to suppress secondary alarms. This can be accomplished by modeling the network as a graph in which each NE is a node and considering the path taken from the NMS to reach each node. If node A can be reached only via node B, A is said to be dependant on node B. If there are alarms from both A and B, the alarm from B is the root cause and the alarm from A is suppressed. In the branch office example in Figure 9.34, nodes R_2, S_1, S_2, and S_3 are dependant on node R_1. Thus, the RCA algorithm presents only the alarm in R_1 to the operator. As the other nodes are not reachable, their status is shown as unknown (grey color) rather then up (green) or down (red).

A dependency relation can be defined on the network elements based on various criteria. One criterion we consider here is *reachability* from the NMS. The status of network element A depends on the status of network element B if A can only be reached via B. The algorithm has two parts. The first part forms a reachability graph from the physical topology. It also takes the full list of status events from the NMS as its input. From this list it determines the status of individual elements in the network. After the execution of the first part, the output is the real status of each element in the network. The real status can be *Up*, *Down*, or *Unknown*. An element with real status *Down* is the root cause for itself (and an alarm will be generated for this element). Nodes that are reachable only via a *Down* node have their status set to *Unknown*.

The FM can also optionally generate alarms for *Unknown* elements. It can indicate for each *Down* node the set of *Unknown* nodes that depend on it. This may be useful for the operator to decide on the order in which to attend to each of several *Down* nodes.

The second part of the algorithm takes each *Unknown* node U and determines the *Down* node D that is on the path from the NMS to node U. This *Down* node D is the root cause for U. The algorithm determines the set of *Unknown* nodes {U} that are dependant on each *Down* node D. The number of nodes in this set gives the operator an indication of how serious the failure of node D is.

The RCA algorithm is efficient. In the worst case, it takes $O(e)$ time where e is the number of edges (links) in the network graph.

In a large network with 1,000s of links or more, it is not feasible to invoke the RCA algorithm for every alarm that is registered. A convenient strategy that can be adopted is to maintain a count of the number of alarms registered since the RCA algorithm was last invoked. When this count exceeds some threshold, the RCA algorithm is run. Since different alarms have different importance, it is preferable to use a weighted count. The weight can depend on the NE and component that generated the alarm, and the severity of the alarm. In addition, there is a maximum delay after which the RCA algorithm is run independent of the number of registered alarms (provided there is at least one pending alarm).

For example, assume that weights are assigned as shown in Table 9.14 and the threshold is 16. If 2 critical alarms occur, the RCA algorithm is triggered. However, it takes 8 consecutive minor alarms or 16 warning alarms to trigger the RCA algorithm.

9.4.7 Distributed Management Approaches

A small network can be managed conveniently by a single NMS. All desired functions are performed by this NMS. In a large network, a single NMS may not be able to handle the load of managing the

Table 9.14 Sample Weights based
on Alarm Security for RCA Invocation
Threshold = 16

SEVERITY	WEIGHT
Critical	8
Major	4
Minor	2
Warning	1

entire network. Especially in a geographically distributed network, the WAN links may have relatively low bandwidth and could become bottlenecks. Hence, it is desirable to have several managers. These managers may all perform similar functions, or they may be functionally specialized. For example, one manager could perform only fault management, while another manager is used only for performance monitoring.

A distributed management application consists of several manager applications running on different management stations. Each manager performs its management functions either by directly interacting with agents or indirectly via other lower-level managers. Distributed management can be classified into categories ranging from centralized management at one end of the spectrum, through weakly distributed, strongly distributed, to cooperative management at the other end [Meyer, 1995].

In the centralized and weakly distributed paradigms, there is a well-defined hierarchy of management stations, and a manager can delegate tasks only to those strictly below it in the hierarchy. In the strongly distributed and cooperative paradigms, horizontal delegation is also allowed.

Another issue is the selection of a suitable management technology to implement the paradigm and whether delegation of management tasks is static or dynamic. For weakly distributed systems, it is customary to have static code running at various lower-level managers. Each manager knows the system being managed and is statically configured to manage it. A lower-level manager can execute a predefined task when requested by a higher-level manager.

The dynamic delegation of management functions to intermediate-level managers allows more flexibility [Meyer, 1995]. Management operations can be instantiated by higher-level managers by downloading or transferring code to remote management stations on the fly.

Multitier Architecture. In choosing a multitier architecture, there is a trade-off between flexibility and ease of implementation and deployment [Vanchynathan *et al.*, 2004]. A strongly distributed or cooperative architecture permits almost unlimited flexibility, while a weakly distributed (hierarchical) architecture is much easier to implement correctly and efficiently. In particular, with the restricted communication and links between managers, it is straightforward to ensure consistency of data that may be replicated in several managers. This is much harder to achieve with strongly distributed designs. Further, most network operators and enterprises have well-defined hierarchical structures for their networks and their personnel.

Topology. We partition the set of elements to be monitored into groups of manageable size based on some criterion, say geographical. A manager process monitors each group and these processes constitute the lowest layer of the management architecture (Figure 9.35).

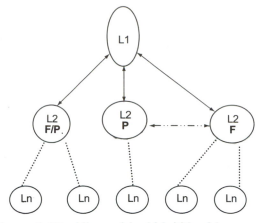

Figure 9.35 Hierarchical Multitier Management

One or more managers that run management processes at higher levels in the hierarchy are a parent of each of these management stations. This concept can be extended to as many layers as required.

To ensure predictable behavior, each cluster of network elements can have at most one parent, i.e., exactly one manager. If we represent each management station by a vertex and draw a directed edge (i, j) between two vertices i and j, if i is managed by j, the topology of the resulting network corresponds to a directed acyclic graph (DAG) [Horowitz, 1995].

9.4.8 Server Platforms

The NMS server requires two software platforms, namely the OS and the DBMS. The choice of these is important as they affect the development effort, performance, security, reliability, and cost of the NMS server. Once the OS and DBMS are chosen, the server design and implementation tend to become specific to these. Changing these at a later date is costly and time-consuming. The platform must be stable, of modest cost, and with a guarantee that it will be supported for the foreseeable future.

A detailed comparison of the available platforms is beyond the scope of this book. We would like to mention the trend of open-source platforms that can compete with commercial platforms in all respects. While in the past the designer of a large and complex software application such as an NMS server was constrained to run it on one of the commercial platforms, today, increasingly we find designers opting for open-source platforms.

Operating System (OS). The OS must support threads, processes, and shared-memory multiprocessors. It must support very large RAM and disk and a variety of peripherals. It must have a good programming interface for access to and control of its functions. It must efficiently support a variety of programming and scripting language chosen by the designers. It must have available a range of third-party software tools, components, and libraries.

Several popular server operating systems today are Linux, various flavors of UNIX (Sun Solaris, IBM AIX, HPUX, MacOS X, FreeBSD) and Microsoft Windows. All of these meet the requirements stated above though to varying degrees. Linux, FreeBSD, and NetBSD are popular open-source server OSs. The others are commercial (Sun Solaris has an open-source version available).

Database Management System (DBMS). The DBMS must efficiently support very large amounts of data. This includes hundreds of tables and 100s of millions of records. The DBMS must support transactions. It must have good administrative tools for creating indexes, recovering from table corruption, taking backups, and especially performance tuning.

As with the OS, the designer has a choice of several high-quality DBMS platforms, both commercial and open source. The viable open-source platforms are MySQL and PostgreSQL. Commercial platforms include Oracle, IBM DB2, Microsoft SQL Server, and Sybase.

9.4.9 NMS Client Design

We now briefly touch on the design of the client application that enables users to access the functions of the NMS. Recall the requirements for diverse users, ease of use and local/remote management capabilities described in Section 9.4.1. Since different users may have to login to the NMS from widely dispersed locations, they need to have the client application software running on their local terminal. Nowadays, the terminal is usually a PC, which is capable of doing substantial processing involved in the UI. This includes providing a window manager, rendering of graphics, generation of audio, etc. Broadly speaking, there are three approaches to the client application: a dumb terminal, a rich client, and a browser-based client. These are elaborated below.

Terminal Client. A "dumb" character-oriented terminal is used to login directly to the NMS. Terminal emulation software such as *xterm* and *putty* may be run on a PC or server and connected to the NMS server via telnet or ssh over a TCP/IP connection. All software functions are performed fully on the server, including editing of commands typed by the user and rendering (color, boldface) of the text on the screen. Terminal clients are useful when the user is at a remote location with access to only low-end terminals, or they are sometimes preferred by veteran administrators and operators for reasons of familiarity. Almost any terminal, PC, or server is capable of being used as a terminal client as is.

Rich Client. In this case, the client PC runs a special client application that is designed to work with the NMS server. The client application is usually GUI based. Besides generic GUI functions such as windows, icons, menus, and a pointer, it may include significant NMS functionality. For example, given a table with the details of the NEs, the client application may be responsible for generating a geographical map and overlaying on it icons for each NE and network link. Likewise, the client may allow the user to sort lists and tables on various criteria without the intervention of the server.

A rich client is usually written in an object-oriented language with good GUI support. Perhaps the most popular language for rich NMS clients is Java, with C++ and C# also being used.

While the rich client can give a very powerful UI and nearly instantaneous response to many user commands, it suffers from two drawbacks, the first being portability. The client application may run on only one OS and sometimes only one version of that OS. Thus, the user has to ensure that his/her PC has the right OS. If the client application is to run on a variety of OS platforms, the NMS vendor has to invest a substantial amount in software development and testing on each of these platforms. This has to be repeated with every new release of the client application.

A second and more serious problem is compatibility with the NMS server. As new versions of the server and client are released, perhaps independently of each other, the user has to ensure that the right version of the client application is installed on the client PC. In some cases, the wrong version simply does not work, which is an annoyance. In other cases, the wrong version appears to work but due to subtle incompatibilities, it performs the wrong functions. For instance, when the server indicates to the client that NEs have failed, the client may display them in green (normal) instead of red due to an incompatibility. This is much more serious as the operator will ignore the fault.

The situation is aggravated when an operator needs to login to several NMS servers in different regional networks. The servers, from the same vendor, may be of different versions. The operator's PC will need to have several versions of the client application installed and the operator would have to run the corresponding client application depending on which NMS server s/he is working with!

Browser or Web Client. The browser or Web client promises to combine the advantages of the terminal and rich clients without their disadvantages. It is rapidly becoming *de facto* for NMS clients (and for many other applications also). The browser client provides all its functionality through the GUI of a Web browser such as Firefox, Internet Explorer, or Safari. (Firefox is open source and runs on almost any OS platform, Internet Explorer runs only on Microsoft Windows, and Safari is supplied with MacOS X. The NMS server includes a Web server to which the user connects via the browser. The NMS server throws up Hyper Text Markup Language (HTML) pages to the browser. For a better user experience, the HTML pages may include some client-side processing through Javascript. Network maps and icons are usually provided using Ajax.

Since there is no software installed on the client PC, there are no issues of version incompatibility between the client and the server. Any client-side NMS processing is done through Javascript code that is downloaded in the HTML page. It is not stored on the disk of the client PC (though it may be cached temporarily to enhance performance).

Today, browsers are ubiquitous. Almost any PC has a good, recent browser installed. Many mobile phones, including some low-end models, can run a browser, though the small screen limits the amount of information that can be presented. Almost everyone who uses a PC and the Internet is familiar with the use of a browser. Hence, the training effort for new users is greatly reduced.

Owing to differences in the way in which different browsers render an HTML page, the problem of portability to different browsers is still an issue, albeit a much smaller one than that of portability of rich client applications. For instance, a data entry form in which the labels and boxes are aesthetically placed in one browser may have some of these GUI components overlapping in another browser. So, the server needs to determine which browser the user is using and feed HTML pages that are tuned to the peculiarities of that browser. Likewise, Javascript code that works on one browser may not work on another browser.

Fortunately, the incompatibilities between browsers are decreasing and are well-documented. Also, there are a variety of open source and proprietary code libraries available that permit the developer to write code that works equally well across a variety of browsers.

9.4.10 Summary: NMS Design

Starting from the requirements for management of a telecom network or a large enterprise network, we derived the architecture for an NMS server. After some general design decisions, we discussed the design of the main modules in an NMS server, the discovery module, PM, and the FM.

The FM is the most complex of the modules in an NMS. This is because it has to deal in real time with a wide range of events that occur at unpredictable times. Rapid fault detection and rectification is the key to the operation of a network. The FM is especially relied upon when there are serious faults in the network. At such a time, the FM would experience a burst in processing requirements. The design of the FM needs to be especially careful to ensure that the NMS itself does not fail due to overload during such periods of severe network problems.

We traced the path of an event through the FM. We explained different methods used to indicate the fault to the operator and the various alarm states. We explored assorted techniques for the correlation of seemingly unrelated events and alarms. These range from the simple matching of fields in event records, to sophisticated AI and graph algorithms.

Finally, we discussed approaches to distributed management. This enables scaling to very large networks. It also mirrors the structure of typical large organizations.

9.5 NETWORK MANAGEMENT SYSTEMS

So far we discussed the use of simple system utilities and tools for management. This was followed by a detailed examination of the design of a high-end NMS server. In the rest of this chapter we will describe several commercial and open-source NMSs. We start with the management of networks, and then cover management of systems and applications. This is followed by enterprise management and telecommunications network management. Finally, we describe approaches for distributed management.

9.5.1 Network Management

A network consists of routers, switches, and hubs connected by network links. Servers, workstations, and PCs are connected to LANs in the network. Various access technologies may be used. In network management, we are primarily interested in the health and performance of the routers, switches, and links. We may also monitor the health of servers.

The first task involved in network management is the **configuration** of the above network elements, their agents, and the NMS itself. This includes discovery of network elements and the topology of the network.

Daily users of NMSs are people in the NOC who do not have the same engineering background as those who designed and implemented the systems. Therefore, ease of use is an important factor in the selection of NMSs. For example, an operator does not constantly sit in front of a monitor and watch for failures and alarms. Thus, when an alarm goes off, it should attract the attention of the operator visibly, audibly, or both. It should present a global picture of the network and give the operator the ability to "drill down" to the lowest level of component failure by successive point-and-click operations of the icon indicating an alarm.

Figure 9.36, Figure 9.37, and Figure 9.38 show hierarchical views of a network testbed at the NMSLab, IIT Madras, which were captured with a CygNet NextGen NMS. (The IP addresses of the nodes have been changed for security reasons.) Figure 9.36 shows the global view with network segments and numerous domains behind routers and gateways. Figure 9.37 is obtained by clicking the mouse (also colloquially referred to as drilling down) on the network segment icon 192.168.9.0 in Figure 9.36 and shows the nodes that are part of that private LAN. The LAN has a switch (SW-11) connected to two routers RTR-1, and RTR-2), and a few other IP hosts. The port details on the switch SW-11 are obtained by drilling down on the SW-11 icon in Figure 9.37. The result shown in Figure 9.38 contains 12 ports, some of which are free.

Next, the **fault management** capability of the NMS must support monitoring of the health of the NEs and links. In an IP network, this is usually done using ICMP ping and SNMP get messages. The NMS reports faults to the operator in a variety of ways depending on the nature, severity, and importance of the fault. It may assist in the rectification of the fault.

The NMS must support **performance management** especially of the expensive WAN links. Planning and management reports keep upper-level management apprised of the status of the network and system operations. Reports in this category include network availability, systems availability, problem reports, service response to problem reports, and customer satisfaction.

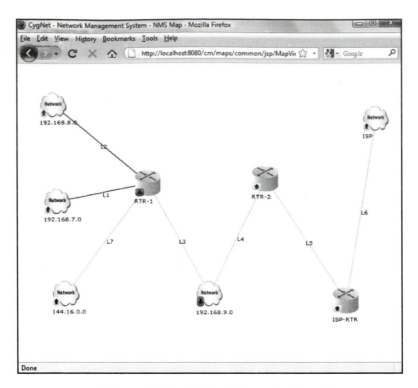

Figure 9.36   Global View of Network

Performance management provides traffic trend reports to enable the network administrator to identify bottlenecks. The administrator can take action to alleviate the bottleneck, such as re-routing traffic via an alternate route, or changing priorities for different classes of traffic. Performance reports help the administrator see long-term traffic trends in order to plan capacity expansion in a timely and cost-effective manner. Trends in traffic should address traffic patterns and volume of traffic in internal networks, as well as external traffic.

Accounting management is probably the least developed function of network management applications. Accounting management could include individual host use, administrative segments, and external traffic.

Accounting of individual hosts is useful to identify some of the hidden costs. For example, the library function in universities and large corporations consumes significant resources and may need to be accounted for functionally. This can be done by using the RMON statistics on hosts.

The cost of operations for the Information Management Services department is based on the service that it provides to the rest of the organization. For planning and budget purposes, this may need to be broken into administrative group costs. The network needs to be configured so that all traffic generated by a department can be gathered from monitoring segments dedicated to that department.

External traffic for an institution is handled by service providers. The tariff is negotiated with the service provider based on the volume of traffic and traffic patterns, such as peak and average traffic. An internal validation of the service provider's billing is a good practice.

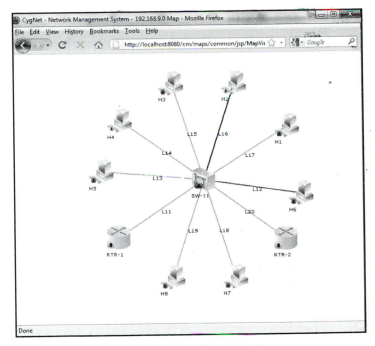

Figure 9.37 Domain View

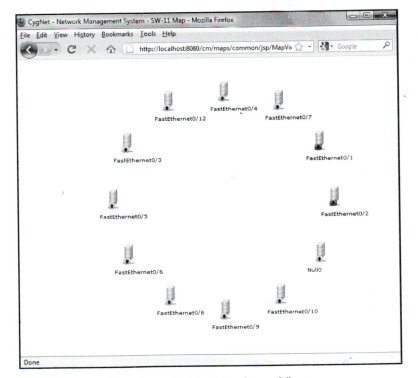

Figure 9.38 Interfaces View

Security management is both a technical and an administrative issue in information management. It involves securing access to the network and the information flowing in the network, access to data stored in the network, and manipulating the data that are stored and flowing across the network. The scope of network access not only covers enterprise intranet network, but also the Internet that it is connected to.

Security management also covers security of the NMS itself. The NMS database contains a wealth of often confidential information about the organization. This must be made available to authorized personnel, but kept away from all others. Likewise, a user of the NMS could reconfigure NEs throughout the network. Hence, login to the NMS must be carefully controlled.

Thus, network management involves the complete **FCAPS** spectrum of application functions defined in Chapter 3. Configuration, fault, and performance management are found in almost every network management deployment. In some cases, the NMS is also used for security and accounting management.

OpenNMS. This is an open-source NMS (http://www.opennms.org), which claims to be the first project aiming to build a complete enterprise-class open-source NMS. OpenNMS is written largely in Java and has a browser-based UI. It is primarily used for managing SNMP devices. It is used to manage small networks of under 25 NEs to large networks with over 80,000 NEs.

The major functional areas covered by OpenNMS are autodiscovery, status polling of NEs, performance polling, and fault management. Reports are provided using the JFreeChart package. Much of the operation of OpenNMS can be customized by the user by means of filters. A filter consists of rules, each of which is essentially a simplified form of an SQL statement. It configures how the component of the NMS behaves. For example, the notification rules control whether or not a received event triggers a notification to the user. Filters can be added to control autodiscovery, to specify the list of IP interfaces that are included in data collection, polling, etc.

Unlike many commercial NMS products, OpenNMS does not have a graphical map for the display of the NEs and their status. The designers of OpenNMS believe that seasoned network administrators prefer to see event lists. OpenNMS provides event lists grouped in various convenient ways. On the main WebUI page there is a "real-time console" (RTC) that reflects the status of categories of devices. These categories reflect groups of devices like database servers, Web servers, etc. However, anything in the database can be used to create a custom category list, and grouping devices by location, building, vendor, IP range, etc., is very common. The categories list follows a basic tenet of OpenNMS; once configured, it should be simple to use and as automated as possible. As new devices are added, the categories automatically update. There is no need for manual customization, such as would be required with a useful map. (There is a group of developers working on a map, so this may become available in due course.)

By default, the FM receives SNMP traps. Other event detectors can be configured through XML configuration files. When an event is accepted, it results in a notification to the user, which can be on-screen, via email, SMS, etc.

In keeping with the philosophy of being utilitarian, OpenNMS has a variety of reports. Most are simple tables with some graphs. They lack the frills that may be attractive to a novice, but contain a wealth of information in a format that is easy for a network administrator to comprehend.

With OpenNMS, the user has the ability to do comprehensive monitoring of a network at the price of just the server hardware. The NMS is customizable by the network administrator without any programming. As with any open-source product, the enterprise has the comfort that it could always get unusual customizations done as the source code is freely available. Currently, OpenNMS supports F, P, and part of C in FCAPS. With the on-going efforts of the developer community, it is likely that other functional areas will be covered in future. Commercial support is also available from the OpenNMS Group for enterprises that need it.

9.5.2   System and Application Management

Network management addresses only the managing of a network (i.e., managing the transport of information). System management deals with managing system resources, which complements network management. For example, *ping* is used to test whether a host is alive. However, we want to know more about the use of system resources on the host, such as the amount of CPU use on the host or whether a specific application is running on the host.

Historically, enterprises had two separate and distinct organizations. The telecommunications department took care of communications, giving rise to network management. The management of information systems (MIS) department took care of the computers, a task that involved system management. However, in the current distributed environment of client/server architecture, the computing depends heavily on the communication network and the distinction has disappeared. System and network management now form a single umbrella, headed by a chief information officer. System and network management are beginning to be considered together as a solution for information management issues and problems. System management tools, which used to be custom developed, are currently available as commercial systems and are being integrated with network management.

System management tools monitor the performance of computer systems. Some parameters that can be monitored are (1) CPU use, which measures the number of processes that are running and the resource consumption of each; (2) status of critical background processes (called *daemons* in UNIX terminology); and (3) application servers such as the Simple Mail Transfer Protocol (SMTP), File Transport Protocol (FTP), and Domain Name Server (DNS). System management may also include backup of server databases, desktop workstations, and operations support systems that support operations such as help desk and trouble ticket tracking.

Several UNIX-based tools can be used to monitor systems. Such tools are constantly evolving and are updated on Web sites that are used to track them. http://www.slac.stanford.edu/xorg/nmtf/nmtf-tools.html is a site active from 1996 that provides a comprehensive list of commercial and open-source network management tools.

High-End System Management. The Computer Associates (CA) Unicenter TNG and Tivoli Enterprise Manager TME 10 are two integrated systems solutions available commercially [ZDNet]. Both solutions offer features that can be classified as high end and thus require the vendor's ongoing active participation. They meet the requirements of large enterprises, particularly as they are offered as integrated solutions, which we will discuss in Section 9.5.3.

Low-End System Management. System management of hosts can be accomplished by installing simple and free public domain software and configuring it to local system management.

Nagios. This is a fairly comprehensive open-source NMS (http://www.nagios.org). The project has been active for over 10 years so it is stable. The design is scalable and extensible.

Nagios provides the basic network management features. These include status and performance polling, fault handling, and configuration management. The FM can indicate faults via a graphical map, color-coded event lists, and email, pager, and cellphone. It allows the administrator to schedule the downtime of hosts, servers, and the network. The reporting feature supports capacity planning.

Unlike other NMSs, Nagios does not have built-in mechanisms for polling. Instead, it relies on external plugins. These can be executables or scripts and hence give substantial flexibility. Nagios by default has support for managing routers, switches, and other IP network components; Windows, Linux, UNIX, and Netware servers; network printers; publicly available services such as HTTP, FTP, SSH, etc. With its extensible design, Nagios has more than 200 community-developed plugins available.

It has a rich UI, which includes a map (unlike OpenNMS described in Section 9.5.1). Sample screenshots are available at http://www.nagios.org/about/screenshots.php. The UI is customizable to each user. This facilitates specialization and also helps maintain security of sensitive information.

As with OpenNMS, Nagios is a good choice for a small organization that cannot afford a big-budget commercial NMS. It is also sufficiently comprehensive and scalable that even large organizations use it. The Nagios Web site claims that it can handle networks of over 100,000 NEs. Given the high overhead of the external polling mechanism, the server hardware would be very expensive if all the 100,000 NEs are polled.

Big Brother. A well-known low-end system management product is Big Brother [MacGuire S]. Although it has very serious limitations in terms of both platforms and functionality, it may be adequate for small and medium-sized company networks.

Big Brother is an example of software that can be implemented with relative ease to manage system resources and is Web based. A central server on a management workstation runs on a UNIX platform and clients on managed objects. Big Brother is written in C and UNIX shell scripts and hence can be run on multiple platforms. The central management station presents the status of all systems and applications being monitored in a matrix of colored cells, each color designating a particular status. It supports pager and email functions that report the occurrence of alarms. Software can be downloaded and modified to meet local requirements for the operations, services, and applications to be monitored.

Big Brother performs the dual function of polling clients and listening to periodic status reports from clients that are UNIX based. Polling checks the network connectivity to any system. Client software periodically wakes up, monitors the system, transmits information to the central server, and then goes back to sleep. Textual details can be obtained on the exact nature of a problem. The systems are grouped for ease of administration.

9.5.3 Enterprise Management

We will next describe the two commercially available integrated solutions to system and network management. The two solutions are offered by two vendors, Computer Associates and Tivoli, the latter has been acquired by IBM. Both partners with several NMS vendors provide integrated solutions.

Computer Associates Unicenter TNG. The CA Unicenter TNG framework [CA] provides infrastructure to support integrated distributed enterprise management. It is based on a client/server architecture having an agent in each host and a centralized workstation. CA provides Unicenter TNG agents that can run on a large number of platforms; and the list continues to increase as the customer base diversifies. Besides TCP/IP and SNMP, the TNG framework supports numerous other network protocols, accommodating a varied enterprise environment.

CA describes Unicenter TNG as a framework comprising three components: Real World Interface, object repository, and distributed services. The Real World Interface presents a visual depiction of managed objects from different user perspectives. Both two-dimensional and three-dimensional presentations are available. The object repository is a management information database that includes multiplicity of data, such as managed objects, metadata class definitions, business process views, policies, topology, and status information. The distributed services link elements at the communications level.

Because of the TNG agents running in the hosts, during autodiscovery the system discovers not just host identifications, but also details of the processor, disk, and other components of the system. The discovered components are presented in a Real World Interface that presents a unified GUI at the higher levels. An object repository stores all the autodiscovered information and any other management information needed to support the Real World Interface. System and network management views are extended to business process views, whereby objects related to an administrative group or functional group can be presented. This approach makes operations easier for human personnel because they do not have to know the technical details behind the operations they are performing.

Event management in the TNG framework includes a rule-based paradigm that correlates events across platforms and presents the resultant alarms at the central console. These events include standard SNMP traps. Standard drilling through layers to detect the lowest level component failure is built in as desktop support.

An additional feature of the TNG framework is calendar management, which provides a shared calendar so that all personnel can view each other's activities. The calendar handles both one-time and periodic activities. Operations such as triggering an alarm pager or email can be programmed according to weekly and weekend shift schedules.

Some of the other notable features of the TNG framework are backup and disaster recovery, customized and canned report generation, and virus detection—all of which can be programmed as part of calendar management activities. In addition to these standard features, numerous optional modules, such as advanced help desk management, Web server management, and software delivery are available.

Tivoli Enterprise Manager. Tivoli's management framework, originally named the Tivoli TME 10 framework, provides system and network management and is in the same class as the Unicenter TNG framework. Tivoli has changed the TME 10 from a two-tier, client/server architecture to a three-tier architecture and has renamed it Tivoli Enterprise Manager. Tivoli claims that the new architecture has increased the capability of handling from 300 to 10,000 managed nodes. The extended three-tier architecture also has a gateway as a middle layer that is designed to handle as many as 2,000 agents. The agent module has been redesigned to consume fewer resources.

Tivoli merged with IBM, allowing it to integrate the features of its systems with IBM's NetView NMS. NetView performs the network management function, and the complementary features of the Tivoli management applications perform the system management functions. The platform is object oriented and uses the standard CORBA-compliant object model for use with diverse and distributed platforms. This feature is somewhat similar to the Sun Enterprise Manager [Sun Enterprise], which also uses the CORBA-compliant OSI object model and standard CMIP protocol. In the management framework, Tivoli management agents reside in the managed host applications. Although the TME Enterprise system does not use SNMP as the management protocol, NetView handles SNMP traps.

The Tivoli Enterprise Manager monitors network, systems, and applications in a distributed architecture, as in most other systems. Event management has a built-in rule-based engine that correlates events and diagnoses problems. It further has an automated or operator-initiated response mechanism to correct problems wherever possible, using a decision support system. Service desk technology is integrated with network and system management technology in the service-level management framework.

Tivoli service management comprises problem management, asset management, and change management. The problem management module tracks customer requests, complaints, and problems. The asset management module handles inventory management. The change management module incorporates and manages business change processes.

The Tivoli Enterprise Manager framework contains an applications manager module (global enterprise manager) that coordinates business applications residing in diverse multiple platforms. An API is provided to permit third-party vendors to integrate their application software into the Tivoli Enterprise Manager framework. The applications manager also measures the response and throughput performance of applications.

The security management module provides encryption and decryption capabilities (optional). A software distribution module automates software distribution and updates. Operations can be scheduled by the workload scheduler module.

9.5.4 Telecommunications Management Systems

Unlike an enterprise network, a telecom network provides commercial services to subscribers. The operator has legal responsibilities to the subscribers. Telecom operators are usually subject to stringent regulations.

Telecommunications network management includes monitoring and managing the network with certain distinctive features. Apart from supporting standard management features such as low level, as well as consolidated, fault and performance management, there are certain features that are specific to telecom:

1. A typical telecommunications network often includes equipment acquired over several years, and a telecommunications NMS must be capable of managing these heterogeneous systems from a single point.

2. Most telecom devices that implement the ITU-T standard protocols (such as CMIP/CMISE) differ in details and this makes development of the management application more complex.

3. Some devices have only an EMS, which often has a proprietary interface, and the NMS must communicate with the EMS rather than with the device agent directly. Thus, often the NMS manages some NEs via an EMS and some directly.

4. Typical telecom networks include multivendor multitechnology equipment, supporting diverse protocols. SDH and related transport technologies (SONET, DWDM, etc.) continue as the de facto technology for delivering reliable and scalable andwidth services over the last decade; and service providers have large amounts of deployed fiber that has been laid out over a period of time.

5. Provisioning of bandwidth is a common and important requirement in telecom networks. Provisioning bandwidth in optical networks in an optimal manner without causing fragmentation of the available bandwidth is a challenge. For example, if there is a requirement to provision an E1 circuit (2 Mbps), it would not be desirable to "break" an STM1 link (64 Mbps) to do the provisioning.

6. A related requirement is the maintenance of the latest inventory in the database so that when there is an incoming bandwidth-provisioning request, reliable and fresh information about the availability of bandwidth can be accessed. Usually, this information is maintained and updated manually. However, a telecom network is a dynamically changing entity, so automatic discovery

with periodic rediscovery to synchronize the inventory database with the actual network is becoming a critical requirement for efficient and optimal management of the network. While autodiscovery of IP networks using ping and/or SNMP is a standard feature in data NMS, the discovery of circuits in telecom networks is a far less straightforward issue.

7. A typical telecom provider assures customers of quality of service via service level agreements (SLAs). In a telecom environment this includes parameters such as call completion rate for voice calls, signal strength on wireless links, call completion for data calls, etc. The management system must provide the support for SLA management.

8. RCA to diagnose the actual source of a problem is another important feature to be supported.

9. Networks tend to be large, often with hundreds of thousands of NEs, and have a wide geographic spread. The telecom operator may have a hierarchical organization with different administrators responsible for different regions of the network. The NMS architecture must be scalable and should support the hierarchy of the operator.

In this section we describe CygNet, a commercial telecom NMS deployed at leading telecom service providers in India. CygNet is the flagship product of NMSWorks Software Pvt. Ltd., a technology company that is a part of the TeNeT (Telecommunications and Networks) group of the Indian Institute of Technology Madras, India.

CygNet NMS is a multivendor multitechnology management system that has been designed to meet the needs of telecommunication management. CygNet architecture accommodates most of the needs of a telecommunications management system.

Architecture of the CygNet Core. Figure 9.39 depicts the architecture of the core CygNet NMS. We describe the major components below.

Managed Element Modeling, Storage, and Depiction The elements server is responsible for this function. Network elements that are managed by the CygNet NMS are stored in the topology (topo) database. Elements to be managed by the CygNet NMS can either be added manually or by automatic discovery. A discovery configurator allows the operator to specify a range of IP addresses for discovering

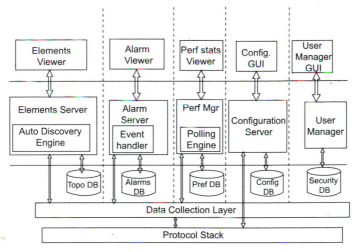

Figure 9.39 Architecture of the CygNet Core

elements, the protocol to be used for discovery, and other such details. A map-based GUI displays the managed elements and the topology of the network, color coded to reflect the status.

Fault Management System The CygNet alarms server is responsible for detecting a problem, correcting it, and restoring the system to normal operation at the earliest. **Fault detection** is done by polling, as well as receiving notifications. Alarms are generated in response to fault conditions in the network, stored in the database, and notifications (visual, audio, email, SMS) sent to capture the attention of concerned persons. The **fault reporting feature** ensures that information regarding a fault condition is disseminated in a meaningful manner to the concerned operators. GUI-based views of current, as well as historical faults, are available. The **fault escalation feature** allows the fault resolution time to be minimized and fault escalation using notifications (traps or TMF 814 notifications), email, or SMS. Multiple events associated with a common fault in a single network element are correlated and forwarded as one consolidated event or alarm by the RCA module described in Section 9.4.6. This minimizes the occurrence of event storms that would result in degraded levels of service.

Performance Management System The function of the performance management module is to manage the performance of individual network elements, links, and services. The PM module performs the following three major functions:

1. Data collection and storage in database.
2. Graphical views of real-time performance statistics.
3. Historical reports of collected data from database.

Configuration Management System The configuration management module in CygNet allows the operator to directly manage and configure network elements using the protocol supported by the network element. Configuration information regarding various network elements is stored in the configuration database.

User Manager This is the authentication and authorization component. CygNet identifies several classes of users with different privileges and access rights. All users have to be authenticated before they log on to CygNet. Role-based access control, idle time-out, and user audit trail are some of the features that this module supports.

Architecture of CygNet as a Telecom NMS. CygNet supports a layered architecture depicted in Figure 9.40 that enables it to be customized for various specific requirements. The custom components

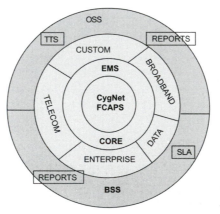

Figure 9.40 CygNet as a Telecom NMS

can be added as overlays to the core product. This also allows CygNet to scale to very large telecom networks.

Telecommunication-specific Subsystems. The CygNet design supports most of the features required for a telecom NMS specified at the beginning of this section. Here we describe some aspects of the design that enable efficient telecom management and also certain components (Mediation Server and Optical Transport Network Management System (OTNMS)) that are customized for this purpose.

CygNet has been designed so that it can be deployed either in a centralized manner or as a multitiered system. This provides a good scalability option when a very large and widely distributed network needs to be managed. Network management traffic can be reduced if lower-level management stations transfer management data to the central server periodically. This deployment strategy also avoids a single point of failure (Section 9.4.7, Figure 9.35).

At the lowest level, the CygNet local manager runs lightweight processes that predominantly collect data. The collected data are analyzed for performance and fault conditions and summarized reports are sent to the central management station. Figure 9.41 depicts this configuration. CygNet supports standard interfaces (TMF 814, SNMP, FTP, SCP (Secure Copy Protocol)) between the local NMS and central NMS. [Vanchynathan *et al.*, 2004].

CygNet supports TMF 814, an NMS–EMS interface defined by the TM Forum, and increasingly adopted as the standard for management of optical transport networks. (TMF 814 is discussed in more detail in Chapter 16. This allows management of newer optical network devices, since many vendors include support for TMF 814 in their EMSs.

There are usually legacy NEs in a network and these either do not have an EMS at all, or even if there is an EMS, it does not support TMF 814. In order to integrate such equipment, the *CygNet Mediation Server* designed for multiple protocol support is used (Figure 9.41). The mediation server of CygNet is a middleware component that is between the NMS (or other OS) and the network. It serves to hide the heterogeneity in EMS interfaces from and provide a uniform TMF 814 interface towards the NMS. The lowermost adaptation layer allows plug-ins to convert proprietary protocols to the format of TMF 814. The middle pre-processing layer performs functions such as event correlation, suppression, filtering, caching, etc. It is a major enabler in bridging legacy and new networks and expedites integration of new equipment into CygNet.

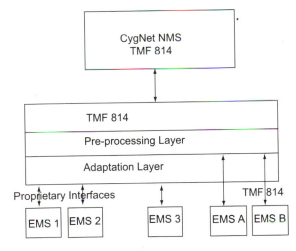

Figure 9.41 CygNet Mediation Server

NMS

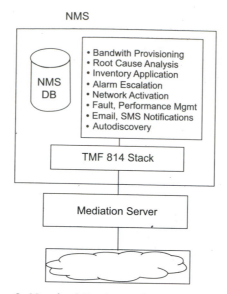

Figure 9.42 Architecture of the CygNet OTNMS

CygNet Optical Transport NMS (OTNMS). This CygNet component is customized for end-to-end management and bandwidth provisioning of optical transport networks. The functional architecture of OTNMS has been designed with a view to making the OTNMS an all-in-one solution for optical network management (Figure 9.42).

It supports automatic, dynamic provisioning of bandwidth services using a path computation algorithm designed to satisfy a maximum number of service requests while optimizing bandwidth use and avoiding fragmentation [Madanagopal, 2007].

The availability of reliable inventory is central to the success of automatic provisioning. The resource inventory database in CygNet stores network and computing equipment, logical resources, and topology. It keeps track of the physical configuration of the network, equipment inventory (cards, ports, etc.), physical connectivity, and logical connectivity of the different network layers. Data in the resource inventory are queried by the provisioning system to satisfy service requests and understand where capacity is available. However, in a typical telecom network, the inventory maintained by the NMS can become out of date for many reasons, including manual network intervention, equipment upgrade, network maintenance, card failures, unaccounted deactivations, etc. Once the inventory is out of date, any design based on this inventory system is unreliable. The CygNet OTNMS supports automatic discovery of NEs, as well as circuits of optical networks with periodic rediscovery. The autodiscovery feature ensures that the inventory can automatically synchronize itself with the network. This requires automatically uploading physical, logical, and service information and correlating it to the normalized internal object models of the inventory database.

The CygNet OTNMS has support for SLA-related performance data collection and storage, and display of SLA reports and threshold alarms to indicate SLA violations. It also uses an RCA module to pinpoint the actual cause of a failure.

Summary

In this chapter we listed a number of utilities that are available on commonly used operating systems such as Linux, UNIX, and Windows. These are invaluable tools in the repertoire of any network manager, and support a significant amount of troubleshooting and traffic monitoring. Some of these tools are based on SNMP, others use assorted protocols such as ICMP or proprietary messages over TCP. We discussed techniques used for monitoring of statistics and the use of MRTG for collecting router traffic statistics.

Focusing on SNMP-enabled devices, the vendor needs to design an MIB that supports remote management of the device. This topic of MIB Engineering was covered in Section 9.3. Several common MIB designs were presented.

Section 9.4 dealt with the design of an NMS server for a large telecom or enterprise network. Motivated by the requirements, we presented a generic architecture. We then covered the detailed design of the important architectural blocks, especially discovery, fault, and performance management. This section draws significantly on our experience in the design of a commercial NMS, viz., CygNet.

Finally, we presented several NMS products, both commercial and open source, which are commonly used for the management of different types of networks and services.

Exercises

1. Execute the commands *nslookup* and *dig* on a host IP address and analyze the results.

    (a) Compare the two results for the common information.
    (b) What kind of additional information do you get from *dig*?

2. Use *dig* to determine the IP address of www.tenet.res.in (or the DNS name that your instructor provides you with).

3. Use *dig* to list all the hosts associated with the domain *tenet.res.in* (or the DNS name that your instructor provides you with).

4. Using *dig*, determine the domain name that corresponds to the IP address 203.199.255.5 (or the one that your instructor provides you with).

5. Ping an international site 100 times and determine the delay distribution and packet loss. Repeat at different times of day and night. Explain any variations.

6. Using *tcpdump* or *wireshark* on an Ethernet interface on a host, capture ten IP packets. Examine their headers and contents.

7. In diagnosing poor network performance—for example, delays—you need to know where the bottleneck is. Use *traceroute* to an international site on another continent and isolate the delay in the path.

8. From a workstation in a segment of your institute's network, discover all other workstations in your segment using a network tool. Substantiate your results with the data gathered by some other means.

9. As a network manager, you are responsible for the operation of a network. You notice heavy traffic in a host that is on a TCP/IP network and want to find out the details.

    (a) What basic network monitoring tool(s) would you use?
    (b) What would you look for in your results?

10. Using an SNMP tool, determine which of the nodes given by your instructor has the longest and shortest up time. Substantiate your result with the gathered data.

11. The function *snmpWalk(subtreeRoot)* returns the values of all the visible OIDs in the subtree rooted in *subtreeRoot*. Using the standard SNMPv1 messages, devise an algorithm for *snmpWalk()*.

12. A switch has several ports each having a different speed. Write a complete SMI definition for the table of port speeds. Assume that the switch OID is {experimental 7}.

13. A node may have several hard disks. Write an SMI definition for the important parameters (brand, type, capacity) of such a set of disks.

14. It is desired to provide username/password protection to a MIB subtree {*enterprises Midas(3794) corDECT(1) config(2)*}. What are the MIB variables that need to be added for this purpose? Draw the MIB subtree and for each variable give its ASN.1 macro definition.

15. It is desired to provide access through SNMP to the database for an NMS course. Design a MIB rooted in {*enterprises NMSWorks(15760) course(10)*} to hold information including the start and end dates of the course, the number of students registered, and the list of reference textbooks. Draw a pictorial representation of the subtree. Write the ASN.1 macro definitions of each node.

16. It is desired to store the roll numbers and final marks for students in an NMS course in an SMI table. Using the nodes {*enterprises NMSWorks (15760) course(10)*} as the base:

   (a) Pictorially draw the subtree of the management information tree.
   (b) Write the complete SMI macro definition for each new node.

17. For a certain trap generated by an agent, it is desired to provide an acknowledgement to the agent that the manager has received the trap. Using only SNMPv1 and SMIv1 without any changes, devise a mechanism to accomplish this.

18. Design a MIB variable *rebootNode*, which a manager can use to reboot the NE. The manager needs assurance that the node has been rebooted. Explain carefully the semantics and write the ASN.1 declaration of the variable.

19. It is desired to manage a traffic light using SNMP. The controller needs to know the count of the number of vehicles that have passed, and be able to change the light between red and green. Sketch the MIB subtree {traffic} for this purpose. For each node in this subtree, write the complete ASN.1 macro.

20. A single-threaded discovery module discovers the subnet 192.168.9.xxx. This subnet contains 20 NEs of which four are routers each having ten interfaces. Each network request from the NMS takes 2 seconds round-trip time. Each failure has a timeout of 30 seconds. Approximately how long will the discovery process take?

21. Write a pseudocode for topology discovery (similar to Figure 9.26). Assume that routers are SNMPv1-enabled with a known community string.

22. With a 1-GHz CPU, the average CPU time taken for status polling is: poll manager 0.6 ms, SNMP stack 0.8 ms. When the poll manager detects a change of status, it informs the FM and writes to the DBMS. The CPU times taken are: FM 1 ms, DBMS 5 ms. Assume that 10% of the polls detect a change of status, and that the CPU power increases linearly with the CPU clock speed.

   (a) What is the minimum CPU speed to handle 1,000 polls/second?
   (b) If the PM, FM, and SNMP are run on one CPU and DBMS on a second CPU, what are the minimum speeds of these two CPUs for 1,000 polls/second? Assume 20% increase in all CPU requirements due to the inter-CPU communication overhead.

23. A data collector polls for 100 OIDs, each on a different NE. When there is a response, the round-trip delay is 1 second per poll. When there is a fault, the timeout is 30 seconds. Assume that 20% of the polls suffer a timeout.

   (a) What is the minimum polling period if the data collector is single threaded?
   (b) What is the minimum number of threads needed to achieve a polling period of 30 seconds?

24. An NMS manages 1,000 large NEs and 100,000 small NEs. For each of the large NEs, it polls 100 OIDs with a polling interval of 5 minutes. For each of the small NEs, it polls two OIDs once an hour.

(a) Estimate the volume of data to be stored in the polled data tables (excluding indexes and temporary space) per day, per week, per month, and per year.

(b) Assume that the network consists of 20 regions each containing 1/20th of the NEs. The following database designs are being considered: one table/NE, one table/region, one table/whole network. In each case, a new table may be created every day, every week, every month.

(c) Draw a table with columns labeled day, week, and month, and one row for each database design. In each cell of the table, enter the number of records/table and the number of tables if data are kept online for 6 months.

(d) The vendor of the DBMS recommends that one table should not contain more than 500 million records and that the DB should not contain more than 1,000 tables. Mark the designs that are feasible according to these criteria. Which one of these designs do you prefer? State your reasons.

25. A telecom network that used to serve 100 million subscribers has 1 million NEs. Suppose the poll manager polls 1% of the NEs for 100 OIDs each at a 5-minute interval and 20% of the NEs for 10 OIDs each at a 15-minute interval. The remaining NEs are polled only for status once an hour.

    (a) Compute the disk space requirements for 1 day, 1 week, 1 month, and 1 year. Assume that the disk space requirement is three times the table size to allow for temporary files

    (b) Suppose the PM also polls the status of each subscriber unit (such as phone, ADSL modem, etc.) once a day. What is the additional disk space requirement?

26. An NMS is connected to a remote network by a 64 kb/s link. There are 1,000 NEs in the remote network, each having 10 OIDs of interest. Assuming 5 OIDs in each SNMP get-request, neatly sketch a curve showing the bandwidth used as a function of the polling period, p. What value of p will result in 20% utilization of the link?

27. In Exercise 26, assume that a regional NMS in the remote network does the polling and once an hour does a bulk file transfer of all the data values only to the central NMS. What value of p will result in 20% utilization of the link? Assume that scp is used and achieves a compression ratio of 50%.

28. An NMS is connected to a remote network by a 64 kb/s link. The NEs in the remote network generate 50 faults/second. Of these, 1% are critical and the others are minor. What fraction of the link bandwidth is used if:

    (a) All fault notifications are sent using SNMP traps?

    (b) Critical fault notifications are sent using SNMP traps, and minor fault notifications are sent once a day using scp? Assume that a trap is of size 100 bytes, and that the information about a fault occupies 8 bytes in a file. Neglect all other overheads.

29. SNMPv1 defines communication only between the manager and the agent. In a network with multiple management servers, communication between them may be necessary. For example, when the operator at one server acknowledges an alarm, the alarm indication should also stop at the other server. Define a mechanism using only SNMPv1 for this purpose.

30. We wish to have two management servers each with a copy of the database for redundancy. There are two approaches.

    (a) Each server independently polls the agents and updates its copy of the database.

    (b) The active server polls the agents and then passes the data onto the passive server.

What are the pros and cons of these approaches? Consider criteria such as load on the agents, network traffic, and loss of data in case of server failure. The consistency of views is an important consideration.

PART III

TMN and Applications Management

Part I reviewed the background for dealing with network management. In Part II, we discussed in detail SNMP management and designing a network management system to manage networks. Part III will address telecommunications management network (TMN) and detail network management applications needed for fault, configuration, accounting, performance, and security functions.

Chapter 10 takes network management to a higher-level management, TMN, based on the OSI model. It addresses five levels of management—network element layer, element management, network management, service management, and business management.

Applications are the focus of Chapter 11. We will first gain a basic understanding of how the tools and systems that we learned in Chapter 9 are used for configuration, fault, and performance management. We will then go into more depth on correlation technologies to localize and diagnose problems that cause multiple alarms. Information security is a very important application in network and system management. Besides basic SNMP security management, you will learn about firewalls and the role of cryptography in authentication and authorization. Accounting and reporting are important to run any business efficiently, including information technology services. We have given special emphasis to report generation. To use tools efficiently, policies need to be established and made operational. Some policies may be automated in management systems, and we will address this at the end of the chapter. We finally cover service level management technology that deals with customer and quality of service.

Telecommunications Management Network

OBJECTIVES

- *Telecommunications management network, TMN*
- *Concept of operations support system, OSS*
- *TMN conceptual model includes:*
  - *Customers*
  - *Service providers*
  - *Network*
  - *Operations support systems, OSSs*
  - *System operators*
- *TMN standards and documentation*
- *TMN architecture*
  - *Functional*
  - *Physical*
  - *Information*

- *TMN service management architecture*
  - *Network element*
  - *Element management*
  - *Network management*
  - *Service management*
  - *Business management*
- *TMN service management*
  - *Operations, administration, maintenance, and provisioning; OAMP*
- *TMN implementation methodologies*
  - *OMNIPoint*
  - *eTOM*

In the second part of the book, we have addressed the principles of network management associated with data communication networks. Data communication networks carry information over long distance and are dependent to a large extent on the telecommunication network, which has evolved from the long-distance telephone network. These networks are owned by public utility companies, which are either long-distance carriers such as AT&T and British Telecom, or local exchange telephone companies, such as Bell Operating Companies. In this chapter, we will discuss the management of telecommunication networks and services provided by these public and private utility companies, and service providers.

The standards for management of the telecommunication network were developed by International Standards Organization as part of ISO management. Hence, it is strongly based on ISO network management, which in turn is based on Common Management Information Protocol (CMIP) and Common Management Information Services (CMIS). Although this chapter addresses telecommunications network management without the requirement of CMIP/CMIS-based management, the reader would have a better appreciation with that knowledge. Toward that goal, OSI network and systems management is presented in Appendix A.

In 1986, the International Telecommunications Union—Telecommunications (ITU-T) proposed the concept of Telecommunications Management Network (TMN) to address interoperability of multivendor equipment used by service providers and to define standard interfaces between the service provider operations. In addition, it also extended the concept of management to include not only management of networks and network elements, but also service functions of service providers. It was envisioned as a solution to the complex problems of operation, administration, maintenance, and provisioning (OAMP) for the telecommunication networks and services.

We will first provide motivation for learning TMN in the next section, and then introduce operations systems, which form the building blocks of TMN, in Section 10.2. Section 10.3 addresses the concept of TMN. TMN is based on a large number of standards, which are listed in Section 10.4. TMN architecture is described in Section 10.5, TMN management service architecture in Section 10.6, and an integrated view in Section 10.7. Implementation issues are dealt with in Section 10.8, including OMNIPoint program that has been developed by the Network Management Forum. The current drive for practical implementation of TMN is handled by TM Forum. The latest development in management technology is covered in Chapter 16.

10.1   WHY TMN?

With the proliferation of SNMP management that has left OSI network management by the wayside, we can ask the question why we are spending time on discussing TMN. Historically, TMN was born out of necessity to extend the private and proprietary, but well-developed network management systems, and make them interoperable. In those days, the large telecommunication organizations referred to the systems that maintained the network and network elements as operations systems. ITU-T formed a working group in 1988 to develop a framework for TMN. ISO was also working on standardizing network management with OSI management framework using CMIP. With globalization and deregulation of the telecommunications industry, the urgency for interoperability of network management systems was strongly felt. With the slow progress of these standards bodies, industry-sponsored groups such as the Network Management Forum started developing standards in parallel to speed up the process.

Unfortunately, the standards and frameworks developed were so complex and expensive to implement using the then-present technology, TMN and OSI network management never got off the ground. However, TMN is the only framework that addressed not only management of network elements, but also the management of network, service, and business. These later issues are so critical in today's business environment with numerous network and service providers (they are not the same as they used to be). Customer service, quality, and cost of business form a three-legged stool [Adams and Willetts, 1996]. You knock out one leg and the stool falls down. TMN framework not only addresses the management of quality of network and network elements, but also service management and business management.

Further, in today's corporate environment, buyouts and mergers demand interoperability and business management. With the work environment going into cyberspace and the Internet facilitating global communications traversing multiple service providers' networks, the exchange of management information has become all the more important. All these motivations have revived the interest in TMN architecture.

It is to be kept in mind that TMN had been developed based on OSI management principles. However, it could be implemented, as is now being done, using other management technology, such as the well established SNMP management as well as newer ones described in Chapter 16. Organizations such as TM Forum are devoting efforts to accomplish this.

10.2   OPERATIONS SYSTEMS

TMN is built using the building blocks of the operations support system. The use of the terminology, operations support system, in the telephone industry was changed to operations system, as it is also used to control the network and network elements. For example, user configurable parameters in the ATM network can be controlled by users via the M3 interface, as we will learn in Chapter 12. The operations system (let us not confuse operations system with operating system) does not directly play a role in the information transfer, but helps in the OAMP of network and information systems. Figure 10.1 and Figure 10.2 present two examples of operations systems that are used in the operation of telephone network and services: trunk test system and traffic measurement system. The terminology of OSS is back in common use again. We will use both terms in this chapter.

The trunk test system shown in Figure 10.1 is used to monitor the loss and signal-to-noise ratio in the trunk transmission system in Bell System. A trunk is a logical entity linking two switching offices.

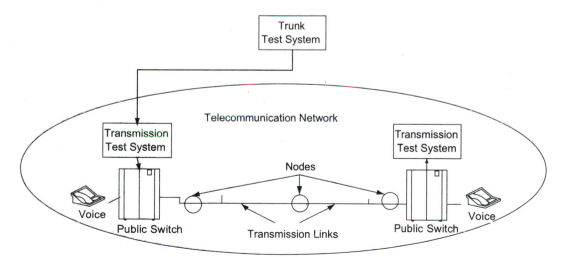

Figure 10.1   Operations Support System for Network Transmission

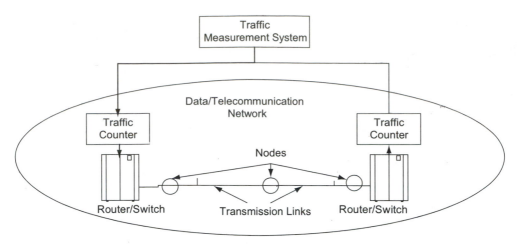

Figure 10.2   Operations Support System for Traffic Measurement

It can seize any available cable facility between the switches while carrying traffic. In order to ensure quality of service, loss and signal-to-noise on the trunks are measured at regular intervals by accessing every trunk at each switching office. This is done from a centralized test center. Any trunk that fails to meet the minimum criteria set for quality control is removed from service. Thus, by removing a trunk out of service as it is failing (but before it actually fails), the customer does not see any degradation of service. The same test system is also used for an on-demand test to track troubles.

Except during popular holidays such as Mother's Day, telephone service is almost always available for communication at any time of the day. This is due to careful planning and implementation of adequate facilities for traffic to be handled without being blocked for lack of facilities. Figure 10.2 shows a traffic measurement operations system, which measures the busy status of switch appearance (access point) on each switch. As the statistics on the number of paths being busy increases, either due to the lack of access points or the lack of adequate trunk facilities, additional equipment is added to reduce blocking.

The above two examples of operations systems illustrate the necessity of the role of operations systems in the OAMP of telecommunication network. They are part of the telecommunications network management activities, and fall under the performance management function of the network management that we have defined under the OSI model in Chapter 4.

10.3   TMN CONCEPTUAL MODEL

From a TMN point of view, the network management system is treated as an operations support system, as shown in Figure 10.3. It manages the data communication and telecommunication network.

We differentiated the data or computer communication network from the telecommunication network in Chapter 1 (see Figure 1.4). Figure 10.3 extends it to TMN, where operations support systems, including the network management system, form a support network. It is logically a separate network, but may or may not be physically separate based on implementation. The telecommunication network in Figure 10.3 consists of network elements of switching exchanges and transmission systems. It is primarily the wide area network of communications. Switching systems include both analog and digital

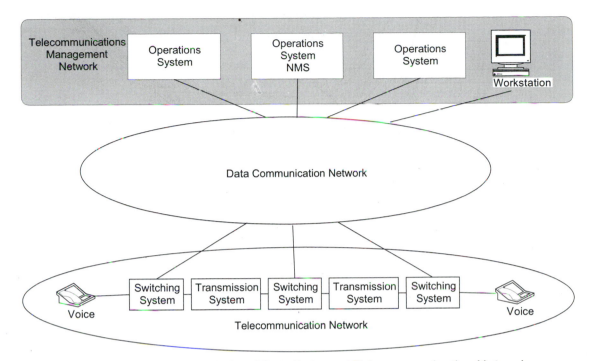

Figure 10.3 TMN Relationship to Data and Telecommunication Networks

switches. And so are the transmission systems of both analog and digital types and include all means of transport facilities including twisted pair, coaxial, fiber optics, and wireless.

Data communication network components consist of LANs, bridges, routers, gateways, and hosts. The workstation shown in Figure 10.3 that is attached to the data communication network is a distinct element of TMN, whose interface we will discuss later.

The TMN in Figure 10.3 is a network in its own right, and not just the management of telecommunication network. (It is TMN and not TNM.) ITU-T Recommendation M.3010 defines TMN as a conceptually separate network that interfaces to one or more individual telecommunication networks at several points in order to send or receive information to or from them and control their operation. It consists of a network of operations systems including a network management system, which, as we stated earlier, is also considered an operations system.

Figure 10.4 shows the TMN conceptual model. Notice that in this model not only are the networks and operations system depicted, but also services and human resources are brought in. The two columns in the figure depict the identical components of the two service providers, A and B.

We identify the following components in Figure 10.4: workstations, operations systems, network, services, and interfaces. Of course, there are the operators who operate on the systems and the customers who use the services.

Customers are provided service by the service provider, and customer service should play a key part in the service provider's business. Thus, service management is an important consideration in conceptualizing the TMN model.

The service provided by the service provider to the customer is telecommunication service, which means that the telecommunication network needs to be operated efficiently and economically. The

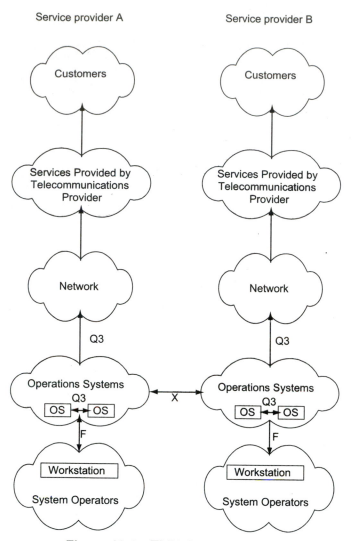

Figure 10.4 TMN Conceptual Model

OAMP on the network needs to be handled in as much of an automated mode as possible to increase the response time and to decrease the cost. Cost considerations lead to business management, which is addressed by the TMN model.

Service management, business management, and network management are all accomplished either partially or totally using the operations systems shown in Figure 10.4. System operators interface with the operations systems using workstations.

The interfaces associated with various functions and services have been standardized in the TMN model. Notice the three interfaces—Q3, F, and X. Q3 is the interface between the operations system and the network element. F is the interface between the workstation and the operations system. Information exchange between operations systems within a TMN is accomplished using the Q3 interface, whereas operations systems belonging to different TMNs communicate over the X interface. We will discuss interfaces in more detail in Section 10.5.

10.4 TMN STANDARDS

ITU-T is the standards body that has developed TMN standards. It is based on the OSI framework. Its scope has been expanded and a good review of it has been published [Sidor, 1995]. The TMN recommendations and scope are summarized in Figure 10.5 [NMF] and Table 10.1. M.3000 document presents a tutorial of TMN. The other documents in the M series address TMN architecture, methodology, and terminology. The Q series addresses the Q interface, such as Q3 and G.733, the protocol profile for the Q interface. These are listed in Table 10.1. Table 10.2 lists some of the study groups that are responsible for various TMN activities.

The other supporting documents are also shown in Figure 10.5. Network traffic management, maintenance, and security are covered in E and M series. The communication protocol, CMIP, and service elements, Common Management Information Service Element (CMISE), are covered in I and X series documents. A discussion of the X series is covered in Appendix A. Please refer to Appendix A of [NMF] for a complete list of the various series in Figure 10.5.

TMN standards define two types of telecommunication resources: managed and operations systems and the interfaces between them [Sidor, 1995, 1998]. Architectural definitions of the communicating TMN entities, their roles in TMN, and their interrelationship are described in M.3010. M.3020 provides an overview. The common services of OAMP functions are defined in M.3200. The functions associated with individual TMN management services are described in M.3200 series. A generic set of TMN management functions, based on OSI management functional areas, is specified in M.3400.

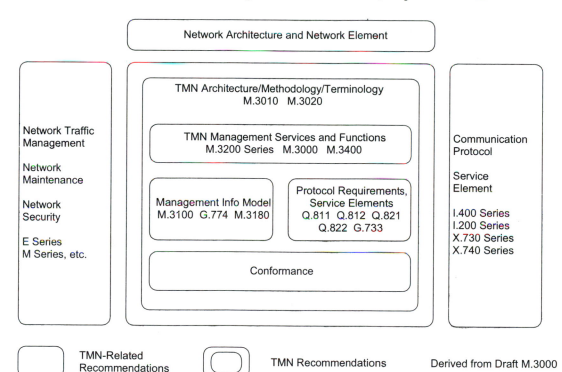

Figure 10.5 TMN Recommendations and Scope

Table 10.1 TMN Documents

M.3000	Tutorial Introduction to TMN
M.3010	Principles for TMN
M.3020	TMN Interface Specifications Methodology
M.3100	Generic Network Information Model for TMN
M.3180	Catalogue of TMN Managed Objects
G.774	SDH Network Information Model for TMN PDH Network Information Model for TMN
M.3200	TMN Management Services Introduction TMN Management Services 1 TMN Management Services n
M.3300	F-interface Management Capabilities
M.3400	TMN Management Functions
Q.811 Q.812	Protocols for the Q Interface
G.773	Protocol Profiles for the Q Interface

Table 10.2 ITU-T Study Groups

STUDY GROUP	STUDY TOPIC	RECOMMENDATION SERIES
SG 2	Traffic management	M series
SG 4	TMN architecture definition Generic network model F-interface	
SG 7	OSI base management standards Data network management and MHS Customer network management	X series
SG 10	User interfaces Specification languages	
SG 11	TMN protocols and profiles Switching and signaling system managed objects ISDN management protocol and information models Intelligent network management UPT management	Q series
SG 13	B-ISDN requirements (transport networks) ISDN	
SG 14	Modem management	V series
SG 15	Transmission system management Transmission system modeling SDH, PDH, ATM management	G series
SG 18	Broadband management requirements	
JRM (JCG)	Overall coordination of TMN	

Management application messages and information models to support OAMP requirements are specified in M.3100 series and G.774. A generic network information model is defined in M.3100 that addresses common solutions for the management of resources of the network such as switching, transmission, and other technologies. OSI management services and CMIS are defined in X.710. TMN-related messages are contained in the information model defining application protocols and support objects, which are covered in Q-series documents.

Communication protocols are addressed in the respective protocol-specific standards documents. The G series addresses those that are not covered in them, but are relevant to TMN, such as SDH network management (G.784).

10.5 TMN ARCHITECTURE

TMN architecture is defined in M.3010 describing the principles for a TMN. There are three architectural perspectives: functional, physical, and information, as shown in Figure 10.6. The functional architecture identifies functional modules or blocks in the TMN environment, including the reference point between them. The requirements for interface are specified. The physical architecture defines the physical blocks and interfaces between them. Information architecture deals with the information exchange between managed objects and management systems, using a distributed object-oriented approach. We will look at each of these three perspectives in the next three subsections. You may also obtain more details from the references [Cohen, 1994; M.3010; NMF; Raman, 1999; Sidor, 1998].

10.5.1 Functional Architecture

M.3010 defines TMN architecture made up of five function blocks: operations systems function, network element function (NEF), mediation function (MF), workstation function (WSF), and Q-adapter function (QAF), as shown in Figure 10.7. Each function block contains a set of functions. There are multiple instances of each function. Thus, for example, there may be many operations systems performing different operational functions in the operations systems' function block. The communication between the function blocks itself is a function, but not a function block, defined as the **TMN data communication function** (DCF). DCF supports the standard transport protocols.

The **TMN operations systems function** (OSF) is implemented in operations systems. As we saw in Section 10.2, operations systems (OS) such as network transmission OS and traffic measurement OS help monitor, manage, and control telecommunication networks and services. Network management, both as a manager and an agent, is also considered to be an OS. This would include MIB in Internet management and naming tree in OSI management as a function of the OSF.

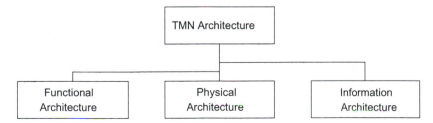

Figure 10.6 TMN Architecture

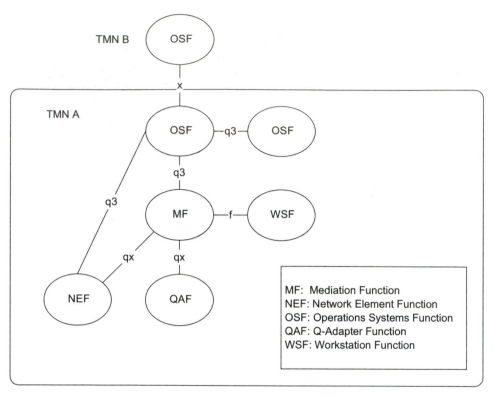

Figure 10.7 TMN Functional Architecture

The **TMN NEF** is concerned with the managed network elements. Network elements themselves are not part of TMN, but are supported by TMN over the standard interfaces. Network elements would include hardware, software, and systems such as hubs, routers, switches, processes, etc. The network management agent and the associated MIB are part of the NEF. Network elements providing information for management, such as packets dropped, collision rate, etc., are considered as part of TMN, i.e., NEF.

The **TMN MF** block addresses the operations performed on the information content passing between the network elements and operations systems. Such operations include filtering, store and forward, protocol conversion, threshold detection, etc. A physical entity in which the MF is implemented can be shared between multiple operations systems and network elements. For example, a remote monitoring device (RMON) can monitor a remote LAN on various parameters such as statistics on users, protocols, and packet loss and report the analyzed data or raw data to accounting and performance management operations systems. In this situation, the RMON device acts as a mediation device performing MF between the network elements on the remote LAN and the operations systems (or network management systems).

The **TMN WSF** provides an interface between human personnel and TMN activities. More specifically, this function addresses the presentation aspect. The conversion function that converts machine-readable information to human-interpretable format in the presentation function belongs in one of the other three function blocks, OSF, MF, and QAF (explained later). This would cover the presentation function such as graphical user interface (GUI) and human–machine interface of workstations.

Communication between the above four functional blocks, OSF, WSF, MF, and NEF, is assumed to be standardized. Of course, this is far from the reality of the world. Therefore, in order to accommodate the legacy functionality as part of TMN, a **TMN QAF** has been defined. This is somewhat similar to a proxy server in SNMP management, where non-SNMP network elements are managed by an SNMP manager via a proxy server. Thus, TMN noncompliant devices are connected to a TMN-compliant system/network using a Q-adapter interface.

Each function in the function block can be considered as providing a service and the service block providing a set of services. An example would be a security management application function as either part of or a stand-alone operations system. As shown in Figure A.13 in Appendix A, there are several security system management functions such as alarm reporting, audit trail, etc. associated with the security functional area. In fact, all five management functional areas of configuration, fault, performance, security, and accounting residing in a network management system would belong to OSF.

Function blocks are designed to be nonoverlapping. However, this does not mean that different function blocks do not use some of the same functions. For example, the MIB is a function that is used by several function blocks that enable them to exchange management information. Another example would be the scheduling function shown in Figure A.13. This could be used by the performance management application to gather traffic statistics, by the configuration system to discover and delete network elements, and by the fault management system to gather errored-seconds on unstable elements.

Notice that the function blocks in Figure 10.7 are connected with interfaces designated by x, q3, qx, and f. These are called TMN service interfaces or simply, TMN interfaces. The TMN interface between function blocks, shown in Figure 10.8, is called a TMN reference point. A reference point can be considered to be a conceptual point of information exchange between function blocks. An interface between a management agent embedded in a network element and a network management system will be a q3 reference point. When a network management system automatically creates a trouble ticket in a trouble tracking system, it is communicating via an x-reference point. When a Web browser interfaces with a Web-based management system, it is accessing an f-reference point. When a TMN-noncompliant switch is managed by a TMN-compliant operations system using a Q-adapter interface, it is interfacing via a qx interface.

Summarizing, some examples of network devices implementing TMN functional components are operations systems, network management system, application, network element, management network agent, management information base, RMON, proxy server, GUI, and Web browser. Remember again that DCF such as SNMP, CMIP, and common object request broker architecture (CORBA) is not included here.

The information exchange going across the TMN reference points can be classified into three classes: q-class, f-class, and x-class. The q-class reference point interfaces to the management application function. In Figure 10.7, the q-class reference point includes both q3- and qx-class TMN reference points. An f-class TMN reference point is an interface between the WSF block and any other function block in TMN. An x-class TMN reference point is an interface between two operations system function (OSF) blocks belonging to two different TMNs, as shown in Figure 10.7. The interface information pertains to functionality of similar nature.

TMN reference points are designated by lowercase letters, q, f, and x, while the associated interfaces in the physical embodiment are identified using uppercase letters, Q, F, and X, as we shall see in the next section.

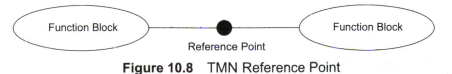

Figure 10.8   TMN Reference Point

10.5.2   Physical Architecture

ITU-T Recommendation M.3010 presents a model for the TMN physical architecture, shown in Figure 10.9. A TMN physical block could be an embodiment of one or more blocks, besides its equivalent function block. For example, an operations system could have its operation function as well as mediation device, which does filtering of information. There are five types of physical blocks representing the five functions discussed in the previous section, excluding the TMN DCF.

Operations systems are embodiments of TMN OSF. It is connected to the mediation device, placing the MF on a data communication network. The data communication network is the physical implementation of DCF, which to repeat, is not a function block, but a TMN function, DCF. The network elements, Q adapter, and workstations reflect their respective TMN functions.

The Q, F, and X TMN interfaces between the physical devices are also shown in Figure 10.9, representing the physical implementation of the respective TMN reference points. The Q3 interface is used

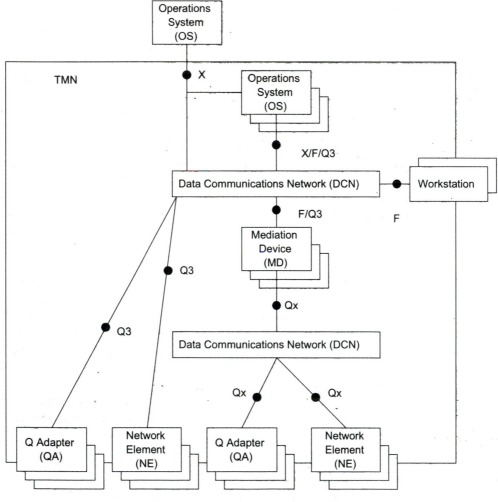

Figure 10.9   TMN Physical Architecture

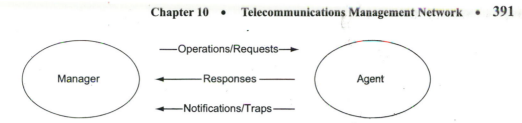

Figure 10.10 TMN Information Architecture

between the OS and either an NE or a QA. The Qx interface is shown between MD and QA/NE. An example of this would be an MD being a proxy server communicating with legacy systems via the QA interface. The F interface is implemented to connect a workstation to TMN. The X interface is between the operations systems belonging to two different TMNs.

10.5.3 Information Architecture

The TMN information architecture initially adopted the OSI management information architecture, CMIP/CMIS, defined in the ITU-T X.700 series and discussed in Appendix A. However, with the wide acceptance of Internet SNMP, extensively covered in our earlier chapters, deployment is in progress using both models in TMN. We have covered both management models in this book. The OSI information model is object oriented and the SNMP model is scalar. Both models are based on the dual roles that entities play in information exchange: manager and agent. Figure 10.10 shows the information exchange between the two types of entities. The manager performs operations or makes requests from an agent. The agent executes the operations on the network elements that it is managing and sends responses to the manager. The agent also sends unsolicited messages to the manager indicating alarm events.

Information models specified by SNMP and OSI management deal with the management of network elements. The TMN information model has been used in specific technology such as ATM and SDH/SONET, which we will cover in Chapter 12.

The information architecture should transport information reliably across the functional boundaries. There are two types of communication services between interfaces: interactive and file oriented. We will discuss the interactive service in Appendix A. It is supported in OSI by CMISE over Remote Operations Service Element (ROSE). In the Internet distributed computing environment (DCE), this will be handled by Remote Procedure Call (RPC). The file-oriented category is supported by File Transfer Access Management (FTAM) in OSI [Raman, 1999] and in the Internet by File Transfer Protocol (FTP). In the OSI model, Association Control Services Element (ACSE) is needed to establish, release, and abort application associations. In the Internet model, this is integrated in RPC presentation service. You may consult the reference [Piscitello and Chapin, 1993] for more details on this subject.

10.6 TMN MANAGEMENT SERVICE ARCHITECTURE

Another functional model of TMN is based on the services provided in a TMN environment. The TMN services are grouped and presented as TMN layered architecture, as shown in Figure 10.11 [M.3400]. This layered architecture is not the same in the strict sense of protocol layered architecture, in that communication can occur between nonadjacent layers.

The lowest layer is the **network element layer** comprising network elements such as switches, routers, bridges, transmission facilities, etc. The next layer, the **network element management layer**,

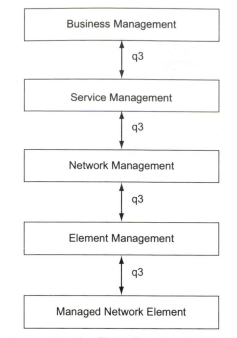

Figure 10.11   TMN Service Architecture

manages the network elements. The third layer is the **network management layer**, which manages the network. The network management functions in this layer would include bandwidth, performance, quality of service, end-to-end flow control, network congestion control, etc. The network element layer and the network element management layer are vendor dependent, whereas the network management layer is not.

The **service management layer** is concerned with managing the services provided by a network service provider to the customer or to another network service provider. This will include services such as billing, order processing, complaints, trouble ticket handling, etc. The top layer in Figure 10.11 is the **business management layer**. This is concerned with managing a communications business, such as fiscal considerations, personnel needs, project management, and customer needs and satisfaction.

We notice that the TMN reference point between the various service layers is q3, which is the standard interface between operations system, network element, and MFs shown in Figure 10.7.

The TMN management services are classified into OSI system management functional areas, which are the five OSI application functions described in Section 3.9. They are configuration management, fault management, performance management, security management, and accounting management. This is presented in Figure 10.12.

10.7   TMN INTEGRATED VIEW

Now that we have discussed various aspects and perspectives of TMN architecture, let us look at the overall picture of how all these fit together. A representation of this is shown in Figure 10.13.

The four TMN management services—business, service, network, and element—are at the top of the hierarchy. They invoke the system management functions defined in the system management functional

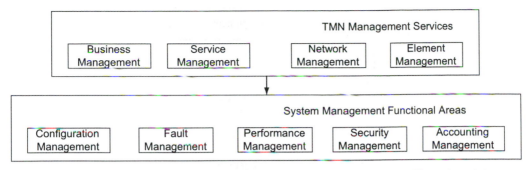

Figure 10.12 TMN Management Services and Management Functional Areas

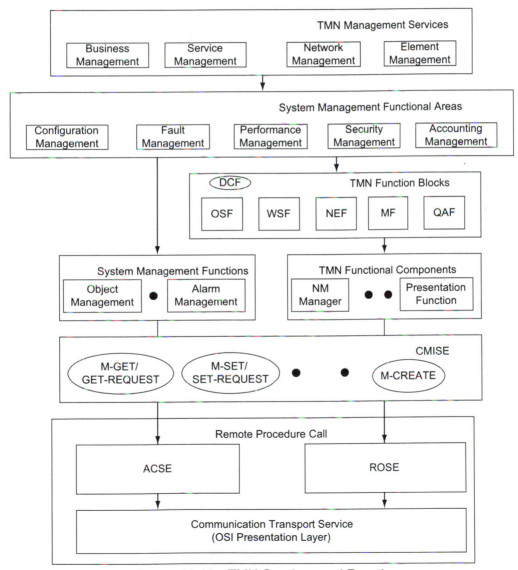

Figure 10.13 TMN Services and Functions

areas. The five components in the system functional areas are the management application functions: configuration, fault, performance, security, and accounting.

The management applications in the system functional areas perform either system management functions or TMN functions. The TMN function blocks, OSF, WSF, NEF, MF, and QAF, constitute the TMN function blocks. The TMN function blocks are made up of TMN functional components such as network management function, MIB, etc. DCF, although not part of TMN function blocks, is included for completeness.

System management functions include functions such as object management, alarm management, etc. System management functions are discussed in Appendix A, Section A.6. In Figure 10.13, we could have embedded the system management functions in TMN function blocks and TMN functional components, but have shown them separately in order to visualize them in a non-OSI environment. TMN has been exclusively associated with the OSI environment and it is only recently that it is being considered in the popular SNMP environment.

System management functions and TMN functions invoke the primitive services. Figure 10.13 shows the OSI primitive services of M-GET, M-SET, etc. Equivalent SNMP services will be GET-REQUEST, SET-REQUEST, etc.

The TMN environment is a distributed environment. The applications communicate remotely with the communication transport service using RPC. In the OSI model, RPC is accomplished with ROSE and ACSE. The former does the remote operation, and the latter establishes and releases the application association. In the SNMP management model, the remote operation is accomplished using RPC and TCP/IP.

10.8   TMN IMPLEMENTATION

Although the TMN concept was proposed in the early 1980s, it has not found wide acceptance for several reasons [Glitho and Hayes, 1995; Raman, 1998]. Some of these are its strong dependency on exclusive OSI network management, high resource requirement, technical complexity, lack of complete standards, popularity and simplicity of SNMP management, and implementation difficulties.

Industry and computer technology were not quite ready in the 1980s to fully implement (or even partially implement) the object-oriented OSI network management due to its complexity. The object-oriented and layered OSI protocol stack demanded processor resources that were beyond the capability of the technology then. However, present-day hardware resources can handle such demands. OSI toolkits are currently available both commercially and as freeware. Using these tools, products have been developed for trouble ticket administration (TMN X interface) and Integrated Digital Loop Carrier (TMN Q3 interface) recently [Raman, 1999].

Object-oriented technology in those years, as for example DCE and CORBA, was not at the same level as it is today. This has revived the work on distributed management environment [Autrata and Strutt, 1994] using the object-oriented approach.

Even with resources and toolkits available, one cannot avoid the legacy systems interfacing with TMN [Glitho and Hayes, 1996]. This is accomplished using either the TMN Q adaptation (TMN QA) interface or adding a new Q (TMN Q3) interface. The choice between the two is based on cost for each approach to accomplish OAMP of a telecommunications network.

There are three forums that have actively promoted the implementation of TMN: ATM Forum (now IP/MPLS Forum), NMF (formerly known as Network Management Forum), and recently TM Forum.

We covered the ATM Forum's application for ATM in Chapter 9. We will now briefly consider NMF's activities. TM Forum's activities are addressed in Section 10.8.2 and in Chapter 16.

10.8.1   OMNIPoint

An example of the realization of TMN architecture is presented in Figure 10.14 [NMF]. The left side of the figure shows the TMN logical layered architecture and the right side a physical realization of it. Each layer consists of several management systems providing the various services. The layered architecture shows the TMN q3 reference points and the physical realization the corresponding Q3 interfaces.

The Network Management Forum, later referred to as NMF, is an industry-sponsored forum. NMF has developed a program called OMNIPoint, which stands for Open Management Interoperability Point.

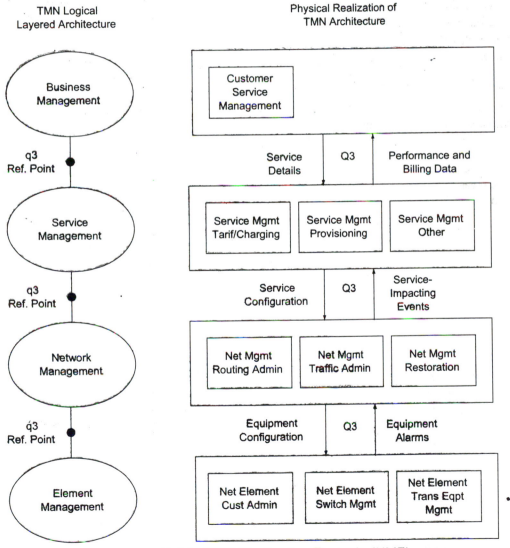

Figure 10.14   TMN Realization Example (NMF)

The objective is to help companies implement management standards across a wide range of suppliers' equipment. It has developed documents [NMF] that specify mapping between the Internet and OSI standards that help TMN implementation in a hybrid management environment.

10.8.2 eTOM

The TeleManagement Forum (TM Forum) is a body whose mission is to align technology with real business, and thus is the next sequential step in the process of TMN implementation. An important goal of the TM Forum is to automate end-to-end the operations that enable delivery of "information, communication and entertainment services," and Enhanced Telecom Operations (eTOM) is the framework to accomplish this mission. eTOM is a framework specification and provides a business process model to the telecommunications industry to define the processes end-to-end. Figure 10.15 depicts the business process architecture defined by eTOM.

The business processes are described in a layered hierarchical fashion, where process at each level can be broken down into lower-level process elements. eTOM is structured in three broad areas or Level 0 processes—Strategy, Infrastructure, and Product (SIP); Operations (OPS); and Enterprise Management (EM). Of these areas, the OPS areas of service management and operations, and resource management and operations come within the purview of network management and address a perspective similar to the functional model covered in Section 3.9. Each Level 0 process in turn contains detailed components at Level 1, 2, etc.

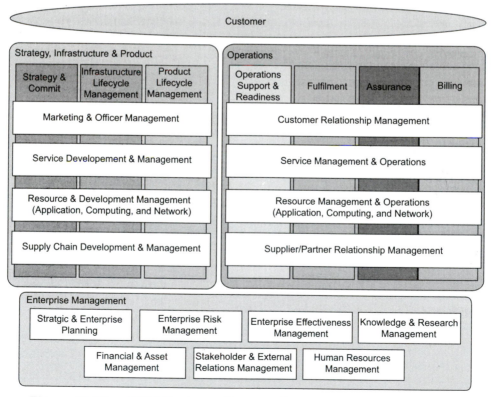

Figure 10.15 eTOM Business Process Framework—Level 0 processes

The ITU-T standard adopts the management service/function approach, while the eTOM framework adopts a business process approach that builds on the management services/functions to develop a reference framework that categorizes all business activities a service provider will use. The main difference between the TMN and eTOM approaches is that the former has been developed starting from networks and network equipment (bottom up) while eTOM is a top-down approach. The eTOM framework has been incorporated in toto within the TMN framework as a set of standards [M.3050.x].

Figure 10.16 depicts the subset of the layers of the eTOM map that are implemented as applications in a typical NMS product alongside a rough correspondence with the more traditional ITU-T-based TMN visualization. While the management functional areas in TMN are referred to as FCAPS (fault, configuration, accounting, performance, and security), they are referred to as FAB (fulfillment, assurance, billing) in eTOM.

The applications in the box of Figure 10.16 are typically implemented as part of an NMS product. Figure 10.17 shows the Level 2 processes for the Level 1 processes of FAB activities in service

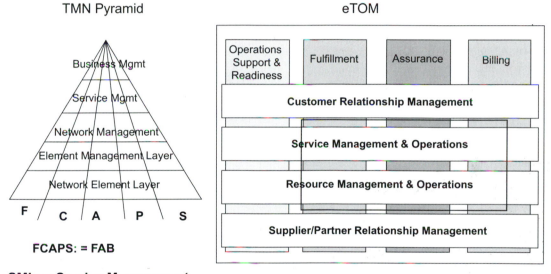

Figure 10.16 eTOM-to-TMN Model

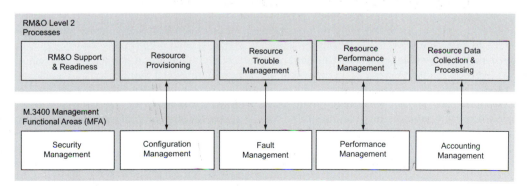

Figure 10.17 eTOM Level 2 Processes-to-M.3400 Function Set Groups

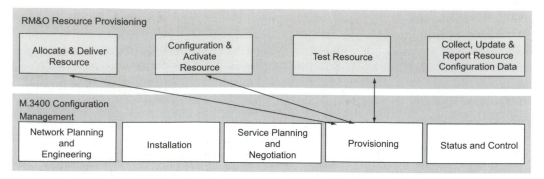

Figure 10.18 eTOM Level 2 Processes-to-M.3400 Configuration Function

management and operations, as well as resource management and operations. Each Level 2 process element is in turn broken down into finer Level 3 elements representing a greater level of detail.

The implementation of the OSI management application functions described in Section 3.9 is covered in detail by ITU-T specifications M.3400. The mapping of these functions to Level 2 eTOM processes is shown in Figure 10.17. There is a one-to-one mapping of four of the five functions, the exception being security management [M.3050 Sup 3]. Figure 10.18 illustrates the mapping of the specific case of configuration function mapped to eTOM Level processes.

Summary

We have presented in this chapter a brief introduction to the complex subject of Telecommunications Management Network (TMN). Although it was proposed by ITU-T in the early 1980s, it is just now becoming a reality due to the advancement of technology and the availability of OSI standards and toolkits.

We learned the role of operations systems in operation, administration, maintenance, and provisioning (OAMP) as they are currently implemented by telecommunication service providers. We defined their role in TMN. Network management system is considered an operations system in the TMN environment.

We defined the concept of TMN consisting of customers, services provided by telecommunication service providers, network, operations systems, and system operators. Due to the multitude of services provided by a multitude of service providers using a multitude of vendor equipment, TMN has proposed reference points between the various components that define standard service interfaces. The original TMN proposal is exclusively OSI standards based.

TMN architecture is presented from three perspectives: functional, physical, and information. The functional architecture is made up of five functions: operations system function (OSF), network element function (NEF), mediation function (MF), Q-adapter function (QAF), and workstation function (WSF). The interface between them is defined by three TMN reference points: f, q3/qx, and x.

TMN physical architecture is the physical manifestation of the functional architecture with the functions implemented in operations systems, mediation devices, network elements, QAFs interfacing with non-TMN legacy systems, and workstations. The data communication function is a distributed function carrying information between function blocks using network management operations, responses, and notifications.

TMN service architecture consists of four layers of management and a fifth layer of network elements. The four layers of management are element management, network management, service management, and business management. We presented an integrated view of all the various components, showing how they all fit together to form the TMN environment. We discussed the issues and recent activities in implementing TMN. We touched upon the recent advancement of technology and tools that have helped the implementation of TMN. The roles played by the three forums–the ATM Forum, the NMF, and TM Forum–were also addressed.

Exercises

1. Shannon's channel capacity theorem provides the following relationship for maximum channel capacity (bits per second) in terms of bandwidth B and signal-to-noise ratio S/N.

$$C = B \log_2 (1+S/N)$$

The S/N in decibels (dB) is related to S/N in power ratio by

$$S/N \text{ in dB} = 10(\log_{10} S/N)$$

The transmission operations system described in Figure 10.1 monitors S/N of a telephone channel with a 3-kHz bandwidth and a channel capacity of 30 kbps. When S/N decreases by 3 dB, the operations system issues a warning alarm and the telephone trunk facility is taken out of service if S/N goes down by 6 dB. Calculate the channel capacity in bps at (a) warning threshold and (b) out-of-service limit keeping the same 3-kHz bandwidth for the telephone channel.

2. Design a traffic measurement operations system that monitors the packet traffic at layer-2 on the nodes shown in Figure 10.2. Assume that all traffic is made up of unicast packets and the links and nodes are such that the packets dropped at any node are primarily due to traffic overload on the node. The system measures the incoming and outgoing packets handled by the data link layer as it interfaces with the physical and network layers. Assume that the system permits the user to set the thresholds for action based on percent packet loss.

   (a) What MIB objects would you monitor?
   (b) Express the threshold parameters for congestion (percent packet loss) on the node as a function of the measured parameters.

3. Figure 10.19 shows a network management environment consisting of a MoM (Manager of Managers) NMS, several agent NMSs that manage individual network domains, and managed network elements. Identify the TMN functions performed by:

   (a) MoM NMS
   (b) Agent NMS
   (c) Managed elements

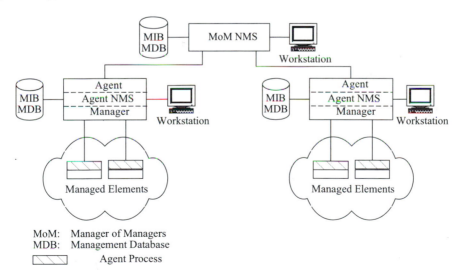

MoM: Manager of Managers
MDB: Management Database
Agent Process

Figure 10.19 Exercise 3

4. A proxy server configuration (Figure 6.46) is used to manage SNMPv1 network elements by an SNMPv2 network management system.

   (a) What TMN function does a proxy server play in an NMS environment?
   (b) Identify the interfaces of the proxy server to the network manager and network elements.

5. In Figure 10.19, identify all:

   (a) TMN reference points
   (b) TMN interfaces

6. Associate M1 through M5 interfaces in ATM management (Figure 10.9 and Figure 10.10) with TMN reference points and TMN service interfaces.

7. CMISE services are listed in Table A.3. Map these services, wherever possible, to SNMPv1 services.

8. Repeat Exercise 7 comparing CMISE and SNMPv2 services.

9. TMN can be applied to ATM switch management using either SNMP or CMIP specifications. Research the ATM Forum specifications referenced in Table 12.3 and identify the OBJECT IDENTIFIERS for the two modules, *atmfM4CmipNEView* and *atmfM4Snmpview*.

10. The ATM objects are defined under the node *informationModule(0)*, which is the subclass of *atmfCmipNEView*. Five managed object classes are defined under the *informationModule*, which are *atmfM4ObjectClass*, *atmfM4Package*, *atmfM4Attribute*, *atmfM4NameBinding*, and *atmfM4Action*. Draw a naming tree for these, explicitly identifying the ObjectID.

11. Figure 10.18 shows mapping of eTOM Level 2 processes-to-M.3400 Configuration Function. Do similar mapping of eTOM Level 2 processes-to-M.3400 specifications for:

    (a) Fault Management
    (b) Performace Management
    (c) Accounting Management

Network Management Applications

OBJECTIVES

- Network management and system management
- Network management
  - Configuration
  - Fault
  - Performance
  - Security
  - Accounting
- Configuration management
  - Configuration management
  - Service/network provisioning
  - Inventory management
- Fault management
  - Fault detection and isolation
  - Correlation techniques for root cause analysis
- Performance management
  - Performance metrics
  - Data monitoring
  - Problem isolation
  - Performance statistics
- Security management
  - Security policies and procedures
  - Security threats
  - Firewall
  - Cryptography: keys, algorithms, authentication, and authorization schemes
  - Secure message transfer methods
- Accounting management
- Report management
- Policy-based management
- Service level management
  - Quality of service, QoS
  - Service level agreement, SLA

The management of networked information services involves management of network and system resources. OSI defines network management as a five-layer architecture. We have extended the model to include system management and have presented the integrated architecture in Figure 11.1. At the highest level of TMN are the functions associated with managing the business, business management.

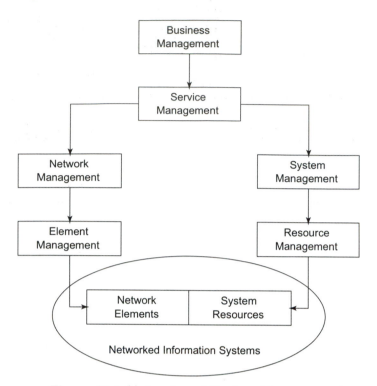

Figure 11.1 Network and System Management

This applies to all institutions, be it a commercial business, educational institute, telecommunications service provider, or any other organization that uses networked systems to manage their business.

An institution is a business that provides either a product or service. In either case, there are service considerations. For example, a product-oriented business has to be concerned with customer service as well as internal services. The service management for a service provider, including a telecommunication service provider, is an absolute necessity. Please see Section 10.8, Figure 10.14 for some of the service applications.

The third layer of TMN deals with network management or system management. Network management manages the global network by aggregating and correlating data obtained from the element management systems. Likewise, the system management aggregates and coordinates system resources by acquisition of data from the resource management systems. The complementary functions of network and system management manage the networked information system composed of network elements and system resources.

Our focus in this chapter will be on network management applications. As we learned in Chapter 3, there are five different categories of applications: configuration management, fault management, performance management, security management, and account management. Others [Leinwand

and Conroy, 1996] have treated the five categories of applications and presented simple and complex tools to manage them.

The subject of configuration management may be looked at not only from an operational viewpoint, but also from engineering and planning viewpoints. In our treatment of configuration management in Section 11.1, we have included network provisioning and inventory management. This is in addition to the configuration of network topology, which is part of traditional network management.

Fault management involves detection of a fault as it occurs in the network, and subsequently locating the source of the problem. We should finally isolate the root cause of the problem. This is covered in Section 11.2.

It is harder to define performance of a network in quantitative terms than in qualitative terms. For example, when a user observes that the network performance is slow, we need to define what slowness is, and which segment of the network is slow. On the other hand, it could be that the application, which could be running on a server, is behaving slowly. We discuss performance management in Section 11.3. We will discuss performance metrics and learn how to monitor a network for performance. Performance statistics play a very important part in network management, and several system tools available for gathering statistics will be covered.

When a fault occurs in a network, either due to failure of a component or due to performance, it may manifest itself in many places. Thus, from a centralized management system, we observe alarms coming from multiple locations. Correlating these alarm events and finding the root cause of the problem is a challenge. We will discuss the various correlation technologies in Section 11.4.

Security in network is concerned with preventing illegal access to information by unauthorized personnel. It involves not only technical issues, but also establishment of well-defined policies and procedures. We will discuss the various issues associated with authentication and authorization in Section 11.5. We will also deal with the establishment of secure (i.e., without illegal monitoring and manipulation) communication between the source and the receiver.

The business health of an institution or corporation depends on well-maintained accounting management and reporting. Reports for management have a different purpose from that of reports generated for day-to-day network operation. There are also reports needed for the user to measure the quality of service to be provided by service level agreement (SLA). These are covered in Sections 11.6 and 11.7

We have addressed the five layers of management with network elements being at the lowest level and business management being at the top. Element management at the second layer maintains the network. Network management at the third level and service management at the fourth level are based not just on technical issues but also on policy issues. Once policies are established, some of them could be implemented in the system. For example, if a network is congested due to heavy traffic, should the network parameters be automatically adjusted to increase bandwidth, or should traffic into the network be decreased. A policy decision that has been made on this can be implemented as part of the management system. We will discuss this in Section 11.8.

Service level management is an important aspect of network and system management. It goes beyond managing resources. It is concerned with the SLA between the customer and the service provider regarding the quality of service of network, systems, and business applications. This is covered in Section 11.9.

11.1 CONFIGURATION MANAGEMENT

Configuration management in network management is normally used in the context of discovering network topology, mapping the network, and setting up the configuration parameters in management agents and management systems. However, as discussed in Section 1.9 and shown in Figure 1.21, network management in the broad sense also includes network provisioning. Network provisioning includes network planning and design and is considered part of configuration management.

11.1.1 Network Provisioning

Network provisioning, also called circuit provisioning in the telephone industry, is an automated process. The design of a trunk (circuit from the originating switching center to the destination switching center) and a special service circuit (customized for customer specifications) is done by application programs written in operation systems. Planning systems and inventory systems are integrated with design systems to build a system of systems. Thus, a circuit designed for the future automatically derives its turn-up date from the planning system and ensures that the components are available in the inventory system. Likewise, when a circuit is to be disconnected, it is coordinated with the planning system and the freed-up components are added to the inventory system. Thus, the design system is made aware of the availability of components for future designs.

An example of a circuit provisioning system is a system of systems developed by Bell System (before it was split), called Trunk Integrated Record Keeping System (TIRKS). TIRKS is used in automated circuit provisioning of trunks. A trunk is a logical circuit between two switching offices and it traverses over many facilities. TIRKS is an operations system in the context of Telecommunications Management Network (TMN) that we dealt with in Chapter 10. Given the requirements of a trunk, such as transmission loss and noise, type of circuit, availability date, etc., as input to the system, the system automatically designs the components of the trunk. The designed circuit will identify transmission facilities between switching offices and equipment in intermediate and end offices. The equipment will be selected based on what would be available in the future when the circuit needs to be installed.

Network provisioning in a computer communications network has different requirements. Instead of circuit-switched connections, we have packet-switched paths for information to be transmitted from the source to the destination. In a connectionless packet-switched circuit, each packet takes an independent path, and the routers at various nodes switch each packet based on the load in the links. The links are provisioned based on average and peak demands. In store-and-forward communication, excess packets can be stored in buffers in routers or retransmitted in the event the packets are lost or discarded. In the connection-oriented circuit requirements, permanent and switched virtual circuit demands need to be accommodated for end-to-end demands on the various links. Network provisioning for packet-switched network is based on performance statistics and quality of service requirements.

Network provisioning in broadband wireless area network (WAN) communication using ATM technology is more complex. The virtual-circuit concept is always used and has to be taken into account in the provisioning process. The switches are cell-based, in contrast to frame-based packet switching. Each ATM switch has knowledge of the virtual path–virtual circuit (VP–VC) of each session connection only to the neighboring nodes and not end-to-end. Each ATM switch vendor has built their proprietary assignment of VP–VC for end-to-end design into the ATM switch. The architecture of end-to-end provisioning of ATM circuits could be either centralized or distributed, and is based on whether the circuit is a permanent virtual circuit (PVC) or a switched virtual circuit (SVC). Commercial products, which provision PVCs across multiple vendor products, have recently been introduced in the market.

11.1.2 Inventory Management

We have addressed the importance of inventory management in circuit provisioning. An efficient database system is an essential part of the inventory management system. We need to be aware of all the details associated with components, which should be accessible using different indices. Some of the obvious access keys are the component description or part number, components that match a set of characteristics, components in use and in spare, and components to be freed-up for future use.

In Section 11.1.1 we cited the example of TIRKS, which is a system of systems. Two of the systems that TIRKS uses are equipment inventory (E1) and facilities inventory (F1). The E1 system has an inventory of all equipment identifying what is currently available and what will become available in the future with dates of availability. Similar information is maintained on facilities by the F1 system. With such a detailed inventory system, TIRKS can anticipate circuit provisioning for the future with components that would be available.

Legacy inventory management systems use hierarchical and scalar-based database systems. Such databases limit the addition of new components or extend the properties of existing components by adding new fields. These limitations can be removed by using relational database technology. Further, new NMSs, such as in OSI CMIP and Web-based management, use object-oriented technology. These manage object-oriented managed objects. An object-oriented relational database is helpful in configuration and inventory management in such an environment.

11.1.3 Network Topology

Network management is based on knowledge of network topology. As a network grows, shrinks, or otherwise changes, the network topology needs to be updated automatically. This is done by the discovery application in the NMS as discussed in Section 9.4.4. The discovery process needs to be constrained as to the scope of the network that it discovers. For example, the *arp* command can discover any network component that responds with an IP address, which can then be mapped by the NMS. If this includes workstations that are turned on only when they are in use, the NMS would indicate failure whenever they are off. Obviously, that is not desirable. In addition, some hosts should not be discovered for security reasons. These should be filtered out during the discovery process so the discovery application should have the capability to set filter parameters to implement these constraints.

Autodiscovery can be done using the broadcast ping on each segment and following up with further SNMP queries to gather more details on the system. The more efficient method is to look at the ARP cache in the local router. The ARP cache table is large and contains the addresses of all the recently communicated hosts and nodes. Using this table, subsequent ARP queries could be sent to other routers. This process is continued until information is obtained on all IP addresses defined by the scope of the autodiscovery procedure. A map, showing network topology, is presented by the autodiscovery procedure after the addresses of the network entities have been discovered.

The autodiscovery procedure becomes more complex in the virtual local area network (LAN) configuration. Figure 11.2 shows the *physical* configuration of a conventional LAN. The router in the figure can be visualized as part of a backbone (not shown). There are two LAN segments connected to the router, Segment A and Segment B. They are physically connected to two physical ports in the router (i.e., there is one port for each segment used on the interface card). They are identified as Port A and Port B, corresponding to Segment A and Segment B, respectively. Both LANs are Ethernet LANs and use hub configuration. Two hosts, A1 and A2, are connected to Hub 1 on LAN segment A and two hosts, B1 and B2, are connected to Hub 2 on LAN Segment B.

Figure 11.3 shows the *logical* configuration for Figure 11.2. The logical configuration is what the autodiscovery process detects. It is very similar to the physical configuration. Segment A corresponds to LAN on Hub 1 with the hosts A1 and A2. It is easy to conceptually visualize this and easy to configure.

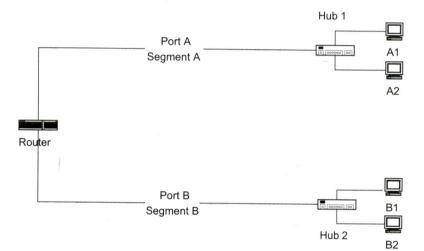

Figure 11.2 LAN Physical Configuration

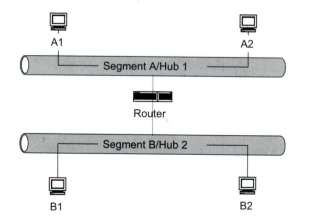

Figure 11.3 Logical Configuration of Two LAN Segments

Let us now contrast Figure 11.2 with Figure 11.4, which shows the *physical* configuration of two virtual LANs (VLAN). We notice that only one physical port, Port A, is used in the router, not two as in the case of a traditional LAN. Hosts A1 and A2 are configured to be on VLAN 1, and hosts B1 and B2 are configured to be on VLAN 2. Although VLAN grouping can be done on different criteria, let us assume that it is done on port basis on the switch. Thus, the two ports marked Segment A on the switch are grouped as VLAN 1. The other two ports, marked Segment B, are grouped as VLAN 2. Thus, Segment A corresponds to VLAN 1 and Segment B corresponds to VLAN 2. We observe that VLAN 1 and VLAN 2 are spread across the two physical hubs, Hub 1 and Hub 2. With a layer-2 bridged network, the VLAN network is efficient. As IEEE 802.3 standards are established and widely adopted, this configuration has been deployed more and more, along with a backbone network.

The *logical* view of the physical VLAN configuration shown in Figure 11.4 is presented in Figure 11.5. We see that Hosts A1 and A2 still belong to Segment A, but are on different hubs. Likewise, Hosts B1 and B2 belong to Segment B. The autodiscovery process would not detect the physical hubs that are identified in Figure 11.5. In many situations, the switch would also be transparent, as there are no IP addresses associated with switch ports. Consequently, it would be harder to associate the logical configuration with the physical configuration.

This makes the network management task a complex one. First, two separate maps must be maintained on an on-going basis as changes to the network are made. Second, when a new component is added and autodiscovered by the system, a manual procedure is needed to follow up on the physical configuration.

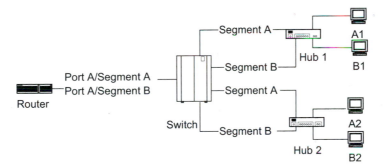

Figure 11.4 VLAN Physical Configuration

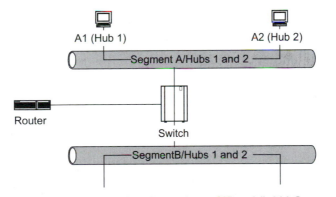

Figure 11.5 Logical Configuration of Two VLAN Segments

In the example above, we talked about grouping of VLAN based on the ports on the switches. We could also group VLAN based on MAC address, IP address, or protocol type. Grouping by IP address has some benefits in the management of VLAN network. The logical grouping of components based on IP network segments makes sense. In addition, as a policy the *sysLocation* entity in a system group should be filled in for easier management.

11.2 FAULT MANAGEMENT

Fault in a network is normally associated with failure of a network component and subsequent loss of connectivity. Fault management involves a five-step process: (1) fault detection, (2) fault location, (3) restoration of service, (4) identification of root cause of the problem, and (5) problem resolution. The fault should be detected as quickly as possible by the centralized management system, preferably before or at about the same time as when the users notice it. Fault location involves identifying where the problem is located. We distinguish this from problem isolation, although in practice it could be the same. The reason for doing this is that it is important to restore service to the users as quickly as possible, using alternative means. The restoration of service takes a higher priority over diagnosing the problem and fixing it. However, it may not always be possible to do this. Identification of the root cause of the problem could be a complex process, which we will go into greater depth soon. After identifying the source of the problem, a trouble ticket can be generated to resolve the problem. In an automated network operations center, the trouble ticket could be generated automatically by the NMS.

11.2.1 Fault Detection

Fault detection is accomplished using either a polling scheme (the NMS polling management agents periodically for status) or by the generation of traps (management agents based on information from the network elements sending unsolicited alarms to the NMS). An application program in NMS generates the **ping** command periodically and waits for response. Connectivity is declared broken when a pre-set number of consecutive responses are not received. The frequency of pinging and the preset number for failure detection may be optimized for balance between traffic overhead and the rapidity with which failure is to be detected.

The alternative detection scheme is to use traps. For example, the generic trap messages *linkDown* and *egpNeighborLoss* in SNMPv1 can be set in the agents giving them the capability to report events to the NMS with the legitimate community name. One of the advantages of traps is that failure detection is accomplished faster with less traffic overhead.

11.2.2 Fault Location and Isolation Techniques

Fault location using a simple approach (we will look at the complex approach using the correlation technology in Section 11.4) would be to detect all the network components that have failed. The origin of the problem could then be traced by walking down the topology tree where the problem starts. Thus, if an interface card on a router has failed, all managed components connected to that interface would indicate failure.

After having located where the fault is, the next step is to isolate the fault (i.e., determine the source of the problem). First, we should delineate the problem between failure of the component and the physical link. Thus, in the above example, the interface card may be functioning well, but the link to the interface may be down. We need to use various diagnostic tools to isolate the cause.

Let us assume for the moment that the link is not the problem but that the interface card is. We then proceed to isolate the problem to the layer that is causing it. It is possible that excessive packet loss is causing disconnection. We can measure packet loss by pinging, if pinging can be used. We can query the various Management Information Base (MIB) parameters on the node itself or other related nodes to further localize the cause of the problem. For example, error rates calculated from the interface group parameters, *ifInDiscards*, *ifInErrors*, *ifOutDiscards*, and *ifOutErrors* with respect to the input and output packet rates, could help us isolate the problem in the interface card.

The ideal solution to locating and isolating the fault is to have an artificial intelligence solution. By observing all the symptoms, we might be able to identify the source of the problem. There are several techniques to accomplish this, which we will address in Section 11.4.

11.3   PERFORMANCE MANAGEMENT

We have already addressed performance management applications directly and indirectly under the various headings. We discussed two popular protocol analyzers, Sniffer and NetMetrix, in Chapter 9. In Section 9.2, we used the protocol analyzer as a system tool to measure traffic monitoring on Ethernet LANs, which is in the realm of performance management. We looked at load monitoring based on various parameters such as source and destination addresses, protocols at different layers, etc. We addressed traffic statistics collected over a period of from hours to a year using the Multi Router Traffic Grapher (MRTG) tool in Section 9.2.4. The statistics obtained using a protocol analyzer as a remote monitoring (RMON) tool was detailed in the case study in Section 8.6. We noticed how we were able to obtain the overall trend in Internet-related traffic and the type of traffic.

Performance of a network is a nebulous term, which is hard to define or quantify in terms of global metrics. The purpose of the network is to carry information and thus performance management is really (data) traffic management. It involves the following: data monitoring, problem isolation, performance tuning, analysis of statistical data for recognizing trends, and resource planning.

11.3.1   Performance Metrics

The parameters that can be attributed to defining network performance on a global level are throughput, response time, network availability, and network reliability. The metrics on these are dependent on what, when, and where the measurements are made. Real-time traffic performance metrics are latency (i.e., delay) and jitter, which are addressed in Section 11.3.4.

These macro-level parameters can be defined in terms of micro-level parameters. Some of the parameters that impact network throughput are bandwidth or capacity of the transmission media, its utilization, error rate of the channel, peak load, and average load of the traffic. These can be measured at specific points in the network. For example, bandwidth or capacity will be different in different segments of the network. An Ethernet LAN with a capacity of 10 Mbps can function to full capacity with a single workstation on it, but reaches full capacity with a utilization factor of 30–40% when densely populated with workstations. This utilization factor can further be defined in terms of collision rate, which is measurable. In contrast, in a WAN, the bandwidth is fully utilized except for the packet overhead.

The response time of a network not only depends on the throughput of the network, but also on the application; in other words, it depends on both the network and system performance. Thus, in a client–server environment, the response time as seen by the client could be slow either due to the server being heavily used, or the network traffic being overloaded, or a combination of both. According to Feldmeir [1997], "the application responsiveness on the network, more than any other measure, reflects whether

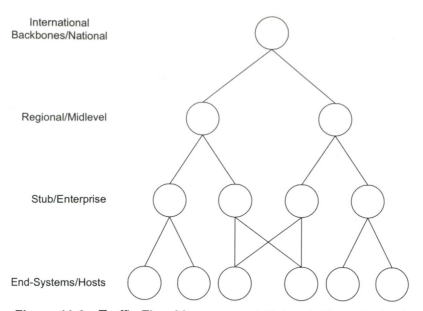

International
Backbones/National

Regional/Midlevel

Stub/Enterprise

End-Systems/Hosts

Figure 11.6 Traffic Flow Measurement Network Characterization

the network is meeting the end users' expectations and requirements." He defines three types of metrics to measure application responsiveness: application availability, response time between the user and the server, and the burst frame rate, which is the rate at which the requested data arrive at the user station.

IETF Network Working Group has developed several Request for Comments (RFCs) on traffic flow measurement. RFC 2063 defines the architecture for the measurement and reporting of network traffic flows. The network is characterized as traffic passing through four representative levels, as shown in Figure 11.6. Backbone networks are those that are typically connected to other networks, and do not have individual hosts connected to them. A regional network is similar to a backbone, but smaller. It may have individual hosts connected to it. Regional hosts are subscribers to a backbone network. Stub/enterprise networks connect hosts and LANs and are subscribers to regional and backbone networks. End systems or hosts are subscribers to all of the above.

The architecture defines three entities for traffic flow measurements: meters, meter readers, and managers. Meters observe network traffic flows and build up a table of flow data records for them. Meter readers collect traffic flow data from meters. Managers oversee the operation of meters and meter readers. RFC 2064 defines the MIB for the meter. RFC 2123 describes NeTraMet, an implementation of flow meter based on RFC 2063 and RFC 2064.

11.3.2 Data Monitoring

Data monitoring in the network for abnormal performance behavior, such as high collision rate in Ethernet LAN, excessive packet drop due to overload, etc., are detected by traps generated by agents and RMON. Performance-related issues are detected primarily using trap messages generated by RMON probes. Thresholds are set for important SNMP parameters in the RMON, which then generate alarms when the pre-set thresholds are crossed. For example, the parameters in the alarm group and the event group in RMON MIB [RFC 1757] may be set for the object identifier to be monitored. The time interval over which the data are to be collected for calculation and the rising and falling thresholds are specified.

In addition, the community names are set for who would receive the alarm. Although we classify such alarms under performance category, they could also be defined under fault category as is done in Section 9.4.6.

NMSs generally report all events selected for display including alarms. Alarms are set for criticality and the icon changes color based on the criticality. Depending on the implementation, the alarm is either automatically cleared when the alarm condition clears or is manually cleared by an operator. The latter case is useful for alerting the operations personnel as to what happened.

11.3.3   Problem Isolation

Problem isolation for performance-related issues depends on the type of problem. As we have indicated before, a high percentage of packet loss will cause loss of connectivity, which could be intermittent. In this situation, monitoring the packet loss over an extended period will isolate the problem. Another example is the performance problem associated with large delay. This may be attributable to an excessive drop of packets. We can identify the source of the packet delay from a route-tracing procedure and then probe for the packet discards at that node. Refer to [Rose and McCloghrie, 1995] for a detailed analysis of the performance degradation cases in various components and media.

As in fault management, problems could occur at multiple locations simultaneously. These could be reported to the central management system as multiple independent events although they may be correlated. For example, an excessive drop in packets in one of the links may switch the traffic to an alternate route. This could cause an overload in that link, which will be reported as an alarm. A more sophisticated approach using the correlation technology is again required here, which we will discuss in Section 11.4.

11.3.4   Performance Statistics

Performance statistics are used in tuning a network, validating of SLA, which will be covered in Section 11.9, analyzing use trends, planning facilities, and functional accounting. Data are gathered by means of an RMON probe and RMON MIB for statistics. Statistics, to be accurate, require large amounts of data sampling, which create overhead traffic on the network and thus impact its performance. One of the enormous benefits of using RMON probe for collecting statistics is that it can be done locally without degrading the overall performance of the network. An RMON MIB contains the history and statistics groups (see Section 8.4) for various media and can be used efficiently to collect the relevant data and store them for current or future analysis.

One application of the results obtained from performance statistics is to tune the network for better performance. For example, two segments of the network may be connected by a gateway and excessive intersegment traffic could produce excessive performance delay. Error statistics on dropped packets on the gateway interfaces would manifest this problem. The solution to resolve this problem is to increase the bandwidth of the gateway by either increasing its capacity or by adding a second gateway between the segments. Of course, adding the extra gateway could cause configuration-related problems and hence reconfiguration of traffic may be needed.

Various error statistics at different layers are gathered to measure the quality of service and to do performance improvement, if needed. Some of the other performance parameters that can be tuned by monitoring network statistics are bandwidth of links, utilization of links, and controlling peak-to-average ratio of inherently bursty data traffic. In addition, traffic utilization can be improved by redistributing the load during the day, with essential traffic occupying the busy hours and non-essential traffic the slack hours, with the latter being store and forward.

An important performance criterion in real-time traffic in broadband service is the latency or delay caused by dispersion in large bandwidth signal. This affects the quality of service due to performance degradation.

Another important statistic, especially in real-time broadband services, is the variation in network delay, otherwise known as **jitter**. This impacts the quality of service (QoS) guaranteed to the customer by the SLA. For example, in a cable modem, a managed object *docsQoSServiceClassMaxJitter* (see the DOCSIS Quality of Service MIB in Table 13.3) is used to monitor the jitter.

Another performance application is validation of SLA between the service user and the service provider. The SLA may require limiting input to the service provider network. If the packet rate is tending toward the threshold of SLA, one may have to control the bandwidth of the access to the service provider network. This can be achieved by implementing application interfaces that use algorithms such as the leaky bucket or the token bucket [Tanenbaum, 1996]. The leaky bucket algorithm limits the maximum output data rate, and the token bucket algorithm controls its average value. Combining the two, we can tune the peak-to-average ratio of the output. Some ATM switches have such interfaces built into them, which are easily tunable. This would be desirable if a service provider's pricing is based on peak data rate usage instead of average rate.

Performance statistics are also used to project traffic use trends on traffic use and to plan future resource requirements. Statistical data on traffic are collected and periodic reports are generated to study use trends and project needs. Thus, trend analysis is helpful for future resource planning.

Statistics can be gathered, as we saw in Section 9.2, on the network load created by various users and applications. These can be used to do functional accounting so that the cost of operation of a network can be charged to the users of the network or at least be justified.

11.4   EVENT CORRELATION TECHNIQUES

We have illustrated some simple methods to diagnose and isolate the source of a problem in fault and performance management. When a centralized NMS receives a trap or a notification, it is called **receiving an event**. A single problem source may cause multiple symptoms, and each symptom detected is reported as an independent event to the management system. Obviously, we do not want to treat each event independently and act to resolve it. Thus, it is important that the management system correlates all these events and isolates the root cause of the problem. The techniques used for accomplishing this are called **event correlation techniques**.

There are several correlation techniques used to isolate and localize fault in networks. All are based on (1) detecting and filtering of events, (2) correlating observed events to isolate and localize the fault either topologically or functionally, and (3) identifying the cause of the problem. In all three cases, there is intelligence or reasoning behind the methods. The reasoning methods distinguish one technique from another.

We will discuss six approaches to correlation techniques. They are (1) rule-based reasoning, (2) model-based reasoning, (3) case-based reasoning, (4) codebook, (5) state transition graph model, and (6) finite state machine model. See Lewis [1999] for a detailed comparison of the various methods.

11.4.1   Rule-Based Reasoning

Rule-based reasoning (RBR) is the earliest form of correlation technique. It is also known by many other names such as rule-based expert system, expert system, production system, and blackboard system. It has a knowledge base, working memory, and an inference engine, as shown in Figure 11.7 [Cronk et al., 1988; Lewis, 1994]. The three levels representing the three components are the knowledge level, the data level, and the control level, respectively. Cronk et al. are also a good source for review of network applications of RBR. The knowledge base contains expert knowledge as to (1) definition of a problem in the network and (2) action that needs to be taken if a par-ticular condition occurs. The knowledge base information is rule-based in the form of **if–then** or **condition–action**, containing rules that indicate which operations are to be performed when. The working memory contains—as working memory elements—the topological and state information of the network being monitored. When the network goes into a faulty state, it is recognized by the working memory. The inference engine, in cooperation with the knowledge base, compares the current state with the left side of the rule-base and finds the closest match to output the right side of the rule. The knowledge base then executes an action on the working memory element.

In Figure 11.7, the rule-based paradigm is interactive between the three components and is iterative. There are several strategies for the rule-based paradigm. A specific strategy is implemented in the inference engine. Choosing a specific rule, an action is performed on the working memory element, which could then initiate another event. This process continues until the correct state is achieved in the working memory.

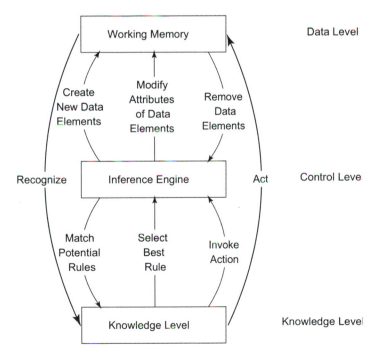

Figure 11.7 Basic Rule-Based Reasoning Paradigm

Rules are made up in the knowledge base from the expertise of the experts in the field. The rule is an exact match and the action is very specific. If the antecedent in the rule does not match, the paradigm breaks and it is called "**brittle**." However, it can be fixed by adding more rules, which would increase the database size and degrade the performance, referred to as **knowledge acquisition bottleneck**. There is an exponential growth in size as the number of working memory elements grows.

In addition, the action is specific, which could cause unwanted behavior. For example, we can define the alarm condition for packet loss as follows:

If packet loss < 10%	alarm green
If packet loss => 10% < 15%	alarm yellow
If packet loss => 15%	alarm red

The left side conditions are the working memory elements, which if detected would execute the appropriate rule defined in the rule-base. As we can see, this could cause the alarm condition to flip back and forth in boundary cases. An application of fuzzy logic is used to remedy this problem [Lewis, 1994], but it is harder to implement.

The RBR is used in Hewlett-Packard OpenView Element Management Framework [Hajela, 1996]. Figure 11.8 is an adaptation of the scenario from [Hajela, 1996] to illustrate an implementation of RBR. It shows a four-layer network. Backbone Router A links to Router B. Hub C, connected to Router B, has four servers, D1 through D4, in its LAN. Without a correlation engine, failure in the interface of Router A will generate an alarm. This fault then propagates to Router B, Hub C, and finally to Servers D1 through D4. It is important to realize that there is a time delay involved in the generation of alarms. In general, propagation of faults and time delay associated with them need to be recognized as such in fault management.

Four correlation rules are specified in Figure 11.9. Rule 0 has no condition associated with it. Rules 1–3 are conditional rules. In order to allow for the propagation time, a correlation window of 20 seconds is set.

The inference engine at the control level interprets the above rules and takes the actions shown in Figure 11.10.

In the above example, it can be observed that only alarm A is sent and others are ignored as long as they arrive within the correlation window. The alarms could even be generated out of sequence.

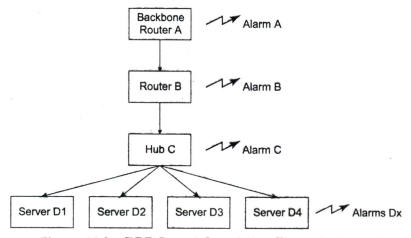

Figure 11.8 RBR-Based Correlation Example Scenario

Rule 0:	Alarm A :	Send root cause Alarm A	
Rule 1	Alarm B	If Alarm A present	Related to A and ignore
Rule 2	Alarm C	If Alarm B present	Related to B and ignore
Rule 3	Alarm Dx	if Alarm C present	Related to C and ignore

Correlation window: 20 seconds.

Figure 11.9 Rules Specifications for the Example in Figure 11.8

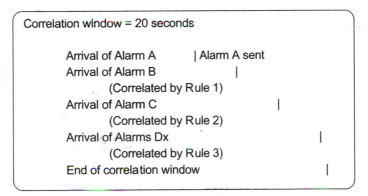

Correlation window = 20 seconds

Arrival of Alarm A | Alarm A sent
Arrival of Alarm B |
    (Correlated by Rule 1)
Arrival of Alarm C |
    (Correlated by Rule 2)
Arrival of Alarms Dx |
    (Correlated by Rule 3)
End of correlation window |

Figure 11.10 Control Actions for the RBR Example of Figure 11.8

However, because of the specification of correlation window size, the inference engine waits before sending alarms B, C, and Dx.

Several commercial systems have been built using RBR. Some examples are Computer Associates TNG and Tivoli TME.

11.4.2 Model-Based Reasoning

An event correlator based on model-based reasoning is built on an object-oriented model associated with each managed object. A model is a representation of the component it models. The model, in the traditional object-oriented representation, has attributes, relations to other models, and behaviors. The relationship between objects is reflected in a similar relationship between models.

Let us picture a network of hubs that are connected to a router, as shown in the left half of Figure 11.11. The right half shows the corresponding model in the event correlator in the NMS. The NMS pings every hub and the router (really a router interface to the backbone network) periodically to check whether each component is working. We can associate communication between the NMS and a managed component as between a model (software object) in the NMS/correlator and its counterpart of managed object. Thus, in our example, the model of each hub periodically pings its hub and the model of the router pings the router. As long as all the components are working, no additional operation is needed.

If Hub1 fails, it is recognized by the H1 model. Let us assume that the H1 model is programmed to wait for lack of response in three consecutive pings. After three pings with no response, the H1 model suspects a failure of Hub1. However, before it declares a failure and displays an alarm, it analyses its relation to other models and recognizes that it should query the router model. If the router model responds that the router is working, only then the Hub1 alarm is triggered. If the router model responds that it

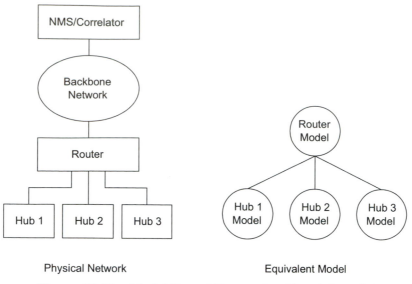

Figure 11.11 Model-Based Reasoning Event Correlator

is not receiving a response from the router, then the Hub1 model deduces that the problem is with the router and not Hub1. At least, it cannot definitively determine a Hub1 failure as long as it cannot communicate with Hub1 because of the router failure.

The above example is modeled after [Lewis, 1999], who presents an interesting scenario of a classroom with teacher. Outside the classroom is a computer network with a router and workstations. Each student is a model (software mirror) of the workstation. The teacher is a model of the router. Each student communicates with his or her real-world counterpart, which is the workstation outside the classroom. The teacher communicates with the router. If a student fails to communicate with his or her workstation, he or she queries the teacher as to whether the teacher could communicate with the teacher's router. Depending on the yes or no answer of the teacher, the student declares a "fail" (yes) or "no-fail" (no) condition, respectively. Model-based reasoning is implemented in Cabletron Spectrum.

11.4.3 Case-Based Reasoning

Case-based reasoning (CBR) overcomes many of the deficiencies of RBR. In RBR, the unit of knowledge is a rule; whereas in CBR, the unit of knowledge is a case [Lewis, 1995]. The intuition of CBR is that situations repeat themselves in the real world; and that what was done in one situation is applicable to others in a similar, but not necessarily identical, situation. Thus, when we try to resolve a trouble, we start with the case that we have experienced before [Kolodner, 1997; Lewis, 1995]. Kolodner treats CBR from an information management viewpoint, and Lewis applies it specifically to network management.

The general CBR architecture is shown in Figure 11.12 [Lewis, 1995]. It consists of four modules: input, retrieve, adapt, and process, along with a case library. The CBR approach uses the knowledge gained before and extends it to the current situation. The former episodes are stored in a case library. If the current situation, as received by the input module, matches one that is present in the case library (as compared by the retrieve module), it is applied. If it does not, the closest situation is chosen by the adapt module, and adapted to the current episode to resolve the problem. The process module takes the appropriate action(s). Once the problem is resolved, the newly adapted case is added to the case library.

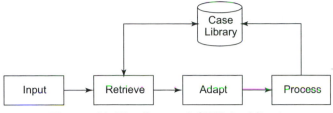

Figure 11.12   General CBR Architecture

Lewis also describes the application of CBR in a trouble-tracking system, CRITTER [Lewis, 1996]. The CRITTER application has evolved into a CBR application for network management named SpectroRx built by Cabletron. When a trouble ticket is created on a network problem, it is compared to similar cases in the case library containing previous trouble tickets with resolutions. The current trouble is resolved by adapting the previous case in one of three ways: (1) parameterized adaptation, (2) abstraction/respecialization adaptation, and (3) critic-based adaptation. The resolved trouble ticket is then added to the case library. We will use the examples given in the reference to illustrate the three adaptation methods.

Parameterized Adaptation. Parameterized adaptation is used when a similar case exists in the case library, but the parameters may have to be scaled to resolve the current situation. Consider the current trouble with file_transfer_throughput, which matches the following trouble ticket in the case library, shown in Figure 11.13.

In the parameterized adaptation of the trouble ticket shown in Figure 11.14, variable F has been modified to F′ and the relationship between network load adjustment variable A′ and F′ remain the same as between A and F. In the default situation, where there is an exact match, F′ and A′ are F and A.

Abstraction/Respecialization Adaptation. Figure 11.15 shows three trouble tickets. The first two are two cases from the case library that matched the current problem we have been discussing. The first option adjusts the network load, and the second option adjusts the bandwidth of the network. The user or the system has the option of adapting either of the two based on restrictions to be placed on adjusting the workload or adjusting the bandwidth. Let us choose the option of not restricting the network load, which implies that we have to increase the bandwidth. We can add this as additional data to the trouble ticket that chooses the bandwidth option and create a new trouble ticket, which is shown as the third trouble ticket in Figure 11.15. This is now added to the case library.

This CBR adaptation is referred to as abstraction/respecialization adaptation. Choosing to adjust bandwidth and not load is a policy decision, which we will discuss in Section 11.8.

Critic-Based Adaptation. The third adaptation, critic-based adaptation, is one where a critic or a craft

Trouble: file_transfer_throughput=F
Additional data: none
Resolution: A=f(F), adjust_network_load=A
Resolution status: good

Figure 11.13   Matching Trouble Ticket for the CBR Example

Trouble: file_transfer_throughput=F′
Additional data: none
Resolution: A′=f(F′), adjust_network_load=A′
Resolution status: good

Figure 11.14 Parameterized Adaptation for the CBR Example

Trouble: file_transfer_throughput=F
Additional data: none
Resolution: A=f(F), adjust_network_load=A
Resolution status: good

Trouble: file_transfer_throughput=F
Additional data: none
Resolution: B=g(F), adjust_network_bandwidth=B
Resolution status: good

Trouble: file_transfer_throughput=F
Additional data: adjust_network_load=no
Resolution: B=g(F), adjust_network_bandwidth=B
Resolution status: good

Figure 11.15 Abstraction/Respecialization Adaptation for the CBR Example

Trouble: file_transfer_throughput=F
Additional data: network_load=N
Resolution: A=f(F,N), adjust_network_load=A
Resolution status: good

Figure 11.16 Critic-Based Adaptation for the CBR Example

person decides to add, remove, reorder, or replace an existing solution. Figure 11.16 shows an example where the network_load has been added as an additional parameter in adjusting the network load, and resolution A is a function of two variables, F and N. This is added as a new case to the case library.

CBR-Based CRITTER. The architecture of CRITTER is shown in Figure 11.17 [Lewis, 1996]. It is integrated with the NMS, Spectrum. The core modules of CRITTER are the four basic modules of the CBR system shown in Figure 11.12: input, retrieve, adapt, and process. There is a fifth additional module, propose, which displays potential solutions found by the reasoning module and allows the user to inspect and manually adapt these solutions.

The input module receives its input from the fault detection module of Spectrum. The process module updates the ticket library with the new experience. The retrieve module uses determinators to retrieve a group of tickets from the library that are similar to an outstanding ticket. The initial set of determination rules is based on expertise knowledge and is built into the determinators module. The application technique is the strategy used by the adapt module. User-based adaptation is the interface module for the user to propose critic-based adaptation.

Comparing RBR and CBR [Kolodner, 1997] distinguishes the differences between RBR and CBR. In RBR, the retrieval is done on exact match, whereas in CBR the match is done on a partial basis. RBR

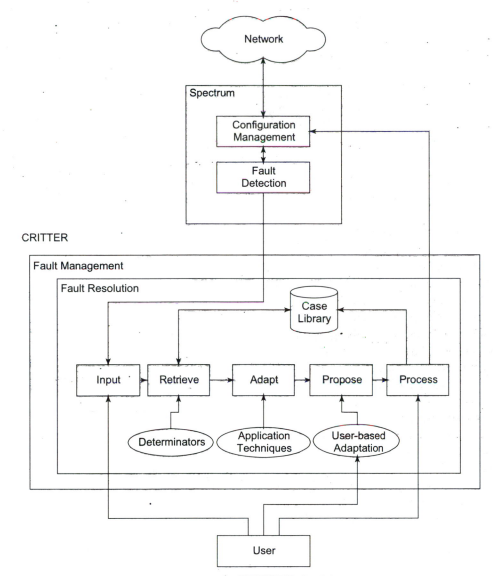

Figure 11.17 CRITTER Architecture

is applied to an iterative cycle of microevents. CBR is applied as a total solution to the trouble and then adapted to the situation on hand.

11.4.4 Codebook Correlation Model

Algorithms have been developed to correlate events that are generated in networks based on modeling of the network and the behavior of network components. Because they are based on algorithms, claims are made that they do not require expert knowledge to associate the events with problems. Although this is true, we still need expert knowledge in selecting the right kinds of input that are to be fed to the correlator to develop an efficient system.

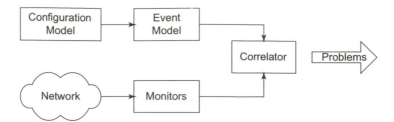

Figure 11.18   Generic Architecture of an Event Correlation System

Figure 11.18 [Kliger *et al.*, 1995] shows the architecture of a model-based event correlation system. We should caution that the "model-based event correlation" should not be confused with the term "model-based reasoning approach" that we discussed in Section 11.4.2. As the heading states, we will refer to this as **codebook correlation**.

Monitors capture alarm events and input them to the correlator. The configuration model contains the configuration of the network. The event model represents the various events and their causal relationships (we will soon define the causality relationship). The correlator correlates the alarm events with the event model and determines the common problems that caused the alarm event.

One of the correlation algorithms based on generic modeling is a coding approach to event correlation [Kliger *et al.*, 1995]. In this approach, problem events are viewed as messages generated by a system and "encoded" in sets of alarms that they cause. The function of the correlator is to "decode" those problem messages to identify the problems. Thus, the coding technique comprises two phases. In the first phase, called the **codebook selection phase**, problems to be monitored are identified and the symptoms or alarms that each of them generates are associated with the problem. (As we stated at the beginning of this approach, this is where expert knowledge is needed.) This produces a problem–symptom matrix. In the second phase, the correlator compares the stream of alarm events with the codebook and identifies the problem.

In order to generate the codebook matrix of problem–symptom, let us first consider a causality graph, which represents symptom events caused by other events. An example of such a causality graph is shown in Figure 11.19. Each node in the graph represents an event. Nodes are connected by directed edges, with edges starting at a causing event and terminating at a resulting event. For example, event E1 causes events E4 and E5. Notice that events E1, E2, and E3 have the directed edges only going out from them and none coming into them. We can identify these nodes as problem nodes and the rest as symptom nodes, as they all have at least one directed edge pointing inward. With problems labeled as Ps and symptoms as Ss, the newly labeled causality graph of Figure 11.19 is shown in Figure 11.20. There are three problem nodes, P1, P2, and P3, and four symptom nodes S1, S2, S3, and S4. We have eliminated

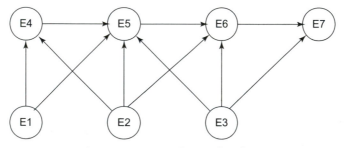

Figure 11.19   Causality Graph

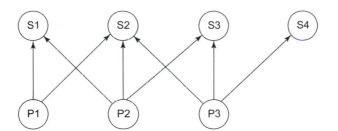

Figure 11.20 Labeled Causality Graph for Figure 11.19

those directed arrows where one symptom causes another symptom, as it does not add any additional information to the overall causality graph.

We can now generate a codebook of problem–symptom matrix for the causality graph of Figure 11.20 (we will drop the qualifier "labeled" from now on). This is shown in Figure 11.21 with three columns as problems and four rows as symptoms.

In general, the number of symptoms will exceed the number of problems and hence, the codebook can be reduced to a minimal set of symptoms needed to uniquely identify the problems. It is easy to show that two rows are adequate to uniquely identify the three problems in the codebook shown in Figure 11.21. We will keep row S1 and try to eliminate subsequent rows, one at a time. At each step, we want to make sure that the remaining codebook distinguishes between the problems. You can prove to yourself that eliminating rows S2 and S3 does not preserve the uniqueness, whereas eliminating either S2 and S4 does. The reduced codebook, called the correlation matrix, is shown in Figure 11.22.

Drawing the causality graph based on the correlation matrix of Figure 11.20, we derive the correlation graph shown in Figure 11.23, which is called the correlation graph.

We will apply the above knowledge to a more general situation of the causality graph shown in Figure 11.24 [Kliger et al., 1995]. Figure 11.24(a) depicts the causality graph of 11 events. Figure 11.24(b) shows the equivalent problem–symptom causality graph. Nodes 1, 2, and 11 show only outgoing directed arrows and are hence identified as problems and the rest of the nodes as symptoms.

We will now reduce the causality graph to a correlation graph. Symptoms 3, 4, and 5 form a cycle of causal equivalence and can be replaced by a single symptom, 3. Symptoms 7 and 10 are caused, respectively, by

	P1	P2	P3
S1	1	1	0
S2	1	1	1
S3	0	1	1
S4	0	0	1

Figure 11.21 Codebook for Figure 11.20

	P1	P2	P3
S1	1	1	0
S3	0	1	1

Figure 11.22 Correlation Matrix for Figure 11.20

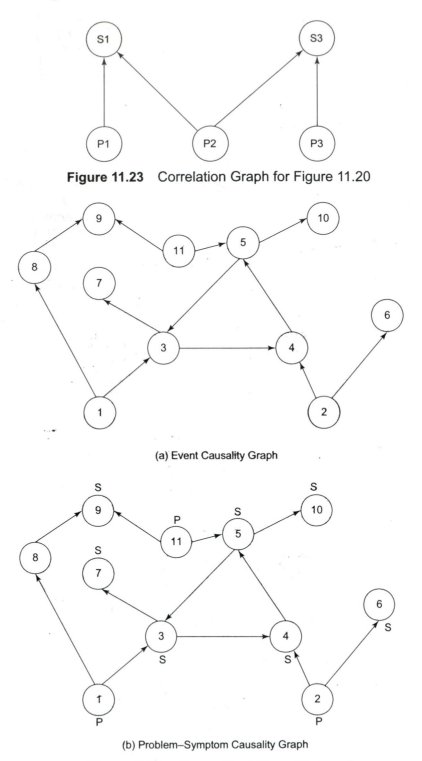

Figure 11.23 Correlation Graph for Figure 11.20

(a) Event Causality Graph

(b) Problem–Symptom Causality Graph

Figure 11.24 Generalized Causality Graph

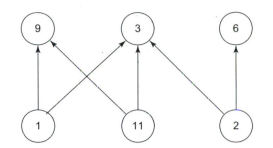

Figure 11.25 Correlation Graph for Figure 11.24

	P1	P2	P11
S3	1	1	1
S6	0	1	0
S9	1	0	1

Figure 11.26 Correlation Matrix for Figure 11.24

symptoms 3 and 5 and hence can be ignored. Likewise, symptom 8 can be eliminated as it is an intermediate symptom node between problem node 1 and symptom node 9, which is also directly related to problem node 11. We thus arrive at the correlation graph shown in Figure 11.25 and the correlation matrix shown in Figure 11.26. Notice that in the particular example the model is unable to distinguish between problems 1 and 11 as they produce identical symptoms in the correlation graph based on the event model.

Further refinements can be made in the codebook approach to event correlation in terms of tolerance to spurious noises and probability relationship in the causality graph. We have derived the correlation matrix to be the minimal causal matrix. Thus, each column in the code matrix is differentiated from other columns by at least one bit (i.e., value in one cell). From coding theory, this corresponds to a Hamming distance of one. Any spurious noise in the event detection could change one of the bits and thus a codeword would identify a pair of problems. This could be avoided by increasing the Hamming distance to two or more, which would increase the number of symptoms in the correlation matrix. Also, the relationship between a problem and symptoms could be defined in terms of probability of occurrence, and the correlation matrix would be a probabilistic matrix.

The codebook correlation technique has been implemented in InCharge system developed by System Management ARTS (SMARTS) [Yemini et al., 1996].

11.4.5 State Transition Graph Model

A state transition graph model is used by Seagate's NerveCenter correlation system. This could be used as a stand-alone system or integrated with an NMS, which HP OpenView and some other vendors have done.

A simple state diagram with two states for a ping/response process is shown in Figure 11.27. The two states are *ping node* and *receive response*. When an NMS sends a ping, it transitions from the *ping node* state to the *receive response* state. When it receives a response, it transitions back to the *ping node* state. As you know by now, this method is how the health of all the components is monitored by the NMS.

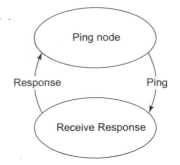

Figure 11.27   State Transition Diagram for Ping/Response

It is best to illustrate with an example of how a state transition diagram could be used to correlate events in the network. Let us choose the same example as in model-based reasoning, Figure 11.11. An NMS is pinging the hubs that are accessed via a router. Let us follow through the scenario of the NMS pinging a hub. When the hub is working and the connectivity to the NMS is good, a response is received for each ping sent, say every minute, by the NMS. This is represented by the top two states, *ping hub* and *receive response*, on the left side of Figure 11.28. Let us now consider the situation when a response for a ping is not received before the next ping is ready to be sent. NMS typically expects a response in 300 milliseconds (we are not pinging some obscure host in a foreign country!). An action is taken by the NMS and the state transitions from *receive response* to *pinged twice* (referred to as *ground state* by NerveCenter). It is possible that a response is received for the second ping and in that situation the state transitions back to the normal *ping hub* state.

However, if there is no response for the second ping, NMS pings a third time. The state transition is now *pinged three times*. The response for this ping will cause a transition to the *ping hub* state. However, let us consider the situation of no-response for the third ping. Let us assume that the NMS is configured to ping three times before it declares that there is a communication failure between it and the hub. Without any correlation, an alarm will be triggered and the icon representing the hub would turn red.

However, the hub may actually be working and the workstations on it may all be communicating with each other. From the topology database, the correlator in the NMS is aware that the path to the hub is via the router. Hence, on failure of the third ping, an action is taken and the system transitions to the *ping router* state. The router is pinged and the system transitions to the *receive response from router* state.

There are two possible outcomes now. The connectivity to the router is lost and no response is received from the router. The system takes no action, which is indicated by the closed loop in the *ping router* state. (How does the router icon turn red in this case?)

The second possibility is that a response is received from the router. This means that the connection to the hub is lost. Now, the correlator in the NMS triggers an alarm that turns the hub icon red.

We notice that in the scenario of a router connectivity failure, only the router icon turns red and none of the hubs connected to it turn red, thus identifying the root cause of the problem.

11.4.6   Finite State Machine Model

Another model-based fault detection scheme uses the communicating finite state machine [Miller, 1998]. The main claim of this process is that it is a passive testing system. It is assumed that an observer agent is present in each node and reports abnormality to a central point. We can visualize the node ob-

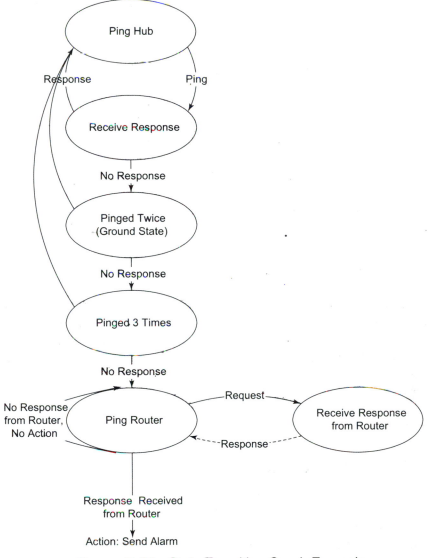

Figure 11.28 State Transition Graph Example

server as a Web agent and the central point as the Web server. An application on the server correlates the events. A failure in a node or a link is indicated by the state machine associated with the component entering an illegal state.

A simple communicating finite state machine for a client–server system is shown in Figure 11.29. It presents communication between a client and server via a communication channel. For simplicity, both the client and the server are assumed to have two states each. The client, which is in send request state, sends a request message to the server, and transitions to receive the response state. The server is currently in the receive request state. The server receives the request and transitions to the send response state. After processing the request, it sends the response and transitions back to the receive request state. The client then receives the response from the server and transitions to the send request state.

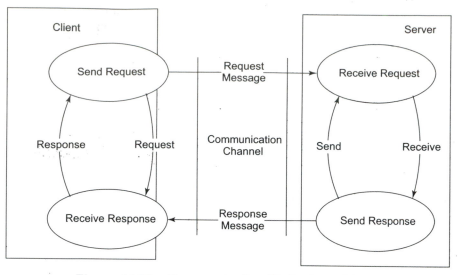

Figure 11.29 Communicating Finite State Machine

If either the client or the server enters an illegal state during the transitions, the system has encountered a fault. For example, after sending a response, if the server does not transition to receive a request state, it is in a failed state. A message is sent to a central location under a fault condition either by the component itself or by the one communicating with the failed component. This is a passive detection scheme similar to the trap mechanism.

We can observe a similarity between the finite state machine model and the state transition graph model with regard to state transitions. However, the main difference is that the former is a passive system and the latter is an active one.

11.5   SECURITY MANAGEMENT

Security management is both a technical and an administrative issue in information management. It involves securing access to the network and information flowing in the network, access to data stored in the network, and manipulating the data that are stored and flowing across the network. The scope of network and access to it not only covers enterprise intranet network, but also the Internet that it is connected to.

Another area of great concern in secure communication is communication with mobile stations. There was an embarrassing case of a voice conversation from the car-phone of a politician being intercepted by a third party traveling in an automobile. Of course, this was an analog signal. However, this could also happen in the case of a mobile digital station such as a hand-held stock trading device. An intruder could intercept messages and alter trade transactions either to benefit by it or to hurt the person sending or receiving them.

In Chapter 7 we covered several of the security issues associated with SNMP management as part of SNMPv3 specifications and discussed possible security threats. Four types of security threats to network management were identified: modification of information, masquerade, message stream modification, and disclosure. They are applicable to security in the implementation of security subsystems in the agent (authoritative engine) and in the manager (non-authoritative engine). The SNMPv3 security subsystem is the User-Based Security Model (USM). It has two modules—an authentication module and a privacy module. The former addresses data integrity and data origin; the latter is concerned with data confidentiality, message timeliness, and limited message protection. The basic concepts discussed in Chapter 7 are part of generalized security management in data communications.

Security management goes beyond the realm of SNMP management. In this section, we will address policies and procedures, resources to prevent security breaches, and network protection from software attacks. Policies and procedures should cover preventive measures, steps to be taken during the occurrence of a security breach, and post-incident measures. Because the Internet is so pervasive and everybody's network is part of it, all government and private organizations in the world are concerned with security and privacy of information traversing it.

In this introductory textbook, we will not be going into the depth of security management that it deserves. For additional information, you are advised to pursue the innumerable references available on the subject [Cooper *et al.*, 1995; Kaufman *et al.*, 1995; Leinwand and Conroy, 1996; RFC 2196; Wack and Carnahan, 1994].

11.5.1   Policies and Procedures

The IETF workgroup that generated RFC 2196 defines a security policy as "a formal statement of the rules by which people who are given access to an organization's technology and information assets must abide." Corporate policy should address both access and security breaches. Access policy is concerned with who has access to what information and from what source. SNMP management addressed this in terms of a community access policy for network management information. An example of access policy in an enterprise network could be that all employees have full access to the network. However, not everyone should have access to all corporate information, and thus accounts are established for appropriate employees to have access to appropriate hosts and applications in those hosts. These policies should be written so that all employees are fully aware of them.

However, illegal entry into systems and accessing of networks must be protected against. The policies and procedures for site security management on the Internet are dealt with in detail elsewhere [RFC 2196; NIST, 1994]. The National Computer Security Center (NCSC) has published what is known as the Orange Book, which defines a rating scheme for computers. It is based on the security design features of the computer. The issues for corporate site security using the intranet are the same as for the Internet and are applicable to them equally. It is a framework for setting security policies and procedures.

The basic guide to setting up policies and procedures is:

1. Identify what you are trying to protect
2. Determine what you are trying to protect it from
3. Determine how likely the threats are
4. Implement measures, which will protect your assets in a cost-effective manner
5. Review the process continuously and make improvements to each item if a weakness is found

The assets that need to be protected should be listed including hardware, software, data, documentation, supplies, and people who have responsibility for all of the above. The classic threats are from unauthorized access to resources and/or information, unintended and/or unauthorized disclosure of information, and denial of service. Denial of service is a serious attack on the network. The network is brought to a state in which it can no longer carry legitimate users' data. This is done either by attacking the routers or by flooding the network with extraneous traffic.

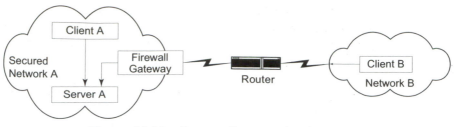

Figure 11.30 Secure Communication Network

Resources to Prevent Security Breaches

We addressed the policies and procedures in the last section. In this section, we will discuss various security breaches that are attempted to access data and systems, and the resources available to protect them.

Figure 11.30 shows a secure communication network, which is actually a misnomer. There is no fully secure system in the real world; there are only systems which are hard and time-consuming to break into, as we shall describe. Figure 11.30 shows two networks communicating with each other via a WAN, which has just one router. Server A and Client A shown in Network A are communicating with each other; and Client B in Network B is also communicating (or trying to communicate) with Server A in Network A.

Let us look at the security breach points in this scenario. Hosts in Network B may not have the privilege to access Network A. The firewall gateway shown in Figure 11.30 is used to screen traffic going in and out of secure Network A. Even if Network B has access permission to Network A, some intruder, for example one who has access to the router in the path, may intercept the message. The contents of the message, as well as source and destination identifications, can be monitored and manipulated, which are security breaches.

Security breaches can occur in the Internet and intranet environment in numerous ways. In most corporate environments, security is limited to user identification and password. Even the password is not changed often enough. This is the extent of authentication. Authorization is limited to the establishment of accounts, i.e., who can log into an application on a host. Besides normal activities of breach, we have to protect against special situations, such as when a disgruntled employee could embed virus programs in company programs and products.

11.5.3 Firewalls

The main purpose of a firewall is to protect a network from external attacks. It monitors and controls traffic into and out of a secure network. It can be implemented in a router, or a gateway, or a special host. A firewall is normally located at the gateway to a network, but it may also be implemented at host access points.

There are numerous benefits in implementing a firewall to a network. It reduces the risk of access to hosts from an external network by filtering insecure services. It can provide controlled access to the network in that only specified hosts or network segments could access some hosts. Since security protection from external threats is centralized and transparent, it reduces the annoyance to internal users while controlling the external users. A firewall could also be used to protect the privacy of a corporation. For example, services such as the utility *finger*, which provides information about employees to outsiders, can be prevented from accessing the network.

When the security policy of a company is implemented in a firewall, it is a concatenation of a higher-level access service policy, where a total service is filtered out. For example, the dial-in service can be totally denied at the service policy level, and the firewall can filter out selected services, such as the utility *finger*, which is used to obtain information on personnel.

Firewalls use packet filtering or application-level gateways as the two primary techniques of controlling undesired traffic.

Packet Filters. Packet filtering is the ability to filter packets based on protocol-specific criteria. It is done at the OSI data link, network, and transport layers. Packet filters are implemented in some commercial routers, called *screening routers* or *packet-filtering routers*. We will use the generic term of packet-filtering routers here. Although routers do not look at the transport layers, some vendors have implemented this additional feature to sell them as firewall routers. The filtering is done on the following parameters: source IP address, destination IP address, source TCP/UDP port, and destination TCP/IP port. The filtering is implemented in each port of the router and can be programmed independently.

Packet-filtering routers can either drop packets or redirect them to specific hosts for further screening, as shown in Figure 11.31. Some of the packets never reach the local network as they are trashed. For example, all packets from network segment a.b.c.0 are programmed to be rejected, as well as File Transfer Protocol (FTP) packets from *d.e.f.0:21* (note that Port 21 is a standard FTP port). The SMTP (email) and FTP packets are redirected to their respective gateways for further screening. It may be observed from the figure that the firewall is asymmetric. All incoming SMTP and FTP packets are parsed to check whether they should be dropped or forwarded. However, outgoing SMTP and FTP packets have already been screened by the gateways and do not have to be checked by the packet-filtering router.

A packet-filtering firewall works well when the rules to be implemented are simple. However, the more rules we introduce, the more difficult it is to implement. The rules have to be implemented in the right order or they may produce adverse effects. Testing and debugging are also difficult in packet filtering [Chapman, 1992].

Application-Level Gateway. An application-level gateway is used to overcome some of the problems identified in packet filtering. Figure 11.32 shows the application gateway architecture. Firewalls F1 and F2 will only forward if data are to or from the application gateway. Thus, the secured LAN is a gateway LAN. The application gateway behaves differently for each application, and filtering is handled by the proxy services in the application gateway. For example, for FTP service, the file is stored first in the application gateway and then forwarded. For TELNET service, the application gateway verifies the

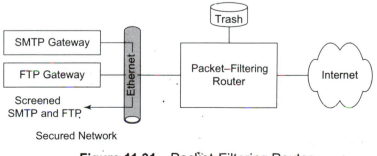

Figure 11.31 Packet-Filtering Router

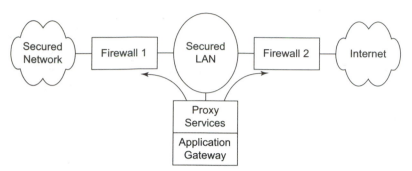

Figure 11.32 Application-Level Gateway

authentication of the foreign host, the legitimacy to communicate with the local host, and then makes the connection between the gateway and the local host. It keeps a log of all transactions.

Firewalls protect a secure site by checking addresses (such as IP address), transport parameters (such as FTP, NNTP), and applications. However, how do we protect access from an external source based on the user, who is using a false identification? Moreover, how do we protect against an intruder manipulating the data while they are traversing the network between the source and the destination? These concerns are addressed by secure communication.

11.5.4 Cryptography

For secure communication, we need to ensure integrity protection and authentication validation. **Integrity protection** makes sure that the information has not been tampered with as it traverses between the source and the destination. **Authentication validation** validates the originator identification. In other words, when Ian receives a message that identifies it coming from Rita, is it really Rita who sent the message? These two important aspects address the four security threats—modification of information, masquerade, message stream modification, and disclosure—mentioned at the beginning of Section 11.5. Besides the actual message, control and protocol handshakes need to be secure.

There are hardware solutions to authentication. However, it is not a complete solution, since the information could be intercepted and tampered with as it traverses from the source to the destination, including the user identification and password.

The technology that is best suited to achieving secure communication is software based. Its foundation lies in cryptography. Hashing or message digest, and digital signature, which we will address soon, are built on top of it to achieve integrity protection and source authentication.

Cryptographic Communication. Cryptography means secret (crypto) writing (graphy). It deals with techniques of transmitting information, for example a letter from a sender to a receiver without any intermediary being able to decipher it. You may view this as the information (letter) being translated to a special language that only the sender and receiver can interpret. Now, cryptography should also detect if somebody was able to intercept the information. Again extending our analogy, if the letter written in a secret language were to be mailed in a sealed (we mean really sealed) envelope, if somebody tampers with it, the receiver would detect it.

The basic model of cryptographic communication is shown in Figure 11.33. The input message, called **plaintext**, is encrypted by the encryption module using a **secret (encryption) key**. The encrypted message is called **ciphertext**, which traverses through an unsecure communication channel, the Internet

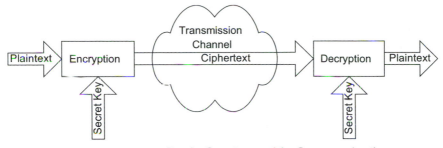

Figure 11.33 Basic Cryptographic Communication

for example. The ciphertext is unintelligible information. At the receiving end, the decryption module deciphers the message with a decryption key to retrieve the plaintext.

The first known example of cryptography is the Caesar cipher. In this scheme, each letter is replaced by another letter, which is three letters later in the alphabet (i.e., key of 3). Thus, the plaintext, *network management*, will read as *qhwzrun pdqdjhphqw* in ciphertext. Of course, the receiver knew ahead of time the secret key (3) for successfully decrypting the message back to the plaintext *network management* by moving each letter back three positions.

Secret Key Cryptography. The Caesar cipher was later enhanced by the makers of Ovaltine and distributed as Captain Midnight Secret Decoder rings. Each letter is replaced by another letter *n* letters later in the alphabet (i.e., key of *n*). Of course, the sender and the receiver have to agree ahead on the secret key for successful communication. It is the same key that is used for encryption and decryption and is called **secret key cryptography**. The encryption and decryption modules can be implemented in either hardware or software.

It is not hard to decode the above ciphertext by an intruder. It would only take a maximum of 26 attempts to decipher since there are 26 letters in the alphabet. Another encryption scheme, *monoalphabetic cipher*, is to replace each letter uniquely with another letter that is randomly chosen. Now, the maximum number of attempts for the intruder to decipher has been increased 26! (26! = 26 · 25 · 24 · …1). However, it really does not take that many attempts as there are patterns in a language.

Obviously, the key is the key (no pun intended) to the security of messages. Another aspect of the key is the convenience of using it. We will illustrate our scenario with Ian and Rita (Ian for initiator and Rita for responder so that it is easy to remember) as users at the two ends of a "secure" communication link. Ian and Rita could share a key, their "secret key," for accomplishing secure communication. However, if Ian wants to communicate with Ted (for third party), they both need to share a secret key. Soon, Ian has to remember one secret key for each person with whom he wants to communicate, which obviously is impractical. It is hard enough to remember your own passwords, if you have several of them, and which systems they go with.

Two standard algorithms implement secret key cryptography. They are Data Encryption Standard (DES) and International Data Encryption Algorithm (IDEA) [Kaufman *et al.*, 1995]. They both deal with 64-bit message blocks and create the same size ciphertext. DES uses a 56-bit key and IDEA uses a 128-bit key. DES is designed for efficient hardware implementation and consequently has a poor performance if implemented in software. In contrast to that, IDEA functions efficiently in software implementation.

Both DES and IDEA are based on the same principle of encryption. The bits in the plaintext block are rearranged using a predetermined algorithm and the secret key several times. While decrypting, the process is repeated in the reverse order for DES and is a bit more complicated for IDEA.

A message that is longer than the block length is divided into 64-bit message blocks. There are several algorithms to break the message. One of the more popular ones is the cipher block chaining (CBC) method. We learned the use of it in USM in SNMPv3 in Section 7.7. There, the message was broken using CBC and then encrypted using DES. Performing such an operation on the message, even on identical plaintext blocks, would result in dissimilar ciphertext blocks.

Public Key Cryptography. We observed that each user has to have a secret key for every user that he/she/it (a program) wants to communicate with. Public key cryptography [Diffe and Hellman, 1976; Kaufman *et al.*, 1995] overcomes the difficulty of having too many keys for using cryptography. Secret key cryptography is symmetric in that the same key is used for encryption and decryption, but public key cryptography is asymmetric with a *public key* and a *private key* (not secret key, remember secret key is symmetric and private key is not). In Figure 11.34, the public key of Ian is the key that Rita, Ted, and everybody else (that Ian wants to communicate with) would know and use to encrypt messages to Ian. The private key, which only Ian knows, is the key that Ian would use to decrypt the messages. With this scheme, there is secure communication between Ian and his communicators on a one-to-one basis. Rita's message to Ian can be read only by Ian and not by anyone else who has his public key, since the public key cannot be used to decrypt the message.

We can compare the use of asymmetric public and private keys in cryptography to a mailbox (or a bank deposit box) with two openings. There is a mail slot to drop the mail and a collection door to take out mail. Suppose it is a private mailbox in a club and has restricted access to members only. All members can open the mail slot with a public key given by the administration to drop their mail, possibly containing comments on a sensitive issue of the club. Any member's mail cannot be accessed by other members since the public key only lets the members open the mail slot to drop mail and not the collection door. The administrator with a private key can open the collection door and access the mail of all the members. Of course, this asymmetric example has more to do with access than cryptography. But, you get the idea!

The Diffe–Hellman public key algorithm is the oldest public key algorithm. It is a hybrid of secret and public key. The commonly used public key cryptography algorithm is RSA, named after its inventors, Rivest *et al.* [1978]. It does both encryption and decryption as well as digital signatures. Both the message length and the key length are variable. The commonly used key length is 512 bits. The block

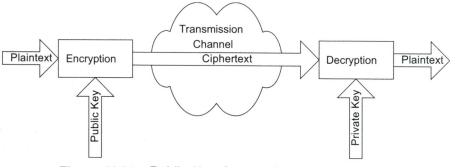

Figure 11.34 Public-Key Cryptographic Communication

size of the plaintext, which is variable, should be less than the key size. The ciphertext is always the length of the key. RSA is less efficient than either of the secret key algorithms, DES or IDEA. Hence, in practice, RSA is used to first encrypt the secret key. The message is then transmitted in one of the secret key algorithms.

Message Digest. Any telecommunications engineer is familiar with the cyclic redundancy check (CRC) detection of errors in digital transmission. This involves calculating a check sum based on the data in the frame or packet at the sending end and transmitting it along with the data. The CRC, also known as *checksum*, is computed at the receiving end and is matched against the received checksum to ensure that the packet is not corrupted. An analogous principle is used in validating the integrity of the message. In order to ensure that the message has not been tampered with between the sender and the receiver, a cryptographic CRC is added with the message. This is derived using a cryptographic hash algorithm, called *message digest* (MD). There are several versions, one of the most common being MD5. We covered the use of MD5 while discussing the authentication protocol in SNMPv3 in Chapter 7. We will look at the use of it in digital signature in the next subsection.

There are different implementations of MD5. In particular, the MD5 utility is used in FreeBSD 2.x (md5sum under LINUX). The utility takes as input a message of arbitrary length producing output consisting of a 128-bit message digest of the input. An example of MD5 utility use is shown in Figure 11.35.

As we can see from the example, the message digest for the string that we entered was generated based on the data received from standard input (from the screen). The FreeBSD version also has a test mode that can be turned on by specifying "-x" as a parameter, as shown in Figure 11.36.

A second algorithm used to obtain a hash or message digest is the Secure Hash Standard (SHS). This has been proposed by the National Institute for Standards and Technology (NIST). It is similar to MD5, but can handle a maximum message length of 2^{64} bits in contrast with MD5, which can handle

```
$ md5
The quick brown fox jumped over the lazy dog
^D
d8e8fca2dc0f896fd7cb4cb0031ba249
```

Figure 11.35 Example of an MD5 Message Digest

```
$ md5 -x
MD5 ("") = d41d8cd98f00b204e9800998ecf8427e
MD5 ("a") = 0cc175b9c0f1b6a831c399e269772661
MD5 ("abc") = 900150983cd24fb0d6963f7d28e17f72
MD5 ("message digest") = f96b697d7cb7938d525a2f31aaf161d0
MD5 ("abcdefghijklmnopqrstuvwxyz") = c3fcd3d76192e4007dfb496cca67e13b
MD5
("ABCDEFGHIJKLMNOPQRSTUVWXYZabcdefghijklmnopqrstuvwxyz012345 6789")
= d174ab98d277d9f5a5611c2c9f419d9f
MD5
("12345678901234567890123456789012345678901234567890123456
78901234567890") = 57edf4a22be3c955ac49da2e2107b67a
```

Figure 11.36 MD5 FreeBSD Version Test Mode Output

an unlimited input length of 32-byte chunks. The SHS produces an output of 160-bit, whereas the MD5 output is 128-bit long.

Some significant features of the message digest are worth mentioning. First, there is a one-to-one relationship between the input and the output messages. Thus, the input is uniquely mapped to an output digest. It is interesting to observe that even a one-bit difference in a block of 512 bits could produce a message digest that looks vastly different. In addition, the output messages are completely uncorrelated. Thus, any pattern in the input will not be recognized at the output.

Another feature of message digest is that the output digest is of constant length for a given algorithm with chosen parameters, irrespective of the input message length. In this respect, it is very similar to CRC in that CRC-32 is exactly 32 bits long. We saw in SNMPv3 that the *authKey* generated by the MD5 algorithm is exactly 16-octet long.

Lastly, the generation of a message digest is a one-way function. Given a message, we can generate a unique message digest. However, given a message digest, there is no way the original message could be generated. Thus, if a password were transmitted from a client to a server, this would protect against somebody eavesdropping and deciphering the password. This could also be used for storing the password file in a host without any human being able to decipher it.

We know that the generation of a message digest is a one-way function. We also know that no two messages could produce identical message digests. Could these two combinations ensure that the message is not tampered in transit by an unauthorized person? The answer is no. This is because if the interceptor knows which algorithm is being used, he or she could modify the message (assuming that he/she decrypts the message), generate a new message digest, and send it along with the modified message. If Ian sent the message to Rita, and Ted modified the message as per the above scenario while in transit, Rita would not know the difference. Additional protection is needed to guard against such a threat, which is achieved by attaching a digital signature to the message.

Digital Signature. In public key cryptography, or even in secret key cryptography, if Rita receives a message claiming that it is from Ian, there is no guarantee as to who sent the message. For example, somebody other than Ian who knows Rita's public key could send a message identifying himself or herself as Ian. Rita could not be absolutely sure who sent it. To overcome this problem, a digital signature can be used. Signed public-key cryptographic communication is shown in Figure 11.37.

The digital signature works in the reverse direction from that of public key cryptography. Ian can create a digital signature using his private key (marked "S" in parentheses in Figure 11.37) and Rita could validate it by reading it using Ian's public key. The digital signature depends on the message and the key. Let us consider that Ian is sending a message by email to Rita. A digital signature, which is a message digest, is generated using any hash algorithm with the combined inputs of the plaintext message and the private key of Ian. The digital signature is concatenated with the plaintext message and is encrypted using Rita's public key (marked "R" in parentheses). At the receiving end, the incoming ciphertext message is decrypted by Rita using her private key. She then generates a message digest with the combined input of the plaintext message and Ian's public key, and compares it with the digital signature received. If they match, she concludes that the message has not been tampered with. Further, she is assured that the message is from Ian, as she used Ian's public key to authenticate the source of the message.

Notice that only the originator can create the digital signature with his or her private key and others can look at it with the originator's public key and validate it, but cannot create it. A real-world analogy to digital signature is check writing. The bank can validate the signature as to its originality, but it is hard to duplicate a signature (at least manually) of the person who signed the check.

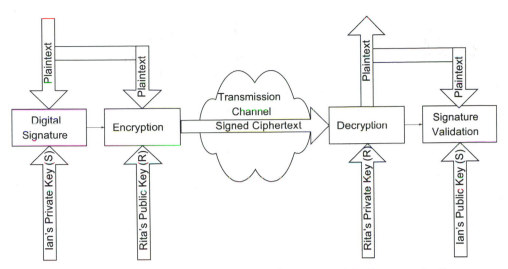

Figure 11.37 Signed Public-Key Cryptographic Communication

Digital signature is valuable in electronic commerce. Suppose Rita wants to place an order with company ABC for buying their router product. She places the order over the Internet with her digital signature attached to it. The digital signature using a public key protects both ABC and Rita regarding the validity of the order and who ordered it. It is even better than using secret key cryptography, since in the latter case, Rita could change her mind and allege that company ABC generated the order using the secret key that they have been using. In public key cryptography, she could not do that.

11.5.5 Authentication and Authorization

Authentication is the verification of the user's identification, and **authorization** is the access privilege to the information. On the Internet without security, the user's identification and password, which are used for authentication, can easily be captured by an intruder snooping on the LAN or WAN. There are several secure mechanisms for authentication, depending on complexity and sensitivity. Authorization to use the services could be a simple read, write, read–write, or no-access for a particular service. The privilege of using the service could be for an indefinite period, or a finite period, or just for one-time use.

There are two main classes of systems, which are of interest to us in the implementation of an authentication scheme. The first is the client–server environment in which there is a request–response communication between the client and the server. The client initiates a request for service to the server. The server responds with the results of the service performed. The communication is essentially two-way communication. In this environment besides authentication (and of course, an integrity check), authorization also needs to be addressed.

The second class of service is a one-way communication environment, such as email or e-commerce transaction. The message transmitted by the source is received by the receiver after a considerable delay—sometimes days if an intermediate server holds up the transaction for a long time. In such a case both the authentication and an integrity check need to be performed at the receiving end.

We will address client–server authentication systems in the next section and the one-way message authentication and integrity protection system in Section 11.5.7.

11.5.6 Client–Server Authentication Systems

We will consider four types of client–server environments and the implementation of authentication function in each: host/user environment, a ticket-granting system, an authentication system, and authentication using cryptographic function.

Host/User Authentication. We have the traditional host and user validation for authentication, both of which are not very secure. They are also not convenient to use. Host authentication involves certain hosts to be validated by the server providing the service. The host names are administered by the server administrator. The server recognizes the host by the host address. If Server S is authorized to serve a client Host C, then anybody who has an account in C could access Server S. The server maintains the list of users associated with Host C and allows access to the user. If John Smith is one of the users in C, and John wants to access the server from another Workstation W, the workstation W has to be authenticated as a client of S. If not, John is out of luck. Further, his name has to be added to the list of users in W to access S. To make the environment flexible, every client with every possible user is added to the server negating the secure access feature!

Let us consider user authentication, which is done by the user providing identification and a password. The main problem with the password is that it is detected easily by eavesdropping, say using a network probe. To protect against the threat of eavesdropping, the security is enhanced by encrypting the password before transmission. Commercial systems are available that generate a one-time password associated with a password server that validates it when presented by the service-providing host. The user uses a unique key each time to obtain the password, such as in the ticket-granting system (next section).

Ticket-Granting System. We will explain the ticket-granting system with the most popular example of Kerberos, which was a system developed by MIT as part of their Project Athena. Figure 11.38 shows the ticket-granting system with Kerberos. Kerberos consists of an authentication server and a ticket-granting server. The user logs into a client workstation and sends a login request to the authentication server. After verifying that the user is on the access control list, the authentication server gives an encrypted ticket-granting ticket to the client. The client workstation requests a password from the user, which it uses to decrypt the message from the authentication server. The client then interacts with the

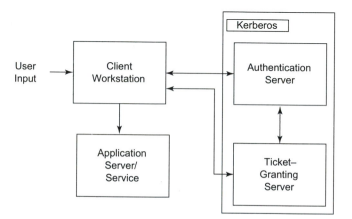

Figure 11.38 Ticket-Granting System

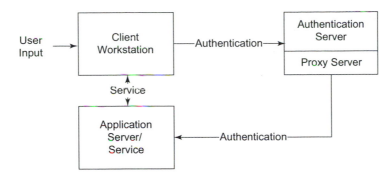

Figure 11.39 Authentication Server

ticket-granting server and obtains a service-granting ticket and a session key to use the application server. The client workstation then requests service from the application server giving the service-granting ticket and the session key. The application server, after validation of the ticket and the session key, provides service to the user. Of course, this processing happens in the background. It is transparent to the user, whose only interaction is with the client workstation requesting application service.

Authentication Server System. An authentication server system, shown in Figure 11.39, is somewhat similar to the ticket-granting system except that there is no ticket granted. No login identification and password pair is sent out of the client workstation. The user authenticates to a central authentication server, which has jurisdiction over a domain of servers. The central authentication server, after validation of the user, acts as a proxy agent to the client and authenticates the user to the application server. This is transparent to the user, and the client proceeds to communicate with the application server. This is the architecture of Novell LAN.

Authentication Using Cryptographic Functions. Cryptographic authentication uses cryptographic functions. The sender can encrypt an authentication request to the receiver, who decrypts the message to validate the identification of the user. Algorithms and keys are used to encrypt and decrypt messages, which we will address now.

11.5.7　Message Transfer Security

The one-way message transfer system is non-interactive. For example, if Rita receives an email from a person who claims to be Ian, she needs to authenticate Ian as the originator of the message, as well as to ensure that nobody has tampered with the message. This could also be the situation in the case where Ian sends a sell order from his mobile station in his car. Ted could intercept the message and alter the number of shares or the price. We will treat all these under the category of secure mail systems.

There are three secure mail systems—privacy-enhanced mail (PEM), pretty good privacy (PGP), and X.400-based mail system [Kaufman *et al.*, 1995]. All three schemes are variations of the signed public-key cryptographic communication discussed in Section 11.5.4 and shown in Figure 11.37. We will describe PEM and PGP in this section. X-400 is a set of specifications for an email system defined by the ITU Standards Committee and adopted by OSI. It is a framework rather than implementation-ready specification. We will also review SNMPv3 secure communication that we covered in Chapter 7 as it bears a close resemblance to the message transfer security.

Privacy-Enhanced Mail (PEM). Privacy-enhanced mail (PEM) was developed by IETF, and specifications are documented in RFC 1421–RFC 1424. It is intended to provide PEM using end-to-end cryptography between originator and recipient processes [RFC 1421]. The PEM provides privacy enhancement services (what else!), which are defined as (1) confidentiality, (2) authentication, (3) message integrity assurance, and (4) non-repudiation of origin. The cryptographic key, called the *data encryption key* (DEK), could be either a secret key or a public key based on the specific implementation and is thus flexible. However, the originating and terminating ends must have common agreement (obviously!).

Figure 11.40 shows three PEM processes defined by IETF: MIC-CLEAR, MIC-ONLY, and ENCRYPTED based on message integrity and encryption scheme. Only the originating end is shown. In all three procedures, reverse procedures are used to extract the message and validate the originator ID and message integrity. The differences between the three procedures are dependent on the extent of cryptography used and message encoding. The **message integrity code** (MIC) is generated as discussed in Section 11.5.4 on digital signature and included as part of email in all three procedures.

The specification provides two types of keys—a **data-encrypting key** (DEK) and an **interexchange key** (IK). The DEK is a random number generated on a per message basis. The DEK is used to encrypt the message text and also to generate an MIC, if needed. The IK, which is a long-range key agreed upon between the sender and the receiver, is used to encrypt DEK for transmission within the message. The IK is either a public or a secret key based on the type of cryptographic exchange used.

If an asymmetric public key is used to encrypt the message, then the sender cannot repudiate ownership of the message. Legal evidence of message transactions is stored in the data, which are used in applications such as e-commerce. Another common characteristic of these procedures is the first step in converting the user-supplied plaintext to a canonical message text representation, defined as equivalent to the inter-SMTP representation of message text. The final output in each procedure is used as the text portion of the email in the electronic mail system.

Figure 11.40(a) shows the MIC-CLEAR procedure and is the simplest of the three. The MIC generated is concatenated with the SMTP text and is inserted as the text portion in the email.

In the MIC-ONLY procedure, shown in Figure 11.40(b), the SMTP text is encoded into a printable character set. The printable character set consists of a limited set of characters that is assured to be present at all sites and thus make the intermediate sites transparent to the message. The MIC is concatenated with the encoded message and is fed to the email system.

Figure 11.40(c) is the most sophisticated of the three procedures. The SMTP text is padded, if needed, and encrypted. A public key is the best choice here, because it guarantees the originator ID. The encrypted message, encrypted MIC, and the DEK are all encoded in printable code to pass through the mail system as ordinary text. They are concatenated and fed to the email system.

Pretty Good Privacy (PGP). Pretty good privacy (PGP) is a secure mail package developed by Phil Zimmerman that is available in the public domain. Figure 11.41 shows the various modules in the PGP process at the originating end. The reverse process occurs at the receiving end and is not shown in the figure. PGP is a package in the sense that it does not reinvent the wheel. It defines a clever procedure that utilizes various available modules to perform the functions needed to transmit a secure message, such as email.

The signature generation module uses MD5 to generate a hash code of the message and encrypts it with the sender's private key using an RSA algorithm. Either IDEA or RSA is employed to generate the encrypted message. IDEA is more efficient than RSA, but secret key maintenance is necessary in contrast to RSA's use of a public key. The encrypted message is compressed using ZIP. The signature is

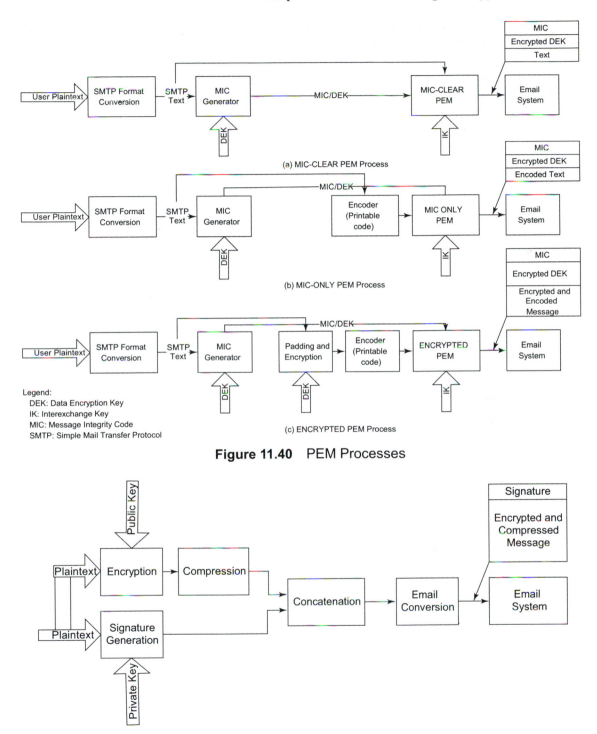

Figure 11.40 PEM Processes

Figure 11.41 PGP Process

concatenated with the encrypted message and converted to ASCII format using the Radix-64 conversion module to make it compatible with the email system.

PGP is similar to ENCRYPTED PEM with additional compression capability. The main difference between PGP and PEM is how the public key is administered. In PGP, it is up to the owner. In PEM, it is formally done by a certification authority (the Internet Policy Certification Authority (PCA) Registration Authority). In practice, PGP is used more than PEM. Both PGP and PEM provide more than a secure mail service. We can send any message or file.

SNMPv3 Security. We dealt with secure transmission in SNMPv3 in Chapter 7. Although an NMS–management agent behaves like a client–server system, the security features are similar to the message transfer cryptography. We will compare the processes studied in Section 7.7 to message transfer cryptography. Figure 11.42 shows a conceptualized representation of Figure 7.13 for an outgoing message.

In an NMS, the user password and authoritative SNMP engine ID (network management agent ID) are used to generate an authentication key by the USM. This is equivalent to the DEK in PEM or the private key in PGP.

Either the authentication key or preferably a different encryption key is used to generate an encrypted *scopedPDU* by the privacy module. This is similar (but not identical) to encryption of the message in PEM and PGP.

The USM module prepares the whole message with the encrypted *scopedPDU* and other parameters. The authentication key and the whole message are used as inputs to generate HMAC, which is equivalent to the signature in PEM and PGP. The authentication module combines the signature and the whole message to output the authenticated whole message. In an incoming message, the authentication module is provided the whole message, authentication key, and the HMAC as input to validate the authentication.

11.5.8 Network Protection from Virus Attacks

In the current Internet environment, we cannot leave the subject of security without mentioning the undesired and unexpected virus attack on networks and hosts. It is usually a program that, when executed, causes harm by making copies and inserting them into other programs. It contaminates a network by importing an infected program from outside sources, either online or via disks.

The impact of virus infection manifests itself in many ways. Among the serious ones are preventing access to your hard disk by infecting the boot track, compromising your processor (an outside source controlling your computer), flooding your network with extraneous traffic that prevents your hosts from using it, etc.

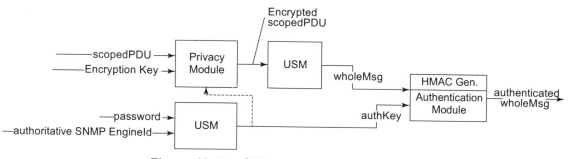

Figure 11.42 SNMP Secure Communication

Generally, viruses are recognized by patterns and virus checkers do just that. Apart from the common sense of preventive measures, it is wise to have the latest virus checkers installed on all your hosts. It should be scheduled to run periodically. It also checks the inputs and outputs of the processor for possible virus infection.

11.6 ACCOUNTING MANAGEMENT

Accounting management is probably the least developed function of network management application. We have discussed the gathering of statistics using RMON probes in Chapter 8 and in Section 11.3.4. Accounting management could also include the use of individual hosts, administrative segments, and external traffic.

Accounting of individual hosts is useful for identifying some hidden costs. For example, the library function in universities and large corporations consumes significant resources and may need to be accounted for functionally. This can be done by using the RMON statistics on hosts.

The cost of operations for an information management services department is based on the service that it provides to the rest of the organization. For planning and budget purposes, this may need to be broken into administrative group costs. The network needs to be configured so that all traffic generated by a department can be gathered from monitoring segments dedicated to that department.

External traffic for an institution is handled by service providers. The tariff is negotiated with the service provider based on the volume of traffic and traffic patterns, such as peak traffic and average traffic. Internal validation of the service provider's billing is a good management practice.

11.7 REPORT MANAGEMENT

We have elected to treat report management as a special category, although it is not assigned a special functionality in the OSI classification. Reports for various application functions—configuration, fault, performance, security, and accounting—could normally be addressed in those sections. The reasons for us to deal with reports as a special category are the following. A well-run network operations center goes unnoticed. Attention is paid normally only when there is a crisis or apparent poor service. It is important to generate, analyze, and distribute various reports to the appropriate groups, even when the network is running smoothly.

We can classify such reports into three categories: (1) planning and management reports, (2) system reports, and (3) user reports.

Planning and management reports keep the upper management appraised as to the status of network and system operations. It is also helpful for planning purposes. Budgeting needs to be done for capital and operational expenses. Table 11.1 lists some of the planning and management reports under different categories. Since the information management services department's main product is service, it is important to keep the management apprised of how the quality of service meets the SLA (more on Section 11.9). Reports on this category include network availability, systems availability, problem reports, service response to problem reports, and customer satisfaction. Trends in traffic should address traffic patterns and volume of traffic in the internal network, as well as external traffic. Information technology is constantly evolving and hence management should be kept apprised of upcoming technology and the plan for migration to new technology. Finally, for budgeting purposes, the cost of operations by function, use, and personnel needs to be presented.

Table 11.1 Planning and Management Reports

CATEGORY	REPORTS
Quality of service/service level agreement	Network availability
	Systems availability
	Problem reports
	Service response
	Customer satisfaction
Traffic trends	Traffic patterns
	Analysis of internal traffic volume
	Analysis of external traffic volume
Technology trends	Current status
	Technology migration projection
Cost of operations	Function
	Use
	Personnel

Table 11.2 System Reports

CATEGORY	REPORTS
Traffic	Traffic load—internal
	Traffic load—external
Failures	Network failures
	System failures
Performance	Network
	Servers
	Applications

The day-to-day functioning of engineering and operations requires operation-oriented reports. Traffic, failure, and performance are the important categories, as shown in Table 11.2. A pattern analysis of these reports will be helpful in tuning the network for optimum results.

Users are partners in network services and should be kept informed as to how well any SLA is being met. Some service objectives are met by joint efforts of the users and the information management services department. Table 11.3 shows some typical user reports. The SLA normally includes network availability, system availability, traffic load, and performance. In addition, users may require special reports. For example, the administration may want reports on payroll or personnel.

11.8 POLICY-BASED MANAGEMENT

We discussed network and system management tools in the last chapter. In this chapter, we covered the application tools and technology geared toward network and system management. For these to be

Table 11.3 User Reports

CATEGORY	REPORTS
Service level agreement	Network availability
	System availability
	Traffic load
	Performance
User-specific reports	User-defined reports

successfully deployed in an operational environment, we need to define a policy and preferably build that into the system, i.e., implement policy management. For example, network operations center personnel may observe an alarm on the NMS, at which time they need to know what action they should take. This depends on what component failed, severity or criticality of the failure, when the failure happened, etc. In addition, they need to know who should be informed and how, and that depends on when the failure occurred and what SLAs have been contracted with the user. We illustrated this with an example of CBR in Section 11.4.3, where a policy restraint was used to increase the bandwidth as opposed to reducing load in resolving a trouble ticket.

As we mentioned in Section 11.5.1 on security management, policy plays an equally important, if not greater, role as the technical area. Without policy establishment and enforcement, security management is not of much use.

Our focus here is not the administrative side of the subject, although it is important, but with the technical aspects of policy implementation in network management. Figure 11.43 is policy management architecture proposed by [Lewis, 1996] for network management. It consists of a domain space of objects, a rule space consisting of rules, a policy driver that controls action to be performed, and action space that implements the actions and attributes of the network being controlled.

The objects in the domain space are events such as alarms in fault management, packet loss in performance, and authentication failure in security management. The objects have attributes. For example, attributes of alarms are severity, type of device, location of device, etc. Attributes of packet loss can be

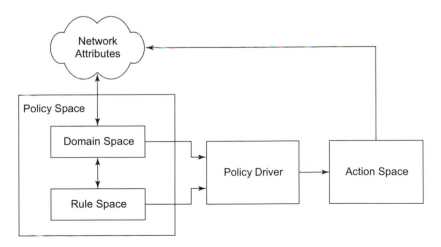

Figure 11.43 Policy Management Architecture

the layer at which packets are lost, the percentage loss, etc. Rules in the rule space define the possible actions that could be taken under various object conditions. It is the same as in RBR, with if–then, condition–action. The policy driver is the control mechanism, which is similar to the inference engine. Thus, the objects in the domain space and the set of rules in the rule space are combined for a policy decision that is made by the policy driver. It is worth bringing the distinction between a rule and policy here. In the operations center, a rule could be that all network failures should be reported to the engineering group. A statement that this applies to the operations personnel at the network management desk makes the rule a policy. Because the responsibility is assigned to specific individuals, failing to do so will be blamed on the person on duty at that time. The action space executes the right-hand side of the rules by changing the attributes of the network and/or executing an external action. In resolving the throughput problem using the CBR technique in Section 11.4.3, we discussed the options regarding the actions to be taken. Whether network load should be controlled or more bandwidth be allocated is a policy decision. This can be implemented as an RBR in the policy rule space. An example of external action could be to page engineering for a severe network failure.

11.9   SERVICE LEVEL MANAGEMENT

Let us keep building a superstructure of telecommunications management to bring us up to date on the technology. We addressed policy management in the last section that ensures the optimal and enterprise-wide consistent use of the network and system management systems. However, the establishment of corporate policy does not stop at the best and consistent use of management tools. The network, systems, and business applications that run on them are there to serve customers, and customer satisfaction is essential for the success of the business [Adams and Willetts, 1996]. Hence, policy management should be driven by service level management, which is the second to the top layer in the TMN model shown in Figure 11.11.

We have illustrated implementing service level management in Chapter 10 on TMN with operations systems. An operations system, in general, does an exclusive or special-purpose function. With the availability of element management and NMSs, it is time for the arrival of a generalized service level management. Service level management is defined as the process of (1) identifying services and characteristics associated with them, (2) negotiating an SLA, (3) deploying agents to monitor and control the performance of network, systems, and application components, and (4) producing service level reports [Lewis, 1999]. Lewis compares the definition of service level management to quality of service (QoS) management defined by the Object Modeling Group (OMG).

The characteristics associated with services are service parameters, service levels, component parameters, and component-to-service mappings. A service parameter is an index into the performance of a service—for example, the availability of a business application for a customer. The business application depends upon various underlying components—for example, network devices, systems, and applications on the systems. Thus, there is a one-to-many mapping between the service parameter and the underlying component parameters. The availability of the business application in the SLA can be defined in terms of the availability of these underlying components. In this case, the availability service parameter is a function of the availability component parameter.

An SLA is a contract between the service provider and the customer, specifying the services to be provided and the quality of those services that the service provider promises to meet. The pricing for the service depends on the QoS commitment.

The objective of service level management is to ensure customer satisfaction by meeting or exceeding the commitments made in the SLA and to guide policy management. In addition, it provides input to the business management system.

Summary

We have learned in this chapter how to apply all the knowledge we have gained in the book to practical situations. We have dealt with the five categories of OSI application functions, namely configuration, fault, performance, security, and accounting.

Configuration management involves, in addition to setting and resetting the parameters of network components, provisioning of the network and inventory management. Operation systems perform the latter functions. Network topology management is concerned with discovery and mapping of the network for operations that can be used to monitor them from a centralized operations center.

Fault detection consists of fault detection and fault isolation. Similarly, performance degradation involves detection and isolation. We dealt with these subjects in a simplistic manner in the early part of the chapter and in a more complex manner in the latter part. We discussed the emerging topic of correlation technology and the various correlation techniques that have been implemented in systems. They correlate events or alarms, which arrive from multiple sources, and determine the root cause of the problem. A knowledge base built upon heuristic experience, as well as algorithmic procedures, is used in such systems, either for the selection of inputs or for reasoning.

While we addressed the issues of performance management, we discussed the performance metrics and the important role of performance statistics in network management.

Security management played a small part in SNMP management, but plays an extremely sensitive and critical role in overall network management. We have dealt with this in detail in this chapter. We covered the importance of policies and procedures. We looked at the various means of how information can be accessed, tampered with, or destroyed. These are done by unauthorized and perverted personnel. We also learned how to protect, if not completely at least partially, against such attacks. In this context, we discussed various authentication and authorization procedures. There are sophisticated cryptographic methods to transport information across unsecured channels to ensure secure communication. We talked about secret and public keys in cryptography to accomplish this. We briefly addressed the issue of how to protect our networks and systems against the growing menace of virus attacks.

From a business management viewpoint, we discussed the methods of using the statistical data gathered from the network to generate accounting applications. Reports play an essential role in the management of information services. We described the three classes of reports: planning and management, system, and user. We gave examples of the types of reports that are useful in each class.

Many of the network and service management decisions are policy based. We discussed how this could be built into the system that would help personnel who are expected to implement those policies.

We brought this chapter to a conclusion discussing service level management. Service level management helps satisfy customer needs. A service level agreement between the customer and the service provider defines the needs of the customer and the commitments of the service provider.

Exercises

1. You are asked to do a study of the use pattern of 24,000 workstations in an academic institution. Make the following assumptions for your study:
   You are pinging each station periodically. The message size in both directions is 128 bytes long. The NMS you are using to do the study is on a 10-Mbps LAN, which functions with 30% efficiency. What would be the frequency of your ping if you were not to exceed 5% overhead?

2. List and contrast the tools available to discover network components.
3. The autodiscovery in some NMSs is done by the network management system starting with an *arp* query to the local router.

   (a) How would you determine the IP address of the local router?
   (b) Determine the local router of your workstation.

4. You are responsible for designing the autodiscovery module of an NMS. Outline the procedure and the software tools that you would use.
5. Redraw Figure 11.4 and Figure 11.5 for VLAN based on IP address.
6. You are the manager of a NOC. Set up a procedure that would help your operators track the failure of a workstation that is on a virtual LAN.
7. What MIB object would you monitor for measuring the collision rate on an Ethernet LAN?
8. Ethernet performance degrades when the collision ratio reaches 30–40%. Explain how you would use the 802.3 MIB [RFC 1398] to measure the collision ratio of an Ethernet LAN. We will define the collision ratio of the LAN as (total number of collisions/number of packets offered to the LAN) measured on the Ethernet interface.
9. Repeat Exercise 7 using an RMON MIB.
10. (a) The trap alarm thresholds are set at two levels—rising and falling. Explain the reasoning behind this.

    (b) Define all the RMON parameters to be set for generating and resetting alarms when the collision rate on an Ethernet LAN exceeds 120,000 collisions per second and falls below 100,000 collisions per second. Use *eventIndex* values of 1 and 2 for event generation for the rising and falling thresholds.

11. Download the MRTG tool and measure the following performance statistics on a subnetwork:

    (a) Current data rate—incoming and outgoing
    (b) Trend over the past 12 months

12. Review RFC 2064 and write a one- or two-page (maximum) report on the NeTraMet flow meter.
13. For Figure 11.8 network configuration, specify:

    (a) RBR rules
    (b) Inference engine actions to accomplish the following:

    Display a red alarm for a failed component.
    Display a yellow alarm for a component that is one layer higher (i.e., one component ahead in its path).

    Display blue alarms on the icons two or more layers higher.
14. Write a pseudocode for MBR to detect failure of the components shown in Figure 11.11.
15. Describe three scenarios that require event correlation and explain clearly why each one needs it.
16. (a) Describe (or select one from Exercise 12) a scenario that clearly requires event correlation.

    (b) Discuss how each method discussed (with the exception of the finite state machine model) would approach the task.
    (c) Evaluate each method.

17. (a) Derive the minimum number of symptoms required to uniquely identify n problems using codebook correlation.

    (b) Draw a chart with the number of problems on the x-axis and the number of symptoms on the y-axis.

18. The causality graph for a network is shown in Figure 11.44.
    (a) Derive a codebook matrix for the causality graph.
    (b) Derive the correlation matrix, which is a minimal codebook.
    (c) Derive the correlation matrix with a Hamming distance of 2.

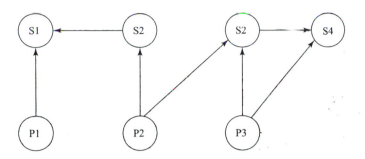

Figure 11.44 Exercise 18

19. (a) Assume that in a monoalphabetic cipher encryption scheme, both alphabet and digits (0–9) can be used interchangeably. Suppose an intruder tries to decipher it knowing the algorithm, but not the key. How many attempts would it take on the average to decipher the message?
    (b) If you are given a powerful computer with a nanosecond instruction period to decipher the message, could you do it in your lifetime? How confident are you with your answer?

20. State three important differences in the characteristics between authentication and encryption algorithms.

21. (a) You own the public key of Ian. What functions of secure email can you perform with that?
    (b) Is it safe for you to include your public key with your email address? Draw a comparison to regular mail.

22. Using md5 utility under FreeBSD 2.x (or md5sum under LINUX), generate a message digest of a file provided by your instructor.

23. Describe the procedure at the originating end when Ian wants to send a secure message using PEM simultaneously to both Rita and Ted. He communicates with Rita using a secret key and with Ted using a public key.

24. Repeat Exercise 23 using PGP.

PART IV

Broadband Network Management

Part IV, and the book, ends by discussing broadband network management and future trends in network management technology. The demarcation of telecommunications and computer communications is becoming increasingly fuzzy in broadband communication. The treatment and influence of ATM, MPLS, and SONET/SDH/DWDM on the WAN segment of broadband network is covered in Chapter 12.

Broadband service to home uses the wired medium of cable, ADSL, and PON for access network from WAN to the customer premises. Management considerations of access networks are discussed in Chapter 13. Other alternatives to bring broadband to home are fixed and mobile wireless access networks, which are addressed in Chapter 14.

Chapter 15 is devoted to Home Networking. There are numerous options available, which include Ethernet LAN, Wireless LAN (WLAN), telephone cable, power line, and IEEE 1394 FireWire™, as well as PANs. We cover the two most popular of these, namely Ethernet LAN and IEEE 802.11-based WLAN and WiFi.

Chapter 16 discusses the evolution of network management technologies to the current and future ones. With the rapid growth of the Internet and Web technology, the industry has migrated to Web-based management. A Web interface to a traditional network management system, such as SNMP, is the early implementation of this technology. We then address embedded Web-based management, Desktop Management Interface (DMI), for managing PCs and servers, and Web-Based Enterprise Management (WBEM) that has been developed by the Desktop Management Task Force (DMTF). You will be introduced to two future management technologies, which are based on CORBA and XML. There has been significant progress in developing new industrial standards in NMS, OSS, and BSS systems recently, which are also addressed.

Broadband Network Management: WAN

12.1   BROADBAND NETWORK AND SERVICES

As new technologies emerge, service providers offer new services to commercial and residential communities using those technologies. In turn, offering of new services by service providers is propelling information technology to new heights. This is especially true in broadband technology. Let us first define what broadband network and services are, which we briefly introduced in Section 2.7.

The broadband network and the narrowband Integrated Services Digital Network (ISDN) are multimedia networks that provide integrated analog and digital services over the same network. Narrowband ISDN is low-bandwidth network that can carry two 56 kilobaud rate channels. The broadband network can transport very high data rate signals. The narrowband ISDN is also known as Basic ISDN.

There are three types of information technology services: voice, video, and data. In the traditional terminology, voice and video services are transported over the telecommunication network. The information may be transported over telecommunication facilities in either an analog or a digital mode. The telecommunication network can be topologically separated into a wide area network (WAN) and local loops. The former serves transportation over long distance between switching offices, and the latter covers the "last mile" from the switching office to the customer premises.

As we saw in Chapter 1, data services are transported over the computer network, which is made up of LANs and WANs. The switches and multiplexers in the telecommunication network are replaced with bridges, routers, and gateways. The computer network uses the facilities of the telecommunication network for transportation over WAN.

The broadband network has several interpretations. One of the chief characteristics of broadband service is the integration of voice, video, and data services over the same transportation medium; in other words, it is multimedia transportation networking. Sometimes, the broadband network is confused with high-speed data network, either dedicated or combined with real-time voice or video, especially in the data traffic arena. However, we limit our definition of the broadband network to those that can handle multimedia service of voice, video, and data. The broadband network is also called the Broadband Integrated Services Digital Network (B-ISDN).

The early form of the integrated services network is the Basic ISDN. It consists of two basic channels: B-channels, 56-kilobaud rate each, combined with an 8-kilobaud signaling channel, D-channel. Together, they are referred to as 2B+D. As we stated earlier, it is also called narrowband ISDN. However, on-line video requires a much larger bandwidth. Besides, voice and video require low latency and latency fluctuations, which are achieved by ATM technology. These necessities have led to the early implementation of broadband ISDN, more succinctly referred to as the broadband network.

The broadband network and service have contributed significantly to advances in three network segments of WAN, access network, and home/customer premises equipment (CPE) network. In the WAN segment, protocols used in addition to IP are the asynchronous transfer mode (ATM), the Synchronous Optical Network (SONET)/the Synchronous Digital Hierarchy (SDH), and Multiprotocol Label Switching (MPLS). The ATM technology can be viewed as a hybrid of circuit- and packet-switched transmission modes. As a switch, the ATM switch makes a physical connection of a virtual circuit. However, the data are transmitted as cells (or packets) unlike in a circuit-switched connection. In Section 2.6 we introduced ATM using cell technology. The data rate of SONET/SDH WAN is an integral multiple of basic OC-1 (Optical Carrier)-1/STS (Synchronous Transport Signal), which is 51.84 Mbps. MPLS, as mentioned in Section 2.6, evolved as the broadband protocol and takes advantage of the high performance of ATM and the richness in features of IP and Ethernet.

Broadband access technology is implemented using one of five technologies. Hybrid fiber coax (HFC) or cable modem technology is a two-way interactive multimedia communication system using fiber and coaxial cable facilities and cable modems. The second technology uses a digital subscriber line (DSL). There are several variations of implementing this, generically referred to as xDSL. For example, ADSL stands for Asymmetric DSL. We will learn about the various DSL technologies in Chapter 13. The third and fourth technologies use wireless transmission from the switching office or the head end to the customer premises. Transmission in the two cases is either terrestrial or via a satellite. The fifth technology is the mobile wireless technology. Mobile wireless technology is deployed as either access technology using GSM (Global System for Mobile Communications)/GPRS (General Packet Radio Service) or CDMA (Code Division Multiple Access), or as a home/CPE network using WiFi (IEEE 802.3) protocol. We will discuss these access technologies in Chapters 13–15.

Figure 2.30, which is duplicated here as Figure 12.1 shows a broadband network. The WAN is MPLS/IP/ATM. The WAN is linked to the customer premises using either optical links, OC-n (Optical Carrier-n)/STS (Synchronous Transport Signal), or a broadband link with emerging access technology (HFC, xDSL, or wireless). The customer network consists of two classes, residential customers and corporate customers with campus-like network. The residential customers are either residential homes or small corporations that use broadband services, but do not require the high-speed access network to WAN. Corporate customers need high-speed access and connect optical or synchronous (E1/T1) links.

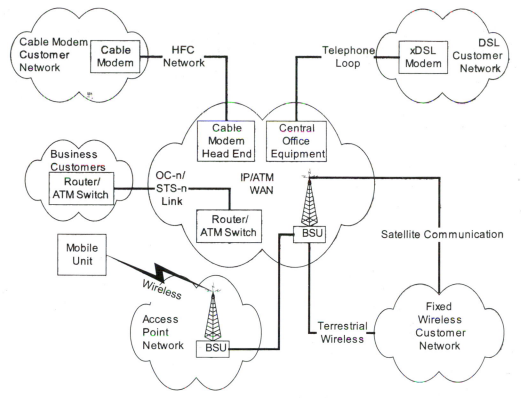

Figure 12.1 Broadband Service Networks

Radio, video (television), Internet Service Provider (ISP), and other service providers constitute the service providers. Multiple services are multiplexed at the central office or the Multiple Service Operator (MSO) head end and are piped to the customer premises via common facilities. The service providers interface with WAN via gateways.

The management of a broadband network is more complex than that of either the conventional computer network, which is mostly based on IP, or the telecommunication network. It is based on MPLS and ATM WAN technology and broadband access technology. An ATM network is based on switches with point-to-point connections (in contrast to one-to-many connections as in broadcast/multicast protocols). It is also a connection-oriented protocol and needs to be integrated in the connectionless Internet environment. These provide challenges to the management of an ATM network. The ATM network is slowly migrating to the MPLS network. However, it is still in extensive use and hence is included here as a broadband WAN. The MPLS protocol can be used with either ATM or IP; and the management requirements and the management information bases (MIBs) are still evolving. We will discuss ATM technology in Section 12.2 and ATM network management in Section 12.3.

12.2 ATM TECHNOLOGY

The ATM has helped bring about the merger of computer and telecommunication networks. There are five important concepts comprising ATM technology [Keshav, 1997]. They are (1) virtual path–virtual circuit (VP–VC), (2) fixed packet size or cells, (3) small packet size, (4) statistical multiplexing, and (5) integrated services. The implementation of these concepts in a network that is made up of ATM switches achieves high-speed network that can transport all three services (voice, video, and data). The desired quality of service is provided to individual streams (unlike the current Internet) at the same time. The network is also easily scaleable. The ATM Forum, an organization that specifies standards for ATM implementation, has also provided a framework for network management, which we will address in Section 12.3.

The subject of ATM is full of acronyms. Hence, we have included a special acronym table, Table 12.1 that contains those that we use here. There are many more acronyms associated with ATM.

Table 12.1 ATM Acronyms

AAL	ATM Adaptation Layer
ABR	Available Bit Rate
AMC	Agent Management Entity
ATM	Asynchronous Transfer Mode
BICI	Broadband Intercarrier Interface
BISDN	Broadband Integrated Services Digital Network
BISSI	Broadband Inter Switching System Interface
CBR	Constant Bit Rate
DS3	Digital Signal 3
DXI	Digital Exchange Interface
ELAN	Emulated Local Area Network
ILMI	Interim/Integrated Local Management Interface
IME	Interface Management Entity
LATA	Local Access and Transport Area
LCD	Loss of Cell Delineation
LE	LAN Emulation
LE ARP	LAN Emulation Address Resolution Protocol
LOF	Loss of Frame
LOP	Loss of Pointer
LOS	Loss of Signal
QoS	Quality of Service
SDH	Synchronous Digital Hierarchy
UBR	Unspecified Bit Rate
UNI	User-Network Interface
VBR-rt	Variable Bit Rate—real time
VBR-nrt	Variable Bit Rate—non-real time
VC	Virtual Channel
VCC	Virtual Channel Connection
VCI	Virtual Channel Identifier
VCL	Virtual Channel Link
VP	Virtual Path
VPC	Virtual Path Connection
VPI	Virtual Path Identifier
VPL	Virtual Path Link

12.2.1   Virtual Path–Virtual Circuit

We learned about the cell transmission mode in Chapter 2. As shown in Figure 2.28(c) and discussed in Section 2.6.4, it combines the best of the circuit- and packet-switched modes of transmission. The packets are all of the same size and are small in size. Each cell has the full bandwidth of the medium, and the cells are statistically multiplexed. The packets all take the same path using the VP–VC concept. This mode of transmission is called the asynchronous transfer mode (ATM) and is one of the fundamental concepts of ATM technology. Let us now look at other aspects of ATM technology.

We discussed in Section 2.4.10 how the VP–VC concept is used in packet switches. Figures 2.27(a) and (b) in Chapter 2 show the distinction between the datagram and the virtual circuit configuration. In ATM technology, the virtual circuit configuration is used. A virtual circuit that has been established between two stations, A and Z, is shown in Figure 12.2. The routing tables in the ATM switches, A, B, and D, associated with this virtual circuit are shown in Figure 12.2. The virtual circuit is first established prior to sending the data. In our example, the virtual circuit is the combination of virtual circuit links VCI-1, VCI-2, VCI-3, and VCI-4. Once the virtual circuit is established, all packets are transported in the sequence in which they were transmitted by the source along the same path for a given session. Thus, packets 1, 2, and 3 transmitted by Station A arrive at Station Z in the correct sequence traversing the same links. Since the path is fixed for the entire session, the transmission rate is considerably increased just as in circuit-switched TDM transmission (Table 12.2).

Although there is enhanced speed of transmission of packets, there is delay associated with pre-establishing the links for the virtual circuit. This delay is reduced by pre-assigning links to a virtual circuit. This is done by grouping a number of virtual circuits between two switches into a virtual path. A virtual

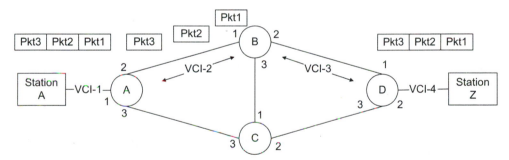

Figure 12.2   Virtual Circuit Configuration

Table 12.2   A–Z Virtual Circuit-Routing Tables

SWITCH	INPUT VCI/PORT	OUTPUT VCI/PORT
A	VCI-1/Port-1	VCI-2/Port-2
	VCI-2/Port-2	VCI-1/Port-1
B	VCI-2/Port-1	VCI-3/Port-2
	VCI-3/Port-2	VCI-2/Port-1
D	VCI-3/Port-1	VCI-4/Port-2
	VCI-4/Port-2	VCI-3/Port-1

path identifier (VPI) comprises virtual circuit identifiers (VCIs). Thus, establishing the route from Station A to Station Z in our example is to do a look-up of the VPI–VCI tables. The price that we pay for adopting this mechanism is that some VCIs may remain idle during non-busy traffic period, and thus waste the bandwidth. However, this wasted bandwidth is a lot less than that for dedicated physical links in a circuit-switched transmission mode.

The VP–VC can be established on a per session basis or on a permanent basis between a pair of end stations that carry large volumes of traffic. In the former case, the circuit is established as and when needed and torn down after the session is over. This is called the switched virtual circuit (SVC). When the connection is established for long periods of time and not switched between sessions, a permanent virtual circuit (PVC) is established.

12.2.2 ATM Packet Size

ATM packets are of fixed size, each 53 bytes long. A fixed-size packet was chosen so that fast and efficient switches can be built. Many switches can operate in parallel if they all perform switching on the same-size packets.

The ATM packet size of 53 bytes has a header of 5 bytes and a payload of 48 bytes. This size was arrived at by optimizing between two factors. The packet size should be as small as possible to reduce the delay in switching and packetization. However, it should be large enough to reduce the overhead of the header relative to the payload.

12.2.3 Integrated Service

The main challenge in integrating the three services is to meet the different requirements of each. Voice and video traffic require low tolerance on variations in delay and low end-to-end (roundtrip) delays for good interactive communication. Once voice data are lost or delayed, real-time communication is garbled and we cannot reproduce it. Thus, it has to be given the highest priority of service in transmission. This is true with the voice portion of the information in video transmission. Further, the voice and video have to be synchronized. Otherwise, it will be like watching a movie with the conversation lagging behind the mouth motion due to wrong threading of the film. Pure video without sound can have less priority than audio.

Data traffic can have a much higher tolerance on latency. It is primarily a store and forward technology and the traffic itself is inherently bursty in nature. However, data speed is important for large data transmission applications, although it has the lowest priority in transmission.

It is possible to set the priority in ATM switches by assigning priority to the different services. This is accomplished by guaranteeing a quality of service (QoS) for each accepted call setup. A traffic descriptor is specified by the user of the service; and the system ensures that the service requested could be met by the virtual circuit that is set up.

There are four main classes of traffic defined to implement quality of service. They are the constant bit rate (CBR), the real-time variable bit rate (VBR-rt), the non-real-time variable bit rate (VBR-nrt), and the available bit rate (ABR). Voice is assigned CBR. Streaming video such as real-time video on the Internet is assigned VBR-rt. The VBR-nrt is applicable to transmission of still images. The IP data traffic gets the lowest bandwidth priority with ABR.

There are two markets for ATM switches using ATM technology, public and private. A public network is the network that is established by the service providers. A private network is primarily a campus network. Network management clearly distinguishes between these two markets, as we shall see in Section 12.3.

12.2.4 WAN/SONET

Although analog high-frequency multiplexing is still in vogue for WAN transportation in legacy systems, digital transmission is the predominant mode of transportation. The basic voice band, 0–4 kHz, is converted to 64 Kbps digital signal universally. However, multiplexing hierarchy of the basic signal has evolved differently in North America, Europe, and Japan. For example, T1 transmission carrier shown in Figure 2.28(a) has a data rate of 1.544 Mbps carrying 24 voice channels. Equivalent of this in Europe is the E1 transmission at a data rate of 2.048 Mbps carrying 30 channels. Thus, whenever digital transmission happens across the "pond" between Europe and North America, there is an expensive conversion involved between the two types of systems.

The digital hierarchy has been brought into synchronization across the world using 155.52 Mbps as the basic data rate in carrier technology using fiber optics. However, the names are different in Europe and North America. In Europe, it is called SDH and in North America SONET. The units of SDH are Synchronous Transport Signal (STS-n) where n is the hierarchical level. The optical carrier starts with the unit of OC-1 (Optical carrier-level 1), which is 51.84 Mbps and thus the basic SONET is level OC-3.

12.2.5 ATM LAN Emulation

It was once considered possible that ATM would be at all desktop workstations. However, this has not been the case and IP over Ethernet has become the most used LAN.

The services provided by ATM differ from conventional LAN in three ways. First, ATM is connection oriented. Second, ATM makes one-to-one connection between pairs of workstations in contrast to the broadcast and multicast mode in conventional LAN. Third, a LAN MAC address is dedicated to the physical network interface card and is independent of network topology. The 20-byte ATM address is not.

In order to use ATM in the current LAN environment, it has to fit into the current TCP/IP LAN environment. Because of the basic differences mentioned in the previous paragraph, although the ATM Forum has developed ATM specifications for LAN emulation (LE or LANE) that emulate services of the current LAN network across an ATM network, it has been discontinued. Hence, we will not discuss this any further.

12.3 ATM NETWORK MANAGEMENT

Broadband network management consists of managing the WAN using ATM technology, as well as access networks from the central office to the home. We will discuss the former in this section. We will discuss access technology management in the next chapter.

WAN facilities are provided by public service providers, who perform the following management functions: operation, administration, maintenance, and provisioning (OAMP). Typically, a large enterprise or corporation services its private network. However, they too use the public service providers' facilities to transport information over a long distance. This is referred to as public network. ATM networks are classified as private and public networks, as shown in Figure 12.3. The standards for the management of each and the interactions between them have been addressed by the ATM Forum, which is an international organization accelerating cooperation on ATM technology. The user interface to the private network is the private user-network interface (UNI), and the interface to the public network is the Public UNI.

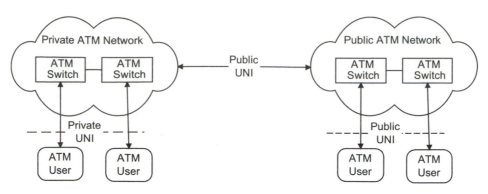

UNI ... User Network Interface

Figure 12.3 Private and Public ATM Network User Network Interfaces

12.3.1 ATM Network Reference Model

The ATM Forum has defined a management interface architecture, ATM network reference model, as shown in Figure 12.4. Private networks are managed by private network managers or private network management systems (NMSs). Public network managers or public network management systems manage the public networks. To distinguish between a human manager and the management system, we will refer to the network manager in the context of a system as the NMS, unless explicitly stated. There are five interfaces between systems and networks. M1 and M2 are, respectively, the interfaces between private NMS and either end user or private network. The end user can be a workstation, ATM switch, or any ATM device. A private ATM network is an enterprise network.

A private NMS can access its own network-related information in a public network via an M3 interface to the public NMS. The public NMS, which manages the public network, responds to the private NMS via the M3 interface with the relevant information or takes the appropriate action requested.

M4 is the interface between a public NMS and a public network. M5 is the interface between NMSs of two service providers. The ATM Forum has not yet specified this interface.

12.3.2 Integrated Local Management Interface

Beside the M-interfaces, Figure 12.4 also shows interfaces between an ATM end user or device and an ATM network, as well as interfaces between ATM networks. These are distinct from the M-interfaces between NMSs and networks or end users. While the M-interfaces provide a top-down management view of network or device, the ATM Forum defines the ATM link-specific view of configuration and fault parameters across a UNI. These are the UNI interfaces presented in Figures 12.3 and 12.4. The specifications for these are contained in the integrated local management interface (ILMI), which we will discuss further in Section 12.3.4.

The "I" in ILMI originally stood for "Interim," not "Integrated." See af.ilmi.0065.000. Its specifications were supposed to have been replaced by IETF specifications. However, it turned out that some were and others were not. Hence, "I" in ILMI now designates Integrated. The ILMI fits into the overall model for an ATM device, as shown in Figure 12.5. The ATM management information is communicated across the UNI or the network-to-network interface (NNI). These interfaces are with ATM devices (end-systems, switches, etc.) that belong to either a private or a public network. Any interface with the

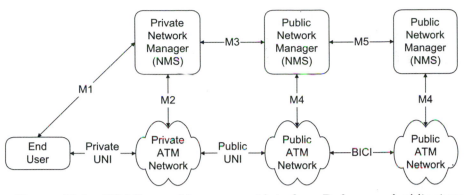

Figure 12.4 ATM Forum Management Interface Reference Architecture

public ATM network is a public UNI or a public NNI. Any interface with a private ATM network is a private UNI or a private NNI. The devices communicate across UNI and NNI via an ATM interface management entity (IME) module in the entity. There are three versions of IME—user, network, and system based on where it is used.

Figure 12.5 shows the various physical connections, virtual connections, and the ILMI communication links between the devices and the networks. The ILMI communication occurs over both physical and virtual links using SNMP or AAL5 protocols. We will discuss the MIB related to management in the following sections.

Two public carrier networks interface with each other via a broadband intercarrier interface (BICI), as shown in Figure 12.4. BICI is also known as network-to-network interface (NNI).

12.3.3   ATM Management Information Base

The MIB and the structure of management of information that are required for the management of the ATM network are specified between two sets of documents defined by IETF and the ATM Forum. The global view of the Internet MIB tree associated with the ATM is presented in Figure 12.6. The two major branches are *mib-2* and *atmForum* (under enterprises). The structure of management information is defined using the ASN.1 syntax. The MIB associated with the ATM is primarily concerned with the ATM sublayer parameters. The parameters associated with higher layers are handled using the standard MIB discussed earlier in Chapter 4. The documents that address the various groups are listed in Table 12.3.

There are five nodes shown under mib-2 in Figure 12.6. We described system and interfaces groups in Chapter 4. the interfaces group has evolved to handle the sublayers, such as ATM; the details are described in RFC 2863. The transmission group contains subgroups for each medium of transmission. The ATM objects, as defined in the *atmMIBObjects* group under *atmMIB*, are specified in RFC 1695.

The *atmForum* group is subnode 353 under the enterprises node. The *atmForum* group contains five subgroups, as shown in Figure 12.6: *atmForumAdmin*, *atmForumUni*, *atmUniDxi*, *atmLanEmulation* and *atmForumNetworkManagement*. The ATM administrative (*atmForumAdmin*) and ATM UNI (*atmForumUni*) groups are defined in the integrated local management interface (ILMI) specification, af-ilmi-0065.000. The ATM DXI (*atmUniDxi*) group is the Data Exchange Interface and is discussed in Section 12.3.9. It is the ATM interface between DTE and DCE and is described in af-dxi-0014.000. The MIB for M4 interface (*atmForumNetworkManagement*) is covered in af-nm-0095.001.

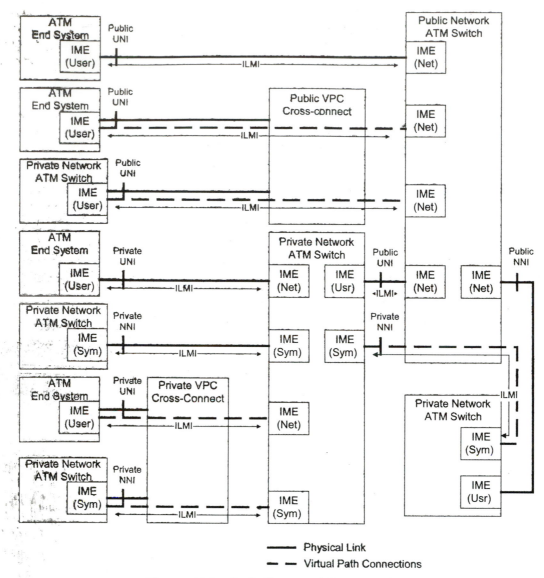

Figure 12.5 Definitions and Context of ILMI

 12.3.4 **Role of SNMP and ILMI in ATM Management**

Although ILMI was conceived as interim specifications, it has become permanent. The ATM network management uses both SNMP MIB and ATM Forum MIB. Figures 12.7 and 12.8 (af-ilmi-0065.000 and Section 4 of UNI) conceptually present the role of the two network management protocols. Figure 12.7 presents the M1 interface. An SNMP agent is shown embedded in an ATM device, and the NMS communicates with it using SNMP protocol and IETF MIB modules. RFC 2863 specifies the interface parameters and types, including the additional tables to manage the ATM sublayer. RFC 1695 specifies the ATM objects. The transport MIB module is dependent on the transmission medium.

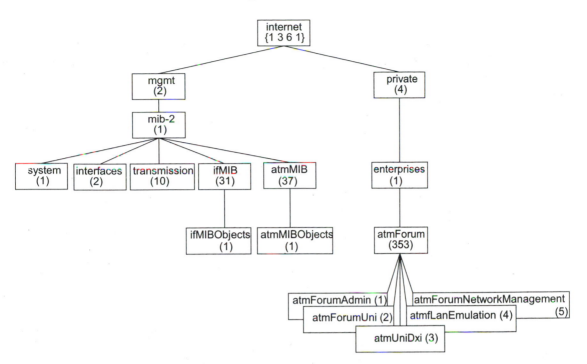

Figure 12.6 Internet ATM MIB

Table 12.3 Internet ATM MIB Groups and Documents

ENTITY	OID	DESCRIPTION	DOCUMENT
system	mib-2 1	System	RFC 1213
interfaces	mib-2 2	Interfaces (modified)	RFC 1213
RFC 1573			
ifMIB	mib-2 31	Interface types	RFC 1573
transmission	mib-2 10	Transmission	RFC 1213
ds1	transmission 18	DS1 carrier objects	RFC 1406
ds3	transmission 30	DS3/E# interface objects	RFC 1407
sonetMIB	transmission 39	SONET MIB	RFC 1595
atmMIB	mib-2 37	ATM objects	RFC 1695
atmForum	enterprises 353	ATM Forum MIB/M3 specification	af-nm-0019.000
		M4 interface	af-nm-0020.000
			af-nm-0020.001
		CMIP specification for M4 interface	af-nm-0027.000
		M4 network-view interface	af-nm-0058.000
		AAL management for the M4 NE View	af-nm-0071.000
		Circuit emulation service internet-working requirements, logical and CMIP MIB	af-nm-0072.000
		M4 network-view CMIP MIB Spec v1.0	af-nm-0073.000
		M4 network-view requirements and logical MIB addendum	af-nm-0774-000

Table 12.3 (continued)

ENTITY	OID	DESCRIPTION	DOCUMENT
atmForumAdmin	atmForum 1	ATM administrative	af-ilmi-0065.000
atmForumUni	atmForum 2	ATM user network interface	af-ilmi-0065.000
atmUniDxi	atmForum 3	Data exchange interface (DXI) specification	af-dxi-0014.000
		Multiprotocol over ATM	af-mpoa-0087.000
		Multiprotocol over ATM Version 1.0 MIB	af-mpoa-0092.000

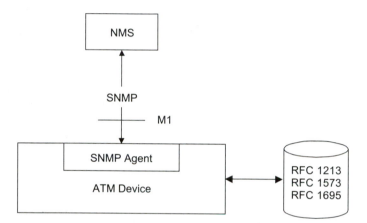

Figure 12.7   SNMP ATM Management (M1 Interface)

Figure 12.8, which shows the M2 interface, comprises the network of two ATM devices. The NMS manages the network with an interface to device A. The ILMI protocol is used for communication between the agent management entity (AME) in device A and the AME in device B. A proxy agent that resides in device A does the translation between ILMI MIB and SNMP MIB.

12.3.5   M1 Interface: Management of ATM Network Element

The M1 interface, as mentioned earlier, is between an SNMP management system and an SNMP agent in an ATM device, as shown in Figure 12.7. Four entities, *ifInNUcastPkts, ifOutNUcastPkts, ifOutQLen*, and *ifSpecific* have been deprecated. The interfaces (interfaces) and *ifMIB* (IF MIB) groups under the *mgmt* node are shown in Figure 12.9. Four tables have been added to handle sublayers. They are shown in Figure 12.9 under *ifMIBObjects*. Table 12.4 gives a brief description of the functions that each table performs.

Figure 12.10 shows the three transmission modes that are used for the ATM. They are DS1 (1.544-Mbps twisted-pair cable), DS3 (44.736-Mbps coaxial cable), and SONET (nx155.52-Mbps optical fiber). DS1 and DS3 are transmitted over T1 and T3 carriers, respectively. Only one of these MIBs

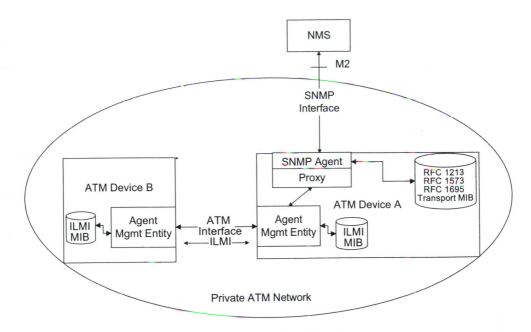

Figure 12.8 Role of SNMP and ILMI in ATM Management (M2 Interface)

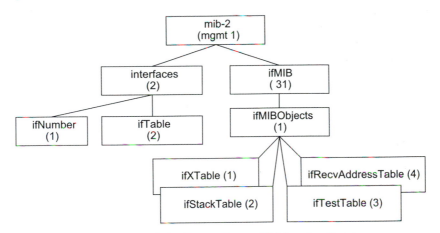

Figure 12.9 Interfaces Group Tables for Sublayers

Table 12.4 Interfaces Group Tables for Sublayers

ENTITY	OID	DESCRIPTION (BRIEF)
ifXTable	ifMIBObjects 1	Additional objects for the interface table
ifStackTable	ifMIBObjects 2	Information on relationship between sublayers
ifTestTable	ifMIBObjects 3	Tests that NMS instructs the agent to perform
ifRecvAddressTable	ifMIBObjects 4	Information on type of packets/frames accepted on an interface

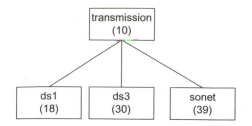

Figure 12.10   Transmission Groups for ATM

needs to be implemented in the agent based on which transmission medium is used. RFCs dealing with transmission group MIB modules are listed in Table 12.3.

Figure 12.11 and Table 12.5 show the ATM MIB objects group. This group contains information to manage the ATM sublayer entities: traffic descriptors, DS3 physical-layer convergence parameters (PLCP), transmission convergence (TC) sublayer parameters, virtual path link/virtual channel link and their associated cross-connect tables, and performance parameters for AAL5 (ATM adaptation layer).

12.3.6   M2 Interface: Management of a Private Network

The M2 interface for ATM management is shown in Figure 12.8. The management information on ATM links between devices is gathered from ILMI MIB. The relative roles of each are shown in Figure 12.8. Detailed UNI and NNI for both private and public interfaces, specified in af-ilmi-0065.000, are shown in Figure 12.5 and were discussed in Section 12.3.2.

The ILMI specifications define the administrative and UNI groups of the ATM Forum MIB. The administrative group defines a general-purpose registry for locating ATM network services such as the ATM name answer server (ANS). Other subgroups under the administrative group have been deprecated and handled by IETF specifications.

Figure 12.12 and Table 12.6 show the ATM UNI MIB object group. They define the management objects associated with the ATM layer and the physical layer. The statistics group is deprecated. The parameters associated with virtual path/virtual connections as well as the adjustable bandwidth rate (ABR) and QoS are covered.

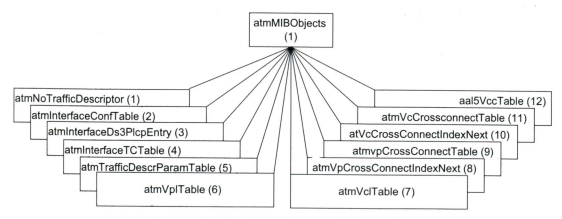

Figure 12.11   ATM Managed Objects Group

Table 12.5 ATM Managed Objects Group

ENTITY	OID	DESCRIPTION (BRIEF)
atmNoTrafficDescriptor	atmMIBObjects 1	ATM traffic descriptor type
atmInterfaceConfTable	atmMIBObjects 2	ATM local interface configuration parameter table
atmInterfaceDs3PlcpEntry	atmMIBObjects 3	ATM interface DS3 PLCP parameters and state variables table
atmInterfaceTCTable	atmMIBObjects 4	ATM TC sublayer configuration and state parameters table
atmTrafficDescrParamTable	atmMIBObjects 5	ATM traffic descriptor type and associated parameters
atmVplTable	atmMIBObjects 6	Virtual path link table
atmVclTable	atmMIBObjects 7	Virtual channel link table
atmVpCrossConnectNext	atmMIBObjects 8	Index for virtual path cross-connect table
atmVpCrossConnectTable	atmMIBObjects 9	Virtual path cross-connect table
atmVcCrossConnectNext	atmMIBObjects 10	Index for virtual channel cross-connect table
atmVcCrossConnectTable	atmMIBObjects 11	Virtual cross-connect table
aal5VccTable	atmMIBObjects 12	AAL VCC performance parameters table

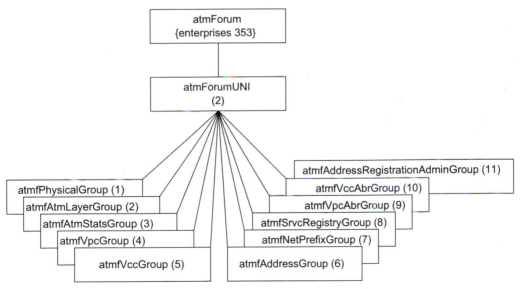

Figure 12.12 ATM UNI MIB Object Group

Table 12.6 ATM UNI MIB Object Group

ENTITY	OID	DESCRIPTION (BRIEF)
atmfPhysicalGroup	atmForumUni 1	Defines a table of physical-layer status and parameter information
atmfAtmLayerGroup	atmForumUni 2	Defines a table of ATM-layer status and parameter information
atmfAtmStatsGroup	atmForumUni 3	Deprecated
atmfVpcGroup	atmForumUni 4	Defines a table of status and parameter information on the virtual path connections
atmfVccGroup	atmForumUni 5	Defines a table of status and parameter information on the virtual channel connections
atmfAddressGroup	atmForumUni 6	Defines the network-side IME table containing the user-side ATM-layer addresses
atmfNetPrefixGroup	atmForumUni 7	Defines a user-side IME table of network prefixes
atmfSrvcRegistryGroup	atmForumUni 8	Defines the network-side IME table containing all services available to the user-side IME
atmfVpcAbrGroup	atmForumUni 9	Defines a table of operational parameters related to ABR virtual path connections
atmfVccAbrGroup	atmForumUni 10	Defines a table of operational parameters related to ABR virtual channel connections
AtmfAddressRegistrationAdminGroup	atmForumUni 11	

12.3.7 M3 Interface: Customer Network Management of a Public Network

M3 is the management interface between the private NMS and the public service provider NMS. It allows the customer to monitor and configure their portion of the public ATM network. The M3 interface specifications are defined in the ATM Forum document af-nm-0019.000. Networks show the typical configuration, how a customer would interact with the public service provider network via the carrier management system. There are two classes of M3 requirements in the figure—status and configuration monitoring (Class I) and virtual configuration control (Class II).

Class I requirements are those which a public network service provider offers to the customer. These include the customer performing monitoring and management of configuration, fault, and performance management of a specific customer's portion of a public ATM network. This service is offered only for PVC configuration. Examples of this service are (a) retrieving performance and configuration information for a UNI link and (b) public service NMS reporting an alarm or trap message to the user NMS on a UNI-link failure.

Class II service provides greater capability to the user. The user can request the service provider to add, delete, or change virtual connections between a pair of customer's UNIs. An example of this would be the customer wanting to establish a new virtual path or increase the number of virtual circuits in a given virtual path.

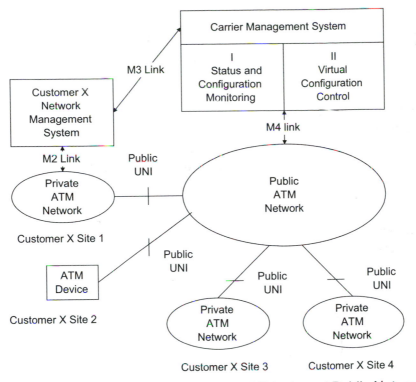

Figure 12.13 Customer Management of Private and Public Networks

A customer network management (CNM) agent residing in the private service provider's NMS provides the M3 service. As mentioned, the service is limited to the portion of the public service provider's network that the user's circuit traverses. If the user's circuit traverses multiple service providers, a separate interface with each provider is needed. The CNM sends requests to the carrier management system (see Figure 12.13), which acts as an agent to the CNM. The carrier management system then invokes the request on the network elements (NE) or other NMS and returns the responses to CNM.

The requirements for M3 and M4 are specified as mandatory or required, conditionally required, and optional. Class I requirements are mandatory, and Class II requirements are optional.

Class I Interface Management Functions. Table 12.7 presents M3 Class I requirements and the MIB groups that are used to obtain the information. The request has SNMP "read-only" capability. The public network service provider should give the CNM customer the ability to retrieve all the information listed in Table 12.7.

Class II Interface Management Functions. M3 Class II functionality is divided into three groups so that the provider can implement one or more subgroups. They are (1) ATM-level subgroup, (2) VPC/VCC-level subgroup, and (3) traffic subgroup.

The ATM-level subgroup should provide the CNM the ability to modify the ATM Level Information Configuration Information.

The VPC/VCC-level subgroup provides the CNM the ability to modify:

1. Virtual path link configuration and status information.
2. Virtual channel link configuration and status information.

Table 12.7 M3 Class I Interface Requirements and MIB

General UNI protocol stack information	System group [RFC 1213],
	interfaces group, including ifTable and ifStackTable [RFC 1213, 2863],
	SNMP group [RFC 1213]
ATM performance information on customer's UNI	ifTable [RFC 2863]
Physical-layer performance and status information	All tables except dsx3ConfigTable [RFC 1407],
	all tables except dsx1ConfigTable [RFC 1406],
	all tables except the configuration tables and VT tables of SONET MIB [RFC 1595],
	atmInterfaceDs3PlcpTable/atmInterfaceTCTable of ATM MIB [RFC 1695]
ATM-level information configuration information	atmInterfaceConfTable of ATM MIB [RFC 1695]
Physical-layer configuration information	dsx3ConfigTable [RFC 1407]
	dsx1ConfigTable [RFC 1406]
	all configuration tables except the sonetVtConfigTable of SONET MIB [RFC 1595]
ATM-layer virtual path link configuration and status information	atmVplTable of ATM MIB [RFC 1695]
ATM-layer virtual channel link configuration and status information	atmVclTable of ATM MIB [RFC 1695]
ATM-layer virtual path connection configuration and status information	atmVpCrossConnectTable and atmVpCrossConnectIndexNext of ATM MIB [RFC 1695]
ATM-layer virtual channel connection configuration and status information	atmVcCrossConnectTable and atmVcCrossConnectIndexNext of ATM MIB [RFC 1695]
ATM-layer traffic characterization (traffic descriptors for customer's UNIs) information	atmTrafficDescrParamTable of ATM MIB [RFC 1695]
Event notifications on ATM link going up or down	warmStart, coldStart, linkUp, linkDown of SNMP group [RFC 1695]

3. Virtual path connection configuration and status information.
4. Virtual channel connection configuration and status information.

The traffic subgroup shall provide the CNM the ability to modify:

1. Traffic descriptors and information objects for virtual channel connections.
2. Traffic descriptors and information objects for virtual path connections.

Table 12.8 presents the M3 Class II requirements and the MIB objects in the ATM MIB group.

12.3.8 M4 Interface: Public Network Management

The management of public ATM network is primarily the responsibility of network service providers—carriers and Postal Telephone and Telegraph (PTT) companies. They have the challenge of not only managing the public network, but also keeping up with new technology. To help this process, ITU-T has

Table 12.8 M3 Class II Interface Requirements and MIB

ATM-level information configuration information	atmInterfaceConfTable in ATM MIB [RFC 1695]
Virtual path link configuration and status information	atmVplTable in ATM MIB [RFC 1695]
Virtual channel link configuration and status information	atmVclTable in ATM MIB [RFC 1695]
Virtual path connection configuration and status information	atmVpCrossConnectTable and atmVpCrossConnectIndexNext of ATM MIB [RFC 1695]
Virtual channel connection configuration and status information	atmVcCrossConnectTable and atmVcCrossConnectIndexNext of ATM MIB [RFC 1695]
Traffic descriptors and information objects for virtual path and channel connections	atmTrafficDescrParamTable in ATM MIB [RFC 1695]

defined M.3010, a five-layer model of operations, telecommunications management network (TMN), which we discussed in detail in Chapter 10. The relationship of ATM to TMN is shown in Figure 12.14. The top two layers, the business management layer and the service management layer, deal with the business and service aspects of TMN and are not addressed by the ATM Forum.

The element layer (EL) contains NEs. The NEs specific to ATM technology are components, such as ATM workstation, ATM switches, ATM transport devices (cross-connect systems and concentrators), etc. The element management layer (EML) manages NEs. The network management layer (NML) has the responsibility to manage the network either directly or via the EML.

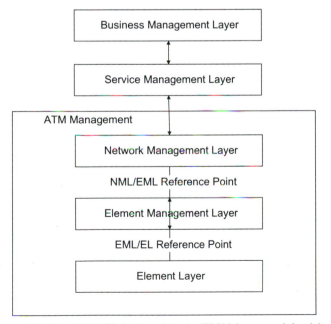

Figure 12.14 ATM Relationship to TMN-Layered Architecture

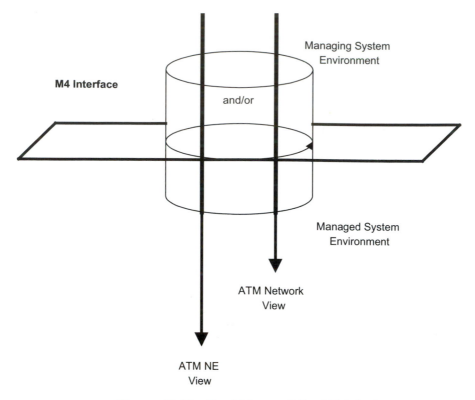

Figure 12.15 Dual Views of the M4 Interface

Figure 12.15 shows the dual view of M4 interface (af-nm-0058.000). Both views are present in the architecture across the M4 interface plane. It should be noted that this is a conceptual view, and the physical connections can be the same for both views.

In the NE-level management architecture, shown in Figure 12.16, the NMS environment, consisting of one or more NMSs, directly interfaces with the ATM NE and manages them. There is a single M4 interface between ATM NE and the NMS environment. The figure shows links between NE, but the NMS directly communicates with each ATM network element. In an actual implementation, it is likely that the NMS is interfacing with another NMS, which is managing the NE, but can still present a network view to the higher-level management system.

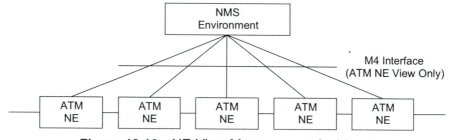

Figure 12.16 NE-View Management Architecture

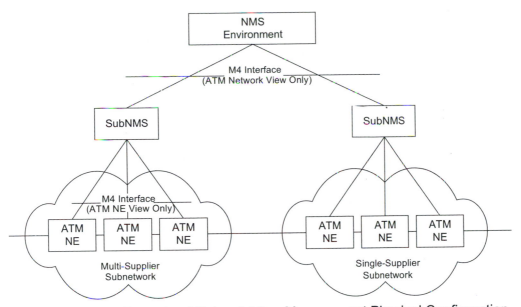

Figure 12.17 Example of Network-View Management Physical Configuration

Figure 12.17 presents an example of network-view management physical configuration. It consists of two ATM networks, one a single-supplier subnetwork and the other a multi-supplier subnetwork. Each subnetwork has its own subNMS managing its NE. In the single-supplier subnetwork shown on the right side, the subNMS has only an ATM NE view. In the multi-supplier subnetwork environment shown on the left side, the subNMS is presented only an ATM NE view, although it may actually be communicating to lower-level NMSs of each supplier. This is similar to the manager-of-manager architecture we discussed in Chapter 4. This is explicitly shown in the figure. Both subNMSs in Figure 12.16 present an ATM network view only to the NMS environment shown at the top. Thus, the top-level NMS sees only the network view of the subnetworks and not the NE view.

The NMS environment can manage both NE and networks, as shown in the architectural view in Figure 12.18. We can visualize such a hybrid situation in some remote ATM devices that do not need to be under a group's NMS, but are managed by an enterprise NMS.

M4 Network Element-View Requirements and Logical MIB. ATM Forum M4 network-element-view specifications support PVCs. Based on the OSI application model, the specifications are confined to configuration management, fault management, and performance management. Basic security features are also included to ensure the authorization and authentication of the user and the protection and privacy of data, while M3 interface responds to queries. The ATM security framework is similar to the security framework discussed for management in Chapter 7. It is covered in af-sec-0096-000. The network management considerations are presented in af-nm-0103.000, which includes security requirements and logical MIB.

The MIB specifications are specified in a logical format in af-nm-0020.000 and updated in af-nm-0020.001. They could be implemented using either CMIP or SNMP protocols. The CMIP specifications are presented on af-nm-0027.000, af-nm-0058.000, af-nm-0071.000, af-nm-0072.000, af-nm-0073.000, and af-nm-0074.000. The SNMP specifications are detailed in af-nm-test-0080.000 and af-nm-0095.001. We will now summarize the protocol-independent specifications of M4 interface and the logical MIB.

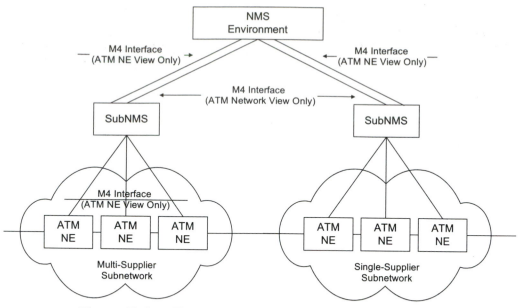

Figure 12.18 Example of NE + Network-View Management

Configuration Management. Configuration management provides the following list of functions to manage NEs:

1. ATM NE configuration identification and change reporting, which involves:
   (a) Operations performed over the craft interface
   (b) Human intervention (removal/insertion of equipment modules)
   (c) Customer control channels (e.g., ILMI)
   (d) Network failures
   (e) Protection switching events
   (f) Sub-ATM NE component initialization
   (g) Secondary effects of atomic operations performed by the management system
2. Configuration of UNIs, BICIs, and BISSIs.
3. Configuration of VPL/VCL termination points and cross-connections.
4. Configuration of VPC and VCC OAM segment end-points.
5. Event flow control—event forwarding discriminator function.

Fault Management. The following set of functions is specified to detect, isolate, and correct abnormal operation:

1. Notifying the NMS of a detected failure.
2. Logging failure reports.
3. Isolating faults via demand testing.

The specific functions are:

1. Failure reporting of the various alarms listed in Table 12.9. The generic troubles that cause the alarm are also listed in the table.
2. Operations, administration, and maintenance (OAM) cell loopback testing.

Table 12.9 Generic Troubles in ATM NEs

ALARM CATEGORY	GENERIC TROUBLE
Communication alarms	Alarm indication signal (AIS)
	Loss of cell delineation (LCD)
	Loss of frame (LOF)
	Loss of pointer (LOP)
	Loss of signal (LOS)
	Payload type mismatch
	Transmission error
	Path trace mismatch
	Remote defect indication (RDI)
	Signal label mismatch
Equipment alarms	Back-plane failure
	Cell establishment error
	Congestion
	External interface device problem
	Line card problem
	Multiplexer problem
	Power problem
	Processor problem
	Protection path failure
	Receiver failure
	Replaceable unit missing
	Replaceable unit problem
	Replaceable unit type mismatch
	Timing problem
	Transmitter failure
	Trunk card problem
Processing error alarms	Storage capacity problem
	Memory mismatch
	Corrupt data
	Software environment problem
	Software download failure
	Version mismatch
Environmental alarms	Cooling fan failure
	Enclosure door open
	Fuse failure
	High temperature
General	Vendor specific

Performance Management. The functions of performance monitoring for an ATM network are:

1. Performance monitoring.
2. Traffic management.
3. UPC (user parameter control)/NPC (network parameter control) disagreement monitoring.
4. Performance management control.
5. Network data collection.

To accomplish these general functions, the following specific functions are specified:

1. Physical-layer performance monitoring.
2. ATM cell-level protocol monitoring.
3. UPC/NPC disagreement monitoring.

Network-View Requirements and Logical MIB. The M4 network view for the management of an ATM public network is concerned with NML information. It addresses the different perspectives of the service providers, each of whom need both network management and service management capabilities.

The ATM Forum document af-nm-0058.000 details the requirements for the ATM network management across the M4 network view interface. The associated MIB is specified in logical form and is not management protocol specific. The functional areas addressed in the specifications are:

1. Transport network configuration provisioning (including subnetwork provisioning and link provisioning).
2. Transport network connection management (including set up/reservation/ modification for subnetwork connection, link connection, trails, and segments).
3. Network fault management (including congestion monitoring and connection and segment monitoring).
4. Network security management.

Managed entities have not been defined in the MIB for meeting all the above requirements.

Transport Network Provisioning/Layered Network Provisioning. The transport network provisioning includes subnetwork provisioning of network nodes and links. Specifically:

1. Subnetwork provisioning: addition and monitoring information on addition, deletions, and changes in NEs and their configuration.
2. Link provisioning: set up, modify, and release subnetwork links.

Subnetwork Connection Management. The M4 network-view managed entities support subnetwork management of reservation and modification of subnetwork connections, link connections, trails, and segments. Specifically, this involves:

1. Point-to-point subnetwork connection: VP–VC subnetwork connection between pair of end points.
2. Multipoint subnetwork connection: Multipoint VP–VC connections between pair-wise end points.
3. Link connection set-up: VP–VC connections between subnetworks.
4. Segment setup: Set up and support VP–VC segment termination end points.
5. Trail setup: Support and set up trails containing information on subnetwork connections and links.

When a part of the ATM trail spans multiple administrative domains, each NMS is responsible for its domain setup and maintains its trails.

Connection Release. The connections release across the M4 interface involves the management of resources to be made available after use. Specifically, the network management should support:

1. Release subnetwork connections and release resources of both point-to-point and multipoint connections.
2. Release link connections between subnetworks.

Subnetwork State Management. The NMS needs to be aware of the operational status of the subnetworks with regard to the network being ready to perform its intended functions, including link connections, trail operational changes, and network components.

Transport Network Fault Management. The M4 interface management is required to report network-view alarms and provide testing capability to isolate the problem. Specifically, this includes:

1. Log network alarms within a subnetwork to be retrieved by the NMS.
2. Autonomously notify failures, such as termination point failures.
3. Provide loopback-testing capability that supports OAM cell loopback along a subnetwork connection or a segment of it.

Network Security Management. The security framework for ATM networks is described in the ATM Forum document af-sec-0096.000. It addresses the security concerns from the perspectives of customers, public communities, and network operators. The main security objectives are (1) confidentiality (confidentiality of stored and transferred information), (2) data integrity (protection of stored and transferred information), (3) accountability (for all ATM network service invocations and for ATM network management activities), and (4) availability (correct access to ATM facilities).

Seven generic threats are considered in the threat analysis of an ATM network. They are (1) masquerade or spoofing (pretence by an entity to be a different entity), (2) eavesdropping (breach of confidentiality by monitoring communication), (3) unauthorized access, (4) loss or corruption of information, (5) repudiation (an entity involved in a communication exchange subsequently denies the fact), (6) forgery, and (7) denial of service (failure to fulfill its functions by an entity or preventing others from fulfilling).

Table 12.10 maps the threats to the objectives. Not all threats affect all security objectives. For example, masquerade and unauthorized access threatens all security objectives, whereas eavesdropping only affects confidentiality of information.

A set of functional security requirements is identified to deal with the generic threats, and security services should be built to address these requirements. Table 12.11 maps the security requirements to the services needed to fulfill them. You may refer to af-sec-0096.000 for specification of each of the services. Security recovery and management of security do not have associated services but are part of the requirements.

The security framework is specifically applied across the M4 interface. The network management M4 security requirements and the logical MIB are documented in af-nm-0103.000. The MIB is defined independent of protocol implementation and is used for the transfer of information across ATM management interfaces. Both resources and services are defined in the MIB as *managed entities* in the ATM network element.

Table 12.10 Mapping of Threats and Objectives

THREAT	CONFIDENTIALITY	DATA INTEGRITY	ACCOUNTABILITY	AVAILABILITY
Masquerade	x	x	x	x
Eavesdropping	x	–	–	–
Unauthorized access	x	x	x	x
Loss or corruption of information	–	x	x	–
Repudiation	–	–	x	–
Forgery	x	–	x	–
Denial of service	–	–	–	x

Table 12.11 Mapping of Security Requirements and Services

FUNCTIONAL SECURITY REQUIREMENTS		SECURITY SERVICES
Verification of identities		User authentication
Peer entity authentication		
Data origin authentication		
Controlled access and authorization		Access control
Protection of confidentiality	Stored data	Access control
	Transferred data	Confidentiality
Protection of data integrity	Stored data	Access control
	Transferred data	Integrity
Strong accountability		Non-repudiation
Activity logging		Security alarm, audit trail, and recovery
Alarm reporting		Security alarm, audit trail, and recovery
Audit		Security alarm, audit trail, and recovery
Security recovery/Management of Security		–

12.3.9 ATM Digital Exchange Interface Management

The Digital Exchange Interface (DXI) is an interface between a Digital Terminal Equipment (DTE) and a Digital Circuit Equipment (DCE) that connects to a public data network. In the ATM network, the public data network is a network of ATM switches. Figure 12.19 shows a high-level view of the DXI interface. Typically, a DTE will be a hub or the router and the DCE is a Digital Service Unit (DSU), which interfaces to an ATM switch. More details on this interface and management of it can be found in the ATM Forum document on Data Exchange Interface Specification, af-dxi-0014.000.

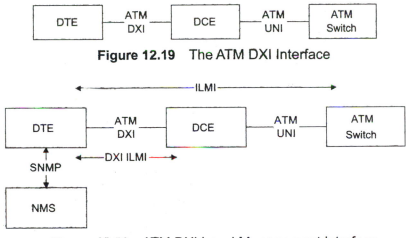

Figure 12.19 The ATM DXI Interface

Figure 12.20 ATM DXI Local Management Interface

Figure 12.20 shows the ATM DXI Local Management Interface (LMI). The ATM LMI defines the protocol for exchange of information across the DXI interface, and supports DXI, AAL, and UNI-specific management information. The LMI protocol supports the SNMP management system and the ILMI Management Entity (IME) running on an ATM switch. The ATM DXI LMI MIB (af-dxi-0014.000) supports IETF ATM MIB and the ATM Forum UNI MIB.

12.4 MPLS NETWORK TECHNOLOGY

Multiprotocol Label Switching (MPLS) is a fast-emerging WAN technology that replaces pure IP and ATM networks [RFC 2702]. It combines the richness of IP and the performance of ATM networks.

12.4.1 MPLS Network

One of the important developments in WAN transport technologies is the evolution of the MPLS protocol from IP and ATM. An IP-based network is feature rich because of its extensive implementation and compatibility with Ethernet LAN. It routes packets intelligently. However, it is slow in performance as it has to open each packet at the layer 3 level to determine its next hop and its output port. The simultaneous transport of real-time and non-real-time traffic is difficult.

In contrast to IP, the ATM protocol is a high-performance cell-based protocol switching cells at the layer 2 level. It is capable of handling real-time and non-real-time traffic simultaneously and thus is superior to the IP-based network. It has been deployed extensively in the WAN. However, its address incompatibility with the popular Ethernet LAN, along with difficult end-to-end circuit provisioning, has limited its usage at the customer premises network and hence related applications.

The MPLS protocol evolved to combine the richness of IP and the performance of ATM networks. It is being deployed in convergent network for broadband services handling real-time and non-real-time traffic simultaneously, thus achieving high quality of service transport. It can be deployed in the legacy network of either IP- or ATM-base. A simplified representation of an MPLS domain network with an ingress MPLS router and an egress MPLS router is shown in Figure 12.21. This shows the MPLS header,

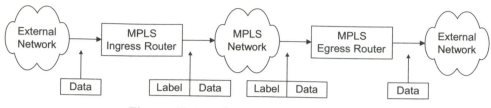

Figure 12.21 Simplified MPLS Network

named label, added between layers 2 and 3 to the packet or cell delivered by the external network to the ingress router and removed by the egress router before delivering to its external router. As we will soon learn, the MPLS header at the output of the MPLS domain may not be the same as the one at the input to the domain.

In general, the packet header contains information to choose the next hop, which comprises information to perform two functions. The first function partitions the entire set of possible packets into a set of forward equivalent classes (FECs). The second function maps each FEC to a next hop. In so far as the forwarding decision is concerned, different packets that are mapped into the same FEC are indistinguishable.

In conventional IP, forwarding is done based on the packets with the same FEC being sent to the next hop on the same port. The FEC is determined by comparing the "longest match" for each packet's destination address, called the address prefix. This is done for each packet at each router. This is shown in Figure 12.22(a). The incoming Packets 1 and 3 generate the same FEC 1 and are transmitted over Port 3. Packets 2 and 4 generate FEC 2 and exit out of Port 4.

In MPLS, the assignment of FEC to packets is done once at the ingress router. All packets that belong to a particular FEC are assigned the same path or paths in the case of multipath routing, leaving the node. This is shown in Figure 12.22(b).

In MPLS, the assignment of FEC to a particular packet is done just once at the ingress router and is encoded in a short fixed value length in the label. Once a packet is assigned to an FEC, no further header analysis is done by subsequent routers; all forwarding is driven by the labels. The label is sent along with the packet. At subsequent hops the label is used as an index into a table, which specifies the next hop and a new label. The old label is replaced with the new label and the packet is forwarded to its next hop, as shown in Figure 12.22.

The MPLS forwarding paradigm has a number of advantages over conventional network layer forwarding. For example, MPLS forwarding can be done by switches that are capable of doing label lookup and replacement, but are either not capable of analyzing the network layer headers or are not capable of analyzing the network layer headers at adequate speed. The reader is referred to RFC 3031 to learn about the various benefits of MPLS that can be applied to broadband services.

Some MPLS routers analyze a packet's network layer header not merely to choose the packet's next hop, but also to determine a packet's "precedence" or "class of service." They may then apply different discard thresholds or scheduling disciplines to different packets. MPLS allows (but does not require) the precedence or class of service to be fully or partially inferred from the label. In this case, one may say that the label represents the combination of an FEC and a precedence or class of service.

MPLS differs from an IP network, where each packet is looked at by each router and is assigned an FEC using the "longest match" for each packet's destination address. This obviously slows down the network data flow process. As IP packets are used by MPLS, the rich features of IP are preserved as the egress MPLS router strips the label and outputs the original IP packet.

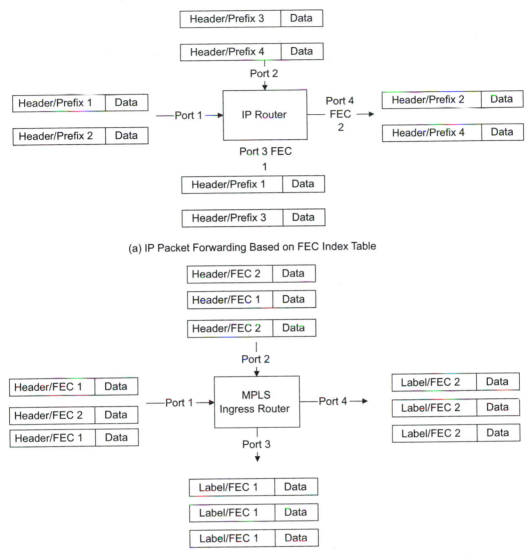

(a) IP Packet Forwarding Based on FEC Index Table

(b) MPLS Packet Forwarding Based on FEC Index Table

Figure 12.22 MPLS Packet Forwarding Based on the FEC Index Table

Let us now ask how does MPLS preserves the efficiency of an ATM. In an ATM, switching is done in layer 2. End-to-end path, "virtual path," containing "virtual circuit" is determined by the VPI–VCI. This establishes a virtual circuit-switched path using "soft" switches. As mentioned earlier, the MPLS router selects the next hop path using a table just as in the ATM switch and hence is efficient.

In the ATM network, a virtual circuit that has been established between two stations, A and Z, is shown in Figure 12.2 The routing tables in the ATM switches, A, B, and D, associated with this virtual circuit are shown in Table 12.2. The virtual circuit is first established prior to sending the data. In our example, the virtual circuit is the combination of virtual circuit links VCI-1, VCI-2, VCI-3, and VCI-4. Once the virtual circuit is established, all packets are transported in the sequence in which they were transmitted by the source along the same path for a given session. Thus, Packets 1, 2, and 3 transmitted by Station A arrive at Station Z in the correct sequence traversing the same links. Since the path is fixed for the entire session, the transmission rate is considerably increased just as in the circuit-switched transmission mode.

In MPLS, packets with input labels are mapped to next hop with output labels. The header in layer 3 is ignored. Once a packet is assigned an FEC, no further analysis is done by subsequent routers. Figure 12.23 illustrates IP routing with Interior Gateway Protocol (IGP) without traffic engineering (TE) and tunnels, and Figure 12.24 illustrates the Interior Gateway Protocol network topology with TE and tunnels implementation [Cisco, MPLS-TE]. The respective routing tables for router R1 are shown in Tables 12.12 and 12.13.

For simplicity, the IP addresses of the routers are designated as i.i.i.i for each router Ri. Table 12.12, representing Figure 12.23, shows the output interface (logical port) and next hop for packets emanating from R1 to Ri. The last column in the table shows the metric of the number of hops from R1 to the destination router. The paths are chosen using IGP. For example, there are two choices for the label-switched path (LSP) from R1 to R4, both of which are shown in Table 12.12. The two paths are R1–R2–R3–R4 and R1–R6–R7–R4. They both have the same metric of 3 hops. The former is transmitted via logical port I1 of R1 and the latter I2 of R2. As can be observed, the router knows only its neighbor router in its routing table.

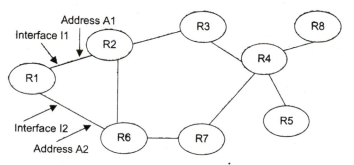

Figure 12.23   Topology without MPLS Tunnels

Table 12.12   R1 Routing Table without Tunnels

DEST	OUTPUT INTERFACE	NEXT HOP	METRIC
2.2.2.2	I1	2.2.2.2	1
3.3.3.3	I1	2.2.2.2	2
4.4.4.4	I1	2.2.2.2	3
	I2	6.6.6.6	3
5.5.5.5	I1	2.2.2.2	4
	I2	6.6.6.6	4
6.6.6.6	I2	6.6.6.6	1
7.7.7.7	I2	6.6.6.6	2
8.8.8.8	I1	2.2.2.2	4
	I2	6.6.6.6	4

Table 12.13 R1 Routing Table
with Tunnels

DEST	0 INTF	NEXT HOP	METRIC
2.2.2.2	I1	2.2.2.2	1
3.3.3.3	I1	2.2.2.2	2
4.4.4.4	T1	4.4.4.4	3 /1
5.5.5.5	T2	5.5.5.5	4/1
6.6.6.6	I2	6.6.6.6	1
7.7.7.7	I2	6.6.6.6	2
8.8.8.8	T1	4.4.4.4	4/2

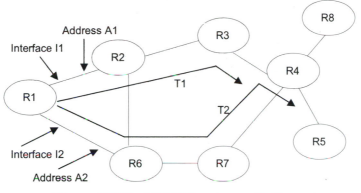

Figure 12.24 MPLS Topology with Tunnels

LSPs for the same topology used in the MPLS protocol with MPLS-TE and tunnels are shown in Figure 12.24, and the routing table in the label-switching router (LSR) R1 is presented in Table 12.13. The LSRs R4 and R5 are directly reached from R1 through tunneling. The transit time delay is low and the throughput is higher as the intermediate routers in the tunnel behave as pass through. The path from R1 to R4 now exits out of the logical port T1 and has the next hop as R4. There are two metrics shown for educational purpose. It is three if no absolute value for the tunnel path metric. If an absolute value, in our case chosen as 1, the value of the metric is 1. For the case of an LSP from R1 to R5, the corresponding metrics are 4 and 1.

12.4.2 MPLS Traffic Engineering

Traffic engineering (TE) is concerned with the performance optimization of operational networks. It includes measurement, modeling, characterization, and control of Internet traffic to achieve specific performance objectives. A major goal of Internet TE is to facilitate efficient and reliable network operations, while simultaneously optimizing network resource utilization and traffic performance. The aspects of TE that are of interest concerning MPLS are measurement and control.

The control capabilities offered by existing Internet interior gateway protocols are not adequate for TE. A popular approach to circumvent the inadequacies of current IGPs is through the use of an overlay model, such as IP over ATM or IP over frame relay. The overlay model extends the design space by enabling arbitrary virtual topologies to be provisioned atop the network's physical topology. The virtual topology is constructed from virtual circuits that appear as physical links to the IGP-routing protocols. The overlay model provides additional important services to support traffic and resource control, including: (1) constraint-based routing at the VC level, (2) support for administratively configurable explicit VC paths, (3) path compression, (4) call admission control functions, (5) traffic shaping and traffic-policing functions, and (6) survivability of VCs. These capabilities enable the actualization of a variety of TE policies. For example, virtual circuits can easily be rerouted to move traffic from over-utilized resources onto relatively under-utilized ones.

For TE in large dense networks, it is desirable to equip MPLS with a level of functionality at least commensurate with current overlay models. Fortunately, this can be done in a fairly straightforward manner. MPLS is strategically significant for TE because it can potentially provide most of the functionality available from the overlay model in an integrated manner, and at a lower cost than the currently competing alternatives. Equally important, MPLS offers the possibility to automate aspects of the TE function.

As defined earlier, a router capable of supporting MPLS is called a label-switching router (LSR) and the end-to-end path of an MPLS circuit is called a label-switching path (LSP). The LSP starts at the ingress router at the head end and terminates at the egress router at the terminating end. As discussed above, the IGP has been extended to engineer intra-area and inter-area traffic [RFC 4105]. Figure 12.25 shows a representation of MPLS-TE implementation [Cisco]. LSRs use IGP extensions to create and maintain a TE link state database that is similar to the one used by the open shortest path first (OSPF)/ intermediate system to intermediate system (IS–IS). It contains TE network topology that is updated by IGP flooding whenever a change occurs. Route is set up by Resource Reservation Protocol-Traffic Engineering (RSVP-TE), and link admission control establishes tunnels that have resources. TE control establishes and maintains links, and the forwarding engine manages the data flow across the LSP.

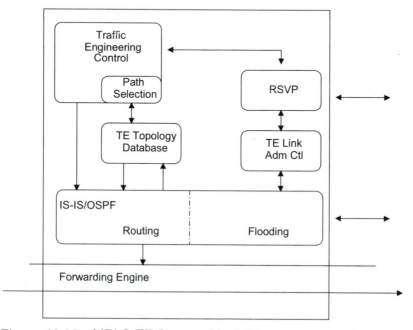

Figure 12.25   MPLS-TE System Block Diagram (Head-End Router)

Figure 12.26   MPLS Shim Header

The control and data planes are separated in MPLS. This permits a variety of signaling protocols to be used for the signal path. This offers flexibility for the implementation of VoIP using the legacy H.323 signaling protocol or Session Initiation Protocol (SIP).

12.4.3   MPLS Label

A label is a short, fixed length, locally significant identifier, which is used to identify an FEC. The label, which is put on a particular packet, represents the forwarding equivalence class (FEC) to which that packet is assigned. The MPLS label is a 4-octet or 32-bit long header and is shown in Figure 12.26. It comprises 20-bit label, 3-bit experimental, 1-bit stack indicator, and 8-bit time-to-live (TTL) information in that sequence. The label is assigned by a downstream router, as we will see later. The experimental bits are used to describe the class of service such as QoS. The stack indicator bit is 0 if it is the bottom of the stack of labels or else it is 1. TTL defines the maximum number of hops.

The MPLS label (or stack of labels) is inserted or "shim"ed between layer 2 and layer 3, as shown in Figure 12.27. Thus, for an IP-based protocol, the MPLS label is inserted between the 802.3 MAC header and the network layer IP header. In the case of the ATM protocol, the MPLS shim without the TTL replaces VPI and VCI fields.

Label switching is the process of extracting information from the label-routing look-up table and creating an outbound label, port, and operations to be performed. The operations are "push a new header," "pop a header off the stack," or "swap a header."

If Ru is the upstream LSR and Rd is the downstream in the LSRs, they may agree that when Ru transmits a packet to Rd, Ru will label the packet with label value L if and only if the packet is a member of a particular FEC F. That is, they can agree to a "binding" between label L and FEC F for packets moving from Ru to Rd. As a result of such an agreement, L becomes Ru's "outgoing label" representing FEC F, and L becomes Rd's "incoming label" representing FEC F. The upstream router packet is assigned the label by the downstream router. Note that L does not necessarily represent FEC F for any packets other than those that are being sent from Ru to Rd. L is an arbitrary value whose binding to F is local to Ru and Rd. Ru and Rd with label L are called a label-binding pair.

The packets "being sent" from Ru to Rd do not imply either that the packet originated at Ru or that its destination is Rd. They include packets that are "transit packets" at one or both of the LSRs. Figure 12.28 shows two upstream LSRs, Ru1 and Ru2, communicating with the downstream LSR Rd. Packet L1 with FEC F and Packet L2 from Ru2 belonging to the same FEC F arrive at downstream LSR Rd. Labels L1 and L2 are "outgoing labels" of Ru1 and Ru2, respectively. They are Rd's "incoming labels." Since they belong to the same FEC, they exit the same port of Rd with the newly assigned Labels L3 and L4 to the next hop from Rd. L3 is assigned by the LSR that is downstream from the Rd shown in Figure 12.28.

In conclusion, MPLS offers the best of IP and ATM network and is well suited for multimedia broadband network. It is currently being deployed by the broadband service providers at a rapid rate.

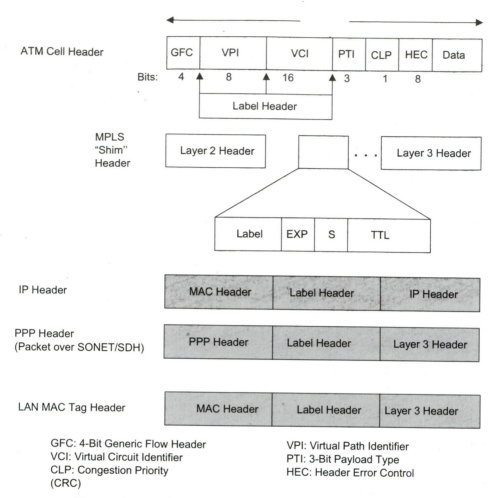

GFC: 4-Bit Generic Flow Header   VPI: Virtual Path Identifier
VCI: Virtual Circuit Identifier   PTI: 3-Bit Payload Type
CLP: Congestion Priority   HEC: Header Error Control
(CRC)

Figure 12.27   Encapsulation of an MPLS-Labeled Packet

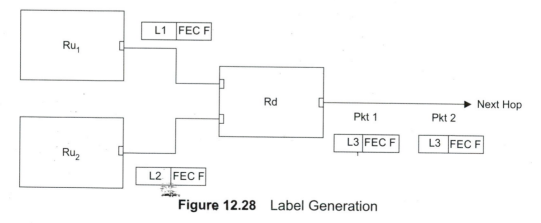

Figure 12.28   Label Generation

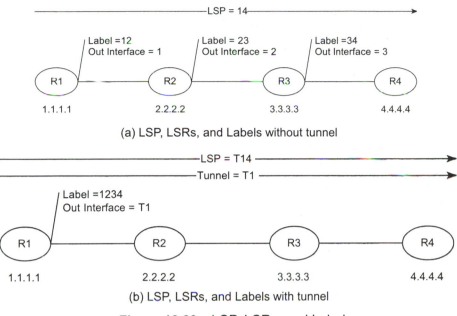

(a) LSP, LSRs, and Labels without tunnel

(b) LSP, LSRs, and Labels with tunnel

Figure 12.29 LSP, LSRs, and Labels

LSP, LSR, LDP, and Label

Let us now try to put together an integrated picture of LSP, LSR, LDP (label distribution protocol), and label in an MPLS network. An LSP comprises the path from ingress to egress router of an MPLS circuit. This is shown in Figure 12.29. It is made up of one or more entries in MPLS-switching tables in each of the LSRs along the LSP path. Each LSR has one input label assigned by the upstream LSR and one or more output labels based on whether a packet is unicast or multicast. An output label is interpreted by the downstream LSR as an input label locally. An input label is used in an LSR to determine the output label(s) and the output interface(s) based on LSP. Thus, the output label 23 tagged by LSR R2 is interpreted by LSR R3 as the input label and is used to tag the output packet with output label 34 and transmit it on output interface 3. The input to output relationship is derived from the cross-connect table of the LSR.

LDP is used by the egress LSR to notify the LSP to all the LSRs that are affected along the LSP's path. An LDP is a set of procedures by which one LSR informs another of the meaning of labels used to forward traffic between and through them. [RFC 3036, 3037] LDP associates an FEC [RFC 3031] with each label it distributes. Two LSRs that use LDP to exchange FEC-label binding information are known as "LDP Peers," and we speak of there being an "LDP Session" between them.

An alternative to LDP, which is distributed architecture, is to use RSVP-TE that has a signaling element built in to distribute the LSP information.

Figure 12.29(a) presents the case of an LSP for the non-tunnel case of transmission from R1 to R4 in Figure 12.23. Figure 12.29(b) shows the case for a tunneled path T1 from R1 to R4 shown in Figure 12.24.

12.5   MPLS OAM MANAGEMENT

In an MPLS network, the data planes and control planes are different. A data plane that carries traffic is used for MPLS OAM (operations, administration, and maintenance). In other words, OAM packets follow the data path. Sections 12.5.2–12.5.6 enumerate the OAM requirements extracted from [Cavendish *et al.*, 2004; Dini *et al.*, 2004; ITU Y1710; Nadeau *et al.*, 2005; RFC 3429, 4377]. The MPLS layer can be visualized as the layer positioned between layers 2 and 3 and hence OAM of MPLS needs to address both networks, namely ATM/MPLS and IP/MPLS. OAM in ATM/MPLS network is briefly addressed and compared with the IP/MPLS network in Section 12.5.1; and the OAM IN IP/MPLS network is covered in greater detail in Sections 12.5.2–12.5.4.

12.5.1   OAM in ATM and MPLS Network

As we have seen, there is commonality between ATM and MPLS in the lower layers. The LSP in MPLS serves the functions of VCC and VCP in the ATM. However, there is a paradigm shift in migrating from ATM OAM to MPLS OAM as illustrated in Table 12.14 [Dini *et al.*, 2004].

The ATM layer is constantly supervised using OAM cells. OAM functions of the ATM layer are accomplished by OAM cell flows being performed for both VC and VP connections. The fault management function is performed by continuity checking, verifying whether a VCC that has been idle for a period of time is still functioning. This is done by sending continuity-check cells along that VCC. Performance management is done by transmitting OAM cells at fixed intervals in both directions for notifying other NEs of detected errors.

MPLS is usually uni-directional and has a tightly coupled relationship between data and control planes. In contrast to ATM, the OAM packets are variable label stack and can be connectionless.

12.5.2   Fault Management of LSP

When an LSP fails to deliver a packet to the egress LSR, the failure can be due to several reasons and cannot always be detected by the MPLS control plane. LSP failures require the testing of specific packet flows, besides failure of the network infrastructure, because in many instances packet flows may get interrupted without network (link/node) failure. Figure 12.30 shows various kinds of plausible fault scenarios. A and B are the intended receivers for A' and B', respectively. Fault (defect) scenarios are: (a) Simple loss of connection, (b) Misconnection, (c) Swapped connection, (d) Mismerging, and (e) Loop/ unintended replication [Cavendish *et al.*, 2004]. In order to ensure that LSP failure is always detected,

Table 12.14 ATM OAM vs. MPLS OAM

ATM OAM	MPLS OAM
Paradigm: Virtual circuits	Paradigm: Label-switched paths
Bi-directional	Usually uni-directional
Established via ATM signaling and management	Established closely tied to control planes
Fixed hierarchy VP–VC	Variable label stack
Connection-oriented	Can be "Connectionless"
Single route	May use ECMP (equal-cost multipath)
No penultimate popping	Penultimate hop popping

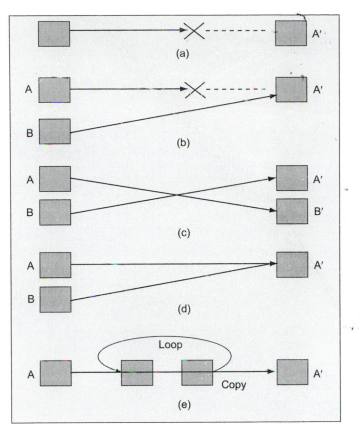

Figure 12.30 MPLS Fault Scenarios

it is important that the OAM packets used travel the same path as regular data packets as the data plane always interacts with the control plane.

There are two distinct methods specified in each of the standards, ITU-T and IETF, for detecting LSP fault detection and recovery. ITU-T Recommendation Y.1711 has standardized connectivity verification (CV) function, whereas bi-directional forwarding detection (BFD) function is specified within IETF.

Connectivity Verification (ITU-T Y.1711). The basic idea of the CV function is to send test packets (CV packets) periodically (one per second) from the ingress LSR to the egress LSR with the identity of the ingress LSR and originating LSP. The egress LSR analyzes the identification information of the received CV packets to detect defects. Figure 12.31 shows the CV packet format. It has two label stack entries. The top label is the same as that in user packets. The second label identifies the OAM packet via a reserved value of 14. The experimental bits, EXP, in the top label, and the OAM label are both set to the highest priority value used across the entire network. The stack bit, S, of the OAM label is set to 1 because it is the bottom label. Moreover, to ensure that CV packets will not go beyond the egress LSR, the MPLS network is treated as one-hop. The function type field indicates the OAM type: a code point 01H is assigned for CV packets. The next two fields, LSR ID and LSP ID, form the LSP trail termination source identifier (TTSI). The TTSI is used to identify the ingress LSR (via the IP address of its output port) and originating LSP (via the LSP ID). The BIP 16 (Byte Interleaved Parity) field is used for error

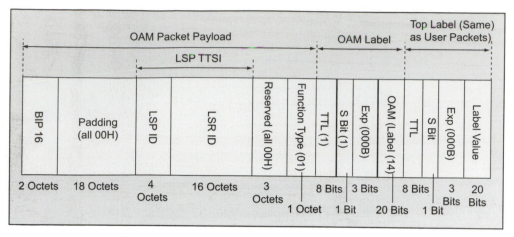

Figure 12.31   Connectivity Verification Packet

detection/correction. The ingress LSR sends CV packets with its TTSI value every second. The egress LSR receives CV packets and analyzes their TTSI values to determine whether they are expected values or not. If the egress LSR receives an expected TTSI, it declares no defect. If it does not receive any CV packet for more than 3 seconds, it declares a loss of connectivity defect (dLOCV), Figure 12.30(a). The egress LSR waits before declaring dLOCV to avoid misdetection of dLOCV due to an OAM packet loss. If there are two consecutive OAM packet losses, the egress LSR may mistakenly declare dLOCV, but this happens very rarely in normal operating conditions. In addition, as an egress LSR waits for 3 seconds, the expected delay variation, which is normally much less than a second, is acceptable. If an egress LRS receives an unexpected TTSI, it declares a TTSI mismatch defect (dTTSI-mismatch), Figure 12.30(b) and (c). If it receives both unexpected and expected TTSI values, it declares a TTSI mismerge defect (dTTSI-mismerge), Figure 12.30(d). If it receives more than five CV packets with expected TTSI values within 3 seconds, it declares excessive reception defect (dExcess), Figure 12.30(e). Before we discuss BFD, we will address LSP ping and LSP traceroute, which are used in BFD.

LSP Ping. LSP ping, which is described in detail in RFC 4379, is modeled after the Internet ping paradigm. The basic idea is to verify that packets that belong to a particular FEC actually end their LSP on an LSR that is an egress for that FEC. This test is carried out by sending a packet (called an "MPLS echo request") along the same data path as other packets belonging to this FEC. An MPLS echo request also carries information about the FEC whose MPLS path is being verified. This echo request is forwarded just like any other packet belonging to that FEC. In the "ping" mode, the packet should reach the end of the path, at which point it is sent to the control plane of the egress LSR, which then verifies whether it is indeed an egress for that FEC.

An MPLS echo request is a (possibly labeled) IPv4 or IPv6 UDP packet; the contents of the UDP packet have the format shown in Table 12.15.

The Version Number is currently 1. The Global Flags field is a bit vector that includes a V flag prescribing the FEC Stack Validation. The Message Type is either echo request (1) or echo reply (2). The Reply Mode can take one of the following values: Do not reply (1), Reply via an IPv4/IPv6 UDP packet (2), Reply via an IPv4/IPv6 UDP packet with Router Alert (3), and Reply via application-level control channel (4). Return Codes and Subcodes are set to zero and are filled in with response codes.

Table 12.15 MPLS Echo Request Packet

Byte 1	Byte 2	Byte 3	Byte 4
Version Number		Global Flags	
Message Type	Reply Mode	Return Code	Return Subcode
Sender's Handle			
Sequence Number			
TimeStamp Sent (seconds)			
TimeStamp Sent (microseconds)			
TimeStamp Received (seconds)			
TimeStamp Received (microseconds)			
TLV			

The Sender's Handle is filled in by the sender and is returned unchanged by the receiver in the echo reply (if any). The Sequence Number is assigned by the sender of the MPLS echo request and can be (for example) used to detect missed replies. The TimeStamp Sent is the time-of-day in seconds and microseconds. TLVs (Type-Length-Value tuples) are of variable length and contain the information on the FEC such as LDP IPv4 FEC.

An FEC connectivity is periodically pinged to ensure that it is active and alive. If the ping fails, one can then initiate a traceroute to determine where the fault lies.

LSP Traceroute. An LSP traceroute is used for hop-by-hop fault localization as well as path tracing. In the "traceroute" mode (fault isolation), the packet is sent to the control plane of each transit LSR, which performs various checks that it is indeed a transit LSR for this path. This LSR also returns further information that helps check the control plane against the data plane, i.e., that forwarding matches what the routing protocols determined as the path. One can also periodically traceroute FECs to verify that forwarding matches the control plane; however, this places a greater burden on transit LSRs and thus should be used with caution.

Bi-directional Forwarding Failure Detection. LSP-Ping [RFC 4379] provides a mechanism for verifying the MPLS control plane against the data plane. This is done by ensuring that the LSP is mapped to the same FEC at the egress, as the ingress. However, BFD cannot be used for verifying the MPLS control plane against the data plane. BFD can be used to detect a data plane failure in the forwarding path of an MPLS LSP.

In the event of an MPLS LSP failing to deliver data traffic, it may not always be possible to detect the failure using the MPLS control plane. For instance, the control plane of the MPLS LSP may be functional while the data plane may be misforwarding or dropping data. Hence, there is a need for a mechanism to detect a data plane failure in the MPLS LSP path [RFC 4377].

BFD is a low-overhead short-duration failure detection mechanism in the forwarding path between two adjacent NEs. A verification packet can be used at any of the protocol layers, which makes BFD a very versatile tool. BFD can provide failure detection on any kind of path and media, such as physical links, virtual circuits, and an MPLS LSP between two pairs of NEs.

To use BFD for fault detection on an MPLS LSP, a BFD session is established for that particular MPLS LSP. BFD control packets are sent along the same data path as the LSP being verified and are processed by the BFD-processing module of the egress LSR. If the LSP is associated with multiple FECs, a BFD session is established for each FEC. For instance, this may happen in the case of next-hop label allocation. Hence, the operation is conceptually similar to the data plane fault detection procedures of LSP-Ping.

If MPLS fast-reroute is being used for the MPLS LSP, the use of BFD for fault detection can result in false fault detections if the BFD fault detection interval is less than the MPLS fast-reroute switchover time. When the MPLS fast-reroute is triggered because of a link or node failure, BFD control packets will be dropped until traffic is switched on to the backup LSP. If the time taken to perform the switchover exceeds the BFD fault detection interval, a fault will be declared even though the MPLS LSP is being locally repaired. To avoid this, the BFD fault detection interval should be greater than the fast-reroute switchover time. An implementation should provide configuration options to control the BFD fault detection interval.

If there are multiple alternate paths from an ingress LSR to an egress LSR for an LDP IP FEC, LSP-Ping traceroute can be used to determine each of these alternate paths. A BFD session needs to be established for each alternate path that is discovered.

A combination of LSP-Ping and BFD can be used to provide faster data plane failure detection and/or make it possible to provide such detection on a greater number of LSPs [Aggarwal *et al.*, 2008]. Periodic LSP-Ping echo request messages should be sent by the ingress LSR to the egress LSR along the same data path as the LSP. This is to periodically verify the control plane against the data plane by ensuring that the LSP is mapped to the same FEC at the egress, as the ingress. The rate of generation of these LSP-Ping echo request messages should be significantly less than the rate of generation of the BFD control packets.

LSP Self-Test. As part of an LSP fault localization procedure for a defective LSP, a self-test can be performed on the data path using self-test protocol. In Figure 12.32, a representation of the self-test is done on LSR-ST with its upstream LSR-U and downstream LSR-D. LSR-ST issues an MPLS data verification request to LSR-U with three hop limitation TTL = 3. LSR-U in turn sends a request to LSR-D via LSR-ST with a TTL = 2 value. The MPLS packet sent by LSR-U is processed as any other labeled packet by LSR-ST and forwarded over to LSR-D. Upon TTL expiration, LSR-D sends a reply to LSR-ST, completing the test. The request and reply messages are special LSP ping messages, optimized for fast processing. There are other fault management aspects such as link management, fault notification, and others, and the reader is referred to [Cavendish *et al.*, 2004].

LSP Fault Localization. Because of the similarity between ATM and MPLS on path definition, some of the OAM concepts can be extended to MPLS. However because of the paradigm shift between the two, there is significant difference between the two protocol-based circuits. Unlike ATM, which defines both segment and end-to-end OAM functions, only end-to-end OAM functions are defined in

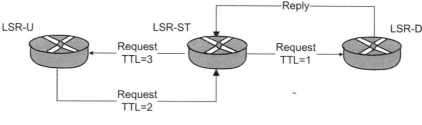

Figure 12.32 LSP Self-Test

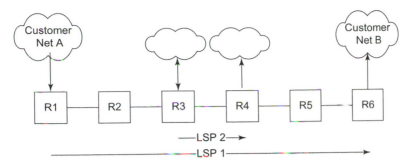

Figure 12.33 LSP Nesting and Fault Localization

ITU-T Recommendation Y.1711 [Y 1711] for MPLS. It may sometimes be necessary to localize a fault to an LSP segment that is part of a longer LSP segment. In this case, the LSPs of the two segments are nested.

Figure 12.33 shows an example with a circuit between customer networks A and B starting at ingressing LSR R1 and ending at egressing LSR R2 with an LSP 1. The LSP 1 traverses a segment from R1 to R6. The figure also shows a subsegment R3 to R4 with LSP 2 that LSP 1 traverses through, which may need to be managed more closely as it may be a higher bandwidth segment with larger bandwidth affecting a larger number of customers. In this situation, LSP 1 is nested with LSP 2. R3 adds or wraps a label L2 on top of L1 associated with LSP 1 and R4 removes or pops label L2. In this situation, both LSP 1 and LSP 2 are managed or only LSP 2 is managed.

It is worth noting that nesting of LSPs may be considered as a factor in configuring circuits paying careful attention to the management needs.

Since LSP specifies end-to-end path, any failure of transmission in the path needs to be localized for OAM function. In the example shown in Figure 12.33, if the fault occurs in R3 to R4 segment, the NMS managing that segment would raise the alarm. However, we need to inform the segments and nodes preceding and following the failed entity of the failure. ITU Recommendation Y.1711 specifies forward defect indication (FDI) and backward defect indication (BDI) as defect information transfer functions in the forward and backward directions, respectively. This could be used to suppress the display of alarms of all NEs except the one that is the root cause of the failure.

12.5.3 Service Level Management

The service level management in an MPLS network involves fault and performance management. In the event of a failure in LSP, the managing NMS localizes the problem by doing root cause analysis of the detected failures in links and nodes. In order to mitigate service to the customers, protection LSPs are con figured either on a local or a global basis. For example, a failure in the link between LSRs R3 and R4 for service between Customer Network A and Customer Network B in Figure 12.33 can be restored by the protection path of LSP 1 on a global basis or the protection path of LSP 2 on a local basis. This is decided based on the SLAs agreed between the service provider and the customers affected by the failure. Any failure detected has to be intimated to the ingress LSR of the LSP, and LSP switching is done based on the recovery policy implemented.

The SLA between the service provider and customers also covers the performance of the LSPs in terms of latency, jitter, and packet loss, especially in real-time service provisioning. The reader is referred to [Nadeau *et al.*, 2005; RFC 3429] for details on the specifications of these, as well as on security and account management.

12.5.4 MPLS MIBs

A range of MIB modules has been developed to help model and manage the various aspects of MPLS networks. These MIB modules are defined in separate documents that focus on the specific areas of responsibility of the modules that they describe [RFC 4221]. The MPLS set of MIBs is complex and consists of tables and managed objects that are inter-related across various MIB modules [Morris, 2004].

The set of MPLS MIB modules mplsStdMIB and the TE Link MIB teLinkStdMIB [RFC 4220] forms the two nodes under the transmission (mib-2 10) managed object node, as shown in Figure 12.34. Tables 12.16 and 12.18, the MPLS Object Identifier (OID) MIB group and the TE Link MIB group, respectively, describe the entities in the MIB groups with their OIDs and brief description of the entities.

MPLS-TC-STD-MIB [RFC 3811] defines textual conventions that may be common to MPLS-related MIB modules. These conventions allow multiple MIB modules to use the same syntax and format for a concept that is shared between the MIB modules.

MPLS-LSR-STD-MIB [RFC 3813] is the heart of the management architecture for MPLS and describes managed objects for modeling an MPLS LSR. It comprises the label-forwarding information base (LFIB) of the LSR and provides a view of the LSPs that are being switched by the LSR in question. Incoming labels on MPLS-enabled interfaces are mapped to outgoing labels on MPLS-enabled interfaces via a managed object called an MPLS cross-connect. MPLS cross-connect entries and their properties are represented in MPLS-LSR-STD-MIB and are typically referenced by other MIB modules in order to refer to the underlying MPLS LSP. For example, MPLS-TE-STD-MIB [RFC 3812] models TE tunnels. These tunnels map to one or more underlying MPLS LSPs. MPLS-TE-STD-MIB refers to the underlying LSPs by pointing to cross-connect entries in MPLS-LSR-STD-MIB.

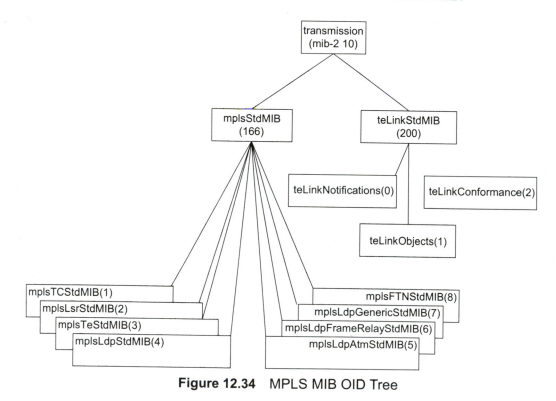

Figure 12.34 MPLS MIB OID Tree

Table 12.16 MPLS Object Identifier (OID) MIB Group

ENTITY	OID	DESCRIPTION (BRIEF)
mplsStdMIB	transmission (166)	MPLS OID group
mplsTCStdMIB	mplsStdMIB (1)	Defines textual conventions
mplsLsrStdMIB	mplsStdMIB (2)	LSR managed objects (MO)
mplsTeStdMIB	mplsStdMIB (3)	Traffic engineered tunnel MO
mplsLdpStdMIB	mplsStdMIB (4)	Label distribution protocol (LDP) MO
mplsLdpAtmStdMIB	mplsStdMIB (5)	MO used with MPLS-LDP-STD-MIB for MPLS/ATM as layer 2
mplsLdpFrameRelayStdMIB	mplsStdMIB (6)	MO used with MPLS-LDP-STD-MIB for MPLS/frame relay as layer 2
mplsLdpGenericStdMIB	mplsStdMIB (7)	LDP per platform label space reserved for other platforms
mplsFTNStdMIB	mplsStdMIB (8)	FTN MO (FEC-to-NHLFE (next hop label forwarding entry)

MPLS-TE-STD-MIB describes managed objects that are used to model and manage MPLS TE tunnels. This MIB module is based on a table that represents TE tunnels that originate from, traverse via, or terminate on the LSR in question. The MIB module provides configuration and statistics objects needed for TE tunnels.

MPLS-LDP-STD-MIB [RFC 3815] describes managed objects used to model and manage the MPLS LDP, one of the MPLS protocols used to distribute labels and establish LSPs [RFC 3036]. This MIB module contains objects common to all LDP implementations. For an LDP implementation that provides standard MIB support, this MIB module provides the core set of objects that are needed, along with one or more of the other LDP MIB modules that are specific to MPLS implementation. It supports the MPLS-LDP-ATM-STD-MIB module if LDP uses ATM as the Layer 2 medium, and supports MPLS-LDP-FRAME-RELAY-STD-MIB if LDP uses frame relay as Layer 2.

The MPLS-LDP-GENERIC-STD-MIB module provides objects for managing the LDP per platform label space and contains tables for configuring MPLS generic label ranges. Although the LDP specification does not provide a way to configure label ranges for generic labels, the MIB module does provide a way to reserve a range of generic labels.

MPLS-FTN-STD-MIB [RFC 3814] describes managed objects that are used to model and manage the MPLS FEC-to-NHLFE (FTN) mappings that take place at an ingress label edge router (LER). An ingress LER is responsible for classifying data and assigning them to a suitable LSP or tunnel. Once data have been classified, it is handed off to an LSP or tunnel through the next hop label forwarding entry (NHLFE). In the case of an IP-to-MPLS mapping, the FEC objects describe IP 6-tuples that represent source and destination address ranges, source and destination port ranges, the IPv4 protocol field or IPv6 next-header field, and the DiffServ code point (DSCP).

12.5.5 Interdependencies of MPLS MIBS

Figure 12.35 presents the relationship between the MPLS MIB modules described. The arrows in the diagram show a "depends on" relationship. A relationship "MIB module A depends on MIB module B"

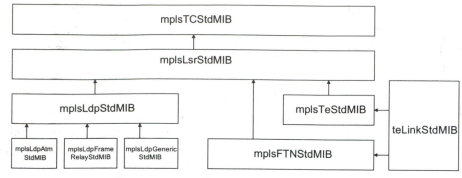

Figure 12.35 MPLS MIBs Dependencies

means that MIB module A uses an object, object identifier, or textual convention defined in MIB module B, or that MIB module A contains a pointer (index or RowPointer) to an object in MIB module B.

It can be observed that all the MIB modules depend on MPLS-TC-STD-MIB. MPLS-LDP-STD-MIB, MPLS-TE-STD-MIB, and MPLS-FTN-STD-MIB contain references to objects in MPLS-LSR-STD-MIB. MPLS-LDP-GENERIC-STD-MIB, MPLS-LDP-ATM-STD-MIB, and MPLS-LDP-FRAME-RELAY-STD-MIB contain references to objects in MPLS-LDP-STD-MIB. MPLS-FTN-STD-MIB contains references to objects in MPLS-TE-STD-MIB.

There are external dependencies of the MPLS MIBs on the interfaces group of IF-MIB [RFC 2863]. We will address these in Section 12.5.7 after we first consider the composition of the MPLS MIBs.

12.5.6 MPLS MIB Group Composition

MPLS MIB groups comprise tables, scalars, and indices and managed objects to issue notifications. Each table in a MIB group can be configured to perform specific functions. Some MIB modules have arbitrary indices and for these, scalars are provided to supply the next available index to generate a row. Scalars serve to specify the range of indices. The indexing is unusual in MPLS-LSR-STD-MIB, and a specific textual convention, *mplsIndexType*, is defined in the LSR MIB module. We will describe MPLS-LSR-STD-MIB here, and the reader is referred to RFC 4221 for details on other MIBs.

Table 12.17 shows the MIB tables with the OID and a brief description of functions. They specify the managed objects to serve the configuration, fault, and performance functions of LSR.

Scalars apply to *mplsInSegmentTable*, *mplsOutSegmentTable*, *mplsXCTable*, and *mplsLabelStack Table*. *mplsMaxLabelStackDepth* defines the maximum size of an imposed label stack supported at each LSR and overrides the specification in MPLS-LSR-STD-MIB. These scalars all use a second textual convention, *mplsIndexNextType*, also defined within MPLS-LSR-STD-MIB. This textual convention allows the "null string," (that is, a string of length one octet with value 0x00). The null string is used to indicate that either write access is not supported or no more indexes are currently available.

mplsXCNotificationsEnable is used to enable and disable notifications from MPLS-LSR-STD-MIB. There are two notifications *mplsXCUp* reports when a cross-connect becomes active and *mplsXCDown* reports when a cross-connect becomes inactive.

12.5.7 Use of Interface Stack in MPLS

The *ifTable* [RFC 2863] contains information on the managed resource's interfaces, and that each sublayer below the internetwork layer of a network interface is considered an interface. The managed

Table 12.17 MPLS LSR Tables

TABLE	OID	FUNCTIONS
Interface configuration	mplsInterfaceTable	Enables MPLS interface
In-segment	mplsInSegmentTable	Enables and monitors LSP segments into LSR
Out-segment	mplsoutSegmentTable	Enables and monitors LSP segments out of LSR
In-segment mapping	mplsInSegmentMapTable	Lookup table for discovery of an in-segment in an in-segment table
Cross-connect	mplsXCTable	Associate in and out segment for an LSP
Label stack	mplsLabelStackTable	Specifies multi-label stacks on LSP
In-segment performance	mplsInSegmentPerfTable	Measures performance of LSP
Out-segment performance	mplsOutSegmentPerfTable	Measures performance of LSP
Interface performance	mplsInterfacePerftable	Measures performance on a per-interface basis.

objects from the interfaces group of IF-MIB are used to manage MPLS tunnels. MPLS MIB modules, MPLS-TE-STD-MIB, and TE-LINK-STD-MIB utilize interface stacking within the interface group.

MPLS-TE-STD-MIB builds on the concept of managing MPLS tunnels as logical interfaces. Thus, an MPLS tunnel managed as an interface is represented as an entry in the *ifTable*. The interrelation of entries in the *ifTable* is defined by the interfaces stack group defined in RFC 2863. When using MPLS tunnels as interfaces, the interface stack table appears, as shown in Figure 12.36. The "Underlying layer" refers to the *ifIndex* of any interface type for which MPLS Internet working has been defined. Examples include ATM, frame relay, and Ethernet.

A detailed listing of the mapping between *ifTable* objects and their use for MPLS tunnels is given in RFC 3812. A few key objects are listed here to provide an overview of the concepts as described in RFC 4221. Each MPLS tunnel is represented by an entry in the *ifTable*. Each tunnel is therefore assigned a unique *ifIndex*. The type of an interface represented by an entry in the *ifTable* is indicated by the *ifType* object. The value that is allocated to identify an MPLS tunnel is 150. The *ifOperStatus* object reflects the actual operational status of the MPLS tunnel and may be mapped from the *mplsTunnelOperStatus* object. It may be considered convenient and good management to set the *ifName* object to reflect the name of the MPLS tunnel as contained in the *mplsTunnelName* object.

Figure 12.37 shows an example of an interface stack when using TE link interfaces. TE-LINK-STD-MIB uses interface stacking to manage TE link interfaces as logical interfaces. In Figure 12.37,

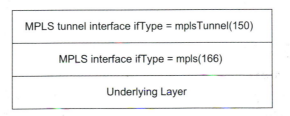

Figure 12.36 Interface Stack Table for an MPLS Tunnel Interface

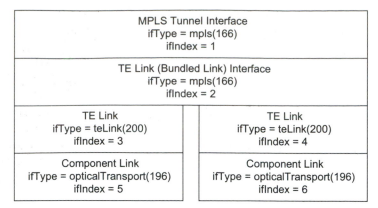

Figure 12.37   Interface Stack Table for a TE Link Physical Interface

"opticalTransport" is an underlying physical optical transport interface. TE link management and bundling can be seen in the levels of interface stacking. Two TE links are defined, each managing an optical transport link. These two TE links are combined into a bundle (see the following section), which is managed as a single TE link interface. This TE link interface supports MPLS and is presented as an MPLS interface. Each TE link interface is represented by a separate entry in the *ifTable*, with a unique *ifIndex*. The type of an interface represented by an entry in the *ifTable* is indicated by the *ifType* object. The value that is allocated to identify a TE Link is 200.

12.5.8   Traffic Engineering Link MIB Group

The TE link MIB group, TE-LINK-STD-MIB, presented in Table 12.18, describes managed objects that are used to model and manage TE links, including bundled links referred to in the previous section, in an MPLS network [RFC 4220]. The TE link feature is designed to aggregate one or more similar data channels or TE links between a pair of LSRs. A TE link is a sub-interface capable of carrying TE MPLS traffic. A bundled link is a sub-interface that bonds the traffic of a group of one or more TE links. Support is provided for configuration of TE parameters associated with TE links. The MIB module is used to monitor the priority-based component link and TE link bandwidth values.

12.5.9   MPLS Example

An LSP for data transmission set up between ingress MPLS router LER-1 and egress MPLS router LER-3 is shown in Figure 12.38. LER-1 receives IP packets from outside of the MPLS network at the

Table 12.18   Traffic Engineering Link MIB Group

ENTITY	OID	DESCRIPTION (BRIEF)
teLinkStdMIB	transmission (200)	MPLS traffic engineered links MO
teLinkNotifications	teLinkStdMIB(0)	Event notifications MO
teLinkObjects	teLinkStdMIB(1)	Traffic engineered link MO
teLinkConformance	teLinkStdMIB(2)	MPLS compliance MIB

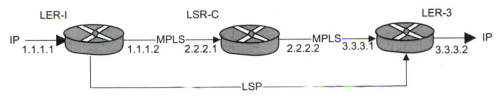

Figure 12.38 MPLS Example with the LSP Path

port with IP addresses 1.1.1.1 and pushes out MPLS packets out of the port (*ifIndex* = 2) with IP address 1.1.1.2 . The egress router LER-3 receives MPLS packets at the port with IP address 3.3.3.1 (*ifIndex* = 1) and puts out IP packets to the external network at the port with IP address 3.3.3.2. The core router LSR-C receives MPLS packets at the port (*ifIndex* = 1) with IP address 2.2.2.1 and pushes MPLS packets out of the port with IP address 2.2.2.2 (*ifIndex* = 2). Each router, in general, can have an *inSegment*, *outSegment*, and a cross-connect *XCTable* as MPLS tables. In our example, the ingress router LER-1 has only *mplsXCTable* and *mplsOutSegmentTable* as the input is not an MPLS packet. The egress router LER-2 has *mplsXCTable* and *mplsInSegmentTable* as the output is IP traffic. LER-3 (owner of the label) assigns a label of 13, which is carried as a single label on the IP/MPLS packet.

mplsInSegmentTable, *mplsOutSegmentTable* and *mplsXCTable* in MPLS LSR MIB [RFC 3813] are used to specify the input segment, output segment, and cross-connect in the three routers shown in Tables 12.19–12.25.

Table 12.19 LER-1 MPLS Out-Segment Table for LSP

mplsoutSegmentIndex	1
mplsoutSegmentInterface	2
mplsoutSegmentPushTopLabel	1
mplsoutSegmentTopLabel	13
mplsoutSegmenttopLabelPointer	0.0 (no external table pointer)
mplsoutSegmentNextHopAddrType	1 (IPv4)
mplsoutSegmentNextHopaddr	2.2.2.1
mplsoutSegmentXCIndex	mplsXCTable.1
mplsoutSegmentOwner	LER-2
mplsoutSegmentTrafficParam	0.0 (for best effort)

Table 12.20 LER-1 MPLS Cross-Connect Table

mplsXCIndex	1
mplsXCInSegmentIndex	0
mplsXCOutSegmentIndex	1
mplsXCLspId	123 (LSP Id forward path from LER-1 to LER-3)
mplsXCLabelStackIndex	0 (only one outgoing label)
mplsXCOwner	LER-1

Table 12.21 MPLS LSR-C Core In-Segment Table

mplsoutSegmentIndex	1
mplsoutSegmentInterface	2
mplsoutSegmentPushTopLabel	True (1) for tunnel
mplsoutSegmentTopLabel	13
mplsoutSegmenttopLabelPointer	0.0 (no external table pointer)
mplsoutSegmentNextHopAddrType	1 (IPv4)
mplsoutSegmentNextHopaddr	3.3.3.1 (Tunnel/LSP destination)
mplsoutSegmentXCIndex	mplsXCTable.1
mplsoutSegmentOwner	LSR-C
mplsoutSegmentTrafficParam	0.0 (for best effort)

Table 12.22 MPLS LSR-C Core Out-Segment Table

mplsoutSegmentIndex	1
mplsoutSegmentInterface	2
mplsoutSegmentPushTopLabel	1
mplsoutSegmentTopLabel	13
mplsoutSegmenttopLabelPointer	0.0 (no external table pointer)
mplsoutSegmentNextHopAddrType	1 (IPv4)
mplsoutSegmentNextHopaddr	3.3.3.1
mplsoutSegmentXCIndex	mplsXCTable.1
mplsoutSegmentOwner	LSR-C
mplsoutSegmentTrafficParam	0.0 (for best effort)

Table 12.23 MPLS LSR-C Core Cross-Connect Table

mplsXCIndex	1
mplsXCInSegmentIndex	0
mplsXCOutSegmentIndex	1
mplsXCLspId	123 (LSP Id forward path from LER-1 to LER-3)
mplsXCLabelStackIndex	0 (only one outgoing label)
mplsXCOwner	LSR-C

12.6 OPTICAL AND MAN FEEDER NETWORKS

Optical transport plays and will continue to play an important role in the future direction of telecommunications network. The transport scheme is used for WAN, as well as extension of WAN to close-to-customer premises in terms of feeder networks that can be considered as part of the broadband access network. The last-mile network for metropolitan area is called the metropolitan area network (MAN).

Table 12.24 MPLS LER-3 In-Segment Table

mplsInSegmentIndex	1
mplsInSegmentInterface	1
mplsInSegmentLabel	0 (if no external LabelPointer)
mplsInSegmentLabelPointer	0.0
mplsInSegmentNPop	1
mplsInSegmentAddrFamily	1 (IPv4)
mplsInSegmentXCIndex	1 (given)
mplsInSegmentTrafficParam	0.0

Table 12.25 MPLS LER-3 Cross-Connect Table

mplsXCIndex	1
mplsXCInSegmentIndex	1
mplsXCOutSegmentIndex	0
mplsXCLspId	123 (LSP Id forward path from LER-1 to LER-3)
mplsXCLabelStackIndex	0 (only one outgoing label)
mplsXCOwner	LER-3

12.6.1 Optical DWDM/SDH Network

The MAN can be defined as that segment of the network that connects the WAN to the broadband access network. There are wired and wireless MANs. While the latter is actually access network for the metropolitan area, the former is concerned with extending the WAN closer to the head end of the access network. We will limit our discussion here to the wired MAN.

The wired MAN has its origin in telephone network as a digital loop carrier where the voice circuits are transported in digital format from the central office terminal (COT) to the remote terminal (RT). This was done employing synchronous optical network (SONET) using synchronous digital hierarchy (SDH). The transmission bandwidth is in multiples of 51.84 Mbps optical carrier Level 1 (OC-1). It is typically from OC-3 (approximately 155 Mbps) to OC-12 (approximately 600 Mbps). With broadband deployment it has gone up to OC-48 (48 x 51.84 Mbps). SONET is implemented as a ring network. The WAN is connected to COT and multiple RTs form a ring with COT, as shown in Figure 12.39.

Another legacy implementation of MAN is to aggregate metro traffic into T1/DS1 (1.55 Mbps) or T3/DS3 (7 T1s) and transport it to WAN. The European equivalent of this is E1/E3. The modulation scheme is time division multiplex (TDM).

Both the above schemes are voice based. The emerging technology for the broadband version of MAN is packet and ring based, but with a dual ring using an efficient MAC protocol, resilient packet ring (RPR) protocol. The ring itself is a dual ring with traffic traversing in opposite directions. If there is a break in one of the rings, such as a fiber cut, all the traffic is routed via one ring with turn-arounds at RTs that are adjacent to the fiber cut. This is shown in Figure 12.40.

Each mode in the ring acts as an add–drop multiplexer (ADM) to add and drop the local traffic, as well as behaving as a pass through for through traffic. RPR is faster than SONET. It is resilient in that

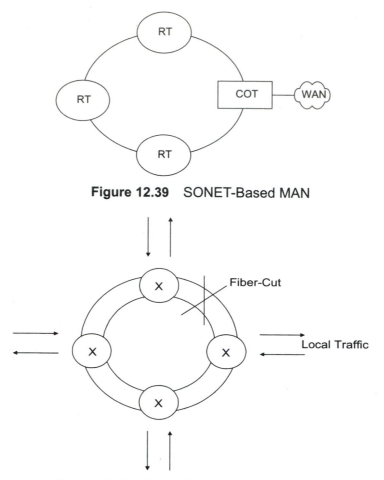

Figure 12.39 SONET-Based MAN

Figure 12.40 Dual Ring with Failure Recovery

it can recover in less than 50 milliseconds, which is 5–10 times faster than SONET. The RPR protocol assures bandwidth fairness and is more efficient for multicast/broadcast. Provisioning in RPR is considerably simpler than in SONET. RPR is IEEE standard 802.17.

RPR specifications are transparent to the physical layer underneath. Thus, the existing infrastructure of SONET rings could be used. The common deployment of the infrastructure uses SDH transport equipment (notice that the device and the technology are both referred to as SDH). The basic transmission rate of SDH is OC-3, 155.52 Mbps (abbreviated to 155 Mbps). The basic SDH ring is referred to as STM-1 (Synchronous Transport Module Level 1). The higher data rate rings are STM-4 (OC-12) and STM-16 (OC-48), which operate at 622.08 Mbps and 2,488.32 Mbps and are deployed using either SONET/SDH transmission or the optical transmission component dense wavelength division multiplexer. Higher data rate signals of OC-48 utilize DWDM technology.

It is worth noting the distinction between SONET/SDH and WDM technologies. Both use optical fiber as the medium. SONET/SDH takes synchronous and asynchronous signals and multiplexes them to a single higher bit rate for transmission at a single wavelength over fiber. It involves conversion from electrical to optical and back to electrical signal each time source signals have to be added or dropped, such as add–drop multiplexing of DS1/E1 sources. On the other hand, WDM is strictly a physical-layer system, and OC-n signals, as well as any SONET signal or ATM signal directly of ATM switches, can be transported over WDM. It is protocol agnostic. The difference between WDM and DWDM is one of density of signal over the fiber.

An optical fiber carrying signals at multiple wavelengths is called a multimode fiber.

In broadband implementation of RPR rings, the RTs house DSL access multiplexers (DSLAMs), and the local traffic shown in Figure 12.40 are DSL access networks carrying multimedia information. The architecture of a hierarchy of metro broadband network using RPR access rings and IP/MPLS metro core network connecting to the Internet via a gateway is shown in Figure 12.41.

12.6.2   SDH Management

We will deal with SDH management only briefly here, and the reader is referred to [Fatato, 1996; ITU G Series; RFC 2558; Wikipedia2]. Most of the SDH-specific management information has been described by ITU in the ITU G.Series Recommendations: [ITU G.774, G.784, and G.831]. It is based on characterization of SDH NEs in terms of functionality and functional partitioning. SONET and SDH have dedicated data communication channels (DCCs) within the section and line overhead for management traffic. Generally, section overhead (regenerator section in SDH) is used. According to ITU-T G.774, there are three modes used for management: (i) IP-only stack, using PPP as a data link; (ii) OSI-only stack, using LAP-D as a data link; and (iii) Dual (IP+OSI) stack using PPP or LAP-D with tunneling functions to communicate between stacks. An interesting fact about modern SONET NEs is that to handle all of the possible management channels and signals, most NEs actually contain a router for routing the network commands and underlying (data) protocols.

ITU G.784 specifies equipment management functions (EMF) for fault management, performance monitoring, and configuration management. Within an STM-N signal there are two DCC channels,

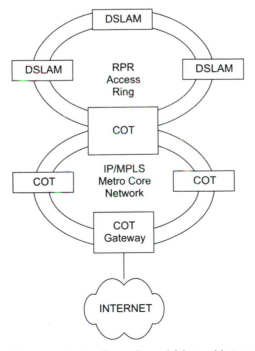

Figure 12.41   Broadband Metro Network

DCCM and DCCR. DCCM is used to forward data over the multiplex sections (using the OSI-routing protocols), and DCCR is used to forward data to the regenerators. DCCM can be regarded as the backbone, while DCCR and LAN are used to interconnect this backbone to equipment that cannot be accessed through DCCM, e.g., regenerators and non-SDH equipment. DCCM and DCCR can be used to carry two independent, possibly proprietary, management applications. An NE can choose to through-connect DCCM on the physical level, or to terminate the DCCM and route the PDUs, while using the DCCR for interconnection within a subnetwork. G.831 specifies the management capabilities of transport network based on the SDH.

Large numbers of alarm and error messages are defined for SDH network fault management. In SDH, these are referred to as defects and anomalies, respectively, and are associated with network sections. The complete failure of a circuit results in a loss of signal alarm (LOS) in the receiving network element. This alarm triggers a chain of subsequent messages in the form of alarm indication signals (AIS). The transmitting side is informed of the failure by the return of an RDI alarm (remote defect indication).

Performance management of SDH equipment is quantified in ITU G.826 by numerous parameters. Of these, there are four commonly used parameters: errored second (ES), severely errored second (SES), background block error (BBE), and unavailable second (UAS). ES is a 1-second time interval containing one or more errored blocks. SES is a 1-second time interval in which more than 30% of the blocks are errored or which contains at least one severely disturbed period (SDP). EB (errored block) is a block containing one or more errored bits. BBE is an errored block that is not an SES. UAS is defined as follows: a circuit is considered to be unavailable from the first of at least 10 consecutive SESs. The circuit is available from the first of at least 10 consecutive seconds which are not SES.

Configuration management involves the management of a large number of parameters. Refer ITU G Series of documents for details.

12.6.3   SONET Transport Hierarchy and ifTables

SDH networks are subdivided into various layers that are directly related to the network topology. SONET/SDH layers are shown in Figure 12.42. The equivalent topological representation is shown in Figure 12.43. The lowest layer is the physical transmission medium, which in our case is fiber. There are line and section segments represented by layers. Each of these three layers is represented by *ifType sonet (39)* managed object in the interfaces group.

A section is a single fiber run that can be terminated by a network element (line or path) or an optical regenerator. The main function of the section layer is to properly format the SONET frames and to convert the electrical signals to optical signals. Section-terminating equipment (STE) can originate, access, modify, or terminate the section header overhead. A standard STS-1 frame is nine rows by 90 bytes. The first three bytes of each row comprise the section and line header overhead.

Line-terminating equipment (LTE) originates or terminates one or more sections of a line signal. The LTE does the synchronization and multiplexing of information on SONET frames. Multiple lower-level SONET signals can be mixed to form higher-level SONET signals. An ADM or digital cross-connect, or MPPS, is an example of LTE.

Path-terminating equipment (PTE) interfaces non-SONET equipment to the SONET network. At this layer, the payload is mapped and demapped into the SONET frame. For example, an STS PTE can assemble 25 1.544 Mbps DS1 signals and insert path overhead to form an STS-1 signal. This layer is concerned with end-to-end transport of data.

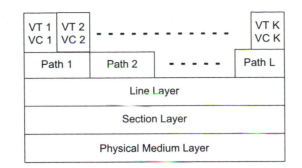

Figure 12.42 SONET/SDH Layers

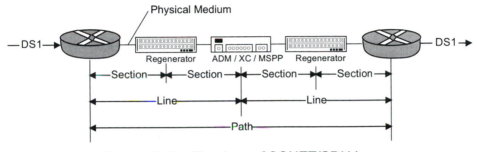

Figure 12.43 Topology of SONET/SDH Layers

The top layer in Figure 12.42 is the virtual container, VC-n, terminology used in ITU and virtual tributary, VT-n, terminology used in North America and Japan. This contains the payload. This is managed object ifType sonetVT (51) in the interfaces group.

The optical interface layers have a hierarchical relationship; each layer builds on the services provided by the next lower layer. Each layer communicates with peer equipment in the same layer and processes information; and then passes it up or down to the next layer. As an example, consider two network nodes that are to exchange DS1 signals, as shown in Figure 12.43.

At the source node, the PTE in the path layer maps 28 DS1 signals and path overhead to form an STS-1 synchronous payload envelope (SPE) and hands this to the line layer. The LTE in the line layer multiplexes STS-1 SPE signals and adds line overhead. This combined signal is then passed to the section layer.

The section layer (STE) performs framing and scrambling and adds section overhead to form an STS-n signal. Finally, the electrical STS signal is converted to an optical signal for the photonic layer and is transmitted over the fiber to the distant node. Across the SONET network, the signal is regenerated in optical regenerators (STE-level devices), passed through an ADM (an LTE-level device), and eventually terminated at a node (at the PTE level). At the distant node, the process is reversed from the photonic layer to the path layer where the DS1 signals terminate.

The terminologies used to describe error conditions on a SONET circuit as monitored and managed by a SONET system are described in [T1.231] or for SDH in ITU recommendation [G.774; G.784; G.831].

12.6.4 WDM Optical Transport Network

We introduced in Section 2.6 optical transport networks using WDM technology as the most flexible and diverse mode of transportation. WDM technology can solve the enormous traffic growth problem evolving through multiple technologies using multiple protocols, as shown in Figure 2.31. For the current high-end transport, we can use IP, ATM, MPLS, or TDM wraped in SONET/SDH frame and transported over the optical physical layer. In course of time, as the IP/MPLS technology advances to handling the real-time and non-real-time QoS as the ATM does, then IP/MPLS can be transported directly over the optical physical medium without the SONET/SDH intermediate layer.

The WDM network management comprises management of NEs and the network configuration. The NEs are similar to the ones shown in Figure 12.43, namely amplifiers or regenerators, add–drop multiplexers (OADMs), and optical cross-connects (OXCs). Optical configuration relates to parameters such as network discovery, connectivity, protection path, etc. The reader is referred to [Liu, 2002] for details on IP over WDM.

◼ Summary

In this chapter we have learned the WAN segment technologies of broadband network and its management. We have specifically addressed ATM, MPLS, optical, and MAN feeder networks.

The ATM is based on cell transmission, which is a hybrid of circuit- and packet-mode transmissions. VP–VCs are established and torn down in this mode. Priorities are assigned to ensure quality of service for voice and video services, which have tight requirements on latency and delay. This has allowed the integrated service to be extended from narrowband ISDN to broadband (B-ISDN) network.

ATM technology has brought the private- and public-switched network services closer together. In fact, they overlap each other. Because of that, the network management functions overlap. Several user interfaces have been specified by the international standards body, ISO, to manage broadband WAN. The ATM Forum has developed ATM MIB that supplements the SNMP MIB developed by IETF.

ISO has identified five M-interfaces to manage the ATM network. M1 manages ATM NE. M2 interface is used to manage private the ATM network. M3 is the interface through which private enterprises can access their domain of the public ATM network and, based on the privilege granted, Class I and Class II can perform limited management of the public network.

The M4 interface defines the management interface of the ATM network for public service providers. They can manage the network at the network element level using the network element view, or at the network management level using the network view. These two views are part of the five-level total management network (TMN) defined by ISO, which we addressed in detail in Chapter 10. Fault, performance, and security management specifications are also addressed in the M4 interface specifications. Circuit provisioning is covered as part of configuration management. M5 is between NMSs of two service providers.

The MPLS network is evolved by using the good performance of the ATM and the rich features of IP. The basic principles of label switching and the LSP routing using LSRs with and without tunnels were covered. TE optimizes the performance of the MPLS network. MPLS label definition and how to generate labels were addressed. Labels could be nested in creating LSPs.

MPLS network management was discussed from the OAM concept. Fault, connectivity verification, MPLS ping and trace-route, and how they are used for BDF failure detection were described. Fault management includes fault localization. Service level management of MPLS was briefly discussed.

MPLS OAM is implemented using the set of MPLS MIBs and TE MIBs. MPLS MIBs are interdependent and their dependencies were illustrated. The MPLS layers are managed using the interfaces group stack and cover data as well as physical layers. We illustrated how to build the basic tables for MPLS routers and network.

Optical fiber medium is used to extend the WAN closer to customer premises. These are called MAN feeder networks and use SONET or SDH ring network. As the name implies, SDH is a digital hierarchy and we briefly covered management of SDH network. SONET/SDH/DWDM are also used as physical-layer protocol for the optical transport of information over a long distance.

Exercises

1. Switched virtual circuit transmission overhead could be high to send a small amount of information. Calculate the minimum time to transmit one ATM cell from Miami to San Francisco on a basic SONET network (OC-3) for the following cases. Assume the distance as 4,500 km and the propagation speed as 300 meters per microsecond.

   (a) Datagram service
   (b) Switched virtual circuit service
   (c) Permanent virtual circuit service

2. Packet-switched transmission of voice affects real-time information due to packetization delay. Packetization delay is defined as the delay caused due to the necessity to buffer all the bits of a packet before it can be processed. Voice signal is normally digitized at 64 kbps rate. Calculate the packetization delay for the packet of the following sizes (use only the information bits).

   (a) One byte
   (b) An Ethernet packet of 1,500 bytes of information
   (c) An ATM cell

3. Although there are numerous benefits of cell transmission for multimedia service, there is penalty in efficiency. Calculate the maximum efficiency (data bytes/(data bytes + overhead bytes) for ATM transmission.

4. Calculate the efficiency of transmission to transmit:

   (a) An Ethernet packet of 1,500 bytes (including the overhead with 6-byte addresses)
   (b) An equivalent data using ATM cells

5. The communication between two ATM switches is broken in a private ATM network. You are troubleshooting the problem from a network management station. What Mx interfaces would you use?

6. In Exercise 5:

   (a) What interfaces MIB would you use from your NMS station to isolate the problem? What MIB objects would you use?
   (b) Can you perform the task using an ATM MIB? What MIB object group would you use and why?

7. The ATM ILMI MIB covers both the physical and virtual configuration of ATM links. How would you use the ILMI MIB to isolate a break in link between physical link failure and virtual link failure?

8. A customer network management is used to look at the QoS classes associated with VCIs across an ATM link interface. What three MIB groups and objects are used to collect the information? Describe the relationship between them.

9. In Figure 12.13, identify the M-interfaces and SNMP and ILMI management systems/agents that are involved to measure the QoS information if the observed interface of the link is:

   (a) In Customer X Site 1
   (b) In Customer X Site 3
   (c) In public ATM network and is connected to Customer X Site 2

10. The network shown in Figure 12.44 is an MPLS network with all routers configured as Label-Switching Routers (LSRs). The paths (LSPs) are determined using TE (Traffic Engineering). Fill in the R2 routing table (a) for paths with no tunnels and (b) for paths with tunnels T1 and T2. The address of each router is x.x.x.x where x is the router number, e.g., 1.1.1.1.

11. An LSP for data transmission is set up between two MPLS routers R1 and R4 with IP addresses 1.1.1.1 and 4.4.4.4, respectively, via tunnel T1, as shown in Figure 12.45. The *outSegment* exits out of R1 on T1 interface out of port 1 (if index =1) and terminates as *inSegment* on port 4 of R4.

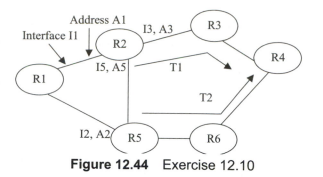

Figure 12.44 Exercise 12.10

R4 (owner of the label) assigns a label of 14, which is carried as a single label (topLabel) on the IP/MPLS packet.

The ingress router R1 contains the *outSegment* and cross-connect components and the egress router R2 contains the *inSegment* and cross-connect components. Use the *mplsInSegmentTable*, *mplsOutSegmentTable*, and *mplsXCTable* in MPLS LSR MIB [RFC 3813] to specify the output segment and cross-connect in R1 and the input segment and cross-connect in R4 .

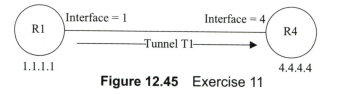

Figure 12.45 Exercise 11

12. Figure 12.38 that shows the example of an LSP is represented in Figure 12.46 with a tunnel interface between LER-1 and LER-3. Generate the appropriate *mplsInSegmentTable*, *mplsOutSegmentTable*, and *mplsXCTable* using RFC 3813 for the three routers.

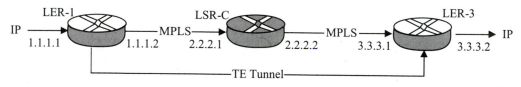

Figure 12.46 Exercise 12

13. How many entries in *ifTable* for SDH Medium/Section/Line Layer will one get for an SDH network element containing two STM-16 ports, two STM-4 ports and eight STM-1 ports? Give the appropriate values for the fields *ifIndex, ifDescr, ifType*, and *ifSpeed* for those entries.

14. How many entries in *if Table* for the SDH paths layer will one get for an STM-4 port in an SDH network element? Give the appropriate values for the fields *ifIndex, ifDescr, ifType*, and *ifSpeed* for those entries.

15. How many possible entries in *ifTable* for the SDH VCs layer will one get for an STM-4 port in an SDH network element? Give the appropriate values for the fields *ifIndex, ifDescr, ifType, ifSpeed*, and *ifPhysAddress* for those entries. For *ifPhysAddress* use the following syntax: j–k–l–m where j, k, l, m represent the VC-4, VC-3, VC-2, VC 12 numbers, respectively.

Note: Use only the relevant numbers; for example, for a VC-3, l and m are not applicable.

16. Draw the SONET/SDH layers—physical medium layer, path layer, and virtual tributary layer as in Figure 12.42 for STM-1 transmission over optical fiber. Assume that the path layer comprises 3 STS-1 links, each carrying exclusively E1, DS1, and DS3 signals. Mark the number of channels in the VT layer.

Broadband Network Management: Wired and Optical Access Networks

OBJECTIVES

- *(Wired) Broadband access networks*
  - *Cable or HFC (hybrid fiber cable) network*
  - *ADSL (asymmetrical digital subscriber line) network*
  - *PON (passive optical network)*
- *Cable access network*
  - *Popular in North American continent*
  - *"Triple play" service can be provided*
  - *DOCSIS (data-over-cable system interface specifications) standards*
- *ADSL*
  - *Predominant throughout the rest of the world*
  - *Uses conventional telephone local loop medium*
  - *Broadband voice and data services*
  - *Adopts IETF and DSL forum standards*
  - *VDSL2 for performance improvement of broadband service*
- *PON*
  - *PON deployment configurations*
  - *Ethernet-based PON, EPON*
  - *EPON protocol architecture*
  - *EPON management*
  - *EPON MIBs*

13.1 BROADBAND ACCESS NETWORK

We learned the general concepts about broadband wide area network (WAN) and services in the previous chapter. We will now address the basics of technologies and management of access networks in this chapter.

As shown in Figure 12.1 in the last chapter, three different types of customers have access to the broadband network. The first type is a corporate or enterprise user who has a campus-wide network. The second type is the service provider. The third type is a residential and small business customer, who has multimedia requirements. However, they typically have neither a sophisticated LAN environment nor large bandwidth requirements in both directions.

In the first customer type, access to broadband WAN for corporate or enterprise customers is accomplished by an optical fiber link from the WAN router or switch to a campus device, which could be either a switch or a router.

The second type of user, a service provider, can be one of several choices: a cable operator, or a local exchange carrier or telephone company, or a multiple system operator (MSO) who multiplexes several services, such as telephony, video, and data services. The interface to the WAN in this case is via a gateway. The physical link between the gateway and the WAN depends on the demographic configuration.

The third type of customer, namely residential and small business office, is the focus of broadband access network and technology. We will address the wired access networks including passive optical network (PON) in this chapter. We will cover wireless access networks in Chapter 14.

Access networks to customer premises from the backbone MPLS/ATM/IP WAN are shown in Figure 13.1. One of the access networks is the OC-n/STS-n links. We discussed the OC–n link in the last chapter and it is shown in Figure 13.1 for completeness. It generally has a router or a switch at either end of the access network. It is primarily used for enterprise connection.

Four categories of access technologies are currently available either in deployable or developmental stage for connection to residential and small and medium business customers. Two access networks that are extensively deployed now are networks based on HFC (Hybrid Fiber Coaxial)/cable modem (CM) and digital subscriber line (DSL). The access network based on either of these two technologies could support the use of voice, video, and data equipment. In the case of a cable access network, information to the CM at the customer site is transmitted via a HFC network from the head end located at an MSO facility. The access network based on DSL uses the existing twisted pair loop facility from the central office to the customer premises. There are various DSL technologies, as we will soon learn, and based

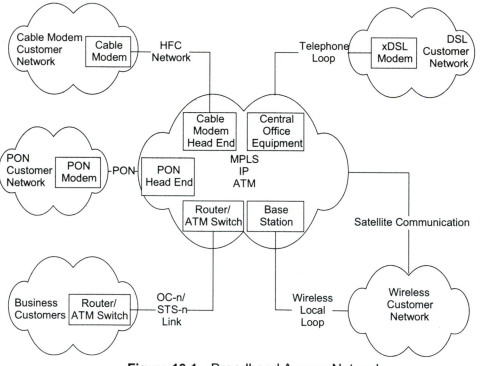

Figure 13.1 Broadband Access Network

on which one is being deployed, that particular type of xDSL modem is used at the customer premises. Corresponding equipment is used at the telephone central office.

Figure 13.1 also shows the third and fourth access networks, which are a wireless customer network and a PON, which are in the early stage of deployment and are trailing behind cable and ADSL. Another method of getting broadband service to home is via a satellite communication network. This is primarily one-way to the customer location and is not easily amenable for interactive broadband communication due to large propagation delay. It is, however, weak in industrial and hard-to-reach rural applications.

An overview of broadband access technology is presented in Section 13.2. CM technology using HFC cable is covered in Section 13.3. Cable access network management is discussed in Section 13.4. Section 13.5 describes Data-over-Cable System Interface Specifications (DOCSIS) standards. We present digital subscriber line technology in Section 13.6 and ADSL in Section 13.7. Section 13.8 covers ADSL management. Section 13.9 describes the enhanced versions of ADSL–ADSL2 and ADSL2+ —as well as VDSL. Sections 13.10 and 13.11 deal with PON technology and management.

13.2 BROADBAND ACCESS TECHNOLOGY

Broadband access technology is still an emerging field. There are four modes of access using four different technologies. As shown in Figure 13.2, they are cable, DSL, wireless, and PON communication. Satellite communication technology is not presented in the figure as it is not deployed as access network to home and SME.

Cable access network technology uses television transmission facilities and CMs and is the most widely deployed access network in North America. Cable access network could be implemented as either one-way with telephony-return or two-way. In the one-way telephony-return configuration, the downstream signal to the customer traverses the cable medium. The return upstream signal from the customer premises is carried over the telephone facilities using a regular modem. Typically, data from a residential customer are significantly less than that to the customer and hence this approach of two- or one-way communication is acceptable. For example, the residential customer may make a request for a movie or download programs from the Internet. Such requests require small bandwidth. The transmission of a movie and digital video, or downloading of the program to the customer site, requires large bandwidth. In a two-way mode of cable access network technology, both upstream and downstream are handled by the HFC medium using CMs.

The DSL has three different implementations and is generally referred to as xDSL, where x stands for asymmetric (A), high-speed (H), or very high data rate (V). All are based on using existing local loop telephone facilities.

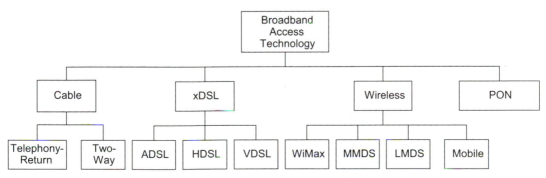

Figure 13.2 Broadband Access Technologies

Wireless access technology uses wireless transmission for the downstream link to the customer site and either wireless or telephony-return for the upstream link from the customer site. Wireless access network can be implemented either as fixed wireless or mobile wireless. Various frequency spectra and technologies are used in wireless transmission. This industry and market are just emerging and the management of wireless access technology is the subject of Chapter 14.

PON technology is technically ready for commercial deployment, but has been delayed due to business considerations of cost and lack of need for large bandwidth to residential customers.

13.3   CABLE MODEM TECHNOLOGY

CM technology, also known as HFC technology, is based on existing cable television (cable TV or CATV) technology. Originally, cable TV systems were built on coaxial cable facilities from the head end of the MSO to the customer premises and used a tree structure. It has since been upgraded in most places today to HFC, where the signal is brought to a fiber node via a pair of optical fibers and then distributed via a coaxial cable to the customer premises. This is shown in Figure 13.3. At the head end, signals from various sources, such as traditional satellite services, analog and digital services using WAN, Internet service provider (ISP) services using a private backbone network, and voice-over-IP service are multiplexed and up-converted from an electrical (radio frequency (RF)) to an optical signal. Communication is one way on the optical fiber. There is a pair of optical fibers from the head end to the fiber node, each carrying one-way traffic in the opposite direction. The optical signal is down-converted to an RF at the

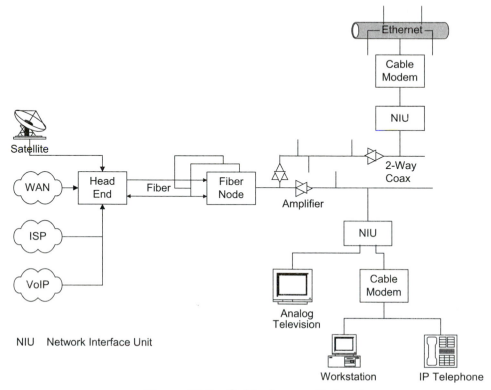

Figure 13.3   Cable Access Network

fiber node and travels over the coaxial cable in a duplex mode. The signal that goes from head end to the customer premises is called the downstream signal or the forward path signal, and the signal going from the customer premises to the head end is called the upstream signal or the reverse path signal.

The broadband signal over the coaxial cable differs from the baseband signal over a pair of wires, for example, a telephone signal of up to 4 kHz. The baseband signal is transmitted over a short distance of up to a few kilometers. The coaxial cable is a shared access medium and is designed to carry signals up to tens of kilometers. The signal is amplified on the way in both directions, as shown in Figure 13.3. A duplex mode of communication is achieved in the United States by transmitting the downstream signal in a high-frequency band, 50–860 MHz, and the upstream signal in the low-frequency band of 5–42 MHz. The downstream signal includes an analog CATV spectrum.

At the customer premises there is a network interface unit (NIU), also referred to as network interface device (NID), which is the demarcation point between the customer network and the service provider network. The analog signal is split at the NIU. The TV signal is directed to the TV and the data to the CM. The CM converts the digitally modulated analog carrier signal to an Ethernet output feeding a PC or an IP telephone either directly or using a home distribution network, such as a LAN. Although most cable service providers offer video and data services, there are several service providers now offering "triple play" service of voice, video, and data in some regions of North America.

The broadband cable access system with the CM can process data at a much faster rate than a conventional telephone modem or integrated services digital network (ISDN). A typical comparative data transmission rate to transmit a single 500 kilobyte message is shown in Table 13.1.

There are several components to be managed in a cable access network. Let us first review the basics of HFC technology to understand the function of the various components to be managed. HFC technology is based on (1) HFC transmission medium and mode; (2) CM at customer premises; (3) cable modem termination system (CMTS) at the head end; and (4) radio-frequency spread-spectrum technique to carry multiple signals over HFC to handle multimedia services of telephony (voice), television (video), and computer communication (data).

13.3.1 Cable Transmission Medium and Modes

The HFC plant consists of multiple pairs of optical fibers to the fiber nodes. Each fiber carries traffic to a fiber node. The head end equipment converts telephony, digital data, digital video, and analog TV signals to optical signals and transmits them to fiber nodes. Each node serves from several hundred to several thousand households. The fiber node is connected to households via a multipoint coaxial cable. As signals are attenuated and dispersed (with frequency), there are amplifiers inserted in the coaxial cables. Since the coaxial cable supports traffic in both directions, in contrast to the fiber that supports one-way, the amplifiers have to be two-way amplifiers, as shown in Figure 13.3. Amplifiers enable coaxial cable systems to be extended to tens of miles. The last section of the HFC plant consists of the section from the coax running along the street to the NIU in the house, referred to as "tap-to-TV" in CATV.

Table 13.1 Comparative Data Transmission Speeds

Telephone modem 28.8 kbps	6–8 minutes
ISDN 64 kbps	1–1.5 minutes
Cable modem 10 Mbps	Approximately 1 second

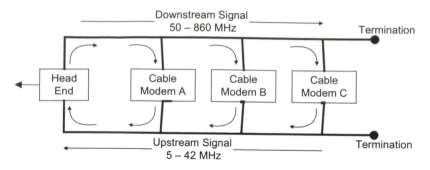

Figure 13.4   Two-way Transmission in a Coaxial Cable

Figure 13.4 shows the architecture of several CMs communicating with each other on a coaxial cable. Although the modems share a common coaxial cable to communicate in both directions, the figure shows the downstream (forward) and upstream (reverse) paths separated to represent the concept clearly. The downstream and upstream paths are separated in the frequency spectrum, downstream signals 50–860 MHz and upstream signals 5–42 MHz. The downstream bandwidth of a channel is 6 MHz, while the upstream bandwidth is variable based on implementation. It ranges from 200 kHz to 3.2 MHz. CMs receive the signal in the downstream signal band and transmit in the upstream signal band. Let us trace the path of Cable Modem B sending a message to Cable Modem A. The message first goes past Cable Modem A (because A cannot pick up the signal from the bottom path in the figure) to the head end, where it is converted to the downstream band frequency and retransmitted. Cable Modem A then sees the message addressed to it from B coming in the downstream (from the top in the figure) and picks it up from the medium. If the message is to be transmitted outside the cable access network, the head end, acting as either a bridge or a router, redirects it appropriately.

Information is carried in the coaxial cable in a shared mode. The unique address and other security features protect the privacy of information for each, as the information can be detected and decoded only by the intended user.

13.3.2   Cable Modem

The CM modulates and demodulates the digital signal from the customer's equipment to the RF signal that is carried on the cable. A similar operation is done at the head end equipment. A single 6-MHz channel in the downstream can support multiple data streams. Different modulation techniques support different capabilities. There are three modes of modulation schemes. They are amplitude shift keying (ASK), frequency shift keying (FSK), and phase shift keying (PSK). Variations and combinations of these schemes are used in CM technology. Of these, the more common modulation techniques used are quadrature phase shift keying (QPSK) and quadrature amplitude modulation (QAM). In order to appreciate how the different modulation schemes accomplish the desired objectives, we need to understand the digital-to-analog encoding schemes, which we will now briefly review.

Figure 13.5 shows the basic concept. A digital signal, for example from a computer, is converted to an analog signal by the modem, in our case a CM. The converted analog signal modulates an RF carrier. The modulated signal occupies a band of frequencies around the carrier frequency, shown as the channel bandwidth. For example, if the digital signal in Figure 13.5 varies at a rate of 1 Mbps, alternating between 0 and 1, its baseband is 1 MHz. It is frequency modulated with a carrier frequency of 100 MHz.

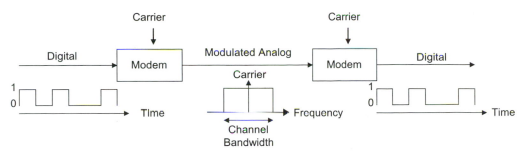

Figure 13.5 Digital-to-Analog Encoding

The modulated RF signal will have a carrier frequency of 100 MHz and a channel bandwidth of 1 MHz. At the receiving end, the receiving modem converts the signal back to the original digital format.

We should clearly understand telecommunication transmission terminology used in managing and evaluating modems. They are bit rate, baud rate, carrier frequency, and bandwidth. The bit rate is the number of bits per second that traverses the medium. The baud rate is the signal units (symbols) per second. The bit rate is baud rate times the number of bits per symbol. In Figure 13.5 the digital signal is shown as binary 0 and 1, i.e., 2 levels (2^1). Hence, the number of bits per symbol is one. The bit rate and the baud rate (symbol rate) are the same in this case.

The input signal could also be quantized into multiple levels, for example, into four levels (2^2). We would then need two bits to represent each signal unit (00, 01, 10, and 11). In this situation, the bit rate would be twice the baud rate. Information is carried as a digital RF signal by modulating the baseband signal by the RF carrier. For example, in the ASK method, the carrier frequency is turned on and off for each bit representing 1 and 0.

The channel bandwidth and data rate depend on the rate at which the signal unit changes and the type of modulation. Thus, for the simple binary case shown in Figure 13.5, bit rate, baud rate, and bandwidth (in Hz) are all the same. For the four-level scheme mentioned earlier, the bandwidth needed for amplitude and phase modulation schemes (which are the ones of interest for us here) can be visualized as the frequency corresponding to the rate at which the signal unit changes, i.e., the baud rate of 10^6. The data rate, as we noted, is twice the baud rate, i.e., 2 Mbps.

In the QPSK modulation, the four levels (00, 01,10, and 11) are represented by the four phase states (0, 90, 270, and 180 degrees). Since PSK is relatively insensitive to external noise amplitude, it is preferred over amplitude modulation (AM) for data transmission at low frequencies, where noise is more predominant. Thus, QPSK is the preferred method of modulation for the upstream signal shown in Figure 13.4. A 6-MHz channel transmitting a signal with QPSK modulation would support a 6×10^6 baud rate and 12 Mbps (2^2 levels or 2 bits, and hence $2 \times 6 \times 10^6$ bps) bit rate capacity.

PSK is limited by the difficulty of detecting small phase shifts. It can be combined with AM to increase the number of levels of a signal. This is called the QAM, *quadrature* indicating the ability to clearly distinguish between levels, and not implying four levels. The number of possible levels is the multiplication of the number of PSK and AM levels. Thus, we can create 16-QAM by combining eight levels of PSK and two levels of AM, or four levels each of PSK and AM. The downstream signal is at a higher frequency band and carries a lot more information than the upstream signal. Since the downstream uses more bandwidth and a spectrally more efficient modulation scheme could be used, it has higher information capacity. QAM is the preferred method of modulation for the downstream signal shown in Figure 13.4. The same 6-MHz signal channel using 16-QAM would require a 24 Mbps (2^4 levels) channel capacity.

A good and detailed treatment on analog-to-digital encoding can be found in [Forouzan, 2006]. We will present a conceptual view of the quantization levels of digital encoding using a two-dimensional constellation diagram. Figure 13.6 shows the constellation diagram for QPSK encoding. The amplitude is maintained constant and the phase is quantized at 0, 90, 180, and 270 degrees corresponding to 00, 01, 10, and 11 levels indicated by s1, s2, s3, and s4, respectively. The absolute values of the phase level can be arbitrary, but they should all be separated in phase quadrature from their neighbors.

Figure 13.7 shows two representations for an 8-QAM encoding scheme. An 8-QAM encoding is accomplished as (amplitude × phase) a combination of 4 × 2 or 2 × 4.

Observing Figure 13.4 and Figure 13.5 together, we notice that signals in upstream and downstream are at different carrier frequencies and hence can be carried on the same medium. CMs transmit and listen at their respective frequencies for duplex operation.

Table 13.2 shows maximum CM speeds [Wikipedia3; National Television System Committee]. The number in parentheses indicates usable data rate in each cable. A 6-MHz channel spacing will allow ten

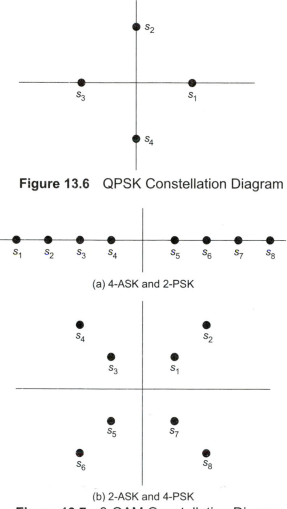

Figure 13.6 QPSK Constellation Diagram

(a) 4-ASK and 2-PSK

(b) 2-ASK and 4-PSK

Figure 13.7 8-QAM Constellation Diagram

Table 13.2 Cable Modem Speeds

	DOCSIS		EURODOCSIS	
Version	Downstream Mbit/s	Upstream Mbit/s	Downstream Mbit/s	Upstream Mbit/s
1.x	42.88 (38)	10.24 (9) Mbit/s	55.62 (50)	10.24 (9)
2.0	42.88 (38)	30.72 (27)	55.62 (50)	30.72 (27)
3.0 4 channel	+171.52 (+152)	+122.88 (+108)	+222.48 (+200)	+122.88 (+108)
3.0 8 channel	+343.04 (+304)	+122.88 (+108)	+444.96 (+400)	+122.88 (+108)

bonded 6-MHz channels as maximum spectrum allocation for DOCSIS 3.0 data. A 60-MHz spectrum allocation could increase with consumer needs and re-allocation of analog TV channels into compressed digital space, leveraging the capability of DOCSIS 3.0 infrastructure to allow for 1 Gbit/s speeds in the future.

HFC uses tree topology, and upstream and downstream transmissions are handled differently. As discussed in Section 13.3.1, the downstream signal on each RF channel is transmitted in the broadcast mode, just as TV broadcast. The upstream signal from each customer's equipment has to be coordinated by the head end equipment.

While downstream traffic in a CM network is a one-to-many configuration, upstream traffic is the opposite, i.e., many-to-one. Multiple subscribers try to access the system simultaneously. Even though a user may not see another subscriber's signal while accessing the medium, there may actually be another subscriber sending information in another branch of the network and signals arriving at the head end will then collide. Users are time-division-multiplexed for the upstream traffic at a different frequency from the downstream traffic by a centralized controller. Such a scheme is called time division multiple access (TDMA).

Interoperability between different vendor products is accomplished by standardizing CM system specifications. There are several groups that have been working on standard specifications for broadband service over cable network. Standards are being developed under the Multimedia Cable Network System (MCNS), the Digital Audio/Video Interoperability Council (DAVIC), IETF, IEEE 802.14 Working Group, and the ATM Forum. The DOCSIS (Data-over-cable service interface specifications) standard that is being developed under MCNS has been adopted as the industry standard. This means we would be able to buy any vendor's CMs and use them for broadband service, just as we buy dial-up modems for dial-up data transmission.

The CM, along with the head end, can handle two-way data traffic over the HFC link. Some CMs are designed as one-way with the return path via telephone link, termed telco return.

The CM is connected to the subscriber PC on an Ethernet LAN interface. Based on the modem, the LAN interface can be either for a single PC connection or to a LAN with multiple PCs. Many CM vendors offer both these options.

Thanks to SNMP standards in network management, most CMs have an SNMP management agent embedded in them, which makes it feasible to remotely manage the CMs. There are also outsourcing companies that manage CM sites for small and medium enterprises (SMEs) and MSOs from remote locations.

13.3.3 Cable Modem Termination System

All CMs terminate on a server, called the CMTS at the head end. The hybrid optical fiber and coaxial cable link (HFC) connect the CMs to the CMTS at the head end. The CMTS provides a number of services to the access network. It is the gateway to the external network from the access network. It multiplexes and demultiplexes the signals from the CMs to interface to the external network.

As we would expect with the topology of a broadband LAN, the upstream and downstream propagation frequencies are different. CMTS performs the frequency conversion. For example, when a CM wants to communicate with another CM in the same access network, the signal goes upstream to the CMTS at the head end. It is converted to the downstream carrier frequency by the CMTS and propagated downstream as a broadcast message. The receiving CM picks up the message by reading the destination address in the message.

From the above two functions, we notice that CMTS does the function of either routing (to the external network) or bridging (intra-access network). The CM system developed by some vendors builds these functions within CMTS. The routing function could also be accomplished by an external router.

CMTS interfaces with operations support systems that serve the function of managing the access network. It also supports security and the access controller system to handle the integrity and security of the access network. We will discuss the architecture and components of CMTS in Section 13.3.5.

13.3.4 RF Spectrum for a Cable Modem

Some key components in broadband services to home are the various aspects of (frequency) spectral decomposition and consequent necessity for spectrum management. Let us first observe the asymmetric configuration to achieve two-way communication. We further notice that the allocation of bandwidth in the two directions is different based on the type of service. Although spectrum usage in HFC extends to 860 MHz, spectrum usage may extend beyond 860 MHz depending on the implementation. Figure 13.8 shows an example of a typical allocation of the CM RF spectrum for different services in the upstream (reverse) and downstream (forward) directions [Ahmed and Vecchi, 1995; Davis, 1998]. The upstream or reverse signal is allocated the low end of the spectrum from 5–42 MHz. The downstream or forward

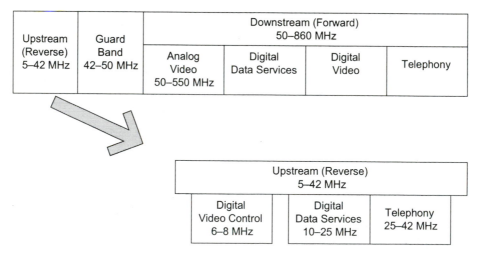

Figure 13.8 Example of a Radio Frequency Assignment

signal is allocated from 50–860 MHz. There is a guard band 42–50 MHz to separate the forward and reverse spectral bands. There are currently variations in the allocation of these from vendor to vendor.

Downstream contains an analog video from 50–550 MHz and is compatible with current TV requirements. Digital data services providing data service to home are offered up to 30 Mbps data rate. It is important to distinguish between bandwidth allocation and data rate. For example, 64-QAM can produce 6 bits per symbol ($2^6 = 64$) and thus a 6-MHz bandwidth that is used for conventional cable channel can produce 36 Mbps (6 bits/symbol × 6 MHz) of data. Digital data services, digital video, and telephony services have bandwidth allocated in both the forward and reverse directions.

Downstream channel bandwidth is 6 MHz, and upstream channel bandwidth is variable based on symbol rate. Toshiba CM, which is DOCSIS compliant, offers upstream channel bandwidths from 200 kHz to 3.2 MHz using QPSK/16-QAM modulation schemes.

CMs are designed to automatically tune themselves to upstream and downstream channel frequencies on initial installation. They listen to downstream data channels from the head end and initiate communication with them. The head end assigns a specific downstream and upstream channel for the CM.

Under noisy conditions, the CM could dynamically switch to different downstream and upstream channels to improve quality of service. Such a feature is called the frequency-agile capability and the CM the frequency-agile CM.

13.3.5 Data-Over-Cable Reference Architecture

The top half of Figure 13.9 shows the system reference architecture of HFC data-over-cable services and interfaces. It is a subset of the HFC network shown in Figure 13.3 portraying a link from the subscriber workstation to the WAN connection. It is made up of head end, HFC link, CM, and subscriber PC. The head end is connected to WAN. Multiple head ends could be connected via the WAN to a regional center head end. In such a case, the local head end may be referred to as the distribution hub. The HFC link consists of fiber links and a coaxial cable, connecting the head end to the CM at the subscriber location.

The bottom half of Figure 13.9 presents an expanded view of the head end. It comprises cable modem termination system (CMTS), switch/router, combiner, transmitter, receiver, splitter and filter, servers, operations support system/element manager, and security and access controller. The CMTS consists of a modulator, *mod*, and a *demodulator*, demod, on the HFC link side, and a network terminator, *network term*, to the switch/router connecting to the WAN and to the Telephone Router Access Controller, *TRAC*. The modulator is connected to the combiner, which multiplexes data and video signals and feeds them to the transmitter. The RF signal is converted to an optical signal in the transmitter. The receiver converts the optical signal down to the RF level and feeds it to the splitter, where the various channels are split. The demodulator in the CMTS demodulates the analog signal back to digital data.

There are servers at the head end that handle applications and databases. The security function (to be described soon) is managed by the security and access controller. The operations support system and the element manager perform the functions of management at various management levels–elements, network, and service.

There are six interfaces indicated in Figure 13.9. Data-over-Cable Service Interface Specifications (DOCSIS) categorizes these into three. They are: (1) data interfaces; (2) operations support system interfaces (OSSIs) and telephony-return interface; and (3) RF and security interfaces. We have listed some of them in Table 13.3. Table 13.3 lists documents associated with the various versions of DOCSIS, namely versions 1.0, 1.1, 2.0, and 3.0. We first focus on DOCSIS 1.0. DOCSIS documents can be downloaded from http://www.cablelabs.com and are not listed in References.

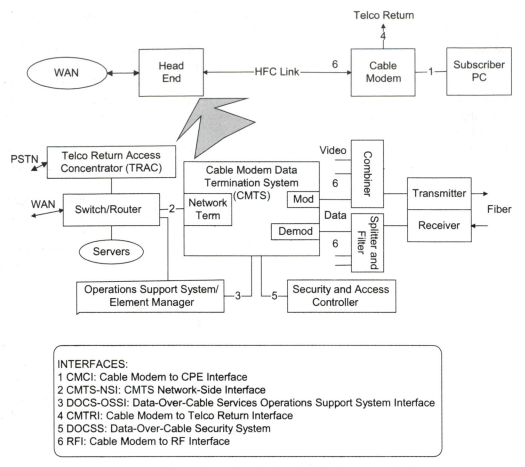

Figure 13.9 Data-Over-Cable System Reference Architecture

There are two interfaces shown in Figure 13.9 in the data interfaces category. They are the CM to the customer premises equipment (CPE) interface (1), and the CMTS-NSI interface (2), which is the network side of the interface of CMTS to the switch/router. SP-CMCI-I10-050408 addresses the CM to customer premises equipment interface (CMCI) specification. CM-SP-L2VPN-I08-080522 and SP-CMTS-NSI-I01-960702 deal with the CMTS—network-side interface specification.

The second category of interfaces is the OSSIs (3), data-over-cable services operations support systems interface (DOCS-OSSI), and the telephony-return interface (4), CM-to-Telco return interface (CMTRI). The element management system is considered an operations support system. Other operations support systems could include administrative systems that manage service and business-layer management, as well as test systems. CM-SP-OSSIv1.1-C01-050907 and CM-SP-OSSIv2.0-I09-050812 are associated with DOCSIS 1.1 and DOCSIS 2.0 specifications. CM-SP-M-OSSI-I07-071206 and CM-SP-OSSIv3.0-I07-080522 address DOCSIS 3.0 specifications. SP-CMTRI-I01-970804 details CM telephony-return interface specifications. RF interface specifications are described in SP-RFIv1-I01-990311 and CM-SP-DRFI-I06-080215 DOCSIS documents.

Table 13.3 HFC/Data-Over-Cable System Documentation

SP-CMCI-I10-050408	Cable modem to customer premises equipment interface (CMCI) specification
SP-CMTRI-I01-970804	CM telephony-return interface specification
CM-SP-L2VPN-I08-080522 SP-CMTS-NSI-I01-960702	CMTS—network-side interface specification
SP-RFIv1-I01-990311 CM-SP-DRFI-I06-080215	RF interface specification
CM-SP-BPI+-I12-050812	Baseline privacy interface specification
CM-SP-OSSIv1.1-C01-050907 CM-SP-OSSIv2.0-I09-050812 CM-SP-M-OSSI-I07-071206 CM-SP-OSSIv3.0-I07-080522	OSS interface specifications
RFC 4639	Cable device MIB
RFC 4547	Event notification MIB
RFC 4546	RF interface MIB
RFC 3083 RFC 4131	Baseline privacy MIB
draft-ietf-ipcdn-qos-mib-07.txt RFC 4323	Quality of service MIB
draft-ietf-ipcdn-tri-mib-00.txt, July 30, 1998	Telephony-return interface MIB for CMs and CMTS
RFC 4036	CMTS for subscriber management

The third category of interfaces is the security system interface (5), Data-Over-Cable Security System (DOCSS), and RF interfaces (6), RFI. There are three security requirements: security system, CM removable security module, and data-over-cable baseline privacy interface (BPI) described in CM-SP-BPI+-I12-050812. Many security and privacy issues associated with shared medium become especially important in CM systems. We have addressed some security and privacy issues in Chapter 7. Privacy issues become more complex in that privacy within customer premises also needs to be considered. This is addressed by Home Cable discussed later in Chapter 15. RF interfaces are between the CM and the HFC network and between the CMTS and the HFC network in the upstream and downstream directions.

MIBs associated with CM systems are described in the various RFCs listed in Table 13.3. RFC 4639 describes the cable device MIB module and RFC 4547 addresses event notification MIB. The QOS MIB module is specified in RFC 4323. RFC 4036 provides a set of objects required for the management of DOCSIS CMTS for subscriber management. The telephony-return interface MIB for CMs and CMTS has stayed in the draft status and has not been standardized.

RFC 4546 specifies the MIB module that provides a set of objects required for the management of DOCSIS-compliant CM and CMTS RF interfaces. The specification is derived in part from the parameters and protocols described in [ITU-T_J.122]. This MIB module is structured as three groups: management information pertinent to both the CM and the CMTS *docsIfBaseObjects*; management information pertinent to the CM only *docsIfCmObjects*; and management information pertinent to the CMTS only *docsIfCmtsObjects*. Tables within each of these groups cover different functions, e.g., upstream queue services, channel characteristics, media access controller (MAC) layer management, etc. Rows created automatically (e.g., by the device according to the hardware configuration) may, and generally will, have a mixture of configuration and status objects within them. Rows that are meant to be created by the management station are generally restricted to configuration (read–create) objects.

RFC 3083 is DOCSIS 1.0 BPI MIB module and deals with management of BPI. It is derived from the operational model described in the DOCSIS BPI Specification DOCSIS 1.0 and is an extension of the RF interface MIB described in RFC 4546. RFC 4131 addresses managed objects for baseline privacy interface plus (BPI+). It specifies a set of objects required for the management of the features of DOCSIS 1.1 and DOCSIS 2.0 CM and CMTS. The specification is derived from the operational model described in the DOCSIS BPI+ specification for DOCSIS 1.1 and 2.0. The original BPI MIB structure has mostly been preserved in the BPI+ MIB.

13.4 CABLE ACCESS NETWORK MANAGEMENT

The cable access network system with CMs (as well as other access networks) is more complex to manage than either computer network or telecommunication network. The management of computer communication network is involved with data layers, the data link layer and above. Telecommunication network management is involved with physical-layer management. Cable access network management is involved with both. A part of the HFC link is fiber and the other part is coaxial cable. There is the complexity of frequency spectrum management. Since cable access technology is under the administration of an MSO, which has to deal with other service providers in close business relationship, the service and business management shown in Figure 10.11 also needs to be addressed.

Figure 13.10 presents protocol-layer architecture of a cable access network system showing both applications and network management components. The head end in the figure is shown connected to a WAN via an MPLS link, and to the HFC via an HFC link. The head end shows both the applications and the SNMP manager in the application layer. The network manager in the head end can also be configured as RMON, if the network management system (NMS) at a regional center is configured as managing multiple head ends. An SNMP agent resides in the CM that monitors both RF and Ethernet interfaces. Communication between the head end and the CM is via the HFC link, containing both fiber and coaxial cable. The interface between the CM and the subscriber PC is an Ethernet interface.

There are two functional areas in the management of a broadband cable access network. They are network maintenance and subscriber (customer) support. In the following sections, we shall focus only

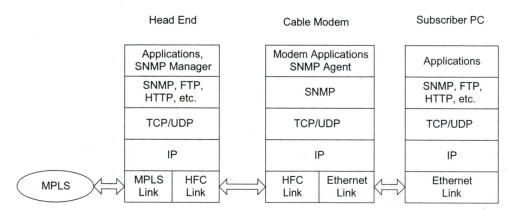

Figure 13.10 Protocol-Layer Architecture in a Cable Access Network System

on network maintenance associated with the element management layer and the network management layer. Customer billing aspects are addressed in DOCSIS 3.0 specifications. Cable access network management involves physical-layer network management and data network management. At the physical layer, management functions include error detection and correction of ingress noise interference, amplifier gains, signal levels at the CMs, and power supply voltages. Data network management functions include traditional configuration, fault, performance, and security management of various components and the network. These are managed using SNMP MIBs.

We can broadly divide cable network management into four components: CM management, CMTS management, HFC link management, and RF spectrum management. We will discuss each of these briefly in the next three subsections.

13.4.1   Cable Modem and CMTS Management

CMs and CMTS can be managed using SNMP management. Different vendors implement the network management function in different ways. Some vendors have CMs and CMTS agents built in them and are managed from a centralized NMS directly. However, others have the network management agent interface built in their head end CMTS, which acquires information on individual modems. An NMS acquires data on CMs and CMTS from the CMTS agent.

Figure 13.11 shows the MIBs associated with CM and CMTS that are relevant to managing CM and CMTS. The MIBs could be grouped into three categories. The first category is the generic set of IETF MIBs, *system {mib-2 1}, interfaces {mib-2 2}* [RFC 1213], and *ifMIB {mib-2 31}* that describes interface types [RFC 2863]. The second category comprises MIBs for the interfaces of CM and CMTS, *docsIfMib*. The *docsIfMib {mib-2.transmission 127}* is a subnode under transmission and includes objects for BPI. The *docsTrCmMIB {mib-2 transmission 128}* specifies the telephony-return (or telco-return) interfaces for CM and CMTS. The third category deals with the set of objects for CM and CMTS. We will now discuss the second and third categories.

Figure 13.12 shows the Data-Over-Cable System (DOCS) Interface MIB that supplements the standard SNMP interface MIBs [RFC 1213, 1573]. The original specifications covered only the CM and CMTS objects, which are the subnodes 1, 2, and 3 under *docsIfMIB*. The updated version is covered in RFC 4546. The baseline privacy MIB, *docsBpiMIB*, has been added later as subnode 5 and contains the same

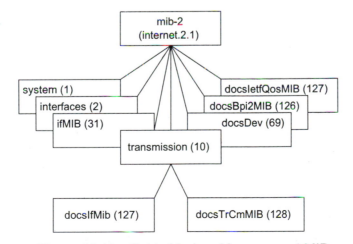

Figure 13.11 Cable Modem Management MIBs

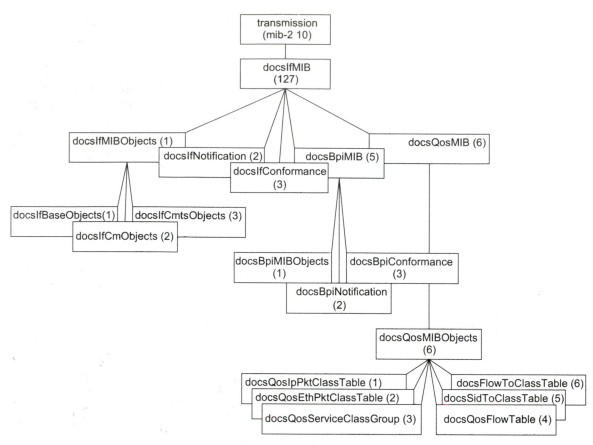

Figure 13.12 DOCS Interface MIB

subgroup structure as nodes 1, 2, and 3 under *docsIfMIB* [RFC 3083, 4131] in Table 13.3. It deals with the privacy issues under security considerations mentioned in Section 13.3.5. Notification subgroups in the interface MIBs are currently placeholders. DOCSIS quality of service MIB, *docsQoSMIB*, is node 6 under *docsIfMIB* and describes control of QoS features for the CM and CMTS [RFC 4323] in Table 13.3.

The DOCS interface objects group, *docsIfMIBObjects*, has three subgroups: base interface objects group that specifies objects common to CM and CMTS; CM interface objects group, *docsIfCmObjects*, which pertains to CM; and CMTS interface objects group, *docsIfCmtsObjects*, which pertains to CMTS.

The RF spectrum has a layered interface similar to that of ATM sublayers. However, the multiple RF channels in the upstream and downstream also need to be specified in this case. Fortunately, specifications of RFC 2863 permit this extension. The layered structure of the RF interface is shown in Figure 13.13. The figure shows an example of one downstream and two upstream channels interfacing to an RF MAC channel on the top user interface, and to the RF physical layer on the service provider interface on the bottom.

The baseline privacy objects group [RFC 3083], *docsBpiMIBObjects*, has eight subgroups, as shown in Table 13.4. The subgroups define the baseline privacy requirements for privacy of CM and CMTS. Specifications include definition of objects, authorization tables, encryption keys, and multicast control tables. Conformance specifications are defined in the *docsBpiConformance* group.

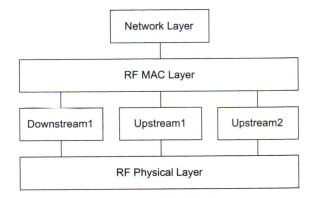

Figure 13.13 RF MAC Interface

Table 13.4 DOCS Baseline Privacy MIB

ENTITY	OID	DESCRIPTION
docsBpiCmObjects	docsBpiMIBObjects 1	Baseline privacy objects for CM
docsBpiCmBaseTable	docsBpiCmObjects 1	Baseline privacy CM base and authorization table
docsBpiCmTEKTable	docsBpiCmObjects 2	Baseline privacy traffic encryption key table
docsBpiCmtsObjects	docsBpiMIBObjects 2	Baseline privacy CMTS objects
docsBpiCmtsBaseTable	docsBpiCmtsObjects 1	Baseline privacy CMTS base table
docsBpiCmtsAuthTable	docsBpiCmtsObjects 2	Baseline privacy CMTS authorization table
docsBpiCmtsTEKTable	docsBpiCmtsObjects 3	Baseline privacy CMTS traffic encryption key table
docsBpiMulticastcontrol	docsBpiCmtsObjects 4	Baseline privacy CMTS multicast control group

DOCSIS BPI+ MIB module (BPI+ MIB) provides a set of objects required for the management of the BPI+ features of DOCSIS 1.1 and DOCSIS 2.0 CM and CMTS. The reader is referred to [RFC 4131] for details on these.

The DOCS quality of service MIB is an extension to the QoS objects defined in *docsIfMIBObjects* and *docsDev*. This has gone through several iterations as described in the ietf document series draft-ietf-ipcdn-qos-mib-NN.txt. It has finally been released as RFC 4323. *docsQosMIB* shown as subnode 6 under *docsIfMIB* is now subnode 127, *docsIetfQosMIB,* under mib-2, as shown in Figure 13.11. There are now 11 subgroups, which are tables, and are shown in Table 13.5. These tables are under *docsQos-MIBObjects,* which is subnode 1 under *docsIetfQosMIB*. Table 13.5 presents the entities, OID, and a brief description of each.

The IP packet classification table describes IP packet classification. Each packet that is either received or routed through may be compared to an ordered list of rules pertaining to the IP (and UDP/IP) packet header. The Ethernet packet classification table serves a similar purpose at the data link layer.

A service class represents a level of service provided by CMTS to a Service Identifier (SID) or to packet flow. SID and flow are associated with exactly one service class. The *docsQosServiceClassTable* describes the set of DOCSIS QoS service classes defined in the managed device. The *docsQosFlowTable* describes the flows in the device. The mapping of service classes to SIDs is contained in the *docsQos-SidToClassTable*. The mapping of flow to service class is described in the *docsQosFlowToClassTable*.

Table 13.5 DOCS QoS MIB

ENTITY	OID	DESCRIPTION
docsQosMIBObjects	docsIetfQoSMIB 1	DOCSIS 1.1 and 2.0 QoS MIB objects
docsIetfQos PktClassTable	docsIetfQosMIBObjects 1	Packet classification configured on the CM or CMTS
docsIetfQos ParamSetTable	docsIetfQosMIBObjects 2	Describes the set of DOCSIS 1.1 and 2.0 QOS parameters in a managed device
docsIetfQos ServiceFlowTable	docsIetfQosMIBObjects 3	Describes the set of DOCSIS-QOS service flows in a managed device
docsIetfQosService FlowStatsTable	docsIetfQosMIBObjects 4	Describes statistics associated with the service flows in a managed device
docsIetfQos UpstreamStatsTable	docsIetfQosMIBObjects 5	Describes statistics associated with
docsIetfQosDynamic ServiceStatsTable	docsIetfQosMIBObjects 6	Describes statistics associated with the dynamic service flows in a managed device
docsIetfQosServiceFlowLogTable	docsIetfQosMIBObjects 7	Contains a log of the disconnected service flows in a managed device
docsIetfQosServiceClassTable	docsIetfQosMIBObjects 8	Contains a log of the disconnected service classes in a managed device
docsIetfQosServiceClassPolicyTable	docsIetfQosMIBObjects 9	Permits mapping a packet to a service class name of an active service flow so long as a classifier does not exist at a higher priority
docsIetfQos PHSTable	docsIetfQosMIBObjects 10	Describes the set of payload header suppression entries
docsIetfQosCmtsMac ToSrvFlowTable	docsIetfQosMIBObjects 11	Provides for referencing the service flows associated with a CM

Figure 13.14 shows DOCS Cable Device MIB (mib-2 69). It provides a set of objects required for the management of MCNS-compliant CM and CMTS. It consists of three groups: *docsDevMIBObjects*, *docsDevNotification*, and *docsDevConformance*.

Table 13.6 summarizes the seven groups under DOCS device MIB objects. The base group extends the MIB-II system group to the CM and CMTS devices. There is a minimum level of access security that is defined in the access table. Software upgrade can be temporarily loaded using SNMP command defined in the software group for test purposes. The server group describes server access and parameters used for initial provisioning and bootstrapping. The event group specifies control and login of events and traps. Trap/notification is to be defined in the notification group, which is currently just a place-holder. The filter group provides objects for both LLC and IP protocol filters.

The conformance group, consisting of groups and compliance groups, addresses conformance and compliance objects.

13.4.2   HFC Link Management

It is extremely important that plant facilities are managed in the HFC system. As mentioned earlier, functioning of CM depends on the signal level strength, which can be neither too high nor too low.

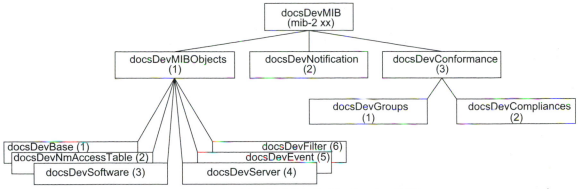

Figure 13.14 DOCS Cable Device MIB

Table 13.6 DOCS Cable Device MIB

ENTITY	OID	DESCRIPTION
docsDevMIBObjects	docsDevMIB 1	Objects of the CM and CMTS device
docsDevBase	docsDevMIBObjects 1	Extends MIB-II system group with objects needed for cable device system management
docsDevNmAccessTable	docsDevMIBObjects 2	Defines the minimum level of SNMP access security
docsDevSoftware	docsDevMIBObjects 3	Provides information for network-downloadable software upgrades
docsDevServer	docsDevMIBObjects 4	Provides information about the progress of the interaction with various provisioning servers
docsDevEvent	docsDevMIBObjects 5	Provides control and logging for event reporting
docsDevFilter	docsDevMIBObjects 6	Configures filters at the link layer and the IP layer for bridged data traffic
docsDevCpe	docsDevMIBObjects 7	CPE IP management and anti-spoofing group on CM

Signal strengths are determined by the gain of amplifiers on the HFC link and source strength at the high end. Thus, controlling parameters of the HFC plant need to be continually monitored to ensure reliability of the CM system. In legacy systems, this is done by implementing transponders that monitor the amplifiers and distribution hubs and telemetry information to the head end. A proxy server is used to convert this into SNMP objects. MIB development in this area is developed by the Society of Cable Television Engineers (SCTE), and the reader is referred to references [SCTE 24-6, 7, and 8].

13.4.3 RF Spectrum Management

Spectrum management system (SMS) is a management system that deals with the management of RF spectrum allocated to different digital services, both in the downstream and upstream. An example of spectral allocation for the various services is represented in Figure 13.8. CMTS vendors provide graphical tools to the allocation of a TV channel spectrum for a cable access network by the service provider.

13.5 DOCSIS STANDARDS

DOCSIS standards have been evolving. Most of the treatment in this chapter has so far been based on the basics of CM technology, which is DOCSIS 1.0. Later standards are oriented toward interoperability and technological improvements in performance and added services. A subset of documents associated with various versions of DOCSIS standards is given in Table 13.3.

13.5.1 DOCSIS 1.0

DOCSIS 1.0, as we just mentioned, focused on basic technology. Each vendor's CM would communicate only with its own CMTS, as communication between them was proprietary. Downstream transmission was TDM broadcast mode and upstream was hybrid of random access, TDMA, and dedicated bandwidth allocation. There was primitive security and privacy provided by the BPI, and QoS features were also limited. *docsIfMib* and *docsTrCmMib* shown in Figure 13.11 form the basis of all managed objects associated with CM technology.

13.5.2 DOCSIS 1.1

There was significant improvement in features in DOCSIS 1.1 compared to DOCSIS 1.0. Eight levels of QoS were defined to handle real-time and non-real-time video and data traffic. Several implementation improvements were introduced that enhanced performance. IP multicast using Internet Gateway Multicast Protocol (IGMP) was specified to handle multicast transmission. SNMPv3 was added to make management data secure. Service assurance was introduced to handle fault management.

Another major enhancement in DOCSIS 1.1 is the introduction of enhanced security as per BPI+. The intent of the BPI+ specification is to describe the MAC-layer security services between CMTS and CM communications. BPI+ security goals are twofold: they provide CM users with data privacy across the cable network, and they provide MSOs with service protection; i.e., prevent unauthorized users from gaining access to the network's RF MAC services. The protected RF MAC data communications services fall into three categories: (1) best-effort, high-speed, IP data services; (2) QoS (e.g., constant bit rate) data services; and (3) IP multicast group services. The earlier BPI specification [ANSI/SCTE 22-2] had "weak" service protection because the underlying key management protocol did not authenticate CMs. BPI+ strengthens this service protection by adding digital certificate-based CM authentication to its key exchange protocol.

13.5.3 DOCSIS 2.0

Two major enhancements in DOCSIS 2.0 are performance improvement and the introduction of IPv6. DOCSIS 2.0 CM support IPv6 provisioning and management. The term 2.0+IPv6 CM is used to represent such CMs. The use of IPv6 allows MSOs to conserve IPv4 addresses. This Technical Report provides guidelines for CM only. DOCSIS 2.0+IPv6 CM is required to support SNMP over IPv6.

Performance improvement is accomplished by providing options to use either TDMA or synchronous CDMA (S-CDMA) MAC protocol in upstream traffic. Note that there is no random access protocol in this version. Downstream traffic is TDM. The management system should support these protocols.

13.5.4 DOCSIS 3.0

DOCSIS 3.0 introduces a number of features that build upon features introduced in previous versions of DOCSIS. They include key new features for OSSI based on requirements established with both the introduction of new DOCSIS 3.0 features and enhancements to management capabilities that are designed to improve operational efficiencies for the MSO. Table 13.7 summarizes new requirements that support new 3.0 features and enhancements to existing management features. The table shows management features along with the traditional network management functional areas (fault, configuration, accounting, performance, and security) for the network elements (NE), CM, CMTS, and the corresponding OSI layer where those features operate.

It needs to be noted that pre-3.0 DOCSIS, network management models used IETF RFCs that were defined to use only IPv4. After the introduction of IPv6, IETF IPv6-compliant MIBs are not backward compatible with IPv4-based MIBs required by pre-3.0 DOCSIS. In contrast, provisioning system backward compatibility is a key requirement for management. To accommodate these two conflicting requirements (backward compatibility and IPv6 support using combined v4/v6 MIBs), DOCSIS 3.0 requires maintaining backward compatibility for provisioning but not monitoring.

Special mention needs to be made for accounting management, which in general includes collection of usage data and permits billing the customer based on the subscriber's use of network resources. CMTS is the NE that is responsible for providing usage statistics to support billing. Subscriber account management interface specification (SAMIS) is defined to enable prospective vendors of CM and CMTS to address the operational requirements of subscriber account management in a uniform and consistent manner.

13.6 DSL ACCESS NETWORK

The main motivating factor to employ xDSL (x digital subscriber line) for access technology in multimedia services is the pre-existence of local loop facilities to most households. Information capacity of a 3,000 Hz analog voice channel of 30 dB signal-to-noise ratio based on Shannon limit is 30,000 bits per second [Tanenbaum, 1996]. However, an unloaded twisted pair of copper wire from the central office to a residence can carry a digital T1/DS1 signal at 1.544 Mbps up to 18,000 feet, and a STS-1 signal at 51.840 Mbps up to 1,000 feet. Thus, Shannon's fundamental limitation of data rate that is prevalent in an analog modem can be overcome by direct digital transmission. This is the basic concept behind xDSL technology, which we will now review. You are referred to numerous books on the subject [e.g., Gorlaski, 2001] for an in-depth treatment.

Distance can be increased for analog telephony if we use loaded cables that compensate for loss and dispersion. However, they cannot support the DSL as the loaded coils attenuate high frequencies. Many modern communities have been cabled with fiber coming to the curb with the digital multiplexer at the end of the fiber. The length limitation of the copper cable in this configuration is practically eliminated. This is being taken advantage of in later releases of xDSL such as very high data rate DSL (VDSL).

Basic asymmetric digital subscriber line (ADSL) architecture consists of an unloaded pair(s) of wires connected between a transceiver unit at the central office and a transceiver unit at the customer premises. This transceiver multiplexes and demultiplexes voice and data and converts the signal to the format suitable for transmission on the ADSL link. Table 13.8 [Broadband Forum] shows various forms of DSL and their characteristics. ADSL 2 and ADSL 2+ are enhancements to ADSL.

Table 13.7 Management Features Requirements for DOCSIS 3.0

FEATURES	MANAGEMENT FUNCTIONAL AREA	OSI LAYER	NE	DESCRIPTION
Multiple upstream channels per port	Configuration	PHY	CMTS	Provisioning physical upstream ports that support multiple upstream receivers according to their capabilities
Plant topology		PHY, MAC (Data link)	CMTS	Provisioning flexible arrangements of US/DS channels for channel-bonding configuration to reflect HFC plant topology
Enhanced diagnostics	Fault	PHY, MAC, network	CMTS	Detailed log of different conditions associated with the CM registration state and operation that may indicate plant problems affecting service availability
Enhanced performance data collection	Performance	PHY, MAC, network	CMTS	IPDR streaming of large statistical data sets such as CMTS CM status information with less performance impact on the CMTS resources
Enhanced signal quality monitoring		PHY	CMTS	Gathers information on narrowband ingress and distortion affecting the quality of the RF signals
Usage-based billing	Accounting	PHY, MAC, network	CMTS	Update SAMIS to 3.0 specification requirements
Enhanced security	Configuration, fault, performance, security	MAC, network	CM/CMTS	Updates to management models to support DOCSIS 3.0 security features
IPv6	Configuration, fault, performance	Network	CM/CMTS	Updates to management models to support IPv6 provisioning, CM IP stack management, CMTS and CM IP filtering requirements
Channel bonding	Configuration, fault, performance	PHY, MAC	CM/CMTS	Update existing management models and include new events to support DS and US channel bonding
IP multicast	Configuration, fault, performance	MAC, network	CM/CMTS	Update existing management modes to support new multicast capabilities such as SSM, IGMP v3, MLD v1, and v2

Table 13.8 DSL Technologies

NAME	MEANING	MAX DATA RATE*	MODE	CABLE	APPLICATIONS
ADSL/ADSL2/ ADSL2+	Asymmetric digital subscriber line	7/12/24 Mbps 0.8/1/1 Mbps	Down Up	1-pair	Most common type
SHDSL	Symmetric high data rate DSL	5.6 Mbps	Duplex Duplex	2-pair	Business connections
VDSL 1 km	Very high data rate digital subscriber line	55 Mbps 15 Mbps	Down Up	2-pair	Triple play (no QoS)
VDSL2- long reach 3 km	Very high data rate digital subscriber line	55 Mbps 30 Mbps	Down Up	2-pair	Triple play
VDSL short reach 500 m	Very high data rate digital subscriber line	100 Mbps	Down Up	2-pair	Triple play

* Max data rate as per broadband forum

Symmetric high data rate digital subscriber line (SHDSL) operates at T1 or E1 data rate in a duplex mode with two pairs of wires [RFC 3276]. The duplex mode is defined as two-way communication with the same speed in both directions. Symmetric HDSL operates with two pairs, one for each direction. SHDSL typically operates at rates from 256 Kb/s to 6 Mb/s upstream and downstream.

VDSL operates asymmetrically. As in ADSL, the downstream signal has a larger bandwidth and is at the high end of the spectrum, whereas the upstream is at the lower end of the spectrum with a lower bandwidth for the signals. VDSL 2 has long- and short-range implementation, the former being asymmetrical and the latter being symmetrical.

13.7 ASYMMETRIC DIGITAL SUBSCRIBER LINE

Among all the xDSLs, the asymmetric digital subscriber line (ADSL) is the technology that is being deployed now in most of the world. A simplified access network using ADSL is shown in Figure 13.15 and consists of an ADSL transmission unit (ATU) and splitter at each end of the ADSL line. The ATU acronym has also been expanded in print as the ADSL transceiver unit as well as the ADSL terminating unit, although ADSL TR-001 defines it as the ADSL transmission unit. The ATU at the central office is ATU-C and the one at the customer residence is ATU-R. The ATU is also called the ADSL modem. The data and video signal from the broadband network is converted to an analog signal by the ATU-C and multiplexed and demultiplexed. The splitter at the central office combines the plain old telephone service (POTS) voice signal and the broadband signal. The reverse process occurs at the splitter and ATU-R at the customer premises (residence). There are modems available that embed the splitter and thus eliminate a separate splitter at the customer site. This configuration is referred to as ADSL-Lite, also known as GLite.

As mentioned above, upstream and downstream signals are placed asymmetrically in the frequency spectrum, as shown in Figure 13.16. The POTS signal is always allocated the baseband of 4 kHz and separated from the broadband signal by a guard band. There are two schemes for separating the upstream and downstream frequency bands: frequency division multiplexing (FDM) or echo cancellation.

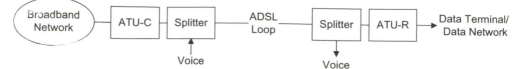

Figure 13.15 ADSL Access Network

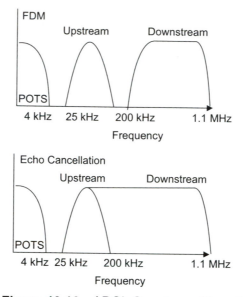

Figure 13.16 ADSL Spectrum Allocation

In FDM, after separating the upstream and downstream bands, each band is then divided into one or more high-speed channels and one or more low-speed channels. In echo cancellation, upstream and downstream bands overlap, but are separated by a technique known as echo cancellation. Using echo cancellation, the low frequency end of the spectrum is made available for downstream, thus increasing the overall downstream spectral band.

Within the upstream and downstream bands, individual channels are allocated a multiple of 4 kHz band using either the standard discrete multitone (DMT) or carrierless amplitude phase (CAP) modulation. The former modulation scheme is more efficient, but more complex and costly. Both schemes are currently in use. You may consult the reference for further details on spectrum allocation schemes [Goralski, 2001].

Standards are addressed by various standards organizations for XDSL including the American National Standards Institute (ANSI). T1-413 is the ANSI standard for XDSL at the physical-layer protocol level. In order to accelerate interoperability and implementation of ADSL, the industry had established a consortium, the ADSL Forum, to address issues associated with end-to-end system operation, management, and security. This organization is now called the Broadband Forum.

Not all residential customers could enjoy the privilege of getting ADSL service. Only those who have direct copper connection from the central office could be served with ADSL. Telephone loop facilities with loaded coils do not qualify for the service. Besides, many newer residential complexes have fiber cable to the neighborhood (FTTN) and twisted pair from FTTN to the residence. For these residences,

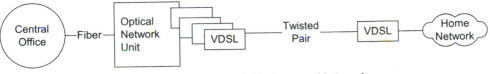

Figure 13.17 VDSL Access Network

telephone companies would offer VDSL service, as shown in Figure 13.17. This has the benefit of providing greater bandwidth. The signal traverses the optical fiber medium from the central office to the optical network unit (ONU) in the neighborhood carrying multiple channels. It is demultiplexed at the ONU and fed through VDSL modems and twisted-pair cable to the residence. A bandwidth of 12.96–55.2 Mbps could be achieved for downstream and up to 15 Mbps for the upstream using a single-pair cable. There are other configurations proposed from ONU to home, which we do not plan to deal with here.

Much of the latest documentation on ADSL is available on TRs published by the ADSL Forum, RFCs released by IETF, and ITU-T standards. The approved documentation list of the ADSL Forum is available in the public domain of the Broadband Forum's Web page, www.broadband-forum.org. Some TRs that are relevant to the basics and management of DSL that we refer to are listed in Table 13.9. ITU-T standards G.xx and RFCs relating to the MIBs are included in the Bibliography at the end of the book.

13.7.1 ADSL Access Network in Overall Network

Broadband Forum's view [TR-001] of how ADSL access network fits into the overall network for broadband services is presented in Figure 13.18. It shows the components of the overall network comprising private, public, and premises network and the role that ADSL access network plays in it. The networking side of the service providers consists of service systems, different types of networks that are behind the access node, the operation systems (OS) that perform the operations, administration, and maintenance (OAM) of the networks and access nodes, and the ATU-Cs. The customer premises network comprises ATU-R, premises distribution network (PDN), various service modules (SM), and terminal equipment (TE). On the bottom of Figure 13.18 are shown five transport modes that depict an evolutionary process from a primitive synchronous transfer mode (STM) to an all ATM mode.

Table 13.9 ADSL Management Documents

TR-001	ADSL Forum System Reference Model	May 1996
TR-005	ADSL Network Element Mgmt	March 1998
TR-015	CAP Line Code-Specific MIB	February 1999
TR-024	DMT Line Code-Specific MIB	June 1999
TR-027	SNMP-based ADSL LINE MIB	September 1999
TR-028	CMIP Specification for ADSL Network Element Mgmt	May 1999
TR-066	ADSL Network Element Mgmt (Update to TR-005)	March 2004
TR-090	Protocol-Independent Object Model for Managing Next Generation ADSL Technologies	December 2004
TR-113	MCM-Specific Managed Objects in VDSL Network Element	December 2005
TR-128	Addendum to TR-090	September 2006

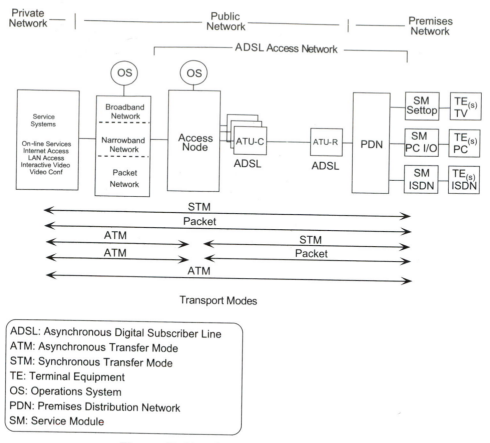

Figure 13.18 Overall Network and ADSL

The service systems are on a private network providing on-line services, Internet access, LAN access, interactive video, and video conference services. The private network interfaces with the public network, which is broadband (such as SONET/SDH), narrowband (such as T1/E1), or packet network (such as IP). The access node is the concentration point for broadband, narrowband data, and packet data. It is either located in the central office or a remote location such as ONU. The access node could include ATU-Cs, such as in a digital subscriber loop access multiplexer (DSLAM). The access network commences at the access node and extends up to PDN in the customer premises.

The premises network starts from the network interface at the output of ATU-R. The PDN, which is part of the home network, could be a choice of a LAN, twisted-pair cable of telephone network, consumer electronics bus (CEBus) which distributes signal over power lines, coaxial cable, optical fiber (in future homes), or a combination of these. SM, such as set-top boxes and ISDN, perform the terminal adaptation functions to the TE.

There are five transport modes presented in Figure 13.18. At the top is what the ADSL Forum termed synchronous transfer mode (STM), which is the bit synchronous transmission mode. An example of this is the bit pipe such as T1/E1, ISDN, or a simple modem. In this mode, the PDN outputs strictly bits out of the SM; and the access node delivers and receives bits to and from the narrowband network.

The second transport scheme is the end-to-end packet mode such as IP packets. In this mode, SM are expected to deliver packets to the ADSL access network through PDN. This is probably one of the most common usages of the Small Office Home Office (SOHO) network. Digital data terminals are interconnected via an Ethernet LAN PDN, and packets are delivered to the ADSL access network via a router. The reverse process occurs at the access node to the network interface.

The next two transport modes are hybrid modes. Output to the network from the access node is the ATM. The SM at the premises network delivers either a bit synchronous output or a packet output. There is a conversion involved in the access node. For example, the access node to the broadband network could be an emulated LAN, wherein IP packets could be transferred as ATM cells to the network.

The fifth, and last, mode of transport scheme is the end-to-end ATM, where SM put out cells instead of packets. We would expect the home network in this case to be wired with optical fiber.

13.7.2   ADSL Architecture

Let us now look at the system architecture details of the ADSL access network presented in Figure 13.15. The ADSL Forum's ADSL system reference model [TR-001] is shown in Figure 13.19. We have already discussed some components in Section 13.7.1. Additional components are splitters at the central office and customer premises, which separate low-frequency telephony from video and digital data. Public-switched telephone network (PSTN) is the switch connected at the central office, while telephones are off the splitter at the customer end. We notice the digital broadcast and network management interfacing with the access node. Digital broadcast is the typical broadcast video. Network management could be treated as one of the operations system components. We will be going into more details on the operations system interfaces and functions in Section 13.8.

Interesting aspects of the ADSL system reference model shown in Figure 13.19 are the interfaces between components of the ADSL network and interfaces between ADSL access network and external networks. There are five basic interfaces: V, U, T, B, and POTS. V_C is the interface between the access node and the network and is usually a physical interface. An interface could have multiple physical connections (as shown in the figure), or multiple logical interfaces can be connected through a physical interface. V_A is the logical interface between ATU-C and the access node. Network management is implemented through the V_C interface. All network monitoring of the central office and the home network component has to go through this interface.

There are several U interfaces shown in Figure 13.19. They are all off the splitters. In fact, these U interfaces may disappear when ADSL-Lite is implemented, although it is highly unlikely for a long time. POTS interfaces are also from the splitters as shown. The B interface is for auxiliary data input; for example, a satellite feed directly into a SM such as a set-top box.

13.7.3   ADSL-Channeling Schemes

There are two perspectives in discussing transport channels in an ADSL access network. The first perspective is the traditional transport bearer channels as they are defined in ISDN. For ADSL transport frames, there are seven "AS" bearer channels defined for the downstream signal operating in a simplex mode. The AS bearer channels are in multiples (one, two, three, or four) of T1 rate of 1.536 Mbps or E1 rate of 2.048 Mbps. In addition to downstream AS channels, there could be three additional "LS" duplex channels carrying the signal in both downstream and upstream directions. The LS bearer channels are 160, 384, or 576 Kbps. The reader is referred to [Goralski, 2000] for a detailed discussion of these. Incidentally, "AS" and "LS" are not specific acronyms.

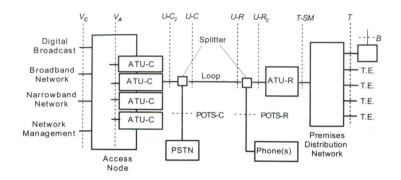

Interfaces:
   B: Auxiliary data input such as a satellite feed to Service Module (TE)
   POTS-C: Interface between PSTN and POTS splitter at network end
   POTS-R: Interface between phones and POTS splitter at premises end
   T: Interface between Premises Distribution Network and Service Modules
   T/SM: Interface between ATU-R and Premises Distribution Network
   U-C: Interface between Loop and ATU-C (analog)
   U-C2: Interface between POTS splitter and ATU-C
   U-R: Interface between Loop and ATU-R (analog)
   U-R2: Interface between POTS splitter and ATU-R
   V_A: Logical interface between ATU-C and Access Node
   V_C: Interface between Access Node and network

   TE: Terminal Equipment
   POTS: Plain Old Telephone Service
   PSTN: Public-Switched Telephone Network

Figure 13.19   ADSL System Reference Model

The second perspective in discussing the channels is how the signal is buffered while traversing the ADSL link. This is represented in Figure 13.20. Real-time signals, such as audio and real-time video, use a fast buffering scheme and hence are referred to as the *fast channel*. Digital data that could tolerate delay use slow buffers that are interleaved between the fast signals. The digital data channel is referred to as the *interleaved channel*. Thus, a physical interface would carry both the fast channel and the interleaved channel and needs to be addressed in the network management of interfaces. We will discuss the interface types of the physical, fast, and interleaved channels more in Section 13.8.

13.7.4   ADSL-Encoding Schemes

ADSL management is dependent on the line-encoding scheme used, and hence we will briefly discuss the two types here. There are two encoding schemes used in ADSL line encoding. They are carrierless amplitude and phase (CAP) modulation and discrete multitone (DMT) technology. Both are based on the QAM scheme that we discussed in Section 13.2. In both cases, the basic approach is to separate the

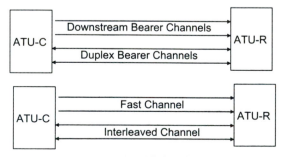

Figure 13.20   ADSL Channeling

POTS band (0–4 kHz), as shown in Figure 13.16. It also shows two views, one that uses FDM to separate the upstream signal from the downstream signal by a guard band. In the second view, upstream and downstream signals overlap, but are distinguished by the echo cancellation technique.

An echoing phenomenon occurs in the telephone system due to crosstalk between neighboring pairs of wires in a bundle. Two signals transmitted from the central office could couple with each other, which is termed *near-end crosstalk*. Two signals traversing in opposite directions could also interfere with each other, which is *far-end crosstalk*. Both of these are mitigated using the echo cancellation technique. The same technique is used to separate the overlapping band between the upstream and downstream shown in the echo cancellation view of Figure 13.16.

Although the ANSI has recommended the use of DMT for ADSL, there currently exist deployed systems that use the CAP system. CAP, as you may recall, is carrierless. In other words, the signal is quadrature amplitude modulated at a specific carrier frequency; the carrier is suppressed at the transmitter, and then sent. The carrier is regenerated at the receiver to detect the signal bits. In CAP, the entire local loop bandwidth (25–200 kHz for upstream or 200 kHz to 1.1 MHz for downstream) is used in the encoding.

In DMT, the entire bandwidth of approximately 1.1 MHz is split into 256 subchannels, each of approximately 4 kHz band. Subchannels 1–6 are used for voice signals and the rest for broadband signals. There are 32 (7–38) upstream subchannels. The number of downstream subchannels is either 250 if echo cancellation is used or 218 if no echo cancellation is performed.

13.8   ADSL MANAGEMENT

The general framework for ADSL management is described in ADSL Forum TR-005 and updated in TR-066. TR-027 presents SNMP-based ADSL Line MIB, and TR-028 contains CMIP specification for ADSL NE management. TR-024 and TR-015 document DMT Line Code-Specific (LCS) MIB and CAP LCS MIB, respectively. Management documentation is specific to ADSL and is a supplement to standard management MIB.

Figure 13.21 shows the ADSL system reference model that is used in the ADSL management framework. It is similar to the one shown in Figure 13.19, but has additional components identifying the switching and physical-layer functions explicitly. Management functions addressed in ADSL-specific documents deal with physical-layer functions. The management of data layers is addressed by the conventional NMSs. Low- and high-pass filters are also explicitly shown in the figure.

13.8.1   ADSL Network Management Elements

ADSL network management deals with parameters, operations, and protocols associated with configuration, fault, and performance management. Security and accounting management are not explicitly dealt with, although these are important management functions and are addressed by other models (for example, SNMP security management discussed in Chapters 7 and 11).

The management of the ADSL network involves the following five NEs: (1) management communications protocol across the network management subinterface of the V interface; (2) management communications protocol across the U interfaces between ATU-C and ATU-R; (3) parameters and operations with the ATU-C; (4) parameters and operations within the ATU-R; and (5) ATU-R side of the T interface. All management functions in the ADSL network are accomplished via the V interface. Thus, the management of elements 2–5 is accomplished via the V interface and not the U interface.

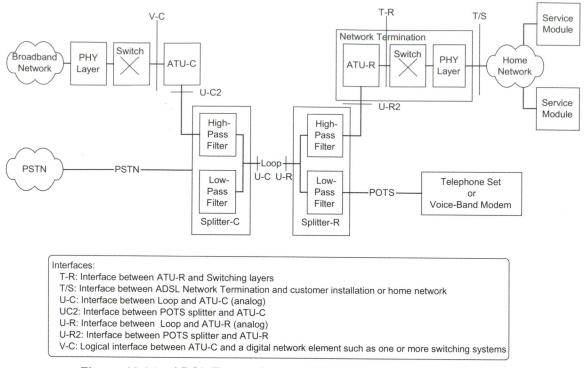

Interfaces:
T-R: Interface between ATU-R and Switching layers
T/S: Interface between ADSL Network Termination and customer installation or home network
U-C: Interface between Loop and ATU-C (analog)
UC2: Interface between POTS splitter and ATU-C
U-R: Interface between Loop and ATU-R (analog)
U-R2: Interface between POTS splitter and ATU-R
V-C: Logical interface between ATU-C and a digital network element such as one or more switching systems

Figure 13.21 ADSL Forum System Reference Model for Management

As discussed in Section 13.7.3, the management function at the physical layer involves three entities: physical channel, fast channel, and interleaved channel. Fast and interleaved channels need to be managed separately. These two use the physical transmission medium that also needs to be managed. Besides the management of physical links and channel parameters, the parameters associated with the type of line coding need to be monitored. We will look at various parameters associated with configuration, fault, and performance management in the next section.

13.8.2 ADSL Configuration Management

Various parameters that need to be managed for configuration are listed in Table 13.10. The table lists the component that the parameter is associated with, as well as whether it pertains to the physical line or fast or interleaved channel. A brief description of each parameter is given in the last column.

It is to be noted that the link could be configured in one of five options: no separation of channels, fast, interleaved, either, or both.

There are five levels of noise margin—from the highest defined by the maximum noise margin to the lowest defined by the minimum noise margin. The transmitted power of the modem needs to be decreased or increased, respectively, based on these thresholds. The transmission rate can be increased if the noise margin goes above a threshold level, which is beneath the maximum noise margin threshold. Similarly, the transmission rate should be decreased if the noise margin falls below a certain threshold, which is higher than the minimum noise margin. Right at the middle of all these thresholds is the steady-state operation. These levels are shown in Figure 13.22.

Table 13.10 ADSL Configuration Management Parameters

PARAMETER	COMPONENT	LINE	DESCRIPTION
ADSL line type	ADSL Line	N/A	Five types: no channel, fast, interleaved, either, or both
ADSL line coding	ADSL Line	N/A	ADSL coding type
Target noise margin	ATU-C/R	Phy	Noise margin under steady state (BER = $<10^{-7}$)
Max. noise margin	ATU-C/R	Phy	Modem reduces power above this threshold
Min. noise margin	ATU-C/R	Phy	Modem increases power below this margin
Rate adaptation mode	ATU-C/R	Phy	Mode 1: Manual Mode 2: Select at start-up Mode 3: Dynamic
Upshift noise margin	ATU-C/R	Phy	Threshold for modem increases data rate
Min. time interval for upshift rate adaptation	ATU-C/R	Phy	Time interval to upshift
Downshift noise margin	ATU-C/R	Phy	Threshold for modem decreases data rate
Min. time interval for downshift rate adaptation	ATU-C/R	Phy	Time interval to downshift
Desired max. rate	ATU-C/R	F/I	Max rates for ATU-C/R
Desired min. rate	ATU-C/R	F/I	Min. rates for ATU-C/R
Rate adaptation ratio	ATU-C/R	Phy	Distribution ratio between fast and interleaved channels for available excess bit rate
Max. interleave delay	ATU-C/R	F/I	Max. transmission delay allowed by interleaving process
Alarm thresholds	ATU-C/R	Phy	15-minute count threshold on loss of signal, frame, power, and error seconds
Rate-up threshold	ATU-C/R	F/I	Rate-up change alarm
Rate-down threshold	ATU-C/R	F/I	Rate-down change alarm
Vendor ID	ATU-C/R	Phy	Vendor ID assigned by T1E1.4
Version No.	ATU-C/R	Phy	Vendor-specific version
Serial No.	ATU-C/R	Phy	Vendor-specific serial no.

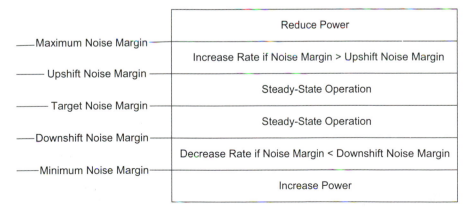

Figure 13.22 Noise Margins

Some modems support rate adaptation modes. There are three modes. Mode 1 is manual in which the rate is changed manually. In mode 2 the rate is automatically selected at start-up, but remains at that level afterwards. The last mode is mode 3 where the rate is dynamic based on the noise margin.

13.8.3 ADSL Fault Management

Fault management parameters are shown in Table 13.11 and should be displayed by the NMS. After the automatic indication of faults, ATU-C and ATU-R self-tests as specified in T1.413 could be used to assist in the diagnostics.

The ADSL line status shows the current state of the line as to whether it is operational, or there is a loss of any of the parameters on frame, signal, power, or link. It also indicates initialization errors. Alarms are generated when the preset counter reading exceeds 15 minutes on loss of signal, frame, power, link, and error seconds.

13.8.4 ADSL Performance Management

Table 13.12 shows the parameters associated with ADSL performance management. Each ATU's performance in terms of line attenuation, noise margin, total output power, current and previous data rate, along with the maximum attainable rate, channel data block length (on which CRC check is done), and interleave delay can be monitored. In addition, statistics are gathered for a 15-minute interval and a 1-day interval on the error-seconds statistics. Two counters are maintained by each ATU for each error condition to measure these. Error statistics are maintained for loss of signal seconds, loss of frame seconds, loss of power seconds, loss of link seconds, error seconds, transmit blocks, receive blocks, corrected blocks, and uncorrectable blocks.

13.8.5 SNMP-based ADSL Line MIB

There are both SNMP- [RFCs 2662, 3440] and CMIP- [TR-016] based specifications that have been developed for ADSL. We will discuss the updated SNMP-based MIB [Table 13.9; RFC 2662; TR-015; TR-024; TR-027] in this section. ADSL SNMP MIB is presented in Figure 13.23.

There are three nodes defined under *adslLineMib {adslMIB 1}*. RFC [2662] specifies *adslMibObjects {adslLineMib 1}*, which are shown in part in Figure 13.23.

Notice that there are complimentary objects for the link in terms of physical and channel objects. For example, there are *adslAtucPhysTable* and corresponding *adslAtucChanTable*. The former specifies

Table 13.11 ADSL Fault Management Parameters

PARAMETER	COMPONENT	LINE	DESCRIPTION
ADSL line status	ADSL Line	Phy	Indicates operational and various types of failures of the link
Alarms thresholds	ATU-C/R	Phy	Generates alarms on failures or crossing of thresholds
Unable to initialize ATU-R	ATU-C/R	Phy	Initialization failure of ATU-R from ATU-C
Rate change	ATU-C/R	Phy	Event generation when rate changes when crossing of shift margins in both upstream and downstream

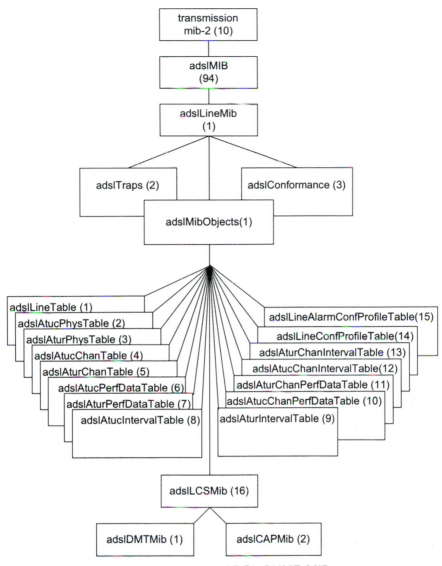

Figure 13.23 ADSL SNMP MIB

a table with each row containing the physical-layer parameters associated with the link on an interface. The latter specifies a table in which each row contains parameters associated with a channel on that interface. These interfaces are defined based on RFC 1213 for *interfaces {mib-2 2}* and RFC 2863 for *ifMIB {mib-2 31}*.

Figure 13.23 contains objects under *adslMibObjects* that pertain to configuration management parameters defined in Table 13.10, fault management parameters defined in Table 13.11, and performance management parameters in Table 13.12.

Table 13.12 ADSL Performance Management Parameters

PARAMETER	COMPONENT	LINE	DESCRIPTION
Line attenuation	ATU-C/R	Phy	Measured power loss in dB from transmitter to receiver ATU
Noise margin	ATU-C/R	Phy	Noise margin in dB of the ATU with respect to the received signal
Total output power	ATU-C/R	Phy	Total output power from the modem
Max. attainable rate	ATU-C/R	Phy	Max. currently attainable data rate by the modem
Current rate	ATU-C/R	F/I	Current transmit rate to which the modem is adapted
Previous rate	ATU-C/R	F/I	Rate of the modem before the last change
Channel data block length	ATU-C/R	F/I	Data block on which CRC check is done
Interleave delay	ATU-C/R	F/I	Transmit delay introduced by the interleaving process
Statistics	ATU-C/R	Phy F/I	15 minute/1 day failure statistics

13.8.6 MIB Integration with Interfaces Group in MIB-2

The ADSL LINE MIB specifies detailed attributes of a data interface. It is integrated with IF-MIB with the following *ifType*(s) relative to ADSL in the following manner:

    adslPhysIf ::= {transmission 94}
    adslInterIf ::= {transmission 124}
    adslFastIf ::= {transmission 125}

Each MIB branch would have the appropriate tables for that interface type and would *augment* the interfaces table with *ifIndex* in *ifEntry* as the accessing index.

Table 13.13 presents the objects needed for ADSL, which are part of the mandatory *ifGeneralGroup* [RFC 2863]. They are applicable to the line, not either end in particular. "NORMAL" means the variable is used normally as specified in MIB-II. Designations "i," "j," and "k" indicate three arbitrary *ifIndex* values corresponding to the physical, interleaved, and fast entries for a single ADSL line.

The *ifStackTable* {*ifMIB.ifMIBObjects 2*}, which is the table containing information on the relationships between multiple sublayers of network interfaces, is used to associate the fast and interleaved channels with the physical line. The top of Figure 13.24 shows the logical representation of the channels. Their relationship with each other and with the higher layer is shown in the bottom of Figure 13.24. The fast channel and the interleaved channel, which are at the same level, are stacked on top of the physical layer. They interface above with a higher layer, for example ATM if ATM is over ADSL.

13.8.7 ADSL Operational and Configuration Profiles

Table 13.14 shows the configuration of the operational file for *ifType* for each modem in setting up the fast and interleaved channels. An *ifIndex* is associated with each channel.

In a typical configuration of an ADSL system, the access node shown in Figure 13.19 has hundreds of ATU-Cs. It would be impractical to provision all the parameters for each ATU-C individually. There are two MIB tables to address this issue—one for configuration profile and another for the performance

Table 13.13 Use of Interfaces Table for ADSL

MIB VARIABLE	PHYSICAL LINE (I)	INTERLEAVED CHANNEL (J)	FAST CHANNEL (K)
ifDescr	NORMAL	NORMAL	NORMAL
ifType (IANA)	94	124	125
ifSpeed	ATU-C line Tx rate	ATU-C channel Tx rate	ATU-C channel Tx rate
ifPhyAddress	NULL	NULL	NULL
ifAdminStatus	NORMAL	NORMAL	NORMAL
ifOperStatus	NORMAL	NORMAL	NORMAL
ifLastChange	NORMAL	NORMAL	NORMAL
ifLinkUpDownTrapEnable	NORMAL (default: Enable)	NORMAL (default: Enable)	NORMAL (default: Enable)
ifConnectPresent	True	False	False
ifHighSpeed	NULL	NULL	NULL

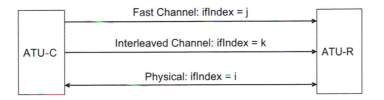

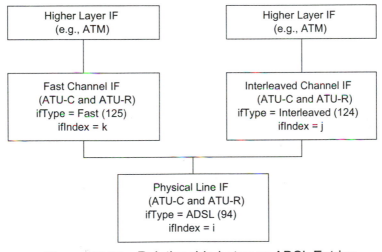

Figure 13.24 Relationship between ADSL Entries

profile. One of the tables is *adslLineConfProfileTable {adslMibObjects 14}*, which contains information on the ADSL line configuration shown in Table 13.10. One or more ADSL lines may be configured to share common profile information. Figure 13.25 shows the dynamic mode, MODE-I, configuration profile scheme. Profile tables are created and indexed 1 to *n*. Each ADSL line interface, with the given

Table 13.14 ADSL Operational Profile for ifType File

LINE TYPE	PHYSICAL	FAST CHANNEL	INTERLEAVED CHANNEL
Number of channels (1)	Yes		Yes
Fast only (2)	Yes	Yes	
Interleaved only (3)	Yes		Yes
Fast or interleaved (4)	Yes	Yes	Yes
Fast and interleaved (5)	Yes	Yes	Yes

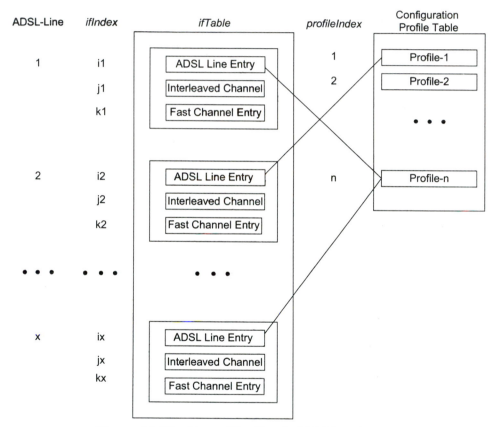

Figure 13.25 Use of Profiles in MODE-I (Dynamic)

value of *ifIndex*, shown ranging from 1 to *x* shares the configuration profiles from 1 to *n*. The three entries for the physical layer, the interleaved channel, and the fast channel for each ADSL line are represented by "i," "j," and "k" as discussed in Section 13.8.6. Only the ADSL line entry contains the pointer to the configuration profile table. The *ifStackTable* [RFC 2863] is used to link channel entries and the corresponding physical layer to acquire the channel configuration parameters.

The second mode, denoted by MODE-II, specifies the static mode of setting up ADSL configuration profile. Each ADSL line interface has a static profile, as shown in Figure 13.26. The ADSL line

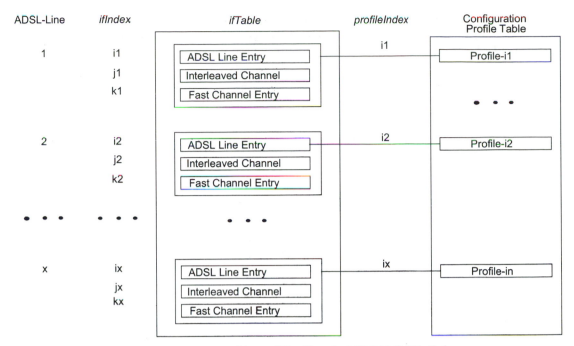

Figure 13.26 Use of Profiles in MODE-II (Static)

interfaces 1 through *x*; each has its own configuration profile i1 through ix, indicated by profile indices i1 through ix.

The alarm profile could also be structured in a manner similar to the configuration profile explained above. That is how the *adslLineAlarmProfileTable {adslMibObjects 15}* is designed.

LCS MIBs for the DMT and CAP ADSL lines are described in TR-024 and TR-015. They are nodes under *adslLCSMib {adslMibObjects 16}*. The tables and other information follow a similar structure and organization similar to that of the ADSL line MIB shown in Figure 13.23 ADSL SNMP MIB as *{adslMib Objects 1-15}*.

Figure 13.23 shows three nodes under *adslLineMib*. The first is the ADSL MIB objects that we have discussed. The other two are traps and conformance groups. These are specified in RFC 2662. Besides the generic traps, alarms are generated by the ATU-C and ATU-R for loss of frame, loss of signal, loss of power, errored seconds threshold, data rate change, loss of link duration threshold, and ATU-C initialization failure. These are specified in *adslTraps* MIB.

13.9 ADSL2, ADSL2+, AND VDSL2

ADSL2 [ADSL2; ITU G.992.3; ITU G. 992.4] adds new features and functionality to improve performance and interoperability. Specifically, improvements include higher data rate, longer reach, rate adaptation, diagnostics, and power-saving stand-by mode. The data rate increase is achieved by improving modulation and coding efficiencies. A downstream data rate of 12 Mbps and an upstream data rate of 1 Mbps can be achieved. A longer reach is accomplished at the expense of lower data rate.

The telephone cable in the local loop contains multiple pairs of 25 or more unshielded twisted pairs. Crosstalk between adjacent pairs degrades performance, as well as causes a drop in calls. In ADSL2, modulation and framing layers are decoupled, which enables the transmission data rate to be changed without affecting the framing layer. Thus, data rate is changed dynamically based on the extent of external disturbing effects of crosstalk and other parameters such as radio, temperature, and water in the binder.

Power saving is accomplished by the ADSL modems operating at three levels—very low-power sleep mode when there is no data transmission, medium-power mode when Internet traffic in the access network is normal; and high-power mode when traffic is heavy such as large file transfer.

ADSL2 provides the ability to split the bandwidth into different channels with different link characteristics for different applications. Thus, real-time voice application can be digitally transmitted as channelized voice over DSL over some channels with low latency and more tolerant error rate, while data can be transmitted over other channels with less stringent latency requirements but more stringent error rate requirements.

ADSL2+ [ITU G.992.5] specifications double the downstream data rate to 2.2 Mbps by limiting the reach to under 5,000 meters. As VDSL does not completely satisfy the needs of triple play service, the Broadband Forum has created VDSL2+, which is a complex protocol and incorporates features and characteristics of ADSL, ADSL2+, and VDSL [ITU 993.2] protocols. The profile of VDSL2 is extracted partially from [ITU G.993.2] and is given in Table 13.15. The performance of VDSL2 deteriorates quickly from a theoretical maximum of 250 Mbit/s at "source" to 100 Mbit/s at 5 kilometers (1,640 feet) and 50 Mbit/s at 10 kilometers (3,280 feet), but degrades at a much slower rate from there. It equals the performance of ADSL2+ at 1.6 kilometers (1 mile).

Performance improvement in DSL has been accomplished by the use of multichannel transmission. In plain vanilla ADSL, we needed to deal with only a single channel, which supports fast, interleaved, or both. The use of multiple channels enabled the assignment of specific latency and error characteristics to each channel to handle real-time and non-real-time data transmission. One of the major impacts is in the bearer channels. The new standards developed allow a flexible configuration of up to four generic channels that can be independently configured with respect to latency. This is shown in Figure 13.27 [TR-O90].

The basic ADSL management framework was developed to meet the needs of the initial set of ADSL technologies [G.992.1; G.992.2] and is shown in Figure 13.28. It is not adequate to meet the next generation models using multichannels. Figure 13.29 shows the revised management model for the next generation technologies. Bearer channel parameters are decoupled from ADSL line parameters into independent profiles.

13.10 PASSIVE OPTICAL NETWORK

The third "wired" broadband access network that we consider is the passive optical network (PON). It is not really wired but the copper is replaced with fiber, although PON can also be implemented on copper. We will only consider an optical fiber medium here. Optical access networks use optical fiber transmission from the central office to the customer premises. The transmission path could have active elements such as regenerative repeaters or amplifiers, in which case it is not a PON. Passive elements such as a beam splitter or a wavelength division multiplexer (WDM) could be present in a PON.

A generic representation of PON is shown in Figure 13.30. It is the segment between the optical line termination (OLT) that is located in the central office (CO) and the ONU equipment that is located in the customer premises (CPE) or home.

Figure 13.31 shows three different schemes of PON. Figure 13.31(a) shows the configuration where fiber is run from an OLT to each ONU. In this case, ONU performs a similar function to the NIU as in

Table 13.15 VDSL2 Profiles

FREQUENCY PLAN	PARAMETER	PARAMETER VALUE FOR PROFILE							
		8A	8B	8C	8D	12A	12B	17A	30A
All	Maximum aggregate downstream transmit power (dBm)	+17.5	+20.5	+11.5	+14.5	+14.5	+14.5	+14.5	+14.5
All	Maximum aggregate upstream transmit power (dBm)	+14.5	+14.5	+14.5	+14.5	+14.5	+14.5	+14.5	+14.5
All	Subcarrier spacing (kHz)	4.3125	4.3125	4.3125	4.3125	4.3125	4.3125	4.3125	8.625
All	Minimum bidirectional net data rate capability (MBDC)	50 Mbit/s	50 Mbit/s	50 Mbit/s	50 Mbit/s	68 Mbit/s	68 Mbit/s	100 Mbit/s	200 Mbit/s
All	Aggregate interleaver and de-interleaver delay (octets)	65,536	65,536	65,536	65,536	65,536	65,536	98,304	1,31,072
All	Maximum interleaving depth (Dmax)	2,048	2,048	2,048	2,048	2,048	2,048	3,072	4,096
All	Parameter (1/S)max downstream	24	24	24	24	24	24	48	28
All	Parameter (1/S)max upstream	12	12	12	12	24	24	24	28

the cable access network. In Figure 13.31(b), the ONU is a passive optical power splitter–combiner, which distributes the signal to multiple homes. The link between OLT and the passive optical splitter–combiner in this case uses Ethernet or ATM protocol. The latter is becoming obsolete. The Ethernet PON is called EPON. The optical signal between ONU and OLT in Figure 13.31(a) and (b) in two directions could be carried on two different wavelengths or on a pair of fibers. Figure 13.31(c) shows the configuration where individual homes are served over different wavelengths. The WDM is the ONU that multiplexes and demultiplexes signals from and to homes.

As we noted, different modes of transmission distribution are used in PON. APON is ATM-based, EPON is Ethernet-based, and PON-GPON is a hybrid that uses EPON and APON systems. The EPON network is also known as EFM (Ethernet in the First Mile). WDM PON is also termed as WPON. For a comparison of the different PONs and their implementation details, you are referred to [Effenberger et al., 2007; Ramaswami, 2002].

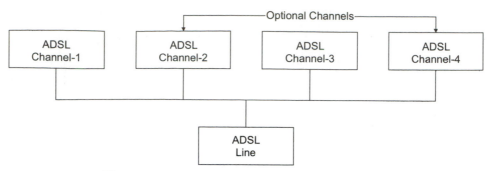

Figure 13.27   Bearer Multichannel Arrangement

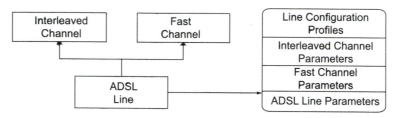

Figure 13.28   Basic ADSL Management Model

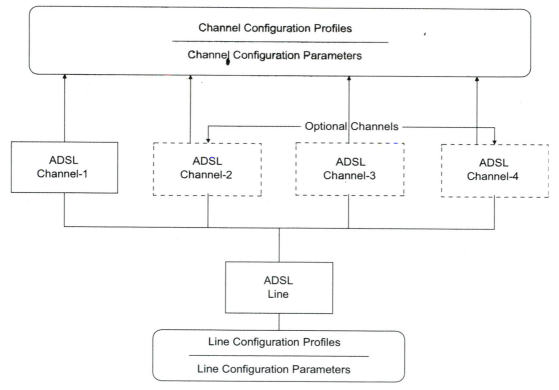

Figure 13.29   Revised Management Framework for a Multichannel DSL

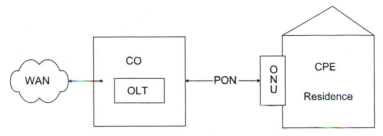

Figure 13.30 Generic PON

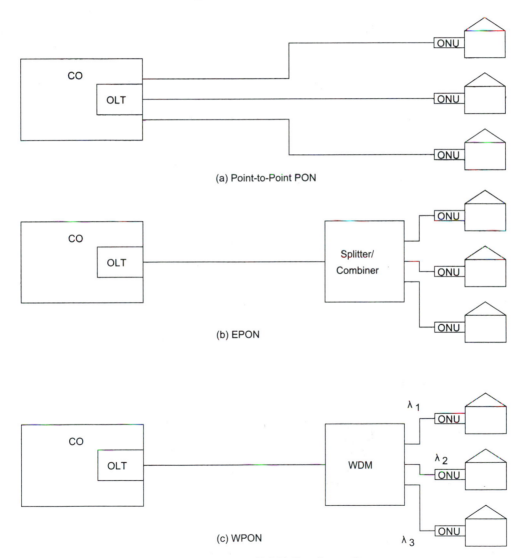

(a) Point-to-Point PON

(b) EPON

(c) WPON

Figure 13.31 PON Configurations

EPON transmission is done using Ethernet packets. Downstream is TDM broadcast mode and upstream is TDMA. The traditional Ethernet LAN was 802.3 protocol. EPON uses packets of variable size. TDM and TDMA use a fixed-window size and hence are not suitable. Hence, 802.3 Ethernet MAC protocol has been enhanced for EFM. We will deal with this when we discuss EPON MIB in the next section. There are no MIBS specified for other PONs.

13.11 PON MANAGEMENT

RFC 4837 details the MAC changes needed and the MIBs associated with them. The EPON configuration in a point-to-point configuration shown in Figure 13.31(a) can be managed by traditional MIBs. However, EPON shown in Figure 13.31(b) has point-to-multipoint and is more complex. [Suryaputra and Squire, 2008] explains this gap in describing OAM for optical access network using an IEEE 802.3ah protocol.

Traditionally, enterprise Ethernet has been managed with IP/SNMP. However, as Ethernet migrates to public networks, IP/SNMP presents several drawbacks. IP/SNMP is not available in EPON, as well as, in general, in carrier class networks. This implies that certain management capabilities are required within the Ethernet layer itself. Requiring the IP network to run just to manage the network could be an unacceptable overhead in terms of the complexity of the equipment and the operational carrier network. We will first address the modification done to IEEE 802.3 for EPON, specified as IEEE 802.3ah, and then address management architecture and MIBs to handle managed objects.

The EPON standard, as defined in 802.3ah, defines the physical media (Layer 1) and the media access (Layer 2) of the EPON interface. EPON is a variant of the gigabit Ethernet protocol for optical access. Optical access topology is based on passive optical splitting topology. The link of a PON is based on a single, shared optical fiber with passive optical splitters dividing the single fiber into separate subscribers.

The EPON protocol architecture, which is a modified version of the gigabit protocol architecture shown in Figure 2.5, is presented in Figure 13.32. New EPON layers are added to Ethernet layerings, as well as some layers have enhanced parameters for EPON. These are identified in the figure. Multipoint control protocol (MPCP) is placed in the MAC control layer, providing the EPON control protocol. The emulation layer, located at the reconciliation sublayer, creates a virtual private path to each ONU. The forward error correction (FEC) layer is located between the PCS and PMA layers, enhancing reach and split performance of the optical link. The virtual links concept is also used to avoid a violation of the IEEE 802.1d bridging rules for peer-to-peer traffic in the PON. Peer-to-peer traffic is traffic between ONUs in the same PON. The OLT cannot preserve the EPON interface as a single interface, connected to N devices, and allow traffic between these devices without violating bridging rules.

802.1d Bridge sublayer is introduced in the MAC layer for peer-to-peer communication between OLT and ONU. OLT has N virtual ports that communicate with N ONUs, which is established through virtual tunneling. Virtual tunneling for an OLT with three ONUs is illustrated in the bottom half of Figure 13.32.

For the management of EPON, IEEE 802.3ah EFM specification defines an optional OAM sublayer just above the Ethernet MAC. This is shown in Figure 13.33. When OAM is present, two connected OAM sublayers between the OLT and ONU exchange OAM frames, which are distinguished from other frames though a combination of the destination MAC address and the Ethernet type/length field. As the OAM packets share usable bandwidth as the payload, it is limited to, at most, 10 frames/second.

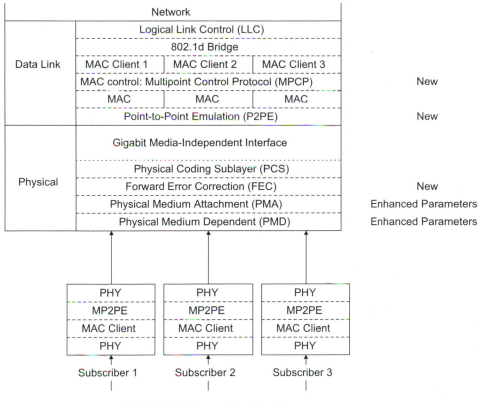

MP2PE Multipoint-to-Point Emulation

Figure 13.32 EPON Protocol Architecture

Figure 13.34 shows an EPON MIB, which is node 155 under *mib-2* [RFC 4837] and Table 13.16 shows the corresponding group. There are two subnodes under *dot3EponMIB, dot3EponObjects* (1), and *dot3EponConformance* (2), which are not shown in the figure. There are four subnodes under *dot3EponObjects*.

MPCP MIB objects, *dot3MpcpObjects {dot3EponMIB* (1)} are MIB objects related to 802.3ah multipoint control protocol attributes. It comprises three tables—*dot3MpcpControlTable* that defines the interface objects used for configuration and status indication, *dot3MpcpStatTable* that defines the statistics of interface objects, and *dot3MpcpControlTable* that defines the operational mode of interface objects.

OMP emulation MIB objects, *dot3EmulationObjects {dot3EponMIB* (2)} are MIB objects defining point-to-point emulation attributes. It comprises *dot3OmpEmulationTable* that defines interface objects used for configuration and status indication; *dot3OmpEmulationStatTable* that defines the statistics interface objects; and *dot3OmpEmulationType* that defines the operational mode of the interface objects.

FEC MIB objects, *dot3EponFecObjects {dot3EponMIB* (3)} are MIB objects related to EPON FEC attributes. It contains *dot3EponFecTable* that defines objects used for configuration and status indication of FEC of the interfaces.

EPON-extended package MIB objects, *dot3ExtPkgObjects {dot3EponMIB* (4)} define MIB objects used for configuration and status indication with extended capabilities of EPON interfaces. You may refer to RFC 4837 for details on these.

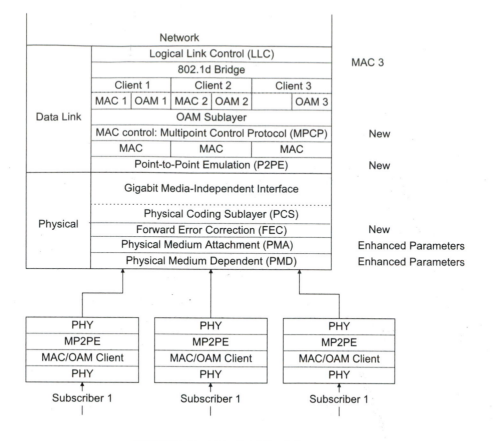

MP2PE Multipoint-to-Point Emulation

Figure 13.33 Managed EPON Protocol Architecture

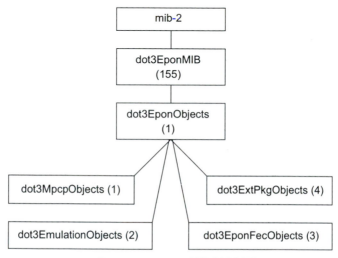

Figure 13.34 EPON MIB

Table 13.16 EPON Group

ENTITY	OID	DESCRIPTION (BRIEF)
dot3EponMIB	Mib-2 155	EPON MAC
dot3EponObjects	dot3EponMIB 1	EPON MIB objects
dot3MpcpObjects	dot3EponMIB 1	802.3ah MPCP attributes
dot3EmulationObjects	dot3EponMIB 2	Point-to-point OMP emulation attributes
dot3EponFecObjects	dot3EponMIB 3	EPON FEC attributes
dot3ExtPkgObjects	dot3EponMIB 4	Configuration and status attributes of extended EPON

Relation of the EPON MIB and Ethernet-like Interfaces MIB. The EPON interface is an Ethernet-like interface. This MIB module extends the objects of the interface MIB [RFC 2863] and the Ethernet-like interfaces MIB [RFC 3635] for an EPON-type interface. Each managed EPON interface and each managed virtual EPON interface would have corresponding entries in the mandatory tables of the Ethernet-like MIB module found in RFC 3635, and in the tables of the interface MIB module found in RFC 2863. Therefore, for instance, the document defines *dot3MpcpRemoteMACAddress* only while assuming that the local MAC address object is already defined in RFC 3635.

The interface MIB module [RFC 2863] defines the interface index (*ifIndex*). The interface index, as specified in RFC 2863, is used in this MIB module as an index to the EPON MIB tables. The *ifIndex* is used to denote the physical interface and the virtual link interfaces at the OLT. The OLT interface and the virtual link interfaces are stacked using the *ifStack* table defined in RFC 2863, and the *ifInvStack* defined in RFC 2864. The OLT interface is the lower layer of all other interfaces associated with virtual links.

Let us consider a specific example of EPON objects of an ONU interface and an OLT interface. Information in the tables is per the logical link ID (LLID). The rows in the EPON MIB tables referring to the LLIDs are denoted with the corresponding *ifIndex*es of the virtual link interfaces.

For example, the values of the interface MIB objects are presented in Table 13.17 and Table 13.18 for an OLT with two registered ONUs. The table below presents the objects of the interface MIB of an ONU in the working mode. ONU_MAC_Address is the MAC address of the ONU EPON interface. The following values will be set in the *ifStack* related to this example: *ifStackHigherLayer* = 100 for the ONU channel and *ifStackLowerLayer* = 1 for the optical channel.

OLT_MAC_Address is the MAC address of the OLT EPON interface. Note that each virtual interface does not have a different physical MAC address at the OLT, as the physical interface is the same. The following values will be set in the *ifStack* table: *ifStackHigherLayer* = 265535, *ifStackLowerLayer* = 2 between the OLT physical interface and its broadcast virtual interface; *ifStackHigherLayer* = 200001, *ifStackLowerLayer* = 2 between the OLT physical interface and its virtual interface of the first ONU; *ifStackHigherLayer* = 200002, *ifStackLowerLayer* = 2 between the OLT physical interface and its virtual interface of the second ONU.

RFC 4878 describes OAM functions on Ethernet-like interfaces, more specifically on EFM. It defines the management objects necessary to integrate OAM functionality into the SNMP management framework. You are referred to the RFC for details on this.

Table 13.17 ONU Interface MIB Example

INTERFACE MIB OBJECT	OPTICAL INTERFACE VALUE	ONU INTERFACE VALUE
ifIndex	1	100
ifDescr	"Interface Description"	"Interface Description"
ifType	ethernetCsmacd (6) 1000base-Px	ethernetCsmacd (6) 1000base-Px
ifMtu	MTU size (1522)	MTU size (1522)
ifSpeed	1000000000	1000000000
ifPhysAddress	ONU_MAC_Address	ONU_MAC_Address

Table 13.18 OLT Interface MIB Example

INTERFACE MIB OBJECT	OPTICAL INTERFACE VALUE	ONU INTERFACE VALUE	ONU INTERFACE VALUE	ONU BROADCAST INTERFACE VALUE
ifIndex	2	200001	200002	265535
ifDescr	"Interface Description"	"Interface Description"	"Interface Description"	"Interface Description"
ifType	ethernetCsmacd (6) 1000base-Px	ethernetCsmacd (6) 1000base-Px	ethernetCsmacd (6) 1000base-Px	ethernetCsmacd (6) 1000base-Px
ifMtu	MTU size (1522)	MTU size (1522)	MTU size (1522)	MTU size (1522)
ifSpeed	1000000000	1000000000	1000000000	1000000000
ifPhysAddress	OLT_MAC_Address	OLT_MAC_Address	OLT_MAC_Address	OLT_MAC_Address

◼ Summary

We have learned the emerging technology of broadband access networks and the management of some broadband access networks in this chapter.

Broadband access technology is primarily focused on bringing multimedia service to residence. We have learned about the three emerging technologies: hybrid fiber coaxial cable (HFC)/cable modem technology, digital subscriber line (DSL) technology, and wireless technology. Of the three, HFC and ADSL are the ones that are in a more mature state of implementation. We have covered those in greater depth both from technology and management aspects.

HFC carries information from the head end to the customer premises via optical fiber and coaxial cables. There are cable modems at the customer sites and a cable modem termination system. Transmission is two-way in most of the implementations, although there are still some one-way downstream and telephony-return upstream systems in use. We learned the management of cable modems and facilities using SNMP management developed by DOCSIS.

ADSL is the most widely implemented configuration of DSL in the United States. HDSL and VDSL are also being introduced, which can handle greater bandwidth and capacity of information. We have covered ADSL technology and the early stage of management of ADSL as specified by the ADSL Forum. The discussion is extended to later DSL technologies.

Two classes of broadband access network using fiber are presented. EPON that belongs to the first class uses the traditional TDM downstream broadcast mode and the TDMA upstream mode of transmission. The MIB developed by IETF is described. Power from the head end is split between various subscribers' ONUs. The second class splits energy from the head end over multiple wavelengths.

Exercises

1. A half-duplex channel is carrying a 2-Mbps signal. Calculate the baud rate and bandwidth in Hz for the following modulated signals:

   (a) ASK (binary)
   (b) PSK (binary)
   (c) QPSK
   (d) 16-QAM

2. The downstream channel bandwidth for the cable modem is 6 MHz. Calculate the bit rate if the signal is:

   (a) QPSK
   (b) 64-QAM
   (c) Draw the constellation diagrams for both (a) and (b)

3. The upstream bandwidth for a cable modem is user settable for the following bandwidth. Calculate the channel data rate that can be accommodated for each case if QPSK is the modulation scheme used:

   (a) 200 kHz
   (b) 800 kHz
   (c) 1.6 MHz
   (d) 3.2 MHz

4. Repeat Exercise 3 for 16-QAM-modulation scheme.
5. Most cable modem manufacturers use QAM (quadrature amplitude modulation) for downstream and QPSK (quadrature phase shift keying) for upstream traffic on HFC. Explain why this is done.
6. Cable modems on the coaxial part of the topology of an HFC configuration shown in Figure 13.3 are a tree structure. Cable modems with Ethernet stations resemble an Ethernet LAN. Contrast an HFC coaxial broadband LAN with a regular Ethernet LAN on:

   (a) Topology
   (b) Downstream protocol
   (c) Upstream protocol

7. Configure a cable modem for the following four upstream and one downstream channels using the *ifTable* and *ifStackTable*. Your answer should present two tables with only the relevant objects in the *ifTable* (index, *ifType*, and *ifSpeed*) and in the *ifStackTable* (*ifStackHigherLayer* and *ifStackLowerLayer*). Refer to Table 13.3 [RFC 4546 RF interface MIB] for additional information.

MAC layer:	10 Mbps	Index 1
Downstream:	10 Mbps	Index 2
Upstream:	6 Mbps (video)	Index 3
	1.5 Mbps (data)	Index 4
	8.0 kbps (telephony)	Index 5
	8.0 kbps (telephony)	Index 6

The *ifType* for each subchannel is:

docsCableMacLayer	127
docsCableDownstream	128
docsCableUpstream	129

The upper layer above the MAC layer and the lower layer below the upstream and downstream layers are designated as "0" in the *ifStackTable*.

8. The QoS table for the cable modem in Exercise 7 is configured with the following priorities: video 4, data 1, and telephony 7. Fill in Table 13.19 for the upstream channels. The "*" in the title stands for "*docsIfQosProf*." Assume that the maximum bandwidth for all channels is 10 Mbps for both upbandwidth and downbandwidth, and the guaranteed bandwidth is the specified bandwidth for each subchannel.

Table 13.19 Exercise 8

*index	*Priority	*MaxUpBandwidth	*GuarUpBandwidth	*MaxDownBandwidth

9. Telephone service providers are now offering ADSL service to home using the existing twisted-pair telephone wires. The signal can be carried up to a maximum of 1-MHz baseband with an S/N (signal power/noise power in ratio) of 30 dB. S/N in decibels (dB) is defined as $10 \log_{10}$ (signal power/noise power). Using MPEG-2 compression techniques, (a) a non-sports video channel can be broadcast at 3-Mbps data rate and (b) a sports video channel at 6 Mbps. Shannon's limitation for information capacity for a channel is given by

$$\text{Maximum bit rate (bits/sec)} = B \log_2(1+S/N),$$

where S/N is in ratio (and not in dB) and B is the bandwidth. How many video channels can simultaneously be transmitted over the line for the two cases?

10. Given a capacity of 1.104 MHz, what is the maximum number of DMT subchannels (at 4.3125 kHz) that can be transmitted over an ADSL channel in both directions?

11. Each subchannel in a DMT is line coded with QAM:

 (a) What is the baud rate in each subchannel?

 (b) The bit rate in each channel can be dynamically varied based on the noise of the channel. The range of operation is 2 bits/baud to 15 bits/baud. What is the range of n in n-QAM modulation?

12. Estimate the number of voice subchannels available for POTS in Figure 13.16, if DMT line coding is used.

13. A 50-Mbyte file is downloaded using FTP from a host attached to a cable modem to a station on an ATU-R. Assume that full bandwidth for the channels is available and the ADSL is a relatively noiseless channel.

14. Repeat Exercise 13 if the download is in the reverse direction.

15. Four tables are involved in the configuration of an ADSL line interface parameters: *ifTable* [RFC 1213], *ifStackTable* [RFC 1573], *adslLineTable*, and *adslLineConfProfileTable* [Table 13.9, TR-027, SNMP-based ADSL line MIB]. Identify the relationship between them and the links (index clause values) that relate them in MODE-I configuration.

16. Repeat Exercise 14 for MODE-II configuration profile.

17. What are the tables involved in the configuration of alarm profile for an ADSL line? Refer to Table 13.9 [TR-027; RFC 2662].

18. A logical view of an EPON is shown in Figure 13.35 with an OLT communicating with two ONUs. The MAC *ifIndex* and speed of each interface is indicated in the figure. Assume that the associated data channel interfaces are corresponding three-digit numbers, e.g., MAC *ifIndex* = 6, associated *ifIndexes* are 6xx.

    (a)   Write the EPON MIB object table and values for the two ONUs as shown in Table 13.17.

    (b)   Write the EPON MIB object table and values for the OLT as shown in Table 13.18.

    (c)   Show all the *ifStack* objects associated with OLT and ONU network elements.

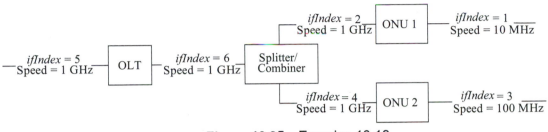

Figure 13.35   Exercise 13.18

19. What EPON MIB object would you use to determine the number of ONUs associated with an OLT?

20. One of the key parameter indicators (KPI) of performance is CRC errors. What is the EPON MIB object that reflects this KPI?

Broadband Wireless Access Networks

We studied basics of broadband (wired) access networks and their management in the previous chapter. We will now look at the basics of broadband wireless access (BWA) networks and how they are managed in this chapter. Wireless access network has a lot of benefits over wired access networks. It is easier to install than cable, asymmetric digital subscriber line (ADSL), and passive optical network (PON) networks. It is more economical as it requires only the installation of a base station (BS). It is easily scalable in that more subscribers can be added by installing more BSs or more sectors in a BS. It is demographically adaptable for both rural and urban communities.

However, the BWA network suffers from some major disadvantages of inadequate bandwidth for broadband, data loss, short and shallow fading, and security threat considerations. Service providers have invested large capital in implementing basic wireless voice network using multiple and proprietary technologies. However, they have been slow in moving to standard and interoperable technologies that could mitigate these deficiencies. All these drawbacks are further complicated by the lack of a common management system that can remotely and centrally manage multiwireless technologies and multivendor products.

The application of wireless technologies can be grouped into three categories. They are personal area networks (PANs), wireless LANs (WLANs), and access networks—metropolitan area network (MAN), GPS/general packet radio service (GPRS), and code division multiple access (CDMA)—and are represented in Figure 14.1.

The PAN is a short-range mobile network that covers a range in the order of tens of feet. It is primarily used for device applications with transmitters and receivers being mobile.

The WLAN, a good example of which is WiFi, is used primarily inside buildings as customer premises equipment (CPE) or home network. It has a reach of several hundreds of meters.

The third category is broadband and narrowband access networks that are deployed as both fixed and mobile networks. Their reach is several kilometers and is deployed outside. Examples of mobile cellular networks are global system for mobile communications (GSM), GPRS, and CDMA [Pahlavan and Krishnamurthy, 2002].

Fixed wireless networks, such as the MAN, are deployed as BWA networks in cities with antennas over the roof top of buildings. This can be deployed as a mesh network. Point-to-multipoint BWA network is deployed using different technologies and using different spectral bands. They are deployed in both metropolitan and rural areas. The third category is the subject of this chapter.

The ever-increasing demand of ubiquity caused by the transition from static to nomadic society is driving wireless technology ahead in general and BWA network technology in particular. We will first look at the basic principles of propagation for wireless transmission in Section 14.1 and understand the current limitations of wireless for broadband transmission. Fixed wireless broadband networks are addressed in

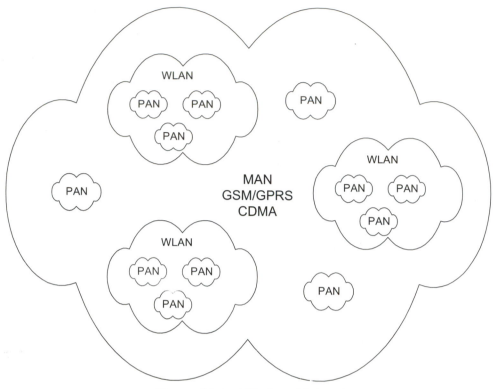

Figure 14.1 Wireless Networks

Section 14.2, and the mobile wireless network is covered in Section 14.3. We have included the very small aperture terminal (VSAT) network in the treatment of broadband access network in Section 14.4 although it meets the requirements of broadband even less than terrestrial wireless systems.

14.1 BASIC PRINCIPLES

Wireless propagation for access network, fixed wireless, also known as wireless local loop (WLL), and cellular mobile wireless are discussed in this section. There are several physical mechanisms to consider in dealing with wireless propagation, which we do not have with propagation through wired networks.

For outdoor propagation, shown in Figure 14.2, the physical mechanisms that we need to consider are line-of-sight (LOS) path, reflection, and diffraction–from ground and other stationary and moving objects–and scattering such as from foliage and buildings.

Let us compare wired media with wireless media. We can list the following three main characteristics of wired media that adversely affect broadband propagation. First is attenuation, which is based on conductivity in copper, or reflection and refraction losses in fiber. The next characteristic is frequency and phase dispersion that are dependent on the refractive index, which in turn is dependent on frequency. The third is time dispersion caused by the speed of transmission, which is dependent on the dispersive refractive index.

Manifestations of the above adversely impacting characteristics of wired media are also present for wireless media. There is attenuation due to absorption by the media, such as water vapor or obstruction of the LOS between the source and the destination such as trees and buildings. There is also decreas-

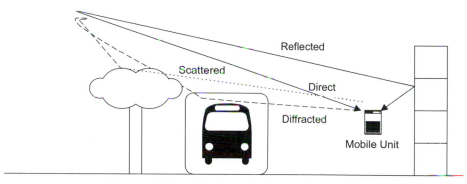

Figure 14.2   Wireless Outdoor Propagation

ing signal strength as we move away from the source antenna since open-space wave propagation is not guided but is divergent. The major cause of frequency, phase, and time dispersion can all be attributed to the signal from the source arriving as multiple signals at the receiver by the multipath. They arrive at the receiver at different times, with changes in frequency and phase, causing interference of short and long duration. If it is a rapid change, it resembles phase, frequency, and time dispersion. If it is gradual and the signal strength degrades, it is called fading. Fading can be slow or rapid temporally or could be spatially fluctuating. Frequency shift is due to Doppler effect when the source or the receiver moves fast with respect to each other.

14.1.1   Free-Space Propagation

Let us first consider the signal strength, which varies with distance from the source in free space. This is shown in Figure 14.3 for an isotropic antenna.

The power at distance d from the source is given by

$$P_r = (P_T / 4\pi d^2) \text{ watts /m}^2 \tag{14-1}$$

where P_r = Received power per unit area and P_T = Total transmitted power.

Figure 14.4 shows configuration of non-isotropic propagation between the transmitter and the receiver antenna of finite size.

For a given effective receiver antenna size, A_R, and receiver efficiency, η_R, the total received power, P_R, for an isotropic transmitter antenna is

$$P_R = \frac{P_T}{4\pi d^2} A_R \eta_R \tag{14-2}$$

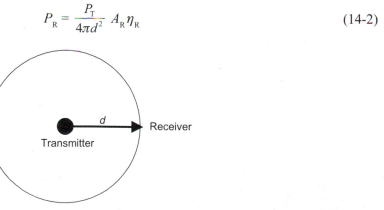

Figure 14.3   Isotropic Antenna Propagation

Figure 14.4 Non-Isotropic Propagation

Now include antenna gain, G_T of transmitter for a finite antenna. Normalizing the effective antenna area A_T with respect to wavelength, λ

$$G_T = \frac{4\pi}{\lambda^2} A_T \eta_T \qquad (14\text{-}3)$$

Multiplying P_T by G_T in Equation (14-2) for the non-isotropic case shown in Figure 14.4, we get

$$P_R = \frac{1}{4\pi d^2} \, P_T G_T A_R \, \eta_R \qquad (14\text{-}4)$$

We can write an equation similar to Equation (14-3) for gain of receiver antenna, G_R. We can then derive the following Equation (14-5) for free-space received power [Schwartz, 2005; Pahlavan and Krishnamurthy, 2002]. This would be valid for the satellite transmission system shown in Figure 14.5

$$P_R = \left(\frac{1}{4\pi d}\right)^2 P_T G_T G_R \qquad (14\text{-}5)$$

Define P_0 = power received at the first meter ($d = 1$ m). Then

$$P_R = P_0 / d^2 = P_0 \, g(d) \qquad (14\text{-}6)$$

where $g(d)$ is the path-loss distance dependence factor.

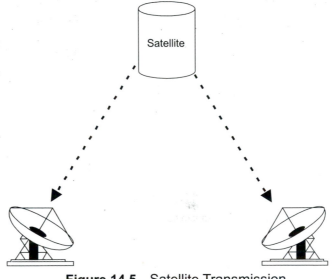

Figure 14.5 Satellite Transmission

In decibels

$$10 \log_{10} P_R = 10 \log_{10} P_0 - 20 \log_{10}(d) \qquad (14\text{-}7)$$

There is a 20-db loss in the signal strength per decade or 6 dB per octave.
Propagation delay/meter = $d/c = 1 / (3 \times 10^8) = 3.3$ nsec/meter

Example:

Let $P_T = 1$ watt

Frequency = 2.4 GHz; $\lambda = 10^8 / (0.8 \times 10^9) = 1/8 = 0.125$ m

$\qquad G_T = G_R = 2.0$

and $\qquad d = 1$ km

$$P_R = \text{Received power} = P_T G_T G_R (\lambda / 4\pi)^2 (1 / d^2)$$
$$= P_T \, 4.0 \, (0.125 /(4 \times 3.14))^2 \, (1/d^2)$$

or

$$P_R = 4 \times 10^{-4} \, (1 / d^2) \text{ watts}$$
$$= 4 \times 10^{-10} \text{ watts}$$

For $d = 1$ m,

$$P_0 = 4 \times 10^{-4} \text{ watts}$$
$$= 0.4 \text{ mW}$$

14.1.2   Two-Ray Propagation

The free-space propagation model derived in Section 14.1.1 can be applied to satellite propagation. However, it does not apply to the terrestrial propagation model. Figure 14.6 shows a simple terrestrial propagation model. The signal travels from the transmitter to the receiver along two paths. The first is a direct path and the other an indirect path caused by ground reflection. If the height of the transmitter and receiver antennas is assumed to be h_t and h_r, it can be shown [Schwartz, 2005] that

$$P_R = P_T G_T G_R (h_t^2 \, h_r^2 / d^4) \qquad (14\text{-}8)$$

where d is the horizontal distance between the transmitter and the receiver.

Comparing Equations (14-5) and (14-8), we observe that the dependency of the received signal power on distance has changed from $1/d^2$ to $1/d^4$. Expressing this in decibels, Equation (14-7) now becomes

$$10 \log_{10} P_R = 10 \log_{10} P_0 - 40 \log_{10}(d) \qquad (14\text{-}9)$$

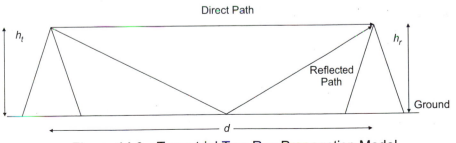

Figure 14.6   Terrestrial Two-Ray Propagation Model

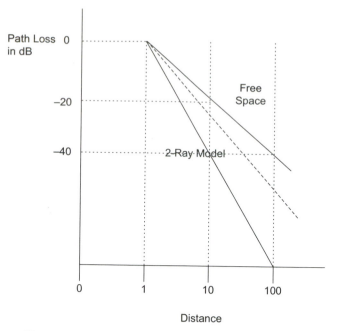

Figure 14.7 Path Loss Depending on Distance

Now, the distance-dependent path-loss factor is 40 dB per decade or 12 dB per octave. Figure 14.7 shows the two cases. In the real world, distance dependency would transition between the two cases as either the distance is increased or the height of the antenna is varied.

Example:

Coverage in cellular network configuration

P_T = Transmitted power from the BS = 1 kW

P_R = Receiver sensitivity = −100 dBm

Path loss at the first meter = 40 dB

Path-loss distance dependency $g(d) = 1/d^n$

P_T in dB = $10 \log_{10} 1,000/0.001$ = 60 dBm

P_R in dB = −100 dBm

Total path loss allowed = 60 − (−100) dB = 160 dB

$$P_0 = 32 \text{ dB}$$

From Equation (14-9)

$$10 \log_{10} P_R = 10 \log_{10} P_0 - 40 \log (d)$$

$$40_{10} \log_{10} (d)_{max} = 160 - 40 = 120 \text{ dB}$$

$$d_{max} = 10^{131/40} \cong 10^3 = 1 \text{ km}$$

Power at the receiver fluctuates due to fading phenomena, which we will soon address. We can generalize the average power received by combining Equations (14-6) and (14-8)

$$P_R = g(d) P_T G_T G_R \qquad (14-10)$$

For free-space wireless

$$g(d) = k_f/d^2 \qquad k_f = (\lambda/4\pi)^2$$

For terrestrial wireless

$$g(d) = k_t/d^4 \qquad k_t = (h_t h_r)^2$$

14.1.3   Fading

Various factors contributing to fading phenomena in outdoor wireless propagation were presented in Figure 14.2. All of them impact the instantaneous value of the received signal that is varying temporally and spatially. The magnitude of the received power fluctuation is caused primarily either by path loss due to absorption and scattering, or due to multipath fading caused by the interference of direct wave with reflected, diffracted, or scattered waves.

The fading phenomenon has both spatial and temporal dependencies. We can classify them into large-scale fading and small-scale fading. The former occurs at a slow spatial rate compared to the wavelength and is generally slow in temporal variation. The latter, namely small-scale fading, occurs at spatial dimension comparable to the wavelength and generally occurs at a more spatially rapid rate compared to large-scale fading. In addition to the above two classifications, there is fading due to Doppler effect in fast-moving mobile units.

Shadow Fading. Large-scale fading, which occurs at relatively long distances compared to wavelength, is also called shadow fading. It is caused due to reflection, scattering, diffraction, meteorological change such as absorption, etc. The fading follows a log-normal (Gaussian) distribution with a standard deviation of 6–10 dB around average power, as shown in Figure 14.8.

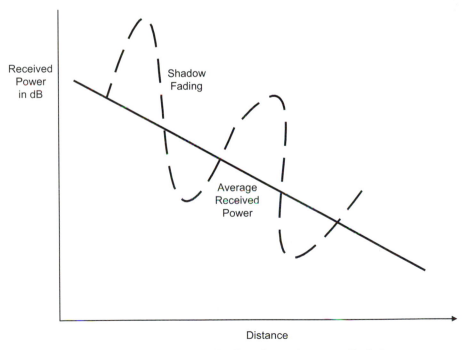

Figure 14.8   Shadow Fading Over Average Path Loss

Cellular Configuration in a Wireless System. Wireless propagation environment can be classified based on the range and range dependency of the BS. An area served by a BS is called a *cell*, and a total wireless system is designed using multiple cells, each cell being served by a BS.

Free-space propagation described earlier, which is applicable to satellite wireless, could cover a very large area spanning hundreds of kilometers depending on the power of the transmitter, height and distance of the satellite, and the beam width of the antennae of the transmitter and the receiver.

Terrestrial wireless propagation can be broadly split into macrocellular areas and microcellular areas.

Macrocells cover an area of a few kilometers to tens of kilometers. These are typically cellular telephony BSs operating at 900 MHz and 1,800–1,900 MHz band. Small-scale fading in the macrocell is empirically found to follow Raleigh distribution.

Microcells typically cover a range of up to a kilometer and operate in the frequency spectrum of up to 11 GHz; commercial deployments include WiFi (2.4 GHz) and WiMax (2.1 GHz). The antennas are at low heights on roof tops and lamp poles in the urban area and hence the cell pattern varies considerably. LOS could be a serious problem in configuration and is overcome by multiple BSs connected in a mesh configuration or implementing orthogonal frequency division multiplexing (OFDM), which is an enabling technology in broadband communications [Schwartz, 2005].

Small-Scale Fading. As we stated earlier, small-scale fading is caused by multipath fading, which is constructive or destructive interference of signals arriving at the receiver traversing different paths and hence at different phases. Moving the receiver by a distance comparable to the wavelength, the signal strength could vary significantly. For example, for the IEEE 802.11b WiFi signal, the data rate could go down from a strong several megabits per second (max. data rate is 11 Mbps) to less than 1 Kbps for displacement in the order of centimeters. Even for a wireless receiver in a stationary state, small-scale fading could occur as the environment fluctuates.

Statistics of the variation of the signal due to small-scale fading depends on the cellular structure of the BSs. In the macrocellular configuration, several multipath rays (5 or 6) interfere with each other and fading distribution follows Raleigh statistics. In microcellular architecture, the direct ray is much stronger than the indirect signal and statistics trend to be Ricean distribution.

Fading Mitigation Techniques. With all the technologies available, although fading could not be completely eliminated, it could be mitigated significantly. One of the techniques used is to spread digital signals out in time by interleaving them. This eliminates loss of adjacent bits of information, i.e., bytes or words of information, and makes it easier to reconstruct the signal using various error correction techniques. This reduces fast fading and possible bursts of noise. It is used in the second-, third-, and fourth- (2G, 3G, and 4G) generation cellular and WLAN systems.

Another technique is to use OFDM using Fourier analysis techniques [Forouzan, 2006; Schwartz, 2005] described in Appendix D. This ensures that each peak or maximum of a digital signal coincides with the valleys or zeros of the rest of the digital signals in the spectrum. This technique is used in all wireless access systems.

A third method is to use the multiple input multiple output (MIMO) technique. This method takes advantage of multipath fading. It uses multiple antennas to transmit and receive the same signals and recover them using correlation techniques. Frequency, spatial, and temporal diversity spread signal can be reconstructed and fading mitigated.

A fourth technique is to introduce equalization in receivers based on a priori knowledge of the distortion of the signal.

14.2 FIXED BROADBAND WIRELESS ACCESS NETWORKS

A fixed BWA network is used to reach subscribers by wireless medium for the last mile and is shown in Figure 14.9. It is a point-to-multipoint network architecture. Broadband information comprising voice, video, and data is multiplexed at the BWA service provider head end and is carried over wired WAN or MAN to the BS from where it is transmitted to subscriber premises. Typical residence and Small Office Home Office (SOHO) subscribers are represented in Figure 14.9. The signal at the subscriber premises is up- and down-converted by transreceiver TR to the baseband signal. The network interface unit (NIU) serves the same function as the NIU in the cable modem system and is the demarcation point between the access network and the subscriber distribution network. At CPE, the network comprises of analog TV and digital network components. The NIU interfaces with either a subscriber station (SS) or a wireless modem (WM), both of which output Ethernet protocol to the CPE distribution network. The former is used with the IEEE 802.16 standard protocol access network. The latter uses a wireless modem termination system (WMTS) at the head end. In this case, the only difference between the fixed wireless system and the cable modem system is the transmission medium of the access network.

Each BS in Figure 14.9 serves several hundred subscribers distributed over multiple sectors. The BS has generally multiple antennas serving multiple sectors. Three or four sectors are common configurations. BSs are spaced depending on the spatial coverage and density of subscribers, as well as the technology used for the access network. We will discuss the various technologies in the next several subsections.

14.2.1 MMDS Network

Multipoint multichannel distribution service (MMDS) is based on point-to-multipoint network architecture. It operates at 2.5–2.686 GHz and carries digital information in the 6-MHz analog TV

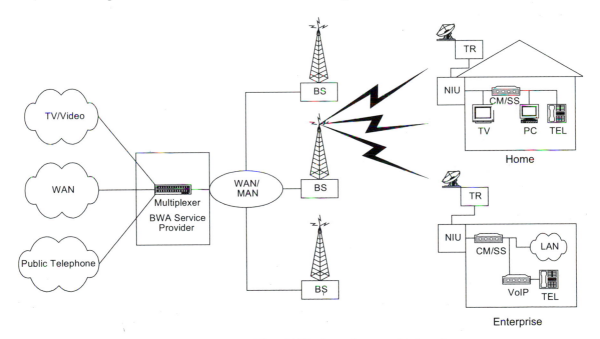

Figure 14.9 Fixed Wireless Access Network

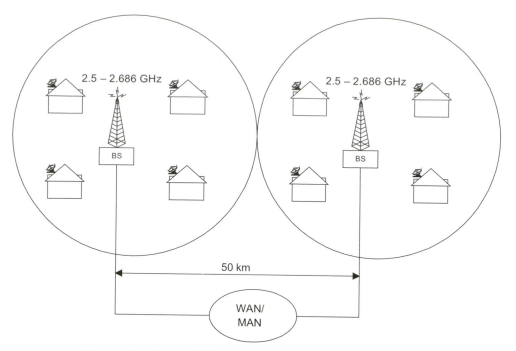

Figure 14.10   Multichannel Multipoint Distribution Service

channel. Well-developed cable access network standards are modified and defined as DOCSIS+ (Data-Over-Cable Service Interface Specifications). We can visualize the MMDS system as the cable modem system with the HFC medium replaced by wireless.

An MMDS broadband system shown in Figure 14.10 comprises a head end, which is the BS, antennas at the head end and at the SS, transreceivers that convert the baseband signal to the microwave signal, and the cable modem at the subscriber end that converts DOCSIS+ protocol to Ethernet protocol for a CPE distribution network. The range of a BS is about 25 kilometers, and hence BSs are separated by about 50 kilometers. The broadband signal is brought to the BSs via WAN or MAN. The range can be extended by having repeater stations, which enables low-powered systems to be used at the SS.

Downstream propagation is TDM broadcast mode and upstream is TDMA transmission. Downstream modulation is QAM and upstream is QPSK. The system is ideal for rural areas. When it is used in the metropolitan area, the LOS is not always good and OFDM modulation is used to mitigate the problem.

14.2.2   LMDS Network

Local multipoint distribution service (LMDS) is a last-mile broadband access network that operates in the K band spectrum, primarily in the 20–40 GHz band. There is no uniformity in the spectral allocation across the world. FCC has allocated the 27.5–29.5 GHz band in the US to LMDS. The architecture of LMDS is the same as MMDS. Its range is shorter than MMDS, about 5 kilometers and hence BSs are separated by about 10 kilometers, as shown in Figure 14.11. One reason for the range limitation is due to the absorption of millimeter waves in the LMDS spectrum by precipitation.

LMDS implementation involves a cluster of cells with a BS in each cell. One of the BSs serves as the coordinating station and acts as the gateway to external networks. As in all fixed BWA networks,

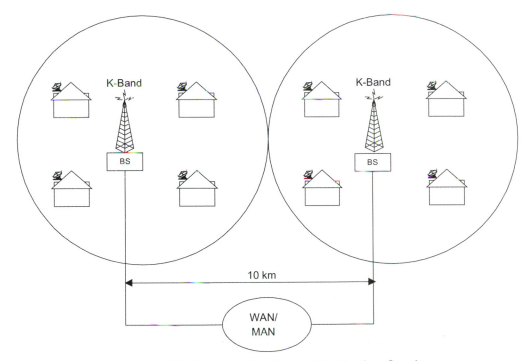

Figure 14.11 Local Multipoint Distribution Service

inter-cell communication is via WAN or MAN. BS to SS communication is TDM downstream and TDMA upstream. In this case, DOCSIS+ standards can be used along with cable modem as the SS.

However, in point-to-point uplink connectivity, other technologies like GPRS are also used. In such cases, the SS and the protocol standards will be different from that of DOCSIS+ standards.

14.2.3 Management of MMDS and LMDS Networks

LMDS (except in exceptional cases mentioned in the previous section) and MMDS have adapted the DOCSIS standards from the cable modem world. As mentioned earlier, the version of DOCSIS modified for wireless broadband is known as DOCSIS+. The management of MMDS and LMDS in these cases can be pictured as the wireless medium replacing the HFC medium, as shown in Figure 14.12. At the head end, CMTS is replaced with a WMTS and the CM is replaced with a WM.

DOCSIS 1.1 and later versions satisfy many requirements of MMDS and LMDS. Security is one of the key considerations. Data-transport security is accomplished under MMDS by encrypting traffic flows between the broadband WM and WMTS located in the BS of the provider's network using Triple Data Encryption Standard (DES).

DOCSIS+ reduces theft-of-service vulnerabilities under MMDS by requiring that the WMTS enforce encryption, and by employing an authenticated client/server key-management protocol in which the WMTS controls distribution of keying material to broadband WMs.

LMDS and MMDS WMs utilize DOCSIS+ key-management protocol to obtain authorization and traffic encryption material from a WMTS, and to support periodic reauthorization and key refresh. Key-management protocol uses X.509 digital certificates, RSA public key encryption, and Triple DES encryption to secure key exchanges between the WM and the WMTS.

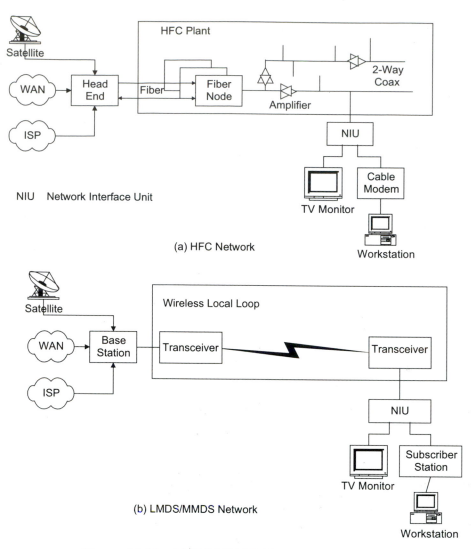

(a) HFC Network

(b) LMDS/MMDS Network

Figure 14.12 LMDS/MMDS Network Management

A second major consideration in specifying DOCSIS+ over DOCSIS is impairment due to radio frequency (RF) impairments. We have discussed various fading phenomena in Section 14.1.3 The QoS of wireless transmission is determined by signal-to-noise ratio (SNR) or carrier-to-noise ratio (CNR).

For downstream performance, CNR in a cable downstream 6-MHz channel should not be less than 35 dB, while the typical multipath (micro-reflections in the cable) should not be greater than 1.5 ms. The upstream performance of SNR in the cable should be less than 25 dB and a typical multipath of less than 1.5 ms. Contrasted with this downstream and upstream performance in wireless propagation, SNR is determined mainly by the transmit level, antenna gain, distance, link budget, interference noise, and the receiver-noise figure and is worse than for cable. More robustness is needed both in the downstream and upstream physical and MAC layers for BWA over cable. DOCSIS+ addresses these by restricting the specifications of DOCSIS [Wilson and Shirali, 2008]. Some of these limitations are mitigated by using OFDM.

MMDS and LMDS will in the future migrate to 802.16 or WiMax standard, which we will consider next.

14.2.4 IEEE 802.16 Network

IEEE 802.16 specifications standardize and achieve interoperability in the WLL system [Eklund, 2002]. An IEEE 802.16-based system is known by several other terminologies—Wireless MAN and WiMax, which is a commercial name given by the industrial consortium WiMax Forum.

An IEEE 802.16-based fixed wireless system is shown in Figure 14.13. The original IEEE 802.16 standard covered 10–66 GHz spectral band. IEEE 802.16a extends the spectral range coverage from 2 to 11 GHz. It is generally deployed as point-to-multipoint architecture, although specifications can be adopted to configure as mesh architecture, as shown in Figure 14.14. Head end transmission is sectionalized with multiple antennas. Transceivers TS convert the RF signal to the baseband as receivers and vice versa as transmitters at both ends. WMTS is at the BS and performs a similar function as CMTS in the cable system. All SSs in a cell terminate at the head end or the BS. The head end allocates bandwidth requested by SS to meet QoS.

The SS performs a similar function as the cable modem but is more complex than the cable modem. It is designed as a highly directional antenna to minimize the transmitter power. The downstream transmission mode is the TDM broadcast mode and the upstream is the TDMA. Upstream and downstream operate in the frequency division duplex mode for bidirectional transmission.

14.2.5 WiMax Network

WiMax specifications are defined by IEEE 802.16d, which is a modification of 802.16a and 802.16c. Some of the limitations due to LOS requirements are mitigated by operating in a lower spectral range

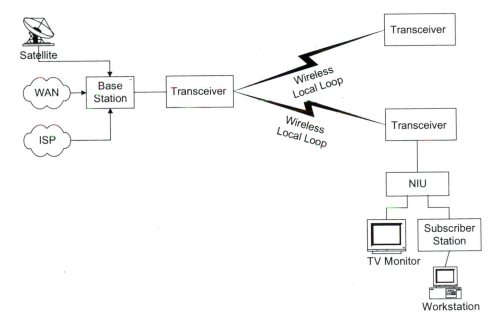

Figure 14.13 IEEE 802.16 Fixed Wireless System

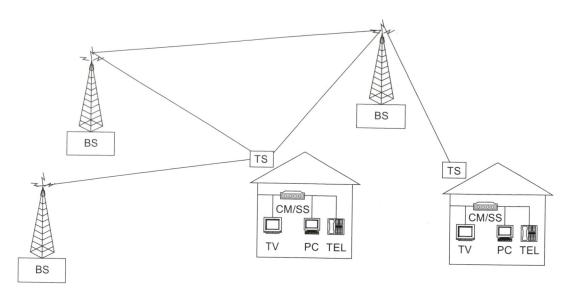

Figure 14.14 WiMax Mesh Network

of 2–11 Gbps. The WiMax Forum has allocated several frequency bands for 802.16d products, both licensed (2.5–2.69 and 3.4–3.6 GHz) and unlicensed spectra (5.725–5.850 GHz).

Multipath phenomenon is taken advantage of to partially mitigate the LOS limitation and, in addition, OFDM technology is used at the PHY layer to improve performance. Channel quality feedback from SS to BS is used to dynamically vary the power and data rate to improve QoS. By using TDMA in the MAC layer, and head end allocating the desired bandwidth to the SSs, the broadband requirement of prioritization of real-time over non-real-time traffic is accomplished.

In a metropolitan area, where antennas are positioned over the roof tops of buildings, the network is configured as mesh network, as shown in Figure 14.14. In this case, obstruction of signal between any two antennas is overcome. If a direct LOS path is not available, the system will redirect traffic through intermediate nodes.

The IEEE 802.16e standard is an extension to the approved IEEE 802.16/16a standard. The purpose of 802.16e is to add limited mobility to the current standard, which is designed for a fixed operation.

14.2.6   Management of Fixed Wireless Access Network

We have addressed the management of MMDS and LMDS in Section 14.2.3. We will now describe management of IEEE 802.16 and IEEE 802.16d, WiMax/Wireless MAN, in this section. The components to be managed are BS, SS, wireless link, and RF spectrum.

Figure 14.15 shows the management reference model of BWA networks [Chou *et al.*, 2004; Dudzinski and Bozier, 2004]. It consists of a network management system (NMS), managed nodes BS and SSs, and a service flow database. The service flow database contains service flow and associated QoS information that have to be populated in BS and SS when service is provisioned, or a mobile SS roams into BS coverage. SSs can be managed directly by NMS, or indirectly through BS, acting as the SNMP proxy. Management information between SS and BS will be carried over second management connection ID (CID) for managed SS. If the second management CID does not exist, SNMP messages will go through another interface in the customer premises. The SNMP agent in the SS can be managed directly or via an SNMP proxy in the BS.

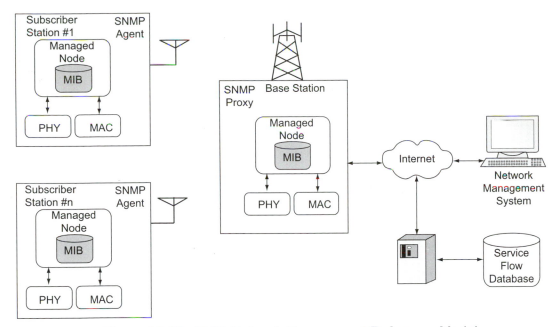

Figure 14.15 BWA Network Management Reference Model

Figure 14.16 shows the MIB structure of *wmanIfMib* for 802.16 and is node 184 under *transmission (mib-2 10)*. It defines the interface table for a wireless MAN interface. Table 14.1 describes some key attributes of BS in the *wmanIfMib*. There are controllers associated with the BS and sectors. The SNMP agent can be implemented in the BS controller or sector controller. There is one entry for each BS if the SNMP agent is implemented in a common BS controller. There is only one entry for the BS sector if the SNMP agent is implemented in the sector controller. This is shown in Table 14.1. The usage table for the SS is shown in Table 14.2.

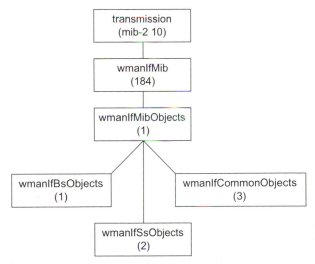

Figure 14.16 WMAN IF MIB

Table 14.1 Usage of ifTable Objects for the Base Station

IFTABLE	IFINDEX	IFTYPE(LANA)	IFSPEED	IFPHYS ADDRESS	IFADMIN STATUS	IFOPER STATUS
BS Sector 1	An ifEntry per BS sector (1)	propBWAp2MP	Null	MAC Address of BS Sector	Administration Status	Operational Status
BS Sector 2	An ifEntry per BS sector (2)	propBWAp2MP	Null	MAC Address of BS Sector	Administration Status	Operational Status
BS Sector 3	An ifEntry per BS sector (3)	propBWAp2MP	Null	MAC Address of BS Sector	Administration Status	Operational Status
Ethernet			Null	MAC Address of BS Sector	Administration Status	Operational Status

Table 14.2 Usage of ifTable Objects for the Subscriber Station

IFTABLE	IFINDEX	IFTYPE (LANA)	IFSPEED	IFPHYS ADDRESS	IFADMIN STATUS	IFOPER STATUS
SS	An ifEntry for SS	propBWAp2MP	Null	MAC Address of SS	Administration Status	Operational Status
Ethernet			Null	MAC Address	Administration Status	Operational Status

wmanIfMibObjects under *wmanIfMib* has three subnodes. *wmanIfBsObjects* (1) has the tables associated with the BS; *wmanIfSsObjects* (2) has the tables associated with the SS; and *wmanIfCommonObjects* (3) has the tables associated with the common objects.

BWA supports various classes of service with various QoS for bearer services. It can be configured for bandwidth negotiation for connectionless service, and with state information, is maintainable for connection-oriented service. It supports ATM traffic categories: CBR, VBR-rt, VBR-nrt, ABR, and Internet categories for integrated and differentiated services.

14.3 MOBILE WIRELESS NETWORKS

Although the wired part of the topology for a cellular mobile network is similar to fixed wireless systems, the topology and characteristics of a wireless segment are very different. Even though today's wireless technology for cellular mobile systems is digital, it is essentially an extension of the voice-based analog system. The 2G technology GSM is primarily used for voice transmission and is essentially circuit switched. The 2.5G networks are GPRS and enhanced data rates for GSM evolution (EDGE) are enhancements to GSM. Voice service uses circuit switching and data service uses packet switching. The 2G networks are TDMA based and 2.5G networks are CDMA based. Standardization and hence interoperability is introduced in 3G networks by ITU-T and is called the universal mobile telecommunication system (UMTS). They are based on CDMA protocol. An IP-based mobile network is a 4G network and is still in its embryonic stage.

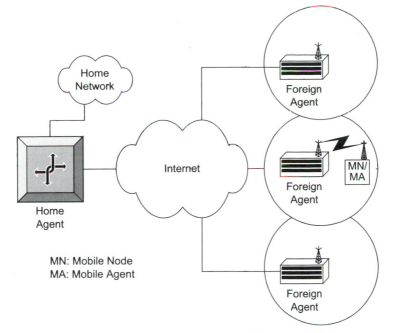

Figure 14.17 Cellular Network

There are numerous ways to structure cells in cellular mobile networks. They are all based on the neighboring (adjacent) cells transmitting at different carrier frequencies. Figure 14.17 shows the architecture of a cellular network. Each mobile node (MN) is associated with a home network with a home agent (HA). It communicates with foreign nodes (FNs), each with its own foreign agent (FA), through the Internet (or WAN/MAN). The MN in turn communicates with the FN using its mobile agent (MA). As the MN transitions from one cell to the next, it is acquired by the FA of the new cell. The FA gets authorization from the MN's home node (HN) before information communication starts.

The management of a 3G and 4G network is more complicated than a fixed wireless network. Some of the issues associated with a cellular mobile network management are listed below:

- Network architecture is a hierarchical LAN architecture
- Mobile computing unit has both hardware and software limitations
- There is bandwidth limitation in reaching the mobile unit
- Mobility of the mobile unit has to be monitored and tracked
- Location of the mobile unit has to be monitored and tracked
- Resource management is complex
- Power in the mobile has to be managed
- Security and privacy management need to be assured
- Broadband QoS needs to be achieved

We will now look at these issues from a management point of view. Most of them are built-in features whose network parameters need to be monitored and managed. One of the technological advances made to manage mobile network is the mobile IP initiative, which we will discuss next.

14.3.1 Mobile IP

Most mobile cell providers currently use proprietary protocol in communicating with mobile units. To make mobile network interoperable, IETF has defined mobile IP [RFCs 2003–2006]. The functioning of mobile IP is analogous to the functioning of call forwarding in telephony. The home telephone with a home telephone number forwards an incoming call to another telephone number that is entered in the home telephone. In mobile network, telephone numbers are replaced by IP addresses, and the mobile IP is not stationary. Notice that this is different from a nomadic unit such as a portable PC. In a nomadic unit, the local unit is assigned a temporary IP address by the local controller such as a wireless access point or an Ethernet hub.

A mobile IP uses two addresses—a fixed home address and a care-of-address that changes with the point of attachment. There are three mobile IP functions performed by three mobile functional entities. They are mobile node, foreign node, and home node. MN is a host or router that changes point of attachment from one network or subnet to another. It has an embedded agent, MA, which does the discovery of an FA in the FN, which is the second entity. The FN is a router in the mobile network that provides services to the MN. The FA, after acquisition of the MA, registers the MN's location with the HA in the HN. The HN is a router on a mobile network that is the home network of the MN. The HA in the HN tunnels packets to and from the HA to the FA care-of-address as the MN roams.

Discovery and registration functions are presented in Figure 14.18. The MN discovers the FA and its care-of-address by the advertisement of the FA. The MN can also discover by its own solicitation. The MN registers the FA with the HA.

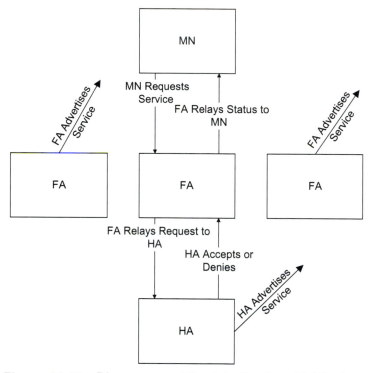

Figure 14.18 Discovery and Registration in a Mobile System

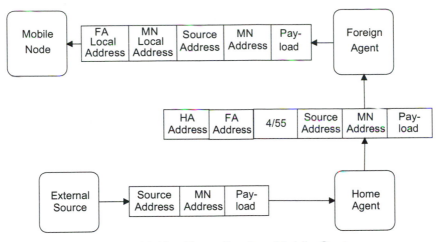

Figure 14.19 Tunneling in a Mobile System

Information flow between the HA and the FA occurs through the tunneling process, as shown in Figure 14.19. An external source attempts to reach an MN through the HA. The MA is transparent to it. The PDU from the external source contains source address, mobile address, and payload. The HA prepends to the PDU home address, foreign address, and protocol number of either 4 or 55, and transmits it to the FA. The number 4 indicates to the higher level that the next header is an IP header with full encapsulation; 55 indicates minimal encapsulation. The FA strips the prepended home and foreign addresses and protocol number and then transmits the PDU to the MN.

Table 14.3 presents mobile IP MIB groups. There are three groups: mobile node, foreign agent, and home agent. Each group is organized as a set of related objects. The relationship is between objects within the same group or across different groups. For example, *mipSystemGroup* spans across all three groups and *maAdvertisementGroup* spans FA and HA groups. *mnSystemGroup* and *faSystemGroup* comprise intra-group-related objects.

Table 14.3 Mobile IP MIB Groups

GROUPS	MOBILE NODE	FOREIGN AGENT	HOME AGENT
Agent			
mipSystemGroup	X	X	X
mipSecAssociationGroup	X	X	X
mipSecViolationGroup	X	X	X
mnSystemGroup	X		
mnDiscoveryGroup	X		
mnRegistrationGroup	X		
maAdvertisementGroup		X	X
faSystemGroup		X	
faAdvertisementGroup		X	
faRegistrationGroup		X	
haRegistrationGroup			X
haRegNodeCountersGroup			X

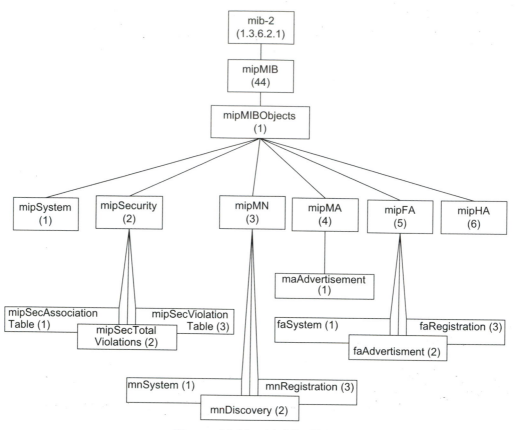

Figure 14.20 Mobile IP MIB

A mobile IP MIB *mipMIB* is shown in Figure 14.20. It is node 44 under mib-2. The entities comprising *mipMIBObjects (mipMIB 1)* and the subnodes under it are presented in Table 14.4.

14.3.2 Mobility Management

We have already learned the important role that mobile IP plays in mobile communication. Mobility management consists of two components, location management and handoff management.

Location management is a two-stage process. First, it enables the network to discover the current attachment point of the mobile user for data delivery. The MA periodically notifies the network of the MN's new access point. The second stage is data delivery. Here the network is queried for the mobile user's location profile and the current position of the mobile host is found.

The second component is handoff (or handover) management that enables the network to maintain a user's connection as the mobile terminal continues to move and change its access point to the network. This is a three-stage process of initiation, connection establishment, and data-flow management. During the initiation stage, either the user (a network agent) or changing network conditions identify the need

Table 14.4   mipMIBObjects

ENTITY	OID	DESCRIPTION
mipMIBObjects	mipMIB 1	Objects under mipMIB
mipSystem	mipMIBObjects 1	Mobile IP system-related parameters
mipSecurity	mipMIBObjects 2	Mobile IP security parameters
mipSecurity AssociationTable	mipSecurity 1	Security association table
mipSecTotal Violations	mipSecurity 2	Total number of security violations in the entity
mipSecViolation Table	mipSecurity 3	Security violation information
mipMN	mipMIBObjects 3	Mobile node group
mnSystem	mipMN 1	Mobile node system information
mnDiscovery	mipMN 2	Mobile node discovery counter on solicitations, advertisements, and moves
mnRegistration	mipMN 3	Mobile node registration table
mipMA	mipMIBObjects 4	Mobile agent group
maAdvertisement	mipMA 1	Mobility agent advertisement configuration table present in both the MN and the FA
mipFA	mipMIBObjects 5	FA group
faSystem	mipFA 1	FA system information
faAdvertisement	mipFA 2	FA advertisement information plus MA advertisement group
faRegistration	mipFA 3	FA visitors list
mipHA	mipMIBObjects 6	HA registration group and mobility binding list

for handoff. In the connection–establishment stage, the network must find new resources for the handoff connection and perform any additional routing operations. The final stage is data-flow control, where delivery of data from the old connection path to the new connection path is maintained.

14.3.3   Resource and Power Management

Resource management deals with scheduling and call admission control (CAC), load balancing between access networks, dynamic control of RF spectrum, and power management. This impacts management of bandwidth to provide multimedia broadband service, as well as handoff between cells to achieve quality of service.

In mobile cellular networks, when a mobile user moves from one cell to a different cell, "handoff" of the user needs to be accomplished without dropping the session. CAC is the process that controls whether an incoming call can be admitted or not. The resource control mechanism has to allocate the limited bandwidth resources to users in an efficient way in order to guarantee the users' QoS requirements. If the handoff target cell does not have enough bandwidth to support this call, the call will be forced to terminate. Handoff calls are commonly given a higher priority in accessing bandwidth resources in order to provide a seamless connection for users. Call dropping during a handoff is mitigated by reserving bandwidth specifically for that function in each cell. For broadband service, handoff management becomes more complicated. The system needs to support, in addition to handoff in the same class of service, multiple classes of service where each class presents different QoS requirements.

Handoff may also need to be done in intra-cell roaming of an MN. If the signal falls below a threshold level of a subscriber's SLA, transmission can be dynamically switched to another frequency that is stronger.

Power management involves multiple components. [Pahlavan and Krishnamurthy, 2002] discusses power control, power-saving mechanisms, energy efficiency, and radio resource management. Power control deals with mechanisms to dynamically control transmitter power to reduce interference. Power-saving mechanisms and energy-efficient designs extend battery life. Radio resource management optimizes transmission by selecting the best spectral components.

Unfortunately, there are no standard MIBs defined for monitoring and managing the above resources. Proxy agents can be developed and used by vendors to implement these requirements.

14.3.4   QoS Management

Third-generation mobile networks, 3G and beyond, are required to transmit voice, video, and data under the specifications of universal mobile telecommunications system (UMTS) developed by the Third Generation Partnership Project [3GPP]. The equivalent of 3GPP for North America is [3GPP2]. The UMTS infrastructure is expected to carry various types of application on the same medium while meeting QoS objectives. The 3GPP has defined four QoS classes (TS 23.107): conversational, streaming, interactive, and background. These are shown in Table 14.5, along with the required delay, delay variation, and bit error rate (BER). Conversation has the most stringent requirements and background tasks such as email have the least.

We have mentioned in the previous two sections the dependency of QoS on mobility and resource management. The QoS discussed here is applicable only between the BS and the mobile stations. QoS

Table 14.5 UMTS QoS Specifications

QOS CLASS	TRANSFER DELAY	TRANSFER DELAY VARIATION	LOW BER	GUARANTEED BIT RATE	EXAMPLE
Conversation	Stringent	Stringent	No	Yes	VoIP, video- and audio-conferencing
Streaming	Constrained	Constrained	No	Yes	Broadcast service, news, sport
Interactive	Looser	No	Yes	No	Web browsing, interactive chat, games
Background	No	No	Yes	No	Email, SMS, TFP transactions

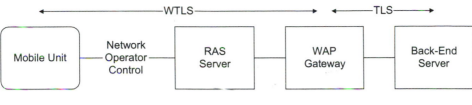

Figure 14.21 Security Management in a Mobile System

on the core network is achieved using wired network methodologies, such as *intserv* (integrated services) or *diffserv* (differentiated services).

14.3.5 Security Management

Security is a major issue in mobile wireless communication. Security requirements for mobile wireless communication involve security in different parts of the network, both wired and wireless. Broadband communication system is based on digital communication technology TDM, TDMA, and CDMA. Air interface security is based on the wireless application.

Wireless application protocol (WAP) and secured socket shell (SSL) are the two approaches that are commonly used for secured wireless communication. Although SSL is used extensively in a wired network, WAP is the common implementation in mobile wireless. It is based on transport layer security (TLS) protocol. It does the normal security functions, which include authentication, authorization, privacy, and address integrity.

Figure 14.21 shows WAP architecture [Howell]. The MN is connected to the WAP gateway through a network operator control and a remote access server. The security protocol used is wireless TLS (WTLS). The TLS protocol is used between the WAP gateway and remote server that the mobile subscriber is trying to access. Most security failures happen in the transition between the two. Robust security can be achieved by careful design and implementation of the WAP gateway using available security tools.

WTLS could be implemented for the wireless leg of the link and SSL could be implemented between the WAP gateway and the remote server. In this case, the WAP gateway module has to perform decryption and encryption, as well as protocol conversion.

3GPP and 3GPP2 have plans to implement IP network. Under that situation, open standard SNMPv3 discussed in Chapter 7, which has built-in security, would be used for mobile network management.

14.4 SATELLITE NETWORKS

14.4.1 VSAT Network

Although satellite communication is currently not ideally suited for broadband communication, it is emerging as one in a limited manner. For example, VSAT (Figure 14.22) is a popular implementation of direct transmission to home (DTH) satellite access network. Some reasons for the revival of DTH are easy implementation, small and highly directional antenna, and video compression technique. It is used as a back-up link for communication by industrial organizations, as well as to set up communication to rural and inaccessible areas such as mountainous regions.

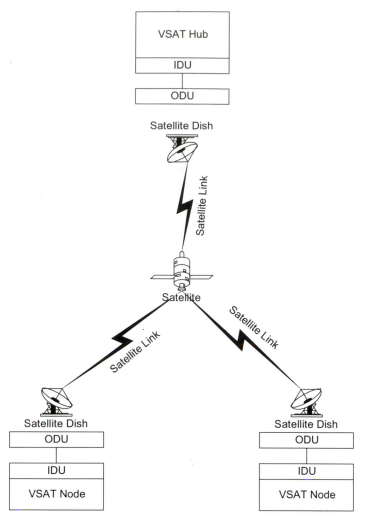

Figure 14.22 VSAT Broadband Links

In the USA, VSAT operates in the Ku- and Ka-bands. In the Ku-band the downlink is in the 12-GHz range and the uplink is in the 14-GHz range. In the Ka-band, the corresponding ranges are 29.5–30 GHz and 19.7–20.2 GHz. Spectral allocations vary from country to country. Both bands suffer from rain absorption and it is worse in the Ka-band than in Ku-band. Although efforts to increase the speed in VSAT systems are in progress, current systems operate at uplink speeds of about 40–60 kbps and downlink speeds of 500 kbps.

The outdoor unit (ODU) consists of a power amplifier and an up-converter feeding into the antenna and low-noise block down-converter receiving signals from the antenna. The signal traverses at intermediate frequency over the coaxial cable between the ODU and the indoor unit (IDU). The IDU includes the following components: modulator, demodulator, frequency synthesizer, encoder, and decoder. The normal interface to the customer network is Ethernet.

Standards are emerging in DTH. Digital video broadcast (DVB) is used for downstream broadcast. Upstream protocol is either DVB-RCS (DVB return channel system) or modified DOCSIS, DOCSIS-S [Steffes, 2005].

VSAT uses geostationary earth orbit and hence appears stationary for the ground station. The signal undergoes frequency conversion and amplification or regeneration in the satellite. The former is called a "bent-pipe" configuration and the latter regeneration configuration. Besides rain attenuation, VSAT also suffers from an end-to-end round-trip delay time of 0.5 seconds; i.e., from one terminal to another and back.

14.4.2   VSAT Network Management

The NMS is usually located at the hub and monitors the hub and nodal site equipment. Management data are acquired over satellite links sharing bandwidth with the payload.

Objects to be managed are parameters associated with the antenna, transceivers, frequency converters, and power amplifiers. Since the total bandwidth available is in the range of 40–500 kbps, assuming a limit of 5% usage for management data, the bandwidth available in the satellite links for management is in the order of a few kilobits per second. The usage of a standard SNMP protocol frame is expensive, and hence efficient proprietary protocols are implemented. Management features and parameters that are implemented are also limited due to bandwidth constraint.

Summary

In this chapter, we addressed the basic principles of wireless communication that are required to understand wireless access networks and their management. The key areas covered are free-space propagation that is applicable to satellite and mobile communications and two-ray propagation that terrestrial wireless access networks are based on. We also discussed the fading phenomenon that separates wireless access networks from those of wired access networks.

We discussed the three major categories of fixed wireless broadband access networks, namely MMDS, LMDS, and IEEE 802.16/WiMax. MMDS has been deployed in rural areas and has adopted wired cable technology defined by DOCSIS standards. LMDS is also based on DOCSIS standards although other technologies such as GPRS are used. Network management of DOCSIS-based MMDS and LMDS has taken advantage of standards developed for the management of cable access networks.

WiMax network is an outgrowth of IEEE 802.16, which is the generalized standard for fixed wireless access networks. This technology is seriously considered for metropolitan access network and will compete with cable and DSL technologies. However, it has been slow in getting deployed due to technical, as well as competitive reasons. MIBs have been specified for this to implement remote network management.

We discussed mobile cellular wireless network primarily from the IP network point of view, although proprietary technologies are mostly used for predominantly voice-based network. Mobile IP plays an important role in the implementation of broadband mobile wireless including management of it. This was addressed in detail.

VSAT was described as emerging DTH technology for broadband access network. It has several advantages and disadvantages for use in broadband communication. Because of its geographical distribution, remote network management system is a necessity. However, due to bandwidth constraint, features of the system are usually limited.

Exercises

1. A satellite is transmitting 10 watts and is positioned at 2 miles over the earth receiver. Assume that the antenna gain of the transmitter and the receiver are each equal to 1.6 and the frequency of operation is at 4.8 GHz. Calculate the power and the latency (propagation delay) of the received signal.

2. A terrestrial wireless point-to-point broadband communication system is established at 2.4 GHz. The height of the transmitter and the receiver antenna is each 50 meters and the separations 10 kilometers. The receiver sensitivity is 10^{-5} watts. Calculate the power needed at the transmitter using a two-ray propagation model. Assume the gain of the antenna as 2 both at the transmitter and the receiver.

3. Latency is a problem for interactive communication via sattelite. Calculate the orbital altitude and round-trip delay time between two stations on the ground communicating via a geostationary satellite. Assume the radius of the orbit is 42,164 kilometers and the radius of the earth is 6,378 kilometers.

4. Fill the *ifTable* objects for a three-sector base station and one subscriber station for each sector shown in Table 14.1 and Table 14.2. The tables should represent reasonable and valid values as they appear in the database of an NMS. Assume that sector 1 is completely functional, sector 2 is under failure condition, and sector 3 is under maintenance mode. All subscriber stations are active.

5. Identify the managed objects and the MIBs that were used to acquire the information in Tables 14.1 and 14.2.

6. (a) What MIB table would you use to measure the QoS of service flow in a fixed wireless system between the base station and the subscriber station?
   (b) Define latency and jitter for service flow in a fixed wireless system
   (c) Write the specific managed objects associated with latency and jitter

7. In designing a mobile network, what is the protocol you would use for:

   (a) Communication between the foreign agent and the mobile agents associated with that cell?
   (b) Communication between the foreign agent and the home agent?

8. In Figure 14.19, assume the home network as a class B network and foreign nodes belonging to a class C network. Fill in the data frame with the appropriate addresses between each pair of nodes.

Broadband Home Networks

In Chapter 1 we introduced the network segment associated with home and customer premises as one of the three segments of broadband network. The customer premises equipment (CPE) network in an enterprise environment is either an IEEE 802.3-based Ethernet local area network (LAN) or an IEEE 802.11-based wireless LAN, also known as WiFi, or a hybrid of both. Home network provides the opportunity to utilize multiple technologies besides Ethernet LAN and WiFi. HomePNA is implemented using a twisted-pair telephone cable medium, HomePlug takes advantage of power line wiring in the house, and cable utilizes the television coaxial cable. FireWire is also a wired medium and is based on IEEE 1394 protocol to transmit high-speed video digital data and Universal Serial Bus (USB) with its own hub for transmitting digital data. Wireless home network technologies include IEEE 802.15.1 Bluetooth and ultra-wide band (UWB) personal area networks (PANs) for short distances. Residential gateway and the home network, which is the CPE network for residences, will be the subject of this chapter.

15.1   HOME NETWORKING TECHNOLOGIES

Home networking technology, or more appropriately technologies, is still in its embryonic stage. We will present here only a brief description of its various components. You are referred to Subramanian [2005a, b] for a detailed presentation.

Figure 15.1 shows higher- and lower-layer protocols in an integrated architecture. The protocols used could be classified into application-layer protocols and transport-layer protocols, with middleware that acts as a gateway between the two. Applications have protocol specifications to handle functions, services, and messages. Transport protocols deal with transport functions belonging to transport, network, MAC, and physical layers. We notice at the application layer that there are four protocols—OSGi, JINI, UPnP, and HAVi. Open Service Gateway Initiative (OSGi) and JINI, which are both based on Java Virtual Machine (JVM) and use Transmission Control Protocol (TCP)/Internet Protocol (IP) for transport and network layers. Universal Plug and Play (UPnP) is based on HTTP and hence HTTP is under UPnP. Home Audio–Video Interoperability (HAVi) and UPnP show IEEE 1394 for the MAC and PHY layers. HAVi is platform and language agnostic, although IEEE 1394 has been adopted as the lower layers. OSGi and JINI use either 802.3 or modified 802.3 with HomePlug and HomePNA or physical layers. X10, Infrared Data Association (IrDA) data, and CEBus are also shown as they do interface with IP.

HAVi architecture is a set of APIs, services, and a wired transport protocol, IEEE 1394. It is intended to interface with multivendor consumer electronic devices and computing devices. HAVi focuses on home entertainment and AV devices.

JINI technology was developed by Sun Microsystems in 1998 for integrating IP-based devices in a computer network, and is based on its Java technology. It is considered as a middleware technology and comprises a set of APIs and network protocols. Its infrastructure enables all devices interoperable irrespective of their operating system and interface constraints.

Application	HAVi	UPnP	OSGi JINI		
			JVM		
Transport/Network		HTTP			
			TCP/IP		
MAC PHY	IEEE 1394		802.3 802.11	Modified 802.3	X10 IrDA
			Ethernet WiFi	HomePlug HomePNA	CEBus

Figure 15.1   Home Network Protocol Architecture

UPnP is architecture for pervasive peer-to-peer network connectivity of smart home wired and wireless devices. It is Microsoft's initiative for home networking and uses Web technologies for device description and control. It also contains a set of APIs, but its strategy is different from that of JINI. JINI APIs are a contract between vendors, and UPnP allows vendors to build the APIs.

OSGi is a residential gateway platform that supports the integration of different home networking technologies and the delivery of different services from service providers. Based on Java technology, different software components, called bundles, can be downloaded remotely to the gateway.

Just as most managed applications are managed as part of the Enterprise Management System using Simple Network Management Protocol (SNMP) agents, residential applications could also have SNMP-like agents built in them. As of now, home network applications are more in a research stage. Application and middleware technologies are based on TCP/IP protocol for the transport and network layers used for transport protocols.

The medium of transport for the home network could be either a wired or a wireless medium, or a hybrid of the two. Wired medium could be any one of the following: copper wire such as power line, twisted pair such as phone line, Cat 3 or Cat 5 Ethernet cable, coaxial cable such as the one used for TV distribution, or optical fiber. Modern homes are being built wired with optical fiber. Wireless transmission is the radio frequency (RF) with single or multiple antennas. Cabling could be hybrid transmission with wired distribution in the home and wireless inside the rooms.

Figure 15.2 shows a comprehensive view of the home network. The access network is one of three choices, namely DSL, HFC, or wireless. Each feed terminates in the respective modem, whose output is connected to a residential gateway. Although a personal computer functions as a residential gateway, in the future this would be a dedicated intelligent device with built-in communication and application modules. In Figure 15.2 the residential gateway has four types of distribution networks connected to it. The USB network has low- and high-speed digital data devices connected to it. The very high-speed digital triple play devices comprise IEEE 1394 network, also known as FireWire® branded by Apple. The third type of network is LAN, the predominant one being wired Ethernet network. Other less popular types of LANs are HomePNA using telephone cable or HomePlug using power line. They could be based on the above-mentioned schemes of either. The fourth home distribution network shown in Figure 15.2 is WiFi, wireless LAN network based on IEEE 802.11. We will next address wired and wireless technologies based on various physical media.

15.2 WIRED HOME DISTRIBUTION NETWORK

Wired transport protocol for transport and network layers is TCP/IP. The lower-layer protocols address physical and MAC layers and there are several choices.

X-10 protocol communicates between the transmitter and the receiver by sending RF bursts–1 millisecond bursts of 120 kHz—over power line wiring. CEBus Standard and Home Plug and Play (HomePnP) devices are capable of communicating with each other over the power line without the need for new wires.

The USB is an alternative to Ethernet as a computer peripheral interface. However, it is data-centric as opposed to multimedia and limited to PC peripheral applications.

USB 1.0	1.5 Mbps	Low speed	Cable length = 3 m
USB 1.1	12 Mbps	Full speed	Cable length = 3 m
USB 2.0	400 Mbps	High speed	Cable length = 5 m

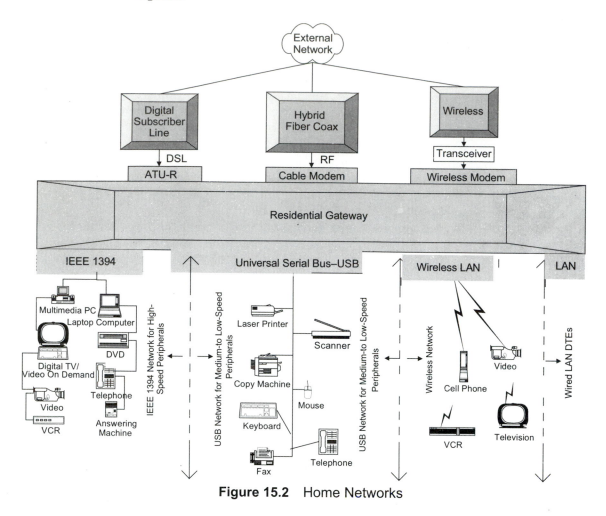

Figure 15.2 Home Networks

IEEE 1394 is more suitable for home networking as it can be applied to audio and video in addition to IP data transmission. It was originally developed as a high-performance serial bus by Apple, known as FireWire. It can be transmitted over copper, as well as fiber, and has the potential of carrying up to 3.2 Gbps.

Cable is prevalent in North America and is extensively used to distribute analog video and data. Digital telephone over cable is being introduced in selected sites by cable service providers. Packet cable being developed by CableLabs will have the capability of delivering and distributing VoIP, video (also digital), and data over cable to and in home.

Home Phoneline Network Alliance (HomePNA) is a technology that can distribute broadband over the phone line in the house. Home Phoneline Networking Alliance was formed in 1998. It is expected to handle data rate up to 10 Mbps and is applicable to phone and low data-rate transmission.

HomePlug, also known as power line communication (PLC), distributes data over power line in the house and is suitable for low data-rate transmission for applications such as electronic device control. Its projected data rate is 10 Mbps.

Since IEEE 802.3 Ethernet is the most popular wired home network today, we will discuss only that here. Most service offerings having modems–residential gateways, cable, and DSL—have multiple

Ethernet outputs. Many home routers have Dynamic Host Configuration Protocol (DHCP)/ Network Address Translator (NAT) built in for handling multiple IP devices. Its primary application is for IP data transmission with limited real-time application.

15.3 ETHERNET MANAGEMENT

We have extensively covered management of Ethernet LANs in earlier chapters. MIBs that address the management of basic Ethernet objects are defined in RFC 1213. Multiple links associated with a given physical interface are handled by layering and use of *ifStackTable* [RFC 2863], although there are no sublayers in the 802.3 Ethernet layer. RFC 3635 supplements the above for the advances made in Ethernet-like interface technology. Some of the salient features are addressed here.

ifRcvAddressTable contains all IEEE 802.3 addresses, unicast, multicast, and broadcast, for which this interface will receive packets and forward them up to a higher-layer entity for local consumption.

MIB [RFC 3635] applies to interfaces that have the *ifType* value *ethernetCsmacd(6)*. It is required that all Ethernet-like interfaces use an *ifType* of *ethernetCsmacd(6)* regardless of the speed that the interface is running or the link-layer encapsulation in use.

ifOctets and packet counts have been redefined. MTU can now accommodate larger than 1,500 bytes. An additional managed object *ifHighSpeed* has been introduced to handle 10 Gigabits per second speed. For current interface types, this will be equal to 1,000,000 (1 million), 10,000,000 (10 million), 100,000,000 (100 million), or 1,000,000,000 (1 billion). *ifHighSpeed* represents the current operational speed in millions of bits per second. For current Ethernet-like interfaces, this will be equal to 1, 10, 100, or 1,000. If the interface has not yet been negotiated to an operational speed, the maximum speed supported by the interface is a default value.

In broadband service, IP telephony allows voice service to be transported over the same infrastructure as data service. This has led to the emergence of Ethernet IP phones, which have similar functions and characteristics as traditional phones. Powering the phone with the same cable used for signal transfer is one of the functions that is now taken for granted. The MIB module defined in RFC 3635 supports management objects required for the management of powered Ethernet devices and ports. In the definition of managed objects [RFC 3621] "pse" stands for power sourcing equipment and "pd" stands for powered device.

Figure 15.3 shows a Power Ethernet MIB [RFC 3621]. The MIB objects group *pethObjects* is categorized into three MIB groups. The *pethPsePortTable* defines objects used for configuring and describing the status of ports on a PSE device. Examples of PSE devices are Ethernet switches that support power Ethernet and mid-span boxes.

The *pethMainPseObjects* MIB group defines management objects for a managed main power source in a PSE device. The Ethernet switch is one example of a box that would support these objects.

The *pethNotificationControlTable* includes objects that control transmission of notifications from the agent to a management application.

Let us now look at wireless transport technologies for the home distribution of broadband service.

15.4 WIRELESS HOME DISTRIBUTION NETWORKS

Once again, the transport and network-layer protocol is the TCP/IP suite. There are three lower-layer wireless groups: IrDA, WLAN/WiFi, and wireless PAN. The IrDA has developed specifications for

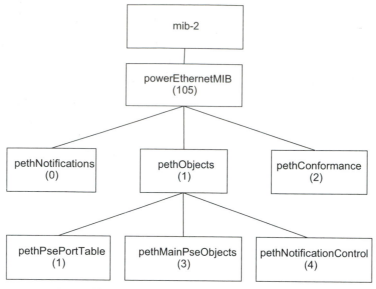

Figure 15.3   Power Ethernet MIB

infrared wireless communication. Application for this technology is short range—between Personal Digital Assistants (PDAs), between PC and hand-held PDA, remote control, etc.

Next to Ethernet LAN, the most popular home network is WLAN. IEEE 802.11a/b/g protocols are in use and we will look at these in detail later in the next section.

There are several wireless PANs, each for a specific application. Bluetooth, specified in IEEE 802.15.1, is in the unlicensed spectrum of 2.4 GHz and is intended for short range. It is in the spectral band as 802.11b/g, which could cause interference. There are IEEE working groups addressing this issue. UWB has been in use for a long time in the defense area and has recently become available commercially. Because of its low-power requirement along with high resistance to noise background, it has high potential as PAN. There are numerous network applications for home devices that require a low data rate, such as appliance control. IEEE 802.15.4 specifications address this area. We will not go into more detail on PANs in our treatment of wireless networks.

15.5   IEEE 802.11/WiFi NETWORK

IEEE 802.11 WLAN standard covers the MAC sublayer and physical (PHY) layer of the open system interconnection (OSI) network reference model, just like wired Ethernet that we discussed in Chapter 2. In the MAC layer, instead of using CSMA/CD, CSMA/CA (Carrier Sensing Multiple Access/Collision Avoidance) is used. CSMA, as we know, is based on the concept of "listening before talking." But instead of implementing collision detection, which is hard to do in wireless architecture, collision avoidance is used. In this method, the transmitting station waits for acknowledgement. If the acknowledgement is not received, it transmits again after "listening before talking" and uses a similar back-off technique as in Ethernet LAN to avoid collision.

IEEE 802.11 is a set of WLAN standards. [Ni *et al.*, 2004] provides a good survey of IEEE 802.11 standards that define PHY and MAC layers. In 1997, IEEE specified three PHY media. They are InfraRed (IR) baseband PHY, a frequency-hopping spread spectrum (FHSS) radio, and a direct sequence spread spectrum (DSSS) radio. All these options support both the 1 and 2 Mbps PHY rate. In 1999, IEEE defined two high-rate extensions: 802.11b in the 2.4-GHz band with data rates up to 11 Mbps, based on DSSS technology, and 802.11a in the 5-GHz band with data rates up to 54 Mbps, based on orthogonal frequency division multiplexing (OFDM) technology. 802.11g extends 802.11b PHY layer to support data rates up to 54 Mbps in the 2.4-GHz band.

The IEEE 802.11 MAC sublayer defines two medium access coordination functions, a basic distributed coordination function (DCF) and an optional point coordination function (PCF). 802.11 can operate both in contention-based DCF mode and contention-free PCF mode and supports two types of transmissions, asynchronous and synchronous. Asynchronous transmission is provided by DCF, whose implementation is mandatory in all 802.11 STAs (stations). Synchronous service is provided by PCF that basically implements a polling-based access. Unlike DCF, implementation of PCF is not mandatory. The reason is that the hardware implementation of PCF was thought to be too complex at that time. Furthermore, PCF itself relies on the asynchronous service provided by DCF. As specified in the standard, a group of STAs coordinated by DCF or PCF is formally called a basic service set (BSS). The area covered by the BSS is known as the basic service area (BSA), which is similar to a cell in a cellular mobile network. There are two different modes to configure an 802.11 wireless network, ad-hoc mode and infrastructure mode. In the ad-hoc mode, mobile STAs can directly communicate with each other to form an independent BSS (IBSS) without connectivity to any wired backbone. In the infrastructure mode, the mobile STAs communicate with the wired backbone through the bridge of access point (AP). Note that DCF can be used both in ad-hoc and infrastructure modes, while PCF is only used in the infrastructure mode.

WiFi is based on IEEE 802.11 protocol. A subset of the standards is shown in Table 15.1. WiFi operates in the 5 and 2.4 GHz public spectrum bands. As mentioned above, 802.11b and 802.11g use the 2.4-GHz ISM (instructional scientific and medical) band and 802.11a uses the 5-GHz band. Security was originally weak in 802.11 and was later enhanced via the 802.11i amendment. 802.11n is a new multi-streaming modulation technique. Other standards in the family (e, f, h, j) are service amendments and extensions or corrections to previous specifications.

Table 15.1   IEEE 802.11 Standards and Amendments

802.11a	54-Mbps data rate at 5.15–5.35 MHz and 5.4–5.825 MHz
802.11b	11-Mbps data rate at 2.4 GHz
802.11e	Addresses QoS issues
802.11f	Addresses multivendor AP interoperability
802.11g	Higher data rate extension to 54 Mbps in the 2.4 GHz
802.11h	Dynamic frequency selection and transmit power control for operation of 5-GHz products
802.11i	Addresses enhanced security issues
802.11j	Addresses channelization in Japan's 4.9-GHz band
802.11k	Enables medium and network resources more efficiently
802.11v	Wireless network management (in preparation)

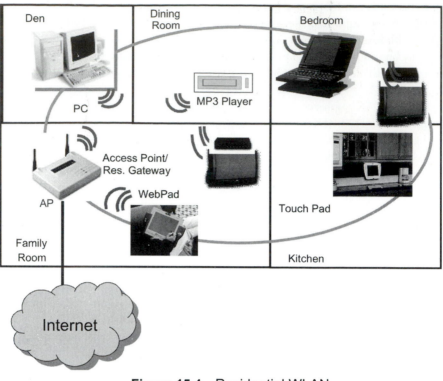

Figure 15.4 Residential WLAN

Figure 15.4 shows how a typical residence is wired on the WiFi network. In wooden houses in Western continents, a single AP or residential gateway could serve the entire house. It is connected to the Internet via an access network. In the Eastern hemisphere and in non-wooden buildings, the CPE distribution network may comprise a hybrid network with wired Ethernet to individual floors or rooms and WLAN as the last link.

We have studied the basics of wireless propagation and some management considerations when we dealt with wireless broadband access network in Chapter 14. Although some implementations of a fixed wireless network have used WiFi protocol, it is inefficient because it is based on random access protocol CDMA/CA, whereas IEEE 802.16 uses deterministic protocol. We will consider in this chapter only those additional aspects that are relevant to WLAN.

There are two modes of configuring WLAN networks, hierarchical and ad-hoc. In the latter, wireless stations are communicating on a peer-to-peer level. Every station can communicate with every other station. There is one beacon station that coordinates data flow. WiFi uses the hierarchical configuration, as shown in Figure 15.5. All wireless stations communicate with each other and with the external network via the controlling device, AP. Figure 15.6 shows the enterprise configuration, which is also applicable to SOHO. In a typical configuration, as shown explicitly in Figures 15.5 and 15.6, the wireless air interface of the AP is IEEE 802.11 and the wired interface is IEEE 802.3.

15.6 IEEE 802.11 NETWORK MANAGEMENT

There are several issues associated with the deployment and the management of WLAN. These include scalability, provisioning, real-time and non-real-time data flow, accessibility range, power management,

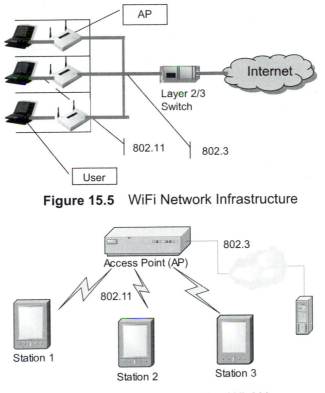

Figure 15.5   WiFi Network Infrastructure

Figure 15.6   Enterprise WLAN

interference from other systems operating in the same spectrum such as Bluetooth, security management, and QoS management. We addressed some of these when we discussed fixed and mobile wireless in the last chapter. Here we will first specifically consider the security and QoS of WLAN and then address how to centrally manage a network of WLANs.

15.6.1   Security Management

Security is a major issue in wireless LAN. Many breaches are more due to negligence on the part of the user not setting up vendor-provided security in the AP. Service providers use proprietary schemes, what is described as the "Walled Garden" approach. Future mobile cell-based system on 3GPP (Third Generation Partnership Project)—3GPP2 in the USA—network will be based on open standard, SNMP.

Security for wireless LAN, WiFi, started with Wired Equivalent Privacy (WEP), which is a scheme trying to replicate the security in the wired network. Since it has a lot of holes, the WiFi consortium developed WiFi Protected Access (WPA) protocol. WPA was made more secure in WPA2, which used IETF 802.11i security. WEP used static weak encryption keys based on RC4 algorithm of typically 40-bit keys. WPA enhanced WEP by using the same RC4 encryption, but adding temporal key integrity protocol (TKIP). WPA2 uses strong AES encryption based on Rijndael algorithm with 128-, 192-, or 256-bit key sizes. Two strong authentication protocols, namely, wireless robust authentication protocol (WRAP) and counter with cipher block chaining message authentication code protocol (CCMP) are added in 802.11i.

Figure 15.7 EAP over Wireless LAN

802.11i data protocols provide confidentiality, data origin authenticity, and replay protection. These protocols require a fresh key on every session. Key management delivers keys used as authorization tokens after channel access is authorized. Key hierarchy comprises pairwise keys and group keys. These are supported by extensible authentication protocol (EAP) over WLAN, as presented in Figure 15.7. Authentication can be approved by either an EMP authenticator or by an external authenticator such as Remote Authentication Dial In User Service (RADIUS).

EAP [RFC 3748, 5247] enables extensible authentication for network access in situations in which the IP is not available. It was originally developed for use with point-to-point protocol with pairwise key. It has subsequently also been applied to IEEE 802.11i. With the use of EAP key derivation, the conversation typically takes place in three phases: discovery (Phase 0); authentication (Phase 1) comprising EAP authentication (Phase 1a) and AAA key transport (optional Phase 1b); and secure association protocol (Phase 2) comprising unicast secure association (Phase 2a) and multicast secure association (optional Phase 2b). Of these phases, phases 0, 1b, and 2 are handled external to EAP. Phases 0 and 2 are handled by the lower-layer protocol, and phase 1b is typically handled by an authentication, authorization, and accounting (AAA) protocol.

15.6.2   Quality of Service Management

The basic specifications of IEEE 802.11 do not satisfy QoS (quality of service) requirements needed for the use of WiFi for broadband service. As we know, broadband comprises real-time voice (voice over IP), video streaming data with/without delay, and non-real-time data. The critical QoS parameters for broadband service are data rate, latency or delay-bound, and jitter. Broadband QoS is severely limited by IEEE 802.11. Both DCF (distributed coordination function) and PCF (point coordination function) MAC sublayers do not meet the requirements of broadband service. Consequently, IEEE 802.11e was developed.

802.11e takes on the characteristics of both DCF and PCF resulting in the development of a hybrid coordination function (HCF). HCF comprises enhanced DCF (EDCF) and HCF-controlled channel access (HCCA). You are referred to [Qiang *et al.*, 2004] for a detailed treatment on this. We will summarize them briefly here.

The HCF introduces quantitative parameters to define and implement QoS in IEEE 802.11e. Data are classified into eight traffic streams (TS) or user priorities (UP) and are further subclassifed into four access categories (AC). Based on the type of service, each service type is assigned a unique combination of UP and AC. This is shown in Table 15.2. These classifications attempt to match the Internet WAN QoS classifications of *intserv* and *diffserv*. EDCF is contention-based channel access. It controls channel access mechanisms. When a frame arrives at the MAC layer, it is tagged with a traffic priority identifier (TID) according to its QoS requirement, which can take values from 0 to 15. Frames with TID values from 0 to 7 are mapped into four AC queues using EDCF access rule. On the other hand, frames

Table 15.2   IEEE 802.11e QoS Table

UP (USER PRIORITY)	AC (ACCESS CATEGORY)	SERVICE TYPE
2	0	Best Effort
1	0	Best Effort
0	0	Best Effort
3	1	Video Probe
4	2	Video
5	2	Video
6	3	Voice
7	3	Voice

with TID values from 8 to 15 are mapped into eight TS queues using the HCF-controlled channel access rule. The reason to separate TS queues from AC queues is to support strict parameterized QoS at TS queues, while prioritized QoS is supported at AC queues. Another main feature of the HCF is the concept of transmission opportunity (TXOP), which is the time interval permitted for a particular STA (station or peer) to transmit packets. During the TXOP, there can be a series of frames transmitted by an STA. TXOP is called either EDCF–TXOP, when it is obtained by winning a successful EDCF contention or polled–TXOP, when it is obtained by receiving a QoS CF-poll frame from the QoS-enhanced AP QAP. The maximum value of TXOP is called TXOPLimit, which is determined by the QAP.

15.6.3   Central Management of WLANs

The use of WLAN has been growing significantly and 802.11 specifications have been standardized. Any vendor's AP can work with any other vendor's WiFi card. However, this applies to only some base set of functions. RFC 3990 defines the problem statement in the configuring and the provisioning of a wireless AP. A survey was conducted and results indicated that terminologies, as well as functions, were divergent and hence it was not easy to define a MIB that could be used to manage an 802.11 network [RFC 4118].

Figure 15.8 and Table 15.3 show high-level presentations of IEEE 802.11 MIB [Kerry and O'Hara, 2002]. An SMT MIB addresses the management of the station. MAC attributes MIB supports access control, generation, as well as verification of frame check sequences (FCSs), and proper delivery of valid data to upper layers. Resource-type attributes MIB addresses attributes related to resources and physical attributes MIB deals with PHY operational information.

As a prelude to developing a MIB that makes all WLAN components, including APs, interoperable, the broad set of AP functions has been divided into two categories: 802.11 functions, which include those that are required by IEEE 802.11 standards, and Configuration and Provisioning of Wireless Access Point (CAPWAP) functions, which include those that are not required by IEEE 802.11, but are deemed essential for control, configuration, and management of 802.11 WLANs on a centrally managed basis. Another term that has caused considerable ambiguity is "access point," which usually reflected a physical box that has antennas, but did not have a uniform set of externally consistent behavior across multiple vendors. To remove this ambiguity, AP has been redefined as the set of 802.11 and CAPWAP functions, while the physical box that terminates the 802.11 PHY is called the wireless termination point (WTP).

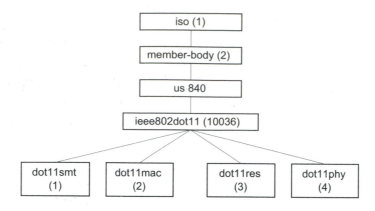

Figure 15.8 IEEE 802.11dot MIB

Table 15.3 IEEE 802dot11 MIB

ENTITY	OID	DESCRIPTION
dot11smt	ieee802dot11 1	Station management attributes: WEP security, power, transmission
dot11mac	ieee802dot11 2	MAC attributes
dot11res	ieee802dot11 3	Resource-type attributes
dot11phy	ieee802dot11 4	Physical attributes

IEEE standards have a well-defined MIB for wireless binding technologies such as 802.11 and 802.16. However, current centralized wireless architectures of most vendors do not use IEEE MIB standards, but use their own private MIBs. The IETF CAPWAP effort is to bring together IEEE and IETF WLAN MIBs and make a wireless LAN network comprising multiple vendor products interoperable.

CAPWAP Protocol [RFC 4564, 5415, and 5416] defines a standard, interoperable protocol, which enables an access controller (AC) to manage a collection of WTPs, as shown in Figure 15.9. The network management system communicates with the AC using the SNMP. The AC communicates with WTP using the CAPWAP protocol. In Figure 15.9 each WTP coordinates the stations in its basic station set (BSS).

In order to make IEEE MIB compatible with IETF CAPWAP MIB, a one-to-one mapping is needed between the two [Yang and Perkins, 2007]. This is accomplished using the abstract interface *ifIndex* in MIB II to a wireless interface, defined as Virtual Radio Interface, with a unique ID. The wireless interface is shown as PHY radio in Figure 15.9 and is assigned a unique ID by the combination of the serial number of WTP and a radio ID for the wireless service in BSS. The left side of the figure shows the one-to-one relationship between *ifIndex* and the virtual radio interface. Thus, in Figure 15.9 for the three WTP virtual interfaces 1, 2, and 3, there are three PHY Radio 1, 2, and 3, respectively, and also corresponding *ifIndex* 1, 2, and 3, respectively. In other words, when AC has interfaces of *ifType* WTP Virtual Radio Interface, it logically represents PHY radio interfaces on the side of WTPs.

RFC CAPWAP-Base-MIB defines MIB modules that can be used to manage CAPWAP implementations. The CAPWAP-Base-MIB module provides information of AC, WTPs, radio and station objects' basic property, and their relationship. The basic idea of CAPWAP-Base-MIB is for the agent to run on AC devices and is not required to be embedded in the WTP device. It follows the same idea as the

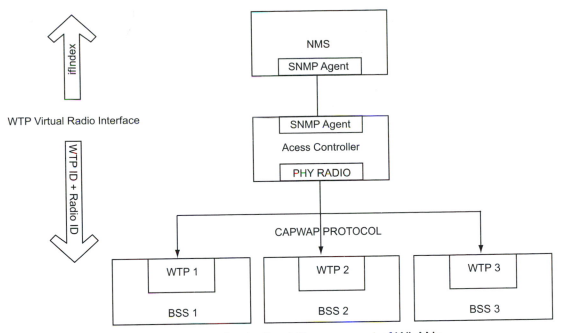

Figure 15.9 Centralized Management of WLANs

CAPWAP protocol, namely centralized control. As a generic mechanism, it is independent of any wireless binding technologies and is defined by an independent MIB file. *ifIndex* [RFC 2863] is used as the common handler for corresponding interfaces in the CAPWAP-Base-MIB and specific wireless technologies MIB modules. The operator could manage and control centralized wireless architectures using multiple MIB standards, while keeping them loosely coupled. Thus, an operator can centrally manage and monitor from AC, WTPs that use CAPWAP protocol parameters.

The CAPWAP-Base-MIB module supports WTP Virtual Radio Interface that enables it to handle bundling of radio channels. According to CAPWAP specifications, WTP Virtual Radio channel in centralized wireless architecture is defined as an ID identifying a specific PHY radio, which is a combination of a WTP and radio (WTP ID + radio ID). In CAPWAP-Base-MIB, this combination can be associated with an *ifIndex*, which is a virtual port. As an abstract interface, "WTP Virtual Radio Interface" could be used by any wireless binding technology such as IEEE 802.11 and 802.16. The table of *capwapRadioBindTable* will indicate the mapping relationship between "WTP id + Radio id" and *IfIndex*.

Figure 15.10 and Table 15.4 present the CAPWAP-Base-MIB, which will be assigned a number by IANA later under mib-2 [Shi *et al.*, 2009]. There are five groups under *capwapBaseMIB*.

capwapBaseAc group defines the access controller objects
capwapBaseWtps the wireless termination point objects
capwapBaseParameters the parameters associated with the base
capwapBasestats the statistics of the system
capwapBaseNotifyVarObjects the objects used only in notifications
There are eight tables—two under AC and six under WTPs presented in Table 15.4.

1. *capwapBaseAcNameListTable* is the AC name list table used to configure the AC name list.
2. *capwapBaseMacAclTable* is the ACL table used to configure stations' Access Control List (ACL).

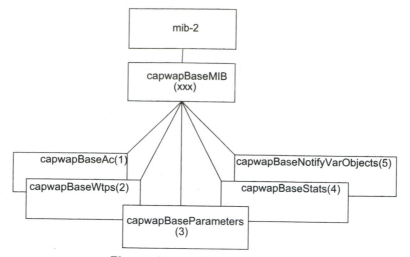

Figure 15.10 CAPWAP-Base-MIB

Table 15.4 CAPWAP-Base-MIB

ENTITY	OID	DESCRIPTION
capwapBaseObjects	capwapBaseMIB 1	CAPWAP MIB objects
capwapBaseAc	capwapBaseObjects 1	Access controller objects group
capwapBaseAcNameListTable	capwapBaseAc 9	Objects that display AC name list
capwapBaseMacAclTable	capwapBaseAc 10	Set of objects that configure station ACL
capwapBaseWtps	capwapBaseObjects 2	Wireless termination point objects group
capwapBaseWtpStateTable	capwapBaseWtps 1	Objects that display WTP CAPWAP FSM state
capwapBaseWtpTable	capwapBaseWtps 2	Objects providing property and configuration information of WTPs in running state
capwapBasewirelessBindingTable	capwapBaseWtps 3	Objects that display mapping relationship between specific interface of "WTP Virtual Radio Interface" ifType and PHY radio
capwapBaseStationTable	capwapBaseWtps 4	Objects providing basic property information on stations
capwapBaseWtpEventsStatsTable	capwapBaseWtps 5	Objects that display WTPs' reboot statistics
capwapBaseRadioStatsTable	capwapBaseWtps 6	Objects that display statistics on radio's behavior
capwapBaseParameters	capwapBaseObjects 3	CAPWAP base parameters group
capwapBaseStats	capwapBaseObjects 4	CAPWAP statistics group
capwapBaseNotifyVarObjects	capwapBaseObjects 5	Objects used only in notifications

3. *capwapBaseWtpStateTable* is WTP's status table used to indicate each WTP's CAPWAP FSM state.

4. *capwapBaseWtpTable* is WTP's table used to provide property and configuration information in detail for WTPs in the running state.

5. *capwapBaseRadioBindTable* is a radio bind table used to indicate the mapping relationship between the logical interface of "WTP Virtual Radio Interface" *ifType* and PHY radio.

6. *capwapBaseStationTable* is a station table used to provide stations' basic property information.

7. *capwapBaseWtpRebootStatsTable* is a WTP reboot statistic table used to collect WTP reboot count, link failure count, hardware failure count, and so on.

8. *capwapBaseRadioStatsTable* is a WTP radio statistic table used to collect radio reset count, channel change count, hardware failure count, etc.

Summary

We presented an overview of various applications and transport technologies that are applicable to the distribution of information in residential and SOHO networks in this chapter. In that context, we looked at various application protocols, transport protocols, and the middleware that acts as the gateway between the two. The treatment of application protocols and middleware is intentionally cursory in nature because they are in the research stage and too early to be considered for central management. However, existing SNMP-like technology could be used to manage them by embedding SNMP-like agents in them.

We reviewed transport infrastructure and protocols for wired and wireless home distribution networks. After reviewing various wired networks, we focused on the most deployed Ethernet network. Management of an IEEE 802.3-based Ethernet network has been dealt with extensively in the book in various chapters. We extended it in this chapter to address very high-data rate at 10 Gbps and modification of the MIB to accommodate that. In the context of IP telephony, IP networks can carry power over the Ethernet cable, and we discussed management aspects of power over the Ethernet network.

Basic principles and some managed aspects of wireless networks were covered when we discussed wireless access networks in the previous chapter. We reviewed in this chapter wireless LANs and PANs. Our in-depth treatment of the basics and management is limited to wireless LAN. WiFi (802.11a/b/g) is based on IEEE 802.11 WLAN. Deployment of WLAN is growing at a rapid rate in residence and in enterprise, as well as in public places. The interoperable protocols of 802.11a/b/g have been standardized; and any wireless client can operate with any vendor's access point. However, implementations of WLANs are not uniform and consequently management aspects are not standardized. We addressed recent initiatives to standardize managed objects and MIBs that are being developed to structure them. Efforts to make IEEE standards compatible with IETF CAPWAP specifications and protocols were covered.

Exercises

1. WLAN is created as an air interface 802.11 from 802.3 Ethernet interface. BSS comprises a set of wireless stations controlled by a wireless termination point (WTP). You have set up your home network using a wireless access point (AP), which is connected to the Ethernet output of ADSL coming into your house.

   (a) What are the two modes of MAC types that the WTP could be configured in?
   (b) Assume that you have a WiFi AP; how is it configured?
   (c) Write the SNMP query to use to validate your answer in (b).

2. In Exercise 1, BSSs are configured in one of three different ways: (1) Autonomous, (2) Centralized, and (3) Distributed mesh configuration [refer to RFC 4118]:

   (a) Describe with high-level block diagrams the three configurations
   (b) What is the module/modules used to configure WTPs in a network of WLANs?
   (c) Show a remote NMS incorporating the configuration control module to manage each infrastructure configuration remotely

3. For *ifIndex* =10, WTP serial number = 01234567, and radio ID =1,

   (a) Write the *capwapRadioBindtable* entities of the table with values
   (b) What is the index you would use to retrieve the *ifIndex* from the table?

4. Create a row in the *capwapWlanTable* for WLAN service interface in Exercise 3 using draft-ietf-capwap-802dot11-mib-04 for

$$MACType = \text{Split-MAC}$$
$$WTPTunnelMode = \text{dot3Tunnel}$$

Advanced Management Topics

OBJECTIVES

- *Next generation NM requirements*
  - *ITU-T*
  - *IETF*
- *Status of current NM technology*
  - *ISO Model: FCAPS*
  - *Product requirements*
- *Limitations of SNMP management*

- *Web-based development*
  - *Early Web-based development*
  - *Web interface and Web management*
  - *Distributed Management Task Force, DMTF*
- *CORBA-based NM technology*
- *XML-based NM technology*
- *Comparison of NM technologies*
- *Recent NM-related standards*

In this chapter we look at new approaches that are emerging for effectively managing Next Generation Networks (NGNs). We discuss the current status of network management technology and the limitations of traditional management technologies (SNMP and OSI) in Section 16.1. We also describe some of the initiatives that were set up to overcome these limitations and see that the attempts were largely fruitless or at most partially successful in addressing some of the operators' requirements.

In the meantime, the rapid growth of the Internet and World Wide Web resulted in Web technology composed of Web server and Web browsers becoming almost universal in the enterprise environment. In Section 16.2 we look at early approaches to Web-based management. The use of Web-based management based on the Hypertext Transfer Protocol (HTTP) started with merely having a Web-based user interface at the client side to display management information. The back end of the management application can use any server-side technology to collect the management information, but the user interface to view management information is Web based. This approach is adopted in most network management tools, including popular tools like multi router traffic grapher (MRTG), HP OpenView Network Node Manager, CygNet, etc. The next step in Web-based management is to have a purely Web-based management system. We discuss the architecture of a purely Web-based management system, based on having an embedded Web server on the network elements that serve management information to clients (Network Management System (NMS) back-end software) using the HTTP protocol, in addition to having a Web-based user interface. We also discuss DMTF, which is a Web-based standard for enterprise management.

In Section 16.3 we discuss the emergence of Common Object Request Broker Architecture (CORBA) as a management technology, particularly in the telecommunications world. Network management increasingly came to be viewed as a distributed application; and CORBA, an object-oriented technology, developed by the Object Management Group (OMG) was recognized as a technology suitable for developing NMS applications. We describe the architecture of an application that uses CORBA for element management. Many standards bodies worked on establishing a standard for CORBA-based management. A popular and widely adopted standard to date is the TM Forum's Multi-Technology Network Management (MTNM) model that is a resource management model for multitechnology and multivendor networks. It allows a service provider to manage various technologies from multiple vendors using a single interface between the NMS and Element Management System (EMS). MTNM has defined TMF 814, a standard that uses CORBA as the NML–EML interface, and that is now widely adopted by industry.

XML and related technologies in the meantime made a big impact on software application development and brought about changes in the design of data networking products and the software systems created to manage them. In Section 16.4 we explain why XML is suitable as a management technology and the status of adoption of XML-based technologies for element management. Some vendor devices have had support for XML-based management since 2000. There has also been extensive research in this front—architectures for XML-based management have been proposed, the impact of using XML on performance has been studied, and prototypes have been developed. We describe the architecture of an XML-based management environment based on this work.

In Section 16.5 we compare the different management technologies based on standard parameters such as information modeling, power of management operations supported, ease of use, maintainability and extensibility, performance, etc.

In Section 16.6 we discuss the current trends and recent standards that have emerged. In keeping with the shift from a network-centric view to a service-centric view of networks, management software is viewed as a collection of applications or Operations Systems (OS) such as NMS, Service Activation system, Root Cause Analysis, etc. In order to deliver the management services efficiently, a service provider's environment has a multitude of applications that are in operation at any given time and the challenge is to integrate the systems so as to provide a unified view, while ensuring that system boundaries are not crossed. A Service Oriented Architecture (SOA) where the interacting components communicate by passing messages over a "message bus" is the well-known solution to this issue. A great advantage of XML-based design is the promise of an SOA for management software and a modular design with reusable, loosely coupled components that communicate over a bus. Multi Technology Operations Systems Interface (MTOSI) is an XML-based specification developed by the TMF that facilitates such development. It is an extension of the MTNM model for integration of management software components via a Web services-based interface. We also describe OASIS, a major standards body for standardizing the use of XML-based and Web services-based system management.

16.1 INTRODUCTION

The evolution of management technologies has remained far behind the evolution of networking technologies. The needs of operators who set up, maintain, operate, and administer networks have also changed. Operators now perceive a need for powerful configuration management support for devices and for an integrated platform for network, system, service, and applications. Moreover, given the service/customer-centric view of the network being taken, there is a strong need for business process automation. The consequence of these changes for existing management techniques has been a fundamental rethinking of management principles and has brought to light the importance of developing standardized management software for easy maintenance and extensibility.

16.1.1 Next Generation NM Requirements

Networks have undergone immense changes from what they were in the middle 1980s to what they are now. Initially, networks delivered basic connectivity services. Devices were simple and had limited capability. Simple Command Line Interface (CLI) served to configure devices. Today, individual network equipments have enormous functional complexity. They are highly intelligent and programmable, thus making configuration a difficult affair. Networks created with such devices can provide an ever-increasing range of services, in response to customer demand. The NGNs look to convergence of multimedia networks and services from all perspectives—voice/video/data, wired/wireless/fiber, etc.–with compressed service lifetimes. The aim is to provide unfettered access for users to networks and to competing service providers for services of their subscribers' choice.

Table 16.1 captures the changing needs. (Source: ITU-T Workshop on NGN jointly organized with IETF, Geneva, 2005.)

16.1.2 Status of Current NM Technology

We can assess the suitability of management technologies based on several criteria. Many of these have been described at length in Chapters 3 and 9. Here we briefly recapitulate and expand on some important factors that play a role in defining the power of a management protocol.

1. Information model: A management technology must allow the network resource to be modeled. The management information model is a representation of the entity that needs to be

Table 16.1 NGN Requirements

ORIGINAL REQUIREMENT	NEW REQUIREMENTS
End-to-end transparency	Packet inspection, NAT
Peer-to-peer	NATs/firewalls/servers
Connectionless	MPLS
Best-effort	Real-time demands, bandwidth demands
User back-off	QoS guarantees
Network empowerment	User empowerment
No flow state	Flow state
Trust	Hackers everywhere
Static addresses	DHCP, mobility
Fairness	QoS
Terminal-to-host	Mass public residential services, multi-terminal, multi QoS
Flat network	Access and core domains
Simple protocol layering	Protocol maze
Research/defence use	Commercialization, competition, consumer choice

managed. It describes the attributes and behavior of such an entity. As we have seen in earlier chapters, TMN provides fully object-oriented comprehensive modeling, while at the other end of the spectrum Simple Network Management Protocol (SNMP) provides very basic modeling capbility. It is important to remember that the expressive power and architectural purity of complex modeling often comes at the cost of ease of implementation.

2. Organization model: This defines the actors, their roles, and the principles of cooperation between them in the process of realizing network management. The familiar manager–agent paradigm is one example. In the manager–agent model, a cluster of managed objects (MOs) is collectively administered by an agent that provides a unique entry point for accessing them, another is the distributed object or the service interface model, in which every MO or interface is accessed individually. Other organization models such as management by delegation, policy-based management, mobile agents, etc. have been proposed by various researchers.

3. Communication model: This defines the communication framework used by the management technology for the exchange of management information. It includes the following aspects:

   a. Data Communication Network (DCN) for a manager to connect with the agent and whether the underlying transport protocol is connection oriented or connectionless

   b. Operations supported for accessing management information

   c. Support for remote configuration. This capability is dependent on the protocol since some protocols impose a size limitation

4. Scalability and flexibility: This attribute determines the capability to scale and handle the management requirement for large networks with a large number of elements. One factor that could impact scalability is the bandwidth overhead imposed by the management technology.

5. Extensibility: Networks are constantly changing—new networking protocols, physical media, and hardware changes are realities that must be dealt with. The network management technology has to be extensible to accommodate these changes without significant changes in the design and code of a network management application. The management technology must be such that new systems can be inducted with little change to the network management software.

6. Cost of development and maintenance of the management application: This is emerging as an important factor in a scenario where networks undergo changes, expansions, and augmentation, and the management software has to cope with this in a timely and cost-effective manner.

7. Performance: This is a critical and practical criterion to evaluate a management technology. Parameters such as the bandwidth used, CPU utilization, response time, and memory utilization determine the efficiency of a technology. A protocol may be very elegant with regard to all the above criteria but if it does not meet performance criteria, it is not usable from a practical perspective.

8. Maturity: The proven qualities and characteristics of a management technology in terms of the above-mentioned factors play a significant part in choosing management protocols.

16.1.3   Limitations of SNMP Management

A major reason for the inadequacy of SNMP is the mismatch in the way the SNMP framework evolved since its inception and the management needs of the community managing large Internet networks. This was recognized over the years and in 2002 an invitational workshop was held between the Internet Engineering Task Force (IETF), the Internet Research Task Force (IRTF), and the Internet Architecture Board (IAB) to bring to the table the management needs of operators. In the ensuing dialogue, several shortcomings of SNMP were identified with respect to what operators really require from a management technology. The perceived shortcomings of the existing framework, as well as the operators' needs, were discussed and documented [RFC 3535]. The objective was to convey the practical management requirements to protocol developers in the IETF so that further development could focus on such requirements. Some of the shortcomings are:

- SNMP is simplistic in respect of data structures and protocol operations. This was an advantage in the late 1980s on devices with limited resources but given the fact that current day devices are intelligent and programmable, this constraint is no longer applicable

- The information model supports modeling of objects using scalar variables and tables of scalar variables. What is referred to as objects actually refers to attributes of an object. There is no support for inheritance and thus information re-use. This makes it difficult to model complex objects. The number of protocol operations was intentionally kept at a minimum. The primitive to retrieve bulk information (getBulk) is not very useful. The SNMP interface is too low-level for end-to-end network management

- Configuration management requirements: Large-scale service providers have extensive backbone networks and need to maintain configuration information in a logical centralized database. Figure 16.1 shows a typical configuration management scenario

- The device should support bulk download of configuration files. At any point in time, the device may contain a number of configuration files but the management application must be capable of activating only one of them. There is a need to schedule configuration operations at specified times. Rollback must be supported to recover from errors. It should also be possible to perform coordinated activation of configurations on several devices at a time, i.e., upload configurations

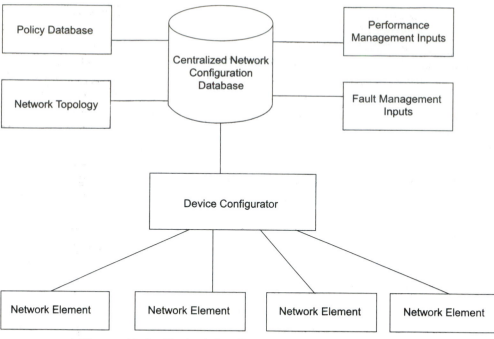

Figure 16.1 Typical Configuration Management Scenario

simultaneously. This is a complicated requirement as network connectivity could get lost while in the midst of an operation, and the protocol should account for such contingencies

Apart from other issues, the choice of User Datagram Protocol (UDP) itself comes with its own limitations and SNMP is proving to be primarily a protocol for fault and performance monitoring, not very suitable for configuration management requirements as detailed.

16.1.4 Evolutionary Approaches to Overcome Limitations

As seen in Chapters 6 and 7, SNMPv2c and v3 resulted in improvements in SNMPv1 in terms of the bulk data transfer facility for tables in SNMPv2c and security in SNMPv3. However, from the perspective of operators' requirements, there were still shortcomings. As a result of the developments described, evolutionary efforts were made to overcome these limitations on three fronts—to improve the data definition language, improve protocol operations, and enhance configuration management capability.

SMIng. The IRTF NMRG developed a new data definition language called SMIng (SMI-next generation), which is more powerful than SMI. It allows arbitrarily nested data structures, facilitates reusability of complex types, and provides an extensibility mechanism. In November 2000, the SMIng effort was moved from IRTF to IETF and a Working Group (WG), SMIng WG, was formed to take the proposal of IRTF and develop a standards track based on it. In the first phase, the objectives for the data definition language were generated and in the second phase, proposals for the language were requested. Of the candidate proposals, two strong contenders remained, one of which was SMIng. These proposals were to be merged and result in a new version of SMI, SMIv3. During this process however, the WG could not arrive at a consensus on some crucial issues and in April 2003, the SMIng WG formally closed down without generating a standards track.

SNMP Protocol Operations Improvements. The main shortcoming in SNMP is the inefficiency in bulk data retrieval. One issue is the overhead due to redundant OID fragments in SNMP Packet Data Units (PDUs). Another problem is the limit on the maximum size of the SNMP PDU (484 bytes) as a result of UDP being the underlying transport protocol. In February 2001, the IETF Evolution of SNMP (EOS) WG was formed to investigate mechanisms for improving the efficiency of bulk information retrieval.

There were three approaches to achieve this: (1) compression of the OID, (2) suppression of redundant and repeated OID fragments, and (3) use of some other protocol such as FTP or HTTP for bulk data transfers.

Several proposals to compress the OID differed in the computational overhead in achieving good compression ratios. Of these, the OID delta compression technique [NMRG] showed promise since it used a light-weight compression algorithm to achieve good compression ratios. Relatively speaking, compression-based approaches found favor compared to suppression, because they did not require major changes in existing protocol operations. The suppression approach requires new protocol operations, and the different approaches used differed in the data selection and filtering mechanisms used. The retrieval of large sections of the MIB using other protocols such as FTP or HTTP did not find favor owing to security issues.

To work around the size limitation associated with UDP, it was proposed that a TCP transport mapping could be defined for the SNMP protocol. The NMRG defined a mapping where a guaranteed minimum size of 8,192 bytes could be transported using SNMP over TCP. Finally, like the SMIng WG, the EOS WG too ended up closing down without reaching consensus in April 2003.

Configuration Management—COPS-PR and SPPI. The IETF Resource Allocation Protocol (RAP) WG defined Common Open Policy Service—Policy Provisioning (COPS-PR) to address shortcomings in SNMP specific to configuration management. The data definition language is Structure of Policy Provisioning Information (SPPI) that is a variant of SMI and the transport is TCP. However, COPS did not meet with market acceptance since it addressed itself to only configuration management shortcomings and that too not completely. Moreover, the improvements offered by COPS can be achieved using the SNMP framework itself. Adopting COPS would involve using yet another management technology that however does not completely meet the operators' requirements. Thus, other technologies came to be actively explored.

16.2   EARLY WEB-BASED DEVELOPMENT

In Chapter 9 we discussed the use of Web technology in system management and presented the example of Big Brother. In this case, information on the processes running on hosts was gathered by using scripted programs (agents) and then sent to a server, which stored it on Web pages. The Web pages were accessed via Web browsers. This method illustrates the use of the Web as a portal in conventional system management. We also discussed the MRTG performance tool, which is used to gather traffic statistics and is based on Web technology. Recall that data are gathered by SNMP counters, analyzed, and then stored in Web pages. These Web pages, stored in Web servers, can be accessed locally and remotely via Web browsers. This method illustrates the use of SNMP network management with a Web–user interface.

16.2.1 Web Interface and Web Management

However, we can go beyond just displaying the information on a Web browser. We can use Web technology to both gather and display data. This is achieved by having an embedded Web server in the device. The device supporting Web-based management needs to have an embedded Web server, HTML pages with the required content, and management applications. Using this approach, a manager with a PC and a browser can connect to the URL of the device Web server and retrieve HTML pages regarding fault information, performance information, etc. and perform detailed configuration operations. Thus, graphical displays of management information can be viewed. This approach suffers from several drawbacks. Map-based representations of the network topology, high-level management functions such as trend analysis, cross-device correlation, notifications, etc. are not possible. Scalability becomes an issue if a management station has to connect individually to devices when thousands of them have to be configured. Thus, although this approach is an improvement over SNMP for configuration management, it was realized that it cannot be a replacement for SNMP.

Since SNMP is a firmly entrenched technology and has advantages for fault and performance monitoring, many network management applications combine SNMP management with Web-based management to combine the advantages of both approaches. It is possible to have a centralized management system with a graphical map-based view of the network topology and use the Web-based interface to connect to the devices using HTTP for detailed configuration management-related operations. In this approach, SNMP is used for fault and performance monitoring and HTTP is used for configuration. Many NMS products use this approach when device support is available.

16.2.2 Web-Based Enterprise Management

The Desktop Management Interface (DMI) is an industry standard generated by the Desktop Management Task Force (DMTF). The task force was formed in 1992 to develop, support, and maintain management standards for PC systems and products. In DMI, MOs with attributes are defined by ASN.1 syntax. Objects are grouped, and multiple instantiations are defined from tables, as in SNMP management. However, the tables do not have all the capabilities of SNMPv2. DMI-MOs may be managed by an SNMP manager, using the DMI MIB shown in Figure 16.2. It is a subnode under *dmtf*, which is in the enterprises branch of the Internet MIB. The two MIBs, *dmtfStdMifs* and *dmtfDynOids*, are reserved for future use by new standard MIBs and remote SNMP/DMI support. The DMI MIB defines MOs, notification, and conformance groups.

In 1996 a consortium of five companies undertook to develop Web-Based Enterprise Management (WBEM) standards, which are designed to integrate existing standards, such as SNMP, CMIP, DMI, and HTTP. There are significant differences between SNMP and DMI. DMTF tried to make them coexist by developing DMI to the SNMP mapping standard [DMI/SNMP], which did not prove to be successful. DMTF was then assigned in June 1998 a broader WBEM task. The goal of the assignment was to unify (not replace) and extend the existing instrumentation and management standards by using object-oriented constructs and design. Then a common management application residing in a Web client could manage network and system components having different management protocol agents via the Internet.

The DMTF has made significant progress in developing WBEM specifications by adopting the **Common Information Model** (CIM), the information-modeling framework developed by Microsoft. The CIM approach is to preserve and extend traditional management information sources, such as SNMP and DMI. The result has been useful for both Internet and intranet services [Heilbronner and Wies, 1997; Hong *et al.*, 1997]. We will use the name Internet in our description.

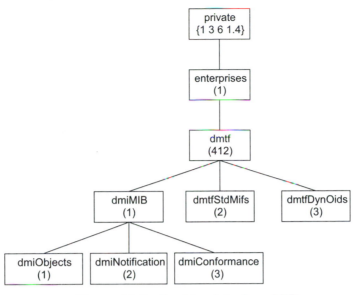

Figure 16.2 Desktop Interface MIB

CIM is an approach to the management of enterprise systems, software, users, and networks. It uses basic object-oriented structures and concepts. A management model is developed that provides a framework for describing the managed environment. A fundamental taxonomy of objects is defined with respect to both classification and association—and with respect to a basic set of classes—that establishes a common framework.

WBEM consists of five components: Web client, Common Information Model Object Manager (CIMOM), CIM schema, specific management protocol providers, and MOs with protocol-specific agents. WBEM architecture is shown in Figure 16.3.

The **Web client** is a Web browser with management applications. The browser uses HTML for presenting management data. The applications could invoke a request to any protocol-specific agent in the MO, as well as process any data coming from any agent. However, the request is issued against an object in the **CIM schema** and is sent to the CIMOM via the HTTP. The management application in the Web client also processes notifications received from CIMOM against objects in the CIM schema. There could be several instances of a Web client on the Internet representing several management systems with manager applications.

The **CIM object manager** forms the heart of WBEM architecture. It mediates all messages among the Web client, MOs, and CIM schema. The messages to and from CIMOM use HTTP as the transport protocol. CIMOM could be implemented as different schemes and in different languages. For example, Microsoft's implementation is Windows Management Instrumentation TM (WMI), which is based on accessing the CIM schema with the Distributed Component Object Model.

CIMOM processes messages from Web clients, as well as those originated by MOs. When CIMOM receives messages from Web clients, it uses the information from CIM schema to determine which protocol system the MO belongs to and switches the message to that protocol provider. It also translates the CIM schema format of the MO to that of the protocol-specific object identification. Thus, an SNMP-specific application may send a get request to a MO, such as a hub, or process a trap received from it. Alternatively, a DMI-specific application may send a set request to a DMI object, such as the hard disk

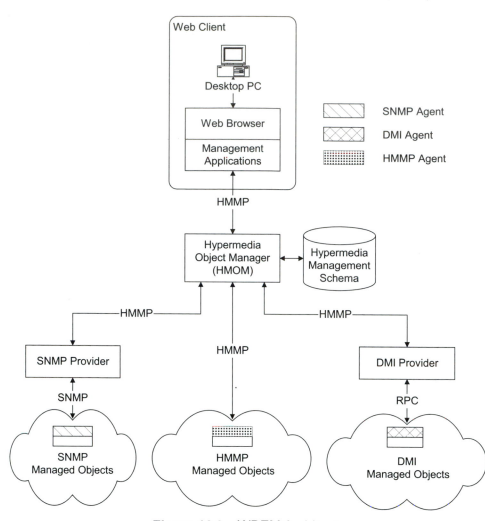

Figure 16.3 WBEM Architecture

on a desktop, or process a disk full notification received from it. These messages pass through CIMOM and the object ID is translated and routed to the appropriate destination.

The **protocol providers** are between CIMOM and the **protocol-specific managed networks**. For example, the SNMP provider is between the CIMOM and the SNMP MOs network, and the DMI provider is between the CIMOM and the DMI-MOs network. The message between a protocol provider and CIMOM uses HTTP, whereas the message between a protocol provider and a management agent in the MO uses the specific management protocol. Thus, the SNMP provider "speaks" HTTP toward CIMOM and SNMP toward the MO. You can visualize the protocol provider as a proxy server. The native case is the one associated with the domain containing CIM-MOs accessed using HTTP protocol. No intermediate protocol provider is needed in this case, which is the ultimate WBEM environment.

Each managed domain contains protocol-specific agents and the components that are being managed by that protocol management system. WBEM architecture uses CIM for MO modeling, XML/WS for management information encoding, and HTTP for transport [Thompson, 1998].

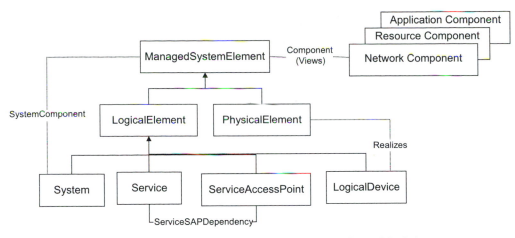

Figure 16.4   Simplified WBEM CIM Core Model

CIM consists of three modules: a core model, common models, and extension models. The **core model** is the high-level framework and is applicable to all management domains. **Common models** are applicable to protocol-specific domains and include information on systems, applications, devices, users, and networks. **Extension models** represent technology-specific extensions of the common models, such as the UNIX or Microsoft Windows operating systems.

A simplified WBEM CIM core model is shown in Figure 16.4 [CIM]. The names are presented as "strings" per model definition. The solid lines indicate the hierarchy or inheritance of the classes; the dashed lines indicate various associations, such as component, system component, realization, and dependency.

In the core model, the Managed System Element is at the top level. The Physical and Logical Elements are subclasses of the Managed System Element. A Physical Element is something that occupies physical space and can be touched and felt. Logical Elements are "realized" by installing Physical Elements. Let us illustrate this distinction with an example of a link between two nodes. The Physical Element is the physical medium (e.g., copper wire or optical fiber), and the Logical Element, the circuit identification, is a path connecting the nodes (IP addresses) at the two ends of the link.

Logical Device, System, Service, and Service Access Point are all subclasses of the Logical Element. A Physical Element can have multiple Logical Elements. For example, a physical interface card in a computer can be loaded with either a network interface software or modem software. In the former case, it is a network interface card Logical Element, and in the latter case it is a modem Logical Element.

System is an aggregate of an enumerable set of Managed System Elements, as shown by the association, *SystemComponent*. Service is a functionality of a logical device, such as print or file service. The Service Access Point represents the management, measurement, and configuration of a Service. For example, using a Service Access Point, a file service can be turned on or off. Dependency relationships exist among the various components shown.

Managed system elements may be viewed as groups of components. We have grouped them into three classifications following the model of [Heilbronner and Weiss, 1997; Hong *et al.*, 1997]. They are network components, resource components, and application components.

16.2.3 Web-Based Interface Management Architecture

Among the earliest research in using Web-based techniques is Web-Based Interface Management Architecture (WIMA) proposed by Martin–Flatin [1999; Martin-Flatin *et al.*, 1999]. WIMA defines a generalized, sophisticated approach to overcome the shortcomings of SNMP, while retaining its strengths. It proposes keeping existing MIBs and the organization model. A push-based management approach is advocated for repetitive tasks such as fault and performance polling. Rather than the SNMP over the UDP communication model, WIMA proposes HTTP over TCP as the communication model. Management information can be encoded in several ways (BER, serialized Java object, XML, etc.) Thus, it is a more generalized architecture, which also supports XML for representation of management information. Flatin demonstrated that XML is especially convenient for distributed and integrated management, for dealing with multiple information models, and for supporting high-level semantics. A unique aspect of WIMA architecture is the support of push-based data transfer from the agent to the manager using HTTP. HTTP is a strictly request–response protocol and the agent at the device cannot send a response without having received a request beforehand. This was overcome in WIMA by an ingenious use of the multipart type of Multipurpose Internet Mail Extensions (MIME) in the context of pushing management information.

The agent sends a single infinite response, with separators embedded in the payload of the HTTP message by using the multipart type of MIME via the embedded HTTP server. It sends one MIME part at each push interval and the MIME separator is interpreted as an end-of-time interval marker. The architecture of a typical agent is shown in Figure 16.5.

In order to implement a WIMA-based architecture, the agent at the network equipment has to have a Web server, a repository to hold the push definitions and schedules, a push scheduler, and a dispatcher. A HTTP server is commonly found in network equipment. The other components have to be explicitly implemented.

HTTP Header	MIME Header	MIME Part Header	Compressed Data	MIME Separator	MIME Part Header	Compressed Data	...

MIME: Multipurpose Internet Mail Extensions

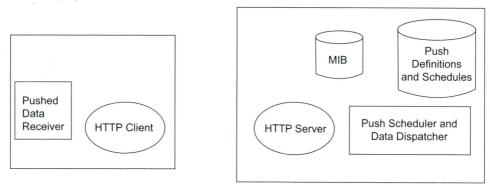

Network Element

Figure 16.5 WIMA Agent Architecture

WIMA has several advantages. The separation of management information model from the communication model provides the flexibility to support a number of management information models. The push-based approach results in reduced bandwidth consumption by the management application. Moreover, the payload can be compressed. The removal of the UDP size constraint means that multiple OIDs can be sent per push cycle.

However, the additional software to be implemented in the network equipment is a costly requirement. Moreover, with this architecture, if there is a network outage, it is the manager's responsibility to detect it and re-establish a connection with the network equipment.

16.3   CORBA-BASED NM TECHNOLOGY

We will now discuss CORBA-based network management, which is based on a distributed network management architecture.

16.3.1   Limitations of TMN-Based Management

In the telecom world, OSI-SM (OSI-Service Management)/TMN (discussed in Chapter 10) was the first management technology to be used in telecom environments. It was found to be comprehensive, but too complex and expensive to be widely adopted and deployed. It was recognized that although the protocol-based approach offered was useful to manage networks, there was a proliferation of application-layer standards and application intercommunication needs to be addressed. Several approaches such as mobile agents, design of active networks, etc. were researched. A significant development was the Open Distributed Processing (ODP) framework for the development of distributed systems. The concepts in distributed systems and distributed computing soon led to the realization that network resources that need to be managed are components of a distributed system that need to communicate with the manager application. Thus, over the second half of the 1990s, a lot of research went into investigating how distributed technologies could be used to build management systems.

16.3.2   Emergence of CORBA-Based Management

The OMG CORBA offers a framework for building fully object-oriented distributed applications and can be considered as a practical realization of the concepts and philosophy of ODP. The potential of CORBA as a management interface was recognized and efforts were soon underway to develop CORBA-based management systems. The heart of the system is the Object Request Broker (ORB) that provides a communication bus for objects to interact over the network. CORBA has the advantage that it can be used as a management technology and can also act as an integrating technology for existing management approaches (building CORBA gateways for existing SNMP/CMIP components).

CORBA as a Management Technology. Considering network management as a distributed application, CORBA satisfies all the criteria to qualify as a management technology.

1. CORBA supports a fully object-oriented approach for information modeling, where network resources are objects that are defined by and accessed through their interface.
2. MOs can be addressed and discovered by a management application using the Naming Service offered by CORBA. The Naming Service provides the ability to bind a name to an object reference, and to later resolve the name to determine the object reference.

3. It supports a client–server-based organization model, with the management application behaving as the client and invoking services from the MOs in the network. A programmatic interface is supported between the manager and the managed elements. Interfaces are specified in the Interface Definition Language (IDL). Methods with any argument and result parameters are possible, providing full flexibility.

4. CORBA supports a Notification Service, an extension of the Event Service, with powerful filtering capability. Both the push and the pull models are supported for event forwarding. This makes event- driven management possible.

Approaches to CORBA as Management Technology. Over the years since the mid-1990s, several approaches have been taken to incorporate CORBA as a management technology [Pavlou *et al.*, 1998; 2004]. While some of these were developed as research prototypes to validate the use of CORBA, standards bodies were constituted to standardize CORBA-based systems. Joint Inter-Domain Management (JIDM) WG set up by NMF/X-Open (now TMF/Open Group—JIDM) was one of the most significant efforts in this direction. One aspect of the JIDM approach is that it attempted to stay close to the TMN approach and attempted re-use of OSI-SM infrastructures. JIDM envisaged the scenarios shown in Figure 16.6 [JIDM].

When using a CORBA-based manager, one option, as pictured in Figure 16.6, is to follow a migratory approach to accommodate existing networks and devices that export traditional management interfaces. This is done by including a generic gateway between the different management technologies. An implementation of the gateway requires the translation of object models from GDMO/ASN.1 to CORBA IDL, a conversion of CMIP protocol data units (PDU) to CORBA, and the reverse conversion of CORBA responses and notifications to CMIP PDUs. In fact, in an attempt to define a standard for network equipment, the JIDM worked on a complete GDMO/ASN.1 to IDL mapping with rules for a compiler that can generate the IDLs from a GDMO specification.

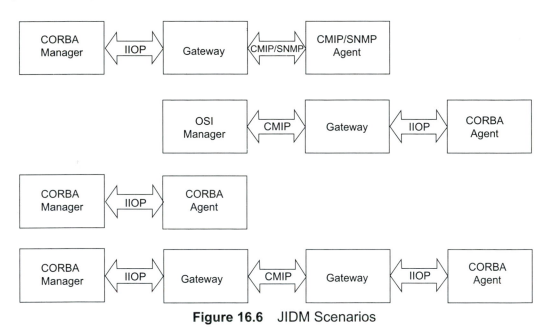

Figure 16.6   JIDM Scenarios

We now look at the architectures of a typical CORBA-based agent as envisaged by JIDM and a CORBA-based manager.

16.3.3   CORBA Agent

A CORBA management agent has a CORBA server and IDL interfaces for each GDMO. In the JIDM scheme, MOs are not structures in a MIB and are all visible at the same level. This implies that each individual NE should have its ORB that handles requests from the management application. The IDL interface of each MO defines the attributes of the MO and the operations supported; and these interfaces are registered in the Interface Repository of the ORB.

However, this approach has problems. The individual MOs do not warrant being considered as CORBA servers—the granularity mismatch in this mapping could result in an inordinately large number of servers and has the potential to pose a scalability problem. ORBs may not be able to handle such large numbers of servers. Lack of support in CORBA for bulk information retrieval is another problem, as a remote method call per attribute accessed is resource intensive. Modeling dynamic entities such as connections as objects is also an expensive approach.

Various researchers proposed other methods to overcome this. One of them is a departure from the approach to provide a syntactic emulation of TMN and design a native CORBA-based interface in the network element that leverages the advantages offered by CORBA. Commonly accessed elements are grouped together so that they can be accessed in a single remote method call. Connections are modeled as a "list" to which new connections can be added, existing ones removed, etc. This approach reduces the number of objects to be handled by the ORB.

16.3.4   CORBA-Based Manager

The design of a CORBA-based manager can realize many of the advantages distributed systems offer. It ensures scalability of the management application by supporting distributed deployment of the components. Figure 16.7 captures the architecture of a typical CORBA-based manager.

Figure 16.8 is an example of the typical components in a CORBA-based network management environment. The CORBA-based manager application has to use OMG-defined interfaces to interact with the CORBA-based agent.

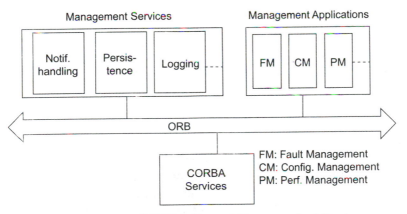

Figure 16.7   CORBA-Based Manager Architecture

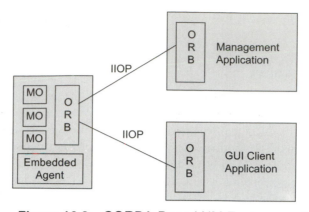

Figure 16.8 CORBA-Based NM Environment

Current Status of CORBA as a Management Technology. Despite the original vision that CORBA would prevail as the technology of choice for distributed network management and the support provided by several vendors, it was challenged by several others such as Java and more significantly Web services that show promise of an all-encompassing distributed management technology. CORBA has turned out to be more popular in the Service and Business Management layers. The need at these layers is more akin to process automation. The requirements for network and system management are different. Large amounts of data have to be retrieved from the devices at frequent intervals; and the technology has to support bulk information retrieval, as well as selective information retrieval. Information has to be real time—especially fault-related information. CORBA does not meet these requirements—especially bulk information retrieval. Moreover, complex devices may have huge numbers of MOs and scalability is a potential issue with the large number of dynamic connections and separate objects with their interfaces. Moreover, HTTP has turned out to be much more popular than CORBA's Internet Inter-ORB Protocol (IIOP) as the communication protocol.

In an interesting development, TMF in its continued quest for standardization developed a standard EML–NML interface for transport networks under the MTNM project. MTNM defines the information exchange between NMS and EMS enabling management of SONET/SDH, DWDM, DSL, Asyn/PDH, Ethernet, and ATM transport networks. The MTNM suite version 3 covers the following items: MTNM Interface Model (TMF 814) as CORBA IDLs, MTNM Information Model (TMF 608) in UML, and MTNM Business Agreement (TMF 513), the latter two being the requirements and use cases.

The TMF 814 standard is increasingly being adopted by equipment vendors as the standard North Bound Interface (NBI) to be supported by EMSs. This standard offers the promise of an integrated "umbrella" NMS that can manage multivendor, multitechnology networks from a central system, as shown in Figure 16.9. The scalability issues raised as a result of managing a large number of complex network elements are addressed by having the NMS communicate with EMS for management. The standard itself is comprehensive and supports autodiscovery, detailed element modeling, fault detection and diagnosis, performance management, configuration management, and provisioning.

The standard recommends that a number of key objects in the network be exposed via this interface. These objects are modeled based on the layered concepts and layer decomposition laid out in ITU G.805. An object model that is based on these concepts is assumed to be used by the EMS. A number of object managers that have services to obtain data about the objects in the network are defined; and the objects modeled by the MTNM standard can be accessed by the NMS using the appropriate Object Manager.

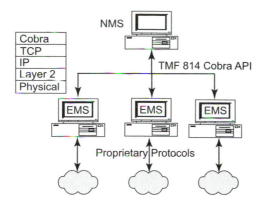

Cobra
TCP
IP
Layer 2
Physical

Figure 16.9 TMF 814-Based NMS and EMSs

In this CORBA-based architecture, the EMS plays the server role, and the NMS acts as the client. The TMF 814-based interface allows the NMS to use the APIs specified in the CORBA IDLs to access management information. The CORBA services that are used along with this specification are Naming Service, Notification Service, and Telecoms Log Service. The Naming Service allows the NMS to address the managed element via the EMS. The Notification Service allows notifications sent by the EMS to be received by the NMS and thereby avoid the overhead of polling. Data retrieval features include multiobject get operations for each type of MO. To reduce the overhead of excessive number of calls, the standard provides the facility to retrieve the names of all objects of a particular type. MTNM supports two ways for bulk data transfer—the iterator interface and ftp. Iterators are used to allow the NMS to deal more easily with retrievals that may return a very large amount of data. They provide a mechanism to retrieve data batch by batch—the ideal size of a batch is specified by the NMS. ftp is used for transferring performance data points from a file.

The MTNM approach is very attractive since the advantages of CORBA-based management can be realized, while eliminating many of the disadvantages of CORBA-based management faced when CORBA is used at the NE level.

16.4   XML-BASED NM TECHNOLOGY

The eXtensible Markup Language (XML) is a meta-markup language standardized by the World Wide Web Consortium (W3C) for document exchange in the Web. It is widely used for a variety of applications including enterprise application integration. It is ideally suited to meet the challenge of application integration since it has strong data formatting and interpretation features. Since it is platform independent, it can be used with almost any programming language (Java, C++, Python, Perl, Ruby, etc.), as long as support tools such as parsers are available.

As we learned in Chapter 9, in a network management application it is important to have a clearly defined management information model, protocols for data exchange, database connectivity, etc. In the approaches we have seen so far, we have seen different base technologies being used quite successfully for these purposes. For example, in the worlds of SNMP and CMIP, protocol definitions are based on ASN.1, databases are often accessible through well-defined ODBC or JDBC APIs, remote procedure calls and remote object access can be defined and realized through CORBA technologies, etc. XML provides a toolkit approach and existing XML-based specifications and their already existing implementations are applicable as building blocks to a wide range of network management aspects as well.

16.4.1   Use of XML and Associated Technologies for NM

1. XML can be used to represent management information: XML is a markup language and is ideally suited to represent arbitrarily complex hierarchical information in a human comprehensible format. Management information modeling of complex network elements can be done effectively. Large chunks of data, as well as atomic information, can be retrieved and the parsing of tagged XML information is much less error prone than extracting such information as ASCII text.

2. XML schema or Document Type Definitions (DTDs) for representing the structure of management information: Just as SNMP uses SMI to formally specify the management information model, XML schema, a purely XML-based standard, can be used to specify the valid grammar for XML documents containing management information. This is especially useful in verifying the integrity of configuration data.

3. Management information transport: TCP and HTTP, which are supported by most network elements, can be used to convey management information to and from the management station. URL can be used to address the network element.

4. DOM (Document Object Model) and SAX (Simple API for XML): Retrieved XML data can be parsed by the tried and tested APIs provided by the DOM and SAX parsers. Management applications can use these APIs for processing the data.

5. XSL (Extensible Style Sheet Language) and XPath (XML Path Language): XSL consists of three components:

    *   XSLT (XSL Transformations), a language for transforming XML documents, used for rearranging, adding and deleting tags and attributes in an XML document
    *   XPath, a language for identifying parts of an XML document
    *   XSL Formatting Objects, a vocabulary for formatting XML documents. XSL is a powerful style sheet and XPath expressions allow efficient queries to an XML document to retrieve data. The two can be used for efficient presentation of management data and recast management data in different lights. XSLTs allow the definition of rules for transforming XML documents to and from other formats such as other XML documents, HTML Web pages, plain text files, Excel sheets, or PDF documents. Together with the filtering capability provided by XPath, these are very powerful tools to process XML-based management information and display them graphically in a GUI. For example, a map-based representation of network elements, drill down capability, statistical processing and display, display of correlated fault information, etc. are naturally supported

6. Configuration management: XML is particularly useful for configuration management and supports a rich set of XML-based configuration options. It can thus be used in provisioning applications, centralized network databases, configuration patch files, and configuration archival.

7. SOAP and WSDL: Higher-level management operations can be defined using Web Services Definition Language (WSDL) and implemented by sending Simple Object Access Protocol (SOAP) messages.

8. Figure 16.10 [Strauss and Klie, 2003] depicts the interrelation between the XML and the associated technologies and tools just discussed.

Thus, XML and associated technologies for which well-tested implementations are available provide the framework needed to build a distributed application like an NMS. Apart from the advantages offered

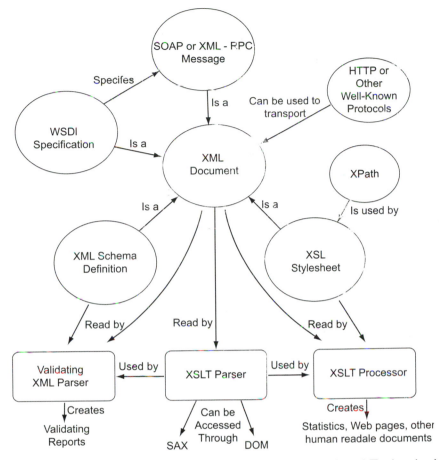

Figure 16.10 Interrelation between XML and Associated Technologies

as a management technology, XML can have a very beneficial effect on the development of network management software, where many of the management operations can be modeled in an XML document. The focus can gradually move from writing codes for management applications to authoring XML documents that represent management operations. Figure 16.11 shows generalized management architecture for using XML in management using the XML toolkit in line with the previous discussion.

16.4.2   XML-Based Management Approaches

Figure 16.12 depicts three possible architectures for XML-based management. The architectures are similar to those we saw for CORBA-based management.

Figure 16.12(a) depicts a purely XML-based approach to network management. Here the NMS is fully XML based and the device also supports an XML interface for manager–agent communication. In the long run, a fully XML-based architecture that affects all entities in a managed network promises the greatest benefits. However, there is a very large installed base of network elements that supports the older protocols. Also, from comparative performance studies conducted by various researchers, SNMP, CMIP, etc. are at a distinct advantage from the efficiency and timeliness points of view. Thus, in the short and medium term, the most pressing needs for the advantages of XML arise on the managers'

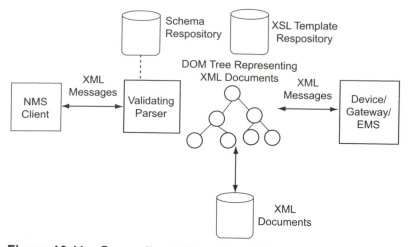

Figure 16.11 Generalized XML-Based Management Architecture

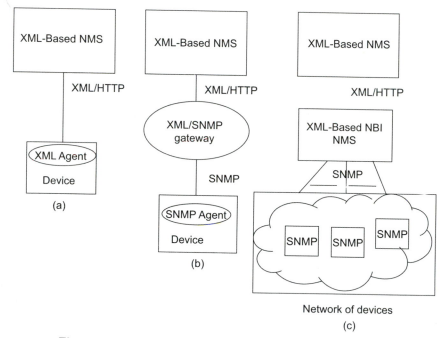

Figure 16.12 Three Specific XML-Based Architectures

side, where operators could take advantage of XML-based processing of their management informa-tion. This situation calls for the integration of managed nodes based on SNMP technology on one side and management systems based on XML technology on the other. The gateway-based architecture in Figure 16.12(b) depicts this approach. The manager application has an XML-based interface to commu-nicate with network elements and is developed leveraging the advantages of XML-based tools. There is a gateway element between the NMS and device that translates between the XML on the managers' side and SNMP on the network element side. Figure 16.12(c) depicts a very attractive approach to XML-based management similar to the approach taken by MTNM. The approach taken by MTNM is that the system facing the network has the flexibility to use any protocol to communicate with the network element. This has the advantage that existing network elements need not undergo sweeping changes to accommodate a totally new technology. Also, lower-level protocols that are more efficient and timely and have a smaller footprint can be used. However, the management application (EMS or NMS) that communicates with the network element directly has to implement a North Bound Interface (NBI), which can communicate with the NMS. This NBI must be XML based. The messages exchanged between the NML and EML are more semantically rich and can correspond to several operations at the lower level. This enables the implementation of SOA and XML messages that can be exchanged between the EMS and the NMS.

16.4.3 Current Status of XML-Based Management

A lot of work has been done in exploring the potential of XML as a management technology. This includes industry initiatives, research initiatives and standards bodies, and industry consortia that are working in this direction.

Vendor Initiatives. Several equipment vendors have added XML support to their devices over a period of time. Leading players such as Juniper Networks, Cisco, 2Wire, etc. already have support for XML-based communication. Juniper Networks was one of the first to support XML for management operations. Support for XML-based management has been incorporated in the network element, as shown in Figure 16.12; and XML-based RPCs can be exchanged between the management application and the network element. An XML RPC consists of a request and the corresponding response, transmitted during a connection-oriented session using any transport protocol. Configuration information can be downloaded, modified, and reloaded. 2Wire has provided XML-based support for provisioning their DSL devices using XML over SSL. This has been submitted to the DSL Forum. Several models of Cisco devices provide an XML-based interface for configuration management. There is support for XML-based export of inventory information.

Research Initiatives. Research groups have investigated how XML can be used for network element management and some have implemented prototypes as proof of concept. They focus on describing the structure of management information as XML documents. In some of the cases this structure is like providing an XML representation of existing SNMP MIBs, and including enhanced operations over this. In this section we describe the proposed approaches of some of the prominent groups and some design decisions that come into the picture [Ju *et al.*, 2002; Menten, 2004; Strauss, 2004; Yoon *et al.*, 2003].

16.4.4 XML-Based Manager

Figure 16.13 shows a schematic representation of the generalized architecture for an XML-based management system. The functional components necessary in an XML-based manager application are described below.

Data collection component: The design of this component is driven by the fact that the communication model used is XML over HTTP. It is possible to use any connection-oriented protocol, but since many such devices already host a Web server and support direct HTTP/HTML-based network management, much of the required infrastructure for Web-based management would already be present. For

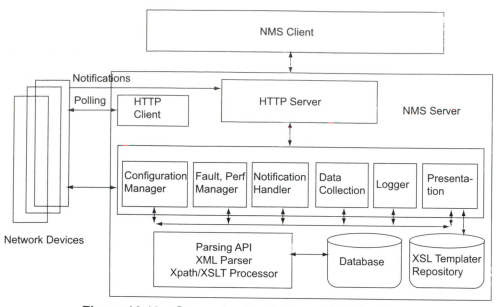

Figure 16.13 Generalized XML-Based NM Architecture

polling-based retrieval of management data, the NMS application has an HTTP client and periodically sends an HTTP request to the device agent for management information. The received response is either processed or stored in the database. For receiving notifications from the device, a Web server is included in the NMS application and a Web client in the device. The Web server is used to receive XML/HTTP notifications from the network element or device/gateway/EMS and to facilitate Web-GUI-based views of management information to operators.

Management information modeling is based on XML; and device characteristics have to be represented as an XML document. Device modeling can either follow the existing SNMP MIB for the device (MIB-Module/Group/Table/TableEntry/RowIndex) or be redesigned and made more expressive and powerful. For example, in the case of architecture shown in Figure 16.12(c), where the XML-based NMS is a manager-of-managers, it would be appropriate to define a suitable XML schema to model the device from a higher-level perspective. Such a perspective would result in a "network-based" view of the network rather than the usual device-centric view.

The **structure of the management data** in the XML documents can be described using either Document Type Definition (DTD) or XML schema. Both approaches are appropriate for most documents, but XML schema are more commonly used.

The **XML documents** in a management application would be of two types—one pertaining to configuring the manager application and the other having device modeling/configuration information. In case the XML management is built on top of SNMP management for example, the device modeling part of the document would be a translation of the device MIB to XML. Several research groups have developed such translators.

Addressing network devices: When the NMS wants to obtain specific information from a particular device, the device is identified by its IP address, the transport protocol is TCP, and the application-layer protocol can be anything: telnet, ssh, HTTP, etc. The most commonly used protocol is HTTP. The XML message received from the network can be analyzed by the manager application using one of several

Xpath Expression for Mib element	Canonical Representation using Xpath	Example
/<M>/<G>/	/<M>/<G>/	RFC 1213—MiB/interfaces
/<M>/<T>/	/<M>/<G>/<T>/	RFC 1213—MIB/interfaces/ifTable
/<M>/<G>/<TE>	/<M>/<G>/<T>/<TE>	RFC 1213—MIB/interfaces/ifTable/ifEntry/1

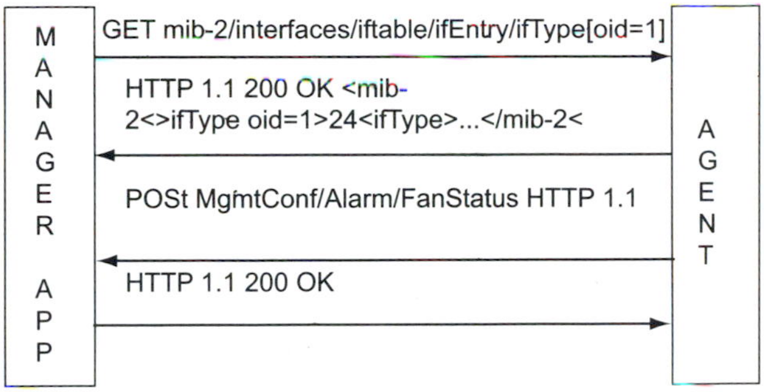

Figure 16.14 · Representation of Management Transactions in XML

options. XML-based technologies also provide several mechanisms for the retrieval of MO information. XPath or XQuery expressions can be used to access specific parts of the XML message. XPath describes a set of elements within an XML document and assumes that the XML document has been parsed into a tree of nodes. XPath allows the specification of a path through the document's element hierarchy, as well as a mechanism for selecting elements from that hierarchy. This is a suitable approach since an XPath expression is the standard way to identify a part of an XML document. SNMP and CMIP OIDs have a nice correspondence with XPath expressions, as shown in Figure 16.14.

Management operations are also represented in an XML document and one question that arises here is which transactions must be represented as attributes and which ones should be XML elements. There are certain rules of thumb that are used when making such a decision. In general, entities that are object-like will be represented as elements, i.e., cases where there will be multiple instances. Data that have a unique value will be represented as attributes. The design must be such that the XML document is easy to read, XML schema for validation is simple, and it is easily searched by an XPath expression.

Management functional applications: This includes applications to achieve the FCAPS functionality. It includes some support applications such as filtering, correlation, logging, etc. Since management information is represented in XML, these must also use some parser such as DOM or SAX. There will also be a repository of XSL templates to render dynamic displays of management information.

16.4.5 XML-Based Agent

The basic component of the XML-based agent is an embedded Web server, some XML processing-related components (XML parser, XPath handler), and the HTTP Client Engine, apart from the standard embedded application that the agent needs to access the current value of data requested and deliver notifications.

Since the components residing on the device are embedded applications and are subject to more resource constraints than the components in the manager application, it is common to write custom

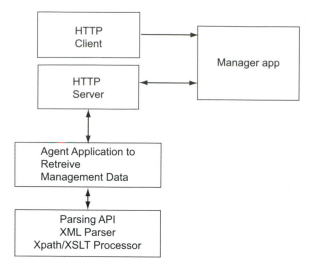

Figure 16.15   XML-Based Agent Architecture

compact XML parsers rather than use DOM or even SAX. For example, in Juniper devices, a custom parser is used to parse data. Figure 16.15 shows the architecture of a typical agent.

A typical request–response transaction between the manager and the agent involves the following operations:

HTTP GET request for the management parameter is sent for data retrieval. An HTTP GET request has a parameter describing the detailed request. The manager identifies the MO as XPath or XQuery expression. HTTP POST is used for configuration operations with the configuration parameters in the body of the POST request.

Validation of the operation using an XML parser and schema is done. Two common readily available parsers are DOM and SAX. DOM parser constructs a tree representation of the entire XML document and is thus memory and processor intensive. SAX parser is an event-driven streaming parser and is more lightweight, but is still resource hungry.

The request is sent to the agent/gateway as an HTTP request via the HTTP client component of the manager application. The agent evaluates the XPath expression and retrieves the latest value of the requested MO.

The response is sent back to the NMS as an XML message, and the data are stored in the NMS database.

A notification or trap is sent via the HTTP client component of the device and is received by the HTTP server in the NMS. It is processed by the concerned management functional application (notification handler in Figure 16.13).

16.4.6   XML-Based Web Services for Management

Web services are the next logical step in which XML-based management is moving since it gives additional structure to XML-based management and defines a machine-independent way for the management application and agent to exchange messages. The Web services standard, developed by the World Wide Web Consortium (W3C), is defined in [W3C] and the following is a brief introduction to Web services.

Web services are an XML-based framework for building distributed applications based on open protocols. The basic Web services platform is XML + HTTP and the Web services platform elements are:

- SOAP (Simple Object Access Protocol)
- WSDL (Web Services Description Language)
- UDDI (Universal Description, Discovery and Integration)

SOAP is a simple XML-based communication protocol for accessing Web services and is designed for use over the Internet. WSDL is an XML-based language for describing Web services and is a W3C standard. WSDL is also used to locate Web services. This document exposes the operations, which parameters to pass to an operation, via which protocols an operation can be accessed, and on which location (i.e., the IP address or domain name) the Web service resides. UDDI is a directory service where organizations can register to search for Web services. It is a directory for storing information of Web service interfaces described by WSDL.

Several researchers [Pras *et al.*, 2004] have done work on using Web services-based element management. The Organization for the Advancement of Structured Information Standards (OASIS) is a standards organization for defining Web services, and several standards such as Management Using Web Services (MUWS), Management of Web Services (MOWS), etc. have emerged. Web services predominantly add-ress systems management.

16.5 COMPARISON OF MANAGEMENT TECHNOLOGIES

In this section we compare the management technologies discussed so far based on the criteria described in Section 16.1.2. There are two factors in making a comparison—the first is with respect to the suitability of the protocols and the other is with respect to the practical usability in terms of performance. It is clear that CORBA and XML are extremely suitable with respect to the parameters mentioned in Sections 16.3 and 16.4.

We now discuss the performance of SNMP, CORBA, and XML in terms of bandwidth, CPU usage, and latency. In literature, the results of the comparison of various protocols have been reported. At a high level, the experimental approach to make the comparison and the conclusions is similar and summarized here. (The details of the experiments and conclusions are outside the scope of this chapter. Interested readers are referred to Drevers [2004] and Pras *et al.* [2004] for more information.)

Experimental setup: An SMP table is selected and experiments are conducted to compare the performance at different data retrieval granularities as shown in Figure 16.16. This will demonstrate the effectiveness of the protocols considered in accessing and returning the data of different sizes and having different structures.

A single instance of an OID, the most atomic entity that can be obtained using SNMP Get is represented in A. Figure B represents a column of the table. For example, if the table is *ifTable*, it represents the value of a single parameter, say *ifInOctets*, for all interfaces in the device. A full row pictured in C represents the values of all parameters for one interface, while Figure D shows retrieval of the entire table.

Findings: Excessive bandwidth consumption is a concern with XML-based solutions. It turns out that for management bandwidth consumption, SNMP consumes the least bandwidth, especially when a single attribute is retrieved. CORBA comes next, while Web services-based management consumes the maximum bandwidth. When multiple MOs are retrieved per request, the difference narrows a little. For such bulk retrievals, SNMP and CORBA are almost at par in terms of bandwidth

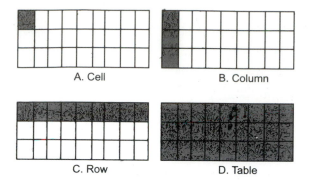

Figure 16.16 Granularities for Performance Comparison

consumption with CORBA performing almost as well, if not marginally better than SNMP, while the bandwidth consumed by Web services can be around eight times as much as CORBA. The bandwidth can be reduced by using compression techniques, but this has an impact on response times. SNMP has the best response times when it comes to retrieval of a single attribute. CORBA shows comparable performance, sometimes even better performance for retrieval of multiple attributes. The response time for Web services-based management is the highest. Table 16.2 is a summary of the comparison of the various protocols.

16.6 RECENT NM-RELATED STANDARDS

From Table 16.2, it is clear that XML as an element management protocol may not be feasible from the point of view of performance. The growing trend now is to use a SOA to build a network management application so that the components in the management ecosystem can communicate with each other. In this section we discuss some of the emerging standards in this area. Some of the prominent standards are MTOSI for management software at service provider premises and OASIS in the areas of systems management.

It is an acknowledged fact that to ensure smooth operations and ensure fast service delivery, service providers need multiple applications that cater to varying requirements. The eTOM map, covered in Chapter 10, specifies the processes, the end-to-end automation of which, results in efficient service delivery. Thus, the individual applications need to be developed using a software architecture that enables seamless integration; and a SOA holds the promise of meeting this requirement. In this section we discuss MTOSI and OASIS, both of which are standards that enable integration of distributed applications using SOA.

MTOSI, a TMF [TMF] initiative, is a standard that provides an integration framework for different applications that result in the automation of some of the key processes in a service provider's environment. These processes, referred to as operations support (OS) functions, are the management functional areas of an NMS (FCAPS), specialized functions such as Root CauseAnalysis, Service Impact Analysis, SLA monitoring, etc. The objective of MTOSI is to extend MTNM using XML/Web services interface to integrate the different OS components using SOA and NGOSS (New Generation OSS) design principles. The initial focus of MTOSI was to develop an OS-to-OS interface that covers the NMS/EMS interface as a special case. This is shown in Figure 16.17 as a component of MTOSI architecture. It is being extended to cater to the more generalized requirement.

Table 16.2 Comparison of Management Protocols

	OSI /CMISE	SNMP	CORBA	XML
Information model	ASN.1/GDMO specifies a fully object-oriented, powerful, comprehensive but very complicated model	SMI/MIBs are basic, simple, but not object oriented, less powerful	CORBA IDLs specify a fully object-oriented model, less powerful than ASN1/GDMO	XML or WSDL documents—powerful, very expressive, flexible
Organization model	Manager–agent paradigm using CMISE as the protocol	Manager–agent paradigm using SNMP as the protocol	Client–server model with programmatic interface between the server and the client	Message-based architecture with XML SOAP-based messages between the server and the client
Communication model	CMISE over OSI protocol stack	SNMP over UDP	CORBA RPC over TCP, IIOP	Usually HTTP over TCP
Service location	N/A	N/A	Inter-ORB-reference (IOR)	Universal Resource Identifier (URI)
Naming, directory	N/A	N/A	Naming service, interface repository	UDDI
Management operations	Very comprehensive, powerful, support for notifications with filtering and scoping	Basic, very few operations, notifications (traps) supported	Powerful, notifications with filtering, somewhat less comprehensive than OSI	No native support for notifications, need was recognized and support has been provided
Support for configuration management	Average	Not satisfactory	Good	Very powerful support
Scalability, flexibility	Scalable	Scalable. Useful for retrieval of small quantities of data from large number of elements rather than bulk data from fewer numbers	Can pose scalability issues at the element management level	Can pose scalability issues at the element management level
Maturity	Mature and time tested	Mature and time tested	Mature. Has been in use since mid-1990s	Relatively new although vendors have been providing support since around 2000

Table 16.2 (continued)

	OSI /CMISE	SNMP	CORBA	XML
Performance	Satisfactory and very efficient for fine-grained operations	Performs well especially for retrieval of atomic data. Very efficient for fine-grained operations	Satisfactory. Not very efficient for fine-grained operations. More efficient when multiple objects are retrieved with a single method call	Poses problems for bandwidth usage, response times, and CPU usage at the NE
Security	CMIP built-in security	SNMPv3	CORBA security service	HTTP/SSL, XML signature

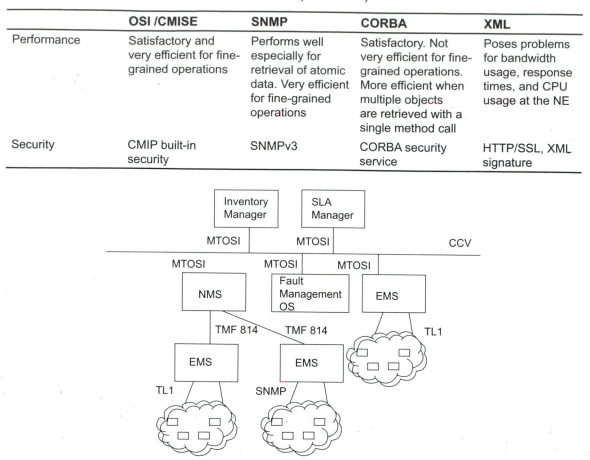

Figure 16.17 MTOSI Architecture

OASIS is a consortium that drives the development, convergence, and adoption of open standards for the global information society. Standards have been defined and adopted in a number of areas including management. The Web Services Distributed Management (WSDM) [WSD] committee defined the architecture and technology to manage distributed resources using Web services and the standard is particularly applicable to systems management. The two applicable standards are Management Using Web Services (MUWS) and Management of Web Services (MOWS).

MUWS addresses the use of Web services as the foundation of a systems management framework. This includes the use of Web services for the interaction between the managed resources and management applications. WSDM also addresses the requirement of managing Web resources like any other resource via the MOWS standard. Figure 16.18 depicts the typical management framework architecture. MUWS is a wire-level specification of how to describe the manageability of a resource using WSDL documents. It provides a mechanism to discover manageable resources and their manageability capabilities. WSDM facilitates Manager to Managed Resource interaction using Web services rather

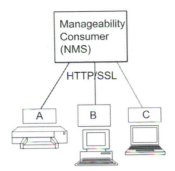

A, B, C: Web Service End Points,
Connection to Manageable Resources

Figure 16.18 Management Framework Architecture

than using some specific management protocol. However, MUWS has not created a new management model—it is able to work with existing standards such as DMTF and SNMP and constitutes a unifying layer on top of existing information models. It specifies how to define XML schema for representing the management information model and how to access the model using Web services.

MOWS defines a model to manage Web services. This includes management-specific attributes to expose properties such as lifecycle state and performance of the Web services. Management operations to monitor/control a Web service itself are specified.

In conclusion, the trend emerging in management application design recognizes that a holistic management system—both from the networks perspective and from the systems perspective—is to be viewed as a distributed system consisting of several loosely coupled applications interacting with managed resources and with each other. These applications typically have an interface to communicate with the managed resources and one to communicate with other applications in the ecosystem. The interface used to communicate with the network tends to be low-level, efficient, and fast and usually managed resource specific. An event-driven bus architecture for conveying exception conditions, supporting one-to-many and many-to-many event dissemination, is required rather than a request–response model. A Web services-based management approach, which allows loosely coupled management applications built around Web services, meets the needs. MTOSI, with its Web services-based interface, plays an important role in the telecom IT environment SOA implementation, while WSDM plays a similar role in systems management.

Summary

In this chapter we reviewed traditional approaches to data communication and telecommunication network management. We saw that the evolution of management technologies did not quite keep pace with the rapid evolution in network technologies and services and consequent operator needs. We identified some shortcomings of SNMP and CMISE/CMIP and discussed approaches taken by the research community to overcome these.

We then discussed the emergence of Web-based management and CORBA as alternative management technologies. We saw that CORBA became popular and was widely adopted in the telecommunication network management environment. The MTNM standard TMF 814, which is CORBA based, is widely adopted as the standard NML–EML interface in transport networks. Web-based management initially just meant having an HTML client, but quickly became very popular, with most devices having a Web server. We saw that WBEM was an early standard and one that prevails to date for System or Enterprise Management. We then discussed the potential of XML as a management technology and described approaches for its use for element management both by vendors and by the research community.

We summarized the pros and cons of the various approaches and finally described the current trends and recent standards. Management systems are to be viewed as distributed systems consisting of several loosely coupled applications interacting with managed resources and with each other. We concluded that in view of the multitude of applications that are needed to keep a service provider's operations running smoothly, seamless integration of these applications to provide a unified view is very important. A Web services-based SOA with the various components communicating over a bus via XML messages is the trend emerging both in telecom and enterprise management. The TMF standard MTOSI in the telecom environment and the OASIS standard WSDM in the enterprise management environment reflect this trend.

▇▇ Exercise

1. What are the disadvantages of SNMP as a configuration management protocol?
2. There are two management stations—one SNMP based and the other CORBA based. The SNMP-based manager does poll-based fault management of a device by sending SNMP requests every 2 minutes. The CORBA-based NMS fault management is fully push based and the NMS receives a notification when there is a fault. The size of the SNMP request and response PDUs is 150 bytes; and the size of a CORBA notification is about 400 bytes. During 1 hour there are 20 alarms. Calculate the bandwidth used in both cases.
3. Consider a CORBA-based modeling of the interface table that uses two approaches—a single method that returns all the interfaces similar to a SNMPGetBulk and separate methods for each interface similar to SNMPGet (a one–one mapping from SMI to IDLs).
   (a) Which of the approaches is more suitable?
   (b) Explain why it is more suitable
4. In a Management system at a Service Provider, it is required to query a device for SysUptime, tcpActiveOpens, tcpPassiveOpens, and tcpAttempts. A designer Anil wants to use SNMP for this while Bina wants to use CORBA (1 method call for SysUptime, 1 for the remaining 3 parameters). Which of their approaches uses less bandwidth? Why?

   This NMS also has to retrieve the ipRouteTable, which has about 10,000 rows. Anil suggests SNMPv2 GetBulk command, while Bina prefers CORBA (1 method to fetch the table). Whose approach results in less bandwidth being used? Why?
5. Suppose a router has 80 interfaces and performance data are to be collected from the interface table. Calculate the average bandwidth used to retrieve 80 rows using SNMPGet, SNMPGetBulk, with and without compression. Also calculate the bandwidth used if Web services are used, with and without compression. Use the following data to calculate bandwidth usage:
   (a) Average size of SNMPGet (request + response) PDU is around 40 bytes and when objects are retrieved using SNMPBulkGet, the average size per object is 20 bytes. Assume that compression with SNMP results in 25% decrease in bandwidth consumption.
   (b) For Web services, every message has a header of size 500 bytes and in the SOAP message, each row in the interface table occupies around 1,000 bytes. Compression results in 75% bandwidth reduction when 80 rows are retrieved.

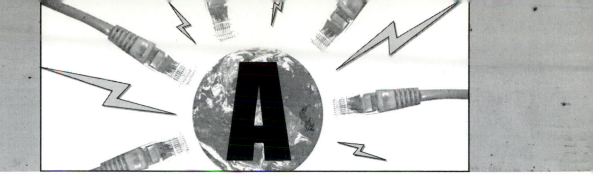

OSI Network and System Management

In Chapter 3 we introduced OSI management, which uses the Common Management Information Protocol (CMIP). Then we discussed its application to the Telecommunications Management Network (TMN) in Chapter 10. We will cover the basic principles of OSI network and system management here. We will describe the management of network resources, including both network elements and the network that connects them. In conjunction with TMN, OSI also addresses management layers above the network—namely, service and business management. You may need to review the basic foundations of OSI in Chapter 3 to follow the material in this appendix.

In contrast to the SNMP management standard, which was intentionally kept simple in concept and implementation, the OSI management standard was developed to be broad and flexible and is based on object-oriented technology. Hence, it turned out to be complex, difficult to understand, and expensive to implement, which is why it has been sparsely deployed. However, the recent availability of object-oriented technology tools and hardware resources, combined with the need for telecommunication management using TMN, have eliminated its implementation impediments.

We will present the complex subject of OSI management by using a simple, easy-to-follow approach. We will compare OSI management to SNMP management wherever appropriate, which will also help you better understand the former.

A.1   OSI MANAGEMENT STANDARDS

Two standards bodies, the International Standards Organization (ISO) and the International Telecommunications Union (ITU), jointly worked on developing standards for network management. Thus, in Table A.1 listing of the various standards documents, two numbers are associated with each entry—an ISO designation and an ITU designation (X-series).

Only a partial list is given in Table A.1; for a more complete list see [Raman, 1998]. The X.700 series covers the general management framework and a systems management overview. The X.710 series covers the communication protocol and service. The Structure of Management Information (SMI) is specified in the X.720 series. An extensive series of documents ranging from X.730 to X.751 addresses numerous application functions.

Table A.1   OSI Systems Management Standards Guide

ISO	ITU	TOPIC
7498-4	X.700	OSI Basic Reference Model Part 4: Management Framework
10040	X.701	Systems Management Overview
9595 9596-1	X.710	Common Management Information Service Definition
9596-2	X.711	Common Management Information Protocol
10165-1	X.720	SMI: Management Information Model
10165-2	X.721	SMI: Definition of Management Information
10165-4	X.722	SMI: Guidelines for the Definition of Managed Objects
10165-5	X.723	SMI: Generic Management Information
10165-6	X.724	SMI: Requirements and Guidelines for ICS Proforma associated with Management Information
10165-7	X.725	SMI: General Relationship Model
10165-9	X.727	SMI: System Management Protocol Machine Managed Objects
10164-1 10164-17	X.730- X.751	Systems Management (specifications for various functions and attributes)

A.2   SYSTEM OVERVIEW

The OSI management system concept is similar to that of SNMP management. After introducing the general concept in Chapter 3, we discussed SNMP management in Chapter 4. Figure A.1 shows the OSI management model, defined in ISO 10040/X.701. The managing system consists of an entity playing the manager role and applications that perform the various functions. The managed system comprises the agent role function and managed objects. The managing system performs various operations, such as get and set, which we covered in discussing SNMP management, on a managed system and receives responses. Notification is similar to the trap in SNMP, but it has a broader role in OSI management. The role of the agent is to perform the operations on managed objects and receive notifications from them. This function is similar to SNMP agent operations on network elements. The communication protocol between the managing system and the managed system is the CMIP, similar to SNMP in SNMP management.

OSI management differs from SNMP management in the way the managed object is defined. In OSI the managed object is object oriented, in contrast to the scalar representation of the managed object in SNMP. We observed the difference between the two perspectives in Chapter 3 (Figure 3.9). A managed object representation in OSI is shown in Figure A.2. As OSI is object oriented, the resources are represented as **managed object classes**. The internal characteristics of a managed object are hidden from the external view, and are specified as **attributes** at the object boundary. The inner **behavior** of the managed object caused by external **operations** is reflected as changes in attributes and is sent out as **notifications**. The operations sent out by the management system as requests requiring responses are part of operations and generate responses by the managed system.

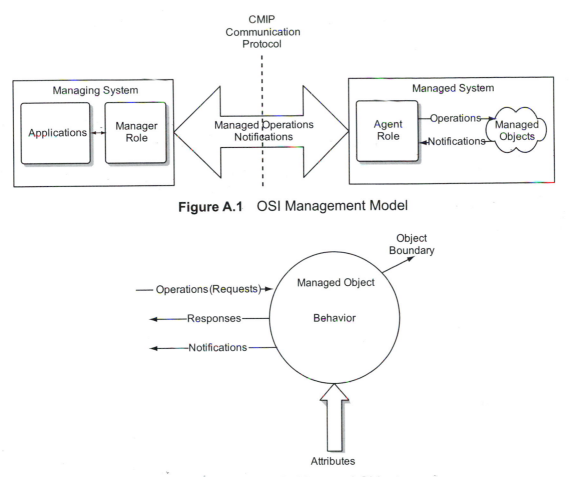

Figure A.1 OSI Management Model

Figure A.2 OSI Managed Object

The OSI management system architecture is shown in Figure A.3. It consists of seven messages representing seven services, called **Common Management Information Service Elements** (CMISEs). The communication protocol used by CMISE is the **Common Management Information Protocol** (CMIP).

All but one, **M-EVENT-REPORT**, are generated by the manager and are represented as solid lines in the OSI manager application layer. They are shown as dashed lines in the OSI agent application layer. The M-EVENT-REPORT is shown as a solid line in the agent layer and as a dashed line in the manager layer. All messages are represented by double arrows in both the manager and the agent layers because messages may elicit or require either response(s) or confirmation. Notice that this approach is different from that of SNMP management, in which all messages are unidirectional.

Messages are generated by application processes and are transferred to the presentation layer via an application entity sublayer in the application layer (more about this later). The other upper layers of the OSI Reference Model consist of presentation and session layers as described in ITU Recommendations X.216 and X.226 for the former and X.215 and X.225 for the latter.

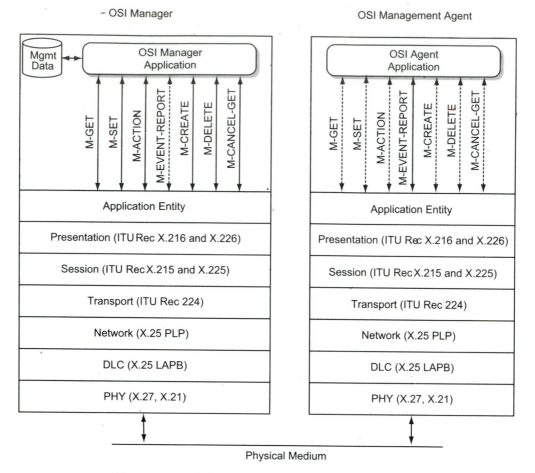

Figure A.3   OSI Management System Architecture

The lower layers of the model may be either connection oriented or connectionless. Numerous choices in the set of lower-layer protocols are available. Figure A.3 shows an example of a set based on X.25 [ITU Recommendation X.25 Protocol, October 1996]. Various profiles can be implemented, including the Internet profile [Raman, 1998].

The **M-GET** service comprises *request* and *response* messages. They are equivalent to get-request and get-response messages in SNMP. The get-next-request could also be included in that the OSI get service is for a management object class and thus includes SNMP multiple scalar managed objects. The M-GET requires a confirmation (response) from the agent. The **M-SET** service enables setting up attribute values in the managed object and may or may not require confirmation. The **M-ACTION** service is used to perform operations in the managed object, and confirmation is optional. An M-GET Request message may be canceled by using the **M-CANCEL-GET** message, which requires confirmation from the agent. The **M-EVENT-REPORT** is akin to the trap message in SNMP, but it has a much broader effect than the few generic alarms in SNMP.

The **M-CREATE** and **M-DELETE** services are used to create and delete object classes, for which there is no equivalent in SNMP. A close analogy in SNMP for these services is creation and deletion of conceptual rows for tabular objects. Both these OSI messages require confirmation from the agent.

A.3 ORGANIZATION MODEL

We explained the OSI organization model in Chapter 3. It comprises the manager system, the agent system, and managed objects. A system can perform the dual role of a manager and an agent, switching from one role to the other dynamically. This approach is significantly different from that of SNMP management, in which the two functions can coexist but are distinct processes.

In the OSI management specifications, managed objects are assigned to groups called *domains*. Such grouping can be done either on an organizational basis or on an administrative basis. When an organizational domain is formed, it consists of a set of managed objects based on functional criteria, such as fault and performance management. The organizational domain may also recognize organizational considerations such as common policies and procedures.

Administrative authority is the basis for an administrative grouping. It determines the creation of and interaction between domains. An administrative grouping may comprise organizational domains.

A.4 INFORMATION MODEL

The OSI information model is based on the abstraction of information on the managed object as seen across the boundary of the managed object by a manager system. (See Figures 3.9(b) and A.2 on the perspective of a managed object.) The schema representing the managed object is used by the manager system and the management agent system to communicate with each other as in SNMP management. Again, the OSI management information model is object oriented and in that regard differs from the SNMP management information model, which is scalar based. The information model deals with the SMI, managed objects and object classes, and management information trees.

A.4.1 Structure of Management Information

The definition of managed objects, syntax based on ASN.1, and the naming convention in the OSI SMI are similar in many ways to the SNMP SMI that we covered in Section 4.7.2. However, because of OSI SMI's object-oriented approach, they differ in content from those in the SNMP SMI.

The concept of managed objects in OSI SMI refers to a group of objects having similar properties, defined as a *managed object class*. We can loosely compare this type of grouping to grouping of managed objects in the SNMP model. However, a managed object class is more than a group of SNMP-managed objects. It is a collection of objects whose attributes and behavior are similar, and it supports a common set of operations and notifications.

A managed object class can be created from other managed object classes, called **packages**, as shown in Figure A.4. It comprises one **mandatory package** and multiple **conditional packages**. A managed class in this structure has the properties associated with the mandatory package and may include properties of conditional packages. For example, a transport class object class would include an OSI transport class 4, applicable to both connection-oriented and connectionless cases, but would include a transport class 0 or 2, only if it is connection oriented. We will address the method of defining the properties of an object class and a package in Section A.4.2.

Managed object classes are obtained by using an *inheritance tree,* as we will show in Section A.4.3. There are three types of trees in OSI management. Besides the inheritance tree, there is a *naming tree* and a *registration tree,* which we will discuss in Section A.4.4. We will cover the *template* for specifying managed objects in Section A.4.5.

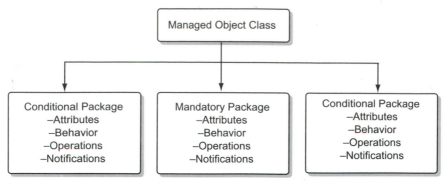

Figure A.4   Structure of a Managed Object Class

Managed Object Class and Instance

A **managed object class** is a group of **managed objects** with common attributes and behavior, can be subjected to similar operations, and emit a set of similar notifications, as previously shown in Figure A.1. The properties of a managed object are defined by a template specifying these characteristics. A managed object is an **instance** of a managed object class with defined values in the template. For example, a hub can be defined as a managed object class, with each hub having different attribute values (e.g., manufacturer, serial number, number of ports, etc.) as an instance of the hub-managed object class. As shown in Figure A.5, the hub is a managed object class having common attributes and two specific hubs as two instances of it. Each instance has different values for hub ID, vendor name, model number, and serial number. They are 10-Mbps Ethernet hubs (*ifType*=6) with 12 ports.

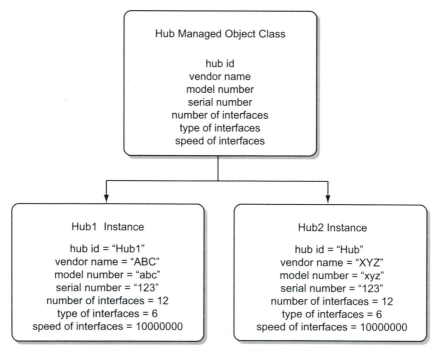

Figure A.5   Example of a Managed Object Class and Instances

Let us now look at the properties (or characteristics) associated with the managed object, which we covered briefly in Chapter 3. The properties of a managed object and object class are interdependent, as we will demonstrate shortly.

Attributes and Attribute Group. Attributes of a managed object include the data types and values associated with it. As discussed in Chapter 3, the basic data types could be either simple or constructed. Unlike SNMP, OSI permits the use of a wider range of ASN.1 data types. For example, multiple values can be associated with attributes by using a SET OF construct.

The value associated with an attribute could be either single- or multiple-valued and is specified according to the syntax rule. The syntax is specified in the ASN.1 language described in Chapter 3.

Attributes have access rules (e.g., read, write, and read–write), which are accomplished with *operations*. Attributes can also be created, deleted, or changed with *operations*.

Attributes can be grouped to form an **attribute group**. Because each attribute value may have different syntax requirements, the attribute group does not follow the syntactical rule.

Behavior. Behavior describes the internal actions of a managed object. It is the glue that holds the properties of a managed object together. Behavior definitions can be specified with attributes and operations and can include notifications. A change in the value of an attribute can generate notification. For example, in an environment with multiple managers performing different functions, such as configuration and performance on a managed system, a change in the configuration made by operations in a configuration management system may affect performance. Hence, the performance management system needs to be sent notifications. Another example is a package, in which two attributes may be related in a constrained manner. In such a situation, an operation on one attribute would cause the behavior to affect the other attribute. We can picture the scenario where the set command is used to administratively turn off an interface, which would behaviorally affect the *get* command that is gathering data on that interface.

Operations. Operations perform actions on attributes and are also called attribute-oriented operations. The **attribute-oriented operations** are *get, set, replace, add,* and *remove*. We will describe the commands and service entities associated with them when we consider the CMIP service element in Section A.5. The *get* operation is a read function. The *set* operation is used to set a value of attributes. The *replace* operation replaces an attribute in a package with any appropriate value or with a default value. The *add* and *remove* operations perform an addition or removal of a member to or from a set (e.g., addition of a member to a group).

Three **object-oriented operations** are used to perform an operation on an object—*action, create,* or *delete*. The *action* operation executes a valid process on the object. Typically, when more than just setting or replacing an attribute value is involved, the *action* operation is used. It could be as complex as running a process that invokes the *behavior*, changes the attributes of a managed class, and invokes multiple *responses* and *notifications*. SNMP management has no equivalent functions.

Notifications. Notifications are similar to traps in SNMP management. They are events generated by the management agent without a command from the management system. However, it is broader in scope than the trap and is generated either by an external or by an internal stimulant. As mentioned under object-oriented operations, notifications may be generated as a side effect. Alarms are also generated and transmitted by managed objects via notifications. Data generated by notifications may also be logged for later utilization and not sent out.

A.4.3   Inheritance

We defined a managed object class as a group of managed objects with common properties. Another way of looking at it is that a managed object is an instantiation of a managed object class, as previously shown in Figure A.5.

We can add attributes to a managed object class and derive a new class, called a *subclass*, which is similar to deriving a data subtype from a data type. The **subclass** is derived from a **superclass** and *inherits* the properties of the *superclass*. All the attributes of a superclass are maintained by a subclass, and more are added to restrict the class of object instances in the subclass.

The three categories of **inheritance—single inheritance, multiple inheritance (polymorphic)**, and **allomorphic**—are shown in Figure A.6, which represents a network containing routers and hubs. At the top of the managed objects is the ultimate superclass, *top*. Hub is superclass of the switched and (regular) hubs. The 10-Mbps regular (non-switched) hub-managed object subclass is derived by single inheritance from the hub superclass. Likewise, the switched 10-Mbps and 100-Mbps hub subclasses are derived by single inheritance from the switched hub superclass. A switched multirate hub that has both 100-Mbps and 10-Mbps port speeds has polymorphic inheritance from its superclasses at the 100-Mbps and 10-Mbps switched hubs. The 10-Mbps uni-LAN hub is the class of hubs that can be configured only as a single LAN. In other words, it behaves as a regular hub and hence is allomorphic with the 10-Mbps regular hub-managed object class.

A.4.4   Management Information Trees

Getting lost in OSI terminology and definitions of the various hierarchical structures—literally losing the forest for the trees—is all too easy. So far we have talked about the development of managed object

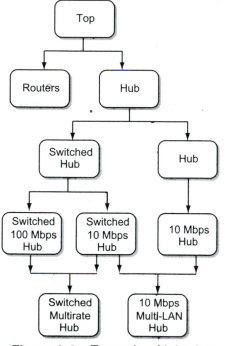

Figure A.6   Example of Inheritance

classes, which is done by using the *inheritance tree.* The object instances have to be uniquely identified, which is done by using the *naming tree.* Once a managed object class has been developed and instances have been given names, they have to be registered with a central authority, which is done by using the *registration tree,* so that they can be universally used.

The Inheritance Tree. The **inheritance tree** defines the relationship between subclasses and superclasses. Because the properties of a subclass are derived from a superclass, a subclass may be considered a subset or specialization of the superclass. We have discussed three categories of inheritance. *Single inheritance* derives its properties from a single superclass. *Multiple inheritance* of a subclass derives its properties from more than one superclass. Care must be taken in developing multiple inheritances so that no conflict exists between the properties of the superclasses being used to derive the subclass. The third category is a special case, called *allomorphism,* in which a subclass derived from multiple superclasses takes on the properties of one of the superclasses. It may be considered as a pointer to a superclass.

The Naming Tree. The **naming tree** is used in the naming of a managed object, which is a specific instance of a managed object class, to give it a unique identification. This procedure is very similar to the OBJECT IDENTIFIER and DESCRIPTOR, using MIB, in SNMP management.

Names are uniquely specified in terms of a **superior** or **context object**. Objects named in terms of another object are called **subordinate objects** and are contained in a **superior object**. Because a subordinate object is contained in a superior object, the naming tree is also called a **containment tree**.

An example of contained managed objects is shown in Figure A.7. The top level of the naming tree is the *root.* Here, *system* is the superior object and *log, alarmRecord,* and *eventforwardingDiscriminator* are objects subordinate to it. Both *log* and *alarmRecord* are subordinated objects under the context name *system.*

A managed object is identified by a name in the naming tree by either its absolute position in the naming tree with a **global name**, such as OSI or with respect to the context object either with a **relative distinguished name** or a **local distinguished name**. Table A.2 illustrates the naming convention for the example shown in Figure A.7. The local context name *system* is used here for illustration. Figure A.7 and Table A.2 present the name attribute of the managed object and the value of the type of that

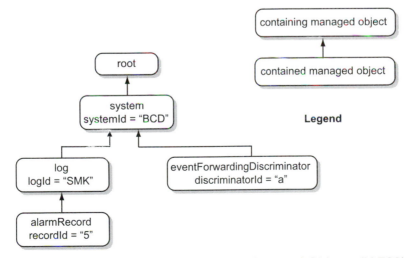

Figure A.7 Example of Contained Managed Objects (X.720)

Table A.2   Relative Distinguished Names Example

RELATIVE DISTINGUISHED NAME	LOCAL DISTINGUISHED NAME
systemId = "BDC"	{ }
logId = "SMK"	{logId = "SMK"}
recordId = "5"	{logId = "SMK", recordId = "5"}

attribute. Thus, the local distinguished name for *alarmRecord* is the sequence of attributes starting with the context name system and is {*logId* = "SMK", *recordId* = "5"}, and the relative distinguished name is *recordId* = "5". The implication is that the relative distinguished name reflects the system context name. Notice that the local distinguished name is a sequence of names and hence is bounded by braces, { }.

A subordinate object under a superior object in a naming tree does not imply that the managed object represented by the subordinate object is contained in the superior object class. The inheritance relationship between superclass and subclass is distinct from the name-binding relationship in the naming tree.

Registration Tree. The **registration tree** is used for officially registering the managed object classes (from the inheritance tree), names of the managed objects (used in the naming tree), attribute definitions, attribute groups, action types, notifications, and packages. The OSI management tree shown in Figure 3.8 has been extended to partially include the registration tree, as shown in Figure A.8. The managed classes, attributes, actions, notifications, and packages developed in the X.700/ISO 10165 series fall under the arc (node) *smi*, structure of management information. It is under the management standard *ms* node. The node *smase* (system management application service entity) and *cmip* are the other two nodes under ms.

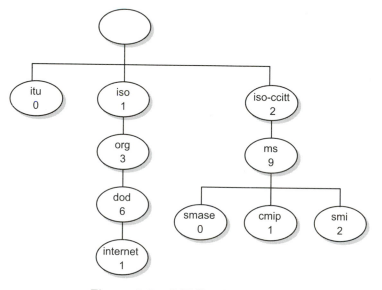

Figure A.8   OSI Registration Tree

A.4.5   Guidelines for Definition of Managed Object Templates

The technique used to specify managed objects in OSI management uses templates and is referred to as **Guidelines for Definition of Managed Objects (GDMO)**. GDMO can be viewed as a set of forms with a list of properties that can be filled with values. See the OSI 10165-4/ITU X.722 standard and Raman [1998] for a detailed discussion of GDMO.

An example of a managed object class using a template for a managed class extracted from X.722 is shown in Figure A.9. The mnemonic name of the managed object class is *lamp*. The MANAGED OBJECT CLASS is the keyword that defines the managed object class.

The DERIVED CLASS identifies the source document and the relationship to either a superclass or subclass. In the example, *lamp* is derived from *top*. It may not always be present, but at least the alternate managed object class in the hierarchy should contain it. Thus, to trace the hierarchy of the managed object class, you may have to trace through a sequence of templates. This procedure is similar to naming of children down the generations in some parts of the world, as in Tamil Nadu, India, where the author was born. The last name of the child (Subramanian in the case of the author) is the given name and the first name is the father's given name. Thus, to trace a name you have to trace through each generation of the family hierarchy.

The construct CHARACTERIZED BY identifies the mandatory packages and properties. In this example, the *lampPackage* is the mandatory package, and the properties associated with it are part of its template definition.

The CONDITIONAL PACKAGES define the optional packages included in the managed object class. The *intensityPackage* is a conditional package and is present only if the defined condition on *resourceSupportsIntensity* is satisfied.

The REGISTERED AS construct defines the official registered name of the managed object class. Here, *lamp* is defined in the registration tree under *gdmoPlusExamplesModule*.

A.5   COMMUNICATION MODEL

We presented the high-level representation of the OSI communication architecture in Section A.2 and Figure A.3. The manager and agent application processes use seven messages to communicate with each other. The application process interfaces with the application entity sublayer that is above the presentation layer. The communication protocol used for intersystem communication is the Common Management Information Protocol (CMIP). The communication model deals with the application entity layer and the intersystem message protocol.

```
lamp  MANAGED OBJECT CLASS
        DERIVED FROM   "ITU-T Rec. X.721 (1992) | ISO/IEC 1Q165-2 : top;
        CHARACTERIZED BY    lampPackage
        CONDITIONAL PACKAGES    intensityPackage PRESENT IF
                (resourceSupportsIntensity(self ()->lampId);
REGISTERED AS
        {gdmoPlusExamplesModule.lampObjectIdentifier managedObjectClass (3)
        lamp(0)}
```

Figure A.9   Example of the OSI Managed Object Class Template

A.5.1 System Management Application Entity

A management application, the System Management Application Process (SMAP) communicates with another management application by invoking System Management Application Entity (SMAE), as shown in Figure A.10. The SMAE comprises several service entity modules. The System Management Application Service Entity module (SMASE) services the five management applications: configuration, fault, performance, security, and accounting.

The CMISE handles the communications function for SMASE, using the CMIP. The Association Control Service Element (ACSE) sets up and coordinates the activities of setting up and releasing an

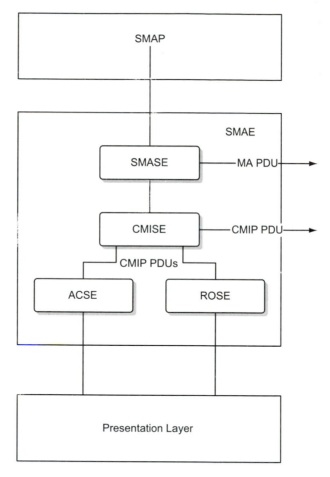

SMAP: Systems Management Application Process
SMAE: Systems Management Application Entity
SMASE: Systems Management Application Service Element
CMISE: Common Management Information Service Entity
CMIP: Common Management Information Protocol
ROSE: Remote Operations Service Element
ACSE: Association Control Service Element

Figure A.10 OSI Network Communications Model

association with the application. Once the association has been set up, the data move from the CMISE to the remote system via the Remote Operation Service Element (ROSE). ROSE issues requests to a remote system and receives responses in an asynchronous mode. In other words, a request may be issued and followed by other requests and the responses correlated with the corresponding requests.

Figure A.11 shows the interoperability of two applications in two remote systems for the OSI network communication model shown in Figure A.10. Communication between SMASE entities exchange management application protocol data units (MA PDU). CMIP PDUs are exchanged between CMISE entities.

Common Management Information Service Elements. We introduced the seven services (or messages) offered by CMISE in Section A.2. The CMISE model consists of two submodels. In the first, the manager sends a command to an agent and may expect one or more responses from the agent, which is called operations. The second submodel is concerned with an unsolicited message from an agent, which may expect confirmation from the manager, and is called notifications.

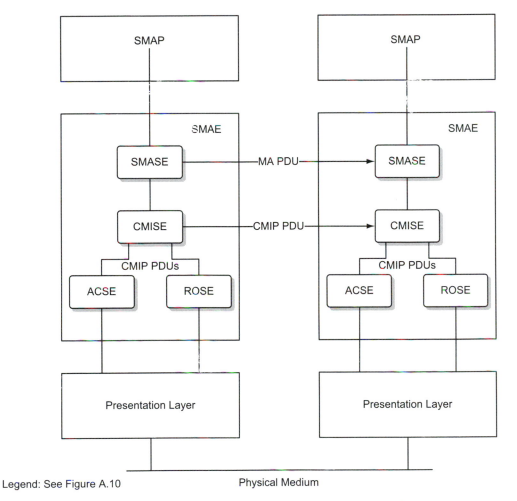

Figure A.11 OSI Interoperability Communication Model

The commands M-GET, M-SET, M-ACTION, M-CREATE, M-DELETE, and M-CANCEL-GET are operations. The event M-EVENT-REPORT belongs to notifications. The M in all the operation and notification command names stands for *management.* The *get, create, delete,* and *cancel-get* operations expect confirmations or responses, called *confirmed services.* A response may be multiple. For example, the GET command associated with a multiple management object class (called *scope*) could invoke multiple responses.

The operations *set* and *action*, as well as the notifications *event-report*, may or may not require responses or acknowledgements. They can be either confirmed or unconfirmed services. The requirement for confirmation depends on the type of operations or notifications, and the data format should specify it. The CMISE services and CMIP operation values are listed in Table A.3, along with a brief description of each service.

Common Management Information Protocol. The CMIP is the communication interface with the CMISE. It generates a PDU for a message. The PDU format generated by CMIP is a modification of the generic ROSE PDU format, and is shown in Figure A.12. The invoke ID field is the PDU identifier and is used in correlating the response. The operation value is determined by the appropriate operation/notification from Table A.3. For example, the *get* operation will have an operation value of 3. The next two fields in the CMIP PDU are the managed object class and the managed object instance. The term *base object* is used in connection with retrieval of multiple objects associated with the scope clause in which multiple objects could be retrieved using the **get** command by specifying a base object. The information field is a group of fields describing operation-specific data.

A.6 APPLICATION FUNCTIONS MANAGEMENT

OSI management had paid specific attention to the development of management applications (functional model), which motivated development of the rest of the OSI management models. Application functions management can be compartmentalized, as shown in Figure A.13, as management application functional areas, system management functions (SMFs), and CMISEs, which we discussed in

Table A.3 CMISE Services and CMIP Operation Values

SERVICE	OPERATION VALUE CONFIRMED/UNCONFIRMED	DESCRIPTION
M-EVENT-REPORT	0/1	Send notifications to another open system
Multiple responses	2	Not a CMISE service, but used with scope
M-GET	3	Retrieve attributes and values from managed objects
M-SET	4/5	Set or modify attributes
M-ACTION	6/7	Initiate action in a managed object
M-CREATE	8	Request an open system to create a managed object
M-DELETE	9	Request an open system to delete managed objects
M-CANCEL-GET	10	Command to cancel a previously sent M-GET service

Invoke Id	Operation Value	Managed/ Base Object Value	Managed/ Base Object Instance	Information

Figure A.12   CMIP PDU

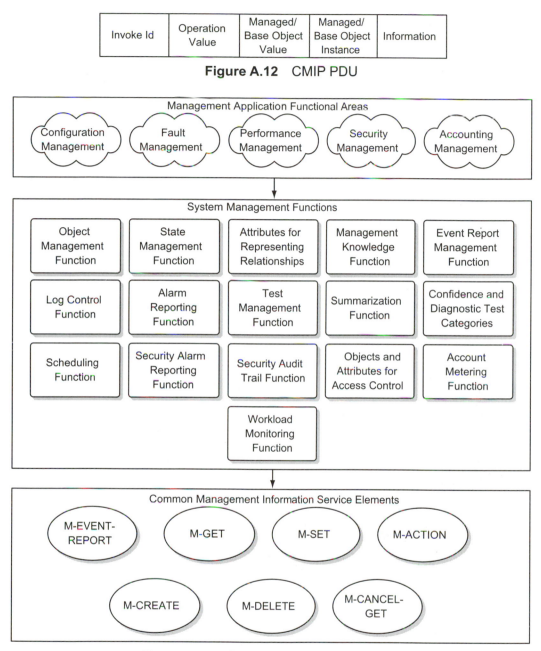

Figure A.13   Functions Management Model

Section A.5. Management application functions invoke SMFs, which in turn utilize the common management information services to execute applications.

The five system application functional areas are configuration, fault, performance, security, and accounting. They are represented as clouds in Figure A.13 because the functional areas overlap. For example, packet loss in a network could be classified under both fault and performance management.

They may even use common management functions. Hence, OSI specifications for SMFs are for primitive service functions.

The SMFs are abstract specifications, more like requirements of the functions needed to implement the applications. They are shown under SMFs in Figure A.13. The purpose of most of the functions can be inferred from the title. The object management function, state management function, and attributes for representing relationships are concerned with the configuration of managed objects. The management knowledge function exchanges information between systems.

The event report management function, log control function, alarm reporting function, test management function, and confidence and diagnostic test categories are oriented toward fault administration and notifications. The summarization function could be used for fault management, as in trouble ticket administration, or for performance management, as with statistics. This function preprocesses and compresses the data prior to transmission.

The SMFs related to security management applications are the security alarm reporting function, security audit trail function, and objects and attributes for access control. The account metering function and workload monitoring function are oriented toward accounting management. The scheduling function is a general SMF used to schedule operations.

The third compartment in Figure A.13 identifies the common management service elements invoked by the SMFs to perform the tasks. They are the seven CMISE services: M-EVENT-REPORT, M-GET, M-SET, M-ACTION, M-CREATE, M-DELETE, and M-CANCEL-GET.

◼ Summary

In this appendix we presented an overview of OSI management. We discussed the complexity and flexibility of object-oriented OSI management and compared it, where appropriate, to the simpler scalar-oriented SNMP/Internet management. OSI management is based on the Common Management Information Protocol/Common Management Information Service Elements (CMIP/CMISE). We identified the service elements of a common management information service and explained how they are used.

Our discussion of the information model dealt with managed object classes and instances. They are derived by using the inheritance tree in the OSI management information model. The naming tree is used to name managed objects, and the registration tree registers the names of managed object classes.

The OSI communication model dealt with the CMISE and CMIP. We looked at the lower- and upper-layer profiles used in OSI management and the role of the Association Control Service Element (ACSE) in establishing and releasing application associations across systems. The Remote Operations Service Element (ROSE) performs the exchange of data after the ACSE has established the associations.

The five management application functional areas of configuration, fault, performance, security, and accounting utilize the system management functions, which in turn invoke the common management information services to execute tasks.

Project Suggestions

B.1   PROJECT STRUCTURE AND EVALUATION

We are presenting a suggestion list for projects to accompany the course. Most of these projects have been undertaken by students in the past 3 years, who have found them interesting. Each project is expected to take 20 to 30 hours of student time. The projects can be done as individual or group projects. If the project is done as a group, there should be a clear distinction of each student's contribution for grading purposes. The group comprises typically 2–4 students. I strongly recommend a presentation of the project to the class by each individual or group at the end of the course. The presentation is limited to 10–15 minutes. Laboratory or software projects are presented to the instructor outside of the presentation.

A possible way of structuring the project is to allow students to pick a project from the list or come up with their own suggestion. The students are expected to select a project and their partners in the first few weeks of the course. An outline of the projects with deliverables is expected during the middle of the quarter/semester. The final report is due a week before the end of the quarter/semester.

The grading criteria for the project are creativity, content, report (organization and completeness), and presentation.

B.2   PROJECTS

1. SNMP is a poll-based network management system:
   There are open-source SNMP stacks available on the Internet. Choose one of them and develop a polling engine for an NMS. The student should do a performance evaluation of the engine.
2. Laboratory setup of a managed LAN with low-end NMS (e.g., OpenNMS):
   Students load PCs with the operating system with TCP/IP stack. They set up multiple LANs using a hub. An NMS is loaded on a PC, which then manages the LANs. Several management applications are practiced.
3. Laboratory setup of a managed virtual LAN with low-end NMS:
   Multiple LANs are set up as VLANs and a network management system is set up to manage them. This project can also be done as a special report expanding the role of VLANs.
4. Set up an enterprise NMS by downloading several of the open-source NMSs available on the Internet. Perform fault and performance management. This usually requires the student to have had some prior experience with a UNIX system. This can be combined with another group setting up the LANs.

5. Configuring system management—Big Brother/Spong:
   Big Brother or Spong can be downloaded and configured to manage systems in local networks. Interesting modifications can be done to the original systems in this project.

6. Web-based management:
   This popular project is done by several groups, each one implementing a different version of Web-based management. This project can be a software development project or a theoretical one in depth.

   A Web interface can be added to an existing SNMP management system. A Web-interface module to an HP OpenView Network Node Manager is available and has been tried in this project. Other variations are possibilities in this approach. The whole project can be done from scratch starting with an SNMP tool.

   For advanced computer science classes, try experimenting with XML schema and CORBA-based NM.

7. Traffic measurement using MRTG:
   MRTG freeware can be downloaded and set up on a host to measure the traffic at an interface of a network component.

8. HFC management:
   This area of network management affords numerous opportunities for hands-on-project if facilities exist. Fault localization is a challenge in this project. A study—both analytical and laboratory, including QoS management for broadband—is an opportunity here.

9. ADSL management:
   A wealth of ADSL projects can be undertaken both as a laboratory project, as well as theoretical study project. In addition, it can be extended to other DSL technologies.

10. Set up a management system for a WiFi network.

11. Use of Tcl/Tk for network management:
    The scripting tool in general is an area of study for a project in network management. Specifically, Tcl/Tk [Zeltserman and Puoplo, 1998] is very useful as a management tool.

12. Event correlation:
    We have dealt with several technologies for event correlation. The implementation of any one would be an interesting project.

13. RMON:
    A simple RMON tool, for example *tcpdump*, can be implemented to do statistical measurement and analysis of the type of traffic.

14. Software simulation:
    Many of the above projects could be simulated using common tools and could be an exciting way to accomplish a laboratory project when the facilities are lacking. Research network simulation tools that are available as freeware to use in this project.

15. Develop an SNMP trap simulator for SNMP versions and acquire them using one of the NMS projects or a commercially available NMS.

Laboratory Tutorial

This tutorial gives a hands-on experience to the students learning basic networking tools and SNMP-based tools.

C.1   NETWORK BASIC TOOLS LAB

Read about functions and the use of the following basic network tool commands. You can invoke **man commandname** to obtain the manual page of a command in a UNIX system.

1. ping
2. traceroute
3. nslookup
4. host
5. dig

Use these commands in the Lab to do the following practice exercises. You may create your own additional exercises and be prepared to discuss them in class.

1. Choose any IP address in your subnet or outside and find the name of the host.
2. Ping at least two public institutions' addresses inside and outside India. Analyse your results and note the significant points.

Execute **traceroute** to the following IP addresses and analyze:
www.gatech.edu
ns1.bangla.net

C.2   SNMP TOOLS LAB

This lab is designed to learn the SNMP-testing tools. Many tools are available on public domain.

- The SNMP test tool is an interactive tool to obtain values of several managed objects, one at a time.
- Get, Get-next, and Set are the SNMP commands that we learned under SNMP architecture/messages. Execution of these will return an SNMP Response message. Pay particular attention to index and instance in this exercise.
- SNMPWalk uses snmpgetnext to trace the entire MIB. A network status command is used to test the status of network connections of a host.

Exercise the following test tools:

- snmptest
- snmpget
- snmpgetnext
- snmpset
- snmptrap
- snmpwalk
- snmpnetstat

C.3   SNMP APPLICATIONS

Apply the SNMP tools you have learned to the following applications.

Application 1: Choose any three hosts and determine which of the hosts has been running the longest.

Application 2: Use SNMP *system* MIB and find all the information about the hosts that you used in Application 1.

Application 3: Acquire the routing table of a router using IP MIB and find out the approximate size of the table.

Application 4: Your instructor has set the snmpd.conf table in a host with different community users accessing different profiles of information from the database.

Inspect the configuration file (/etc/snmpd.conf) for the SNMP daemon running on the host. Attempt an snmpwalk using each of the community names it defines. Compare the amount of information available with each.

Application 5: Your instructor will give you MIB views for different groups of users. Modify the snmpd.conf table to implement those views.

Spread Spectrum Technology: OFDM

Orthogonal Frequency Division Multiplexing (OFDM) is a modulation scheme that comprises multicarrier, multisymbol, and multirate techniques using spread spectrum technology. It is converged technologies of spread spectrum, Fast Fourier Transform (FFT), and multiple input multiple output (MIMO) antennae.

Broadband services require transmission of modulation of broadband signal at a high digital data rate. Due to frequency selective fading, the digital pulses in the time domain are spread out, interfering with neighboring digits and thus causing inter-symbol interference (ISI). This is shown in Figure D.1.

The basic principle of operation of OFDM is to divide the broadband-modulated carrier into narrowband segments. All the narrowband segments are transmitted in parallel over subcarrier channels. Since the fading is flat over a narrow band, there is less distortion of the signal and hence, less ISI. Instead of modulating a single carrier at the rate of R symbols per second (sps), each of the N subcarriers separated by about R/N Hz are modulated and each symbol is transmitted at R/N sps. This is shown in Figure D.2. Figure D.2(a) shows the single carrier modulation, and Figure D.2(b) shows the multicarrier for the same digital signal. Figure D.3 shows the system representation of multicarrier multisymbol OFDM at the transmitting end. The multicarrier system could be further improved by making each subcarrier orthogonal to others.

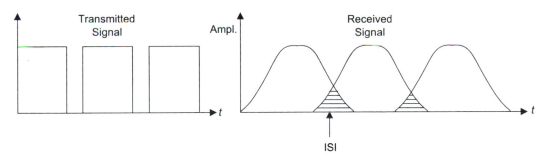

Figure D.1   Inter-Symbol Interference (ISI)

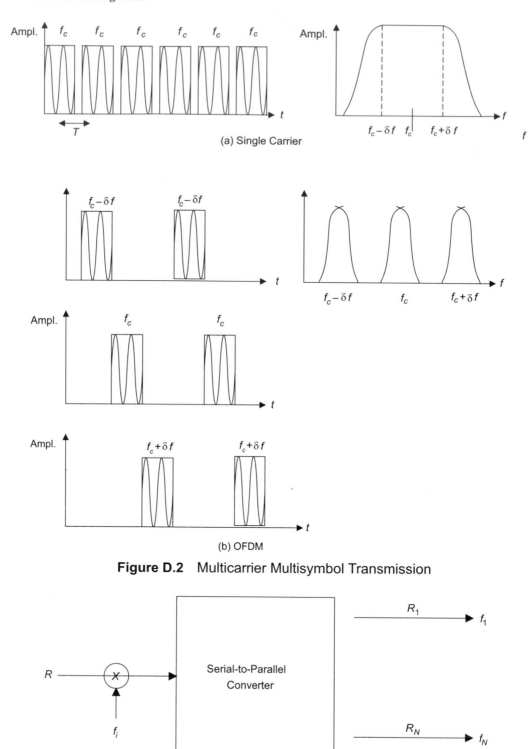

Figure D.2 Multicarrier Multisymbol Transmission

Figure D.3 Multicarrier Multisymbol System

D.1 FOURIER TRANSFORMATION

Any periodic signal $x(t)$, which repeats itself with a period T, can be decomposed into an infinite number of frequency components with fundamental frequency

$$f_o = 1/T_0 \quad \text{and} \quad \omega_0 = 2\pi f_0 = 2\pi/T_0$$

and its harmonics

$$f_n = n/T_0 = nf_0 \quad \text{where } n = 1, -2, \ldots \quad \text{and}$$

$$\omega_n = n\omega_0 = n2\pi f_0$$

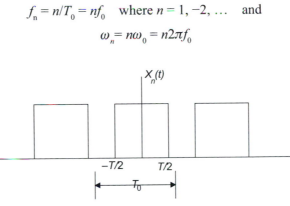

(a) Pulse train

(b) Sinc function

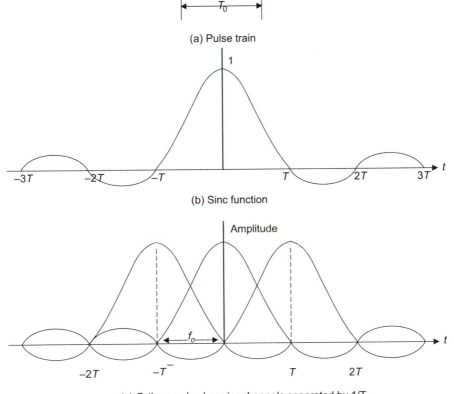

(c) Orthogonal subcarrier channels separated by 1/T

Figure D.4 OFDM

The decomposed representation in the frequency spectrum is defined as the Fourier series. The Fourier series can be written as:

$$X(t) = a_0/2 + a_1 \cos \omega_1 t + a_2 \cos 2\omega_1 t + \cdots + b_1 \sin \omega_1 t + b_2 \sin 2\omega_1 t + \cdots$$

where a_n and b_n are coefficients of harmonic terms.

Figure D.4 (a) shows a pulse train $x_n(t)$ of amplitude A, pulse width T, and periodicity of T_0. This can be shown using Fourier analysis [Forouzan, 2006]:

$$X_n(t) = \sum_{n=\infty}^{\infty} C_n(e^{j\omega nt}) \, dt$$

where

$$C_n = (AT/T_0) \sin (\pi nT/T_0) / (\pi nT/T_0) = (AT/T_0) \, \text{sinc} \, (nT/T_0)$$

We define a sinc function, where

$$\text{Sinc} \, (nT/T_0) = \sin\pi \, (nT/T_0)/\pi(nT/T_0)$$

The value of the sinc function $\sin (\pi x)/(\pi x)$ equals 1 at $x = 0$ and equals 0 at $x = 1, 2, 3,...$, which are integral multiples of T. The sinc function is shown in Figure D.4 (b). The Fourier spectrum of $x_n(t)$ is often used as a measure of the signal bandwidth $1/T$ in Hertz for a pulse train with pulse width T.

We can observe from Figure D.4(b) that if the subcarrier frequencies are separated by the periodicity $f_c = 1/T$, they will all be orthogonal to each other. This is the basic concept of OFDM. The multicarrier transmission, classified as OFDM, mitigates ISI.

Trademarks

ITEM	(REGISTERED) TRADEMARK OF
AdvanceStack	Hewlett-Packard Company
Big Brother	Big Brother Software
CiscoWorks	Cisco Systems, Inc
CRITTER	Cabletron Systems
CygNet	NMSWorks Software Pvt. Ltd.
FireWire	Apple Computer
HP 9000	Hewlett-Packard Company
HP AdvanceStack Assistant	Hewlett-Packard Company
InCharge	System Management ARTS
Internet Explorer	Microsoft Corporation
Java	Sun Microsystems, Inc.
Microsoft Windows	Microsoft Corporation
NerveCenter	Seagate Software
NetMetrix	Hewlett-Packard Company
NetView	IBM Corporation
Network Node Manager	Hewlett-Packard Company
OpenView	Hewlett-Packard Company
Real World Interface	Computer Associates, Inc.
RSA	RSA Data Security, Inc.
Sniffer	Network Associates
Spectrum	Cabletron Systems
Sun Sparc	Sun Microsystems, Inc.
TME 10 / NetView	Tivoli Systems, Inc.
Unicenter/TNG	Computer Associates, Inc.
UNIX	AT&T Bell Laboratories
Windows Management Instrumentation	Microsoft Corporation
Windows	Microsoft Corporation

Acronyms

3GPP	Third Generation Partnership Project
3GPP2	Third Generation Partnership Project in US
AAA	Authentication, Authorization, and Accounting
ACSE	Application Control Service Element
ADSL	Asymmetric Digital Subscriber Line
ANSI	American National Standards Institute
ASK	Amplitude Shift Keying
ASN.1	Abstract Syntax Notation One
ATM	Asynchronous Transfer Mode
ATU	ADSL Transmission Unit
ATU-C	ATU at the Central Office/Network End
ATU-R	ATU at the Remote/Customer Premises End
BWA	Broadband Wireless Access
BER	Basic Encoding Rules
BER	Bit Error Rate
BERT	Bit Error Rate Tester
BISDN	Broadband ISDN
CAP	Carrierless Amplitude Phase modulation
CAPWAP	Configuration and Provisioning of Wireless Access Point
CBC	Cipher Block Chaining
CBR	Case-Based Reasoning
CCITT	International Telegraph and Telephone Consultative Committee
CEBus	Consumer Electronic Bus
CIM	Common Information Model
CIMOM	CIM Object Manager
CLI	Command Line Interface
CLTS	Connectionless Transport Service
CMIP	Common Management Information Protocol

CMIS	Common Management Information Service
CMISE	Common Management Information Service Element
CMTS	Cable Modem Terminating System
COM	Component Object Model
COPS	Common Open Policy Service
CORBA	Common Object Request Broker Architecture
COTS	Connection-Oriented Transport Service
CPE	Customer Premises Equipment
CSMA/CA	Carrier Sensing Multiple Access with Collision Avoidance
CSMA/CD	Carrier Sensing Multiple Access with Collision Detection
DBMS	Database Management System
DCE	Data Circuit-Terminating Equipment
DCE	Distributed Computing Environment
DCF	Distributed Communication Function in TMN
DCF	Distributed Coordination Function in 802.11
DCN	Data Communications Network
DCOM	Distributed Component Object Model
DDD	Direct Distance Dialing
DES	Data Encryption Standard
DHCP	Dynamic Host Configuration Protocol
DLL	Data Link Layer
DMI	Desktop Management Interface
DMTF	Desktop Management Task Force
DOCS	Data-Over-Cable System
DOCSIS	Data-Over-Cable System Interface Specifications
DOM	Document Object Model
DTE	Data Terminating Equipment
DSL	Digital Subscriber Line
DSLAM	Digital Subscriber Line Access Multiplexer
DWDM	Dense Wavelength Division Multiplexer
EAP	Extensible Authentication Protocol
EGP	External Gateway Protocol
EIA	Electrical Industries Association
ELAN	Emulated Local Area Network
EMS	Element Management System, Enterprise Management System

EPON	Ethernet PON
eTOM	Enhanced Telecom Operations Map
FCAPS	Fault, Configuration, Accounting, Performance, and Security
FDDI	Fiber Distributed Data Interface
FEC	Forward Error Correction
FSK	Frequency Shift Keying
FTAM	File Transfer and Access Management
FTP	File Transfer Protocol
FTTN	Fiber to the Neighborhood
GDMO	Guidelines for Definition of Managed Objects
GMPLS	Generalized MPLS
GUI	Graphical User Interface
HAVi	Home Audio–Video Interoperability
HCF	Hybrid Control Function
HDSL	High Data Rate Digital Subscriber Line
HFC	Hybrid Fiber Coaxial cable
HMAC	Hashed Message Access Code
HTML	Hypertext Markup Language
HTTP	Hypertext Transfer Protocol
IAB	Internet Advisory Board
IANA	Internet Assigned Numbers Authority
ICMP	Internet Control Message Protocol
IDEA	International Data Encryption Algorithm
IDL	Interface Definition Language
IEEE	Institute of Electrical and Electronic Engineers
IETF	Internet Engineering Task Force
IGP	Internal Gateway Protocol
IIOP	Internet Inter-Orb Protocol
ILMI	Integrated Local Management Interface
IP	Internet Protocol
IPC	Inter-Processor Communication
IrDA	Infrared Data Association
IRTF	Internet Research Task Force
ISDN	Integrated Services Digital Network
ISO	International Organization for Standardization

ITU	International Telecommunications Union
ITU-T	ITU—Telecommunications Sector
JDBC	Java Database Connectivity
JDMK	Java Dynamic Management Kit
JIDM	Joint Inter-Domain Management
JMAPI	Java Management Application Interface
JVM	Java Virtual Machine
JMX	Java Management Extensions
LAN	Local Area Network
LANE	Local Area Network Emulation
LLC	Logical Link Control
LMDS	Local Multipoint Distribution Service
MAC	Medium Access Control
MAN	Metropolitan Area Network
MBR	Model-Based Reasoning
MCNS	Multimedia Cable Network System
MD	Message Digest
MF	Mediation Function in TMN
MIB	Management Information Base
MIME	Multipurpose Internet Mail Extensions
MIMO	Multiple Input Multiple Output
MIT	Management Information Tree
MMDS	Multichannel Multipoint Distribution Service
MOM	Manager of Managers
MOTIS	Message Oriented Text Interchange Standard
MPLS	Multiprotocol Label Switching
MRTG	Multi Router Traffic Grapher
MSO	Multiple Systems Operator
MSSP	Multiservice Switching Platform
MTNM	Multitechnology Network Management
MTOSI	Multitechnology Operations System Interface
MUWS	Management Using Web Service
NAT	Network Address Translator
NGN	Next Generation Network

NGOSS	New Generation OSS
NID	Network Interface Device
NIU	Network Interface Unit
NMF	Network Management Forum
NMS	Network Management System
NOC	Network Operations Center
OAM	Operation, Administration, and Maintenance
OAMP	Operation, Administration, Maintenance, and Provisioning
OASIS	Organization for the Advancement of Structured Information Services
OC	Optical Carrier
ODBC	Open Database Connectivity
OFDM	Orthogonal Frequency Division Multiplexing
OLT	Optical Line Termination
ONU	Optical Network Unit
OS	Operations System
OS	Operating System
OSF	Operation System Function in TMN
OSF	Open Systems Foundation
OSGi	Open Service Gateway Initiative
OSI	Open System Interface
OSPF	Open Shortest Path First
OSS	Operations Support System
PAN	Personal Area Network
PBX	Private Branch eXchange
PCI	Protocol Control Information
PCF	Point Coordination Function
PDU	Packet Data Unit
PEM	Privacy Enhanced Mail
PGP	Pretty Good Privacy
PING	Packet Internet Groper
PON	Passive Optical Network
PPP	Point-to-Point Protocol
QAF	Q-Adapter Function in TMN
QoS	Quality of Service
RADIUS	Remote Authentication Dial In User Service

RBR	Rule-Based Reasoning
RF	Radio Frequency
RFC	Request for Comments
RIP	Routing Information Protocol
RMI	Remote Method Invocation
RMON	Remote Monitoring
ROSE	Remote Operation Service Element
RPC	Remote Procedure Call
RSA	Rivest, Shamir, and Adleman (Cryptographic Algorithm)
SDH	Synchronous Digital Hierarchy
SDU	Service Data Unit
SGMP	Simple Gateway Monitoring Protocol
SHS	Secure Hash Standard
SLA	Service Level Agreement
SMAE	System Management Application Entity
SAX	Simple API for XML
SMAP	System Management Application Process
SMASE	System Management Application Service Entity
SMF	System Management Function
SMI	Structure of Management Information
SMTP	Simple Mail Transport Protocol
SNCIP	Subnetwork-Independent Convergence Protocol
SNDAP	Subnetwork-Dependent Access Protocol
SNDCP	Subnetwork-Dependent Convergence Protocol
SNMP	Simple Network Management Protocol
SOA	Service Oriented Architecture
SOAP	Simple Object Access Protocol
SONET	Synchronous Optical NETwork
SPF	Shortest Path First
STS	Synchronous Transport Signal
TCP	Transmission Control Protocol
TDM	Time Division Multiplexing
TDMA	Time Division Multiple Access
TE	Traffic Engineering
TMF	TeleManagement Forum

TMN	Telecommunications Management Network
TR	Token Ring
UDDI	Universal Description, Discovery, and Integration of Web Services
UDP	User Datagram Protocol
UI	User Interface
UNI	User Network Interface
UPnP	Universal Plug and Play
USB	Universal Serial Bus
URL	Universal Resource Locator
USM	User-Based Security Model
UWB	Ultra-Wide Band
VACM	View-Based Access Control Model
VDSL	Very High Data Rate Digital Subscriber Line
VLAN	Virtual Local Area Network
VT	Virtual Terminal
W3C	World Wide Web Consortium
WAN	Wide Area Network
WBEM	Web-Based Enterprise Management
WBM	Web-Based Management
WCS	Wireless Communication Service
WEP	Wired Equivalency Protocol
WPA	WiFi Protected Access
WiFi	Trade name for Wireless LAN
WIMA	Web-Based Integrated Management Architecture
WiMax	Worldwide Interoperability for Microwave Access
WLAN	Wireless LAN
WSDL	Web Services Definition Language
WSF	Workstation Function in TMN
WMI	Windows Management Interface
XML	Extensible Markup Language
XPath	XML Filter
XSL	XML Style Sheet
XSLT	XML Transformer to Other Documents

Glossary

Abstract Syntax Notation (ASN.1)   A formalized syntax language used to define managed objects.

Access Mode   The MIB access privilege defined in an SNMP agent based on community name to a network element—read only or read-write.

Access Policy   A pairing of an SNMP community name with an SNMP community profile is defined as SNMP access policy.

Accounting Management   Administration of cost allocation of the usage of network resources.

Agent Module   A management software module resident in a network component that can be queried for information by another software module resident in network manager. The agent module can also generate and transmit information in an unsolicited manner. These are called notifications (traps in SNMPv1).

Aggregate Managed Object   A group of related managed objects. It is represented by a conceptual table of rows, each row comprising a list of scalar managed objects. The columns of the table are columnar objects, with each row being an instance of the entry. This group is distinct from MIB groups.

Amplitude Shift Keying (ASK)   A digital-to-analog modulation scheme in which the carrier is amplitude modulated.

Application Control Service Element (ACSE)   Sets up and coordinates the activities of setting up and releasing an association with an application. This is used in conjunction with ROSE in OSI management.

Asymmetric Digital Subscriber Line (ADSL)   Digital subscriber line that carries multimedia information from the central office to the customer premises. The downstream and upstream frequencies are different, hence the term asymmetric.

Asynchronous Transfer Mode (ATM)   A cell-based technology that is used to transport digital data. A switch that switches ATM protocol is called ATM switch.

ATM Forum   An industry-sponsored international organization accelerating cooperation on ATM technology.

ADSL Transmission Unit (ATU)   ATU is an ADSL modem. ATU-C is located at the central office and ATU-R is at the remote (customer premises) site.

Authentication Key   A secret key derived from a chosen password of the user (SNMPv3) that is used in authenticating the legitimacy of the user accessing a secure system.

Autodiscovery   In a network management system, the process of discovering the components of a network automatically, usually using the ping commands. This is done when the system is turned on and during maintenance on a scheduled basis.

Basic Encoding Rules (BER)   The encoding rules used to code ASN.1 syntax defined objects. SNMP message is encoded in BER using type, length, and value (TLV).

Beacon   A management enabling stations to establish and maintain communications in an ad-hoc wireless network in an orderly fashion.

Bridge   A device that connects two LANs at the data link layer.

Broadband Networks   Broadband networks are multimedia networks that provide integrated services of voice, video, and data over the same medium. It is the short form for broadband ISDN (BISDN). The network comprises WAN using ATM technology and the local loop based on cable, digital subscriber line, and wireless technologies. The services offered are referred to as broadband services.

Cable Modem   A device used in broadband services that modulates and demodulates from the customer equipment to the radio frequency signal that is carried on the cable.

Case-based Reasoning   A paradigm used in network management that is based on comparing a problem to previously encountered cases to derive the cause of the problem.

Cipher Block Chaining Method of Data Encryption Standard (CBC-DES)   A symmetric encryption protocol recommended in SNMPv3 for secure communication.

Codebook   In network management, codebook is a matrix of problems and symptoms that is generated modeling the network. Multiple symptoms are correlated to isolate the root cause of the problem.

Common Management Information Protocol (CMIP)   OSI standard management protocol, which is object-oriented.

Common Management Information Service (CMIS)   A management service function provided in OSI management that uses CMIP protocol. CMISE is a CMIS Element.

Community   Pairing of two SNMP entities that can communicate with each other is called an SNMP com-munity and is given a name *community name*. All SNMP entities with the same community name can communicate with each other. A pairing of MIB view with SNMP access mode is called *community profile*.

Compliance   Defined in SNMPv2 as the minimum set of modules and mandatory groups that should be implemented in an SNMP entity for it to be declared compatible with SNMP.

Configuration Management   Setting and changing of configuration of networks and network components.

Conformance   SNMPv2 defines conformance in units of OBJECT-GROUPS. The SNMP conformance of a product is specified including compliance modules and additional OBJECT-GROUPS.

Common Object Request Broker Architecture (CORBA)   CORBA standard provides a communication bus for distributed applications to interact over the network.

CORBA Management Technology   Object-oriented CORBA-based technology for implementation of distributed management application architecture.

CORBA Agent   A server with IDL interfaces for each GDMO.

CORBA-based Manager   A network manager with distributed management applications.

Counter   An SNMP application-wide data type, whose value is a non-negative integer. Its value is monotonically increasing and wraps around when it reaches a maximum value.

Customer Premises Equipment (CPE)   Any equipment in the customer or subscriber premises, which is connected to the service provider network. The CPE network interfaces to the service provider network at the "demarcation point."

Dense Wavelength Division Multiplexer (DWDM)   Wavelength Division Multiplexer is add–drop Optical signal multiplexer. DWDM was developed for erbium-doped fiber amplifiers (EDFAs), which is an economical system.

DESCRIPTOR   Defines a unique mnemonic name for an object type and begins with lower case letter.

Digital Subscriber Line Access Multiplexer (DSLAM)   A device at the central office that multiplexes several ATU-C modems.

Digital Subscriber Line (DSL)   Transmission link (loop) between the central office and the customer premises that carries information in a digital format. There are several implementations of DSL: Asymmetric DSL, in which the upstream and downstream bands are different; HDSL is high data rate DSL, which offers symmetric service at a higher data rate; VDSL, very high data rate DSL is asymmetric at a very high data rate (up to 52 Mbps).

Digital Over Cable System Interface Specifications (DOCSIS)   Specifications for cable modem access technology approved by the MCNS industry consortium.

Discovery   A process in network management system that discovers network elements and builds an inventory of network elements and links. See autodiscovery.

Dynamic Host Configuration Protocol   Converts and dynamically allocates global IP address to local IP address in local networks.

Element Management System (EMS)   Lowest level in management hierarchy that manages the network elements directly.

Emulated LAN (ELAN)   Emulated LAN is an ATM network configured as a LAN and coexists with Ethernet LAN.

Ethernet   A LAN based on bus architecture that uses CSMA/CD medium access protocol and operates at 10 Mbps speed. Fast Ethernet functions at 100 Mbps and Gigabit Ethernet at 1 Gbps.

eXtensible Markup Language (XML)   A markup language for document exchange in the Web.

Fast Channel   In ADSL, the channel that handles audio and real-time video with fast buffers.

Fault Management   Detection and isolation of the problem causing the failure in the network.

Fiber Distributed Data Interface (FDDI)   A LAN based on token-ring technology that uses fiber medium and operates at 100 Mbps. It can be implemented as either a single or a dual ring configuration.

Forward Equivalent Class (FEC)   FEC is used to map forwarding of a packet to a next hop port in a router.

Gateway   A router that connects two networks and can perform protocol conversion.

Gauge   An SNMP application-wide data type, whose value is a non-negative integer. Its value can move either up or down and pegs at a maximum value.

Get-Bulk-Request   An SNMP message issued by the manager to an agent to retrieve a group of managed objects and their values in bulk.

Get-Next-Request   An SNMP message issued by the manager to an agent to retrieve the object ID and the value of the next managed object in the MIB.

Get-Request   An SNMP message issued by the manager to an agent to retrieve the value of a managed object.

Get-Response   An SNMP message issued by an agent to a manager in response to either a get or set request message. It is simply called response in SNMPv2.

Guidelines for Definition of Managed Objects (GDMO) The technique that is adopted to specify managed objects in OSI management using templates.

Half Bridge/Half Router Provides a method to connect a LAN via a bridge to a router. This configura-tion is deployed for access to service provider by small office–home office customer on an as-required basis using a dial-up link.

High Data Rate Digital Subscriber Line (HDSL) Digital subscriber line that operates in duplex mode at T1 or E1 rate.

HMAC Protocols The authentication protocols used for authentication scheme in security management. It is based on hashing algorithm (H) to derive message access code (MAC). Two common algorithms used in SNMP security management are HMAC-MD5-96 and HMAC-SHA-96.

HomePlug HomePlug, also known as PLC (Power Line Communication), distributes data over power line in the house.

HomePNA HomePNA (Home Phoneline Network Alliance) is a technology that can distribute broadband over the phone line in the house.

Hub A LAN in a box. It is a hybrid of star topology with either Ethernet or token-ring configuration inside the hub.

Hybrid Fiber Coaxial Cable (HFC) Technology The HFC technology is based on multimedia services provided over the television cable system. It is also called cable modem technology.

Inform-Request An SNMPv2 message from a manager to another manager.

Inheritance In OSI network management, managed object classes are inherited from other managed objects. There are several categories of inheritance, such as single inheritance and multiple inheritance.

Instructional Scientific and Medical Service (ISM) A wireless transmission system that operates over two frequency bands (902–928 MHz) and (2400–2483.5 MHz) with a range of 0.5 and 15 miles, respectively.

Integrated Local Management Interface (ILMI) A management interface between two ATM interface management entities (IMFs) that provides view of configuration and fault parameters across user network interface (UNI).

Integrated Services Digital Network (ISDN) Integrated voice and digital services over a single medium. Narrow-band ISDN, referred to as basic rate, carries two channels. Broadband ISDN, or simply broadband services, is a cell-based technology at high data rate.

Interleaved Channel In ADSL, the channel that handles data signal, which can tolerate latency and hence interleaved between the fast channel signal.

Internet A worldwide network that is based on TCP/IP suite of protocols.

IpAddress An SNMP application-wide data type that defines four groups of dotted decimal notation of IPv4.

Java Management Extensions (JMX) A Java-based management architecture proposed by Sun Microsystems.

Label Distribution Protocol (LDP) LDP is the protocol used by egress LSR to notify LSP to all the affected routers.

Label Switching Path (LSP) End-to-end path of an MPLS circuit.

Label Switching Router (LSR) A router capable of supporting MPLS protocol.

Local Area Network (LAN)　A LAN is a shared medium serving many DTEs located in close proximity, as in a building or a campus environment.

Local Multipoint Distribution System (LMDS)　A wireless transmission system that operates over two frequency bands (27,500–28,350 MHz) and (31,000–31,000 MHz) with a range of about 3 miles.

M-ACTION　An OSI management service element that performs operation in managed objects and sends confirmations on an optional basis.

Managed Object　Commonly, a network element that can be managed remotely by network management system. In TCP/IP-based network management, it consists of object type and object instance. A rigor-ous definition of a managed object is that it is a node in the MIB that could be either a physical or a logical entity.

Managed Object Class　An object-oriented definition of managed objects in OSI network management.

Management Information Base (MIB)　A management information tree containing Internet management objects. A management object holds a unique position and ID in the MIB. The portion of the MIB that a network element permits an SNMP agent to access is called MIB view.

Management Information Tree　A hierarchical tree structure used to organize managed objects and object classes. It is called MIB.in SNMP and naming tree or containment tree in OSI.

Management Using Web Services (MUWS)　Use of Web services for a system management framework.

Management of Web Services (MOWS)　Management model to manage Web services.

M-CANCEL-GET　An OSI management service element that cancels a request message.

M-CREATE　An OSI management service element that creates a management object class.

M-DELETE　An OSI management service element that deletes a management object class.

Media Access Control Protocol　Lower sublayer protocol in OSI layer 2 that interfaces with the physical layer protocol.

Metropolitan Area Network (MAN)　It can be defined as that segment of the network that connects the wide area network to the broadband access network. There are wired and wireless MANs. While the latter is actually access network for the metropolitan area, the former is concerned with extending the WAN closer to the head end of the access network.

M-EVENT-REPORT　An OSI management service element that generates unsolicited notifications to another open system.

M-GET　An OSI management service element that retrieves attributes and values from managed objects.

MIB Browser　An SNMP tool to browse through the MIB. It is also called MIB walk.

M-interface　Five interfaces M1–M5 are defined between network management system and either private or public networks for management of telecommunication networks including ATM networks.

MODULE-IDENTITY　An ASN.1 macro that describes the semantics of an information module in ASN.1 syntax.

M-SET　An OSI management service element that sets or modifies attributes of managed objects.

Multichannel Multipoint Distribution Service (MMDS)　A wireless transmission system that operates over the frequency band of 2500–2686 MHz with a range of up to 35 miles.

Multiple Systems Operator (MSO) MSO is a service provider, which owns and operates several cable television systems and used to provide primarily cable TV service. MSOs are now providing broadband services over cable.

Multiprotocol Label Switching (MPLS) Network MPLS is a WAN technology that replaces IP and ATM networks. It combines the richness of IP and the performance of ATM networks

Multiprotocol Label Switching (MPLS) Label A label is a short, fixed length, locally significant identifier, which is used to identify a FEC.

Multitechnology Network Management (MTNM) A management system that manages network of multitechnology multivendor network elements.

Multitechnology OSI (MTOSI) A TM Forum standard for framework for OS-OS integration.

Network Address Translator Converts global IP to local IP address.

Network Interface Device/Unit (NID/NIU) A device at the customer premises, which is the demarcation point between the customer network and service provider network.

Network Management System (NMS) A platform that houses the network manager module. It monitors and controls the network components from a centralized operation.

NMS Server A platform in which NMS software runs in a server–client architecture.

NMS Client A client platform, which accesses NMS server remotely and performs operations on it. An HTML browser can be used as an NMS client.

Network Operations Center (NOC) A centralized operation to monitor and manage the network using network management tools and systems.

NOTIFICATION-TYPE An ASN.1 macro of notification, which is an event or alarm generated by a network management agent and sent to a network management system in SNMPv2 and SNMPv3. It is termed as TRAP-TYPE in SNMPv1.

OAMP (Traditionally OAM&P) Operations, Administration, Maintenance, and Provisioning functions in the telecommunications industry.

Object An object type, and associated instance.

Object Identifier Identifies an object type and is a node in the MIB. It is described in terms of a sequence of numbers or DESCRIPTORs that describes its position in the MIB, or abbreviated by the name of a reference object type followed by a sequence of numbers from that node.

Object Type The component of the managed object that is defined by SMI and in the MIB. In TCP/IP management, it consists of an object identifier defined by ASN.1 syntax OBJECT-TYPE, and encoded using BER. It does not include object instance.

Open Service Gateway Initiative (OSGi) A residential software platform that acts as a gateway to residential network. It supports integration of different home networking technologies and delivery of different services and components, called bundles, from service providers.

Operations System (OS) Operations system, in the telecommunications industry, is used to control the network and network elements. The term is used in ADSL technology and TMN. The operations system does not directly play a role in the information transfer, but helps in the OAMP of network and information systems.

Optical Carrier (OC) The data rate unit of SONET (OC-n) digital hierarchy in the USA. The data rate is 51.84 Mbps.

Optical Line Termination (OLT) Termination point at the central office of PON link.

Optical Network Unit (ONU) Demarcation point between access network and home network in PON. The ONU may contain a passive or active element that divides access network into individual subscriber cables.

Passive Optical Network (PON) Fiber access network in broadband system.

Performance Management Monitoring and management of performance parameters of network and network components.

Personal Area Network (PAN) There are several wireless personal area networks, each for a specific application and primarily used at residences for short range. Bluetooth is the most popular one, which is specified in IEEE 802.15.1 and is in the unlicensed spectrum of 2.4 GHz. PAN with network control applications for home devices that require low data rate, are specified in IEEE 802.15.4

Phase Shift Keying (PSK) A digital-to-analog modulation scheme in which the phase of the carrier signal is modulated.

Ping A network tool to test the connectivity to a remote device.

Protocol Converter A node in a network, which does protocol conversion at layers above the network layer. It is similar to the gateway, which does protocol conversion at the network layer.

Proxy Server An SNMP device that converts any protocol to an SNMP-compatible MIB and protocol. It is also used to convert SNMPv1 to SNMPv2 protocol.

Quadrature Amplitude Modulation (QAM) A digital-to-analog modulation scheme in which the carrier is modulated with a combination of amplitude and phase modulation. It is used in HFC and ADSL access technologies.

Quadrature Phase Shift Keying (QPSK) A digital-to-analog modulation scheme in which the phase of the carrier signal is modulated based on four levels of the signal represented by four phase states. It is used in HFC technology.

Rediscovery Periodic check by NMS for the configuration change in the network.

Remote Monitoring (RMON) Remotely monitoring the network with a probe is termed RMON. The monitored information, gathered and analyzed by RMON, is transmitted to a remote network management system. RMON1 deals with the data link control layer and RMON2 covers all the higher layers.

Remote Operation Service Element (ROSE) Issues request to remote system and receives responses in an asynchronous mode. This module is used in conjunction with ACSE in OSI management.

Residential Gateway The gateway component that is between the access network and home network. It handles primarily the communication interface and can also have application modules in it.

Response An SNMP message in SNMPv2. See Get-response.

Root Cause Analysis (RCA) RCA correlates multiple alarms from a single fault, localizes the problem, shows the primary alarm, and suppresses secondary alarms.

Router A device that does the routing function of packets in a network.

Rule-based Reasoning An if-then paradigm used in network management that is based on comparing a problem to previously encountered situations to arrive at the source of the problem.

Security Management Securing legal access to network resources and protecting the information during transfer of data from modification of information, masquerade, message stream modification, and disclosure.

Service Level Agreement (SLA)   SLA is a part of a service contract where the level of service, such as service availability and performance, is formally defined and agreed upon between the service provider and subscriber or customer.

Set-Request   An SNMP message from a manager to an agent to set the parameters of a network element.

Simple Network Management Protocol (SNMP)   Internet/TCP-IP-based network management protocol.

Single Line Digital Subscriber Line (SDSL)   A high data rate digital subscriber line in which two-way duplex communication occurs over a single twisted pair.

SNMP Framework   Defines a version of SNMP and comprises subsystems and models. SNMP Frameworks are specified for SNMPv1, SNMPv2, and SNMPv3.

Source Routing Bridged Network   A network based on token-ring bridges, in which the source node determines the path of the packet.

Spectrum Management System   In HFC link management, a system that deals with the management of RF spectrum allocated to different digital services, both in the upstream and downstream.

Structure of Management Information (SMI)   Definitions for the structure of management information. It defines managed objects and their characteristics, as well as the relationship between the objects.

Switch   A device that switches analog and digital data.

Synchronous Digital Hierarchy (SDH)   The name used in Europe for the digital hierarchy that is used in ATM network. The data rate is an integral multiple of 51.84 Mbps. Equivalent name in United States is SONET.

Synchronous Optical Network (SONET)   The name used in United States for the digital hierarchy (OC-n) that is used in ATM network. The basic SONET rate (OC-3) is 155.52 Mbps and is three times that of the basic optical carrier (OC-1) of 51.84 Mbps. Equivalent term in Europe is SDH.

Synchronous Transport Signal (STS)   The data rate unit of SDH (STS-n) digital hierarchy in Europe. The data rate is 51.84 Mbps.

System Network Architecture   IBM proprietary network architecture.

Tcpdump   A network tool to monitor the IP packets in a network. A similar tool is called a sniffer.

Telecommunications Management Network (TMN)   The management of telecommunications network was developed by International Standards Organization as part of ISO management. Hence, it is strongly based on ISO network management.

Topology   A map of the interconnections between routers and switches. Topology representation is done at the network layer (layer 3) or the data link layer (layer 2).

Time Division Multiplexing (TDM)   Mode of transmission in which signals are assigned time-divided slots in multiplexing in TDM systems.

Time Division Multiple Access (TDMA)   TDMA is normally used for carrying information from multiple stations to the head end. The individual station information is multiplexed with others under the control of the head end.

TimeTicks   An SNMP application-wide data type, which measures time in units of hundredths of a second.

TMF 814   A standard protocol between EMS and NMS that is specified by the TM Forum.

Traceroute   A UNIX network tool to test the route to a remote device. A similar tool in Microsoft Windows in *tracert*.

Traffic Engineering (TE)   Configuration of traffic flow that is concerned with performance optimization of operational networks.

Transparent Bridged Network   A network of Ethernet-based bridges with a tree topology.

Transport Control Protocol/Internet Protocol (TCP/IP)   A suite of transport-layer/network-layer protocols that forms the basis for Internet network.

Trap   An alarm or an event generated by a management agent and sent unsolicited to a network management system.

Ultra Wide Band (UWB)   A personal area network carrying information in a very high bandwidth spectrum at 3–10 GHz band that is least impacted by noise.

Universal Serial Bus (USB)   A high data rate serial interface out of PC. USB hub multiple interfaces from a single interface.

User-based Security Model (USM)   The security subsystem specified in SNMPv3 that is based on the traditional user name concept.

Very High Data Rate Digital Subscriber Line (VDSL)   VDSL is similar to ADSL and operates at a very high data rate over shorter lines.

Very Small Aperture Terminal (VSAT)   VSAT is direct transmission to home using geosynchronous satellite. It is more used to access difficult-to-access remote sites and back-up link by service providers.

View-based Access Control Model (VACM)   The access control scheme defined in SNMPv3 that is more secure and flexible than the simple access policy defined in SNMPv1.

Virtual LAN (VLAN)   Virtual LAN is a LAN that is based on switched hub technology and enables sta-tions to be assigned to different LANs administratively. They are not restrained by the physical configuration of LAN networks.

Web-based Enterprise Management (WBEM)   A project undertaken by Desk Top Management Task Force to bring different management systems under one umbrella using Microsoft object-oriented framework, Common Information Module.

Wavelength Division Multiplexer (WDM)   is multiplexing at optical wavelength and is identical to fre-quency division multiplexing at (relatively) lower frequencies. Information can be transmitted over multiple wavelengths using multiple transmission protocols.

WiFi   Commercial name for WLAN using IEEE 802.11a/b/g protocols.

WiFi Protected Access (WPA)   Enhanced security protocol for WiFi network.

Wired Equivalency protocol (WEP)   Early version of security protocol for WiFi network.

Wireless LAN   Wireless LAN with IEEE 802.11a/b/g interface.

WiMax   (Worldwide Interoperability for Microwave Access) A common name for Wireless Metropolitan Area Network (MAN) using IEEE 802.16 protocol.

XML-based Network Management   A management architecture comprising XML-based agent in devices and XML-based NMS with communication transported using XML over HTTP.

REFERENCES

3GPP: Standards organization associated with ITU.

3GPP2: Standards organization in North America.

802.11 1999: IEEE 802.11 WG, Reference number ISO/IEC 8802-11:1999 (E) IEEE STD 802.11, 1999 edition. International Standard [for] Information Technology—Telecommunications and Information Exchange Between Systems—Local and Metropolitan Area Networks—Specific Requirements—Part 11: Wireless LAN Medium Access Control (MAC) and Physical Layer (PHY) Specifications, 1999.

802.11e: IEEE 802.11 WG, Draft Supplement to Standard for Telecommunications and Information Exchange Between Systems—LAN/MAN Specific Requirements—Part 11: Wireless Medium Access Control (MAC) and Physical Layer (PHY) Specifications: Medium Access Control (MAC) Enhancements for Quality of Service (QoS), IEEE 802.11e/Draft 4.2, February 2003.

Adams, Elizabeth K. and Willetts, Keith J., *The Lean Communications Provider: Surviving the Shakeout Through Service Management Excellence*, New York: McGraw-Hill, 1996.

ADSL2: ADSL2 and ADSL2+—The New ADSL Standards, *DSL Forum White Paper*, March 25, 2003.

Aggarwal, R., Kompella, K., Nadeau, T., and Swallow, G., "BFD for MPLS LSPs", draft-ietf-bfd-mpls-07.txt, June 20, 2008.

Ahmed, Masuma and Vecchi, Mario P., "Definitions of Managed Objects for HFC RF Spectrum Management Version 2.0," *RF Spectrum Management MIB*, April 21, 1995.

AT&T 1977: AT&T: *Telecommunications Transmission Engineering, Vol. 3, Networks and Services*, 2nd Edition, Winston-Salem, NC: American Telephone and Telegraph Co., 1977.

Autrata, Matthias and Strutt, Colin, "DME Framework and Design," *Network and Distributed Systems Management*, Morris Sloman (ed.), Workingham, England: Addison-Wesley, 1994.

Bahrami, A., *Object Oriental Systems Development*, Irwin McGraw-Hill, 1999.

Bhattacharya, K., Rani, N. Usha, Gonsalves, Timothy A., and Murthy, Hema A., "An Efficient Algorithm for Root Cause Analysis," in *Proceedings of the NCC-05 11th National Conference on Communications*, IIT Kharagpur, India, January 2005, pp. 447–451.

Black, Uyless, *Network Management Standards*, 2nd Edition, McGraw-Hill, Inc., 1995.

CA: "Unicenter TNG Framework," *Computer Associates*, Available from: http://www.cai.com/products/unicent/framework/tng_framework_overview.htm, 1997.

Cassel, Lillian N. and Austing, Richard H., *Computer Networks and Open Systems—A Top-Down Approach*, Available from: http://www.csc.vill.edu/~cassel/netbook, 1996.

Cavendish, Dirceu, Ohta, Hiroshi, and Rakotoranto, Hari, "Operations, Administration, and Maintenance in MPLS Networks," *IEEE Communications Magazine*, October 2004.

Chapman, D. Brent, "Network (In)Security Through IP Filtering," in *USENIX Security Symposium III Proceedings*, Baltimore, MD, September 14–16, 1992.

Chou, Joey, *et al.*, "MAC and PHY MIB for WirelessMAN and WirelessHUMAN BS and SS," *IEEE C802.16mgt-04/04r1*, July 7, 2004.

CIM: Desktop Management Task Force, "Common Information Model: Core Model White Paper, Version 2.0," Available from: http:///www.dmtf.org/, 1999.

Cisco/MPLS-TE: "Advanced Topics in MPLS-TE Deployment," *Cisco Systems White Paper*, 2002.

Cisco/RMON: Available from: http://www.cisco.com/warp/public/cc/cisco/mkt/enm/cwsiman/tech/rmon2_wp.html.

Cohen, R.S., "The Telecommunications Management Network," *Network and Distributed Systems Management*, Morris Sloman (ed.), Workingham, England: Addison-Wesley, 1994.

Cooper, Frederic J., *et. al.*, *Implementing Internet Security*, New Indianapolis, IN: Riders Publishing, 1995.

Cozens, Simon, "Beginning Perl," Available from: http://www.perl.org/books/beginning-perl.

Cronk, R., Callahan, P., and Berstein, L., "Rule-based Expert Systems for Network Management Operations: An Introduction," *IEEE Network Magazine*, September 1988.

Davis, A.W., "Cable Modems: A High-Bandwidth Solution to Internet Access," Desktop Video Communications, January–February 1998.

Diffe, W. and Hellman, M.E., "New Directions in Cryptography," *IEEE Transactions on Information Theory*, Vol. 22, No. 6, 1976.

Dini, Petre, Hasan, Masum Z., Morrow, Monique, Parr, Gerard, and Rolin, Pierre, "IP/MPLS OAM Challenges and Directions," *0-7803-8836-4/04/IEEE*, 2004.

DMI/SNMP: "DMI to SNMP Mapping Standard," *Desktop Management Task Force*, Version 1.0, Available from: ftp://ftp.dmtf.org or http://www.dmtf.org, November 1997.

Drevers, Thomas, "Performance of Web Services-Based Network Monitoring," *Thesis for a Master of Science Degree in Telematics*, University of Twente, Enschede, The Netherlands, January 5, 2004.

Dudzinski, Krzysztof and Bozier, Michele, "Extension of wmanIfMib for Improved Manageability of 802.16d," *IEEE c802.16f-04/03*, October 28, 2004.

Effenberger, Frank, Kramer, Glen, and Hesse, Bernd, "Passive Optical Network Update," *IEEE Communications Magazine*, March 2007.

Eklund, Carl, Marks, Roger B., Stanwood, Kenneth L., and Wang, Stanley, "IEEE Standard 802.16: A Technical Overview of the WirelessMAN™ Air Interface for Broadband Wireless Access," *IEEE Communications Magazine*, June 2002.

Fatato, Massimo, "Modeling Telecommunications Networks' Transmission Systems," *IEEE Communications Magazine*, March 1996.

Feldmeir, John, "Network Traffic Management," *Unix Review*, November 1997.

Forouzan, Behrouz A., *Data Communications and Networking*, 4th Edition, New Delhi, India: Tata McGraw-Hill, 2006.

G.774.01: G.774.01 SDH Performance Monitoring for the Network Element View.

G.774.02: SDH Configuration of the Payload Structure for the Network Element View.

G.774.03: SDH Management of Multiplex Section Protection for the Network Element View.

G.774.04: SDH Management of Subnetwork Connection Protection from the Network Element View.

G.774.05: SDH Management of the Connection Supervision Functionality (HCS/LCS) for the Network Element View.

G.774: SDH Information Model for the Network Element View.

G.784: Synchronous Digital Hierarchy (SDH) Management.

G.831: Management Capabilities of Transport Network Based on the SDH.

Gast, Matthew, *802.11 Wireless Networks: The Definitive Guide*, 2nd Edition, O'Reilly Media, Inc., 2005.

Glitho, Roch H. and Hayes, Stephen, "Approaches for Introducing TMN in Legacy Networks: A Critical Look," *IEEE Communications Magazine*, September 1996.

Glitho, Roch H. and Hayes, Stephen, "Telecommunications Management Network: Vision vs. Reality," *IEEE Communications Magazine*, March 1995.

Gonsalves, T.A., Jhunjhunwala, A., Murthy, Hema A., *et. al.*, "CygNet: An Integrated Management for Modern Telecom Networks," in *Proceedings of the NCC-2000 6th National Conference on Communications*, Delhi, India, January 2000.

Goralski, Walter, *ADSL and DSL Technologies*, New York, NY: McGraw-Hill, 2001.

Hajela, Sujai, "HP OEMF: Alarm Management in Telecommunications Networks," *Hewlett-Packard Journal*, October 1996.

Heilbronner, Stephen and Wies, Rene, "Managing PC Networks," *IEEE Communications Magazine*, October 1997.

Hong, James Won-Ki, *et. al.*, "Web-Based Intranet Services and Network Management," *IEEE Communications Magazine*, October 1997.

Horowitz, E., Sahni, S., and Mehta, D., "Fundamentals of Data Structures in C++," W.H. Freeman, 1995.

Howell, Ric, "WAP Security," Available from: www.vbxml.com/wap/articles/wap_security.

ITU G.992.3: ITU-T Recommendation G.992.3, Asymmetric Digital Subscriber Line Transceivers 2 (ADSL2), Approved 2005.

ITU G.992.4: ITU-T Recommendation G.992.4, Splitterless Asymmetric Digital Subscriber Line Transceivers 2 (Splitterless ADSL2), Approved 2005.

ITU G.992.5: ITU-T Recommendation G.992.5, Asymmetric Digital Subscriber Line (ADSL) Transceivers—Extended Bandwidth ADSL2 (ADSL2plus), Approved 2005.

ITU G.993.2: ITU-T Recommendation G.993.2, Very High Speed Digital Subscriber Line Transceivers 2 (VDSL2), Approved 2006.

ITU X.25: ITU-T Recommendation X.25, Approved October 1996.

Jagadish, C. and Gonsalves, T.A., "Distributed Control of Event Floods in a Large Telecom Network," *International Journal of Network Management*, 2009a.

Jagadish, C. and Gonsalves, T.A., "Distributed Control of Performance Traffic with Accuracy Objects," *International Journal of Network Management*, 2009b.

JIDM: Available from: www.opengroup.org/external/jidm/.

JMX WP: "Java Management Extensions White Paper," Available from: http://java.sun.com/products/Java-Management/, June 15, 1999.

Ju, H.T., Choi, M.J., and Hong, J.W., "EWS-based Management Application Interface and Integration Mechanisms for Web-based Element Management," *Journal of Network and Systems Management*, Vol. 9, No. 1, 2001, pp. 31–50.

Ju, H.T., Choi, M.J., Han, S.H., Oh, Y.J., Yoon, J.H., Lee, H.J., and Hong, J.W.K., "An Embedded Web Server Architecture for XML-based Network Management," in *Proceedings of the IEEE/IFIP Network Operations and Management Symposium (NOMS 2002)*, Florence, Italy, April 2002, pp.1–14.

Kaufman, Charlie, Perlman, Radia, and Speciner, Mike, *Network Security: Private Communication in a PUBLIC World*, Upper Saddle River, NJ: Prentice-Hall PTR, 1995.

Kerry, Stuart J. and O'Hara, Bob, "IEEE 802.11 Management Information Base," members.cruzio.com/~jeffl/crud/IEEE802dot11-MIB, November 2002.

Keshav, S., *An Engineering Approach to Computer Networking: ATM Networks, The Internet, and The Telephone Network*, Reading, MA, Addison-Wesley Publishing Company, 1997.

Kliger, S., Yemini, S., Yemini, Y., Ohsie, D., and Stolfo, S., "A Coding Approach to Event Correlations," in *Proceedings of the Fourth International Symposium on Integrated Network Management*, Munich, Germany, 1995.

Kolodner, Janet, *Case-base Reasoning*, San Mateo, CA: Morgan Kaufman Publishers, Inc., 1997.

Larmouth, John, *Understanding OSI,* University of Salford, Available from: http://www.salford.ac.uk/iti/books/osi, November 1997.

Leinwand, Allan and Conroy, Karen Fang, *Network Management: A Practical Perspective*, 2nd Edition, Addison Wesley Longman, Inc., 1996.

Lewis, Lundy, "A Case-based Reasoning Approach to the Management of Faults in Communication Networks," in *Proceedings of the IEEE Infocom '93*, Vol. 3, San Francisco, CA, March 28–April 1, 1993.

Lewis, Lundy, "A Fuzzy Logic Representation of Knowledge for Detecting/Correcting Network Performance Deficiencies," *Network Management and Control*, Frisch, Ivan T., Malek, Manu, and Panwar Shivendra S. (eds), Vol. 2, New York and London: Plenum Press, 1994.

Lewis, Lundy, *Managing Computer Networks: A Case-based Reasoning Approach*, Norwood, MA: Artech House Publishers, 1995.

Lewis, Lundy, "Implementing Policy in Enterprise Networks," *IEEE Communications Magazine*, January 1996.

Lewis, Lundy, *Service Level Management for Enterprise Networks*, Norwood, MA: Artech House Publishers, 1999.

Lidie, Steven and Walsh, Nancy, *Mastering Perl/TK*, O'Reilly Associates, 2002.

Liu, Kevin H., *IP over WDM*, John Wiley & Sons, 2002.

M.3010: (CCITT) ITU_T Recommendation M.3010, "Principles of Telecommunications Management Network (TMN)," December 1991.

M.3020: (CCITT) ITU_T Recommendation M.3020, "TMN Management Services: Overview," 1992.

M.3040: ITU-T Recommendation M.3400, TMN Management Functions, 2000.

M.3050 Sup 3: ITU-T Recommendation M.3050 Enhanced Telecom Operations Map (eTOM) Supplement 3 eTOM to M.3400 Mapping.

M.3050.0: ITU-T Recommendation M.3050.0, Enhanced Telecom Operations Map (eTOM)—Introduction, 2004.

M.3050.1: ITU-T Recommendation M.3050.1, Enhanced Telecom Operations Map (eTOM)—The Business Process Framework, 2004.

M.3050.2: ITU-T Recommendation M.3050.2, Enhanced Telecom Operations Map (eTOM)—Process Decompositions and Descriptions, 2004.

M.3050.3: ITU-T Recommendation M.3050.3, Enhanced Telecom Operations Map (eTOM)—Representative Process Flows, 2004.

M.3200: ITU-T Recommendation M.3200, TMN Management Services and Telecommunications Managed Areas: Overview, 1997.

MacGuire, Sean, "Big Brother: A Web-based Systems and Network Monitoring and Notification System," Available from: http://www.maclawran.ca/bb/bb-info.html.

Madanagopal, R., Rani, N. Usha, Gonsalves, T.A., "Path Computation Algorithms for Dynamic Service Provisioning in SDH Networks," in *Proceedings of the 10th IEEE/IFIP International Symposium. Integrated Network Management (IM 2007)*, Munich, Germany, May 2007, pp. 206–215.

Martin-Flatin, J.P., Bovet, M., Hubaux, J.P., "Active Technologies for Network and Service Management," Stadler, R. and Stiller, B. (eds), in *Proceedings of 10th IFIP/IEEE International Workshop on Distributed Systems: Operations and Management (DSOM '99)*, Zurich, Switzerland, 1999, pp 164–178.

Martin-Flatin, J.P., Push vs. Pull in Web-based Network Management, Sloman, M., Mazumdar, S., and Lupu, E. (eds), in *Proceedings of IFIP/IEEE International Symposium of Integrated Management (IM '99)*, Boston, MA, May 1999.

Maurer, Herman A., *Data Structures and Programming Techniques*, Translated by Camille C Price, Englewood Cliffs, NJ: Prentice-Hall, Inc., 1977.

Menten, Lawrence E., Bell Laboratories, "Experiences in the Application of XML for Device Management," IEEE Communications Magazine, July 2004.

Meyer, K., Erlinger, M., Betser, J., Sunshine, C., Goldszmidt, G., and Yemini, Y., "Decentralizing Control and Intelligence in Network Management," in *Proceedings of the 4th International Symposium on Integrated Network Management*, Munich, Germany, May 1995.

Miller, Raymond E., "Passive Testing of Networks Using a CFSM Specification," in *Proceedings of the 1998 IEEE International Performance, Computing, and Communications Conference,* February 1998.

Morris, Stephen, *Network Management, MIBs and MPLS: Principles, Design and Implementation*, Pearson, 2004.

Nadeau, Thomas D., Morrow, Monique, Swallow, George, and Satoru, Matsushima, *Operations and Management Requirements for Multiprotocol Label Switched Networks*, Available from: draft-ietf-mpls-oam-requirements-07.txt, December 2005.

Ni, Qiang, Romdhani, Lamia, and Turletti, Thierry, "A Survey of QoS Enhancements for IEEE 802.11 Wireless LAN," *Journal of Wireless Communications and Mobile Computing*, Vol. 4, No. 5, 2004, pp. 547–566.

NIST, "Keeping Your Site Comfortably Secure: An Introduction to Internet Firewalls," Available from: http://csrc.ncsl.nist.gov/nistpubs/800-10.ps, December 1994.

NMF, "A Technical Strategy: Implementing TMN using OMNIPoint", *Network Management Forum*, 1994.

NMRG, "Delta OID Compression Techniques: Internet Drafts Produced by the IRTF NMRG", Available from: http://www.ibr.cs.tu-bs.de/projects/nmrg/.

Oetiker, Tobias and Rand, Dave, "Multi Router Traffic Grapher," Available from: http://ee-staff.ethz.ch/~oetiker/webtools/mrtg/mrtg.html.

Pahlavan, Kaveh and Krishnamurthy, Prashant, "Principles of Wireless Networks," New Delhi, India: Pearson, 2002.

Pavlou, George, Aidarous, S., and Plevyak, T. (eds), "OSI Systems Management, Internet SNMP and ODP/OMG CORBA as Technologies for Telecommunications Network Management," *Telecommunications Network Management: Technologies and Implementations*, IEEE Press, 1998.

Pavlou, George, Flegkas, Paris, Gooveris, Stelios, and Liotta, Antonio, "On Management Technologies and the Potential of Web Services," University of Surrey, *IEEE Communications Magazine*, July 2004.

Perkins, David and McGinnis, Evan, *Understanding SNMP MIBs,* Upper Saddle River, NJ: Prentice-Hall PTR, 1997.

Piscitello, David M. and Chapin, A. Lyman, *Open Systems Networking: TCP/IP and OSI,* Reading, MA: Addison-Wesley Publishing Company, 1993.

Pras, Aiko, Drevers, Thomas, van de Meent, Remco, and Quartel, Dick, "Comparing the Performance of SNMP and Web Services-based Management," *Etransactions on Network and Service Management*, Fall 2004.

Raman, Lakshmi G., "OSI Systems and Network Management," *IEEE Communications Magazine*, March 1998.

Raman, Lakshmi G., *Fundamentals of Telecommunications Network Management*, Piscataway, NJ: IEEE Press, 1999.

Ramaswami, Rajiv and Sivarajan, Kumar N., *Optical Networks: Practical Perspective*, 2nd Edition, New Delhi, India: Morgan Kaufman Publishers, 2002.

RFC 854: Postel, J. and Reynolds, J.K., "Telnet Protocol Specifications," May 1, 1983.

RFC 1155: Rose, M. and McCloghrie, K., "Structure and Identification of Management Information for TCP/IP-based Internets," May 1990.

RFC 1157: Case, J., Fedor, M., Schoffstall, M., and Davin, J., "A Simple Network Management Protocol," May 1990 (Historic).

RFC 1212: Rose, M. and McCloghrie, K., "Concise MIB Definitions," March 1991.

RFC 1213: Rose, M., "Management Information Base for Network Management of TC/IP-based Internets: MIB-II," March 1991.

RFC 1215: Rose, M., "A Convention for Defining Traps for Use with the SNMP," March 1991.

RFC 1253: Baker, F. and Coltun, R., "OSPF Version 2 Management Information Base," August 1991.

RFC 1284: Cook, J., "Definitions of Managed Objects for the Ethernet-like Interface Types," December 1991.

RFC 1285: Case, J., "FDDI Management Information Base," January 1992.

RFC 1354: Baker, F., "IP Forwarding Table MIB," July 1992.

RFC 1398: Kastenholz, F., "Definitions of Managed Objects for the Ethernet-like Interface Types," January 1993.

RFC 1406: Baker, F. and Watt, J. (eds), "Definitions of Managed Objects for the DS1 and E1 Interface Types," January 1993.

RFC 1407: Cox, T.A. and Tesink, K., "Definitions of Managed Objects for the DS3/E3 Interface Type," January 1994.

RFC 1421: Linn, J., "Privacy Enhancement for Internet Electronic Mail: Part I—Message Encryption and Authentication Procedures," February 1993.

RFC 1422: Kent, S., "Privacy Enhancement for Internet Electronic Mail: Part II—Certificate-based Key Management," February 1993.

RFC 1423: Balenson, D., "Privacy Enhancement for Internet Electronic Mail: Part III—Algorithms, Modes, and Identifiers," February 1993.

RFC 1424: Kaliski, B., "Privacy Enhancement for Internet Electronic Mail: Part IV—Key Certification and Related Services," February 1993.

RFC 1493: Decker, E., *et al.*, "Definitions of Managed Objects for Bridges," July 1993.

RFC 1513: Waldbusser, S., "Token Ring Extensions to the Remote Network Monitoring MIB," September 1993.

RFC 1695: Ahmed, M. and Tesink, K. (eds), "Definitions of Managed Objects for ATM Management Version 8.0 Using SMIv2," August 1994.

RFC 1748: McCloghrie, K. and Decker, E., "IEEE 802.5 Token Ring MIB Using SMIv2," December 1994.

RFC 1757: Waldbusser, S., "Remote Network Monitoring Management Information Base," February 1995.

RFC 1901: SNMPv2 Working Group, Case, J., McCloghrie, K., Rose, M., and Waldbusser, S., "Introduction to Community-based SNMPv2," January 1996. (Historic).

RFC 1903: SNMPv2 Working Group, Case, J., McCloghrie, K., Rose, M., and Waldbusser, S., "Textual Conventions for Version 2 of the Simple Network Management Protocol (SNMPv2)," January 1996.

RFC 1904: SNMPv2 Working Group, Case, J., McCloghrie, K., Rose, M., and Waldbusser, S., "Conformance Statements for Version 2 of the Simple Network Management Protocol (SNMPv2)," January 1996.

RFC 1905: SNMPv2 Working Group, Case, J., McCloghrie, K., Rose, M., and Waldbusser, S., "Protocol Operations for Version 2 of the Simple Network Management Protocol (SNMPv2)," January 1996.

RFC 1906: SNMPv2 Working Group, Case, J., McCloghrie, K., Rose, M., and Waldbusser, S., "Transport Mappings for Version 2 of the Simple Network Management Protocol (SNMPv2)," January 1996.

RFC 1907: SNMPv2 Working Group, Case, J., McCloghrie, K., Rose, M., and Waldbusser, S., "Management Information Base for Version 2 of the Simple Network Management Protocol (SNMPv2)," January 1996.

RFC 1908: SNMPv2 Working Group, Case, J., McCloghrie, K., Rose, M., and Waldbusser, S., "Coexistence Between Version 1 and Version 2 of the Simple Network Management Protocol (SNMPv2)," January 1996.

RFC 2003: Perkins, "IP Encapsulation Within IP," October 1996.

RFC 2004: Perkins, "Minimal Encapsulation Within IP," October 1996.

RFC 2005: Solomon, "Applicability Statement for IP Mobility Support," October 1995.

RFC 2006: Cong, D., Hamlen, M., and Perkins, C., "The Definitions of Managed Objects for IP Mobility Support using SMIv2," October 1996.

RFC 2021: Waldbusser, S., "Remote Network Monitoring Management Information Base Version 2," January 1997.

RFC 2063: Brownlee, N., Mills, C., and Ruth, G., "Traffic Flow Measurement: Architecture," January 1997.

RFC 2064: Brownlee, N., "Traffic Flow Measurement: Meter MIB," January 1997.

RFC 2074: Bierman, A., "Remote Network Monitoring MIB Protocol Identifiers," January 1997.

RFC 2104: Krawczk, H., Bellare, M., and Canetti, R., "HMAC: Key-hashing for Message Authentication," February 1997.

RFC 2123: Brownlee, N., "Traffic Flow Measurement: Experiences With NeTraMet," March 1997.

RFC 2196: B. Fraser, "Site Security Management," September 1997.

RFC 2205: Braden, R., Zhang, L., Berson, S., and Herzog, S., "Resource ReSerVation Protocol (RSVP)," September 1997.

RFC 2274: Blumenthal, U., and Wijnen, B., "User-based Security Model (USM) for Version 3 of the Simple Network Management Protocol (SNMPv3)," January 1998.

RFC 2358: Flick, J. and Johnson, J., "Definitions of Managed Objects for the Ethernet-like Interface Types," June 1998.

RFC 2474: Nichols, K., Blake, S., Baker, F., and Black, D., "Definition of the Differentiated Services Field (DS Field) in the IPv4 and IPv6 Headers," December 1998.

RFC 2558: Tesink, K., "Definitions of Managed Objects for the SONET/SDH Interface Type," March 1999.

RFC 2573: Levi, D., Meyer, P., and Stewart, B., "SNMP Applications," April 1999.

RFC 2574: Blumenthal, U. and Wijnen, B., "User-based Security Model (USM) for Version 3 of the Simple Network Management Protocol (SNMPv3)," April 1999,

RFC 2575: Wijnen, B., Presuhn, R., and McCloghrie, K. "View-based Access Control Model (VACM) for the Simple Network Management Protocol (SNMP)," April 1999.

RFC 2578: SNMPv2 Working Group, Case, J., McCloghrie, K., Rose, M., and Waldbusser, S., "Structure of Management Information for Version 2 of the Simple Network Management Protocol (SNMPv2)," April 1999.

RFC 2579: McCloghrie, K., Perkins, D., Schoenwaelder, J., and Braunschweig, T.U., "Textual Conventions for SMIv2," April 1999.

RFC 2580: McCloghrie, K., Perkins, D., Schoenwaelder, J., and Braunschweig, T.U., "Conformance Statements for SMIv2," April 1999.

RFC 2662: Bathrick, G. and Ly, F., "Definitions of Managed Objects for the ADSL Lines," August 1999.

RFC 2702: Awduche, D., Malcolm, J., Agoguba, J., O'Dell, M., and McManua, J., "Requirements for Traffic Engineering Over MPLS," September 1999.

RFC 2863: McCloghrie, K. and Kastenholtz, F., "The Interfaces Group MIB," June 2000.

RFC 2864: McCloghrie, K. and Hanson, G., "The Inverted Stack Table Extension to the Interfaces Group MIB," June 2000.

RFC 3031: Rosen, E., Viswanathan, A., and Callon, R., "Multiprotocol Label Switching Architecture," January 2001.

RFC 3036: Andersson, L., Doolan, P., Fredette, A., and Thomas, B., "LDP Specification," January 2001.

RFC 3037: Thomas, B., and Gray, E., "LDP Applicability," January 2001.

RFC 3276: Ray, B. and Abbi, R., "Definitions of Managed Objects for High Bit-Rate DSL—2nd Generation (HDSL2) and Single-Pair High-Speed Digital Subscriber Line (SHDSL) Lines," May 2002.

RFC 3410: Case, J., Mundy, R., Partain, D., and Stewart, B., "Introduction and Applicability Statements for Internet Standard Management Framework," December 2002.

RFC 3411: Harrington, D., Presuhn, R., and Wijnen, B., "An Architecture for Describing SNMP Management Frameworks," December 2002.

RFC 3412: Case, J., Harrington, D., Presuhn, R., and Wijnen, B., "Message Processing and Dispatching for the Simple Network Management Protocol (SNMP)," December 2002.

RFC 3413: Levi, D., Meyer, P., and Stewart, B., "Simple Network Management Protocol (SNMP) Applications," December 2002.

RFC 3414: Blumenthal, U. and Wijnen, B., "User-based Security Model (USM) for Version 3 of the Simple Network Management Protocol (SNMPv3)," December 2002.

RFC 3415: Wijnen, B., Presuhn, R., and McCloghrie, K., "View-based Access Control Model (VACM) for the Simple Network Management Protocol (SNMP)," December 2002.

RFC 3418: Presuhn, R., Case, J., McCloghrie, K., Rose, M., and Waldbusser, S., "Management Information Base (MIB) for the Simple Network Management Protocol (SNMP)," December 2002.

RFC 3429: Ohta, H., "Assignment of the 'OAM Alert Label' for Multiprotocol Label Switching Architecture (MPLS) Operation and Maintenance (OAM) Functions," November 2002.

RFC 3440: Ly, F. and Bathrick, G., "Definitions of Extension Managed Objects for Asymmetric Digital Subscriber Lines," December 2002.

RFC 3535: Schoenwaelder, J., "Overview of the 2002 IAB Network Management Workshop," May 2003.

RFC 3584: Frye, R., Levi, D., Routhier, S., and Wijnen, B., "Coexistence Between Version 1, Version 2, and Version 3 of the Internet-standard Network Management Framework," August 2003.

RFC 3621: Berger, A. and Romascanu, D., "Power Ethernet MIB," December 2003.

RFC 3635: Flick, J., "Definitions of Managed Objects for the Ethernet-like Interface Types," September 2003.

RFC 3728: Ray, B. and Abbi, R., "Definitions of Managed Objects for Very High Speed Digital Subscriber Lines (VDSL)," February 2004.

RFC 3748: Aboba, B., Blunk, L., Vollbrecht, J., Carlson, J., and Levkowetz, H., "Extensible Authentication Protocol (EAP)," June 2004.

RFC 3811: Nadeau, T. and Cucchiara, J., "Definitions of Textual Conventions (TCs) for Multiprotocol Label Switching (MPLS) Management," June 2004.

RFC 3812: Srinivasan, C., Viswanathan, A., and Nadeau, T., "Multiprotocol Label Switching (MPLS) Traffic Engineering (TE) Management Information Base (MIB)," June 2004.

RFC 3813: Srinivasan, C., Viswanathan, A., and Nadeau, T., "Multiprotocol Label Switching (MPLS) Label Switching Router (LSR) Management Information Base (MIB)," June 2004.

RFC 3814: Nadeau, T., Srinivasan, C., and Viswanathan, A., "Multiprotocol Label Switching (MPLS) Forwarding Equivalence Class to Next Hop Label Forwarding Entry (FEC-To-NHLFE) Management Information Base (MIB)," June 2004.

RFC 3815: Cucchiara, J., Sjostrand, H., and Luciani, J., "Definitions of Managed Objects for the Multiprotocol Label Switching (MPLS), Label Distribution Protocol (LDP)," June 2004.

RFC 3990: O'Hara, B., Calhoun, P., and Kempf, J., "Configuration and Provisioning for Wireless Access Points (CAPWAP) Problem Statement," February 2005.

RFC 4070: Dodge, M. and Ray, B., "Definitions of Managed Object Extensions for Very High Speed Digital Subscriber Lines (VDSL) Using Multiple Carrier Modulation (MCM) Line Coding," May 2005.

RFC 4105: Le Roux, L., Vasseur, J.-P., and Boyle, J., "Requirements for Inter-area MPLS Traffic Engineering," June 2005.

RFC 4118: Yang, L., Zerfos, P., and Sadot, E., "Architecture Taxonomy for Control and Provisioning of Wireless Access Points (CAPWAP)," June 2005.

RFC 4220: Dubuc, M., Nadeau, T., and Lang, J., "Traffic Engineering Link Management Information Base," November 2005.

RFC 4221: Nadeau, T., Srinivasan, C., and Farrel, A., "Multiprotocol Label Switching (MPLS) Management Overview," November 2005.

RFC 4377: Nadeau, T., Morrow, M., Swallow, G., Allen, D., and Matsushima, S., "Operations and Management (OAM) Requirements for Multiprotocol Label Switched (MPLS) Networks," February 2006.

RFC 4379: Kompella, K. and Swallow, G., "Detecting Multiprotocol Label Switched (MPLS) Data Plane Failures," February 2006.

RFC 4564: Govindan, S., Cheng, H., Yao, Z.H., Zhou, W.H., Yang, I.., "Objectives for Control and Provisioning of Wireless Access Points (CAPWAP)," July 2006.

RFC 4837: Khermosh, L., "Managed Objects of Ethernet Passive Optical Networks (EPON)," July 2007.

RFC 4878: Squire, M., "Definitions and Managed Objects for Operations, Administration, and Maintenance (OAM) Functions on Ethernet-like Interfaces," June 2007.

RFC 5247: Aboba, B., Simon, D., and Eronen, P., "Extensible Authentication Protocol (EAP) Key Management Framework," August 2008.

RFC 5415: Calhoun, P., Montemurro, M., and Stanley, D., "CAPWAP Protocol Specification," March 2009.

RFC 5416: Calhoun, P., Montemurro, M., and Stanley, D., "CAPWAP Protocol Binding for IEEE 802.11," March 2009.

RFC CAPWAP Base MIB: Shi, Y., Shi, Y., Elliott, C., and Zhang, Y., "CAPWAP Protocol Base MIB," Available from: draft-ietf-capwap-base-mib-03, November 1, 2008.

Rivest, R.L., Shamir, A., and Adelman, L., "A Method for Obtaining Digital Signatures and Public-key Cryptosystems," *Communications of the ACM*, February 1978.

Rose, M.T., *The Simple Book: An Introduction to Network Management*, Upper Saddle River, NJ, Prentice-Hall PTR, 1996.

Rose, Marshall T. and McCloghrie, Keith, *How to Manage Your Network Using SNMP*, Upper Saddle River, NJ, Prentice Hall PTR, 1995.

Schwartz M: Schwartz, Mischa, "Mobile Wireless Communications," Cambridge: Cambridge University Press, 2005.

SCTE 24-6: ANSI/SCTE 24-6 2006 IPCablecom Part 6: IPCablecom Management Information Base (MIB) Framework.

SCTE 24-7: ANSI/SCTE 24-7 2006 IPCablecom Part 7: Media Terminal Adapter (MTA) Management Information Base (MIB) Requirements.

SCTE 24-8: ANSI/SCTE 24-8 200 6 IPCablecom Part 8: Signaling Management Information Base (MIB) Requirements.

Shi, Y., *et al.*, "CAPWAP Protocol Binding MIB for IEEE 802.11, "Available from: draft-ietf-capwap-802dot11-mib-04, May 30, 2009.

Sidor, David J., "Managing Telecommunications Networks Using TMN Interface Standards," *IEEE Communications Magazine*, March 1995.

Sidor, David J., "TMN Standards: Satisfying Today's Needs while Preparing for Tomorrow," *IEEE Communications Magazine*, March 1998.

Stallings, William, *SNMP, SNMPv2, SNMPv3, and RMON 1 and 2,* Reading, MA: Addison-Wesley Publishing Company, Inc., 1998.

Steffes, Paul G. and Stratigos, Jim, "Satellite Technologies Serving as Last Mile Solutions," *Access Technologies for Multimedia Communications,* Jayant, Nikil (ed.), Florida: CRC Press, 2005.

Strauss, F. and Klie, T., "Towards XML Oriented Internet Management," in *Proceedings of the 8th IFIP/IEEE International Symposium Integrated Network Management*, Goldszmidt, G. and Schonwalder, I. (eds), Colorado Springs, CO, March 2003, pp. 505–518.

Subramanian, Mani, "Home Networking: Market Drivers, Technologies, and Business Models," *IEEE Tutorials*, November 2005a.

Subramanian, Mani, "Wireless Broadband: Status, Challenges, and Solutions," in *EntNet@Supercom 2005, IEEE International Enterprise Networking & Services Conference*, Chicago, June 7, 2005b.

Sun Enterprise: "Solstice Enterprise Manager 2.1—A Technical White Paper," Copyright 1994–1998, Sun Microsystems, Inc., Palo Alto, CA.

Suryaputra, Stephen and Squire, Matthew, "IEEE 802.3ah OAM Helps Bridge Ethernet Management Gap," *CommsDesign*, Available from: http://www.commsdesign.com/design_corner/showArticle.jhtml?article ID=31000001, October 2, 2008.

T1.231: Draft American National Standard for Telecommunications—Digital Hierarchy—Layer 1 In-service Digital Transmission Performance Monitoring, T1M1.3/93-005R2, July 1993.

Tanenbaum, Andrew S., *Computer Networks*, 3rd Edition, Upper Saddle River, NJ: Prentice-Hall PTR, 1996.

Tanenbaum, Andrew S., *Modern Operating Systems,* 3rd Edition, New Delhi, India: Prentice-Hall, 2007.

Thompson, J. Patrick, "Web-based Enterprise Management Architecture," *IEEE Communications Magazine*, March 1998.

Tivoli: A series of product and technical documents, Available from: http://www.tivoli.com/.

TMF: Available from: www.tmforum.org.

Vanchynathan, A.G.K., Rani, N. Usha, Charitha, C., and Gonsalves, T.A., "Distributed NMS for Affordable Communications," in *Proceedings of the NCC-04 10th National Conference on Communications*, IISc, Bangalore, India, 2004, pp. 346–351.

W3C: "W3C: World Wide Web Consortium," Available from: http://www.w3.org.

Wack, John P. and Carnahan, Lisa J. "Keeping Your Site Comfortably Secure: An Introduction to Internet Firewalls," *NIST Special Publication 800-10*, U.S. Department of Commerce, National Institute of Standards and Technology, Gaithersburg, MD, 1994.

Wikipedia1: Gigabit Ethernet

Wikipedia2: Synchronous Optical Networking

Wikipedia3: Cable Modem

Wilson, Eric K. and Shirali, Chet, "Adapting DOCSIS for Broadband Wireless-access Systems," *CommsDesign*, October 29, 2008.

WSD: Available from: www.oasis-open.org.

X.208 (1988): ITU-T Recommendation X.208, "Specification of Abstract Syntax Notation One (ASN.1)," 1988.

X.209 (1988): ITU-T Recommendation, "Specification of Basic Encoding Rules for Abstract Syntax Notation One (ASN.1)," 1988.

Y1710: ITU-T Recommendation Y.1710, "Requirements for OAM Functionality in MPLS Networks."

Y1711: ITU-T Rec. Y.1720, "Protection Switching for MPLS Networks", September 2003.

Yang, Shi and Perkins, David T., "CAPWAP Protocol and Dot11 Binding MIB," in *IETF 70th*, Vancouver, December 3, 2007.

Yemini, S.A., Kliger, S., Mozes, E., Yemini, Y., and Olsie, D., "High Speed and Robust Event Correlation," *IEEE Communications Magazine*, May 1996.

Yoon, J.H., Ju, H.T., and Hong, J.W., "Development of SNMP-XML Translator and Gateway for XML-based Integrated Network Management," *International Journal of Network Management*, Vol. 13, 2003, pp. 259–276.

ZDNet: "Task Masters: Network Monitoring Tools," ZDNet UK, Available from: http://www.microsite.co.uk/tivoli/tme, 1998.

Zeltserman, Dave and Puoplo, Gerard, *Building Network Management Tools with Tcl/Tk*, Upper Saddle River, NJ: Prentice-Hall PTR, 1998.

RFC: Request for Comments.

Index